THE ULTIMATE GUIDE TO
LESBIAN & GAY
FILM AND VIDEO

THE ULTIMATE GUIDE TO
LESBIAN & GAY
FILM AND VIDEO
EDITED BY JENNI OLSON

NEW YORK/LONDON

First published 1996 by
Serpent's Tail, 4 Blackstock Mews, London N4 2BT
and 180 Varick Street, 10th floor, New York, NY 10014

Library of Congress Catalog Card Number: 95–72972

A full catalogue record for this book can be obtained from the British Library on request

Cover and text design by Rex Ray
Printed in the USA by R. R. Donnelley & Sons Company

"The fact is I am quite happy in a movie, even a bad movie. Other people, so I have read, treasure memorable moments in their lives."
—Walker Percy

This book is dedicated to the memory of my friend and colleague, Mark Finch (1961–1995), and to the memory of my mother, Erma Olson (1926–1995).

CONTENTS

1   Acknowledgments/About This Book
4   How to Use This Book

6   Centenary of Cinema: Frameline's Lesbian & Gay Top Ten Survey

11   Alphabetical Film and Video Catalog
288   Alphabetical Catalog of Clip Shows and Special Presentations

      Indexes:
296   Lesbian features
296   Gay features
298   Cogender features
299   Bisexual features
299   Transgender features
299   Lesbian shorts
302   Gay shorts
307   Cogender shorts
308   Bisexual shorts
308   Transgender shorts
309   Index of Subjects
331   Index of Directors

336   Distributor Directory
364   A Cinema of One's Own: A Brief History of the
      San Francisco International Lesbian & Gay Film Festival by Susan Stryker
371   Checklist for Programming
381   International Directory of Lesbian & Gay Film and Video Festivals
386   U.S. and U.K. Lesbian & Gay Mail Order Home Video Distributors
387   Bibliography

Acknowledgements/About This Book

This volume originated as my B.A. thesis project at the University of Minnesota. It was born in 1989 as a comprehensive lesbian filmography under the auspices of Jacqueline Zita and the University of Minnesota Women's Studies Department, with the assistance of a grant from the Undergraduate Research Opportunity grant program. Additional support was provided by Brad Theissen and Minneapolis-based GAZE Media.

On a 1991 visit to Frameline's San Francisco International Lesbian & Gay Film Festival and to the festival's bustling old Dolores Street office, it became clear to me that this was where the project belonged. The filmography and I soon found a home in the dark corner where the water cooler used to be when Tom di Maria hired me as guest curator for the 1992 film festival (where I stayed on as festival codirector until 1994). I am ever grateful to Tom for believing in me and for bringing me to San Francisco to fulfill my dreams. His early fund-raising for the project brought in much needed support from the Morgan R. Pinney Trust and the Stanley Cornfield Fund. The project's first dedicated Frameline intern, Cheryl Gariepy, hit on the idea of narrowing our focus to include only films and videos that had been shown in the festival (amended again later to include a sampling of other major feature films); at which point I also decided to expand beyond the lesbian focus of the project to include gay, bisexual, and transgender works as well. I want to thank Cheryl and the project's other early intern, Jennifer Morris, for their perseverance in developing the filmography into what you see before you.

For assistance in the early stages of developing the structure of the book and trying to find a publisher, my special thanks go to: John Miller-Monzon at Baseline, Robin Stevens, Mary Wings, Peter Fowler, and to Janis Plotkin, Deborah Kaufman, and Marc Smolowitz at the San Francisco Jewish Film Festival. For believing in the project enough to take on the job of editing and publishing it, I thank Amy Scholder and Ira Silverberg, and Serpent's Tail Ltd. My thanks also to the book's designer Rex Ray, and to copy editor Myia Williams. And for their assistance with the seemingly endless stream of data entry, thanks to: Mandana Auladini, Leo Chang, Diane Davis, Kathy Fretz, Kara Hughes, Lisa Kuhne, Cate Latchford, Alexis Lezin, Michelle Mattos, Karin Michalski, Tanya Miller, Michelle Patterson, Chandra Pugh, Elizabeth Rubin, Pamela August Russell, Laurie Sirois, Sara Whiteley, and Amy Yunis, with special thanks to Monica Nolan and Sanford Steadman. Special thanks also for assistance, support, and advice to: Tom Abell, Al Baum, Desi del Valle, Richard Dyer, Nancy Fishman, Marc Geller, Tim Highsted, Larry Horne, Jim Hubbard, Marc Huestis, Jeff Lunger, Lara Mac, Danny Mangin, Stuart Marshall, Ric Mears, Anita Monga, Raymond Murray, Dan Nicoletta, Louise Rafkin, Melissa Rasmussen, Tom Reilly, Rink, Stafford, Jim Van Buskirk, Andrea Weiss, Gary Wilson, and Sande Zeig. And for her very thorough lesbian and gay film and video bibliography, thanks to Tanya Miller.

For moral and financial support of this project and for being my pal, thanks to Judith Halberstam. And, for her infinite love and support, thanks to my girlfriend, Julie Dorf.

I will always be grateful to my stepfather, Charles Gorder, for inspiring my childhood love of the movies. I would also like to acknowledge my gratitude to the three men who inspired and cultivated my early interest in queer cinema: the late Vito Russo whose book *The Celluloid Closet* changed my life; Peter Lowy, who was the first director of New York's Lesbian and Gay Film Festival; and Michael Lumpkin, the first (and now current) director of the San Francisco International Lesbian & Gay Film Festival.

About the Text

Most of the film and video descriptions herein were taken directly from the catalogs of the San Francisco International Lesbian & Gay Film Festival and were written by the festival programmers. In cases where no other description was available, some blurbs were taken from distribution catalogs. The majority of technical information about each title (year, country, format, running time, etc.) was taken directly from the original published festival catalogs or from festival files. In some cases information was determined from distribution catalogs, books, periodicals, and other anecdotal sources.

The majority of film descriptions in this book were written by the programmers of the San Francisco International Lesbian & Gay Film Festival, with the assistance of individual guest curators and film critics. The following acknowledgements include the program staff and all of the individual catalog contributors for every year of the festival. Thanks to: Paul Bollwinkel, Berne Boyle, Aarin Burch, John Canaly, Suzy Capo, Lawrence Chua, Community United Against Violence, Jay Ruben Dayrit, Vic De La Rosa, Desi del Valle, Nikos Diaman, Thomas di Maria, Cecilia Dougherty, Linda Farin, Mark Finch, Andre Fischer, Nancy Fishman, Dave Ford, Annette Forster, Kathy Geritz, Greg Gonzalez, Ed Halter, Robert Hawk, Glen Helfand, Marc Huestis, Marcus Hu, Maria Kellet, David Kim, Penni Kimmel, Karl Knapper, Liz Kotz, Paul Lee, Quentin Lee, Michael Lumpkin, Jeffrey Lunger, Ming Yuen S. Ma, Sande Mack, Daniel Mangin, Erica Marcus, Ric Mears, Lynette Molnar, Jay Moman, Jennifer Morris, Meena Nanji, Boone Nguyen, Paul Nichols, Dan Nicoletta, Susanne Ofteringer, David Olivares, Jenni Olson, Mark Page, David Robinson, John W. Rowberry, Vito Russo, Michelle Sophia Sabol, Sarah Schulman, Steve Seid, Jaime Smith, Marc Smolowitz, Aaron Shurin, Scott Simmon, Wayne Smolen, Britt Tennel, Laura Thielen, Paul Thurston, David Waggoner, Darlene Weide, Mary Wings, Jeffrey Winter, John Wright, Sande Zeig, and Phil Zwickler.

Additional film critiques and reviews were solicited in order to highlight some of the important films of the last two decades, which for one reason or another, were not shown in the festival. The following writers brought a breadth of perspectives and insights to the amazing array of queer films in this volume: Justin Chin, Lawrence Chua, Mark Finch, Susan Gerhard, Eric Gutierrez, Judith Halberstam, Dennis Harvey, William Jones, Karl Knapper, Daniel Mangin, Elizabeth Pincus, B. Ruby Rich, Marlon Riggs, Cherry Smyth, Susan Stryker, and Randy Turoff. The author's initials are noted following each of their entries in the book.

Words cannot express my vast gratitude and indebtedness to Frameline and to the film and video makers, distributors, festival staff, colleagues, and volunteers who made these nineteen years of the festival possible. Let this volume be a testament to their dedication and vision.

Lastly, sadly, with deep love, I thank my dear friend and colleague, the late Mark Finch. In the three years that we worked together and became friends he taught me more than I ever thought I could know about life, love, and running a film festival. Let your absence be the latest shape of your being felt forever . . . (Rainer Maria Rilke).

—Jenni Olson
San Francisco, October 6, 1995

How to Use This Book

It is my hope that this book will be of interest and of use to gay and lesbian cineastes, consumers wanting more information about a title that is now available on home video, students, researchers, film and video makers, and to programmers who want to bring these films and videos to wider audiences. The primary purpose of this book is to provide useful critical and descriptive commentary as well as distribution and source data on lesbian and gay films and videos, and also to provide vital information to assist programmers in determining appropriate films for their audiences. While this is not a comprehensive catalog of lesbian and gay film and video, the two-thousand-plus titles herein—the majority of which were presented in Frameline's San Francisco International Lesbian & Gay Film Festival—reflect a very thorough overview of the last twenty years of queer film and video production, and, in the inclusion of retrospective and archival titles, a glimpse at the entire history of gay and lesbian cinematic representation.

The primary body of this text is organized in alphabetical listings by film or video title. In the case of foreign films and videos, English-translated titles are cross-listed, with the full information given under the original language title listing only. In this alphabetical directory of films and videos, each title listing features standard production information (title, director, country of origin, year of release, running time, format, etc.), along with information about the U.S. and U.K. distributor, followed by a one-word descriptive classification, and a brief description, review, or synopsis. Unless otherwise specified, all films and videos are with sound. Films of less than sixty minutes running time are considered shorts; longer than sixty minutes, features. Both U.S. and U.K. distribution sources are listed if there are separate distributors; if only a U.S. (or U.K.) source is listed, contact that source to find out about distribution information for other territories. In some cases, the U.K. home video (sell-thru) source is listed when there is no U.K. nontheatrical distributor. The abbreviation "n.a." is cited if no source is available. Please see the Distributor Index for more complete information.

The descriptive classifications preceding the synopses are intended as a general guide to more concisely characterize each film or video, and may sometimes be insufficient indicators of a film's complexity. I will use the following terms for these classifications: documentary, experimental, narrative, other. Many films and videos defy traditional descriptions, hence the category "Other."

The subject index at the back of the book should also be a helpful guide for readers searching for titles dealing with particular topics.

Also included here is a separate listing of the many clip shows and special programs that have been presented at the festival over the years, as well as a sampling of the results of Frameline's 1993 Centenary of Cinema survey, which polled some 250 lesbian and gay media professionals, asking them to list their top ten films.

For readers interested in obtaining further information about lesbian and gay film and video, a bibliography is included at the end of the volume. Other appendixes include the Checklist for Programming, the Directory of Lesbian and Gay Mail-Order Home Video Sources, and the Directory of International Lesbian & Gay Film Festivals. Film indexes are also included in the categories of: gay feature, lesbian feature, cogender feature, bisexual feature, transgender feature, gay short, lesbian short, cogender short, bisexual short, transgender short; as well as indexes by subject and director.

The Ultimate Guide to Lesbian & Gay Film and Video is now also available online. The databases that were used to create this book are the primary content of popcornQ, a new online website dedicated to facilitating access to resources and information about lesbian, gay, bisexual, and transgender moving images, promoting awareness about film and video preservation, and providing networking and communications tools for lesbian, gay, bisexual, and transgender film and video professionals. popcornQ can be reached by e-mail at: popcornQ@aol.com, on the world wide web at: http://www.popcornQ.com, or by snail mail at: popcornQ 584 Castro St., #550, San Francisco, CA 94114. Or you can call (415) 252-6285, or fax (415) 252-6287.

Centenary of Cinema: Lesbian and Gay Top Ten Survey

The Top Ten Films of All Time, according to 200 lesbian and gay film and video makers, curators, and critics:

1. Vertigo (Alfred Hitchcock, 1958, USA)
2. Sunset Boulevard (Billy Wilder, 1950, USA)
3. The Times of Harvey Milk
   (Robert Epstein, 1984, USA)
4. La Dolce Vita
   (Federico Fellini, 1960, ITALY/FRANCE)
5. Jeanne Dielman (Chantal Akerman, 1975, BELGIUM/FRANCE)
6. Citizen Kane (Orson Welles, 1941, USA)
7. Imitation of Life (Douglas Sirk, 1959, USA)
8. The Wizard of Oz
   (Victor Fleming, 1939, USA)
9. Thelma & Louise (Ridley Scott, 1991, USA)
10. Law of Desire
    (Pedro Almodovar, 1987, SPAIN)

[Surveys were sent to 250 men and 200 women. Results were compiled from 210 completed surveys (70% men, 30% women). Thanks to all the people who aided in compiling this unique perspective on the shape of lesbian and gay media today.]

The following sampling of responses from Frameline's 1993 survey of lesbian and gay media professionals offers a cheeky riposte to all those dreary Top Ten critics' lists, where Citizen Kane comes out #1 again and again. Respondents were also asked to say what film (or filmmaker) has most influenced their work. Here, then, are a few of the most interesting lists from some our brightest queer film critics, programmers, film and video makers:

Marta Balletbò Coll
(filmmaker: Intrepidissima, Costa Brava)
400 Blows (Frânçois Truffaut)
Citizen Kane (Orson Welles)
The Conformist (Bernardo Bertolucci)
Casablanca (Michael Curtiz)
Cabaret (Bob Fosse)
Ninotchka (Ernst Lubitsch)
Nosferatu (F.W. Murnau)
Metropolis (Fritz Lang)
Gone With the Wind (Victor Fleming)

Some Like It Hot (Billy Wilder)

Influence: Nestor Almendros

Susana Blaustein Munoz
(filmmaker: Susana, Las Madres de Plaza del Mayo)
The Berlin Affair (Liliana Cavani)
Hiroshima Mon Amour (Alain Resnais)
Anne Trister (Lea Pool)
The Night Porter (Liliana Cavani)
Sophie's Choice (Alan J. Pakula)
La Strada (Federico Fellini)
La Dolce Vita (Federico Fellini)
The Exterminating Angel (Luis Bunuel)
Matador (Pedro Almodovar)
The Law of Desire (Pedro Almodovar)

Influence: Alain Resnais

Kate Bornstein
(author: Crossing the Gender Divide)
All That Jazz (Bob Fosse)
Nashville (Robert Altman)
Cabaret (Bob Fosse)
The Producers (Mel Brooks)
Siesta (Mary Lambert)
Housekeeping (Bill Forsyth)
Juliet of the Spirits (Federico Fellini)
The Crying Game (Neil Jordan)
The Seven Samurai (Akira Kurosawa)
Z (Costa Gavras)

Influences: It's a tie between Bob Fosse and Robert Altman

Lawrence Chua
(film critic: Village Voice, Bomb)
Imitation of Life (Douglas Sirk)
The Color of Pomegranates (Paradjanov)
King of Children (Chen Kaige)
Vertigo (Alfred Hitchcock)
Butterfly and Flowers (Euthana Mukdasanit)
Sex Garage (Fred Halsted)
Teorema (Pier Paolo Pasolini)
Viva Mexico (Sergei Eisenstein)
Who's Afraid of Virginia Woolf? (Mike Nichols)
Ali: Fear Eats the Soul (Rainer Werner Fassbinder)

Influence: Yasujiro Ozu

Desi del Valle
(actress and filmmaker: Cruel, Costa Brava)
Poison (Todd Haynes)
Full Metal Jacket (Stanley Kubrick)
How to Kill Her (Ana Maria Simo)
Body Beautiful (Nguzi Onwurah)
Two Lies (Pam Tom)
Women on the Verge of a Nervous Breakdown
(Pedro Almodovar)
Anything by Sadie Benning
Daughters Of The Dust (Julie Dash)
The films of Jane Campion
Rope (Alfred Hitchcock)

Influence: Alfred Hitchcock

Mark Finch
(former Director, San Francisco International
Lesbian & Gay Film Festival)
Marnie (Alfred Hitchcock)
Imitation of Life (Douglas Sirk)
Sunday, Bloody Sunday (John Schlesinger)
A Reason To Live (George Kuchar)
Pink Narcissus (Anonymous)
Death In Venice (Luchino Visconti)
Without You I'm Nothing (John Boskovitch)
My Beautiful Laundrette (Stephen Frears)
Casta Diva (Eric de Kuyper)
La Jetee (Chris Marker)

Influences: Alfred Hitchcock, Douglas Sirk,
Chantal Akerman, George Kuchar, Irwin Allen

Nigel Finch
(filmmaker: Stonewall)
Battleship Potemkin (Sergei Eisenstein)
Performance (Nicolas Roeg)
Sunset Boulevard (Billy Wilder)
Some Like It Hot (Billy Wilder)
The Godfather (Francis Ford Coppola)
Rumblefish (Francis Ford Coppola)
Beauty and the Beast (Jean Cocteau)
Snow White and the Seven Dwarfs (Walt Disney)
Kind Hearts and Coronets (Robert Hamer)
The Ladykillers (Alexander Mackendrick)

Influence: Francis Ford Coppola

Constantine Giannaris
(filmmaker: A Place In The Sun)
Un Chant d'Amour (Jean Genet)
Citizen Kane (Orson Welles)

The Conformist (Bernardo Bertolucci)
The Gospel According to St. Matthew (Pier Paolo
Pasolini)
Imitation of Life (Douglas Sirk)
Mother India (Mehboob Kahn)
Ali: Fear Eats the Soul (Rainer Werner
Fassbinder)
Teorema (Pier Paolo Pasolini)
Rebel Without a Cause (Nicholas Ray)
The Philadelphia Story (George Cukor)

Influence: Pier Paolo Pasolini

Judith Halberstam
(film critic and author: Skin Shows: Gothic Horror
and the Technology of Monsters)
Blade Runner (Ridley Scott)
The Birds (Alfred Hitchcock)
Ran (Akira Kurosawa)
Flaming Ears (A. Hans Scheirl)
The Silence of the Lambs (Jonathan Demme)
The Cabinet of Dr. Caligari (Robert Wiene)
A Touch of Evil (Orson Welles)
Thelma & Louise (Ridley Scott)
Do the Right Thing (Spike Lee)
M (Fritz Lang)

Barbara Hammer
(filmmaker: Dyketactics, Nitrate Kisses)
Woman of the Dunes (Hiroshi Teshigahara)
Meshes of the Afternoon (Maya Deren)
Maedchen In Uniform (Leontine Sagan)
Bambi (Walt Disney)
Pierrot Le Fou (Jean-Luc Godard)
The Bitter Tears of Petra Van Kant (Rainer
Werner Fassbinder)
Act of Seeing with One's Own Eyes (Stan
Brakhage)
Privilege (Yvonne Rainer)
Gently Down the Stream (Su Friedrich)
Poison (Todd Haynes)

Influences: Alain Resnais and Abigail Childs

Tim Highsted
(Programmer, London Film Festival)
Pandora's Box (G.W. Pabst)
Peeping Tom (Michael Powell)
Fireworks (Kenneth Anger)
King Kong (Merian C. Cooper)
Nosferatu (F.W. Murnau)
Imitation of Life (Douglas Sirk)

October (Sergei Eisenstein)
Destry Rides Again (George Marshall)
Cabinet of Dr. Caligari (Robert Wiene)
Act of Seeing with One's Own Eyes (Stan Brakhage)

Influences: Kenneth Anger, Douglas Sirk

Marcus Hu

(producer and distributor: The Living End, Frisk)
Vertigo (Alfred Hitchcock)
Touch of Evil (Orson Welles)
Taxi Driver (Martin Scorsese)
Ace in the Hole (Billy Wilder)
Last Year at Marienbad (Alain Resnais)
Double Indemnity (Billy Wilder)
Black Sunday (Mario Bava)
Badlands (Terrence Malick)
Carrie (Brian De Palma)
Hellzapoppin (HiCi Potter)

Influence: Roger Corman

Vivian Kleiman

(filmmaker: My Body's My Business)
A Woman under the Influence (John Cassavettes)
Tongues Untied (Marlon Riggs)
Angry Harvest (Agnieszka Holland)
The Times of Harvey Milk (Rob Epstein and Jeffrey Friedman)
Sans Soleil (Chris Marker)
Bitter Tears of Petra Von Kant (Rainer Werner Fassbinder)
Citizen Kane (Orson Welles)
Love Streams (John Cassavettes)
Minnie & Moskowitz (John Cassavettes)

Influence: John Cassavettes

Richard Kwietniowski

(filmmaker: Flames Of Passion)
Written on the Wind (Douglas Sirk)
Madame de . . . (Max Ophuls)
Brief Encounter (David Lean)
Now Voyager (Irving Rapper)
Jeanne Dielman (Chantal Akerman)
Peeping Tom (Michael Powell)
Slow Motion (Jean-Luc Godard)
Vertigo (Alfred Hitchcock)
Chinatown (Roman Polanski)
Blue Velvet (David Lynch)

Influences: Chantal Akerman, Hollis Frampton, Ernst Lubitsch, John Smith, Preston Sturges, Genet's Un Chant d'Amour

Bruce La Bruce

(filmmaker: No Skin Off My Ass, Super 8 1/2)
The Ladies Man (Jerry Lewis)
A Woman under the Influence (John Cassavettes)
Chelsea Girls (Andy Warhol)
Interiors (Woody Allen)
La Dolce Vita (Federico Fellini)
Persona (Ingmar Bergman)
La Notte (Michaelangelo Antonioni)
A Bout De Souffle (Jean-Luc Godard)
McCabe and Mrs. Miller (Robert Altman)
The Birds (Alfred Hitchcock)

Influence: Jerry Lewis

Paul Lee

(programmer and filmmaker: These Shoes Weren't Made For Walking)
La Dolce Vita (Federico Fellini)
Black Lizard (King Fukasaku)
Ju Dou (Zhang Yimou)
Law of Desire (Pedro Almodovar)
In the Realm of the Senses (Nagisa Oshima)
Carmen (Carlos Saura)
Dark Eyes (Nikita Mikhalhov)
My Beautiful Laundrette (Stephen Frears)
Betty Blue (Jean-Jaques Beineix)
The Rocky Horror Picture Show (Jim Sharman)

Influence: The earlier work of Pedro Almodovar (before Law of Desire).

Daniel Mangin

(film critic: San Francisco Weekly)
Greed (Erich Von Stroheim)
Touch of Evil (Orson Welles)
La Strada (Federico Fellini)
Late Spring (Yasujiro Ozu)
Maedchen In Uniform (Leontine Sagan)
Nashville (Robert Altman)
Trouble in Paradise (Jim Jarmusch)
Pather Panchali (Satyajit Ray)
Some Like It Hot (Billy Wilder)
Five Easy Pieces (Bob Rafelson)

Influence: Federico Fellini and Billy Wilder

Pratibha Parmar
(filmmaker: Khush, Warrior Marks,
Memsahib Rita)
Raging Bull (Martin Scorcese)
Citizen Kane (Orson Welles)
Johnny Guitar (Nicholas Ray)
Pakeeza (Kamal Amrohi)
Umrao Jaan (Muzaffar Ali)
Women on the Verge of a Nervous Breakdown
(Pedro Almodovar)
Thelma & Louise (Ridley Scott)
Rue des Casa Negres (Euzhan Palcy)
Blade Runner (Ridley Scott)

Influence: Derek Jarman

A. Hans Scheirl
(filmmaker: Flaming Ears)
Singapore Sling (Nicos Nicolaidas)
Blood of a Poet (Jean Cocteau)
Night Porter (Liliana Cavanni)
Eraser Head (David Lynch)
Tetsuo I+II (Shinya Tsukamoto)
Kings of the Road (Wim Wenders)
Repulsion (Roman Polanski)
Dangerous Liaisons (Stephen Frears)
Thundercrack! (Curt McDowell)
Nekromantik 2 (Jorg Buttgergeit)

Influence: Jean Cocteau

Wieland Speck
(filmmaker and programmer:
Berlin International Film Festival)
Zelig (Woody Allen)
The Misfits (John Huston)
From Here To Eternity (Fred Zinneman)
It Is Not The Homosexual That Is Perverse But
The Society In Which He Lives (Rosa von
Praunheim)
Together Alone (Paul Castalenetta)
Les Enfants Terribles (Jean Cocteau)
Mala Noche (Gus Van Sant)
Myra Breckenridge (Mike Sarne)
Ludwig II (Luchino Visconti)
Manhattan Underground (Peter De Rome)

Influences: Every single one of the ones I adore
(impossible to name).

Gus Van Sant
(filmmaker: My Own Private Idaho, To Die For)
Clockwork Orange (Stanley Kubrick)
Thoroughly Modern Millie (George Roy Hill)
Fellini's Roma (Federico Fellini)
Last Tango in Paris (Bernardo Bertolucci)
The Last of England (Derek Jarman)
The Birds (Alfred Hitchcock)
Suddenly Last Summer (Joseph L. Mankiewicz)

Influence: Stanley Kubrick

Todd Verow
(filmmaker: Frisk):
Death of Maria Marenblad (Werner Schroeter)
Beauty No. 2 (Andy Warhol)
Repulsion (Roman Polanski)
Divine Atrocities (Kim Cristy)
Querelle (Rainer Werner Fassbinder)
A Zed and Two Noughts (Peter Greenaway)
Weekend (Jean Luc Godard)
Scorpio Rising (Kenneth Anger)
Belle de Jour (Luis Bunuel)
Last Year at Marienblad (Alain Resnais)

Influence: Andy Warhol

John Waters
(filmmaker: Pink Flamingos, Serial Mom):
The Wizard of Oz (Victor Fleming)
Faster Pussycat, Kill! Kill! (Russ Meyer)
Brink of Life (Ingmar Bergman)
L'argent (Marcel L'Herbier)
The Tingler (William Castle)
In the Year of 13 Moons (Rainer Werner
Fassbinder)
Chelsea Girls (Andy Warhol)
8 1/2 (Federico Fellini)
Boom! (Joseph Losey)
Viridiana (Luis Bunuel)

Influences: Walt Disney, Douglas Sirk, Andy
Warhol, George and Mike Kuchar, Ingmar
Bergman, Russ Meyer

Andrea Weiss
(filmmaker and author: Vampires and Violets)
A Midsummer Night's Dream (Max Reinhardt)
Sunset Boulevard (Billy Wilder)
Jeanne Dielman (Chantal Akerman)
Night of the Hunter (Charles Laughton)
Maedchen In Uniform (Leontine Sagan)

One Way or Another (Sarah Gomez)
God's Country (Louis Malle)
Suddenly Last Summer (Joseph L. Mankiewicz)
Before Stonewall (Greta Schiller)
Gaslight (George Cukor)

Influences: Derek Jarman, Yvonne Rainer, Ulrike
Ottinger, Emile de Antonio

David Weissman
(filmmaker: Beauties Without a Cause,
Complaints)
Dersu Uzala (Akira Kurosawa)
Juliet of the Spirits (Federico Fellini)
Once Upon a Time in the West (Sergio Leone)
Apocalypse Now (Francis Ford Coppola)
Sunset Boulevard (Billy Wilder)
Modern Times (Charlie Chaplin)
Chinatown (Roman Polanski)
Casablanca (Michael Curtiz)
The Wizard of Oz (Victor Fleming)
Pee Wee's Big Adventure (Tim Burton)

Influences: Federico Fellini, Charlie Chaplin,
Andy Warhol

Yvonne Welbon
(video maker: Sisters in the Life)
Sugar Cane Alley (Euzhan Palcy)
Daughters of the Dust (Julie Dash)
Finding Christa (Camille Billops)
Entre Nous (Diane Kurys)
Flower on a Rainy Night (Wang Tong)
Color Adjustment (Marlon Riggs)
The Crying Game (Neil Jordan)
The Terrorizer (Yang De Chang)
Deutchland Spielel (Sharon Couzin)
It's a Wonderful Life (Frank Capra)

Influence: Julie Dash

Alphabetical Film and Video Catalog

A
B
C
D
E
F
G
H
I
J
K
L
M
N
O
P
Q
R
S
T
U
V
W
X
Y
Z

A.I.D.S.C.R.E.A.M.
Dir. Tartaglia, Jerry
1988 USA English
6 mins. 16mm color Experimental
Dist. (U.S.): Canyon Cinema
An examination of AIDS fear, desexualization of homosex and dissolution of gay identity.

Absence of Us, The
Dir. Pike, Pamela
1986 USA English
19 mins. video color Experimental
Dist. (U.S.): Pike, Pamela
A tape that explores the politics of words and the significance of names. Fingers tracing letters written on walls. A hand holding a pen as it fills the pages of a diary. A woman's voice reverberating. This is a personal commentary about what it means to be a lesbian out in society.

Absolutely Positive
Dir. Adair, Peter
Prod. Cole, Janet
1990 USA English
87 mins. video color Documentary
Dist. (U.S.): Frameline
The U.S. government estimates that there are between 1 and 1.5 million Americans currently infected with HIV. Within ten years, researchers believe, half will get serious illnesses and within sixteen years, half will develop AIDS. In spite of immense media coverage, there has been little exploration of this, the largest group affected by the epidemic. Yet HIV seropositives share—along with those with full-blown AIDS—both the terror and the stigma of the disease. Most people infected with HIV learn to cope with the psychological uncertainty of knowing they may get sick at any time. *Absolutely Positive* is the story of how eleven men and women are living with this news. *Absolutely Positive* was a recipient of Frameline's 1991 Film/Video Completion Fund.

Abuse
Dir. Bressan, Arthur
1982 USA English
94 mins. 16mm color Narrative
Dist. (U.S.): Frameline Archive
When other gay filmmakers were starting to invent stories of middle-class monogamy, Bressan turned up with *Abuse*, a queer kind of love story between a filmmaker and a 14-year-old child abuse victim. On *Abuse* (he said): "In 1975, when I met the real Thomas Carroll, I had no idea of making a movie about him, child abuse, or our relationship. Only after we became friends, then lovers, and finally ex-lovers, did I see a powerful film in his story. My straight and gay friends criticized me for my sexual involvement with Thomas. Some felt I was exploiting him, others believed he was using me simply to get away from his abusive parents. I listened to my friends but—like Larry, the filmmaker in the movie—I did not follow their advice. Instead, Thomas and I wound up living in San Francisco. I made *Abuse* because I thought it was a unique, compelling story about people and things that don't usually get into American feature films."

Achilles
Dir. Purves, Barry J.C.
Prod. Holberton, Glenn
1995 Great Britain English
11 mins. 35mm color Narrative
Dist. (U.K.): Channel 4 Television
An animated retelling of the Greek tragedy.

Across the Rubicon
Dir. Friedberg, Lionel
Prod. Friedberg, Diana
1987 South Africa English
54 mins. video color Documentary
Dist. (U.S.): Zepra International
Pieter-Dirk Uys is a South African female impersonator/caricaturist whose finely-wrought satirical touring show elucidates apartheid while lampooning it. Uys walks a thin line between censorship and arrest as he occasionally steps out of characters that include P.W. Botha, Desmond Tutu, and Margaret Thatcher to deliver pointed attacks on apartheid and the South African government. Uys's popularity with both white and black audiences insulates him somewhat from government interference, but he describes his balancing act as being "like doing the tango in front of a firing squad." *Across the Rubicon* brilliantly portrays the humor and grace with which Uys makes his contribution to the fight against apartheid.

ACT UP at the FDA
Dir. Spiro, Ellen
1988 USA English
13 mins. video color Documentary
Dist. (U.S.): Spiro, Ellen
ACT UP's closing down of the FDA in October 1988 is dramatically recorded by Ellen Spiro.

Acting Up for Prisoners
Dir. Slade, Eric and Mic Sweeney
1992 USA English
27 mins. video color Documentary

Dist. (U.S.): Frameline
An empowering chronicle of ACT UP's campaign for adequate health care for HIV-positive women at Frontera prison.

Actions Speak Louder Than Words
Dir. Kwietniowski, Richard
1992 Great Britain English
22 mins. video color Documentary
Dist. (U.S.): Frameline
Dist. (U.K.): Alfalfa Entertainments, Ltd.
Six deaf performers—three women, three men—are brought together to devise staged pieces based on their experience of gay and deaf cultures intersecting, and the highly politicized nature of both in Britain. The result is a diverse, assertive collage, ranging from advice on how to seduce a librarian (in silence, of course), to the importance of short hair in visibly proclaiming your lesbianism and deafness; plus an essential beginner's guide to sexual signing. Shot entirely in British Sign Language, with subtitles for the hearing.

Ad, The
Dir. Tate, Jennifer
1995 USA English
13 mins. 16mm color Narrative
Dist. (U.S.): Tate, Jennifer
An Africanesque lesbian finds what she wants only after she stops looking for it.

Adios, Roberto
Dir. Dawi, Enrique
1985 Argentina Spanish
90 mins. 35mm color Narrative
Dist. (U.S.): Altermedia
The first gay film to be produced by the newly uncensored Argentine cinema, *Adios, Roberto* is a witty entertaining comedy about the initiation into homosexuality of a young man with a macho reputation.

Recently separated from his wife, Roberto moves in with Marcelo, who eventually reveals his homosexuality. His first experience with gay sex occurs (as it so often does) after a drunken night out. Afterwards, Roberto feels the shame and guilt expected of him in a Catholic society.

Despite his concern for his young son and the reactions of those around him, Roberto soon begins to realize that he did enjoy his encounter with Marcelo and to question the damnations of his ex-wife, former fiancée, and priest (who punches Roberto after hearing his confession). Seeking analysis to help sort things out, Roberto begins to experience a barrage of ghosts past and present intertwining in revealing and amusing ways. Finally, he realizes that a choice must be made.

Adrian's Montag (Adrian's Monday)
Dir. Redding, Dominick, and
Benjamin Redding
1994 Germany German
9 mins. 16mm b&w Narrative
Dist. (U.S.): Twinbrothers Filmproduktion
A provocative skinhead fantasy set in a locker room.

ADS Epidemic, The
Dir. Greyson, John
1987 Canada English
5 mins. 16mm color Experimental
Dist. (U.S.): Frameline
A safe-sex music video.

Adventures of Priscilla, Queen of the Desert, The
Dir. Elliot, Stephan
1994 Australia English
102 mins. 35mm color Narrative
Dist. (U.S.): Swank Motion Pictures
Fabulous costumes, marvelous location shooting, and a great retro soundtrack in this feel-good film about two queens and a transsexual road-tripping across the Australian Outback to an obscure resort town are unfortunately marred by racist representations of Aborigines and a stunningly misogynistic barroom encounter with a butch woman. Fast-forward through the offensive parts and enjoy the spectacle. (S.S.)

Aesthetics and/or Transportation
Dir. Minahan, Dan
1987 USA English
14 mins. video color Experimental
Dist. (U.S.): Kitchen, The
Dan Minahan's peculiar take on art critic Gregory Battock (a woman reads Battock's essay; he's in Puerto Rico with his boyfriend).

Affairs of Love, The
(see *Cosas del Querer, Las*)

Affengeil (Life Is Like a Cucumber)
Dir. Von Praunheim, Rosa
1990 Germany German
87 mins. 35mm color Documentary
Dist. (U.S.): First Run Features
Rosa von Praunheim's best film yet is a homage to larger-than-life actress Lotti Huber (most

recently, star of von Praunheim's film, *Anita— Dances of Vice*). She describes her careers as dancer, wife, restaurateur, concentration camp prisoner, and full-time eccentric. Full of gay humor and bruised egos, *Affengeil*—it means something like "apeshit"—is a generous, affectionate, and lively movie.

Affirmations
Dir. Riggs, Marlon
1990 USA English
10 mins. video color Other
Dist. (U.S.): Frameline
Anecdotes and affirmations on black gay male identity are presented in this empowering tape from the maker of *Tongues Untied*.

Afflicted
Dir. Guttman, Amos
1985 Israel Hebrew
25 mins. video color Narrative
Dist. (U.S.): Third Ear, The
Guttman's best short film, *Afflicted* tells the story of a young, closeted Israeli man who visits a drag bar one night in search of sexual expression.

After Stonewall
(see *Out on Four: Episodes 5 & 6*)

After the Break
Dir. Guzman, Mary
1992 USA English
13 mins. 16mm b&w Narrative
Dist. (U.S.): Frameline
Personalities clash in a lesbian therapy group.

After the Game
Dir. Gray, Donna
1979 USA English
19 mins. 16mm b&w Narrative
Dist. (U.S.): Gray, Donna
Dist. (U.K.): Cinenova
The touching story of two women discovering their true feelings for each other.

After the Revolution
Dir. Thynne, Lizzie
1993 Great Britain English
27 mins. video color Documentary
Dist. (U.K.): Piranha Productions
After the Revolution documents the effect sexual repression has had on gays and lesbians in the former Czechoslovakia. Maria Dunková and Sonia Pompová and other lesbian and gay couples tell how they found each other and the struggles they have gone through to maintain their relationships. Lizzie Thynne's Channel Four production

also examines the impact the new gay movement has had on this newly liberated country.

After the War You Have to Tell Everyone about the Dutch Gay Resistance Fighters
Dir. Muller, Klaus
1991 Netherlands Dutch
60 mins. video color/b&w Documentary
Dist. (U.S.): United States Holocaust Memorial Museum
While many historians have written about the Dutch Underground, the participation of gay and lesbian heroes has been virtually ignored. In this fascinating and emotional film, director Klaus Muller acknowledges these heroic contributions.

Afternoon Breezes
(see *Kazetachi No Gogo*)

Age 12: Love With A Little L
Dir. Montgomery, Jennifer
1991 USA English
23 mins. video color Experimental
Dist. (U.S.): Women Make Movies
An experimental narrative that looks at the relationship between adolescent sexual experiences and the formation of lesbian identity.

Age of Dissent
Dir. Parry, William
1994 Great Britain English
55 mins. video color Documentary
Dist. (U.K.): Maya Vision
Age of Dissent captures the yearlong battle to change British legislation about the gay age of consent. It includes a visit to Russia, where homosexuality was recently legalized.

Agora
Dir. Kinney, Robert, and Donald Kinney
1992 USA English
73 mins. video color Narrative
Dist. (U.S.): Video Data Bank
Agoraphobia is a neurotic condition in which the individual harbors an intense fear of public places. The true agoraphobe lives in seclusion, hidden from view, closeted from the popular discourse. In the ribald hands of look-alikes Robert and Donald Kinney, known for their twinning adaptations of *Stephen* and *The Maids*, this neurotic complex becomes an expansive metaphor for social repression.

At a bland Midwestern motel, five desperate people have sought refuge from their hostile surroundings. Crab (Charles Louis), the desk clerk, is a troubled young gay man, suffocating in his small town. In room seven, Swallow (Donald Kinney), an escaped con, takes poorly to his newfound confinement, even though his outlaw lover Jack (Randy Rovans) tries to calm him with affection. In the adjoining room, Katch (Kerry Snyder), just dishonorably discharged from the military, has lost the uniformity that kept her contained; Joy (Tammy Hopkins), her lover, wants to flee the Midwest and enter the ranks of the larger gay community.

Using a hyped-up soaper sensibility with some dizzy art direction, the Kinneys have made a punchy drama that depicts social conformity as a subtle brand of psychological incarceration. *Agora* is the Motel Hell of repressed activity.

AIDS: A Priest's Testament
Dir. McAnally, Conor
1987 Ireland English
52 mins. video color Documentary
Dist. (U.S.): Strongbow Marketing
Shot in the U.S. for Irish television, *AIDS: A Priest's Testament* is the story of Father Bernard Lynch, an Irish-born priest and psychotherapist who set up an AIDS ministry in New York. Father Lynch is a daring, eloquent, and passionate missionary who discusses with startling honesty the pressures that have brought him close to the edge of his physical and spiritual limits as he conducts his ministry.

AIDS in the Barrio
Dir. Biella, Peter and Frances Negron
1991 USA English
30 mins. video color Documentary
Dist. (U.S.): West Glen Films
An X-ray of social conditions in Philadelphia's barrio.

AIDS Movie, The
Dir. Durrin, Ginny
1986 USA English
26 mins. video color Documentary
Dist. (U.S.): Durrin Films
An AIDS education film for youth featuring three people with AIDS who share what it's like to live with the disease and how to protect against it.

AIDS Show, The
Dir. Epstein, Robert and Peter Adair
1986 USA English
58 mins. video color Documentary
Dist. (U.S.): Adair & Armstrong
The AIDS Show video began in 1985 when Bay Area filmmakers Robert Epstein and Peter Adair decided to collaborate on a film about AIDS: "We

talked for a long time about doing a documentary that looked at the impact of AIDS on our community—not a medical film, but one that would address the more intangible, invisible effects. Then a friend suggested we see a play at a local community theater. It was called *The A.I.D.S. Show.* "

The initial inspiration for *The A.I.D.S. Show*, an acronym for "Artists Involved in Death and Survival," came in 1984 when Theater Rhinoceros founder Allen Estes and two colleagues envisioned a series of theater pieces to be presented at the time of the Democratic convention to focus public attention on AIDS. Under the direction of Leland Moss, the play—a collection of music, satire, dramatic monologue, and comedy sketches—became a smash hit at the Theater Rhinoceros. When the theater decided to mount a new, updated version in the fall of 1985, (co-directed by Moss and Douglas Holsclaw), Adair and Epstein decided to follow its development from the initial auditions through its premiere.

The result is a moving, beautifully photographed combination of theater and documentary that captures the incredible excitement of live theater and intensifies the power of the play's messages. Robert Epstein is the Oscar-winning director of *The Times of Harvey Milk* and codirected *Word Is Out* and *Greetings From Washington D.C.* Peter Adair codirected *Word Is Out* and directed *Stopping History.*

Winner of the 1986 San Francisco International Lesbian & Gay Film Festival Audience Award for Best Documentary.

AIDS/ARC Vigil
Dir. Gaffney, Cynthia
1986 USA English
30 mins. video color Documentary
Dist. (U.S.): Gaffney, Cynthia
A documentary on the eight-month-old AIDS/ARC vigil at San Francisco's U.N. Plaza where people with AIDS and ARC have chained themselves to the Federal Building to publicize the need for increased federal response to the crisis.

Airport
Dir. Dunkhorst, Silke, and Manuela Kay
1994 Germany German
33 mins. video color Narrative
Dist. (U.S.): Take Off Productions
An adventurous group of stewardesses discover the joys of group sex in the bathroom while in between flights.

Al Margen del Margen (Beyond Outcasts)
Dir. Arocha, Ivan and Hernandez, David
1992 Cuba English
35 mins. video color Documentary
Dist. (U.S.): Arocha, Ivan and Hernandez, David
An expanded version of a 13-minute short screened in 1991, *Beyond Outcasts (Al Margen del Margen)* has since been labeled "counterrevolutionary" by the Cuban government. It is a shocking critique of Cuba's AIDS policy.

aletheia
Dir. Trang, Tran T. Kim
1994 USA English
16 mins. video color Experimental
Dist. (U.S.): Third World Newsreel
Blindness, sex, desire, and violence is examined in this stark video which foregrounds the practice of eyelid alteration among some Asian women.

Alfalfa
Dir. Kwietniowski, Richard
1987 Great Britain English
9 mins. 16mm color Other
Dist. (U.S.): Frameline
Dist. (U.K.): British Film Institute
One of the year's most exuberant short films, *Alfalfa* is a gay dicktionary, a fag's thesaurus for those in the know (that's you, honey). You can dish about it—and you will—but you can't really find a name for it. The Queen's English from A to Z; state of the tart, queer as Christmas, and British as a bent penny.

Algie the Miner
Prod. Guy-Blaché, Alice
1912 USA English
10 mins. 35mm b&w Narrative
Dist. (U.S.): Library of Congress
In *Algie the Miner*, a 1912 one-reeler from pioneer producer Alice Guy-Blaché, a young man (Billy Quirk doing something of a limp-wristed "nance" routine) is obliged to prove machismo to his prospective father-in-law. Off to the West he goes, learning first that one does not thank gunslingers by kissing them.

Alicia Was Fainting
Dir. Olivé-Bellés, Núria
1994 USA English
37 mins. 16mm color Narrative
Dist. (U.S.): Olivé-Bellés, Núria
This bittersweet coming-of-age featurette from Spanish filmmaker/choreographer Núria Olivé-Bellés tells the story of a fourteen-year-old girl dealing with her mother's death, the onset of womanhood, and with her own awakening sexuality. Preparing to graduate from elementary school, Alicia must now part with her best friend and blood-sister Margarite. Resistant to the idea of traditional women's roles, Alicia works in a butcher shop where, amidst the hanging meat and bones, she daydreams about her mother and writes letters to Margarite.

Alkali, Iowa
Dir. Christopher, Mark
1995 USA English
17 mins. 16mm color Narrative
Dist. (U.S.): Christopher, Mark
Set on an expansive bean farm on the Fourth of July, all-American Jack Gudmanson discovers the reason his father has long since disappeared. Skillfully crafted, this film is one of the most beautiful in this year's Festival, both cinematically and emotionally.

All Day Always
Dir. Wolfe, Kathy, and Irene Young
1988 USA English
4 mins. video color Other
Dist. (U.S.): Wolfe Video
A Deidre McCalla music video.

All Fall Down
Dir. Foiles, Stacey
1993 USA English
30 mins. 35mm color Narrative
Dist. (U.S.): Women Make Movies
In this powerfully crafted family drama, two sisters travel to their mother's home on the second anniversary of their brother's suicide. Dark memories of their childhood come to the surface when Virginia, a lesbian, and her sister Amanda struggle through the issues of guilt and truth around the secret of their grandfather's death.

All Of Me
Dir. Wilhelm, Bettina
1990 Germany German
76 mins. 16mm color Narrative
Dist. (U.S.): Bettina Wilhelm Filmproduktion
Orlanda is a person between male and female. His/her profession is diseuse, a performer who entertains with songs and speeches in the German tradition of the '20s and '30s. To escape from loneliness, as well as to play with taboos, Orlanda decides to marry her friend Elizabeth. On a concert tour in Warsaw, which also serves as a honeymoon, both the newlyweds fall in love with a charming young Polish man.

This quite special marriage offers material for comedy as well as melodrama, cleverly commented on by Orlanda's songs. Georgette Dee as Orlanda is playing him/herself. The gender ambiguity that characterizes Dee makes it impossible to see these characters as simply straight, gay, or lesbian. Mechtild Grossmann displays a talent for both comedy and tragedy that she hasn't used before, and while *All Of Me* is meant to be fun, it has a serious side as well. Like *Seduction: The Cruel Woman*, in which these two actresses played the parts of Frederike and Wanda, respectively, the film is also embedded in the German tradition that, with wit and insight, explores ways to play with gender roles in film.

All Out Comedy
Dir. Zachary, Bohdan
1993 USA English
78 mins. video color Other
Dist. (U.S.): Zachary, Bohdan
Laugh out loud at Bay Area comedians Scott Capurro, Marilyn Pittman, Tom Ammiano, and Karen Ripley—taped live at Josie's Cabaret and Juice Joint in San Francisco.

All the Time
Dir. Scovill, Ruth
1992 USA English
4 mins. video color Other
Dist. (U.S.): Scovill, Ruth
A moving, Dionne Warwick inspired salute to some of our lesbian and gay heroes.

All You Can Eat
Dir. Brynntrup, Michael
1993 Germany German
5 mins. 35mm color Other
Dist. (U.S.): Brynntrup, Michael
A clever tribute to porn performers and front of film warnings.

Alleged, The
Dir. Slane, Andrea
1992 USA English
16 mins. video color Experimental
Dist. (U.S.): Chicago Filmmakers
Andrea Slane presents a barrage of tabloid television stories of "real-life" violence and tragedy as she works through her own expressions of grief, guilt, anger, and regret around the circumstances of her 20-year-old brother's suicide.

Alone Once Again
Dir. Becerra, Andrew
(Eagle Creek Youth Center)

Prod. Ming-Yuen S. Ma and Julia Meltzer
1995 USA English
1 mins. video color Other
Dist. (U.S.): Hourglass Productions
In *Alone Once Again*, a young filmmaker/poet thrills the audience with romantic and profound images of gay youth.

Alone Together:
Young Adults Living With HIV
Dir. Okazaki, Steven
1995 USA English
18 mins. 35mm color Documentary
Dist. (U.S.): Farallon Films
In this poignant documentary, young adults talk about what it is like to be HIV-positive and how it has changed their lives.

Alphabit Land: The Backyard Tour
Featuring Wigstock '89
Dir. Canalli, John
1990 USA English
28 mins. video color Other
Dist. (U.S.): Canalli, John
Alphabit Land, John Canalli's introduction to his low-key lifestyle in New York's hottest ghetto, explodes into drag delirium with scenes from Wigstock, an annual '60s-styled spectacular located in Tompkins Square Park.

Alpsee
Dir. Muller, Matthias
1994 Germany German
15 mins. 16mm color Experimental
Dist. (U.S.): Canyon Cinema
Matthias Muller's fantastic tale in which the daily aspects of life take on grand significance for a young boy.

Alternative Conceptions
Dir. Sunley, Christina
Prod. Sunley, Christina, and Vicki Funari
1985 USA English
36 mins. video color Documentar
Dist. (U.S.): Women Make Movies
Lesbian motherhood through donor insemination is the subject of this supportive tape about a controversial subject. *Alternative Conceptions* makes sense of some of the medical, legal, and social issues surrounding insemination: Is it difficult to become pregnant using this method? Does a sperm donor have any legal rights to the child? How do the mothers explain the "facts of life" to their children?

Ⓐ
Ⓑ
Ⓒ
Ⓓ
Ⓔ
Ⓕ
Ⓖ
Ⓗ
Ⓘ
Ⓙ
Ⓚ
Ⓛ
Ⓜ
Ⓝ
Ⓞ
Ⓟ
Ⓠ
Ⓡ
Ⓢ
Ⓣ
Ⓤ
Ⓥ
Ⓦ
Ⓧ
Ⓨ
Ⓩ

Always On Sunday
Prod. Gay Girls Riding Club
1962 USA English
20 mins. 16mm b&w Narrative
Dist. (U.S.): Tremaglio Productions
This spoof of *Never On Sunday* was the first film made by a group of gay men who frequented a Los Angeles gay bar, The Brownstone, for Sunday brunch. Organized by Ray Harrison, the group spent their Sunday mornings horseback riding (hence their name). *Always On Sunday* was filmed at The Brownstone in one Sunday, and the group went on to make four more films: *The Roman Springs on Mrs. Stone*, *What Really Happened to Baby Jane*, *All About Alice*, and *The Spy on the Fly*, screening them at the Brownstone to great acclaim. Rarely seen today, and never widely shown outside Los Angeles' gay bars, these films, made at a time when our lives were universally portrayed as tragic, remain a unique affirmation of the pleasure and joy gay people take in their lives. Titles on this evening's program also include: *The Roman Springs on Mrs. Stone* and *What Really Happened to Baby Jane*.

Amazing Grace
Dir. Gutman, Amos
1992 Israel Hebrew
95 mins. 35mm color Narrative
Dist. (U.S.): Midbar Films
A naive Israeli teenager falls in love with a 30ish HIV-positive musician. Full of illusions and delusions, Jonathon is desparate for love but still smarting from a short-lived affair with his handsome contemporary, Miki. Jonathon's family members—an ex-hippie mother, druggie sister, and straight-as-an-arrow brother—are tolerant, but have problems of their own to confront. Enter the enigmatic Thomas, just back from New York and hiding his medical condition from his constantly bickering mother and grandmother—and also from Jonathon, their downstairs neighbor. "I don't want to get used to something I'll lose tomorrow," Jonathon tells Thomas; he has no idea how high the stakes are in this fateful encounter.

A casual yet candid story about love in the age of AIDS, into which Gutman weaves observations of the family, gay relationships, and mortality . . . all with amazing grace.

Ambiman
Dir. Hanson, Mark
1983 USA English

3 mins. S8mm color Other
Dist. (U.S.): n/a
Part of the 1983 Super 8 Gay Festival.

Amblyopia (Points of View)
Dir. Stambrini, Monica
1994 Italy Italian
4 mins. 16mm color Narrative
Dist. (U.S.): Stambrini, Monica
Martino is practically a man when, during an eye test, the optometrist and his mother discover that he never saw things quite in the same way they have.

Amelia Rose Towers
Dir. Farkas, Jackie
1992 Australia English
11 mins. 35mm b&w Narrative
Dist. (U.S.): Australian Film, Television & Radio School
A wonderfully quirky fairy tale about a very tall girl who wishes she were small.

American Fabulous
Dir. Dakota, Reno
1991 USA English
120 mins. video/16mm color Documentary
Dist. (U.S.): First Run Features
Adding to a hearty tradition of ascerbic gay folklore, *American Fabulous* is the very oral biography of Jeffrey Strouth, a wild, storytelling homosexual whose unglamorously picaresque life makes for compulsively addictive narratives that are unbelievable, hilarious, and movingly tragic.

From a thronelike position in the backseat of a 1957 Cadillac, Strouth indulges in an autobiographical yakfest while the uninspiring landscape of Columbus, Ohio, provides a moving backdrop. He recounts a life so relentlessly melodramatic that, as he says, "nobody could make this up, and if they did, why would they want to?" Between cigarettes Strouth tells us about his first gay friend, the toothless "Myth Earl"; his psychopathic, abusive father; being kept, at 14, by a kindly 400-pound drag queen with a closet full of faux denim leisure suits; his passion for sex and drugs; and just about all the poop on the East Village club scene.

Like a queeny, white-trash Kerouac, Strouth's most poignant moments take place on the road. To hear his epic of hitchhiking from Ohio to Hollywood with a mincing, Tallulah Bankhead groupie boyfriend, a tiny yapping dog, and a finch in a cage is classic Americana, alone worth entering this tragicomic universe.

As indulgent as its subject, the tape's

two-hour length may send you out screaming, but if you can stick with it—and I suggest you do—Strouth emerges as an admirably uncompromising "free spirit" who has more than earned his endearing bitchiness.

Winner of the 1991 San Francisco International Lesbian & Gay Film Festival Audience Award for Best Video.

American Shooting Numbers 1, 2 and 3
Dir. Haas, George Robert
1981 USA English
10 mins. 16mm Other
Dist. (U.S.): n/a
Three frightening vignettes about violence and hatred in American society.

Among Good Christian Peoples
Dir. Saalfield, Catherine
1991 USA English
23 mins. video color Experimental
Dist. (U.S.): Frameline
Dist. (U.K.): Cinenova
Among Good Christian Peoples ex-plores some of the historical, emotional, and social interpretations of Jacqueline Woodson's personal essay "Growing Up Black and Gay Among Good Christian Peoples." The video combines Woodson reading her own compelling essay with footage shot in Pixel Vision (using a Fisher-Price camera) imaging childhood memories through interviews, and adults play-acting by reading a children's Bible and having slumber parties.

This video received a grant in 1991 from Frameline's Film/Video Completion Fund.

Among Men
Dir. Speck, Wieland
1980-91 Germany German
80 mins. 16mm color Narrative
Dist. (U.S.): Frameline
A package of five boy's stories by Wieland Speck, who made the 1987 gay favorite *Westler: East of the Wall*. As with *Westler*, all of Speck's short films deal with that fine space between reality and fantasy, a space only bridged by desire; it's Genet for the next generation. In *David, Montgomery & I* (made in San Francisco in 1980), a daydreamer struggles with his romantic cravings. There's more sleepless nights and fevered dreaming in *The Sound of Fast Relief*, an inventive drama about a big city, a room, and a fantasy somebody put in it. Plus *Chez Nous* and *November*, a four-minute short made for Britain's Channel Four TV, but never broadcast. The program ends with *Room 303*, a wordless, poignant series of flashbacks from a dying lover's bedside.

An All-American Story
Dir. Keitel, John
1992 USA English
21 mins. 16mm color Narrative
Dist. (U.S.): Keitel, John
A sharp, funny snapshot of the filmmaker as a young gay man, attending a Stanford reunion and shocking himself more than his straight pals.

An Empty Bed
Dir. Gasper, Mark
1988 USA English
56 mins. 16mm color Narrative
Dist. (U.S.): Yankee-Oriole Company
An Empty Bed is a day in the life of Bill Frayne, a gay man in his mid-'60s living alone in Greenwich Village. During the course of this typical day, he encounters people, objects and places, that stir and revive memories from his past. Told largely through flashbacks, the film is a time tapestry where past and present weave together to form a poignant and graceful picture of one man's life.

An Individual Desires Solution
Dir. Brose, Lawrence
1986 USA English
16 mins. 16mm color/b&w Experimental
Dist. (U.S.): Filmmaker's Cooperative
An Individual Desires Solution is about two lovers. One struggles to survive, the other to understand.

Analstahl (Anal Steel)
Dir. Fockele, Jorg, et al
1992 Germany German
15 mins. video color Narrative
Dist. (U.S.): HFF Munchen
A zany, violent tale from a Hamburg filmmaking collective.

Anastasia and the Queen of Hearts
Dir. Atkins, Sharon, and Vaneska Kluck
1994 USA English
5 mins. video color Other
Dist. (U.S.): Atkins, Shawn
An animated love story.

Anatomy of Desire
Dir. Monette, Jean-Francois
Prod. Wilson, David
1995 Canada English
50 mins. video color Documentary
Dist. (U.S.): National Film Board of Canada
Starting with Simon LeVay's current hypothala-

Ⓐ
Ⓑ
Ⓒ
Ⓓ
Ⓔ
Ⓕ
Ⓖ
Ⓗ
Ⓘ
Ⓙ
Ⓚ
Ⓛ
Ⓜ
Ⓝ
Ⓞ
Ⓟ
Ⓠ
Ⓡ
Ⓢ
Ⓣ
Ⓤ
Ⓥ
Ⓦ
Ⓧ
Ⓨ
Ⓩ

mus theory, *Anatomy of Desire* examines the role that science has played in shaping society's understanding of homosexuality throughout the 20th century. Using insightful interviews, medical films and photographs, 1950s educational films, and other historical footage, this documentary makes important links between today's rush to find the cause for homosexuality with the biological determinism that has been used throughout time to single out and oppress different segments of society. Most striking is the footage of the Nazis who used biological theories to bolster their racial hygiene propaganda that sent tens of thousands of gays and lesbians to their deaths in Nazi concentration camps. This important film documents society's continued need to have science define and possibly someday control our very existence.

And the Band Played On
Dir. Spottiswoode, Roger

1993 USA English
100 mins. 35mm color Narrative
Dist. (U.S.): Swank Motion Pictures

We stood warned, going into two and a half hours of the HBO version of Randy Shilts's *And the Band Played On* at the Castro Theater in San Francisco. "As you're watching," the esteemed gay actor and English knight Sir Ian McKellen told us, "imagine someone whose only information about AIDS comes from Jesse Helms and Howard Stern." It was a polite enough disclaimer ("Save your antagonism for the Rush Limbaughs," he also said), but not necessarily easy advice to follow.

Keeping McKellen's arms-length intro in mind, I tried to imagine that the dewy-eyed people leaving the theater were crying about AIDS for the first time. But it didn't work.

Some of the lessons Randy Shilts hands out in *And the Band Played On* have already been turned into public policy (the closing of the bathhouses); others have been made into public property. Since the book's 1987 publication, we've seen *Longtime Companion*, a change of administration, and a shift in public concern about healthcare policy. The kind of corruption Shilts documents in *And the Band Played On* has shown up in as distant parts of pop culture as *The Fugitive*: health care is a business, not a hospice. It's bureaucracy, not individuals, that is evil. It's not necessarily news.

But *And the Band Played On*, an HBO movie, isn't looking for complexity; it's looking for a hero. It's convenient for the dramatic structure of the film—and it works to create sympathy for its own story. Don Francis (played by Matthew Modine) with the Centers for Disease Control and Prevention, like his mythic male compatriots in Hollywood film, is doing overtime in compassion, leaving jelly doughnuts uneaten on the diner counters, spending sleepless nights thinking, and settling for Chinese takeout in late-night sessions trying to get this "Gay Related Immune Deficiency" thing figured out. Lily Tomlin, as the cantankerous Dr. Selma Dritz of the San Francisco Department of Public Health, is on a righteous crusade, cruising the gay bathhouses, confronting the secret STD-doctors of the closeted elite, looking for solutions, providing the necessary outbursts. And Ronald Reagan is the worthy villain, at the top of the bureaucracy heap, announcing an increase in defense spending as Dr. Don scrapes away in his lab, looking for meager funds for a new electron microscope.

It's not a story we would have seen on TV during the Bush years, when something like *Longtime Companion* was content to simply shore up sympathy for victims rather than move on to doling out the blame. It's not the only story that should be seen. But, as you watch the final five minutes, when the AIDS toll is counted, when images of the AIDS quilt are juxtaposed against the Liz Taylor–Elton John spokespeople and homeless people with AIDS, you don't need to imagine a Helms-and-Stern-type viewing audience to see why this TV movie should exist.

Ian McKellen received an Emmy nomination for his performance. (S.G.)

Anders als die Anderen
(Different from the Others)
Dir. Oswald, Richard

1919 Germany German
45 mins. 35mm b&w Narrative
Dist. (U.S.): UCLA Film and Television Archive

Anders als die Anderen is a powerful story of the blackmail of a gay violinist. Paul (Conrad Veidt) at first tries to change his sexual orientation through hypnosis but when that proves ineffective he consults a sexual specialist. He is told that his desires are completely natural and that he should stop paying his blackmailer. This long-lost silent classic was made as a plea for an end to Germany's notorious Paragraph 175 which outlawed homosexual acts between men. Conrad Veidt went on to star in *The Cabinet of Dr. Caligari*, *Casablanca*, and many other films.

Andy Makes a Movie

Dir. Torbet, Bruce

1967 USA English
21 mins. 16mm color Documentary
Dist. (U.S.): Filmmaker's Cooperative
This pop movie about Warhol includes appearances by Henry Geldzahler, Edie Sedgwick, and The Velvet Underground.

Andy the Furniture Maker
Dir. Oremland, Paul

1986 Great Britain English
40 mins. video color Documentary
Dist. (U.K.): Kinesis Films
"I came from a place where you either get a married and get a mortgage, or die on a motorcycle before 18," admits Andy the furniture maker in an aside that's a cue for "Summertime" on the soundtrack and the beginning of a brilliantly upbeat sketch on sex and rebellion.

Andy gives equal time to its subject's life and work. His stubborn, austere furniture is celebrated, historically and anecdotally. Oremland's film caused a small censorship scandal at Channel 4, not so much for its subject as for its sex-positive attitude. Andy is the ideal TV tease—"a bit lippy"—with one eye always scanning for offscreen reaction. "Being a rent boy boring? It's fucking tedious. I don't get an erection when someone wraps a 20 pound note around it. Takes a bit more than that to get me excited." Hypnotic.

Andy Warhol
Prod. Blackwood Productions

1973 USA English
53 mins. 16mm color Documentary
Dist. (U.S.): Blackwood Productions
A look at the art and life of Andy Warhol, featuring narration by Warhol and his contemporaries including Viva, Emile de Antonio, Bridgit Polk, and Paul Morrissey. With excerpts from his films, including *Bike Boy*, *Chelsea Girls*, *Women in Revolt*, *Trash*, *Lonesome Cowboys*, and *I, a Man*.

Angel
Dir. Katakouzinos, George

1982 Greece Greek
120 mins. 35mm color Narrative
Dist. (U.S.): Greek Film Centre
Based on a real criminal case, *Angel* is about a young gay man working the streets as a transvestite prostitute to support his macho sailor lover. The tragedy that unfolds—set in an Athens tourists rarely see—is both beautifully structured and grim. *Angel* has become one of the most successful films in Greek history. Katakouzinos has collaborated with Agnes Varda and Costa-Gavras and has directed several short films, including the award-winning *Nights*. *Angel* is his first feature.

Winner of the 1984 San Francisco International Lesbian & Gay Film Festival Audience Award for Best Feature.

Angel of Woolworths, The
Dir. Black, Julie X.

1994 USA English
10 mins. 16mm color Narrative
Dist. (U.S.): Black, Julie X.
A photobooth romance.

Angelic Conversation, The
Dir. Jarman, Derek
Prod. Mackay, James

1984 Great Britain English
78 mins. 35mm color Experimental
Dist. (U.K.): British Film Institute
Derek Jarman brings to his films a painter's eye, and with it the technical ingenuity by means of which he has devised, out of the marriage of film and video, a whole new palette of visual effects. An example is the characteristic, stroboscopic style of his most recent films—analysing motion into successions of still images not unlike Muybridge or Marey sequence photographs. Jarman has devised a novel technique to attain the effect. The action is first filmed with a stop-motion camera at the rate of around 3 frames per second. The moving image is then reconstituted by projecting at the same rate, and recording from the screen to video. (It is characteristic of Jarman's practical approach to film problems that he is as delighted by the economy of celluloid the device acheives as by the visual conquest.) In the case of *The Angelic Conversation*, the process of successive transfer from Super-8 to low-band video to high-band video to 35mm film obtained the striking textured effect of the images. Jarman's distinctive color effects are produced by processing black-and-white images on video. To achieve particular effects he will sometimes deliberately trick and confuse the electronic equipment—for example, by substituting a bright green gel for the white card ordinarily required for color correction. At the first sight characterized by a system of repetition, *The Angelic Conversation* never succumbs to monotony. The repetitions tend in fact to be variations which serve to concentrate the attention and heighten the significance of small gesture: the

Ⓐ Ⓑ Ⓒ Ⓓ Ⓔ Ⓕ Ⓖ Ⓗ Ⓘ Ⓙ Ⓚ Ⓛ Ⓜ Ⓝ Ⓞ Ⓟ Ⓠ Ⓡ Ⓢ Ⓣ Ⓤ Ⓥ Ⓦ Ⓧ Ⓨ Ⓩ

climactic homoerotic love scene achieves powerful effect just through chaste and tender touching and twining of hands. More than earlier films,
this one demonstrates the meeting of cineast and
painter that gives special character to Jarman's
most successful work. Every image is arresting
for its compositions, its use of mass and shadow,
and of color that is sometimes so elusive that you
are momentarily uncertain whether you see it or
not. Jarman paints in light.

Anguished Love
Dir. Akarasainee, Pisan
1987 Thailand Thai
105 mins. 35mm color Narrative
Dist. (U.S.): Thai Motion Picture Producers
Association
Anguished Love begins with the funeral of
Somying Daorai, who killed himself at the end of
The Last Song when his lover, Boontherm, went
straight. Boontherm, now living with his ex-les-
bian wife, appears at the funeral, enraging
Somying's drag queen friends, who vow revenge.
As luck would have it, Somying has a twin broth-
er, who is brought in to plot Boontherm's demise.

Unfortunately for the vengeful drag
queens, Somnuek (Somying #2) is just as sus-
ceptible to Boon's charms as Somying #1 and
quickly falls in love with his brother's ex.
Meanwhile, the ex-lesbian wife, Orn, is about to
suffer another of the lapses that so enraged her
mother in *The Last Song*. She consults with a few
of her girlfriends (at what may be the first Thai
lesbian potluck ever filmed) and somehow tracks
down her ex-girlfriend Praew, who since having
lost Orn has been living as a semi-lunatic in a
"smelly" part of town.

Alongside all of this is a subplot
about a pudgy gay aristocrat who on a whim bor-
rows money from his lesbian sister to purchase
the Tiffany Club, where Somying formerly sang, a
sort of Drag Queen Central in Pattaya. The club
owner was the Bangkok Post reviewer's favorite:
"Easily the most delightful character . . . his
tantrums are hilarious . . . his promiscuity is both
rollicking fun and a satirical view of the gay
lifestyle. He likes every good-looking boy in sight.
He wears several rings to give away to new partners and is always loaded with cash in the event
he has to buy off other men to take their
boyfriends away from them. What a character!"

As before, we must warn that the
subtitling is occasionally problematic. Prepare to
be lost now and again, but in between enjoy the
les/gay fun.

Anita Bryant: Pie-in-the-Face
Dir. Unknown
1977 USA English
4 mins. 16mm color Documentary
Dist. (U.S.): Olson, Jenni
One of Anita Bryant's "Save Our Children" television news conferences is zapped by a pie-wield-
ing gay activist. A historic document of political
strategy.

Anne Trister
Dir. Pool, Lea
Prod. Frappier, Roger, and Claude Bonin
1985 Canada French
115 mins. 35mm color Narrative
Dist. (U.S.): Telefilm Canada
Dist. (U.K.): British Film Institute
An often melancholy, deliberate work, *Anne
Trister* (triste means sad, in French) is the story
of Anne, a young Jewish painter, who, as the
films opens, is burying her father and grieving
deeply. She decides to leave her boyfriend and go
to Quebec for an indeterminate visit. She looks
up an acquaintance, Alix, a 40-year-old child
psychologist, and moves in with her. Thin, dark,
intense, Anne is obviously adrift; Alix is more
mature and settled, a handsome woman with an
elegant apartment, arrogant boyfriend, and beautiful clothes.

Anne finds herself an enormous studio space, and begins to create a detailed,
abstract mural, from floor to ceiling. This aspect
is the more interesting and unique in the film—
to literally watch the design develop, as Anne
works on a rickety scaffolding with tape, sponges,
and paint, alone with her vision. Director Lea
Pool sets up parallel situations in *Anne Trister*:
Alix is working with an aggressive, difficult child,
Sarah, whose behavior often resembles Anne's.
And when Anne is distraught with Alix at one
point she tries to destroy her magnificent mural.

This is not a fully realized lesbian
love story at all, though both women discard their
boyfriends and acknowledge their need for each
other. And presumably they end up together, following Anne's coming to terms with the loss of
her father. The pace is often frustrating—one
wants the women to be together—but their reluctance and doubts are somehow realistic, especially considering the disparity in their professions and ages, and their former sexual preference.

Annie
Dir. Treut, Monika

1989 Germany English
10 mins. 16mm color Documentary
Dist. (U.S.): First Run Features
Dist. (U.K.): Out On a Limb
Annie, in which sex entertainer Annie Sprinkle transforms herself from plain Jane to a very provocative lady, takes the meaning of "graphic depiction" one step further—to "gynecological," speculum included.

Annie was released in 1993 as part of *Female Misbehaviour* (see separate entry), a package of four short films by Monika Treut.

Anniversary, The
Dir. Christensen, Garth
1995 U.S.A. English
14 mins. 16mm color Narrative
Dist. (U.S.): Christensen Productions
First-time filmmaker Garth Christen-son's *The Anniversary* is a romantic comedy that will charm your socks off. Set in a typical Manhattan apartment building, two couples get their anniversary dates mixed and tensions build. As their spouses prepare fabulous meals, the nosy new neighbor Nancy is trying to be friendly, but only adds to the confusion.

Another Way
(see *Egymasra Nezve*)

Anthem
Dir. Riggs, Marlon
1990 USA English
9 mins. video color Other
Dist. (U.S.): Frameline
Marlon Riggs's new experimental music video politicizes the homoeroticism of African-American men. With images—sensual, sexual, defiant—and words intended to provoke, *Anthem* reasserts our "self-evident right" to life and liberty in an era of pervasive antigay, antiblack backlash and hysterical cultural repression.

Antonia's Line
Dir. Gorris, Marleen
Prod. De Weers, Hans, Antonino Lombardo, and Judy Counihan
1995 Netherlands/Belgium/Great Britain Dutch
93 mins. 35mm color Narrative
Dist. (U.K.): Sales Company, The
The latest feminist allegory from Holland's renowned Marleen Gorris. *Antonia's Line* continues the feminist allegorical themes of Gorris's earlier works (*A Question of Silence*, *Broken Mirrors*, *The Last Island*) as a woman looks back on her life and the lives of her daughter, grand-daughter, and great-granddaughter. Her daughter happens to be a lesbian.

Gorris's vivid characterizations of the denizens of a small Dutch town includes lots of awful, brutal men and wonderful, free-spirited women who play out a violent battle of the sexes throughout the late-20th century. (J.O.)

Anxiety of Inexpression and the Otherness Machine
Dir. Lee, Quentin
1992 USA English
53 mins. video color Experimental
Dist. (U.S.): Lee, Quentin
In *Anxiety of Inexpression and the Otherness Machine*, Lee collapses genres (is this documentary? twisted fiction? or just media-addled autobiography?) along with modesty (is this porn? erotic deconstruction? or just full-blown narcissism?). The ever-peering camcorder captures Lee with friends, family, and especially in brazen repose with his lover. As if in retaliation to the stern image, each sequence is ruptured by self-conscious meditations on the construction of ethnicity and the self within Western culture. *Anxiety of Inexpression* is a cultural travelogue about a gay twenty-something in the deconstruction zone.

Apartment Zero
Dir. Donovan, Martin
1989 Great Britain English
114 mins. 35mm color/b&w Narrative
Dist. (U.S.): n/a
Part black comedy and part erotic thriller, this debut feature film from Argentinian director Martin Donovan revolves around the relationship that develops between Adrian (Colin Firth), an introverted film buff, and his mysterious new roommate Jack (Hart Bochner). Adrian, smitten with the charismatic and apparently omnisexual Jack, welcomes him into his apartment and develops a peculiarly obssessive relationship with him.

Looking like a young Warren Beatty, Bochner swaggers into the hearts, and apartments, of each tenant in Adrian's building. The two nosy elderly women who live downstairs invite him over for a drink and a bit of gossip after he rescues a cat; the drag queen on the second floor has him over after he saves her from being attacked by a man in a movie theater; the macho stud next door gazes longingly into Jack's eyes over a glass of wine at his place; and the lonely wife across the hall leaves her door open for Jack to come in and seduce her. Taking

Ⓐ Ⓑ Ⓒ Ⓓ Ⓔ Ⓕ Ⓖ Ⓗ Ⓘ Ⓙ Ⓚ Ⓛ Ⓜ Ⓝ Ⓞ Ⓟ Ⓠ Ⓡ Ⓢ Ⓣ Ⓤ Ⓥ Ⓦ Ⓧ Ⓨ Ⓩ

Brando, Dean, and Clift as models for his macho posing, Bochner treads the line between caricature and homage. In sunglasses, T-shirt, and tight jeans Bochner displays a charismatic presence which plays brilliantly against Colin Firth's endearingly neurotic Adrian.

References to film history (and, specifically, to gay film history) provide an intriguing backdrop and commentary on the action of the film. In Adrian's apartment, photographs of gay actors (Charles Laughton, Montgomery Clift, James Dean) adorn his living room. And in the movie theater he owns, he runs films like *Compulsion*, Orson Welles's classic psychodrama based on the famous Leopold/Loeb murder case. The sadistic homoerotic relationship between Leopold and Loeb, as it was portrayed in *Compulsion*, is subtly suggestive of the strange relationship between Adrian and Jack.

The erotic tension between the two protagonists is the driving force of the film. And, although the final "consummation" of that tension is far from a happily-ever-after walk into the sunset, it is perversely romantic (along the lines of Hitchcock) in its affirmation of the bond between them. (J.O.)

Aquavitae
Dir. Jopp, Vanessa
1994 Germany German
7 mins. 35mm color Documentary
Dist. (U.S.): Filmschool Munich
In *Aquavitae* director Vanessa Jopp shows a transgender male-to-female self reflecting on the creative potential and limitations of gender.

Aqueles Dois
Dir. Amon, Sergio
1985 Brazil Portuguese
85 mins. 35mm color Narrative
Dist. (U.S.): Embrafilme
Raul, extroverted and funny, has just left a frustrating marriage and spends his time playing sad music in the small flat he shares with a pet canary. Saul is shy, bitter and relentlessly critical of the world around him. He recently attempted suicide. Both men are very lonely and very heterosexual. But when they meet on the first day of work at a government agency, they become drawn to each other and develop a deep, very close friendship. While there is nothing overtly sexual about their relationship they soon discover the extent of their society's homophobia when their colleagues decide that they are gay.

Twenty-five-year-old director Sergio

Amon has created a thought-provoking study of male bonding that beautifully blurs the line between heterosexual and homosexual friendship and affection. *Aqueles Dois* is a production of Roda films, one of the most original and exciting film production companies in Brazil.

Arlene Raven—April '79
Prod. Blumenthal, Lyn, and Kate Horsfield
1979 USA English
40 mins. video color Documentary
Dist. (U.S.): Video Data Bank
A documentary about the life of Arlene Raven, lesbian poet, historian, and cofounder of the Women's Building in Los Angeles.

Armistead Maupin Is a Man I Dreamt Up
Dir. Meynell, Kate
Prod. Clarke, Kristiene
1992 USA English
60 mins. 16mm color Documentary
Dist. (U.K.): BBC TV
Armistead Maupin Is a Man I Dreamt Up is an affectionate portrait of San Francisco, and of the man whose *Tales of the City* have inspired thousands to come here. Maupin relates a life story more bizarre than his fictional characters' (including his meeting Richard Nixon), while local eccentrics and ex-colleagues dish and praise lavishly. Beautifully put together for BBC television by Kate Meynell and Kristiene Clarke, *Armistead Maupin* is also a filmmaker's fascinating attempt to get at the myth and meaning of San Francisco. Appropriately, the mood is capped with music by the Gay Men's Chorus.

Army of Lovers: or Revolt of the Sex Perverts
Dir. von Praunheim, Rosa
1979 Germany English
104 mins. 16mm color Documentary
Dist. (U.S.): Exportfilm Bischoff & Co.
A challenging and controversial film that asks serious questions about gay politics in America, *Army of Lovers* charts the progress of what director Praunheim sees as a losing battle. His images form a picture of a movement talking to itself as he examines the stridencies of political and social extremes within the gay movement. Through a series of interviews interspersed with newsreel footage, still photo montages, and snippets of marches and rallies we are consistently asked to redefine and reexamine the nature and purpose of gay liberation. "Radicalism died in 1973," a grim-voiced narrator intones while

onscreen the former executive director of the National Gay Task Force, Bruce Voeller, is seen on the street wearing a suit and tie. NGTF is described, conversationally, as a "conservative, elitist organization." Anita Bryant, Stonewall, San Francisco's 1977 Gay Freedom Day Parade, and cynical scenes of the cult worship of superstar women by gay men are all included in this radical documentary that has been both praised and condemned by feminists, lesbians, gay men, and straights.

In an interview with Montreal gay publication *Le Berdache*, director Praunheim made his intentions clear: "It's too easy to show homosexuals as victims. To get out of the situation of victim you have to struggle. Gays have been used to hiding and playing a passive role. They are also passive politically . . . when they saw my films, many gays felt hatred and anger for the first time, though it was directed at men and at the films. But that's the reaction I wanted. It's a very important step forward."

Featuring music by the Tom Robinson Band.

Art of Mirrors, The
Dir. Jarman, Derek
1973 Great Britain English
10 mins. 16mm color Experimental
Dist. (U.K.): Basilisk
"*Art of Mirrors* . . . was a breakthrough film for Jarman. In it are the themes and images that reoccur throughout his work. The theatrical positioning of characters . . . , the mesmerized cinema of gestures to his early painting . . ."
—Michael O'Pray

Asa Branca (A Brazilian Dream)
Dir. Batista, Limongi Djalma
1982 Brazil Spanish
90 mins. 35mm color Narrative
Dist. (U.S.): Embrafilme
Djalma Limongi Batista's first feature is a sensual, simple story full of provocative ideas and imagery that have met considerable resistance in Brazil, a country where there are no greater idols than soccer players. *Asa Branca* is the story of a young, handsome, champion athlete who is gay. While this film of homosexual repression and attraction has been publicly condemned by Brazil's soccer establishment, it has nevertheless won major Brazilian film awards as well as a special prize at the 4th Festival des Trois-France. Batista made several short experimental, erotic films as a student at the University of São Paulo

before beginning work on *Asa Branca*.

Ash and Hatred
Dir. Seyger, Israel, and Ido Ricklin
1990 Israel Hebrew
5 mins. 16mm color Other
Dist. (U.S.): Seyger, Israel
Two songs from Israeli lesbian singer Sharon Ben-Ezer.

Assassination
Dir. Gillbergh, Gregory
1994 USA English
28 mins. 16mm color Narrative
Dist. (U.S.): Production Pictures
A New York short story for anyone who has ever experienced awkward moments between appetizers and entrées. Filmed in fake documentary-style flashback, six guests recount the fateful events leading up to one incident. Hugely enjoyable, dry as a martini, *Assassination* is light on gay calories but high in unsaturated style.

Assassination of Anita Bryant, The
Dir. Boyle, Bernie
1977 USA English
3 mins. S8mm color Other
Dist. (U.S.): n/a
A symbolic comedy, nonviolent, of course.

Assembly at Dyke High
Dir. Scooter
Prod. Scooter
1986 USA English
21 mins. video color Other
Dist. (U.S.): n/a
A video of a live performance by the fabulous Dyketones. Great fun, humor, music, and costumes. Lesbian versions of some of the classic pop hits of the past. Poodle skirts and horn-rimmed glasses. Wishful fantasies about favorite female vocalists. Outrageous entertainment.

Assumption, The
Dir. Trubuhovich, May
1993 New Zealand English
4 mins. 16mm color Other
Dist. (U.S.): New Zealand Film Commission
An animated homage to some surprising lesbian icons.

At Home
(see *Babi-It*)

At Home with the Stars
Dir. Westmoreland, Joe
1984 USA English

Ⓐ
Ⓑ
Ⓒ
Ⓓ
Ⓔ
Ⓕ
Ⓖ
Ⓗ
Ⓘ
Ⓙ
Ⓚ
Ⓛ
Ⓜ
Ⓝ
Ⓞ
Ⓟ
Ⓠ
Ⓡ
Ⓢ
Ⓣ
Ⓤ
Ⓥ
Ⓦ
Ⓧ
Ⓨ
Ⓩ

12 mins. video color Documentary
Dist. (U.S.): Westmoreland, Joe
Joe Westmoreland's hilarious *At Home with the Stars* features Patsy Cline and Yma Sumac.

Attendant, The
Dir. Julien, Isaac
1993 Great Britain English
8 mins. 16mm color Experimental
Dist. (U.S.): Frameline
Dist. (U.K.): British Film Institute
The Attendant is older, wiser, black, and works in an art museum, where—with a young white gay boy as his erotic memory—he sees a nineteenth-century painting of slaves in chains come to life.

Audience
Dir. Hammer, Barbara
1982 USA English
33 mins. 16mm b&w Documentary
Dist. (U.S.): Canyon Cinema
Filmed in San Francisco, London, Toronto, and Montreal, lesbian/feminist filmmaker Barbara Hammer explores her audiences, their reactions, their hopes, and their feelings.

Automating
Dir. Behdarvand, Pej
1988 Iran Arabic
6 mins. 16mm color Experimental
Dist. (U.S.): Frameline
A study in human form.

Automolove
Dir. Castro, Rick
1992 USA English
4 mins. video color Other
Dist. (U.S.): Castro, Rick
A sexy guy and his car.

Automonosexual
Dir. Barens, Edgar A.
1988 USA English
3 mins. 16mm b&w Experimental
Dist. (U.S.): Chicago Filmmakers
Automonosexual comes across like a cartoon made from xeroxed Bruce Webers. Edgar Barens shoots his own body in more ways than one. He plays with industrial sounds and metaphors while discovering a new way to photograph an act usually reserved for porn films.

Avonden, De (Evenings, The)
Dir. Van den Berg, Rudolf
1989 Netherlands Dutch
120 mins. 35mm color Narrative
Dist. (U.S.): Netherlands Ministry of Culture

In this alternately arch, mesmerizing, and poignant yarn about fading adolescence and personal transformation, Dutch director Rudolf Van den Berg knits together Oedipal tangles and flickering friendships with a sly dream logic that's both entrancing and terrifying. *The Evenings* is based on renowned gay author Gerard Reve's same-name novel. (Reve also wrote the book that became the movie *The Fourth Man.*) *The Evenings* follows 23-year-old clerk and nascent writer Frits van Etgers through the six days preceding New Year's Eve of 1947. A Holden Caulfieldish figure, Frits is obsessed with time, thinning hair, the dark, sanity, belly-button lint, and a handsome schooldays chum. He endures hilarious meals with his flatulent, deaf father and demandingly eager-to-please mother, with whom he lives. He lurks around public pools with his demented friend Duivenis, a greasy-haired boy torture fantasist. And he stumble through parties, offices, school reunions, and various sexual encounters with the vivid fear and defensive cynicism of a true neurotic.
    Director Van den Berg imagistically threads together themes of coming out, the soul-slaughtering nature of family relationships, and the paradoxically suffocating and freeing nature of time's passage. Along the way he whimsically depicts the ribald sensitivities of a Dutch town gripped by the Christmas spirit. Yes the film's surface comedy only highlights the claustrophobic angst that haunts Frits's dreams—and thus, his lonely life. He has a secret to tell; the film's tension lies in whether or not—and how—he'll tell it. Van den Berg deftly drags us through each of Frits's sexually charged, anxiety-fraught daydreams, irrevocably revealing the desperation of Frits's flight to freedom and his fight for metamorphosis. Even the bathos-heavy denouement, which follows a sidesplitting climactic family meal, fail to mute the film's redemptive power. Frits's ultimate act of communication mirrors our own, perhaps hidden desire to convey ourselves to what sometimes seems a deaf and uncaring world. With Thom Hoffman, Rijk de Gooijer, Viviane de Muynck, Pierre Bokma

Avskedet (Farewell, The)
Dir. Niskanen, Tuija-Maij
1980 Finland/Sweden Finnish
90 mins. 35mm color Narrative
Dist. (U.S.): Finnish Film Archive
Written and directed by women, this powerful story of self-discovery portrays a young lesbian's recollection of, and recovery from, a painful and

lonely childhood. Set in the stale, repressive home of a middle-class Finnish family on the eve of World War II, *Avskedet* follows Valerie from childhood to independence. Faced with cold indifference from her parents, she turns toward her governess for affection. When Valerie eventually finds love with another woman, her father brutally denounces her. She finally breaks free of her family and joins the theater, where she finds her own strength, self-love, and the power to heal.

Awakening of Nancy Kaye, The
Dir. Hershey, Ann
1986 USA English
46 mins. video color Documentary
Dist. (U.S.): Hershey, Ann
A powerful and moving documentary about a disabled woman who is dying of cancer. Her friends admit she can be a difficult person at times and there are emotional issues between her and her family which must be resolved. Yet despite the seriousness of this subject, what are also shown are some of the transcendent qualities of the human spirit which emerge during a time of trial.

Awkward for Years
Dir. Wolfley, Brad
1994 USA English
6 mins. video color Other
Dist. (U.S.): Wolfley, Brad
Exploring the possibilities of adolescent sexuality.

B.U.C.K.L.E.
Dir. Saalfield, Catherine, and Julie Tolentino
1993 USA English
11 mins. video color Other
Dist. (U.S.): Frameline
A few tips on how to pick up girls at The Clit Club in New York City.

Babi-It (At Home)
Dir. Sagalle, Jonathan
1991 Israel Hebrew
29 mins. video color Documentary
Dist. (U.S.): Frameline
In *Baba-It*, director Jonathan Sagalle shares the story of Alex and his older lover Gershon. Both men are playwrights; both men are not equally successful. Yet they manage to maintain a long-time companionship, negotiating sex and love in ways which are all too familiar.

Bachvirus, Het (Bach Virus, The)
Dir. Verhoeven, Robert, and Arnold Vogel
1993 Netherlands Dutch
40 mins. video color Documentary

Dist. (U.S.): Lagestee Film BV
The Bach Virus could only be made in the Netherlands. It's an extraordinarily frank documentary about three gay pedophiles.

Baja Fantasy
Dir. Walters, Jamie
1984 USA English
4 mins. video color Other
Dist. (U.S.): n/a
An exciting juxtaposition of ideas, where we discover daydreaming or reality; both are inviting ways to spend your mind. Starring Jamie Walters himself.

Balancing Factor
Dir. House, Carrie
1993 USA English
33 mins. video color Documentary
Dist. (U.S.): House, Carrie H.
An experimental documentary about Native Gay/Lesbians sharing their regard for balance. Prior to the onslaught of Euro-Americans, Native Gays held special roles. Today these roles still have cultural and environmental significance.

Balcony, The
Dir. Strick, Joseph
1963 USA English
84 mins. 35mm color Narrative
Dist. (U.S.): Kino International
In a nameless revolution-torn country, war goes on, but for brothel boss Shelley Winters it's business as usual. Variety dubbed Winter's character "a lesbian letch" for her on-screen dry kissing with bookkeeper Lee Grant; Peter Falk and Leonard Nimoy bring a surprising degree of muscularity to their roles as the bordello's fantasy-fueled customers. Hardly Genet's ferocious, cynical sexual-political stageplay, but Hollywood at its weirdest and most intriguing.

Ballad of Little Jo, The
Dir. Greenwald, Maggie
1993 USA English
120 mins. 35mm color Narrative
Dist. (U.S.): Films Incorporated
Spring 1993: In the wake of Maggie Greenwald's *The Ballad of Little Jo* and Gus Van Sant's *Even Cowgirls Get the Blues*, the air began to swirl with new tumbleweeds that got this critic thinking new thoughts about female Westerns: what they are, the genre to which they claim to belong, and the reasons why the road to putting cowgirls on the screen leads to such a rough ride.

Enter Maggie Greenwald. Greenwald

Ⓐ
Ⓑ
Ⓒ
Ⓓ
Ⓔ
Ⓕ
Ⓖ
Ⓗ
Ⓘ
Ⓙ
Ⓚ
Ⓛ
Ⓜ
Ⓝ
Ⓞ
Ⓟ
Ⓠ
Ⓡ
Ⓢ
Ⓣ
Ⓤ
Ⓥ
Ⓦ
Ⓧ
Ⓨ
Ⓩ

says she had wanted to make a Western ever since she was a child. Indeed, there's something childishly fairytale-like about *The Ballad of Little Jo*, not at all what you'd expect from the butched-up, rugged, cross-dressing Western the press kit describes. Suzy Amis plays an Eastern society woman who slips up and gets herself pregnant. In short order, she's exiled from her family and community (i.e., the East) to the horrors of poverty, vulnerability, attempted rape, and betrayal (i.e., the West). Traversing the frontier on her own, without protection, she realizes that there's only one way a woman can survive the West: to disappear into manhood. So she cuts off her hair, cuts a scar in her face, changes her clothes, and presto, Josephine is Jo, without even the benefit of the now-fashionable surgical assistance. Little Jo finds the town of Ruby City, where "he" passes, becomes a miner and then a sheepherder, and finally a settled rancher; Jo fights the cattle interests and becomes "just one of the guys" all the way—until death reveals her secret. Greenwald chooses a journey-of-the-innocent structure, and whenever the going gets rough, hey-donny-donny music surges onto the soundtrack and a montage of images tries to move the narrative along to its next high point. I guess that's the "ballad" part of the title.

It's obvious early on that *Ballad* is not a film "about" cross-dressing or sexual transgression, nor about Little Jo's psychology or inner life. Rather, what Greenwald offers is a view of the West from the perspective of a changeling, a creature whose alteration of herself also alters her (and our) experience of the frontier and the kinds of life it dictates to its inhabitants. Greenwald's view of Little Jo's transformation as lack rather than gain is certainly disappointing to viewers in search of lesbian prehistory or convincing butch behaviour (especially so because the film is based on an actual woman, Jo Monaghan, whose true gender was only discovered posthumously). The film does better on what must have been more comfortable ground for its director: the ever presence of male violence—against other men and, in its sexual form, against women—and the absence of female options.

Greenwald wants to immerse us in the brutality of the "real" old West, but along the way she stumbles on to something much more interesting and unexpected: the interplay of race and gender. David Chung plays Tinman, an ailing Chinese worker whom Jo rescues from lynching and takes on as a hired hand. A fellow outsider to the white male West, he immediately detects Jo's true gender and they become secret lovers. While Greenwald seems pretty unconscious of the stereotypes of feminised Asian masculinity that she finds it convenient to deploy here, the scenes of Amis and Chung making love are truly hot, with his long hair and her Nautilised body played for counterpoint. They're also *Ballad's* most transgressive scenes, suggesting the exchange of roles and the interplay of dominance and submission that Greenwald is so loathe to explore in any same-sex pairings.

Actually, Greenwald comes close to doing just that—but the scenes involve Jo and a man, not a woman. Ian McKellen is cast in a minor role as Percy, a woman-hater whose intimate affection for the male Jo turns to rage when he discovers the truth. I don't know whether Greenwald's casting of McKellen here is ironic, iconic, or subtextual red herring, but it's an interesting spin. Jo, however, is ultimately more rancher than cowpoke. For the ever-elusive figure of the cowgirl, look elsewhere.

Cowgirls' Revenge

"Ha!" said Jelly with dramatic disdain. "Movies. There hasn't been a cowgirl in Hollywood since the days of the musical Westerns. The last movie cowgirl disappeared when Roy and Gene got fat and 50. And there's never been a movie about cowgirls. . . . Cowgirls exist as an image. The idea of cowgirls prevails in our culture. Therefore, it seems to me, the fact of cowgirls should prevail. . . . I'm a cowgirl. I've always been a cowgirl. Caught a silver bullet when I was 12. Now I'm in a position where I can help others become cowgirls, too. If a girl wants to grow up to be a cowgirl, she ought to be able to do it, or else this world ain't worth living in."

Enter Gus Van Sant. The infamous Bonanza Jellybean (henceforth Rain Phoenix) delivers this speech in the original Tom Robbins novel, and most of it has made it into the film as well. But perhaps I'm getting ahead of the story. For everyone who postdates the '70s, know that *Even Cowgirls Get the Blues* concerns the adventures of one Sissy Hankshaw (that's Uma Thurman to you), born with giant thumbs and a consequent talent for, uh, hitchhiking. Sissy, star model for the Yoni Yum line of female-hygiene products, is dispatched by her employer, the arch-decadent Countess (John Hurt), to his Rubber Rose dude ranch cum health spa, where he has similarly dispatched a team of German admen to shoot a commercial of her cavorting in nature, in this case, in a pas de deux with a flock of whooping cranes.

Alas, the Rubber Rose manager Miss Adrian (Angie Dickinson) has her hands full, battling a crew of ornery cowgirls who aim to overthrow the patriarchy and restore the ranch, its clients, and herds to the natural state of equilibrium of cowgirls and nature. Oh, and overlooking all the action from his mountain home is the Chink, a Japanese-American escapee from a World War II internment camp misnamed by a renegade group of Native Americans called the Clock People who rescued him from a snowbank. Add to that a serious side-plot concerning the whooping cranes, peyote, the FBI, and a certain Delores Del Ruby (Lorraine Bracco) and you can begin to imagine what Van Sant has taken on. Or can you? The film managed to divide critics by both gender and generation, and only the goddess could have predicted what a mass audience would have made of it. My guess is that it's an instant cult film. For sure, it's the craziest, most gender-bending, transgressive Western that's ever made it to the screen. But remember that this is a film based on a novel that originally appeared in 1976 in serial form in a magazine called *High Times*—and it bears all the marks of its time of origin. For all the buzz, two decades long, regarding *Cowgirls* as a classic feminist text, on closer examination it's no such thing.

The Robbins novel surprises the faulty memory with its determined heterosexuality and male-centered narrative: the narrator is constantly inserting himself into the action and finally even awards himself a central role in the plot. This was great literary fun, but rather undermines the conceptions of the novel as a dyke playground. Instead, it's true to its time, offering a reminder of what sexual liberation, heterosexual-style, was like. Robbins even has Bonanza Jellybean explain all the girl-girl sex to Sissy as just a man-shortage thing. The cowgirls on the Rubber Rose Ranch? "There's not a queer among 'em," declares Bonanza.

Gus Van Sant, bless his soul, has changed things a bit. In fact, he's taken almost every bit of heterosexuality out of the movie (except the Chink, but that's another story) and queered things up. *Cowgirls'* cameos alone are a tip-off that this is no normative biopic: Roseanne Arnold as a palm-reading psychic who angers little Sissy's mother by predicting "lots and lots and lots of women" in her child's future; River Phoenix as a guru-seeking hippy who tells Uma how "bummed out" he and his pals were by the Chink's shaking his wanger at them; William Burroughs as a random pedestrian worried about how gloomy the sky looks.

Bonanza and Sissy fall so sweetly in love that it nearly gave me an acid-flashback to the earliest days of innocence of lesbian-feminism. The cowgirls' debates over group action and gender-appropriate strategies made me remember the worst nightmares of consciousness-raising groups and collective decision-making. My favorite line? "This furniture's too masculine!" The showdowns between Miss Adrian and Delores are hysterical reminders of how the women's movement divided women, with femininity pitted against revolution as either/or decisions. The whole plot of the whooping cranes is probably as good a fantasy as any regarding the origins of eco-feminism.

It may, though, be ahead of its time. Or maybe Gus stumbled on his way to the '70s revival and landed, not in a Robbins-replay commercial dream, but rather in a genuine lesbian-feminist movie. If so, while popular Richard Linklater picks up accolades for *Dazed and Confused*, his bland-revival party movie, Van Sant may suffer the critical scorn usually reserved for women directors. No matter: *Cowgirls* is irresistible fun. But is it a Western? Only a fraction of the film actually takes place at the Rubber Rose ranch: the rest of it transpires in the sites of Sissy's childhood, or in the New York apartments of the Countess or Sissy's erstwhile suitor Julian and his Beautiful People friends, or in one of the mysterious Clock-works, or on the road, à la *My Own Private Idaho*.

Ah, but the Rubber Rose scenes that are there allow us to begin to imagine what a female Western might look like, if one could ever really be made. If, say, *Johnny Guitar* could borrow Susan Sarandon and Geena Davis from *Thelma & Louise* (the closest thing to a female Western so far) and imagine them shooting not at each other but at the good ole boys just outside the circle of firelight. You see, I suspect that the only way a female Western could ever be devised, one that could take advantage of the formulas and retain the magic of the genre, would be to replace race (cowboys versus Indians) with gender (cowgirls versus varmits).

I like to imagine Julie Christie, retrieved from the archaic world of *McCabe and Mrs. Miller*, set into a newfangled Western where she could kick her opium habit and get on with the next chapter. Hey, no one said it would be easy. (B.R.R.)

Ballad of Reading Gaol
Dir. Kwietniowski, Richard
1988 Great Britain English
12 mins. 16mm color Other
Dist. (U.S.): Frameline
Dist. (U.K.): British Film Institute
A unique visual interpretation of Oscar Wilde's defense testimony ("The love that dare not speak its name . . .").

Ballot Measure Nine
Dir. McDonald, Heather
1994 USA English
75 mins. video color Documentary
Dist. (U.S.): Zeitgeist Films
Ballot Measure Nine is a fast-paced crash course in homophobic legislation and the religious right that details Oregon's 1992 antigay ballot.

Bar Girls
Dir. Hoffman, Lauran
1995 USA English
95 mins. 35mm color Narrative
Dist. (U.S.): Orion Classics
Writer/producer Lauran Hoffman dishes up L.A.-style lesbian love drama to rival the theatrics of "Melrose Place": Big hair, prime-time—style punch lines, tacky sets—only the hot topless middle-class lesbian sex puts this film in another ratings category. Not that *Bar Girls*—originally a play before it became a film, directed by Marita Giovanni, really cares. The story of Loretta—who's fallen for Rachel, who also likes J.R., who ends up getting it on with Loretta instead of Rachel—*Bar Girls* is a comedy that isn't seeking to revolutionize the world, it just wants to have a drink with it. (S. G.)

Bar Time
Dir. Kalmen, Michael
1979 USA English
24 mins. video color Narrative
Dist. (U.S.): n/a
A San Francisco soap opera.

Bar Yoga
Prod. Deep, Meaningful, Sincere Performance Art Company
1984 USA English
10 mins. video color Other
Dist. (U.S.): n/a
Excellent talk-show satire. Biting parody on the human condition, and the faux pas we'd like to see.

Bare

Dir. Tien
1991 Canada English
15 mins. video color Documentary
Dist. (U.S.): Video Out
Bare uses the documentary form to explore an unconventional subject matter—women who shave their heads. Three women talk about various personal experiences, touching on issues of identity and retaliation over the stereotyping of women of color, and how they use shaving as a personal, political action to achieve empowerment.

Barely Human
Dir. Reinke, Steve
1992 Canada English
4 mins. video color Experimental
Dist. (U.S.): Reinke, Steve
Canadian Steve Reinke takes brief images from gay porn and turns them into something lyrical and resonant.

Bashing
Dir. Lamble, David
1991 USA English
10 mins. video color Documentar
Dist. (U.S.): Lamble, David
America's Most Wanted: Bashing is a powerful, angry-making collage of antigay hate crimes.

Basic Instinct
Dir. Verhoeven, Paul
1992 USA English
127 mins. 35mm color Narrative
Dist. (U.S.): Films Incorporated
Queer Nation and queer journalists have expressed outrage at contemporary representations of gays and lesbians in Hollywood mainstream films. Little has appeared in print to date that takes issue with the general denouncement of a homophobic industry which, the critics claim, is intent upon inspiring murderous desires in their largely heterosexual audiences. But, I think, the protests against *Basic Instinct* and *The Silence of the Lambs* are missing the point.

It seems to me that we are at a peculiar time in history, a time when it is becoming impossible to tell the difference between homophobia and representations of homophobia. We might read the emergence of cultural watchdogs like Queer Nation as a sign that people are confused about representation, about interpretation, about the difference between depiction and stereotyping. In the example of *The Silence of the Lambs*, it is quite possible to argue that

Buffalo Bill, the murderer who skins his female victims in order to build "a woman suit," is not reducible to "homosexual," or "transsexual"; he is simply a man at odds with gender identity. Indeed, Buffalo Bill could be another victim of the heterosexist culture which believes that anatomy is destiny.

In the more recent case of *Basic Instinct*, the signs of homophobia and misogyny are even more difficult to read. After all, like *Thelma & Louise*, this is a film about women who kill, women who stand up to male aggression, manipulate male sexuality, and refuse to be bullied into some kind of conventional submission. Furthermore, *Basic Instinct* pays careful attention to the issue of representation by making the heroine a writer, a novelist who plots murders that then occur in real life. The police and police psychiatrists (almost all men) are confused by the relationship between fiction and truth: did the murderer plot the novels to give herself the perfect alibi ("I am not stupid; I wouldn't depict a murder and then enact it, it would be too obvious")? Or did she become so enamored with her fictions that she feels compelled to carry them out?

Basic Instinct is a smart enough film not to resolve the problem of the relationship between representations and actions. It is enough that this relationship emerges as strained and contested. Queer Nation, of course, thinks they know exactly what the terms of this relationship are and so they began their protests before the film had even been completed! At a time when our government seems all too eager to censor depictions of alternative sexualities because, supposedly, they are dangerous and may produce perversion, it is extremely problematic for the gay community to counterprotest "straight" representation. Being too literal-minded, indeed, puts us right in the trenches with antiporn groups and censors who think that there is a simple and unitary relation between seeing and doing, fantasy and reality, perversion and corruption.

While I understand that Hollywood harbors all kinds of homophobic sentiment and closeted hatred, I do not think that it does us any good to police mainstream representations of queer characters. Also, it is quite possible that these "queer" protests conceal differences between gay male audiences and lesbian audiences. It would be interesting to find out if as many lesbians were offended by *The Silence of the Lambs* and *Basic Instinct* as gay men. After all these are both films featuring strong female

characters in positions of great power. It is possible that the so-called offensive images provoke outrage largely from men because men are not used to seeing women hunt and stalk male prey.

I would like to offer a slightly different reading of *Basic Instinct* since I viewed it as a film about the objectification of men, and even as a film about the "lesbianization" of straight sex. Catherine Tramel, you will notice, has a long-term relationship with a woman Roxie and fucks men for fun while Roxie watches. Michael Douglas's character is obviously threatened by the bonds between women which seem almost to turn him into a sex toy, a body attached to a dildo, in fact. In one scene he encounters Roxie in the bathroom after he has finished fucking Catherine. He asks her to talk to him "man to man" but his fake bravado falters as he learns that Catherine likes Roxie to watch her sexual encounters with men. Douglas is naked, Roxie is clothed, and it is he who looks fragile and vulnerable. In a way, this scene inverts the homophobic triangle of heterosexual pornography which portrays two women having sex while a man looks on. Now, the dyke lover watches the heterosexual sex for her own enjoyment. Furthermore, Douglas is hardly a symbol of virile domination. Douglas, in fact, is positively feminized in the film.

So, let me be the first to "out" Michael Douglas: to end all further speculation, Michael Douglas is definitely a lesbian. He still seems a little behind the times, however, since he seems to think that one date, one fuck, means he should marry his lover, but Catherine has ways of fixing his nostalgia; she carries an ice pick along with her on dates and is sure to brandish it whenever he starts talking about marriage and kids and a happy ever after.

Douglas actually "comes out" in the movie on the night when he follows Catherine to a dance club. In the club he wears a rather low-cut sweater that shows just enough of his cleavage. The sweater comes off later and Catherine pays serious attention to his small but firm breasts. On the morning after the night before, Michael follows Catherine to her Marin hideout. It is obvious he is feeling vulnerable so he wears his butchest outfit—501s, a sweater, and a bomber jacket. Later that day, he forces his rival, Roxie, to drive her car off the road and gets ready to replace her as Catherine's lesbian lover.

All the women in *Basic Instinct*, (and some of the men apparently) are lesbians. They also all seem to be in on some violent conspiracy to kill men. In fact any man in the film who ever

(A)
(B)
(C)
(D)
(E)
(F)
(G)
(H)
(I)
(J)
(K)
(L)
(M)
(N)
(O)
(P)
(Q)
(R)
(S)
(T)
(U)
(V)
(W)
(X)
(Y)
(Z)

utters a misogynist comment seems to end up with an ice pick in the brain. What exactly are the protesters in Queer Nation and elsewhere angry about then, given that this film punishes misogyny and suggests that beneath all heterosexual relations lies a complicated web of sexual relations between women? The protesters claim, of course, that Hollywood never gives us any positive images of gay men and lesbians; Hollywood, they claim, will only show queers as killers and psychopaths.

But what about the positive depictions? We tend to consider films like the recent *Fried Green Tomatoes* as "positive," as gay or lesbian sensitive. I will go out on a limb here and say that I would rather see lesbians depicted as outlaws and destroyers than cozy, feminine, domestic, tame lovers. *Fried Green Tomatoes* has been given awards by GLAAD and other gay and lesbian groups for its "outstanding depiction of lesbians in a film." Well, I may have looked away for a moment but I didn't see any lesbians in that film. I saw two women "friends" who were close and affectionate but who never kissed, never really touched. At least in *Basic Instinct* women kissed and fondled each other. The Idgie character in *Fried Green Tomatoes* was totally unconvincing as the hard-drinking, card-playing, whore-visiting butch of the novel. In the novel, Idgie is often mistaken for a boy; the film erases all of Idgie's fundamental masculinity, and it does so precisely because her butchness would have suggested the lesbian nature of the relationship.

Invisibility, in fact, can often do much more damage than visibility. But we do not hear about protesters outraged by the invisible butch and the muted lesbianism in *Fried Green Tomatoes* because this movie is a feel-good film (despite the fact that it too implicates lesbians in the killing of men) and we think of it as "positive." Positivity and negativity, finally, are obviously not the best standards to use when measuring the political impact of any given representation. We need to be more creative in our interpretations, more willing to use Hollywood and quicker to "out" straight actors as the lesbian wannabes that they really are. (J.H.)

Basic Instincts
(see *Frau und Geschlecht*)

Basic Necessities
Dir. Miller, Tanya
1993 USA English
10 mins. video color Experimental
Dist. (U.S.): Miller, Tanya
Basic Necessities is an impactful poetic narrative exploring the effects of sex work on a lesbian couple.

Basket Case
Dir. Huestis, Marc
1978 USA English
15 mins. S8mm color Narrative
Dist. (U.S.): Outsider Enterprises
The Wizard of Oz meets *Carrie* on the streets of San Francisco.

Bathroom Gender
Dir. Ashley, Carol, and Kathy Clarke
1990 USA English
7 mins. video color Experimental
Dist. (U.S.): Clash Pictures
Dist. (U.K.): Cinenova
Recalling early gender limitation/formation, two women enact male bathroom rituals with style and fun.

Battle of Tuntenhaüs, The
Dir. Bashore, Juliet
1991 Great Britain English
24 mins. video color Documentary
Dist. (U.K.): Maya Vision
Lesbians and gays from around the world have created a variety of housing situations that reflect their lifestyles, as well as their social and political status. Tuntenhaüs—literally the "house of queers"—was, until recently, a squat in East Berlin. This gritty verité documentary follows the thirty gay men of Tuntenhaüs through the dark days of anarchy and riots that followed German reunification.

BD Women
Dir. Blackman, Inge
Prod. Edwards, Deanne
1994 Great Britain English
20 mins. video color Documentary
Dist. (U.K.): Jane Balfour Films
The teaching of black history has been traditionally male and the teaching of women's history has been traditionally white. If you're a black-identified lesbian, where do you go to learn about your history? The subjects of Inge Blackman's *BD Women* suggest it is possible to create one's own history. This stylish documentary gives a thorough overview of how black lesbians in Great Britain and the Carribean cope with identity and sexuality in a queer community that typically overlooks racism.

Be Careful What Kind of Skin You Pull Back, You Never Know What Kind of Head Will Appear

Dir. Bruning, Jurgen
1994 Germany German
26 mins. video color Experimental
Dist. (U.S.): Jurgen Bruning Filmproduktion
"Skinheads are the macho clones of the '90s," declares one interviewee featured in the film. Be Careful is a provocative essay about the eroticism—and political antecedents—of the gay skinhead lifestyle.

Be My Valentine

Dir. Sandler, Carl
1995 USA English
10 mins. video color Documentary
Dist. (U.S.): Sandler, Carl
A lyrical documentary about the ways young gay men look for love and acceptance.

Bears in the Hall

1994 Canada English
5 mins. video color Other
Dist. (U.S.): n/a
What you should do if you encounter a bear, in Bears in the Hall.

Bears Will Be Bears

Dir. Spero, Chuck
1995 USA English
4 mins. video color Other
Dist. (U.S.): Spero, Chuck
Another bear video from the groundbreaking Lions & Tigers & Chubs & Bears program.

Beauties without a Cause

Dir. Weissman, David
1986 USA English
7 mins. 16mm color Narrative
Dist. (U.S.): Frameline
Four lawless drag queens prepare for a night of light crime.

Beauty, Fame, Wealth, and Tears

Dir. Gundlach, Dan
1983 USA English
3 mins. S8mm color
Dist. (U.S.): n/a
Part of the 1983 Super 8 Gay Film Festival.

Because Reality Isn't Black and White

[work in progress]
Dir. Anderson, Kelly
1992 USA/Cuba English
9 mins. video color Documentary
Dist. (U.S.): Anderson, Kelly
Because Reality Isn't Black and White is about the reality of lesbian and gay life in Cuba.

Because the Dawn

Dir. Goldstein, Amy
1988 USA English
40 mins. 16mm color Narrative
Dist. (U.S.): Women Make Movies
The smoky feel of film noir and the sultry rhythms of swing music frame a mysterious and romantic vampire tale in Because the Dawn, a new film by Amy Goldstein, the award-winning director of Commercial for Murder.

Marie has been alive for centuries— living off her victims' blood. Her thirst is driven by a desire to be recognized by the light of day and to feel more a part of the world around her.

At dusk in a cemetery overlooking Manhattan she sees a disheveled, good-looking photographer, Ariel. Through her camera, Ariel catches sight of Marie and is captivated. The exquisitely erotic relationship that develops between the women takes place against an evocative backdrop of New York City at night.

Edwige Belmore (the vampire Marie) is a French recording artist and cabaret performer who plays the saxophone, sings, models, and has acted in numerous films. Sandy Gray (Ariel) has appeared in Francis Coppola's One from the Heart and Mel Brooks's To Be or Not To Be, among other films.

Because This Is About Love

Dir. Ong, Shu Lee
1990 USA English
28 mins. video color Documentary
Dist. (U.S.): Filmmaker's Library
A documentary that looks at marriage in the lesbian and gay community. Shu Lee Ong's Because This Is About Love profiles six same-sex couples who have made lifelong commitments through some form of marriage. Through interviews and footage of actual ceremonies, Because This Is About Love reveals why some same-sex couples would want to marry despite the lack of legal and social support.

Because We Must

Dir. Atlas, Charles
1989 Great Britain English
50 mins. video color Experimental
Dist. (U.S.): Electronic Arts Intermix
Dist. (U.K.): Channel 4 Television
Because We Must starts with Michael Clark puk-

Ⓐ Ⓑ Ⓒ Ⓓ Ⓔ Ⓕ Ⓖ Ⓗ Ⓘ Ⓙ Ⓚ Ⓛ Ⓜ Ⓝ Ⓞ Ⓟ Ⓠ Ⓡ Ⓢ Ⓣ Ⓤ Ⓥ Ⓦ Ⓧ Ⓨ Ⓩ

ing on the camera lens. Clark is the epitome of London's post-punk arty gay scene; like Derek Jarman, he's become increasingly both outspoken politically and respected professionally. *Because We Must* is a recording of the same-name show that first played at Sadlers Well, London, in 1989, put together with canny style by director Charles Atlas (who made the earlier Clark portrait, *Hail the New Puritan*, shown at the 1987 festival). Onstage: Marilyn lookalikes pose while a girl with a chain saw decapitates a colleague, all to a Chopin sonata. Backstage: Clark gives a lipsticky smile to the camera, and runs about changing his Leigh Bowery and Bodymap costumes every two minutes. The show hops backward in time to the sixties, from a comic, queeny cover of Ebony and Ivory, to T-Rex, Blue Meenies, and psychedelia—with a pitstop for pub-set Cockney songs and choreography. Strange by even British standards, *Because We Must* is possibly the queerest thing in this year's festival.

Bedtime Stories
Dir. Hammer, Barbara
1989 USA English
33 mins. video color Experimental
Dist. (U.S.): Hammer, Barbara
I: The Wet Dream—Questions of seduction, viewer/viewed, and personal stories are collaged in this heavily postproduced account of a "hot tub relationship."

II: The Erotic Intellect—Shot in Garbo's Hairdressing Salon, Hammer suggests intellectual stimulation to be as provocative as overt sexuality.

III: Clip, Grab, and Paint—A sunstroke delirium as the videographer identifies with Georgia O'Keeffe and her radio obituary using a frame buffer and computer program for paintbrush and easel.

Bedtime Stories [work in progress]
Dir. Friedrich, Su
1994 USA English
10 mins. video color Other
Dist. (U.S.): Friedrich, Su
A quick glimpse at Su Friedrich's forthcoming feature-length tale of growing up lesbian.

Beefcake Cheesecake
Dir. unknown
1983 USA English
13 mins. video color Other
Dist. (U.S.): n/a
Archival '50s porno, well edited, that will be cherished forever.

Before Stonewall
Dir. Schiller, Greta, and Robert Rosenberg
1985 USA English
87 mins. 16mm color Documentary
Dist. (U.S.): Frameline
From the sexual experimentations of the roaring twenties, to the scapegoating of homosexuals during the McCarthy era, to the developement of the early homophile rights movement, *Before Stonewall* presents a unique portrait of the history of the homosexual experience in America. Archival research director: Andrea Weiss; narrated by Rita Mae Brown.

Before the Act
Dir. Butler, Kenneth
1987 Great Britain English
25 mins. 16mm color Documentary
Dist. (U.K.): British Film Institute
A documentary about the 1967 Sexual Offences Act in England, which decriminalized homosexuality between consenting males over the age of twenty-one.

Behind Every Good Man
Dir. unknown
1965 USA English
20 mins. 16mm color Documentary
Dist. (U.S.): Stevenson, Jack
A peek at the life of a black transvestite from the 1960s.

Behind Glass
Dir. Van Ieperen, Ab
1981 Netherlands Dutch
69 mins. 16mm color Narrative
Dist. (U.S.): Frameline
Behind Glass deals with the tensions that can arise in a homosexual relationship between two people of very different social and cultural backgrounds. The film revolves around David, Thomas and Marina. David makes information programs for radio. Thomas is a window washer and is taking a correspondence course. Marina has a daughter and is a close friend of David. Wanting nothing more than to be happy, David and Thomas find their lives disintegrating into a series of small wars over class, education, money, and sex.

Behind the Fence
Dir. Chamberlain, Robert F.
1980 USA English
4 mins. S8mm color
Dist. (U.S.): n/a

A glimpse of the boy next door . . .

Being at Home with Claude
Dir. Beaudin, Jean
1992 Canada French
84 mins. 35mm color Narrative
Dist. (U.S.): Strand Releasing
Dist. (U.K.): Dangerous To Know
Based on the controversial stage play by Rene-Daniel Dubois, *Being at Home with Claude* is everything New Queer Cinema was hyped up to be, and wasn't. Queer criminality meets aching romanticism in a daring, moving illustration of Wilde's sober maxim: "each man kills the thing he loves." Opening with a stunning montage sequence in which the man is, literally, fucked to death, the mystery of the film is not whodunit, but why. A hustler (Roy Dupuis) confesses to the murder, but the law, in the shape of an unarmed police inspector (Jacques Grodin) requires a motive. What follows is an extended dialogue between a gay outlaw and the voice of a shocked society. The prospect of 84 minutes in the company of two main characters enclosed by a single set might not sound like a bag o' thrills but there is more drama to be found than in many other recent gay movies. The lead performances are superb, the direction is tighter than a hustler's vest, and if the opening scene doesn't have you gasping for breath, you're probably dead already.

Bel Ragazzo
Dir. Bensoussan, George
1986 Italy French
12 mins. 35mm color Narrative
Dist. (U.S.): Unifrance Film
A young Italian stops at a filling station on the freeway, and having some time to kill, telephones a friend. He recounts his adventures as a hustler, but in doing so a sudden awareness causes him to reconsider certain values that had escaped him, bringing him face-to-face with himself.

Belle
Dir. Achten, Irma
1993 Netherlands Dutch
99 mins. 35mm color Narrative
Dist. (U.S.): Holland Film Promotion
This stunning debut feature from Dutch lesbian filmmaker Irma Achten portrays the life story of Belle, a woman in search of herself and the meaning of life. Crisply photographed and poetically constructed, this tender tale follows in the footsteps of Dutch director Annette Apon's 1989 magical-realist feature, *Crocodiles in Amsterdam*.
Drawing on operatic and poetic conventions, director Achten presents Belle as a sort of Everywoman who confronts the ethical, existential, and moral issues of modern times. The haunting existential figure of "The Man" appears at critical moments in Belle's life to remind her of her mortality. A feminist cross between *Citizen Kane* and *Wings of Desire*, Belle never wavers from its woman-focused center. Belle's lifelong commitment to her lover, Marthe, is the emotional linchpin of her life. But when Belle's desperate desire for independence mutates into an obsession with power and control, she pushes Marthe out of her life. Although Belle marries as a means to independence ("I never had any illusions, I can do exactly what I like"), her repressed love for Marthe continues to influence her life.

Beloved Murderer
Dir. Kull, Heidi
1993 Germany German
8 mins. video b&w Narrative
Dist. (U.S.): Frameline
Two lesbian hit women are hired to bump each other off in Heidi Kull's darkly romantic animated film noir.

Beneath the Surface
Dir. Johns, Jennifer
1993 USA English
26 mins. 16mm color Experimental
Dist. (U.S.): Johns, Jennifer
A portrait of the filmmaker's struggle to come to terms with her mother's death from breast cancer.

Bent Time
Dir. Hammer, Barbara
1984 USA English
22 mins. 16mm color Experimental
Dist. (U.S.): Canyon Cinema
Dist. (U.K.): London Filmmaker's Co-op
In *Bent Time* Barbara Hammer attempts to capture in pictures the scientific theory that light rays curve at the outer edges of the universe, leading scientists to theorize that time bends.
Released by Facets Multimedia in the U.S. along with four of her other short films as a feature-length package, *Perceptual Landscapes: The Films of Barbara Hammer, Volume III*.

Berenice Abbott:
A View of the 20th Century
Dir. Wheelock, Martha and Kay Weaver
1993 USA English
57 mins. 16mm color Documentary
Dist. (U.S.): Ishtar Films

Ⓐ Ⓑ Ⓒ Ⓓ Ⓔ Ⓕ Ⓖ Ⓗ Ⓘ Ⓙ Ⓚ Ⓛ Ⓜ Ⓝ Ⓞ Ⓟ Ⓠ Ⓡ Ⓢ Ⓣ Ⓤ Ⓥ Ⓦ Ⓧ Ⓨ Ⓩ

A portrait of one of the richest careers in the history of photography. The 92-year-old Abbott shines as she talks about her life, her work, and her circle of friends which included such famous artists and writers as James Joyce, Andre Gide, and Janet Flanner. Focusing on Abbott's prolific work as an artist, the film also reveals clues about her relationships with women, including such notable contemporaries as Djuna Barnes and Edna St. Vincent Millay. Extensive archival film footage and photographs are complemented by interviews with scholars, as filmmakers Martha Wheelock and Kay Weaver trace the fascinating life of this remarkable lesbian of the twentieth century.

This thorough and engaging biography traces Abbott's life from her Ohio roots, to her days in Paris during the '20s, her documentation of New York in the '30s, her landmark studies of science in the '50s, and her portraits of small town America. *Berenice Abbott: A View of the 20th Century* reveals the life of one of our greatest woman artists, who not only endured—but triumphed—writing books, patenting inventions, teaching at prestigious universities, and giving the world a grand body of work.

Berlin Affair, The
Dir. Cavani, Lilliana
1985 Italy/West Germany English
121 mins. 35mm color Narrative
Dist. (U.S.): MGM Classics
Berlin in the late thirties, Louise von Hollendorf, wife of a high-ranking diplomat, idly whiles away her days at cocktail parties, playing tennis, in painting and drawing classes. But her privileged upper-class lifestyle is shaken when she meets Mitsuko Matsigae, the young attractive daughter of the Japanese amabassador, who arouses emotions in Louise that she has never felt before. After their torrid love affair begins, Mitsuko's male lover attempts to blackmail them, then Heinz, Louise's husband, gets involved in the ménage, with Mitsuko playing husband against wife against blackmailer, so nobody knows who Mitsuko really loves. The sex scenes between the women are some of the most beautiful in the film, with hair tugging and the knotting and unknotting of both bodies and silk. The hetero-humping scenes come off a poor second. Director Liliana Cavani (*The Night Porter*) combines treachery, sleeping powders, poisons, and international intrigue for a sensationalistic, pretentious, and often ludicrous yet thoroughly entertaining movie experience.

Bertrand Disparu (Bertrand Is Missing)
Dir. Mimouni, Patrick
1986 France French
44 mins. 35mm color Narrative
Dist. (U.S.): Les Films du Labyrinthe
In Paris, Bertrand, 12, runs away from home. While trying to steal something to eat in a supermarket, he meets Boris who saves him from getting into trouble and lets him stay at his home. Boris is an odd sort of man and Bertrand an odd sort of boy. They gradually become acquainted . . .

Winner of the 1988 San Francisco International Lesbian & Gay Film Festival Audience Award for Best Short Film.

Bete Noire
Dir. Hunt, Victoria
1994 Australia English
15 mins. 16mm b&w Narrative
Dist. (U.S.): Frameline
Bete Noire takes a film noir shot at girls, guns, and ventolin.

Betty Kaplowitz
Dir. Marie, Pat
1979 USA English
8 mins. video color Documentary
Dist. (U.S.): n/a
In performance.

Betty Walters Show, The
Dir. Brune, Charles
1983 USA English
45 mins. video color Other
Dist. (U.S.): n/a
A scathing parody of Barbara Walters. In this edition she remembers her four favorite interviews: Tallulah Bankhead, Greta Garbo, Mae West, and Joan Crawford. It is video history.

Between Two Worlds
Dir. Nash, Mark
1993 Great Britain English
27 mins. 16mm color Narrative
Dist. (U.K.): British Film Institute
A white boy and his shrink: Mark Nash's *Between Two Worlds* features Jason Durr—the white punk in Isaac Julien's *Young Soul Rebels*—as Graham, who, when not working in a flower shop, develops an intense relationship with Dr. Ludwig, his Czechoslovakian analyst. Graham thinks he might be gay; Paul, the florist's owner, definitely is.

Beyond Gravity
Dir. Maxwell, Garth
1988 New Zealand English

48 mins. 16mm color Narrative
Dist. (U.S.): Frameline
Dist. (U.K.): Dangerous To Know
Richard is a reserved, thoughtful lab technician with an obsessive interest in astronomy—he fantasizes about the destruction of the Earth by the Sun. Johnny is so eccentric and unpredictably romantic that he seems to have come from another planet. This may be why they are drawn to each other in *Beyond Gravity*, the offbeat, charming story of the chaotic love that develops between these mismatched young New Zealanders. While Richard initially finds Johnny's relentless pursuit disruptive and unappealing (he has recently broken up with a lover and says he's not ready for a new romance), the dark, handsome Italian proves impossible for Richard to resist.

Beyond Imagining: Margaret Anderson & the Little Review
Dir. Weinberg, Wendy
1991 USA English
30 mins. 16mm color Documentary
Dist. (U.S.): Women Make Movies
The Oscar-nominated *Beyond Imagining: Margaret Anderson & the Little Review* is about a remarkable woman whose *Little Review* published work by Gertrude Stein, Djuna Barnes, Emma Goldman, and many other great writers. This profile of Anderson's life, loves, and work details her extensive travels and her "romantic friendships" with coeditor Jane Heap and singers Georgette Leblanc (with whom she is buried) and Dorothy Caruso (Enrico's widow).

Beyond Outcasts
(see *Al Margen del Margen*)

Beyond/Body/Memory
Dir. Dosanjh, Neesha
1993 Canada English
5 mins. video color Experimental
Dist. (U.S.): n/a
Beyond/Body/Memory uses body movement and gesture to express a woman's struggle with and emergence from the effects of child abuse on her sense of self and sexuality.

Bi-Ways
Dir. Shimazaki, Paul and Prescott Chow
1993 USA English
5 mins. video color Other
Dist. (U.S.): San Francisco AIDS Foundation/Prevention Dept.
A bizarre commentary on the cult of cuteness.

Bicentennial Movie, A
Dir. Ward, Ken
1977 USA English
7 mins. S8mm color Other
Dist. (U.S.): n/a
Two conflicting views of our late (great?) two-hundredth birthday by a novice filmmaker. A verité classic.

Biennale Apollo
Dir. Bussotti, Sylvano
1989 Italy Italian
6 mins. 35mm color Other
Dist. (U.K.): Basilisk
Biennale Apollo is a short, Venice-set musical, with John Janssen and Enzo F. Carabba.

Big Fat Slenderella
Dir. Boschman, Lorna
Prod. Western Front
1993 Canada English
15 mins. video color Other
Dist. (U.S.): Video Out
Big Fat Slenderella is a humorous and fast-paced look at dieting from the fat person's point of view. Interviews with fat persons are juxtaposed with commercial spoofs that satirize the mainstream obsession with dieting.

Big Time Wrestlers from Hollywood
Dir. Hunt, Hubbard
1950 USA English
5 mins. 16mm b&w Other
Dist. (U.S.): Stevenson, Jack
Big Time Wrestlers from Hollywood stars June Adair, "The Battling Ballerina" versus Lynn O'Conner, "The Lovely Terror."

Bigger Splash, A
Dir. Hazan, Jack
1973 Great Britain English
105 mins. 16mm color Documentary
Dist. (U.S.): n/a
A portrait of British artist David Hockney.

Bike Boy
Dir. Warhol, Andy
1967 USA English
110 mins. 16mm b&w Narrative
Dist. (U.S.): Museum of Modern Art
Young working-class motorcyclist Joe Spencer is everyone's object of desire. But he's decidedly out of his element in the sophisticated world of Warhol's superstar friends—Viva, Ingrid Superstar, Brigid Polk, and Ed Weiner.

Ⓐ Ⓑ Ⓒ Ⓓ Ⓔ Ⓕ Ⓖ Ⓗ Ⓘ Ⓙ Ⓚ Ⓛ Ⓜ Ⓝ Ⓞ Ⓟ Ⓠ Ⓡ Ⓢ Ⓣ Ⓤ Ⓥ Ⓦ Ⓧ Ⓨ Ⓩ

Bill and Ted's Homosexual Adventure
Dir. Freeman, Chris and Jon Ginoli
1993 USA English
4 mins. video color Other
Dist. (U.S.): Pansy Division
A porno music video.

Bill Pope: Portrait of a Native Son
Dir. Pope, Bill
1985 USA English
22 mins. video color Documentary
Dist. (U.S.): n/a
An autobiographical account by a gay San Franciscan covering his childhood in the city, his memories of the '60s, and experiences in the Peace Corps in Latin America, as well as his response to being diagnosed with ARC and what he has been doing since that time.

Billy Turner's Secret
Dir. Mayson, Michael
1990 USA English
26 mins. 16mm color Narrative
Dist. (U.S.): Frameline
Billy and Rufus live together and share everything, except Billy's secret—he's gay. Rufus just isn't ready to deal with it. A hip black comedy about street attitudes and coming to terms with the big picture.

Bird in the Hand
Dir. Nelson, Melanie and Catherine Saalfield
1992 USA English
25 mins. video color Narrative
Dist. (U.S.): Frameline
Dist. (U.K.): Cinenova
Portrays a jealous triangle. Simone and Kaye are lovers trying desperately to escape New York City and the reality of their friend Ayo's abusive relationship.

Birds of a Feather
(see Sech Wie Pech & Schwefel)

Birthday Party
Dir. Reiter, Jill
1994 USA English
9 mins. video color Other
Dist. (U.S.): Reiter, Jill
A drag queen mom throws her dyke daughter a surreal sweet sixteen party where the entertainment includes a tattooed gay boy go-go dancer and a human piñata that ejaculates presents when caressed.

Birthday Party at Repitition Cafe, The
Dir. Levy, Wendy
1992 USA English
14 mins. 16mm color Narrative
Dist. (U.S.): Crazy Heart Films
A lesbian struggles to overcome her grief over the death of a gay male friend.

Birthday Tribute to Dame Edna Everage, A (BBC Arena)
Dir. Jebb, Julian
1984 Great Britain English
60 mins. video color Documentary
Dist. (U.K.): BBC TV
As much a parody of the typical BBC documentary style as an extravagant curtsy to Dame Edna Everage, Housewife Superstar. The Dame is known here largely through her network special broadcast late last year; in Britain s/he is a household name. This 1984 birthday tribute—subtitled La Dame Aux Gladioli: The Agony and Ecstasy of Edna Everage—is a deeply probing investigative profile of one of the world's spookiest celebrities.

Bisexual Kingdom, The
Dir. Schroder, Elizabeth G.
1987 Canada English
22 mins. video color Narrative
Dist. (U.S.): V-Tape
The Bisexual Kingdom, where girl meets girl, still likes boy, and all hell breaks loose.

Bit of Scarlett, A
Dir. Weiss, Andrea
Prod. Dobbs, Rebecca
1995 Great Britain English
70 mins. 35mm color/b&w Other
Dist. (U.K.): British Film Institute
Andrea Weiss's dynamic new feature creates a unique personal look at gay and lesbian images in the history of British cinema and culture. Rare and fascinating footage is brought to light in this vivid exploration.

Bitter Old Queens [work in progress]
Dir. Huestis, Marc
1995 USA English
15 mins. video color Documentary
Dist. (U.S.): Outsider Enterprises
About the perils and pitfalls of growing older as a gay man with HIV.

Bitter Strength: Sadistic Response Version
Dir. Nurudin, Azian

1993 USA
3 mins. video color Experimental
Dist. (U.S.): Nurudin, Azian
Another amazing experimental S/M pixel scene from Azian Nurudin.

Bittersweet
Dir. Brave, Alice B.
1992 USA English
16 mins. video color Narrative
Dist. (U.S.): House O' Chicks
After a long day at the dungeon, a dominatrix comes home to her slave.

Black and White in Color
Dir. Julien, Isaac
1992 Great Britain English
5952 mins. video color Documentary
Dist. (U.K.): British Film Institute
Black and White in Color documents the involvement of black people in British Broadcasting from its earliest days. This tangy two-parter offers a concise social history of English race relations as well as some distinctly campy blasts from the past.

Part One deals with British TV from the BBC's 1936 opening night (featuring American song and dance duo Buck and Bubbles) through "the excitement and variety of negro entertainment" to the late '50s. In Part Two, Julien investigates the rise of social realism and the achievements of Channel Four in the '80s and '90s. (Hanif Kureishi describes the development of *My Beautiful Laundrette*.)

Black and White in Color is a fascinating counterpoint to Marlon Riggs's *Color Adjustment*, which tackled similar terrain in relationship to American TV. Julien's remarkable raid on the archives proves that there's more to British broadcasting than Masterpiece Theatre.

Black Bag: Gender Bender
Dir. Postman, Laurens
1993 Great Britain English
25 mins. video color Documentary
Dist. (U.S.): Yoyo Film Video & Theatre Productions
An episode from a British series devoted to black issues, called Black Bag. This one—*Gender Bender*—is a short portrait of Winston, England's answer to Ru Paul and a dead ringer for Naomi Campbell. "I'm not a drag queen, I'm a gender illusionist," says Winston; we get to join him on a fabulous Mahogany-style photo shoot, as well as on-stage at London's hot club, Kinky Gerlinky.

Black Body
Dir. Harris, Thomas Allen
1992 USA English
5 mins. video color Experimental
Dist. (U.S.): Third World Newsreel
Thomas Allen Harris explores racism and the black body in this impactful video.

Black Lizard, The
(see *Kuro Tokage*)

Black People Get Aids, Too
Dir. Pounds, Cedric
1987 USA English
23 mins. video color Documentary
Dist. (U.S.): Multicultural Prevention Resource Center
Black health care professionals discuss AIDS causes, offer advice on safe sex and IV drug use in this tape for blacks, presently one-quarter of those with AIDS.

Black Sheep Boy
Dir. Wallin, Michael
1995 USA English
35 mins. 16mm color Experimental
Dist. (U.S.): Wallin, Michael
Michael Wallin's voyeuristic *Black Sheep Boy* explores the sexual thrill and emotional obstacles inherent in looking at and eroticizing boys barely on the edge of being legal. These are "boys who open like flowers, boys who look like they could murder." Their tough street clothes, the cool way they undress before his self-conscious camera, their cocky attitudes broken only by an occasional boyish smile, the extreme close-ups on their bulging crotches: these images expose a lingering purity, a freshness untainted by the burdens of adulthood. But as Wallin's poetic narration reveals, such unspoiled virtue is a fantasy that cannot long be sustained, and a pair of clean white Jockeys becomes more than just a metaphor for young sexual energy. It becomes a poignant reminder of that which is lost in the aftermath of these erotic encounters, when all that's left is the space between boy and man.

Black Widow
Dir. Rafaelson, Bob
1987 USA English
102 mins. 16mm/35mm color Narrative
Dist. (U.S.): Films Incorporated
Reading mainstream films subversively, lesbians have often constructed heroines who do not officially belong to them. The persistence of the dyke invention of lesbian heroines urged me to

Ⓐ Ⓑ Ⓒ Ⓓ Ⓔ Ⓕ Ⓖ Ⓗ Ⓘ Ⓙ Ⓚ Ⓛ Ⓜ Ⓝ Ⓞ Ⓟ Ⓠ Ⓡ Ⓢ Ⓣ Ⓤ Ⓥ Ⓦ Ⓧ Ⓨ Ⓩ

reconstruct a mainstream Hollywood movie, a psychological thriller, in which the best thrills happen only if you impose a lesbian reading. At the time of its release, *Black Widow* met with mixed (let's say heterosexual) press reviews, keen dyke response privately, and severe dismissal from some dykes in public. For several reasons, I believe *Black Widow* is ripe for another spin. While I do not wish to argue that *Black Widow* is ultimately a progressive text, it does reveal ambivalences in the patriarchal order and the heterosexist gaze and opens spaces for a transgressive lesbian sexual subject.

Sharon Stone's character in *Basic Instinct* may be distinctly antifeminist, but was cited popularly as a lesbian heroine.

Black Widow lends itself to a similar kind of ironic reinvention. Here we have a rich, young, beautiful woman, the eponymous Catherine (Teresa Russell) who picks up and poisons her husbands with the skill of a brain surgeon. She is discovered and sought after by a rather dowdy and workaholic federal agent, Alex (Debra Winger), who needs a bit of hands-on excitement. It's a classic chase movie, with the familiar, and so compelling, ugly duckling motif thrown in. What is less familiar is that not only are there two female protagonists, but that Alex develops an obsession with Catherine far beyond the call of duty.

The psychological motivation is thin. When Alex tells her boss that "no one knows why anybody does anything," the gate opens and the psychiatrist has bolted, leaving the field of supposition totally accessible for a dyke interpretation of motivation. Alex's reply, which deflects her boss's concern that she is obsessed with Catherine, acts as a comic cypher for all the times dykes have no answers for the "why." "Why do you always have to have your hair so short? Why don't you ever wear a dress? Why do you have to be so public about it? Why do you enjoy licking pussy?" Alex may be obsessed, but she's not going to see a doctor. She has become a hunter.

Teresa Russell as Catherine is young, stiff, bereaved, and stylish, conjuring up the image of Catherine Deneuve, not only in *Belle de Jour*, but also in the later and much more dyke-embedded *The Hunger*. As a widow, however, Catherine is not upset enough, which the spectator may read as a betrayal or as an opening for a story of female revenge, of a husband killed because he deserved it, murdered because he tried to thwart his much younger wife. Catherine

is already constituted as a "bad girl," therefore, ripe for transgressive lesbian identification.

To Catherine men are disposable. She swots up enough specialized knowledge to catch her professional mate, exposing hetero-desire as being as superficial and simple to mimic as a game show. Alex, by contrast, is contructed as operating in an adolescent presexual state of distraction. Her reluctance to socialise with her male colleagues (except when playing cards) reinforces the trope of Alex as a lesbian who doesn't know it. Yet. *Black Widow* is a slow time-bomb of a movie whose formula is charmingly predictable and whose lesbian subtext is so unimaginable to itself that its frissons have endless repercussions. As soon as lesbianism is suggested it is quickly denied. (C.S.)

Blauer Dunst (Blue Smoke)
Dir. Keske, Klaus
1983 Germany German
86 mins. S8mm b&w Narrative
Dist. (U.S.): Syrup Productions
A dark and moody story of petty thieves, gay lovers, lesbian lust, waterfront bars and murder. *Blue Smoke* is a nostalgic new Super-8 feature from Berlin made in the tradition of Cocteau, Genet, and the early German silents. With its stylishly grainy photography and claustrophobically intimate scale, director Keske's film may actually be more true to the atmosphere of Genet's *Querelle* than Fassbinder's overblown production.

Blicklust
Dir. Brehm, Dietmar
1992 Austria German
15 mins. 16mm color Experimental
Dist. (U.S.): Sixpack Films
An arty found-footage horror film made from worn-out Super-8 S/M porno and surgery footage.

Blond Fury
Dir. Sobel, Lee Bennett
1995 USA English
45 mins. video color Narrative
Dist. (U.S.): Sobel, Lee Bennett /Garage Rock Pictures
Two trashy New Jersey housewives take to the road in *Blond Fury*. When they think their husbands have been kidnapped, they arm themselves and set off in hot pursuit. Unlike the stars of *Thelma & Louise*, however, these two wind up falling in love with each other. After picking up an Aileen Wuornos look alike, our heroines realize their husbands have been cheating on them and

give them a good taste of *Blond Fury*.

Blood and Roses
Dir. Vadim, Roger
1960 Italy English
74 mins. 35mm color Narrative
Dist. (U.S.): Films Incorporated
Annette Vadim stars as the sexy Carmilla in this lush and provocative Italian-made feature. Seduced by her lesbian vampire ancestor who takes over her body, the lusty Carmilla first jumps a young maid, and then her beautiful cousin. Although the cousin is engaged to be married, the women make eyes at each other throughout the film (in that Euro-soft-porn sort of way), and director Roger Vadim plays up every lesbionic inch of it. Not as dirty as the Hammer Studio's lesbian vampire movies (*The Vampire Lovers*, *Twins of Evil*, and *Lust for a Vampire*), much more lively and very well produced. (J.O.)

Blood Sisters: Leather, Dykes and Sadomasochism
Dir. Handelman, Michelle
1995 USA English
75 mins. video color Documentary
Dist. (U.S.): Handelman, Michelle
Michelle Handelman's long awaited documentary about the political activities and sexual choices of women in the leather S/M community. Using a combination of documentary, personal histories, artistic visions, and media imagery, this film focuses on nine central figures who represent a diverse cross-section of the leather S/M community. Handelman documents a series of competitions held throughout the country by the women's leather S/M community. By following these women and cutting between their personal lives, political activities, and candid interviews, *Blood Sisters* provides an in-depth picture of the leather S/M community. Graphic footage of actual play also gives us a greater understanding of the nature of the intensity of the bonds that exist between these women. Mixing both experimental and traditional documentary styles, Handelman draws us deeper into this often misunderstood community and gives us a more intelligent and less sensationalistic view of the reality behind these women's lives. Starring Tala Brandeis, Wickie Stamps, Amy Marie Meek, Pat Califia, and Skeeter, with music by Coil, Chris and Cosey, Frightwig, and the Lucy Stoners.

Blow Job, The
Prod. Mears, Ric, T.K. Perkins, and David Waggoner
1977 USA English
3 mins. S8mm color Experimental
Dist. (U.S.): n/a
Just something to get us started. A Persistence of Vision group effort. Drawn by Stephen Iadereste.

Blow Job (Warhol, Andy)
Dir. Warhol, Andy
1963 USA English
35 mins. 16mm color Experimental
Dist. (U.S.): Museum of Modern Art
Blow Job, originally shown unadvertised in 1963, later found unlisted in gay porn theaters, now receives its Castro coming-out in brand new prints. A would-be James Dean in a black leather jacket is sexually serviced by someone outside the frame. He lolls his head back, scratches his nose, seems bored, and then bucks about a bit in one of cinema's most eloquent and extensive close-ups (over half an hour long!). Hypnotic, tawdry, sublime.

Blue
Dir. Jarman, Derek
1994 Great Britain English
76 mins. 35mm color Experimental
Dist. (U.S.): Zeitgeist Films
Derek Jarman's *Blue* is a self-portrait made during the latter stages of his time as a "person with AIDS," when his "mind [was] as bright as a button, my body falling apart." Not counting its titles, *Blue* consists of 70-plus minutes of cobalt-blue celluloid, but it would be wrong to think of the film as a purely formal experiment. Its soundtrack—music and spoken-word—is narrative, coherent, and highly accessible. *Blue* washes over one, powered by Jarman's vivid language (by turns moody, maudlin, poetic, and profound), the sonorous voice of Nigel Terry (Tilda Swinton and John Quentin also participate) and Simon Turner's elegiac score. Despite the blank screen, pictures do emerge, a reminder of imagery's connection to the imagination. (D.M.)

Blue Boys
Dir. Marshall, Stuart
1992 Great Britain English
25 mins. video color/b&w Documentary
Dist. (U.K.): Maya Vision
Distinctive, clever history of British obscenity laws, from the maker of 1990s *Over Our Dead Bodies*.

Ⓐ Ⓑ Ⓒ Ⓓ Ⓔ Ⓕ Ⓖ Ⓗ Ⓘ Ⓙ Ⓚ Ⓛ Ⓜ Ⓝ Ⓞ Ⓟ Ⓠ Ⓡ Ⓢ Ⓣ Ⓤ Ⓥ Ⓦ Ⓧ Ⓨ Ⓩ

Blue Distance
Dir. Mikesch, Elf
1983 Germany German
22 mins. 35mm color Experimental
Dist. (U.S.): Mikesch, Elfi
Blue Distance is set in a train compartment. An androgynous woman thinks of letters a lady wrote to a gentleman about the necessity of separation and the desire for a casual encounter in the future. Another woman, a mirror image of the first, disrupts her reverie. After she leaves it is unknown whether the first woman's wish was about the man with whom an encounter will never take place or about the woman with whom it has just happened.

Blue Smoke
(see *Blauer Dunst*)

Bob Diva's
Dir. Diva, Bob
1985 USA English
15 mins. video color Other
Dist. (U.S.): n/a
Definitely not for the squeamish, as we research everything from Enema Bandits to Bye Bye Birdie.

Bob Ross
Dir. Holloran, Jim
1979 USA English
7 mins. video color Documentary
Dist. (U.S.): n/a
An interview.

Bodies In Trouble
Dir. Bociurkiw, Marusia
1991 Canada
15 mins. video color Experimental
Dist. (U.S.): Frameline
A video about the lesbian body under siege. Short vignettes describe a specifically lesbian erotic language and sense of the absurd that exists alongside danger. By talking about the threat the new right poses to lesbian and feminist groups, *Bodies In Trouble* becomes a call to action. By describing lesbian humor, eroticism, and social space (the bars, the bedrooms, the streets), it also attempts to evoke what it is that's funny, sexy, and charming about lesbian existence.

Bodily Functions [work in progress]
Dir. Taylor, Jocelyn
1994 USA English
13 mins. video color Experimental
Dist. (U.S.): Taylor, Jocelyn

A little sneak peek at the latest project from Jocelyn Taylor.

Body of Dissent:
Lesbian and Gay Mennonites and
Brethren Continue the Journey
Dir. Bridge Video Productions
1994 Canada English
39 mins. video color Documentary
Dist. (U.S.): Bridge Video Productions
Examines the struggles of lesbian and gay Mennonites by presenting insightful interviews, as well as historical background on the Mennonite church.

Bogjavlar (Damned Queers)
Prod. Almer, Gunnar, Nils Gredeby, Lars Gustafsson, Staffan Hallin, Hakan Hede, Sten Ake Hedstrom, Olle Holm, Anders Naslun, and Pelle Pettersson
1978 Sweden Swedish
21 mins. 16mm color Other
Dist. (U.S.): UCLA Film and Television Archive
We who made *Damned Queers* are a group of radical gays. Some of us live in the commune, mentioned in the film. The idea to *Damned Queers* was born as a reaction to current gay images in films. We are experts on our own reality and wanted to describe it. We made *Damned Queers* as a group production, where all of us supplied experience, ideas, and practical work. Most of us had no earlier experience of filmmaking. The aim of *Damned Queers* is to give gay people a positive and balanced film to identify with and get strength from for cooperation and to fight against oppression. We hope to make the heterosexual audience think about their fear of homosexuality and do something about that. We also see the film as discussion material in sexual politics, sex roles, and homosexuality.

Bondage
Dir. Treut, Monika
1983 Germany English
20 mins. 16mm color Documentary
Dist. (U.S.): First Run Features
Bondage was made from, among other things, footage that Monika Treut filmed in New York with women of the LSM (Lesbian Sex Mafia/Lesbian Sado-Masochists) for her film In Search of the Libertine Women of Today. The statements of Carol form the core of the film. She speaks about her sexuality, her love of bondage, her desire for pain, which she shows in front of the camera. Her talking is interrupted by assembled impressions: intersections and subways pass

through a chained female body.

Released in the U.S. and U.K. as part of a package of four of Treut's short films under the title *Female Misbehaviour*.

Boot
Dir. Collins, David and Ian Jarvis
1992 Canada English
6 mins. video color Narrative
Dist. (U.S.): Collins, David
Describes one subway rider's fantasy about striking back.

Borderline
Dir. MacPherson, Kenneth
1930 Great Britain English
80 mins. 16mm b&w Narrative
Dist. (U.K.): British Film Institute
A rare, silent Paul Robeson picture, *Borderline* was recently rediscovered by the British Film Institute. Paul Robeson (1898–1976) was a major star with both black and white audiences from the 1920s until the mid '40s. Gay film historian Richard Dyer describes Robeson's achievements as many and complex: the best-known and most successful male singer of Negro spirituals; performer of the definitive *Othello* (in 1943); star of Hollywood's 1935 *Showboat*.

In 1930 he made *Borderline*, a fascinating piece of melancholy and passion, which—while not exactly gay-explicit—is full of lesbian and gay undercurrents. It's an energetically edited, elliptical melodrama about interracial love, set in a small Swiss village inn.

Robeson's role is strangely emblematic. He is the object of adoration for the inn's slim, elegant, overanxious pianist. Robeson is also friendly with the cigar-smoking lesbian owner of the inn and her barmaid lover. The film's sexual ambiguity is explicable in terms of its artistic milieu as much as codes governing what could and couldn't be said.

Bisexual writer/director Kenneth MacPherson was part of the avant-garde group associated with the film journal *Close-Up*, which had just published a special issue on the Harlem Renaissance, blacks, and film. *Close-Up* was also caught up in the tide of new critical ideas coming from psychoanalysis and feminism; *Borderline's* themes and formalist style also reveal this influence.

Born In Flames
Dir. Borden, Lizzie
1983 USA English
90 mins. 16mm color Narrative

Dist. (U.S.): First Run Features
Dist. (U.K.): Cinenov
A worldwide lesbian-feminist classic, *Born In Flames* presents a tale of feminist activism set in an imagined future, ten years after a socialist revolution. This independent feature has a cinema verité quality that lends the story the raw power of documentary while conveying a hopeful fantasy of women of different races and sexual preferences working together against oppression.

Both
Dir. Child, Abigail
1989 USA English
5 mins. 16mm color Experimental
Dist. (U.S.): Child, Abigail
Abigail Child's camera creates a small masterpiece in Both. It is a richly textured film that is simultaneoously revealing and mysterious as a study of the nude in light and movement.

Both
Dir. De La Rosa, Vic
1993 USA English
8 mins. 16mm b&w Documentary
Dist. (U.S.): Frameline
A painfully honest retelling of a romance between two HIV positive San Francisco men.

Both of My Mom's Names Are Judy
Prod. Lesbian and Gay Parents Association
1994 USA English
10 mins. video color Documentary
Dist. (U.S.): Lesbian and Gay Parents Association
Both of My Mom's Names Are Judy was created by the Lesbian and Gay Parents Association as a tool for elementary school educators. A diverse group of children (ages 7–11) tell us what it is like to have lesbian and gay parents.

Bottom
Dir. Chiu, Terry
1994 USA English
7 mins. video color Experimental
Dist. (U.S.): Chiu, Terry
Terry Chiu's *Bottom* is a dramatic, suggestive glimpse at expected roles and sexual stereotyping of the gay Asian male, which makes an offer of escape through rejection of white male desire.

Boy Next Door: A Profile of Boy George
Dir. Kidel, Mark
1993 Great Britain English
50 mins. video color Documentary
Dist. (U.K.): Kidel, Mark

Ⓐ
Ⓑ
Ⓒ
Ⓓ
Ⓔ
Ⓕ
Ⓖ
Ⓗ
Ⓘ
Ⓙ
Ⓚ
Ⓛ
Ⓜ
Ⓝ
Ⓞ
Ⓟ
Ⓠ
Ⓡ
Ⓢ
Ⓣ
Ⓤ
Ⓥ
Ⓦ
Ⓧ
Ⓨ
Ⓩ

Mark Kidel's portrait of Boy George is a hypnotic story of narcissism and neediness, drugs and drag. *Boy Next Door* covers nine years, from Culture Club's sudden success through George's rebirth as a solo celeb. Along the way, there's tons of amazing archive footage, some very queer fashions, a gripping interview with B.G.'s ex, Jon Moss, and a sign of salvation. Looking back on it all, a candid George concludes, "Being gay is my only saving grace."

Boy! What A Girl!
Dir. Leonard, Arthur
1945 USA English
70 mins. 16mm b&w Narrative
Dist. (U.S.): Em Gee Film Library
This rediscovered all-black-cast musical stars Tim Moore ("The Kingfish" on the popular '50s "Amos 'n' Andy" television series) as a butch queen pursued by three men with marriage on their minds. Black comedy team Patterson and Jackson costar, along with a musical lineup that includes the Slam Stewart Trio, Sid Catlett Orchestra (with a cameo by Gene Krupa), Deek Watson and His Brown Dots, Ann Cornell, and the International Jitterbugs.

Although Herald Pictures was a white production company, *Boy! What a Girl!* was made for the contemporary black audience, and featured some of the best black musical and comic talent of the day. The acting is less than naturalistic at times—and the plot less than subtle—but these were characteristics of most of the big studio musicals of the '40s.

A Harlem tenement is home to the film's collection of entertainers. The plot revolves around a pair of small-time producers trying to stage a show, while wooing the daughters of the show's wealthy backer. The romantic element in this romantic comedy is heterosexual; the comedy element, however, is eminently queer. When the show's other backer doesn't arrive from "Gay Paree," the producers enlist the talents of a bald, cigar-smoking female impersonator to masquerade as "Madame Deborah." Class emerges rather strangely as the defining stereotypical element in this convoluted comedy of errors.

Boy Who Fell In Love, The
Dir. Skeet, Brian
Prod. Benson, Ian
1994 Great Britain English
20 mins. 16mm color Narrative
Dist. (U.K.): Christmas Pictures Ltd.
Brian Skeet's oddly poetic *The Boy Who Fell In*

Love is a tale of an HIV positive young man, his lover who died from AIDS, and axolotls—the larval stage of a species of salamander which give birth and die while still physically immature.

Boy with Cat
Dir. Richie, Donald
1966 Japan English
6 mins. 16mm b&w Experimental
Dist. (U.S.): Frameline Archive
The youth in question is prevented from onanistic euphoria by the inquisitiveness of his feline companion.

Boys from Brazil
Dir. Davidson, John Paul
1993 Brazil/Great Britain English
69 mins. video color Documentary
Dist. (U.S.): n/a
Boys from Brazil is an amazing, moving, and in-depth diary of a small group of Rio drag queens and "travesties."

Boys in the Band, The
Dir. Friedkin, William
1970 USA English
100 mins. 35mm color Narrative
Dist. (U.S.): Swank Motion Pictures
Dist. (U.K.): British Film Institute
The first Hollywood film entirely about homosexuality. From our lengthy historical distance this depressing gay birthday party is an amusing "period piece."

Boys on the Side
Dir. Ross, Herbert
1995 USA English
117 mins. 35mm color Narrative
Dist. (U.S.): Swank Motion Pictures
From the look of its promotional campaign—as a "touching" story about "the kind of lifelong friendships, intense feelings, and unconditional love that's always cherished by women and often envied by men"—this *Thelma & Louise* take-off is a six-car pileup waiting to happen. But in spite of the multiple twists this overconceived road-trip comedy/melodrama delivers in its path from New York to Pittsburgh to Tucson, Arizona, covering most political issues in between—it actually does a miraculous job of evading disaster.

It's the story of three women flung together by fate—Whoopi Goldberg (Jan), Mary-Louise Parker (Robi), and Drew Barrymore (Holly), representing, respectively, three demographics (African American, WASP, white trash) and three different sexual approaches (lesbian, repressed heterosexual, expressed heterosexual)—breaking the law and bonding, venturing through three different cities and at least as many genres.

It opens with a down-and-out Whoopi Goldberg answering an ad to go cross-country with the terminally white real estate agent Mary Louise Parker and picks up Drew Barrymore, the beaten-down wife of a Pittsburgh addict, along the way. What begins as a buddy-flick-transitioning-to-road-movie takes a left toward physical comedy before it quickly skids off into melodrama, takes a short rest stop in the world of courtroom drama, and eventually finds a parking place in the redemptive Movie of the Week genre.

But *Boys* manages to juggle its caustic one-liners with deadly serious dialogue—it has to: Parker has AIDS; Barrymore is pregnant; Goldberg's in love with a straight woman—someone's committed a murder. And they're all having a pretty good time. It's only through the power of personality and the combined talents of its cast members that the movie manages to keep its head above comedy to become *Beaches* with a radical agenda and workable soundtrack (including Joan Armatrading, Melissa Etheridge, Bonnie Raitt—and cameos by the Indigo Girls). In spite of its sometimes high school yearbook look, 1995's *Boys on the Side* was welcome tragicomedy in a world filled with *Forrest Gump*s. (S. G.)

Boys/Life
Dir. Roth, Phillip B.
1989 USA English
10 mins. 16mm b&w Narrative
Dist. (U.S.): Roth, Phillip B.
Boys/Life shoots scenes from New York's Jack-Off Club and 24 hours of all-male kissing on the streets of Manhattan with the Radical Faeries. It's blunt and beautiful.

Brazilian Dream, A
(see *Asa Branca*)

Breaking the Silence
Dir. Chait, Melanie
1985 Great Britain English
62 mins. 16mm color Documentary
Dist. (U.K.): Cinenova
As a companion piece to *Choosing Children* this documentary from England seems to indicate that that country is behind the United States in recognizing lesbian mothers. The optimism of the former film is replaced by poignant interviews with divorced lesbians who have lost their children in *Breaking the Silence*. British courts in

reality are no more conservative than their American counterparts in Peoria. Lesbian mothers everywhere are still being forced to relinquish their children. Yet what can be sadder than the look on a woman's face when she relates how she trusted her husband (after all, she had lived with him for ten years), until the day he walked into court and condemned her as an unfit mother for loving another woman?

Breast Exam
Dir. Keller, Lynn, Donna Shepard, and Kay Turner
1994 USA English
17 mins. video color Other
Dist. (U.S.): Girls In The Nose
Girls in the Nose do a rocking live version of their song "Breast Exam," and a diverse group of lesbians share with us their feelings on breast health and beauty.

Brenda and Glenda Show, The [excerpt]
Dir. Belverio, Glenn
1991 USA English
11 mins. video color Other
Dist. (U.S.): Belverio, Glenn
The Brenda and Glenda Show is New York City's terrifying contribution to the realm of queer broadcasting.

Bridgette
Dir. Perko, Brian
1994 USA English
5 mins. video color Other
Dist. (U.S.): Pussy Tourette
A music video from the notorious Pussy Tourette.

Bright Eyes
Dir. Marshall, Stuart
1986 Great Britain English
85 mins. video color Experimental
Dist. (U.S.): Video Data Bank
In this three-part tape made for Channel 4, Britain's showcase for innovative and experimental work, videographer Stuart Marshall thoughtfully examines the historical and social factors influencing current reactions to AIDS and homosexuality. The first of this impressive tape compares 19th-century British attitudes toward disease to present ones. Marshall focuses on a particularly sensational tabloid story about a person with AIDS in order to demonstrate how inbred bias against homosexuality in media coverage of AIDS ruthlessly obscures the medical aspects of the crisis. The tape argues against the misrepresentation of AIDS as a "gay disease," implicitly

Ⓐ Ⓑ Ⓒ Ⓓ Ⓔ Ⓕ Ⓖ Ⓗ Ⓘ Ⓙ Ⓚ Ⓛ Ⓜ Ⓝ Ⓞ Ⓟ Ⓠ Ⓡ Ⓢ Ⓣ Ⓤ Ⓥ Ⓦ Ⓧ Ⓨ Ⓩ

suggesting that AIDS be seen as a disease that affects human beings, some of whom are gay.

The second part of *Bright Eyes* is a stylized comparison of the treatment of gays by the Nazis and others to police/governmental actions against homosexuals today. The poetic rhythms of the language of persecution underscore the pervasiveness of homophobia in contemporary society.

Political activist and person with AIDS Michael Callen concludes the third part of *Bright Eyes* by recreating a dramatic speech he made in front of New York legislators. Callen vigorously asserts the need for more funding for research and care for those with AIDS.

Brincando El Charco:
Portrait of a Puerto Rican
Dir. Negron-Muntaner, Frances
1994 USA English and Spanish
57 mins. 16mm color Other
Dist. (U.S.): Women Make Movies

In Frances Negron-Muntaner's film *Brincando El Charco*, a young Latina artist serves seven years of exile in Philadelphia. When her father dies suddenly, Claudia copes with detachment. While she considers her obligation to a family who abandoned her because she is a lesbian, Claudia spends her days photographing and documenting other Latina/o gays. Her gay white publishing agent, however, discourages Claudia from pushing "the people-of-color issue" onto the rest of the community. Although she steers clear of becoming too involved in her lawyer girlfriend's political activism, Claudia copes inwardly with the effects of what has happened to her people politically since the colonialization of Puerto Rico. Race, language, birthplace, and economics surface as fractures in a culture as diverse as the world itself. As a light-skinned, island-born, mainland-living, bilingual lesbian Claudia struggles for a place on the spectrum.

Brincando El Charco offers extensive and sensitive coverage of a community still rarely seen in cinema today. "The only time we make the news is when we kill somebody." Included is actual footage from the first ever gay and lesbian Pride march in Puerto Rico. Carefully crafted, this film deserves each of the three filmmaking genres it encompasses—narrative, documentary, and experimental—anything less would stifle its provocativeness. A rich and fulfilling work offering a tender view of feminine sexuality.

"Here's a marvel—a tender, funny, knowing tale of cultural dysphoria that spans genre with a gusto rarely seen on the big screen." (E.P.)

Brinco, O (The Earring)
Dir. Flavia Moraes
1989 Brazil Spanish
6 mins. 35mm color Narrative
Dist. (U.S.): Film Cinematografica

A droll Brazilian short on the theme of an incriminating earring.

Broadcast Tapes of Dr. Peter, The
Dir. Paperny, David
1994 Canada English
50 mins. video color Documentary
Dist. (U.S.): Canadian Broadcasting Corporation (Toronto)

From Canada, *The Broadcast Tapes of Dr. Peter* is a deeply moving compression of TV programs recorded by an articulate doctor dying of AIDS; it was nominated for a 1994 Best Documentary Academy Award.

Broken Goddess
Dir. Dallas
1969 USA No Dialogue
29 mins. 16mm b&w Other
Dist. (U.S.): Conboy, Teresa

Broken Goddess features Warhol superstar Holly Woodlawn. It is a beautiful black-and-white salute to both silent films and the Woodlawn image; she lounges beside fountains, looking ravishing while Debussy plays on the soundtrack. *Broken Goddess* is camp in the richest sense, and truly moving.

Broken Mirrors
(see *Gerbroken Spiegels*)

Brown Sugar Licks Snow White
Dir. Vachal, Robin, and Suzi Silbar
1992 USA English
4 mins. video b&w Experimental
Dist. (U.S.): Video Data Bank

A video dealing with interracial relationships. Part of *Those Fluttering Objects of Desire*, released in the U.S. on a twenty-minute compilation with *Vanilla Sex*, *What's the Difference between a Yam and a Sweet Potato?*, and *I've Never*.

Buddies
Dir. Bressan, Arthur J., Jr.
1985 USA English
81 mins. 16mm color Narrative
Dist. (U.S.): Films Incorporated
Dist. (U.K.): British Film Institute

Buddies, the first American film to dramatize the AIDS crisis, is an intensely personal story of a 32-year-old Californian dying of AIDS in a Manhattan Hospital and the 25-year-old New Yorker who starts as his volunteer counselor and becomes his greatest friend.

Writer/director Arthur Bressan Jr. includes factual information about AIDS, but more importantly shows that love and caring is also a major part of this tragedy. "I made this movie," Bressan says, " because I had to make it. This one came from my heart . . . It is a very small movie about the landscape of the heart and caves within us."

Robert, the patient, and David, his "buddy," resist one another at first, but, as time goes by and their hospital visits become more personal, the men share thoughts and experiences that touch them both.

Since Frameline presented the world premiere in 1984, *Buddies* has played to audiences around the world and received critical acclaim—both for the fine performances of Geoff Edhold and David Schacter, and the no-nonsense, gut-wrenching emotion of the film.

Built for Endurance
Dir. Verow, Todd
1993 USA English
7 mins. 16mm b&w Experimental
Dist. (U.S.): Strand Releasing
A tall and torrid story by Todd Verow.

Bump and Grind It
Dir. Rubnitz, Tom
1986 USA English
3 mins. video color Other
Dist. (U.S.): Video Data Bank
Part of the Tom Rubnitz Marathon (*A Dozen Tapes, Wigs Included*).

Bumps
Dir. Carlton, Wendy Jo
1993 USA English
18 mins. video color Other
Dist. (U.S.): Carlton, Wendy Jo
A charming account of the life of an STD.

Burden of Dykes
Dir. Chamberlain, Anne
1994 USA English
12 mins. 16mm color Other
Dist. (U.S.): Chamberlain, Anne
A spoof of the misrepresentations that arise when sexism, homophobia, and cinema collide.

Burning, The
Dir. Jubela, Joan
1984 USA English
1 mins. video color Other
Dist. (U.S.): Jubela, Joan
Short, but terrific.

Bus Stops Here: Three Case Histories, The
Dir. Zando, Julie, and Jo Anstey
1990 USA English
27 mins. video b&w Experimental
Dist. (U.S.): Video Data Bank
Perhaps Zando's darkest work to date, *The Bus Stops Here: Three Case Histories* is a troubling look at three women's struggle with male authority figures. Like all her works, it's deeply sensitive to the power embedded in its own relationship to the viewer. Zando explores storytelling forms and the power of the camera to direct and control the viewer's attention, expectations, and desires.

Buscando un Espacio: Los Homosexuales en Cuba (Looking for a Space)
Dir. Anderson, Kelly
1993 USA Spanish
38 mins. video color Documentary
Dist. (U.S.): Filmmaker's Library
Director Kelly Anderson steers a thoughtful course between the myths and stereotypes about Cuban culture.

Bust-Up
Dir. Cook, Cathy C.
1989 USA English
7 mins. 16mm color Experimental
Dist. (U.S.): Chicago Filmmakers
In *Bust-Up*, an offscreen visitor comes to tea with an anglophile queen, who, like the film's style, suddenly takes a horror-movie turn for the worse.

But No One
Dir. Friedrich, Su
1982 USA No Dialogue
9 mins. 16mm color Experimental
Dist. (U.S.): Friedrich, Su
A rarely seen film from Su Friedrich—*But No One* incorporates a range of images interspersed with the text of an unsettling dream poem.

Butch Patrol!
Dir. Paci, Myra
1990 USA English
5 mins. video color Other
Dist. (U.S.): Paci, Myra
Long-haired pretties are being snatched and

Ⓐ Ⓑ Ⓒ Ⓓ Ⓔ Ⓕ Ⓖ Ⓗ Ⓘ Ⓙ Ⓚ Ⓛ Ⓜ Ⓝ Ⓞ Ⓟ Ⓠ Ⓡ Ⓢ Ⓣ Ⓤ Ⓥ Ⓦ Ⓧ Ⓨ Ⓩ

clipped right on the street by a gang of no-nonsense dyke toughies. Not for the hair-squeamish.

Butch Wax
Dir. Lane, Jennifer
1994 USA English
7 mins. video color Other
Dist. (U.S.): Light Box
Butch Wax looks at our adult female-to-male cross-dressing tendencies.

Butch/Femme in Paradise
Dir. Boschman, Lorna
1988 Canada English
5 mins. 16mm color Narrative
Dist. (U.S.): Women In Focus
Humor and eroticism. Women on the beach.

Butterfly Kiss
Dir. Winterbottom, Michael
Prod. Baines, Julie
1994 Great Britain English
85 mins. 35mm color Narrative
Dist. (U.K.): Sales Company, The
"You're not Judith," protests Eunice, a psychotic drifter traipsing along the back highways of England in Michael Winterbottom's *Butterfly Kiss.* In her search for an elusive Judith and a love song she can't name, Eunice encounters Miriam, a naive gas station attendant with an empty life of pumping gas, caring for her senile mother, and eating tinned food.

Miriam falls in love with Eunice and follows her on a long distance killing spree, covering up her bloody trail. If Miriam doesn't understand her lover's madness, she comes to at least empathize with it and in the end, experience a taste of it. Winterbottom infuses this otherwise terrifying descent into murderous obsession with a warped humor. But for all the promise of two dangerous dykes on the lam, *Butterfly Kiss* is curiously devoid of any real passion or affection. Its cold, gray tones and its clinical grasp of space subvert its dramatic potential.

Madness may be the way that women come to possess language and power in patriarchy, but in *Butterfly Kiss* madness is used to strip its characters of any sense of agency. The result is a film that provokes little more than condescending pity and a fleeting sense of shock. (L.C.)

By Attrition
(see *L'Usure*)

Caesura
Dir. Fitz, Tracey

1981 USA English
10 mins. 16mm color Other
Dist. (U.S.): n/a
Family bonds, how they hold us, and how we break them.

Caged
Dir. Cromwell, John
1950 USA English
91 mins. 35mm b&w Narrative
Dist. (U.S.): Swank Motion Pictures
From the *Cinema News and Property Gazette*, 1950: "Harrowing account of experiences of first-offender in women's prison. Powerful overall indictment of conditions that may possibly exist in American institutions, the picture dwells incessantly on varied types that people this sordid scene: crime-soaked females cut off from common decencies; sadistic matron open to bribes; kindly prison superintendent struggling for sweeping reforms; elderly vice-queen who organizes paroles. Gripping narration almost overpowering in realism of terrible conditions and slow decline of inmates' decent feelings. Superb line-up of sensitive portrayals, backed by sympathetic direction that never strikes a jarring note. Excellent production quality. First-rate dramatic entertainment that deserves wide exhibition, though hardly recommended for squeamish tastes." With Eleanor Parker, Hope Emerson, Jan Sterling, Agnes Moorehead.

Caged is pure '50s Hollywood. It features a sadistic matron with unstated lesbian feelings—a clear creation of male attitude, simultaneously humiliating and lusting after her charges. The inmates have the look and demeanor of maturing starlets instead of hardened criminals, and it's sanitized of any substantial lesbian content, while including titillating shower room scenes. But *Caged* offers the best aspects of Hollywood vehicles. It's well cast: Agnes Moorehead plays the warden, Eleanor Parker is pretty convincing, and Hope Emerson received an Oscar nomination for her portrayal of the sadistic guard. In addition, this black-and-white feature is wonderfully, noirishly lit.

Calamity Jane
Dir. Butler, David
1953 USA English
101 mins. 35mm color Narrative
Dist. (U.S.): Kit Parker Films
Doris Day stars as every tomboy's hero! She's the fast-shootin', tough-talkin', cross-dressin' (real-life lesbian cowboy) Calamity Jane! Saddle up

and come on down for lots of rootin'-tootin' fun for the whole lesbian and gay American family.

Of course, we know enough about the real Calamity to ignore the film's heterosexualized narrative and read it the other way around—which is easy enough when Calamity brings sexy Katie Brown to Deadwood and they move in together and paint "Calam & Katie" in a big heart on their front door!

Calamity Jane also happens to be a great old-fashioned musical with a bunch of spunky song and dance numbers—including "Whip Crack Away," "My Secret Love" and Dick Wesson's fantastic drag performance of "I've Got a Hive Full of Honey"—all in a brilliant, newly refurbished 35mm Technicolor print.

Unfortunately, the film is less than enlightened on the subject of Native Americans, reflecting Hollywood's stereotypes of the time. Doris Day unwittingly notes the injustice of the conquest of the Native American land as she admires the landscape, saying "No wonder the injuns fight so fierce to hang onto this country."

California New Wave
Dir. Rees, Joe
1979 USA English
20 mins. video color Documentary
Dist. (U.S.): n/
Punk with a passion.

Call Me Your Girlfriend
Dir. Farthing, Cheryl
1992 Great Britain English
21 mins. video color Documentary
Dist. (U.K.): Alfalfa Entertainments, Ltd.
An on-the-road profile and intimate glimpse of the remarkable British lesbian singer Rita Lynch.

Camp Christmas
Dir. Gordon, Caz, Frances Dickenson, and Alasdair McMillan
1993 Great Britain English
51 mins. video color Other
Dist. (U.K.): Film Four International
How queer can TV be? Look no further than *Camp Christmas*, a holiday special broadcast on Britain's Channel 4 TV. "What rhymes with Como but is never seen on TV at Christmas?" asks the press notes. Aiming to be a genuinely sincere gather-round-the-fireplace sort of thing, *Camp Christmas* actually ends up being a unique summit of queer talent. Melissa Etheridge and Andy Bell are hosts to a lineup that includes Armistead Maupin, Quentin Crisp, Pierrre et Gilles, Col. Margrethe Cammermeyer, Sir Ian McKellen, and Lea DeLaria (who gets to say the word "pussy" on primetime TV).

One interesting footnote: The British press were so upset by the idea of *Camp Christmas* that they called upon church leaders to organize an advertiser boycott!

Can You Say Androgynous?
Dir. Cowell, Laura
1990 Canada English
2 mins. video color Other
Dist. (U.S.): Cowell, Laura
If you've ever been mistaken for a boy you'll identify with the dry humor and unmistakable style of *Can You Say Androgynous?*

Can't Help Lovin Dat Man
Dir. Umen, Alex
1995 USA English
8 mins. video color Other
Dist. (U.S.): Umen, Alex
A romp through the life and times of transvestite jazz musician Billy Tipton.

Can't Stop the Music
Dir. Walker, Nancy
Prod. Carr, Allan
1980 USA English
124 mins. 35mm color Narrative
Dist. (U.S.): Swank Motion Pictures
Produced by Allan Carr after the unlikely success of *Grease, Can't Stop the Music* was designed to broaden the appeal of '70s gay icons, The Village People. It is probably one of the strangest films of the '80s. On the one hand, it was promoted as the family musical movie phenomenon of the decade, and accordingly The Village People were scrubbed clean of their gay image (and the American Dairy Association sponsored a nationwide tie-in). On the other hand, the movie is chock-full of faggy in-jokes and nancy-boy behavior. Despite the (barely credible) central heterosexual romance, it's impossible to see it as anything but a queer treat. Besides, any movie with cameos of June Havoc, Barbara Rush, and Paul Sand must know a thing or two about gay credibility.

Can't Take That Way from Me
Dir. Adams, Kevin
1992 USA English
13 mins. video color Other
Dist. (U.S.): Chicago Filmmakers
A horrific, powerful analysis of a queer-bashing. Grand Prize Winner: 1992 Visions of the U.S. Awards.

Ⓐ Ⓑ Ⓒ Ⓓ Ⓔ Ⓕ Ⓖ Ⓗ Ⓘ Ⓙ Ⓚ Ⓛ Ⓜ Ⓝ Ⓞ Ⓟ Ⓠ Ⓡ Ⓢ Ⓣ Ⓤ Ⓥ Ⓦ Ⓧ Ⓨ Ⓩ

Can't You Take a Joke?
Dir. Dun, Viki

1989 Australia English
26 mins. 16mm color Narrative
Dist. (U.S.): Women Make Movies
Dist. (U.K.): Cinenova

Amanda Drax, a cartoonist whose pet character is a lady detective, is engaged by a mysterious woman to recover her lost sense of humor. This witty lesbian comedy uses the style of film noir to explore the ideal of love at first sight.

Cana, Em
Dir. Zeida, Garcey, Launes Santos and Lemos Santos

1994 Brazil Portugese
4 mins. video color Other
Dist. (U.S.): MIX Brasil

Highlights the presence of gays and lesbians in Brazilian society.

Cancer in Two Voices
Dir. Phenix, Lucy Massie

1993 USA English
43 mins. 16mm color Documentary
Dist. (U.S.): Women Make Movies

Acclaimed at the 1994 Sundance and Berlin Film Festivals, Lucy Massie Phenix's *Cancer in Two Voices* addresses one of the most urgent and underrepresented health care issues facing women today. This deeply moving film documents the struggle and courage of a lesbian couple dealing with one partner's breast cancer. As an intimate home-movie journal, *Cancer in Two Voices* deals with their anger and grief, sexuality and friendship, and the painful process of confronting death.

Candlelight Vigil, A
Prod. Jabaily, Barbara

1988 USA English
8 mins. video color Documentary
Dist. (U.S.): Jabaily, Barbara/KBDI-TV

Barbara Jabaily's *A Candlelight Vigil* documents a candlelight vigil held in Denver to protest Colorado's funding of contact tracing instead of research or services for people with AIDS.

Cap Tourmente
Dir. Langlois, Michel

1993 France French
115 mins. 16mm color Narrative
Dist. (U.S.): Cinepix Inc.

Intensely luscious Roy Dupois (the hustler in *Being at Home with Claude*) stars as a hunky ne'er-do-well who returns home to his claustrophobic family after a long absence. Turns out that both his mother (Andree Lachapelle) and Sister (Elise Guilbault) both seem to want to sleep with him; things aren't helped when an old friend (Gilbert Sciotte) arrives, causing chaos for the polymorphously perverse clan.

The first of two ripe family dramas in this year's festival (the other is *Under Heat*), *Cap Tourmente* is a striking and award-winning first feature from Montreal screenwriter Michel Langlois, who has previously collaborated with Lea Pool. For a gay audience, the main appeal may be Dupois's on-screen charisma (or "jeans ad posturing" as Variety cattily described it), but *Cap Tourmente* is also interesting for its seamless incorporation of homosexuality as one of many options for this seductive house of horrors.

The plot of *Cap Tourmente* is not really the point; it's about confrontations with the sexual undertow of family life. The performers bring the film to life. Besides Dupois's convincing irritating infantilism, Lachapelle is thrilling—in a Jeanne Moreauish way—as the world-weary mother. Moody and austere, maddening and moving, *Cap Tourmente* is a film which positively spins between the sententious and the subversive.

Carmelita Tropicana
Dir. Troyano, Ela
Prod. Bejar, Alfredo

1993 USA English
30 mins. 16mm color Narrative
Dist. (U.S.): First Run Features

Though staged in New York, *Carmelita Tropicana* draws on a cultural history that encompasses much of Latina life. Ela Troyano's hilarious film makes a sumptuous stew of Puerto Rican lesbians, colonial betrayals, tragic Spanish ballads, and contemporary class consciousness. In *Carmelita Tropicana*, ethnic identity is improvised around loyalties, affection, and the common burden of a morena among men.

Winner of the 1994 San Francisco International Lesbian & Gay Film Festival Audience Award for Best Short Film.

Carrie
Dir. Vaguely, Tony

1993 USA English
6 mins. video color Other
Dist. (U.S.): n/a

A queer excerpt from *Carrie*, the twisted version.

Carrington

Dir. Hampton, Christopher

Prod. Shedlo, Ronald, and John McGrath

1995 Great Britain/France English
126 mins. 35mm color Narrative
Dist. (U.K.): PolygGram Film International

"*Carrington* details the unsettling but engrossing partnership between renowned writer Lytton Strachey and obscure painter Dora Carrington. He follows them through 17 years of affairs and scandal, celebrating a love that would not be bound by social mores, sexuality, or death.

Strachey, a committed homosexual, met Carrington in 1915, when he spotted her bounding about a garden. They were rarely apart again. Strachey continued to dally with young men, and Carrington pursued myriad liaisons, even marrying one of Strachey's lovers to keep Strachey near her. . . .

This splendid film is highlighted by superb performances from two of the world's finest actors: Emma Thompson, and Jonathan Pryce, whose portrayal of Strachey's biting wit won him Best Actor laurels at Cannes this year."

—Suzanne Weiss,
Toronto International Film Festival

Casta Diva

Dir. De Kuyper, Eric

Prod. Frans Rasher Film

1983 Netherlands Dutch
107 mins. 16mm b&w Experimental
Dist. (U.S.): Netherlands Information Service

Casta Diva examines man in his relationship with his body: while washing, while dressing, while undressing, before and after exertion; but always in solitude. Each individual is totally absorbed by what he is doing. In these everyday surroundings movements develop their own choreography—the window cleaner, the man washing. *Casta Diva* is mainly a silent film. Sometimes the silence is broken by pathetic screams and sobbing. Opera! Theatrical song full of pathos contrasts starkly with the intentional triviality of the image; lyrical and musical effusiveness contrast with the insistent "objectivity" of the camera.

Castro at 18th

Dir. Boyle, Bernie

1977 USA English
3 mins. S8mm color Other
Dist. (U.S.): n/a

A time study, shot single frame, Saturday, June 11th, 1 p.m. to 2 p.m.

Castro Cowboy

Dir. Kates, Nancy

1992 USA English
7 mins. 16mm b&w Documentary
Dist. (U.S.): Kates, Nancy

This portrait of ex–Marlboro man Christian Haren dubs him the Castro Cowboy.

Castro—The Video

Prod. Vieira, Mark A.

1986 USA English
37 mins. video color Narrative
Dist. (U.S.): n/a

This is a first installment of a soap opera showing the Castro as a Gothic, sleazy neighborhod where danger and duplicity lurk. Assorted characters include the innocent new boy in town, a streetwise detective, a pair of lesbian astronauts, a bitchy male couple, and an alcoholic landlord. Sylvester sings the theme song wearing enough jewelry to sink the Missouri.

Cat and the Canary, The

Dir. Metzger, Radley

1978 Great Britain English
98 mins. 35mm color Narrative
Dist. (U.S.): n/a

Upscale '60s softcore director Radley Metzger (who helmed the kitsch lesbian-schoolgirl classic *Therese and Isabelle*) made this comic thriller as his sole mainstream bid. It flopped. But there are pleasures here worth an off evening's perusal, especially since pulp genre features have so seldom incorporated gay characters as a matter of course. When an elderly, rich curmudgeon dies, his potential heirs are gathered for the will reading. But murder and intrigue inevitably arise during the long, stereotypically stormy night. Carol Lynley screams a lot as the nominal heroine; more amusingly, Olivia Hussey and Honor Blackman make a swank, unapologetic lesbian couple, while Edward Fox is one very camp police inspector. The bad news: homicidal mania is blamed at last on sadistic gay male lovers. The good news: everything here seems to be a sophisticated, ironic joke, by and for deviants of every stripe. (D.H.)

Cat Nip

Dir. Taylor, Amanda

1995 USA English
14 mins. 16mm color Other
Dist. (U.S.): Taylor, Amanda

Amanda Taylor's *Cat Nip* looks at her family's myths and how they intertwine with the stereotypes of lesbians and cats.

Ⓐ Ⓑ Ⓒ Ⓓ Ⓔ Ⓕ Ⓖ Ⓗ Ⓘ Ⓙ Ⓚ Ⓛ Ⓜ Ⓝ Ⓞ Ⓟ Ⓠ Ⓡ Ⓢ Ⓣ Ⓤ Ⓥ Ⓦ Ⓧ Ⓨ Ⓩ

Catalina
Dir. O'Haver, Tommy
Prod. Shah, Byron
1995 USA English
6 mins. 16mm b&w Narrative
Dist. (U.S.): O'Haver, Tommy
An amusing story of a gay man's problematic attraction to a straight surfer boy.

Caught Looking
Dir. Giannaris, Constantine
1991 Great Britain English
35 mins. 16mm color Narrative
Dist. (U.K.): Maya Vision
A sexy and subversive comedy about gay men's stereotypical sexual fantasies; it's built around a new virtual reality home computer game in which the player can select any historical period or location, and then insert himself into the action. *Caught Looking* was originally made for Channel Four's Out Series, but—unsurprisingly—deemed too explicit for mid-evening television.
Best Gay Filmmaker of the Year (1992) by British magazine *Gay Times*. Teddy Bear Prize for Best Gay Short (1992) at the Berlin Film Festival.

Cavale
Dir. Fritsch, Luc
1987 France French
10 mins. 35mm color Narrative
Dist. (U.S.): Fritsch, Luc
Diane, a lesbian, becomes involved in a dispute between her friend Valerie, who she has been in love with for a long time, and Valerie's lover, Romain.

Cell Mates
Dir. Fontaine, Richard
1968 USA English
11 mins. 16mm color Other
Dist. (U.S.): Fontaine, Richard
A Richard Fontaine physique short, *Cell Mates*, stars muscle buddies Wayne Johnston and Bob Watson.

Celluloid Closet, The
Dir. Epstein, Rob, and Jeffrey Friedman
1995 USA English
102 mins. 35mm color/b&w Documentary
Dist. (U.S.): Sony Pictures Classics
Rob Epstein and Jeffrey Friedman's adaptation of Vito Russo's groundbreaking book, *The Celluloid Closet* is narrated by Lily Tomlin. The feature-length overview of homosexuality and Hollywood is long on fascinating archival footage and industry anecdotes, if a bit short on deep socio-historical context and analysis—with Tomlin's participation in the project reflecting a peculiar irony. (J.O.)

Central Park
Dir. Zeig, Sande
1994 USA English
9 mins. 16mm b&w Narrative
Dist. (U.S.): Artistic License Films
Two women enjoy a dreamlike encounter in a rowboat.

Cerebral Accident
Dir. Derry, Charles
1986 USA English
28 mins. 16mm color Narrative
Dist. (U.S.): Derry, Charles
Dreams, memories, and death are imaginatively treated in a compelling barrage of visual and aural imagery as a young gay man sits at the bedside of his dying father.

Certain Grace, A
Dir. Nettelbeck, Sandra
1992 USA English
40 mins. 16mm color Narrative
Dist. (U.S.): Frameline
Zelda meets Alice and they begin to work together on a photography project. Their relationship develops, and Zelda's boyfriend starts to think Zelda is spending too much time with Alice. As the erotic tension between Zelda and Alice heightens, a large poster of Michelle Shocked looms prominently on the kitchen wall.
Winner of the 1992 San Francisco International Lesbian & Gay Film Festival Audience Award for Best Short Film.

Chaero
Dir. Hayes, Matt
1988 Ireland English
15 mins. 16mm color Narrative
Dist. (U.S.): Frameline
Dist. (U.K.): Hayes, Mat
Two Dublin youths inhabit their own autonomous teenage world where adult moods have no sway, cigarettes are the standard unit of currency, and alcohol the usual means of escape.

Chameleon
Dir. Syed, Tanya
1990 USA English
4 mins. 16mm color Experimental
Dist. (U.S.): London Film Makers Co-op

A stark, visceral exercise in sight and sound.

Chance of a Lifetime
Dir. Lewis, John
Prod. Jacobs, Raymond and GMHC
1986 USA English
45 mins. video color Narrative
Dist. (U.S.): Gay Men's Health Crisis
What happens when the hot man you have invited over for dinner is making advances you are too afraid to respond to because you haven't dealt with AIDS panic yet. That is the sitcom beginning of this gay male erotic drama which shows that even New York guys still want to have fun and are doing it safely with condoms. Included is a guest appearance by Casey Donovan.

Chance, The
Dir. Eichorn, Christoph
1982 Germany German
12 mins. 35mm b&w Narrative
Dist. (U.S.): Eichorn, Christoph
The filmmaker plays multiple roles in this parody of a chorus girl becoming the star of the show.

Change
Dir. Philpott, Ger
Prod. Sheehan, Brian
1995 Ireland English
13 mins. 16mm color Narrative
Dist. (U.K.): Sheehan, Brian/Caspar Films
Ger Philpott's lyrical *Change* is an award-winning film from Ireland in which a man lovingly remembers his lover who died of AIDS. At the same time, he attempts to come to terms with religious and familial oppressions. A sometimes erotic, sometimes sad love story, this unusual film builds a moving portrait of strength and tenderness.

Change the Frame
Dir. Rey, Cristina
1995 USA English
93 mins. 16mm color Narrative
Dist. (U.S.): Fearless Productions Inc.
With lesbian films being all the rage in Hollywood, it is reassuring to know that independent films like *Change the Frame* are still managing to get made. Director/producer Cristina Rey's first feature film is a whimsical and realistic portrayal of love, growing up, and life's direction. Rey focuses her camera on the lives of a couple living in a small college town in the Colorado Rockies. Angela (Stephani Shope), is a college graduate working at a hot dog cart who one day realizes she has put her art career on hold while waiting for her girlfriend Rachel (Cristina Rey) to finish graduate school. Rachel, meanwhile, is too busy with school to realize Angela has become frustrated with her life and their relationship. The arrival of a flirtatious singer from San Francisco helps to distract Angela from the reality of her relationship, but she soon realizes that she must reassess her life goals and priorities. Their relationship begins to suffer under the intense pressure Angela is feeling to make changes in her life. It is a pleasure to finally see a feature film that so honestly captures some of the common experiences we have all shared in our relationships. Finally, a film that takes lesbian relationships seriously.

Changer: A Record of the Times, The
Dir. Reid, Frances and Judy Dlugacz
1991 USA English
60 mins. video color/b&w Documentary
Dist. (U.S.): Wolfe Video
In 1975 Cris Williamson recorded *The Changer and the Changed* for Olivia Records, the first national women's recording company. *The Changer* went on to become one of the all-time best-selling albums on an independent label.

Whether you lived through the sisterhood of the '70s or were merely a gleam in your mother's partner's eye, this documentary video is heartwarming and highly entertaining. Color footage from a 1990 Williamson concert in Berkeley is interspersed with clips and stills from the '70s and '80s. The cast reads like a who's who of women's music: Cris Williamson, Margie Adam, Meg Christian, Holly Near, Vicki Randle, and Bonnie Raitt.

The black-and-white footage of early recording sessions is priceless: flannel shirts and overalls never looked so good! Holly Near, looking back at the early days of Olivia and women's music says, "It felt like summer camp, but it also felt courageous and brave." So, to you venerable women of the '70s and '80s, and to you lipsticky gals of the '90s, here's a chance to enjoy a retrospective of Williamson's throaty voice and the early years of women's music.

Changes
Dir. Miggins, Billy
1977 USA English
7 mins. S8mm color Experimental
Dist. (U.S.): n/a
I wanted to make a film dealing with feminism, bureaucracy, and gayness that would reflect a

Ⓐ Ⓑ Ⓒ Ⓓ Ⓔ Ⓕ Ⓖ Ⓗ Ⓘ Ⓙ Ⓚ Ⓛ Ⓜ Ⓝ Ⓞ Ⓟ Ⓠ Ⓡ Ⓢ Ⓣ Ⓤ Ⓥ Ⓦ Ⓧ Ⓨ Ⓩ

number of emotions. This is my first serious film.

Changing Our Minds:
The Story Of Dr. Evelyn Hooker
Dir. Schmiechen, Richard
Prod. Haugland, David
1992 USA English
75 mins. 16mm color/b&w Documentary
Dist. (U.S.): Frameline

For lesbians and gay men, our history is still an undiscovered country. In *Changing Our Minds*, director Richard Schmiechen—producer of the Academy Award–winning *Times of Harvey Milk*—brings to film the compelling historical story of the trailblazing psychologist whose research proved that homosexuality is not a mental illness. It's a powerful and affecting drama, moving from the 1940s to the present day, using archival footage and illuminating interviews.

Eye-opening period films and photos evoke the repressive period of her research: lesbian and gay love was illegal, and hysteria over the McCarthy hearings prompted the prosecution of "perverts." For decades the medical community had been using appalling treatments on gay men and women: lobotomy, castration, hysterectomy, and electroshock therapy. Through her friendship with a student who introduced her to Los Angeles' secret gay world, Dr. Hooker began pioneering studies which resulted—in 1974—in the removal of homosexuality from the American Psychiatric Association's official list of mental disorders.

Changing Our Minds is a brilliant tribute to an important pioneer whose work has impacted the lives of all American lesbians and gay men.

Winner of the 1992 San Francisco International Lesbian & Gay Film Festival Audience Award for Best Documentary.

Chant d'amour, Un
Dir. Genet, Jean
1950 France French
26 mins. 35mm b&w Experimental
Dist. (U.S.): Filmmaker's Cooperative
Dist. (U.K.): British Film Institute

"*Un Chant d'amour* was made shrouded in the anonymity of pornography, and was intended for the eyes of private collectors only. Yet it has regularly demonstrated the ability of a film to elude the control of its maker in a way unlike any other medium, to become [what Tony Rayns called], 'the most famous gay short film in European history.' . . . Like both Genet's literature and his lifestyle, his only completed film became a cause célèbre of criminality and homosexuality."
—Jane Giles, *The Cinema of Jean Genet: Un Chant d'amour*
"There's no smoke without fire; *Un Chant d'amour* is a communion in which Jean Genet takes us into the prison in order to liberate us from it." —Derek Jarman

Charming Mutt
Dir. Reinke, Steve
1993 Canada English
1 mins. video color Other
Dist. (U.S.): V-Tape
Short-attention-span gay humor.

Chasing the Moon
Dir. Suggs, Dawn
1991 USA English
4 mins. video color Experimental
Dist. (U.S.): Third World Newsreel
Using dream sequences and flashback, a black woman memorizes one night's haunting experiences. Poetic film language helps her escape.

Cheap Skates:
The Hardly-Cardigan Affair
Dir. Ebert, Matt
1994 USA English
15 mins. 16mm color Narrative
Dist. (U.S.): Ebert, Matt
The true story behind the Tonya Harding/Nancy Kerrigan headlines.

Chicken Elaine
Dir. Rubnitz, Tom
1983 USA English
2 mins. video color Other
Dist. (U.S.): Video Data Bank
Part of the *Tom Rubnitz Marathon (A Dozen Tapes, Wigs Included)*.

Chicken Hawk
Dir. Sideman, Adi
1994 USA English
60 mins. 16mm color Documentary
Dist. (U.S.): Stranger Than Fiction Films
A raw, American-made essay about the North American Man/Boy Love Association wavers between caution and voyeurism. Its chief virtue is in furnishing more information for a debate that will clearly continue.

Chicks in White Satin
Dir. Holliman, Elaine
1993 USA English

27 mins. 16mm color Documentary
Dist. (U.S.): University of Southern California—
School of Cinema
Chicks in White Satin, by Los Angeles–based
filmmaker Elaine Holliman, documents the mar-
riage of two southern California Jewish lesbians.
The two women receive mixed support from their
families, wear bridal gowns, and reinvent tradi-
tion in this loving and intelligent portrait of a
commitment ceremony.
        Winner of the 1993 San Francisco
International Lesbian & Gay Film Festival
Audience Award for Best Short Documentary.

Chickula: Teenage Vampire
Dir. Robinson, Angela
Prod. Malder, Kristina
1995 USA English
4 mins. video color Other
Dist. (U.S.): Robinson, Angela
A lesbian vampire wreaks havoc in *Chickula:
Teenage Vampire*.

Chinaman's Peak: Walking the Mountain
Dir. Wong, Paul
1992 Canada English
25 mins. video color Experimental
Dist. (U.S.): Video Out
This film is not ostensibly about homosexuality. It
is a hybrid narrative that progresses from an
investigation into the naming of a geographical
site to the remembrance of forebearers and lost
friends, linked conceptually by the Chinese practice of Hanng San—walking the mountain—a ritualistic act that provides continuity between the
past, present, and future, between the living and
those in the spirit world. However, the act of
mourning here evokes the parallel in lesbian and
gay communities of remembering those who are
lost to the AIDS pandemic.

Chinese Characters
Dir. Fung, Richard
1986 Canada English
22 mins. video color Documentary
Dist. (U.S.): Video Data Bank
Chinese Characters explores the relationship of
gay Asians to male erotica by juxtaposing cultural
and sexual icons and sound. A serene landscape
and traditional music. A rapid change of
wardrobe which suggests the myriad possibilities
of costume. Scenes from classic pornos.
Interviews of Asian men talking about significant
sexual experiences.

Cholo Joto

Dir. Robles, Augie
1993 USA English
12 mins. video color Documentary
Dist. (U.S.): Robles, Augie
Gay life from a Latino perspective: *Law of Desire*,
Low Riders, Catholic eroticism, Castro St. racism,
machismo, and narcissism.

Choosing Children
Dir. Chasnoff, Debra and Kim Klausner
1984 USA English
45 mins. 16mm color Documentary
Dist. (U.S.): Frameline
Dist. (U.K.): Cinenova
How does a lesbian couple go about having a
baby? First, they should see this documentary. It
can qualify as a how-to film but is also a candid,
and often funny, examination of six lesbian-head-
ed families that have the same problems as
"ordinary" families—problems of money, division
of responsibilities, lack of time, etc. Through
excellent editing, *Choosing Children* covers an
impressive range of topics from novel methods of
getting pregnant to the legal aspects of adoption
and custody rights. It even grants screen time to
the children themselves and addresses the issue
of whom they think should be called "mommy"
and why. Obviously, not all lesbians want to
become mothers, but this provocative film has
something of interest for everyone, and covers
social issues which concern us all.

Christopher Isherwood:
Over There on a Visit
Dir. Wallis, Alan
1976 Great Britain English
30 mins. 16mm color Documentary
Dist. (U.S.): n/a
A portrait of the writer.

Chubs & Bears [work in progress]
Dir. Outcalt, John
Prod. Rosenthal, Andrew
1996 USA English
18 mins. video color Documentary
Dist. (U.S.): Rosenthal, Andrew /Sputnik
Productions
Chubs & Bears is a work-in-progress screening of
the first-ever Bear documentary. This film takes
an unflinching look at [self-defined] gay sub-
groups such as "chasers"—men who desire large
men; "gainers"—men who want to gain excess
weight; and "bears"—men who are . . . well,
Bears.

Ⓐ
Ⓑ
Ⓒ
Ⓓ
Ⓔ
Ⓕ
Ⓖ
Ⓗ
Ⓘ
Ⓙ
Ⓚ
Ⓛ
Ⓜ
Ⓝ
Ⓞ
Ⓟ
Ⓠ
Ⓡ
Ⓢ
Ⓣ
Ⓤ
Ⓥ
Ⓦ
Ⓧ
Ⓨ
Ⓩ

Chuck Solomon: Coming of Age
Dir. Huestis, Marc
1986 USA English
58 mins. video color Documentary
Dist. (U.S.): Cinema Guild

Chuck Solomon: Coming of Age is a video cele-bretion of a remarkable man and his equally remarkable community. Last March 10 at the California Club, San Franciscans gathered to pay tribute to Chuck Solomon, a major figure in the San Francisco gay theater community for the past decade. The gala dinner party was highlight-ed by a staged tribute featuring some of San Francisco's most talented entertainers, including the San Francisco Mime Troupe, comic Tom Ammiano, the cast of The AIDS Show, and singer Esmerelda.

Coming of Age captures the excite-ment of that evening and includes interviews with Chuck and over twenty of Chuck's loved ones—friends and family—focusing on why Chuck has affected so many lives in the past and how he continues to inspire so many with his strong commitment to living. Chuck Solomon was diagnosed with AIDS in October 1985. This video is a tribute to him, his work in the theater, and to the community that his life has brought together.

Cities of Lust
Dir. Ferrera-Balanquet, Raul
1993 USA English
30 mins. video color Documentary
Dist. (U.S.): Ferrera-Balanquet, Raul

Cities of Lust addresses issues of relationships, desire, and ethnicity among African-American and Latino gay men. Filmed on location in Merida, Chicago, and at the last year's San Francisco International Lesbian and Gay Film Festival, the tape works best of all as a vivid description of racism and of the social obstacles to romantic fulfillment.

City of Lost Souls
(see *Stadt der Verlorenen Seelen*)

Civil Enough
Dir. Freeman, Marilyn
1994 USA English
1 mins. video color Other
Dist. (U.S.): Freeman, Marilyn/Olympia Pictures

A clever pair of pro queer public service announcements.

Claire of the Moon
Dir. Conn, Nicole
Prod. Kuri, Pam
1992 USA English
90 mins. 35mm color Narrative
Dist. (U.S.): Strand Releasing
Dist. (U.K.): Dangerous To Know

Like many people interested in the future of les-bian film, I went to my local Landmark theater to watch the recent lesbian-produced and lesbian-directed feature film: *Claire of the Moon*. I can only call my viewing experience devastating (at best). This film ranks up there with *Switch* and *It's a Wonderful Life* in the "worst films of all times" category. Give it an award for "Worst Non-Action Film With No Sex, No Effects, And No Clue." Give it two.

My question is this: why weren't the Queer Nation protesters who filled the streets during the shooting of last year's *Basic Instinct* picketing outside of *Claire of the Moon*? If you want to protest negative images of lesbians, if you want to intervene in the way that Hollywood sells lesbianism to the mainstream, if you want to raise your voice against heterosexist representa-tions of alternative sexualities, if you care about the future of lesbian film, then *Claire of the Moon* must be stopped! As a friend pointed out to me, an ice-pick scene would have been all too welcome in this dreary and predictable feature.

If I were to say "tampax commercial" to you, I would be coming close to describing the emotional pitch and formal complexity of *Claire of the Moon*. Let me set the scene: uptight thera-pist and bad-girl slut are roommates at a women writers' retreat. The other writers represent a not very diverse group of stereotypes: the racist and homophobic southern belle, the mousy house-wife, a new-age spiritualist, and a pushy liberal type. The whole deal is run by a butch-femme couple. Therapist is haunted by a lost love (a patient); slut agonizes over her waning heterosex-uality. Slut and therapist hate sharing a space together and they bring out the best and worst in each other (make that the worst and the worst). Slut reveals sensitive side as she shows her piano-playing skills (although the sound synch was off so she was often playing Chopin without moving her hands); therapist reveals wild side of herself by drinking and saying the "shit" word or even the "F" word occasionally. As you can imag-ine, this scenario is a panoply of erotic possibili-ty. Not! (J.H.)

Clean Fun with Sally Alley
Dir. Meyer, Keli, and Melissa Dopp
1993 USA English
10 mins. video color Other

Dist. (U.S.): Scratch & Sniff Videos
This is your dream lesbian talk show.

Clearing, The
Dir. Bistecis, Alexis
1993 Great Britain English
8 mins. 35mm color Experimental
Dist. (U.S.): Bistecis, Alexis
A brief stroll through London's infamous Hampstead Heath in the company of Derek Jarman.

Cliche in the Afternoon
Dir. Huestis, Marc
1977 USA English
10 mins. S8mm color/b&w Narrative
Dist. (U.S.): Outsider Enterprises
Dedicated and/or with apologies to my love life, Joseph von Sternberg, *Swept Away*, and every other flawless tacky B movie I've ever seen.

Clinic, The
Dir. Stevens, David
Prod. LeTet, Robert, and Bob Weis
1982 Australia English
93 mins. 35mm color Narrative
Dist. (U.S.): Satori Films
The Clinic sends up a day's worth of routine medical exercises in a Sydney STD dispensary with a wealth of energy, humor, and nail-on-the head characterizations of ordinary people in an all too ordinary bind. Prime focus is on Dr. Eric Linden (Chris Haywood), who has to put up with— besides the usual run of troubled and demanding clients—traumatized colleagues, the awful anticipation of meeting his lover's parents and a priggish intern. This well-wrought seriocomic film is the brainchild of director Stevens, who scripted *Breaker Morant*, and cinematographer Ian Baker, who lensed *The Chant of Jimmie Blacksmith* and *The Devil's Playground*—a tour de force from Down Under.

Clips from Kelly's Porn Movie
Dir. Link, Matthew
1991 USA English
6 mins. video color Documentary
Dist. (U.S.): Link, Matthew
A wild ride through the trials and tribulations of Kelly's (our favorite male Madonna) first romp in the world of glamour porno.

Clones In Love
Dir. Biello, Michael
1985 USA English
5 mins. video color Other
Dist. (U.S.): n/a

A heavy-handed, well-thought-out criticism on our ever-changing, ever-interesting evolution of what's desirable.

Closet, The
Dir. Tiffenbach, Joe
1985 USA No Dialogue
20 mins. 16mm color Other
Dist. (U.S.): Frameline Archive
The Closet is Tiffenbach's best known work. In a blackened room a naked young man is given the massage of his life by a handsome body builder. The film is silent.

Closing Numbers
Dir. Whittaker, Stephen
1993 Great Britain English
95 mins. 35mm color Narrative
Dist. (U.K.): Film Four International
Anna (Jane Asher) and Keith (Tim Woodward) have been married for many years. Suddenly, she is spiraled into a world of homosexuality and HIV . . .

    Closing Numbers is a commanding inspection of homophobia, infidelity, and compassion, from the director of *Portrait of a Marriage*. Asher is superb as the housewife who reluctantly befriends her husband's lover (Patrick Pearson, as one of the most level-headed gay characters you've ever seen on the screen) and his dying friend Jim (Nigel Charnock, another standout). Fans of classy drama will find many other pleasures too. A thoroughbred in an increasingly large stable of AIDS dramas, Closing Numbers proves that biology counts for nothing: home is where the HIV is.

Club des Femmes (Women's Club)
Dir. Deval, Jacques
1936 France French
90 mins. 16mm b&w Narrative
Dist. (U.S.): Em Gee Film Library
Dist. (U.K.): British Film Institute
The rarely seen comedy, *Club des Femmes*, is set in an all-women's hotel in Paris, established to provide an environment for women to interact and support one another. The main characters include an attractive lesbian, a young dancer with a healthy sex drive, a foreign student who becomes involved in a prostitution ring, and a man whose masculinity isn't threatened by dressing in drag.

    With traces of the classic American screwball comedy, *Club des Femmes* expresses a variety of sexual attidudes. In this 1936 film we find a principal character who is clearly a lesbian

Ⓐ Ⓑ Ⓒ Ⓓ Ⓔ Ⓕ Ⓖ Ⓗ Ⓘ Ⓙ Ⓚ Ⓛ Ⓜ Ⓝ Ⓞ Ⓟ Ⓠ Ⓡ Ⓢ Ⓣ Ⓤ Ⓥ Ⓦ Ⓧ Ⓨ Ⓩ

but not defined stereotypically. Alice's tragedy is arguably not being a lesbian, but being in love with another woman who is unable to understand or return her affection.

Club des Femmes had a brief run in New York in 1937. However, it was a much shorter version with all nudity suppressed and large chunks of footage and subplots cut out. Key words were removed from the dialogue and subtitles were manipulated to reinterpret relationships. In spite of these changes, the film was still considered as too racy for the general public and never received national release.

Clue
Dir. Mathias, Gisela
1994 Brazil Portugese
2 mins. video color Other
Dist. (U.S.): MIX Brasil
Clue expresses the deep sense of loss caused by AIDS.

Coal Miner's Granddaughter
Dir. Dougherty, Cecilia
1991 USA English
90 mins. video color Narrative
Dist. (U.S.): Women Make Movies
This hysterically funny epic about a brutally realistic American family does for lesbians what John Waters did for Baltimore.

While disrupting everything audiences expect about plot and acting, director Cecilia Dougherty grabs our emotions on her own terms. Her sharp and skillful original visual style recreates moments, like memories, that will resonate with an audience's own deeply felt emotions about family, illness, and sexuality.

Video artist Leslie Singer plays the protagonist Jane Dobson. Under the thumb of her sleazy, evil father (brilliantly portrayed by novelist Kevin Killian), Jane is not the hero of her own life. She's simply there. But when Jane escapes from the structured narrative of her family back in Lancaster, Pennsylvania, *Coal Miner's Granddaughter* opens up into the impressionistic world of her sexuality, laughing aloud throughout.

Dougherty continues the work of her earlier videos *Kathy*, *Claudia*, and the much acclaimed *Grapefruit*, to insist on the highly charged sexuality and power of ordinary women. She enjoys how we really make love. Her camera makes all the posing and artificiality that have become staples of lesbian erotica seem tepid and silly. Dougherty's camera jumps right into the fray to the tune of "Total Abandon."

Coconut/Cane & Cutlass
Dir. Mohabeer, Michelle
1994 Canada English
30 mins. 16mm color Experimental
Dist. (U.S.): Women Make Movies
Incorporating a rich, poetic style with elements of dance, personal history, and ethnographic documentary, Michelle Mohabeer reflects on her Indo-Caribbean heritage, exile, and sexual and cultural identity.

Cold Bath
Dir. Orr, Steve
Prod. Orr, Steve
1994 USA English
5 mins. video color Documentary
Dist. (U.S.): St. Orr Healing Arts
Steve Orr's *Cold Bath* is a poignant look at one day in the life of a male prostitute whose clients don't know he is dying from AIDS.

Color Box
Dir. Smolen, Wayne
1977 USA English
4 mins. S8mm color Experimental
Dist. (U.S.): Mears, Rik
A test for motion by painting on film. With much respect, I borrowed the title from the 1935 film.

Colour Eyes
(see *Irome*)

Colour Wind
(see *Iro Kaze*)

Columnburium
Dir. Navarre, Alan
1979 USA English
8 mins. video color Experimental
Dist. (U.S.): n/a
Depression.

Comedy in Six Unnatural Acts, A
Dir. Oxenberg, Jan
1975 USA English
26 mins. 16mm color Other
Dist. (U.S.): Frameline
Dist. (U.K.): Cinenova
Oxenberg toys with stereotypical notions about lesbians in her historic, funny, anarchic *A Comedy in Six Unnatural Acts*.

Coming Out
Dir. Carow, Heiner
1989 Germany German
109 mins. 35mm color Narrative
Dist. (U.S.): DEFA

Dist. (U.K.): Dangerous To Know

The first significant gay movie from East Germany opened on a historic night last fall. Given its controversial subject and difficult production history, *Coming Out* was expected to excite its first night crowd in East Berlin; nevertheless, director Heiner Carow hadn't anticipated what happened next. The applause and party atmosphere continued out on the streets after the screening, where people were already shouting and celebrating. *Coming Out's* premiere had coincided with the night the Berlin Wall came down. Even without this profound political backdrop, Carow's tale of socialist sexuality would seem extraordinary. Produced by the state studio DEFA (which kept a discreet distance from the project), and cloaked by the inevitable which-actor's-queer? curiosity, *Coming Out* clearly had a struggle just to see it to the screen.

It's a classic story—a sort of Marxist, modern-day *Maurice*. Schoolteacher Philipp finds himself distracted from his colorless romance with colleague Tanja by the attention of a teen he meets in a concert ticket line. Haunted by memories of his schooldays' desire for gay pal Jakob— and his parents' plea to stay on the straight and narrow—Philipp becomes torn between his two lovers, and risks losing both. Philipps' predicament propels him into the city's gay scene.

Heiner Carow shot *Coming Out* largely at real East Berlin bars and back alleys; outside of the Super-8 segments in Wieland Speck's *Westler*, this is a first and last look at gay locations and gay life before the Wall fell. Even separated from its historic circumstances, educational ambition, and fascinating cultural tourism, *Coming Out* stands as a moving and passionate story, honestly told.

Coming Out of the Iron Closet
Dir. Peloso, Larry, and Imre Sooaar
1995 USA Russian
40 mins. video color Documentary
Dist. (U.S.): Peloso, Larry
Coming Out of the Iron Closet visits several Soviet bloc countries and has many captivating interviews with political activists, entertainers, transsexuals, and one very supportive mother of a gay son. You won't want to miss the scenes at the gay nude beach in Moscow or the opening of their first-ever state sanctioned gay nightclub!

Winner of the 1995 San Francisco International Lesbian & Gay Film Festival Audience Award for Best Video.

Coming Out under Fire
Dir. Dong, Arthur
1994 USA English
90 mins. 16mm color/b&w Documentary
Dist. (U.S.): Zeitgeist Films
Based on the book of the same name by Allan Berube, who cowrote the documentary, *Coming Out under Fire* interviews 10 gays and lesbians who served in the military during the Second World War. Intercut with declassified military "education" films and newsreels, the interviews form a grave counterpoint to the campy, wholly ludicrious and sometimes painful stock footage where homosexuals were portrayed as darkly psychologically malevolent individuals. That the film focuses on gays and lesbians who served in World War II also neatly places contemporary national debates about gays in the military into some historical perspective. The issue is not gays in the military, Dong says, but how government works and how it treats a group of people.

With documentaries of this sort, what is left out and what doesn't make the cut is as interesting as what is presented. Dong had interviewed two African-American lesbians who had served in the Second World War. However, they declined to appear on camera as they were afraid they would lose their pension benefits.

While some people might find the idea of the military somewhat repellent, there are some quite real economic factors that govern a person's decision to "come out" or to even join the military; and perhaps the two women's decisions pointedly illustrate this.

Of the ten interviews in the film, only one asked that his identity not be revealed. The result is the man speaking in silhouette, a grim reminder of the psychological trauma of coming out that some people still grapple with. But with the current national debate about the subject and the accompanying media attention, some of the interviewees who had chosen to remain behind a pseudonym in Berube's book decided to allow the filmmaker to use their real names for the film. (J.C.)

Commercial for Murder
Dir. Goldstein, Amy
1985 USA English
15 mins. 16mm color Other
Dist. (U.S.): Picture Start c/o Film Library
A battle of the sexes, and the drag queen wins. Released in the U.S. as part of the collection, *Sexuality in the '90s.*

(A) (B) (C) (D) (E) (F) (G) (H) (I) (J) (K) (L) (M) (N) (O) (P) (Q) (R) (S) (T) (U) (V) (W) (X) (Y) (Z)

Common Flower, A
Dir. Bartoni, Doreen
1992 USA English
26 mins. 16mm color Narrative
Dist. (U.S.): Bartoni, Doreen
A Common Flower presents a touching portrayal of two older women in love. Paula plans to go to Russia with her lover, Sylvia. When Sylvia dies, Paula prepares to make the trip alone.

Common Loss
Dir. Haynes, Doug
1981 USA English
15 mins. 16mm color Experimental
Dist. (U.S.): n/a
Cut-out animation techniques are used to create a delightful, yet alarming picture of the conditioning and repression faced by individualists in a world of conformists.

Communication from Weber
Dir. Gates, Robert F.
1988 USA English
14 mins. 16mm color Documentary
Dist. (U.S.): Chicago Filmmakers
A fascinating look at Albert Michael Weber, described by the filmmaker as a "derelict-politico/artist-collagist/communicator" who lives "on the edge of society" in a small hotel room in Montgomery.

Complaint of the Empress, The
Dir. Bausch, Pina
1990 France / Germany German
108 mins. 35mm color Experimenta
Dist. (U.S.): Cinemien
This is a film by a person who knows how actors and actresses can evoke emotions with their bodies: the famous German choreographer Pina Bausch. The emotional energy and grotesque helplessness of the human being are also themes in her innovative work in dance and theater, but The Complaint of the Empress is not based on one of her plays, nor is it a conventional film. Instead of a traditional story, it links scenes about vain attempts and lost wishes. The erotic, the pathetic, and the despairing are all crucial elements in her humor and drama. A drunk woman recites a love poem in a streetcar. A woman in a bunny suit stumbles through a plowed field, her strapless suit slipping down under her breasts. Two men dance the tango on three legs—the fourth is held as an arm around the partner's shoulder. There is a poetic sensuality in Bausch's imagery and the music that accompanies it. The Complaint of the Empress might be a controversial film for a lesbian and gay film festival. Indeed, it doesn't offer any clear-cut views on lesbian or gay sexuality or existence. But it does open up fixed ideas about gender and sexual categories by working with and through the sexually and culturally determined language of the body, creating a new and appropriate cinematic approach in the process.

Complaints
Dir. Weissman, David
1990 USA English
6 mins. 35mm color Other
Dist. (U.S.): Weissman, David
Thirty-two of David's close personal friends sing about those things that tick them off.

Complaints of a Dutiful Daughter
Dir. Hoffman, Deborah
1994 USA English
42 mins. 16mm color Documentary
Dist. (U.S.): Women Make Movies
Deborah Hoffman's Complaints of a Dutiful Daughter gives a jarring account of her own struggle with her mother's Alzheimer's. It's a fascinating look at memory, aging, and self. As her mother's condition worsens, she becomes more accepting of her daughter's lesbianism. Through interviews, answering machine messages, home movies, and photographs, Hoffman constructs an emotional and heartening overview of another all too common (and often untalked about) contemporary health issue. Nominated for a 1994 Academy Award for Best Documentary.
Winner of the 1994 San Francisco International Lesbian & Gay Film Festival Audience Award for Best Documentary.

Complete St. Veronica, The
Dir. Hoyt, Dale
1986 USA English
5 mins. video color Documentary
Dist. (U.S.): Hoyt, Dale
Performer Winston Tong stars.

Complicated Flesh
Dir. Dunye, Cheryl, and Kristina Deutsch
1993 USA English
14 mins. video color Experimental
Dist. (U.S.): Two Faced Production
Reflections on an interracial relationship.

Comrades In Arms
Dir. Marshall, Stuart
1990 Great Britain English

52 mins. 16mm color Documentary
Dist. (U.S.): Filmmaker's Library
Dist. (U.K.): Maya Vision
Stuart Marshall is gaining a reputation for putting the homo back into history. After squaring up to Weimar and wartime Germany in last year's *Desire*, Marshall and his dedicated documentary team move back to Britain. *Comrades In Arms* (commissioned, like *Desire*, as part of Channel Four's *Out On Tuesday* and shown here separately in 16mm) describes homosexual life during the Second World War. Six lesbians and gay men narrate their experiences of sleeping and serving with the British Armed Forces. "It's a cliché, isn't it, when they say that there's nothing like the friendships you form in wartime—but it's perfectly true. You never meet it again in any form of life." Instead of stories of persecution and oppression, the film's interviewees recall a riotous time. In that typically English manner, most people were left alone to get on with their business as long as they were fairly discreet, and as long as the authorities weren't forced to recognize them officially. The blackout clearly had its advantages. *Comrades In Arms* matches the stories with a new take on clips from classic combat movies. Marshall has also shot new Hollywood-style scenes that restore the romance and bravado of lesbian and gay men's contribution to the war effort. A complement to Allan Berube's recent book on the American forces, *Comrades* rippingly reveals the spunk and gay spirit behind wartime Britain's stiff upper lip.

Red Ribbon Award Winner: 1991 American Film and Video Festival.

Conceicao
Dir. Jabour, Roberto
1993 Brazil Portugese
10 mins. video color Other
Dist. (U.S.): MIX Brasil
Features a TV Globo all-star cast in a story of two drag queens adopting a cat in Rio de Janeiro.

Conception, The
Dir. Sigal, David
Prod. De La Harpe, Martine
1995 USA English
20 mins. 16mm color Narrative
Dist. (U.S.): Sigal, David
The Conception brings together a pregnant straight teen, a gay man with relationship problems, and a lesbian couple desperately trying to get pregnant. This determined couple tries everything, including adoption, procreation, bribery, and immaculate conception. None of these options seem to work until they get a little help from a friend.

Condomnation
Dir. Chamberlain, Anne
1992 USA English
8 mins. 16mm color Documentary
Dist. (U.S.): Chamberlain, Anne
A lesbian safe-sex message.

Condoms Are a Girl's Best Friend
Dir. Kay, Eric
1991 USA English
4 mins. video color Other
Dist. (U.S.): Memory Lane
From Chicago, comedienne Memory Lane stars in this socially relevant music video.

Confessions of a Pretty Lady (BBC Arena)
Dir. Clarke, Kris, and Sarah Mortimer
1993 Great Britain English
70 mins. 16mm color Documentary
Dist. (U.K.): BBC TV
Follow Sandra Bernhard as L.A. dykes on bikes escort her through the streets of tinsel town in this world premiere screening of *Confessions of a Pretty Lady*. Old home movies and interviews with Sandra Bernhard's mother, aunt, and uncle give a personal touch to Kris Clarke and Sarah Mortimer's colorful and sexy portrait of the controversial ("there are different ways of being a feminist") comedienne. This engaging documentary (from the makers of the hit, *Armistead Maupin Is a Man I Dreamt Up*) features candid interviews with Bernhard, Martin Scorcese, Paul Mooney, *The Advocate* editor Jeff Yarborough, and yes, Camille Paglia. Extensive footage of Bernhard's celluloid performances in *King of Comedy*, *Without You I'm Nothing*, and *Sandra After Dark* are complemented by exhilarating live footage of her "Giving 'Til It Hurts" show at Madison Square Garden.

Connan the Waitress
Dir. Addy, Mark
1985 USA English
7 mins. video color Narrative
Dist. (U.S.): n/a
You'll never complain about bad service again after experiencing this excessive parody of the restaurant of your darkest nightmares.

Consequence, The
(see *Konsequenz, Die*)

Ⓐ
Ⓑ
Ⓒ
Ⓓ
Ⓔ
Ⓕ
Ⓖ
Ⓗ
Ⓘ
Ⓙ
Ⓚ
Ⓛ
Ⓜ
Ⓝ
Ⓞ
Ⓟ
Ⓠ
Ⓡ
Ⓢ
Ⓣ
Ⓤ
Ⓥ
Ⓦ
Ⓧ
Ⓨ
Ⓩ

Continuum 2
Dir. Mears, Ric
1972 USA English
7 mins. S8mm color Experimental
Dist. (U.S.): Mears, Ric
This film grew out of a desire to take a piece of music, graph out its beats and rhythms, and set animation to it, which would hopefully resemble some of the hallucinations I would see while listening to music when stoned. One minute of the film is actually animated, and it took almost six months to make. This is the second "real" film I made, while still living in Alabama, with no other teacher but Lenny Lipton's book *Independent Filmmaking*, which I recommend highly.

Cool Gleam
Dir. Wehren, Rixanne
1987 USA English
6 mins. video color Other
Dist. (U.S.): Freelance Video
Starring the Emerald Art Ensemble.

Cool Hands, Warm Heart
Dir. Friedrich, Su
1979 USA No Dialogue
17 mins. 16mm b&w Experimental
Dist. (U.S.): Canyon Cinema
Su Friedrich's perceptive *Cool Hands, Warm Heart* takes women's private rituals directly to the streets (of lower Manhattan).

Copenhagen: Gay Capitol of Denmark
Dir. unknown
1960 USA English
8 mins. 16mm b&w Documentary
Dist. (U.S.): Olson, Jenni
A campy, condensed travelogue of Copenhagen.

Corps Perdu, A (Straight to the Heart)
Dir. Pool, Lea
1988 Canada French
90 mins. 35mm color/b&w Narrative
Dist. (U.S.): Alliance International
Lea Pool's latest feature (she made the arty lesbian love story *Anne Trister*) is a depiction of the breakup of a decade-long ménage-a-trois involving one woman and two men. It's the tale of a photographer, Pierre, who returns to Montreal after an alarming assignment in Nicaragua only to find that both boyfriend and girlfriend have left him. He broods, he remembers (lots of black-and-white flashbacks), and—after brief and frustrating encounters with each of his former lovers—he tentatively begins a new relationship with Quentin, a young deaf-mute. *Straight to the*

Heart is adapted from a novel by French author Yves Navarre, whose writing always weaves in gay themes and characters; like Navarre, the film matches form and feeling perfectly. Lea Pool's lyrical style suits those introspective moments we've all felt at the end of a relationship. At the same time, she treats Pierre's bisexuality with a cool matter-of-factness, at least until he takes up with his new lover. Then the movie becomes detailed and affectionate in describing the practical problems they face. *Straight to the Heart* is always haunting and affecting.

Cosas del Querer, Las (Affairs of Love, The)
Dir. Chavarri, Jaime
1990 Spain Spanish
100 mins. 35mm color Narrative
Dist. (U.S.): Iberoamerica Films
A highly entertaining drama set in 1940s Madrid. It follows the fortunes of three vaudeville performers: handsome Juan, who plays piano for his passionate girlfriend Pepita, and her onstage partner, flamboyant Mario.

    The life of a gay man in the forties, and the power of music—the two main themes of the film—are both carefully choreographed by director Jaime Chavarri. Like Pepita, Mario is in love with straight man Juan (this is the *Fabulous Baker Boys* bit); rebuffed, he happily moves his attention to a string of lovers. After an affair with a young nobleman, whom Mario spurns, the nobleman's mother concocts a nasty revenge. A throwback to the pre-Almodovar days of Spanish cinema, *The Affairs of Love* is a gorgeous, completely un-self-conscious cinematic pleasure.

Cosmic Demonstration of Sexuality, A
Dir. Frilot, Shari
1992 USA English
15 mins. video color Experimental
Dist. (U.S.): Third World Newsreel
From the personal to the global, black women reflect on their bodies, sexuality, and the cosmos in the sexy, funny, and empowering "Lesbian's Guide to the Galaxy."

Cost of Love, The
Dir. Kwietniowski, Richard
1991 Great Britain English
2 mins. 16mm color Other
Dist. (U.S.): Frameline
A photo-romance featuring events that may become illegal in Britain under Clause 25 of the Criminal Justice Bill.

Costa Brava
Dir. Balletbò-Coll, Marta
1995 Spain English
92 mins. 35mm color Narrative
Dist. (U.S.): Balletbò-Coll, Marta
Catalonia's Marta Balletbò-Coll is a multi-talent-ed force who both directs and acts in *Costa Brava*, a sweetly melancholic love story rife with cheery, *Annie Hall*-ish eccentricity. Resembling an out-of-the-closet Rosie O'Donnell (imagine that), Balletbò-Coll is Anna, a monologuist and Barcelona tour guide who ricochets through the movie dropping sardonic asides and juicy bon mots. Then she meets Montserrat (San Francisco's fabulous Desi del Valle) a visiting scientist with a knack for seismic analysis and, naturally, the earth moves. What's special about the picture is its understatement, its comic tim-ing, its savvy framing. Indeed, *Costa Brava* is almost avant-garde in execution; the camera cuts away, jarringly, just before each caress, and cap-tures the fabled city of Barcelona through frac-tured glimpses of balconies and rooftops.

Winner of the 1995 San Francisco International Lesbian & Gay Film Festival Audience Award for Best Feature. (E.P.)

Count Me In
Dir. Patterson, Rebecca
1991 USA English
6 mins. video color Other
Dist. (U.S.): Dovi, Lori
A lyrical lesbian music video featuring Judith Kate Friedman.

Covert Action
Dir. Child, Abigail
1985 USA English
10 mins. 16mm color Experimental
Dist. (U.S.): Canyon Cinema
Celebrated filmmaker Abigail Child checks in with *Covert Action*, in which she subverts home movies to explore the contradictions of sexual existence, after which "one's own 8mm child-hood souvenirs become forever fraught with alarming possibilities."

Craig's Wife
Dir. Arzner, Dorothy
1936 USA English
78 mins. 35mm b&w Narrative
Dist. (U.S.): Films Incorporated
The horrors of heterosexuality. As the only openly lesbian director in Hollywood in the 1930s, Dorothy Arzner made a wonderful collection of "women's pictures" featuring such strong female stars as Katharine Hepburn, Joan Crawford, and Rosalind Russell. *Craig's Wife* is a disturbing proto-feminist melodrama/murder mystery (remade with Joan Crawford as *Harriet Craig* in 1950). Here, Roz Russell stars as Harriet Craig, the anal-retentive control queen of the century. A scathing commentary on the institution of mar-riage, *Craig's Wife* maps the tragic demise of a woman who has married a man she doesn't love. As she matter-of-factly tells her niece, Ethel: "I saw to it that my marriage was a way to emanci-pation. I had no private fortune, no special train-ing—so the only road to independence for me was through the man I married. I married to be independent."

Arzner presents Harriet as a victim of a society in which women must essentially prosti-tute themselves to men (by marrying them) in order to live. Harriet accepts this fact of life and is determined to have all of the superficial mid-dle-class happiness and stability she fears she cannot live without. Although her controlling demeanor seems at first villainous, her vulnera-bility is subtly conveyed, and in the end she emerges as a truly tragic figure.

Creation of Adam
Dir. Pavlov, Yuri
1993 Russia Russian
93 mins. 35mm color Narrative
Dist. (U.S.): Intercinema Agency
Andrey (Alexander Strizhenov) is disconsolate. His marriage is on the rocks (his wife thinks he is gay), and there's more trouble in store when he helps a young gay man escape from some local queer-bashers. But a work visit from a charismat-ic, wealthy businessman turns Andrey's life around. "I have come to teach you one thing . . ." he whispers, "To love."

Like a drunken mix of *It's A Wonderful Life* and *Apartment Zero*, *Creation of Adam* is also staggeringly bold. Although Andrey and Philip kiss and even sleep together, their relationship is never named; in fact, it's clearly meant to be metaphoric. Their homosexuality exists entirely at the visual level; for example, you can tell Philip is gay because he wears eye-liner and sharp clothes.

An absorbing and unique story, as a gay film from Eastern Europe *Creation of Adam* is a true breakthrough.

Crimes Against Nature
Dir. Dundas, Edward

Ⓐ Ⓑ Ⓒ Ⓓ Ⓔ Ⓕ Ⓖ Ⓗ Ⓘ Ⓙ Ⓚ Ⓛ Ⓜ Ⓝ Ⓞ Ⓟ Ⓠ Ⓡ Ⓢ Ⓣ Ⓤ Ⓥ Ⓦ Ⓧ Ⓨ Ⓩ

1977 USA English
90 mins. video b&w Documentary
Dist. (U.S.): Cinematherapy, Inc.
In 1977, the Gay Men's Theatre Collective of San Francisco commisioned a videotape of their landmark play, *Crimes Against Nature*, in hopes of gaining funding for a film that never panned out. A three-camera, forty-hour shot produced this vibrant translation of the testaments and self-discovery of a group of gay men.

Described in the '70s as a "*Chorus Line* for gay people," *Crimes Against Nature* remains vital today as a communal disclosure of roles gay people adopt in order to survive in a world that devalues homosexual feelings.

The play features individual actors delivering revealing monologues, during which the other memebers of the collective play background roles (parents, schoolmates, etc.). One by one the actors detail the ways in which they have buried their true selves in order to survive and be accepted in the world: repression; drug use; shyness; being agreeable; putting experiences into "little boxes"; acting "butch"; and so on.

An inspiring courage informs the sometimes humorous, sometimes painful testimony of the men, each of whom occupies the unsettling region between intellectual and emotional transformation. Exceptional performances convey the suspense involved in treading such dangerous psychological ground.

Clever staging raised the original theatrical production above mere confession and director Edward Dundas imaginatively weaves his camera into the play's action to create an intimacy that the viewer fully shares. Dundas's videotape recreates the emotion, humor, ritual, and pathos that characterized the play.

The world premiere of *Crimes Against Nature* is one of the "must see" programs of this year's festival. As a record of a popular and important play produced in a bygone era, this tape has obvious historical value. Its message about the urgency of authenticity speaks directly to the present.

Crimes of Passion
(see *Out On Four: Episodes 1 & 2*)

Crocodiles in Amsterdam
(see *Krokodillen in Amsterdam*)

Cross Body Ride
Dir. McMahon, Jeff
1988 USA English
13 mins. 16mm color Experimental

Dist. (U.S.): McMahon, Jeff
Two men dance a sensual duet.

Cross Your Heart
Dir. Richter, Suzy
1993 Canada English
13 mins. video color Experimental
Dist. (U.S.): Richter, Suzy
Suzy Richter's *Cross Your Heart* is a gritty Toronto dyke tale of obsession.

Crows
Dir. Menahemi, Ayelet
1987 Israel Hebrew
45 mins. 16mm color Narrative
Dist. (U.S.): Crows/Big Girl
A piercing authentic look at the life of homeless youngsters who lead a strange, commune-like life in a colorful garbage sanctuary amidst an ignoring Tel-Aviv. This is viewed through the eyes of Maggie, a naive but tough seventeen-year-old, who leaves her home in the province, comes to the big city, and is taken in by a group of young homosexuals.

Cruel
Dir. Del Valle, Desi
1994 USA English and Spanish
20 mins. 16mm b&w Narrative
Dist. (U.S.): del Valle, Desi/Chula Pictures
Cruel reflects on the agonizing conclusion of a Latina lesbian relationship.

Cruising
Dir. Friedkin, William
1980 USA English
106 mins. 35mm color Narrative
Dist. (U.S.): Films Incorporated
If I were a film about a murderer of S/M men cruising through urban Gaymerica, I wouldn't want to have been born in 1980, bracketed by 1979's White Night Riots and 1981's new "gay" disease. But the year Ronald Reagan beat Jimmy Carter in a landslide election—the year I was trying to figure out how to curl my bangs into feathers—also happened to be the year a lot of ink was spilled over William Friedkin's film *Cruising*. There was plenty to be angry about in 1979–1980, when tempers flared, protest erupted, and headaches followed. It's only strange that so much of that anger focused on this movie.

In retrospect the *Cruising* flap of the late '70s looks to be more about bad timing than bad intentions. The film is—and was—a sympathetic film about part of a subculture Mapplethorpe and the NEA eventually helped to make famous. *Cruising*-land is a place where gay victims are innocent and detectives (imagine) want to help. It features the sweet humor of undercover cop Al Pacino, in leather, entering a bar called Precinct 9 and facing a crowd of men all in police drag, then being kicked out by a doorman for being too cuddly. The film shows a man who, through a series of hot encounters with men in dark bars and alleys, is transformed from his too-happily-married condition to a confused, self-questioning state. And it has stuff some people only wish they could reminisce about: 1980s pseudo—'fros, play-cuffs, bandanas.

Then there is the issue itself, which has aged just about as gracefully as the film. The implication that people who practice S/M like to move from play to murder would have been frightening in the early '70s, when gays and non-gays alike were mistakenly looking at sadistic murders, like the ones Dean Corll committed, as an extension of S/M culture.

But Friedkin's movie doesn't connect those dots. His film never got much of a chance to imply anything, good or bad. It got buried by yield signs coming from all directions (family movie chains that wouldn't show it, protesters who didn't want it made or seen, viewers who were scared by it).

But now that S/M has moved out to the suburbs, now that AIDS and the new strain of right-wing misanthropy have taken its place in the protest pantheon, it would seem like at least one part of the world should be ready, finally, to appreciate the beauty of Al Pacino's naked butt on screen. Apparently not. (S.G.)

Crushed Lilies
Dir. Jankowski, T.
1983 USA English
40 mins. video color Other
Dist. (U.S.): n/a
A woman reflects upon her lover, and the near loss of her own life through an attempted suicide. Totally subjective, this is a point of view piece: a postromantic perception of psycho-sexuality.

Crying Game, The
Dir. Jordan, Neil
1992 USA English
112 mins. 35mm color Narrative
Dist. (U.S.): Films Incorporated
This film is a brilliant and thrilling sexual mystery, a blockbuster that exposes queer and mainstream audiences alike to an attractive fantasy of alternative sexuality. Some writers in the gay press criticized Neil Jordan for shrouding his film in secrecy during its opening run. However, as viewers will know by now, the secrecy does not merely participate in heterosexist power structures by making transvestism a guilty secret, the secrecy was integral to the pleasure of the film itself. In fact, not knowing some anatomical facts about the protagonist Dill is all-important to the film's construction of a complex web of gender, race, sexuality, and nationality.

Dill, of course, the woman with whom the male protagonist (Fergus) falls hopelessly in love, is anatomically male. There all all kinds of clues that let the discerning or queer viewer in on this secret and yet the narrative is able to maintain the illusion of Dill's femininity for the viewer who cannot tell the difference. Dill's transvestism, then, allows for at least two viewing experiences and this is why it works on both mainstream heterosexual audiences and queer audiences.

The fact that Dill is anatomically male throws all other identities in the film into doubt. In fact the film is a scathing critique of identity politics; accordingly, its backdrop—IRA terrorism—must be read in the light of this critique. If gender identities are uncertain, and if sexual instincts often lead us astray, then how much less reliable are concepts like national identity? This point is made very well in the opening sequence that shows IRA members kidnapping an English soldier who happens to be black. Jody, the soldier, points out the irony of his position by saying that, because of pervasive racism, most English people would not be comfortable with the idea of a black icon of Englishness.

The homoerotic bond that develops between Fergus and Jody in the film's beginning seems vaguely offensive while we still think that Jody and Fergus are straight. These scenes of course resonate with many homoerotically charged moments in film history and so it is particularly satisfying that the early homoeroticism builds to an extremely queer pitch as Fergus searches out Jody's lover, Dill, after Jody is killed. Dill is Jody's revenge; Dill is the snare that awaits all literal readings of bodies, sexes, races, nationalities. Dill attracts Fergus and then reveals to Fergus the possibility of misdirecting desire. Biology in this film, of course, is not destiny because Fergus seems to desire Dill in spite of his belief in his own unwavering heterosexuality.

Dill's performance of femininity is awesome. Dill simply is a woman; she is sexy as a

Ⓐ
Ⓑ
Ⓒ
Ⓓ
Ⓔ
Ⓕ
Ⓖ
Ⓗ
Ⓘ
Ⓙ
Ⓚ
Ⓛ
Ⓜ
Ⓝ
Ⓞ
Ⓟ
Ⓠ
Ⓡ
Ⓢ
Ⓣ
Ⓤ
Ⓥ
Ⓦ
Ⓧ
Ⓨ
Ⓩ

woman and strangely pathetic when Fergus cuts her hair and makes her dress up as a boy in order to disguise herself at the end of the film. Femininity in this film is always powerful (the female terrorist is the IRA's most lethal weapon) and masculinity is oddly manipulable and unstable. When Fergus cuts Dill's hair off to make her into a sad looking boy, it appears that masculinity or maleness is defined as castration. When Fergus reappears at the end in full drag and with her hair grown out, she is restored to feminine glory.

The Crying Game takes queer film to another level because it allows the viewer to see how s/he participates in constructions of identity. We, the viewers, stabilize Dill's ambiguity into "female," we demand that characters be read according to rigid codes of identification. But essentialism is not only misguided, it can lead us to oppose or validate certain performances for all the wrong reasons. Essentialism, the belief in biological sex, the desire to stabilize ambiguous sexualities, can be dangerous. (J.H.)

Cumulus Nimbus
Dir. Giritlian, Virginia
1973 USA English
5 mins. 16mm color Other
Dist. (U.S.): Canyon Cinema
Cumulus Nimbus features the musing of a woman wondering if she is gay.

Cunt Dykula
Dir. Kuhne, Kadet
1993 USA English
1 mins. video color Other
Dist. (U.S.): Frameline
A silent safe-sex horror spoof. Released in the U.S. as part of She's Safe, a feature-length package of lesbian safe-sex videos.

Cupid's True Love
Dir. Steinman, Connie
1987 USA English
10 mins. 16mm b&w Narrative
Dist. (U.S.): Connie Boy Productions
A lesbian cupid on a crusade to get the world to love her way.

Current Flow
Dir. Carlomusto, Jean
1990 USA English
5 mins. video color Documentary
Dist. (U.S.): Frameline
Released in the U.S. as part of She's Safe, a lesbian safe-sex video package.

Cut Sleeve
Dir. Diamon, Nikos
1992 USA English
24 mins. video color Documentary
Dist. (U.S.): Persona Video
Kitty Tsui and other Bay Area interviewees speak about the experience of being gay and Asian.

Cutting the Edge of a Free Bird
Dir. Bryan, Ann Marie J.
1993 USA English and American Sign Language
15 mins. 16mm color Narrative
Dist. (U.S.): Deafvision Filmworks
In Ann Marie Bryan's Cutting the Edge of a Free Bird a deaf, African-American lesbian wants to go to NYU, but her mother wants her to go to Gallaudet University for the deaf.

Cuz' It's Boy
Dir. Saalfield, Catherine
1994 USA English
13 mins. video color Other
Dist. (U.S.): Kitchen, The
Dist. (U.K.): Cinenova
Lesbian reflections on the case of Brandon Teena.

Da Da Da
Dir. Mongovia, Jack
1982 USA English
3 mins. 16mm color Other
Dist. (U.S.): n/a
Elaborately detailed, colorful, and humorous animation.

Daddy and the Muscle Academy
Dir. Pohjola, Ilppo
1992 Finland Finnish and English
55 mins. 16mm color Documentary
Dist. (U.S.): Zeitgeist Films
Tom of Finland was one of the gay world's few authentic icons. His hypermasculine drawings have had a lasting influence—not only on the visual appearance of gay men (the '70s clone look, the fetishism of leather)—but also on their self-understanding. Daddy and the Muscle Academy combines interview material with Tom and hundreds of his drawings, with testifying "Tom's men," from Drummer daddies to fellow artists. Ilppo Pohjola's controversial film also includes some steamy, invented sequences—a sort of journey to the center of Tom's psyche. Daddy and the Muscle Academy gets so close to the mystique of Tom of Finland, you can smell the leather.

Dadshuttle, The
Dir. Donaghy, Tom
Prod. Stremmel, Michael
1995 USA English
23 mins. 16mm color Narrative
Dist. (U.S.): Stremmel, Michael
A young man makes a futile attempt to come out and disclose his partner's HIV status to his elderly father in Michael Stremel's *The Dadshuttle*.

Damned If You Don't
Dir. Freidrich, Su
1987 USA English
42 mins. 16mm b&w Experimental
Dist. (U.S.): Frameline
Damned If You Don't is a portrait of a young nun fighting a losing battle against her sexual desires, then suddenly awakened by the persistent attentions of a beautiful neighbor. The film combines narrative and experimental elements and draws on historical documents, among them testimony from the trial of a 17th-century abbess accused of lesbian relations with another nun. The film also makes much use of *Black Narcissus*, a "classic" nun film in which the "bad" nun admits her desire for a man and therefore dies. In *Damned If You Don't* not only does the nun finally admit her desire but finds great pleasure.

    Damned If You Don't engages viewers in the act of sexually desiring nuns. The highly ironic deconstruction of the narrative of the classic film *Black Narcissus* opens up the space to tell the true story of a 17th-century nun accused of lesbian relations. This exploration of attraction of nuns for a lesbian is completed when the main character seduces, disrobes, and makes love to a contemporary nun.

Damned Queers
(See *Bogjavlar*)

Damned, The
Dir. Visconti, Luchino
1969 Italy/Germany English
155 mins. 16mm/35mm color Narrative
Dist. (U.S.): Swank/Kit Parker
"Soon he would become the 2nd most powerful man in Nazi Germany" smirked the original ads, over a photo of Helmut Berger in poutiest Marlene-the-Blue-Angel cabaret drag. Visconti's operatic tendencies began to bloat with this once "controversial" multinational epic, in which a Teutonic clan's moneyed decadence is offered as partial explanation for the rise of Hitler's Ultimate Evil. Dirk Bogarde grimaces from the conscience strain; Baroness/monster-mother Ingrid Thulin frets incestuously over gender-confused trouble child Berger. The infamous Nazi gay-slaughtering "Night of the Long Knives" is staged as a postorgy slumber-party-cum-bloodbath. Good for a few howls, though the cumbersome length (and pace) suggests everybody really thought they were making a Serious Artistic Statement. (D.H.)

Dance Macabre
Dir. Prouveur, Jean Michel
1993 Great Britain English
13 mins. 16mm color Experimental
Dist. (U.K.): Out On A Limb
A salute to angels by photographer/filmmaker Jean-Marc Prouveur.

Dance, The
Dir. Hubbard, Jim
1992 USA English
8 mins. 16mm color Experimental
Dist. (U.S.): Hubbard, Jim
A delicate short about the intimate relationship between musicians Dan Martin and Michael Biello.

Dance with a Body, A
Dir. Stanley, Anie
1991 USA English
2 mins. 8mm color Experimental
Dist. (U.S.): Stanley, Anie
A Dance with a Body goes under the skin to explore the truthfulness of flesh.

Dancing in Dulais
Dir. Lesbian and Gay Support the Miners Group
1986 Great Britain English
25 mins. video color Documentary
Dist. (U.S.): Converse Pictures
The South Wales miners' strike of 1984–1985 saw the formation of a curious alliance between a plucky group of young homosexuals from London and miners in Dulais Valley. In *Dancing in Dulais*, an initial wariness on the part of the young gays, the miners, and the miners' families gives way, through sometimes delicate interactions, to a loving and purposeful solidarity. The unembellished videography captures well this fascinating-to-witness union of two disparate yet ultimately kindred groups. The "Pits and Perverts" benefit concert features the Bronski Beat.

Dancing Is Illegal
Dir. Nicoletta, Daniel
1978 USA English
6 mins. S8mm color Documentary

Ⓐ Ⓑ Ⓒ Ⓓ Ⓔ Ⓕ Ⓖ Ⓗ Ⓘ Ⓙ Ⓚ Ⓛ Ⓜ Ⓝ Ⓞ Ⓟ Ⓠ Ⓡ Ⓢ Ⓣ Ⓤ Ⓥ Ⓦ Ⓧ Ⓨ Ⓩ

Dist. (U.S.): Nicoletta, Daniel
Footage of the Machine Worship sequence of *Sci-clones*, an Angels of Light production.

Dandy Dust [trailer]
Dir. Scheirl, A. Hans
1995 Great Britain English
8 mins. Super 8 color Narrative
Dist. (U.K.): Scheirl, A. Hans
A sensuous cyborg fantasy.

Danger Girl, The
Dir. Sennett, Mack
1916 USA No Dialogue
26 mins. 16mm b&w Narrative
Dist. (U.S.): Em Gee Film Library
Gloria Swanson stars in this madcap hetero melo-drama. She wants the boy, but he wants the other girl. Gloria dons male persona and seduces the other girl to get her out of the way. Although it ends heterosexually-ever-after, it's full of trans-gender fun and girl-girl tension.

Dangerous Bliss
Dir. Carla Wolf
Prod. Lock Up Your Daughters
1994 Canada English
7 mins. video color Other
Dist. (U.S.): Video Out
In Carla Wolf's *Dangerous Bliss*, the pleasurable edges of butch and femme intertwine in a spiral of velvet and Levis.

Dangerous When Wet
Dir. Bonder, Diane
1994 USA English
5 mins. video color Experimental
Dist. (U.S.): Frameline
A sensuous story of first orgasm and the language of pleasure.

Danny
Dir. Benavides, Cady Abarca
1993 Peru Spanish
18 mins. 35mm b&w Narrative
Dist. (U.S.): Benavides, Cady Abarca
Cady Abarca's *Danny* is a moody, intense, and disturbing black-and-white short about the melancholy friendship between a teen boxer and a homosexual hairdresser in Lima, Peru.

Dare to Be Butch
Dir. Sloan, Tamela
Prod. Sloan, Tamela
1994 USA English
17 mins. 16mm color Other
Dist. (U.S.): Sloan, Tamela
In *Dare to Be Butch*, Tamela Sloan explores the roots of gender identification and reflects on her childhood and how being raised by her lesbian mother and her partner has influenced her.

Dark Habits
(see *Entre Tinieblas*)

Darker Side of Black, A (BBC Arena)
Dir. Julien, Isaac
1994 Great Britain English
55 mins. 16mm color Documentary
Dist. (U.S.): Filmmaker's Library
Dist. (U.K.): BBC TV
Director Isaac Julien travels to Jamaica and investigates the world of rap, ragga and homo-phobia. In 1992 Jet Star Records released a sin-gle by Buju Banton called "Boom Boom Bye Bye," in which he demanded that all lesbians and gays should be shot. It wasn't long before this attitude found the support of Shabba Ranks and other musicians. In *A Darker Side of Black*, Ranks and Banton get to justify their theories, alongside opinions from Michael Manley (former prime minister of Jamaica), Michael Franti (Disposable Heroes of Hiphopcricy), Ice Cube, and cultural commentators Cornell West and Trisha Rose.
    "Julien captures views from across the black diaspora—moving his camera between London, the Caribbean and America. Like all his work, the investigation is rich and provocative, yet it scorns any tinge of easy judgement."
    —Cynthia Rose, *The Guardian* (London)

Darkness of My Language, The
Dir. Afram, Silvana
1989 Canada English
4 mins. video color Experimental
Dist. (U.S.): Women Make Movies
A lyrical love letter, this tape examines cultural identity and colonialism from the point of view of a Brazilian woman living in Canada.

Daughters of Darkness
Dir. Kumel, Harry
1971 France/Germany/Spain
87 mins. 35mm color Narrative
Dist. (U.S.): n/a
One of the most stylish horror films of the 1970s, this lesbian vampire epic masterfully combines traditional horror elements with outrageous, often ludicrous, wit. It also expresses feminist themes and is decidedly antimale, despite being directed by a man, Belgian writer-director Harry Kumel. A sadistic male chauvinist and his beautiful new bride miss their boat to England and check into a

deserted seaside hotel in modern-day Belgium. A mysterious woman arrives with a young companion who is both servant and lover. The mystery woman claims to be Elizabeth Bathory, the name of the "Bloody Countess" who lived and murdered scores of virgins for their blood three centuries before. She becomes attracted to the bride and sets out to take her away from her new husband. *Daughters of Darkness* moves from campy to sexy to horrifying and does it all with amazing originality. Kumel makes great use of sound, music, color (red especially), clothes, character placement, and wierd camera angles. The creepy husband's mother is played out by a man-director Fons Rademakers who makes a memorable contribution to this horrifying, undeniably fun cult classic.

David Hockney's Diaries
Prod. Blackwood Productions
1973 USA English
28 mins. 16mm color Documentary
Dist. (U.S.): Blackwood Productions
The English painter David Hockney has been keeping albums of snapshots since 1967, when he decided to clear his closet of hundreds of loose pictures. Slowly turning the pages of these personal albums, which constitute his diaries, Hockney explains that the snapshots are more than mere chronicles of his friends and travels; they provide the compositional elements on which his paintings and graphic works are based.

David, Montgomery und Ich
Dir. Speck, Wieland
1980 Germany German
16 mins. 16mm color Narrative
Dist. (U.S.): Frameline
Bowie, Clift, and a really bad nightclub singer form the imagery in this somber film about sexual frustration. Released as part of *Among Men*, a feature-length package of five short films by Wieland Speck.

David Roche Talks to You about Love
Dir. Podeswa, Jeremy
1985 Canada English
22 mins. 16mm color Other
Dist. (U.S.): Canadian Filmmakers Distribution Centre
One man's wry and very personal perspective on life, love, and romance.
    Winner of the 1985 San Francisco International Lesbian & Gay Film Festival Audience Award for Best Short Film.

Day in the Life of Edmund White, A
Dir. Cory, Bill
1993 USA English
37 mins. video b&w Other
Dist. (U.S.): Cory, Bill
America's best-known gay novelist, now resident in Paris, tries to prepare for a dinner party but is interrupted by fantasies about his personal trainer, an anonymous sex date, and a ghastly lunch with the countess. Director Bill Cory composes this clever comic chronicle as a series of saucy vignettes, which spoof the image of the American in Paris.

Dead Boys' Club, The
Dir. Christopher, Mark
1992 USA English
25 mins. 16mm color Narrative
Dist. (U.S.): Frameline
Dist. (U.K.): British Film Institute
Awkward, nerdy Toby is visiting his New York cousin Packard, who gives him a pair of shoes previously owned by his recently deceased lover. When Toby dons the shoes, he's transported to a world of promiscuity, disco music, hot guys, and glitter balls. Released in the U.S. as part of a feature-length package of gay short films, *Boys Shorts: The New Queer Cinema*.
    Winner of the 1992 San Francisco International Lesbian & Gay Film Festival Audience Award for Best Short Film.

Dead Dreams of Monochrome Men
Dir. Hinton, David
1990 Great Britain English
60 mins. video b&w Other
Dist. (U.K.): RM Associates
Wild, cruisy sex, that staple of gay male identity, is not what it used to be. The added bonus issue of mortality has made it quirkier, riskier, and more enticingly forbidden. Its inherent dysfunctionality, however, has never seemed steamier than in the salaciously arty *Dead Dreams of Monochrome Men*. In this surprisingly homoerotic British television (!) version of a dance/performance piece by the London-based DV8 Physical Theatre, anonymous sex is sweat-soaked, serious business with arousing, if somber, consequences. But, like the real thing, getting there is too delicious to do without.
    Filmed in starkly lit, anguish- and muscle-enhancing black and white, *Dead Dreams* looks like a living George Platt Lynes photograph set in a fevered, prisonlike bar world, pulsating with wordless sexual narratives, twitchy erotic

Ⓐ Ⓑ Ⓒ Ⓓ Ⓔ Ⓕ Ⓖ Ⓗ Ⓘ Ⓙ Ⓚ Ⓛ Ⓜ Ⓝ Ⓞ Ⓟ Ⓠ Ⓡ Ⓢ Ⓣ Ⓤ Ⓥ Ⓦ Ⓧ Ⓨ Ⓩ

appetites and well-shorn, hunky men. DV8's extremely physical choreography, while at times almost acrobatic, is appropriately rooted in urban sexual realism. Seamlessly woven into the "dance" are universally recognizable cruising rituals, cigarette smoke, boot licking, S/M, jockey short fetishes, and not-so-dry humping.

Easily transcending the stigmas of both dance and television with its use of angst-ridden sexual truth, *Dead Dreams of Monochrome Men* ultimately posits an unlikely, white hot link between performance art and performance anxiety.

Deadly Deception
Dir. Chasnoff, Debra
1991 USA English
29 mins. 16mm color Documentary
Dist. (U.S.): Tara Releasing
Debra Chasnoff's 1991 Academy Award–winning documentary, *Deadly Deception* is a powerful indictment of General Electric's nuclear weapons development in the United States. The film offers a disturbing documentation of GE's destruction of the environment and disregard for human lives in its release of radiation, dumping of toxic wastes, and continued development of nuclear weapons. It's a remarkable, lesbian-made documentary.

Deaf Heaven
Dir. Levitt, Steve
1993 USA English
25 mins. 35mm color Narrative
Dist. (U.S.): Frameline
Steve Levitt's *Deaf Heaven* is about AIDS, angels, faith, and the Holocaust; it is also an accomplished and affecting drama about a young man tending to his dying lover.

Winner of the 1993 San Francisco International Lesbian & Gay Film Festival Audience Award for Best Short Film.

Dear Boys
(see *Lieve Jongens*)

Dear Rock
Dir. Walsh, Jack
1992 USA English
18 mins. video color Experimental
Dist. (U.S.): Walsh, Jack
To sir with love: an intentionally digressive letter to Rock Hudson.

Death in Venice, CA
Dir. Ebersole, P. David
1994 USA English

30 mins. 16mm color Narrative
Dist. (U.S.): First Run Features
Dist. (U.K.): Dangerous To Know
In P. David Ebersole's immensely pleasurable *Death in Venice, CA*, our modern-day Dirk Bogarde finds himself forced to confront desires Thomas Mann could only dream of. Handsome 40ish introvert Mason Carver, a scholar of romantic love, takes a break in Venice and is suddenly plunged into a passion he has studied but never known—with drop-dead gorgeous 18-year-old Sebastian Dickens.

Death of a Writer in Two Parts (A Comedy of Sorts)
Dir. Russell, Pamela August
1995 USA English
9 mins. video color Other
Dist. (U.S.): Russell, Pamela August
A lesbian comedy about the hardships of writing fiction and keeping your characters in check.

Death of Dottie Love, The
Dir. Verow, Todd
1991 USA English
7 mins. 16mm color Experimental
Dist. (U.S.): Strand Releasing
A vampy, noirish seduction, it is a visual orgy of mutilated film emulsion.

Death Of Mikel, The
(see *La Muerte De Mikel*)

Death Watch
Dir. Morrow, Vic
1967 USA English
88 mins. 35mm color Narrative
Dist. (U.S.): Castle Hill Productions
The Murderer, The Thief and The Homo: Director Vic Morrow keeps the cipherlike characterizations but brings a cinematic quality to Genet's one-set stage play. Leonard Nimoy (who coproduced the film with Morrow) is the small-time thief who battles with queer Paul Mazursky over illiterate, muscular king convict Michael Forest. The three are constant cellmates so things turn a bit twitchy, talky, and tense. *Deathwatch* is a bold gay-themed mainstream movie which vanished rapidly on release and has never been screened since. We're preceding its parole with a brand-new print of Genet's only film, *Un Chant d'amour*.

DeAundra Peek's High Class Hall O'Fame Theater
Dir. Richards, Dick

1991 USA English
10 mins. video color Other
Dist. (U.S.): Richards, Dick
DeAundra Peek's High Class Hall O'Fame Theater
displays the talents of Atlanta's own DeAundra
Peek.

Dedicated to Those Days
Dir. Perkins, T.K.
1977 USA English
6 mins. S8mm color Experimental
Dist. (U.S.): n/a
I have been living and working and going to
school in the city for three years; currently I'm
enrolled in film school at San Francisco State.
This film was inspired one morning while on my
way to work.

Defect [unfinished]
Dir. Navarro, Ray
1990 USA English
20 mins. video color Documentary
Dist. (U.S.): Saalfield, Catherine
Defect is about Latino gay male culture.

Defectors: My Vacation
Dir. Medbury, Vinton W.
1984 USA English
6 mins. video color Other
Dist. (U.S.): n/a
A prophetic, well produced, very different rock
video that succeeds in affecting time and space
as perceived by the viewer.

Deflatable Man, The
Dir. Bettell, Paul
1988 Great Britain English
24 mins. 16mm color Experimental
Dist. (U.S.): Frameline
Dist. (U.K.): Basilisk
A ceremony of love, humor, spontaneity, and sexuality. Raw, unadulterated life, free from the con-
stricts of society.

Delius
Dir. Seyger, Israel, and Ido Ricklin
1988 Israel Hebrew
3 mins. 16mm color Other
Dist. (U.S.): Seyger, Israel
Two boys on some rocks with a video camera.

Deliver Us from Evil
Dir. Paradis, Marc
1987 Canada French
9 mins. video color Experimental
Dist. (U.S.): Videographe, Inc.
An early work from one of Canada's most cele-

brated experimental gay video makers.

Denajua: I Like My Name
Dir. Wehling, Susan
1993 USA English
28 mins. video color Documentary
Dist. (U.S.): Wehling, Susan
Transcending the "so what's it like to be a transsexual?" documentary genre, *Denajua, I Like My
Name* is a moving portrait of a charming fashion
designer who happens to be a male-to-female
transsexual.

Depart to Arrive
(see *Weggehen um Anzukommen*)

Deputy, The
(see *Diputado,II*)

Derek Jarman, Know What I Mean
Dir. Postma, Laurens
1988 Great Britain English
52 mins. 16mm color Documentary
Dist. (U.K.): Yoyo Film Video & Theatre
Productions
This documentary blends Derek Jarman's own
films, paintings, and poetry with original material
to give a starling poetic image of a controversial
artist's life and work. From the home counties of
the 1950s to the Slade, from the Royal Opera
House to Ken Russell, from feature films to the
Florence Opera House, the film portrays Jarman's
humor and humanity which transcends the controversy that surrounds him, making his dilemma
in Margaret Thatcher's Britain of the 1980s both
poignant and desperate.

Descent
Dir. Charles, Spenger
1992 USA English
14 mins. video color Narrative
Dist. (U.S.): Charles, Spenger
Descent paints a nightmarish vision of porcelain
and castration.

Desert Hearts
Dir. Deitch, Donna
1986 USA English
90 mins. 16mm color Narrative
Dist. (U.S.): Samuel Goldwyn Company
Dist. (U.K.): British Film Institute
Based on the novel *Desert of the Heart* by Jane
Rule, this romantic classic tells the story of
Vivian (Helen Shaver) and Cay (Patricia
Charbonneau) as they meet and fall in love in
Reno, Nevada, in the 1950s. Intelligent, fun,
and sexy, *Desert Hearts* has earned its place as a

Ⓐ
Ⓑ
Ⓒ
Ⓓ
Ⓔ
Ⓕ
Ⓖ
Ⓗ
Ⓘ
Ⓙ
Ⓚ
Ⓛ
Ⓜ
Ⓝ
Ⓞ
Ⓟ
Ⓠ
Ⓡ
Ⓢ
Ⓣ
Ⓤ
Ⓥ
Ⓦ
Ⓧ
Ⓨ
Ⓩ

landmark lesbian film. This print is subtitled for the hearing-impaired.

Desert of Love
Dir. Lambert, Lothar
1986 Germany German
70 mins. 16mm b&w Narrative
Dist. (U.S.): Altermedia

One of the most prolific European gay directors, Lothar Lambert began making underground films in the 1970s. Since then he has grown as both an actor and a director, though his films still create a certain amount of controversy. New Yorkers still remember the angry reaction to his *Fucking City*, a film that was called one of the ten best of 1982 by the *Village Voice*. His *Paso Doble*, about a bizarre German family's Spanish vacation (shown at the festival in 1985) was his first mainstream success. *Desert of Love*, a bitter, funny look at the failures of human relationships has been called both his rawest and cruelest film, and a clever pastiche. The story centers around a director's ruined film—most of which was inadvertently destroyed at the lab. It is a wild mosaic of startling imagery including a safe-sex foot-fucking scene with toes in a condom, a woman flasher, and a woman voyeur in a wheelchair who comments on the street life near a public toilet. *Desert of Love* is a challenging, highly original work from one of Germany's most exciting gay talents.

Deserter
(see *Lipotaktis*)

Desire
Dir. Marshall, Stuart
Prod. Dobbs, Rebecca, and Maya Vision
1989 Great Britain English
90 mins. 16mm color Documentary
Dist. (U.K.): Maya Vision

Stuart Marshall's forceful film (separately commissioned, but screened in Britain as part of—and the most watched episode of—Channel Four's lesbian and gay magazine series) isn't just about the Holocaust. Subheaded *Sexuality in Germany 1910–1945*, it digs up a whole deal of stories leading to the Nazi extermination of lesbians and gay men, the body and nature worship cult; the deification of same-sex friendship; the growth of gay bars; the persecution of sexual radicals—Marshall's interviews add up to a sharp analysis of the anxieties and inconsistencies in the rise of Nazism. Of course the massacre is a hideous and appalling historical fact. But *Desire* aims to get more out of the death toll than anger

and upset. Marshall's earlier tape (shown at the 1987 festival), *Bright Eyes*, was partly about the relation between AIDS and the Holocaust. Here he strikes a less complicated and didactic pose. If the concentration camps can teach anything, the ground has to be raked thoroughly and soberly. So on-screen women and men recall anecdotes of a pre-Nazi Berlin life like lost friends, and Marshall stitches them together in a compelling patchwork. Innovative and illuminating, *Desire* is an instance of outstanding gay research.

Desperate Remedies
Dir. Main, Stewart, and Peter Wells
1993 New Zealand English
93 mins. 35mm color Narrative
Dist. (U.S.): Swank Motion Pictures

Something for everyone! *Desperate Remedies* is an insanely campy bodice-ripper about a turn-of-the-century lipstick lesbian and the ridiculously handsome men who seek to defame her. Trapped in the dispiriting New Zealand harbor town of Hope, Dorothea Brook, a draper of distinction, finds her discreet life with companion Anne turned upside down when immigrant Lawrence arrives.

Dorothea wants Lawrence to marry her opium-addled sister Rose; Rose wants to marry flamboyant queen Fraser; Lawrence wants to devour Dorothea, who's in love with Anne; Anne wants Dorothea to enter a marriage of convenience with a sleazy local politician. Life in Hope is more complicated than a week at "Melrose Place."

Orlando on acid, *Querelle* cross-dressed by *Barbarella*, *Vogue* meets *Queen Christina* . . . it's very easy to get excited about *Desperate Remedies*; the film positively inspires giddiness. Plot points aside, *Remedies* is driven by a rampantly operatic score, eye-popping color, and a generous, demented gay sensibility. A tale of lesbian triumph, peopled by *Playgirl* pin-ups, and directed by New Zealand's most important gay filmmakers (Stewart Main and Peter Wells made the far more serious *Death in the Family*, which we screened in 1987), *Desperate Remedies* is the perfect way to mark the end of Lesbian and Gay Freedom Day.

Destiny/Desire/Devotion
Dir. Dar, Zahid
1994 Great Britain English
10 mins. 16mm color Narrative
Dist. (U.K.): Dar, Zahid
A bittersweet British short.

Devotion

Dir. Kaplan, Mindy
Prod. Battishill, Arlene
1994 USA English
120 mins. 35mm color Narrative
Dist. (U.S.): Northern Arts Entertainment

k.d. lang lookalike Jan Derbyshire plays Sheila Caston, an aspiring lesbian stand-up comedian who is about to get her big break in the business. Sheila has been living happily with her lover of four years, Julie, in a beautiful seaside home. Returning from an out-of-town comedy engagement, she is offered the starring role in a new TV sitcom by a husband-and-wife producing team. All is well until Sheila comes face to face with the woman behind the offer. Catching Sheila by surprise, the mysterious producer turns out to be her long-lost first love, Lynn, who reappears after a fifteen-year absence. Through a series of flashbacks, we realize that Lynn, while battling her own internalized homophobia had rejected Sheila's advances, causing her to become suicidal. Unable to put the past behind her, Sheila must decide whether she is still in love with the elusive Lynn. The two do their best to keep their past relationship a secret, but emotions boil to the surface and their prospective mates begin to suspect. Lynn becomes obsessed with Sheila and buys a date with her for $1,200 at a charity benefit. Sheila on the other hand starts to withdraw and become introspective. She spends many an evening vigorously rowing in a tied-up boat that can go nowhere while her career and her committed relationship are put on hold. Eventually her partner gives her an ultimatum and Sheila must choose between her past and present loves.

Devotions

Dir. Broughton, James
1983 USA English
20 mins. 16mm color Experimental
Dist. (U.S.): Canyon Cinema

Devotions celebrates images of the gay community and gay relationships in a masterful visual and poetic montage.

DHPG Mon Amour

Dir. George, Carl M.
1989 USA English
12 mins. video color Documentary
Dist. (U.S.): n/a
Dist. (U.K.): London Filmmakers Co-op

DHPG Mon Amour is a document of personal activism. David Conver is an AIDS patient who has taken control of his own treatment by choosing an alternative drug therapy. On the surface, this tape is about coping, about the need for love and support, and even evokes aspects of quiet heroism. Mixed with videomaker Carl M. George's love of lounge music and a good dose of self-consciousness in the voice-over, however, the private drudgery of coping becomes an affirmative dissemination of information and encouragement.

Dialogo

Dir. Pino, Haydee
1991 Venezuela Spanish
10 mins. 16mm color Narrative
Dist. (U.S.): Ashkenazi

Dialogo is a moving monologue about sexuality as imagined by a Venezuelan drag queen.

Diamanda Galas: Judgement Day

Dir. Fax, Fred
1993 USA English
60 mins. video color Documentary
Dist. (U.S.): n/a

The work of Diamanda Galas—the diabolical siren of the uber-avant-garde—explores pain, madness, isolation, obsession, death, and despair in the context of the AIDS community. A classically trained pianist and industrial-strength singer with a three-and-a-half octave range, Diamanda reinterprets gospel and blues standards in this extraordinary film/performance.

DiAna's Hair Ego: AIDS Info Up Front

Dir. Spiro, Ellen
1990 USA English
29 mins. video color Documentary
Dist. (U.S.): Women Make Movies
Dist. (U.K.): British Film Institute

DiAna's Hair Ego: AIDS Info Up Front is the inspiring story of a South Carolina town that took the initiative in getting educated about AIDS. It all started when DiAna, who runs a local beauty salon, became curious about AIDS and went looking for information. Not the type to keep anything to herself, she gradually involved her customers, their families, and the local school system in a program of grassroots AIDS education. DiAna emerges as a compulsive organizer, a brilliant educator, a great friend across communities, and the best hairdresser in town.

These films are direct explorations of the injustice that exists in the world of living with AIDS. In *Hair Ego*, it is the willful dissemination of misinformation that kills. Beauty parlor owner DiAna is seething below the surface (and what a fancy surface: the permanents, the curlers—a veneer of true camp hilarity). The idea exposed is

A B C D E F G H I J K L M N O P Q R S T U V W X Y Z

this: People can't talk about sex in South Carolina, so thousands will die in ignorance. DiAna is a hero. She opens her life and does something to counter the misinformation. From her hair-do parlor she hands out safe sex info and free condoms. Director Ellen Spiro has made a loving portrait of a passionate mission, a drama about a single fight in the face of South Carolina bigotry.

Dick Tricks
Dir. Oshiro, Resa
1993 USA English
12 mins. video color Other
Dist. (U.S.): Oshiro, Resa
A variety of penile prestidigitations.

Different from the Others
(see *Anders als die Anderen*)

Ding Dong
Dir. Hughes, Todd
Prod. Ebersole, P. David
1995 USA English
40 mins. video color Narrative
Dist. (U.S.): Ebersole, P. David
In *Ding Dong*, Todd Hughes turns the negative gay stereotypes of such blockbuster films as *The Silence of the Lambs* and *Basic Instinct* on their heads. Honey and Slim are two successful door-to-door cosmetic salesladies who just happen to be lesbian lovers. When two investigative reporters try to do an exposé on them, they discover yet another shocking secret about the duo. Like most lesbians these days, they are serial killers! That's when the action begins in this hilarious spoof.

Dinner with Malibu
Dir. Carnoy, Jon
1992 USA/France English
13 mins. 16mm color Narrative
Dist. (U.S.): Andre Duchaine Films
In Jon Carnoy's *Dinner with Malibu*, Tommy's father is about to chow down with his new girlfriend, but Tommy knows something about her that dad doesn't.

Diputado, II (Deputy, The)
Dir. de la Iglesia, Eloy
1980 Spain Spanish
110 mins. 35mm color Narrative
Dist. (U.S.): Strand Releasing
The Deputy is a taut and gripping political thriller about a gay man high in the ranks of the Spanish Socialist party. Roberto Orbea (Jose Sacristan),

married to a loyal and beautiful wife, is well-respected by his colleagues and is in line for one of the party's top positions. While in prison for political offenses, however, he became involved with a young hustler. Later, out of prison, he makes contact with the hustler and, drawn to the lower-class world to which he is so politically committed, he falls in love with another teenage boy, Jaunito. As their relationship develops we realize that Jaunito is part of a blackmail plot by a neo-fascist group out to get Orbea. Director Eloy de la Iglesia, who cowrote *The Deputy*, successfully blends the political turmoil of 1970s Spain (often using well-known incidents) with the personal story of a man's struggle, both as a Socialist and a homosexual. *The Deputy* is one of the most challenging and controversial films to come out of post-Franco Spain.

Disappearing Act
Dir. Ferebee, Gideon
1992 USA English
8 mins. video color Experimental
Dist. (U.S.): n/a
A moving statement about daily loss, adapted from Chasen Given's short poem.

Disco Years, The
Dir. King, Robert Lee
1992 USA English
30 mins. 16mm color Narrative
Dist. (U.S.): Strand Releasing
A sexy and honest teen coming-out story set in the time of pet rocks, gas lines, and macramé—yes, the '70s. High School student Tom's sexual passions are stirred in a gym class by tennis champ Matt (played by Steve Rally, a recent Playgirl model). Sex, tension, and lots of tennis games follow.

Released in the U.S. as part of *Boys Life*, a feature-length package of three gay shorts.

Disco's Revenge
(see *Out On Four: Episodes 3 & 4*)

Displaced View, The
Dir. Onodera, Midi
1988 Canada English
52 mins. 16mm color Documentary
Dist. (U.S.): Women Make Movies
Displaced View is the latest film by Midi Onodera, a third-generation Japanese Canadian (Sansei). Most Sansei grew up unaware of the unique history of their people. The film traces a personal search for identity and pride within that

history. Through an examination of the emotional and cultural links between the women of one family, the processes of the construction of memory and the reconstruction of history are revealed. The film is a celebration of the acceptance of self, not only as a Japanese Canadian, but as woman, person of color, lesbian, immigrant.

Divine Bodies
Dir. Roycht, Charlene
1995 Canada English
4 mins. video color Documentary
Dist. (U.S.): V-Tape
We are given an up-close view of lesbian body builders Robin Chesky and Chris Dahl in *Divine Bodies*.

Djune/Idexa
Dir. Milstead, J.D. Salome
1994 USA English
9 mins. 16mm b&w Experimental
Dist. (U.S.): Milstead, J.D. Salome
A hypnotic ode.

Do Not Listen
Dir. Jubela, Joan
1984 USA English
5 mins. video
Dist. (U.S.): Jubela, Joan
Purely visual, painfully artistic.

Do You Know What I Mean
Dir. McClain, Allen
1977 USA English
6 mins. S8mm color Documentary
Dist. (U.S.): n/a
Coming out is a triumph of personal liberation over oppressive societal pressure to conform. For many gay women and men, coming out is relatively easy. For others it is a tormenting struggle. This film portrays a gay man experiencing this internal conflict.

Do You Mind?
Dir. Stephans, Elizabeth
1992 USA English
11 mins. video color Documentary
Dist. (U.S.): Stephens, Elizabeth
Speaking of desire.

Do You Think that a Candidate Should Live Like This?
Dir. Montgomery, Jennifer
1992 USA English
3 mins. video color Experimental
Dist. (U.S.): Montgomery, Jennifer

An intimate and nosy perspective on the apartment of lesbian poet and Presidential candidate Eileen Myles.

Doctors, Liars and Women
Dir. Carlomusto, Jean, and Maria Maggenti
1988 USA English
22 mins. video color Documentary
Dist. (U.S.): Gay Men's Health Crisis
New York women react to a *Cosmopolitan* article stating unprotected heterosexual vaginal intercourse constitutes little risk for women. Grassroots protest gains media attention and confrontation with the article's author. A primer on political action that elucidates many of the medical facts as well.

Does Your Mother Know?
Dir. Littleboy, Helen
Prod. Brown, Shauna, and Cheryl Farthing
1994 Great Britain English
18 mins. video color Documentary
Dist. (U.K.): Piranha Productions
Young gays and lesbians talk about growing up in the '90s on this irreverent documentary.

Doll House
Dir. Hammer, Barbara
1984 USA English
4 mins. 16mm color/b&w Experimental
Dist. (U.S.): Canyon Cinema
In *Doll House* Barbara Hammer captures an echo of the militant feminism that informed her earlier work.
  Released in the U.S. along with four of her other short films as a feature-length package, *Lesbian Humor: The Films of Barbara Hammer, Volume I*.

Doll Shop
Dir. Rasmussen, Christine
1991 USA English
11 mins. 16mm color Narrative
Dist. (U.S.): Frameline
A woman's realization of her attraction to a coworker prompts a fantastic reverie in this stop-motion animated short.

Domestic Bliss
Dir. Chamberlain, Joy
Prod. Newsreel Collective Ltd.
1984 Great Britain English
52 mins. 16mm color Narrative
Dist. (U.S.): Women Make Movies
Dist. (U.K.): Cinenova
The conflicts in this carefully observed and know-

Ⓐ Ⓑ Ⓒ Ⓓ Ⓔ Ⓕ Ⓖ Ⓗ Ⓘ Ⓙ Ⓚ Ⓛ Ⓜ Ⓝ Ⓞ Ⓟ Ⓠ Ⓡ Ⓢ Ⓣ Ⓤ Ⓥ Ⓦ Ⓧ Ⓨ Ⓩ

ing comedy/drama center around the relationship of Diana, a successful doctor, and her lover, Emma, a divorced woman with a ten-year-old daughter. Diana invites Emma and daughter to live with her in her comfortable London home. They all get more than they bargained for, including visits from Emma's ex-husband, Emma's best friend Amelia, who arrives with baby and dog, and a next-door neighbor who has a bad habit of locking herself in the bathroom and crawling through Diana's window. Diana, loving but inflexible, is torn between her love for Emma and her need for structure and tranquillity. Full of bright dialogue and a genuine chemistry between the excellent cast, the film depicts lesbians in a way rarely seen in the movies.

Don't Forget You're Going To Die
(see *N'oublie pas que tu vas mourir*)

Don't Look Up My Skirt Unless You Mean It
Dir. Vachon, Christine, and Marlene McCarty
1994 USA English
5 mins. video color Narrative
Dist. (U.S.): KVPI
From Marlene McCarty and 1994 Frameline Award–winner Christine Vachon, the video with the title that says it all, *Don't Look Up My Skirt Unless You Mean It.*

Don't Make Me Up
Dir. Tuft, Sarah
1986 USA English
4 mins. video color Experimental
Dist. (U.S.): Tuft, Sarah
Sarah Tuft's *Don't Make Me Up* is a snappy, musical request of Madison Avenue.

Don't Touch (Hors limite)
Dir. Roques, Philippe, and Eric Slade
1991 USA English
8 mins. video color Other
Dist. (U.S.): Roques, Phillippe
Exploring the forbidden—men touching men.

Dona Herlinda Y Su Hijo (Dona Herlinda and Her Son)
Dir. Hermosillo, Jaime Humberto
Prod. Ponce, Manual Barbachano
1985 Mexico Spanish
90 mins. 35mm color Narrative
Dist. (U.S.): Cinevista
This year's opening night feature is a sophisticated social comedy directed by Jaime Humberto Hermosillo, one of Mexico's most daring, original

filmmakers.

Dona Herlinda is a wealthy, fantastically manipulative widow living in Guadalajara who quietly accepts her son Rudolfo's affair with a handsome young music student, Ramon. After she invites Ramon to live with her family ("Rudolfo has such a big bed," she says) the situation becomes hilariously complicated by Rudolfo's marriage of convenience to Olga, a feminist and employee of Amnesty International.

Dona Herlinda's comedy lies in watching Dona Herlinda flawlessly manipulate the people in her life while maintaining a Nancy Reagan–like facade of cool detachment. Despite all the possibilities for disaster the characters in this film react to unbelievable situations with deadpan nonchalance. Jaime Humberto Hermosillo has directed twelve features—most dealing with the conventions and petty concerns of middle class society. *Dona Herlinda* is his third collaboration with producer Manual Barbachano Ponce, one of Mexico's most important independent film producers.

Based on a story Hermosillo read in a Guadalajara newspaper, *Dona Herlinda* has met with some interesting reactions in Mexico. According to Hermosillo: "The most disturbing thing about the film to some of the 'machista' audience has not been the sex in the film but the tenderness—it's so tender, the relationship between the men, and some cannot accept that. I think that's terrible."

Donna e Mobile, La
Dir. Maggenti, Maria
1994 USA English
5 mins. video color Narrative
Dist. (U.S.): Maggenti, Maria/Smash Pictures
A short story about a hot Italian babe.

Doom Generation, The
Dir. Araki, Gregg
1995 USA English
85 mins. 35mm color Narrative
Dist. (U.S.): Samuel Goldwyn Company
Araki's alleged first "heterosexual movie" is just as homoerotic as *The Living End*, if not more so. It's an over-the-top road movie determined to out-shock *Natural Born Killers*, as punky L.A. teens Amy (a foul-mouthed Rose McGowan) and Jordan (Keanu-ish James Duval) cross paths with slightly psycho, very sexy Xavier Red (Johnathan Schaech). Blood, tears, and sweaty bisexual chemistry soon soaks the screen. This seemed the last word in envelope-pushing at the time of

its release, the movie your grandma would rather fellate a crucifix than watch to its outré end. Yet Araki is so hell-bent on shocking an imagined bourgeoisie that, for more jaded viewers, it all comes off as a harmless bad-taste joke. And a very stylish one, too. One thing Araki is quite serious about: his sex scenes (whatever their gender configuration) sport a genuine, groin-levitating tension that megabuck major-studio "erotic thrillers" would die for. Featuring cameo appearances by such pop icons as Heidi Fleiss, Christopher ("Brady Bunch") Knight, Lauren ("Love Boat") Tewes, Perry Farrell, Margaret Cho, and Amanda Bearse. (D.H.)

Dorian Gray Im Spiegel Der Boulevardpresse (Dorian Gray in the Mirror of the Popular Press)
Dir. Ottinger, Ulrike
1984 Germany German
150 mins. 35mm color Narrative
Dist. (U.S.): Exportfilm Bischoff & Co.
Oscar Wilde's *The Picture of Dorian Gray* has been the inspiration for numerous film and television interpretations—some have been horribly literal translations of his classic horror tale while others have used the story as a jumping-off point. Director Ulrike Ottinger, one of Germany's leading lesbian filmakers, uses Wilde's work as the basis for an exploration of the function of the media in the modern world. Visually and thematically, *Dorian Gray in the Mirror of the Popular Press* owes less to Wilde's novel than it does to the traditions of Germany's expressionistic cinema.

Dr. Mabuse (played by Delphine Seyrig), the president of a multinational press conglomerate, has an unscrupulous plan for the company's expansion. She wants to use her company to create a human being that she can shape and control according to the corporation's requirements.

Enter Dorian Gray, a wealthy and handsome young man (played by female actress/model Veruschka von Lehndorff) who Mabuse leads on a nightmare journey through the city. "We shall let him experience everything the reader does not dare to dream, " she explains. At the premiere of an opera the self-obsessed Dorian Gray meets his mirror image on stage, leading to the central question in this bizarre, startling, and masterfully made film: will Dorian Gray become Dr. Mabuse's victim or her best disciple?

Dorothy Arzner: A Profile

(BBC The Late Show)
Prod. Beavan, Clare
1993 Great Britain English
15 mins. video color Documentary
Dist. (U.K.): BBC TV
This overview of Arzner's life and works discusses her status as a lesbian director in Hollywood's Golden Age during which she worked with such strong female stars as Katharine Hepburn, Rosalind Russell, and Joan Crawford. Produced for the nightly BBC TV arts program, "The Late Show."

Dos Jorges, Los
(see *Two Georges, The*)

Dottie Gets Spanked
Dir. Haynes, Todd
1993 USA English
27 mins. 16mm color Narrative
Dist. (U.S.): Zeitgeist Films
Todd Haynes exceeds the dazzling dementia of *Superstar* and *Poison* with *Dottie Gets Spanked*, a perverse nod to his own childhood infatuation with "The Lucy Show." A young boy enters a limitless erotic world through the miracle of modern television. *Dottie Gets Spanked* is being screened here in tribute to producer Christine Vachon, this year's Frameline Award winner, and it was commissioned for broadcast on public television as part of the five-part series, "TV Families."

Double Entente
Dir. Lawrence, Jacquie
1994 Great Britain English
11 mins. 16mm color Narrative
Dist. (U.K.): Lawrence, Jacquie
Fantasy and reality mix in *Double Entente.*

Double Exposure
Dir. Slater, Jeanne
1989 USA English
18 mins. 16mm color Narrative
Dist. (U.S.): Fireball Films
In Jeanne Slater's erotic *Double Exposure*, a photographer and her model are drawn together in their first taste of lesbian longing. With exquisite photography by Susan Plack, Slater emphasizes the difference between gay and straight relations in sensuous and often clever detail, always keeping an edge of desperation in her characters' drastic passage.

Double Strength
Dir. Hammer, Barbara
1978 USA English

Ⓐ Ⓑ Ⓒ Ⓓ Ⓔ Ⓕ Ⓖ Ⓗ Ⓘ Ⓙ Ⓚ Ⓛ Ⓜ Ⓝ Ⓞ Ⓟ Ⓠ Ⓡ Ⓢ Ⓣ Ⓤ Ⓥ Ⓦ Ⓧ Ⓨ Ⓩ

20 mins. 16mm color Experimental
Dist. (U.S.): Canyon Cinema
A poetic study of the stages of a lesbian relationship between two women performance artists, from honeymoon, to struggle, to breakup, to enduring friendship. Released in the U.S. along with four of her other short films as a feature-length package, *Lesbian Sexuality: The Films of Barbara Hammer, Volume II.*

Double the Trouble, Twice the Fun
Dir. Parmar, Pratibha
1992 Great Britain English
25 mins. video color Documentary
Dist. (U.S.): Women Make Movies
A tale about one man's search for his community. That the man is Indian, gay, and disabled leads to some revealing confrontations; Pratibha Parmar brings to her latest film—made for Channel Four's *Out*—the same wit and richness seen in her acclaimed earlier work *Khush.*

Double Trouble
Dir. Aynes, Tony
1991 Australia English
24 mins. video color Documentary
Dist. (U.S.): Aynes, Tony
"I don't think there were any," is the constant refrain of white Australia on the subject of lesbian and gay Aborigines. *Double Trouble* proves them wrong with insight and a sharp edge of humor. Young urban Aboriginals—and older men and women from rural backgrounds— describe their first sexual experience, the racism of the white gay scene, and the contradictions of living in collision between the third and first world.

Down on the River
Dir. Stevens, Ylonda
1991 USA English
6 mins. video color Documentary
Dist. (U.S.): Frameline
Released in the U.S. as part of *She's Safe*, a feature-length package of lesbian safe-sex videos.

Downey Street
Dir. Ward, Ken
1977 USA English
6 mins. S8mm color Experimental
Dist. (U.S.): n/a
A class assignment to capture the character of a street in San Francisco. I chose the street I've always wanted to live on.

Dozens, The
Dir. Dall, Christine, and Randall Conrad

1981 USA English
78 mins. 16mm color Narrative
Dist. (U.S.): Calliope Film Resources
The Dozens is the story of Sally Connors, a young working-class woman who returns to a Boston community after a time in a state prison for economic crimes. Among those who eagerly and not-so-eagerly await her return are her husband who, although he has not maintained their relationship during her incarceration, expects Sally to reunite with him, and a mother, whose refusal to accept reality has led her to tell people Sally's been in the hospital for two years. The closeness and comfort she had found within the community of female prisoners, and especially with her woman lover in prison, has been suddenly withdrawn. In its place is the cold impersonality of the city, the sextyped expectations of mother and husband, and the paternalistic eye of the parole officer. As the film progresses, these forces chip away at Sally's independence, but she demonstrates a rebellion, determination, and spirited humor that make her truly a feminist heroine.

Dr. Jekyll and Sister Hyde
Dir. Baker, Roy Ward
Prod. Fennel, Albert, and Brian Clemens
1971 Great Britain English
95 mins. 35mm color Narrative
Dist. (U.S.): Orion Classics
The queerest Hammer horror film ever has plenty of schlock style, conflating the Victorian mad scientist story with a gender-fuck Jack-the-Ripper plot in which the good doctor inadvertently turns himself into a woman while pursuing immortality, then kills prostitutes to extract their hormones in order to live forever. A surprisingly sophisticated film that raises moral dilemmas of Faustian proportions. (S.S.)

Dr. Paglia
Dir. Treut, Monika
1992 Germany/ USA English
23 mins. 16mm color Documentary
Dist. (U.S.): First Run Features
In Monika Treut's short documentary, *Dr. Paglia*, Camille's egomaniacal, self-acknowledged obsession with herself is punctuated by her relentless barrage of attacks on contemporary feminists, concluding with characteristic bile, "Let them suck raw eggs and eat my dust." Paglia is a difficult figure in current, queer culture: she has appealed strongly to gay men while receiving ambivalent reactions from lesbians—celebrating gay male culture (Paglia's Ancient Greeks) while

deriding lesbian sexual politics. She illustrates the thorny alliance between gay men and lesbians. Released as part of *Female Misbehaviour*, a feature-length package of four films by Monika Treut.

Dracula's Daughter
Dir. Hillyer, Lambert
1936 USA English
70 mins. 16mm color Narrative
Dist. (U.S.): Swank Motion Pictures
This sequel to Dracula is much better than the original. Dracula is dead, and his smart, cultured daughter (Gloria Holden) is not interested in carrying on her father's evil ways. She seeks the advice of a doctor (Otto Kruger) to help her cure her vampirism. Showing her human side, she falls in love with him, and sets out to wrest him away from his fiancée as her bloodlust becomes too difficult to control.

This version is far superior to the Lugosi original in conveying the sexuality implicit in the vampire legend. The film's most famous scene has Holden painting (she's also an artist) a young, depressed streetwalker (Nan Grey). She is attracted to the half-naked girl and ends up seducing her with her eyes and draining her blood. There wouldn't be a more explicit lesbian scene in a vampire film until Roger Vadim's *Blood and Roses*, made 24 years later.

Drag Attack
Dir. Soldo, Mario, and Ken Kruger
1994 Austria German
14 mins. 35mm color Other
Dist. (U.S.): Soldo, Mario
Drag Attack follows two too glamorous drag queens on their globe-trotting expedition.

Drag in for Votes
Dir. Gomez, Gabriel, and Elspeth Kydd
1991 USA English
17 mins. video color Documentary
Dist. (U.S.): Kydd, Elspeth
From Chicago, a field report on Joan Jett Black's 1991 campaign for mayoral election. Queer Nation candidate Joan is shown hard at work, lobbying at late-night gay clubs, and carefully expounding her political philosophy.

Drag on a Fag
Dir. Stagias, Nikolaos and Arlene Sandler
1992 USA English
5 mins. video color Experimental
Dist. (U.S.): Sandler, Arlene
All smokes and poses.

Drag Queen Marathon, The
Dir. Rubnitz, Tom
1986 USA English
6 mins. video color Other
Dist. (U.S.): Video Data Bank
Drag queens ditch Nikes for spikes as they romp through New York in Rubnitz's *Drag Queen Marathon*, which features a moving haiku by the sensitive Hapi Phace. Part of the *Tom Rubnitz Marathon (A Dozen Tapes, Wigs Included)*.

Drama in Blond
Dir. Lambert, Lothar
1984 Germany German
81 mins. 16mm color Narrative
Dist. (U.S.): Altermedia
A funny, highly original work from Germany's underground film hero, Lothar Lambert, *Drama in Blond* is a thoughtful study of conflicting worlds. A shy, reclusive bank clerk in his mid-thirties discovers the dazzling, and for him, alien, world of cabaret entertainment and learns a lot about himself in the process. With the help of an outgoing young collegue, Gerhardt learns to rid himself of an oppressive older sister and fulfills a desire to explore and become part ot the cabaret scene. He dresses as a woman, diligently practices lip-syncing and then completely bungles his debut at the notorious Travesty Club. Surviving this ordeal he then develops a major, heartbreaking crush on Reinhard, the club's middle-class, hunky technician. Through these funny and touching situations Lambert—in an uncharacteristically lighthearted style—offers interesting contrasts between the bourgeois and the bohemian, the narrow-minded and the permissive, and between conformity and unfulfilled sexuality.

Drama of the Gifted Child, The
Dir. Dougherty, Cecilia
1992 USA English
10 mins. video color Experimental
Dist. (U.S.): Dougherty, Cecilia
The Drama of the Gifted Child tries to understand the role of the lesbian within the lesbian and gay community.

Dream A40
Dir. Reckord, Lloyd
1965 Great Britain English
15 mins. 16mm b&w Narrative
Dist. (U.S.): Frameline Archive
A sad black-and-white fantasy about how self-oppression can strangle a relationship. Part *Orphee* and part kitchen-sink drama, it's a '60s

Ⓐ Ⓑ Ⓒ Ⓓ Ⓔ Ⓕ Ⓖ Ⓗ Ⓘ Ⓙ Ⓚ Ⓛ Ⓜ Ⓝ Ⓞ Ⓟ Ⓠ Ⓡ Ⓢ Ⓣ Ⓤ Ⓥ Ⓦ Ⓧ Ⓨ Ⓩ

British curio by West Indian filmmaker Lloyd Reckord.

Dream Come True
Dir. Breitling/Birchum
1985 USA English
17 mins. video color Documentary
Dist. (U.S.): n/a
A glittery, behind-the-scenes look and concise documentation of the official Gay Miss America contest.

Dream Machine, The
Dir. Jarman, Derek, Cerith Wyn Evans, John Maybury, and Michael Kostiff
1982 Great Britain English
32 mins. 16mm color Experimental
Dist. (U.K.): Basilisk
A phantastic meditation on William Burroughs and Brion Gysin.

Dreamgirls
Dir. Longinotto, Kim, and Jano Williams
1993 Great Britain/Japan Japanese and English
50 mins. 16mm color Documentary
Dist. (U.S.): Women Make Movies
Girls from all over Japan dream of attending Takaruzuka Music School and Theatre. An all-girl school, the young woman must either play female or male parts. While their training for these roles is elaborate, the shcool is equally concerned with their training to be good wives. The young women who have played male parts speak of "knowing" better a man's needs, while another who has only played women's roles complains of never getting to escape being a woman.

The school's performances are pure Hollywood fantasy and the almost all-women audience is there to escape. They eagerly stand in line for hours to deliver love notes to the "male" star, described by one fan as less coarse than "real" men. This fascinating depiction of gender construction and the gap between dreams and reality, reveals that the female role has been learned well both on and off stage, but without providing the promised happily-ever-after.

Dreams of Passion
Dir. Burch, Aarin
1989 USA English
5 mins. 16mm color Experimental
Dist. (U.S.): Women Make Movies
The exploration of desire is also a form of activism, and *Dreams of Passion* is a brief, expressive performance of love and desire between two black women.

Dressed in Blue
(see *Vestida De Azul*)

Drifting
(see *Nagua*)

Drip: A Narcissistic Love Story
Dir. Dickenson, Frances
1994 Great Britain English
14 mins. video color Narrative
Dist. (U.K.): Arts Council of Great Britain
Drip is Frances Dickinson's imaginative and zany *Strictly Ballroom* on a budget.

Du Darst (Truth or Dare) [excerpt]
Dir. S.A.F.E. Productions
1991 Germany German
10 mins. video color Documentary
Dist. (U.S.): Frameline
Lesbian safe-sex in Germany.

Dual of the Senses
Dir. Arnesen, Heidi
1991 USA English
3 mins. 16mm b&w Narrative
Dist. (U.S.): Frameline
Cross-dressing gives a hetero twist to an encounter between a gay man and a lesbian.

Dumbshit
Dir. Bull, Marilyn
1995 USA English
3 mins. video color Experimental
Dist. (U.S.): Bull, Marilyn
A Pixel Vision and HI8 collage set to original music by the artist.

Dura Mater
Dir. Bush, Lainard E.
1981 USA English
11 mins. 16mm color Experimental
Dist. (U.S.): n/a
A silent experimental film that mixes images of eroticism and daily life.

Dykes Rule
Dir. Patierno, Mary, and Harriet Hirshorn
1994 USA English
10 mins. video color Documentary
Dist. (U.S.): Patierno, Mary
Dykes rule.

Dyketactics
Dir. Hammer, Barbara
1974 USA English
4 mins. 16mm color Experimental
Dist. (U.S.): Canyon Cinema

Dist. (U.K.): Cinenova
Hammer's *Dyketactics* is the original "lesbian commercial" (many were convinced about the product!). Released in the U.S. along with four of her other short films as a feature-length package, *Lesbian Sexuality: The Films of Barbara Hammer, Volume II.*

Eagle Shooting Hero
Dir. Lau, Jeffrey
1994 Hong Kong Cantonese
116 mins. 35mm color Narrative
Dist. (U.S.): Rim Film Distributors
We can't seem to resist bringing you at least one gender-bending Hong Kong film. This year we have Jeffrey Lau's *Eagle Shooting Hero*, a wacky spoof of just about every Hong Kong film you have ever seen which stars just about every major Hong Kong actor, including Brigitte Lin from *The East Is Red* and Leslie Cheung from *Farewell My Concubine*. Don't even try to follow the plot in this silly comedy as the characters constantly swap sex roles, only adding to the confusion. It involves two evil cousins trying to take over a kingdom, a search for an all-powerful kung-fu manual, a young male priest (played by a woman) who is in love with his murdered master, and an emperor who wants to achieve nirvana, but in order to do so must persuade another man to tell him he loves him. With all this gender bending and the usual astounding displays of kung-fu mastery, you won't want to miss this hilarious send up of Hong Kong films. Starring Brigitte Lin, Leslie Cheung, Tony Leung, Maggie Cheung, and Joey Wong.

Early Patterns
Dir. Mears, Ric
1971 USA English
10 mins. S8mm color/b&w Experimental
Dist. (U.S.): Mears, Ric
Exploring textures and patterns in nature.

Earring, The
(see *Brinco, O*)

East Is Red, The
Dir. Lee, Raymond, and Ching Siu-Tung
1993 Hong Kong Cantonese
95 mins. 35mm color Narrative
Dist. (U.S.): Rim Film Distributors
Time, space, gravity, narrative continuity, narrative conceptions about good and evil, and character identity are all shifting, ambiguous threads in the world of *The East Is Red*—a world governed by an other-worldly set of rules. In other words, if you can't keep up with the story, just let it go. Played out against the conflicts of the Ming dynasty, *The East Is Red* features spectacular land and sea battle sequences among the Hans, the Sun Moon Sect, the Spaniards, and the Japanese Ninjas. These abundantly violent, wildly choreographed, and edited battles are highlighted by Asia's flying needles and by the protagonists' ability to fly like superhero acrobats as they fight. There's also one very hot (unpleasantly concluded, but hot while it lasts) lesbian love scene. And although Asia is referred to as male, the character is played by a woman. There's no denying the relationship between Snow and Asia, and in the film's queer logic one can't help but read Asia the Invincible as the first transsexual lesbian superhero. A fantastically choreographed, genderfuck Kung-Fu period piece, this sequel to *Swordsman II* starts in a-blink-and-you'll-miss-it recap of its prequel. The film's protagonist, Asia the Invincible, vacillates between hero and villain throughout the film; Asia's gender and sexual orientation are equally complex.

East River Park
Dir. Leonard, Zoe
1992 USA English
6 mins. 16mm b&w Experimental
Dist. (U.S.): Frameline
Zoe Leonard's *East River Park* documents AIDSphobia in the form of a duel between two graffiti writers.

Easy Garden, The
Dir. Stanley, Anie
1994 U.S.A. English
9 mins. video color Experimental
Dist. (U.S.): Stanley, Anie
A lyrical silent montage of urban images, interspersed, naturally, with erotic ones.

Easy Money [work in progress]
Dir. Geffner, David
Prod. Geffner, David
1995 USA English
15 mins. video color Documentary
Dist. (U.S.): Little Turk Films
An intimate and compassionate view inside the world of male prostitutes living and working in Los Angeles.

Eat This
Dir. Willging, Chris, and Halle Hennessey
1992 USA English
7 mins. 16mm b&w Other
Dist. (U.S.): Hennessey, Halle and Willging, Chris

Ⓐ Ⓑ Ⓒ Ⓓ **Ⓔ** Ⓕ Ⓖ Ⓗ Ⓘ Ⓙ Ⓚ Ⓛ Ⓜ Ⓝ Ⓞ Ⓟ Ⓠ Ⓡ Ⓢ Ⓣ Ⓤ Ⓥ Ⓦ Ⓧ Ⓨ Ⓩ

Eat This is an angry bad girl diatribe from Halle Hennessey and Chris Willging.

Ecce Homo
Dir. Tartaglia, Jerry
1989 USA English
7 mins. 16mm color Experimental
Dist. (U.S.): Canyon Cinema
Jerry Tartaglia's canny *Un Chant d'amour* re-mix.

Eclipse
Dir. Podeswa, Jeremy
Prod. Frieberg, Camelia, and Jeremy Podeswa
1994 Canada English
95 mins. 35mm color/b&w Narrative
Dist. (U.S.): Strand Releasing
Dist. (U.K.): ICA Projects
As the cosmic phenomenon of a solar eclipse draws near, ten individuals find one another in this powerfully erotic reexamination of what drives us to seek emotional and sexual solace. The eclipse acts as a metaphor for their electrifying sexual couplings. Much like the Moon and the Sun, the couples are constantly jockeying for position in the sexual and emotional games they play.

Educate Your Attitude (Fresh Talk)
Dir. Marshall, Teresa, and Craig Berggold
1992 Canada English
30 mins. video color Documentary
Dist. (U.S.): Frameline
In *Educate Your Attitude (Fresh Talk)*, thirty young Canadians (gay and straight) express themselves to the camera after attending a ten-day workshop on youth and sexuality. In this excerpted version, lesbian and gay youth talk frankly and directly, discussing race, sex, intimacy, abuse, body image, coming out, and emotional aspects of their lesbian and gay sexuality.
Red Ribbon Award Winner, American Film & Video Festival.

Edward II
Dir. Jarman, Derek
1991 Great Britain English
90 mins. 35mm color Narrative
Dist. (U.K.): British Film Institute
Traditional productions of Christopher Marlowe's play *Edward II* tend to focus on jealousy, murder, and court intrigue, but Derek Jarman's painterly film version emphasizes the sexual and political ramifications of the love affair between "queer" Edward (Steven Waddington) and Piers Gaveston (Andrew Tiernan). Jarman probes the historical roots of homophobia in *Edward II*, and makes inescapable connections to the present with Annie Lennox's music-videoish performance of Cole Porter's "Ev'ry Time We Say Goodbye" and footage of Act-Up-like demonstrations. Tilda Swinton won the best actress award at the 1992 Venice Film Festival for her role as Edward's jealous wife. (D.M.)

Eggsplantsia
Dir. Fontenot, Heyd
1992 USA English
13 mins. video color Narrative
Dist. (U.S.): Fontenot, Heyd
A giddy snapshot of an especially excruciating house party.

Egymasra Nezve (Another Way)
Dir. Makk, Karoly
1982 Hungary Hungarian
107 mins. 35mm color Narrative
Dist. (U.S.): Hungarofilm
Based on a popular, partly autobiographical novel, *Another Way* traces the developing relationship between Eva, a sparrowlike but determinedly uncompromising journalist from the provinces who is overtly lesbian, and Livia, a beautiful, restless fellow journalist unhappily married to an army officer.
Director Karoly Makk's considerable achievement here is his interweaving of two controversial themes—lesbianism and political repression—into the historic context of the still-sensitive period following the 1956 Hungarian uprising. *Another Way* skillfully treats the lesbian affair as a mirror for a wider discussion of public and private freedom. More specifically, the film follows the precarious path of journalists in the post-1956 "consolidation" period between commitment and compromise. Makk triumphs in evoking astonishingly sensitive performances from Polish actresses Jadwiga Jankowska-Cieslak (winner of the Best Actress Prize at the 1982 Cannes Film Festival) and Graznya Szapolowska as the tormented couple whose characterizations vividly intensify the impact of the film's controversial sexual and political themes.

8mm Lesbian Love Film
Dir. Corzine, Georgina
1992 USA English
4 mins. video color Other
Dist. (U.S.): Corzine, Georgina
Georgina Corzine's catchy little music video tells the bisexual biography of a San Francisco girl and all her cute friends.

Eileen Myles: An American Poem
Dir. Kirsch, Andrea
1987 USA English
3 mins. 16mm color Other
Dist. (U.S.): Myles, Eileen
Eileen Myles comes out politically.

Ein Mann Wie Eva (Man Like Eva, A)
Dir. Gabrea, Radu
1983 Germany German
92 mins. 16mm/35mm color Narrative
Dist. (U.S.): Cinevista
Dist. (U.K.): British Film Institute
A brilliant cinema-á-clef on the life and filmmaking of Rainer Fassbinder. *A Man Like Eva* tells the story of a director (Eva) and his company holed up in a dilapidated rented villa, trying desperately to finish his remake of Camille before the money runs out. Bullying and seducing his cast, Eva ditches his male lover for his leading lady, only to set his lustful sights on his leading man. Former Fassbinder actress Eva Mattes creates an electrifying portrait in the lead role. Swaggering and staggering behind leather vest, sunglasses, and beard in one of the most cross-gender acting performances ever. Fassbinder's squalid personal life, his cruelty and manipulation are contrasted to the glamour being created in front of the camera. Director Gabrea has created a spellbinding drama sure to generate controversy reguarding the truth about Fassbinder. True or not, it stands on its own as a brilliant film.

Elegant Spanking, The
Dir. Beatty, Maria and Rosemary Delain
Prod. Beatty, Maria
1995 USA English
30 mins. video color Narrative
Dist. (U.S.): Beatty, Maria
Maria Beatty and Rosemary Delain's highly erotic film *The Elegant Spanking*, beautifully details the S/M relationship between a mistress and her majd. We are treated to an aesthetic subversion of sexual perversion as mistress and maid indulge in punishment, seduction, submission, spanking, strapping, piss drinking, spike heel and foot worship.

Elegy in the Streets
Dir. Hubbard, Jim
1990 USA English
29 mins. 16mm color Experimental
Dist. (U.S.): Hubbard, Jim
Jim Hubbard's *Elegy in the Streets* uses silence as forcefully as Warren Sonbert's *Friendly*

Witness plays with sound. It's a gorgeous, wordless pan across several years of ACT-UP demos and Pride marches, combined with rural and domestic footage of the filmmaker's dying friend. Hubbard has, as usual, processed the film himself; his control of color gives a spooky emphasis to some scenes and washes them with the quality of old photos. *Elegy* is about the connections and discontinuities between personal loss, public mourning, and collective action; it demands and rewards concentration.

Elevator Girls in Bondage
Dir. Calma, Michael
1972 USA English
20 mins. 16mm color Narrative
Dist. (U.S.): n/a
A short film featuring the 1970s San Francisco drag troupe, The Cockettes.

Emergence
Dir. Parmar, Pratibha
1986 Great Britain English
18 mins. video color Documentary
Dist. (U.S.): Women Make Movies
Emergence focuses on four black and Third World women artists whose work addresses the diasporan experience, including Audre Lorde and Palestinian performance artist Mona Hartoum.

Empire State
Dir. Peck, Ron
1986 Great Britain English
104 mins. 35mm color Narrative
Dist. (U.S.): Vidmark
Moments from Ron Peck's first feature since the landmark *Nighthawks* have as much sign-of-the-times significance as his early desultory schoolteacher, cruising the shadows in a ceaseless search for fulfillment. Only the times that Peck now chronicles in his sassy soap opera thriller are both more bleak and more energetic. Here's a movie in which American businessmen crave S/M and the worst nightmare for East End rent boys is a stock market downturn, all set to the beat of a Communards (et al.) soundtrack. In other words: the best of times, the worst of times.

    Empire State started life as an epitaph for contemporary Britain in the fashion, if not the style, of *My Beautiful Laundrette* and *Letter to Brezhnev*. Whereas these earlier unhappy valentines revel in nuance and nitty gritty, Peck picks a different path from social realism. Not so much a sideswipe at Thatcher's rotten landscape as a last-gasp lunge at the throat: Characters have names like ciphers in a Jackie

Ⓐ Ⓑ Ⓒ Ⓓ Ⓔ Ⓕ Ⓖ Ⓗ Ⓘ Ⓙ Ⓚ Ⓛ Ⓜ Ⓝ Ⓞ Ⓟ Ⓠ Ⓡ Ⓢ Ⓣ Ⓤ Ⓥ Ⓦ Ⓧ Ⓨ Ⓩ

Collins novel (The Journalist, The Businessman, The Boxer) and endure the disaster movie denouement in a suffocating, panoramic dockside nightclub.

Through a broad cartoonish quality, Ron Peck achieves a visual pastiche and political satire along the lines of his film *What Can I Do With a Male Nude?*; especially successful in a breezy, teasing opening full of the iconography of '40s thrillers. Sometimes overambitious, *Empire State*'s problems are also offset by its unique gay tone: Jimmy Somerville on the soundtrack, a riot of rent boys, and a set-piece workout to rival *Can't Stop the Music*.

Enchanted

(see *Verzaubert*)

Entre Tinieblas (Dark Habits)
Dir. Almodovar, Pedro
1983 Spain Spanish
113 mins. 35mm color Narrative
Dist. (U.S.): Cinevista
Dist. (U.K.): Metro Tartan

Yolanda Bell, a young "bolero" singer who enjoys taking drugs, daring and ambiguous, sees her boyfriend Jorge die before her own eyes from an overdose of heroin laced with strychnine that she brought him. Their relationship was of mutual destruction and rather uptight dependency. Scared, she decides to disappear. She seeks refuge in a convent run by the "Humble Redeemers" whose Mother Superior told her about her admiration one night when she went to see her sing at the "Molino Rojo."

For years now, the Humble Redeemers have tried to save young girls leading a wild life. Lately, the community is going through a crisis: very few girls seem to want to be redeemed. Thus, Yolanda is most welcomed, especially by the Mother Superior, a cross between Saint John Bosco and Jean Genet, whose fascination for evil pushes her to become an accomplice and a friend to all the young girls who have passed by the convent.

Yolanda allows the Mother Superior to trap her, and starts reliving with her the same kind of self-destructive game that she was playing with Jorge. A game from which heroin is not absent . . .

The members of the commmunity, five nuns and a chaplain, lost in the midst of the huge deserted convent, have unconsciously evolved towards a strange, even autonomy that they will have to defend against the order established by a new Mother General, the highest authority in their order.

The party to celebrate the Mother Superior's name-day, to which nuns from the other convents have been invited, will become a real battlefield.

Ernesto
Dir. Samperi, Salvatore
1979 Italy Italian
95 mins. 35mm color Narrative
Dist. (U.S.): Frameline Archive

Salvatore Samperi's delicious, amoral tale about a cunning lad's social and sexual rise-and-rise. Set in Trieste in the last years before World War II, *Ernesto* is a subtle, sensual comedy about class and circumstance.

Our relentless hero is bored with business school and dreams of being a world famous violinist. He also yearns for something else besides strings, and flirts with a handsome laborer (played by Michele Placido, who won the Best Actor Award at the 1979 Berlin Film Festival for this role). But his brief adventure with the laborer is really a ruse for bigger ambitions.

Ernie and Rose
Dir. Huckert, John
1982 USA English
30 mins. 16mm color Narrative
Dist. (U.S.): n/a

A completely original film about two aging men sharing their lives together, *Ernie and Rose* is at once a touching document and a subtle, brilliantly satiric look at sexual role playing.

Erotic in Nature
Dir. Rothermund, Christen Lee
Prod. Tigress Productions
1985 USA English
40 mins. video color Narrative
Dist. (U.S.): n/a

Some call it erotica, some call it smut. We won't pretend that this new phenomenon isn't controversial, but sex videos made by lesbians for lesbian audiences have finally arrived. As far as visual entertainment is concerned, it has good production values, better-than-average acting, and an effective soundtrack consisting of original music with limited voice-overs.

Erotique
Dir. Borden, Lizzie, Monika Treut, and Clara Law
1994 USA/Germany/Hong Kong English

90 mins. 35mm color Narrative
Dist. (U.S.): Group 1
Clearly aimed at hip straight audiences, this high-gloss package of feminist erotica showcases the latest work of three talented women filmmakers, including festival favorites Monika Treut (*My Father is Coming*, *The Virgin Machine*) and Lizzie Borden (*Born in Flames*), alongside Hong Kong director Clara Law (*Autumn Moon*). *Erotique* is an interesting and ambitious experiment, bringing the combined ideas of *Cosmo*, *Playgirl*, and *On Our Backs* to the silver screen.

Lizzie Borden's *Let's Talk About Sex* (cowritten by San Francisco's own Susie Bright) follows the erotic entanglement of a spunky, bisexual Latina phone-sex worker and her sleazy male client. Borden and Bright also include some nice queer characters in the background: the gay sex-line manager and the protagonist's best friend, a dyke cop.

Monika Treut's *Taboo Parlor* is the stylish adventure of a pair of lusciously predatory, lipstick lesbians. With cameo appearances by musician Tanita Tikaram and Marianne Sagebrecht (*Bagdad Cafe*), *Taboo Parlor* echoes the look of Madonna's Open Your Heart peepshow video as it offers up a smart twist on *Basic Instinct*.

And lastly, in Clara Law's beautiful *Wonton Soup*, Hong Kong provides the backdrop for a straight couple's erotic encounters and reflections on Chinese identity.

Erte
Dir. unknown
1970 USA English
28 mins. 16mm color Documentary
Dist. (U.S.): n/a
A portrait of the artist's life and work.

ESP: Vision
Dir. Kelly, Joe
Prod. Paull, Craig
1994 USA English
9 mins. video color Other
Dist. (U.S.): Paull, Craig
Joe Kelly's *ESP: Vision* about the murder of supermodels as witnessed through the eyes of the killer, à la *The Eyes of Laura Mars*.

Esplada, A
Dir. Raballa, Marcela
1994 Brazil Portugese
1 mins. video color Other
Dist. (U.S.): MIX Brasil
A short, short from Brazil's dynamic MIXBrasil

program.

Etc.
Dir. Boyle, Bernie
1977 USA English
6 mins. S8mm color Other
Dist. (U.S.): n/a
Scraps, maybe.

Eunuchs: India's Third Gender
Dir. Yorke, Michael
1991 Great Britain English
40 mins. 16mm color Documentary
Dist. (U.K.): BBC TV
Harish yearns to be a woman, but has a wife and two children. His best friend Kiran was castrated four months ago; "I thought it would be better if Kiran got castrated," says his truck driver boyfriend, "So he could wear a petticoat." *Eunuchs: India's Third Gender* is a new documentary (made for BBC television) about the people who are man and woman in one body. There are more than half a million eunuchs—or hijiras—in India; they are variously despised and revered, and they are all granted the power to bless and curse. Three years in the making, Michael Yorke's film easily captures the pleasures and painful contradictions of a living alternative to Western ideas about gender.

Eurotrash
Prod. Rapido Productions
1994 Great Britain English
22 mins. video color Other
Dist. (U.K.): Channel 4 Television
"It's the rudest telly show ever!" screamed Britain's *Sun* newspaper when Channel Four TV's cheeky magazine series hit the airwaves. Now see for yourself, as we bring Eurotrash to America.

Jean-Paul Gaultier (yes, Jean-Paul Gaultier) and Antoine de Caunes are the cohosts of this uniquely British send-up of everything embarrassing and low-brow about European culture: Sylvia Kristel's movie career, soap-opera themed vacations, Bjorn Borg designer underwear. The special pleasure for gay audiences lies in the campy rivalry between Gaultier and de Caunes; Gaultier wins hands-down in the skirt department.

Even Cowgirls Get the Blues
Dir. Van Sant, Gus
1994 USA English
110 mins. 35mm color Narrative
Dist. (U.S.): Films Incorporated
Please see under *The Ballad of Little Jo* for B.

Ⓐ
Ⓑ
Ⓒ
Ⓓ
Ⓔ
Ⓕ
Ⓖ
Ⓗ
Ⓘ
Ⓙ
Ⓚ
Ⓛ
Ⓜ
Ⓝ
Ⓞ
Ⓟ
Ⓠ
Ⓡ
Ⓢ
Ⓣ
Ⓤ
Ⓥ
Ⓦ
Ⓧ
Ⓨ
Ⓩ

Ruby Rich's entry.

Evenings, The
(see *Avonden, De*)

Everlasting Secret Family, The
Dir. Thornhill, Michael
1988 Australia English
94 mins. 35mm color Narrative
Dist. (U.S.): Kino International
This provocative and daring new work from Australia employs an excellent cast, Arthur Dignam and Mark Lee (Gallipoli), to tell the story of a secret homosexual society. A wealthy senator, Dignam, is chauffeured to a private boy's school to select his next lover. Having surveyed the crop of handsome youths, he picks a blond, Mark Lee. Several encounters are arranged between the two, and eventually, Lee is inducted into a private group of older homosexual men in high places and their young lovers. To further his career, the senator marries and has a son. Lee stays around and works as a companion for the senator's son.

Lee becomes concerned about his fading youth and seeks the assistance of a doctor who succeeds in keeping him forever young. As the senator's son comes into his manhood, he too falls in love with Lee and is also inducted into the secret family. Lee now has both, father and son. An original and oddly surreal film which could well become the next gay cult classic.

Every Conceivable Position: Inside Gay Porn
Dir. Beavan, Clare
Prod. Merck, Mandy
1992 Great Britain English
50 mins. video color Documentary
Dist. (U.K.): Fulcrum Productions
A sharp sixty-minute documentary, commissioned—amazingly—for BBC television. It's a fresh and thoughtful program about the modern lesbian and gay porn industry, as well as being a good deal of fun (the film's makers were allowed to use clips, so long as genitals weren't visible). Included are behind-the-scenes interviews with current-day stars, producers, and commentators, including Al Parker, Chi Chi LaRue, and San Francisco's own Susie Bright, filmed in a bubble bath.

Evil Thoughts
Dir. Hammond, Joe
1993 USA English
5 mins. video Other

Dist. (U.S.): San Francisco AIDS Foundation/ Prevention Dept.
Joe Hammond's computer-animated safe-sex short.

Evolution Of a Sex Life
Dir. Gaffney, Cynthia
1988 USA English
15 mins. video color Other
Dist. (U.S.): Gaffney, Cynthia
Cynthia Gaffney irreligiously traces the evolution of her sex life, from its baptism all the way to . . . the Revelation.

Excerpts from the Far East
Dir. unknown
1985 USA English
30 mins. video color Other
Dist. (U.S.): n/a
Obscure bondage techniques and much more that practically verge on a story line.

Excess Is What I Came For
Dir. Gignac, Paula, and Kathleen Pirrie-Adams
1994 Canada English
8 mins. video color Documentary
Dist. (U.S.): Gignac, Paula
Excess Is What I Came For is a beat-driven, flesh-filled document of the nocturnal paradise that was Toronto's The Boom Boom Room.

Execution: A Study of Mary
Dir. Mikesch, Elfi
1979 Germany German
28 mins. 35mm color Experimental
Dist. (U.S.): Cinemien
Inspired by the life of Mary Stuart, *Execution* is an expressionistic film about passion, love, innocence, and death. Instead of portraying her as a pawn in anonymous history, Elfi Mikesch depicts her as a woman who was abused by her family. The images are wondrously ominous compositions of hatred, intrigue, and madness, drawing attention to the subjectivity that generates such drama.

Exits
Dir. Diaz, Ramona S.
1992 USA English
10 mins. video color Documentary
Dist. (U.S.): Diaz, Ramona S.
A frank discussion of mortality, this thoughtful documentary conveys a lesbian couple's process of dealing with one partner's cancer diagnosis and subsequent death.

Exposure

Dir. Mohabeer, Michelle
1990 Canada English
8 mins. 16mm color Documentary
Dist. (U.S.): Women Make Movies
An experimental documentary exploring issues of
race, sexuality, and cultural identity. A dialogue
between two lesbians of color intercut with photographs, paintings, and writings of African-
American, African-Caribbean, and Japanese-
Canadian women writers.

Extramuros
Dir. Picazo, Miguel
1985 Spain Spanish
120 mins. 35mm color Narrative
Dist. (U.S.): Frameline
We've tried for five years to bring *Extramuros* to
San Francisco. It's an extraordinary lesbian love
story which has only been screened twice in the
States before. In 16th-century Spain, crushing
taxes, war, and disease reign, forcing people
either to emigrate, join the army, or enter a religious order. But even behind convent walls.
women struggle with poverty and the prospect of
being flung back into the world—that is, until
one nun, Sor Angela, hits upon the idea of faking
stigmata with the aid of her lesbian lover. Pedro
Almodovar's woman-on-the-verge, Carmen Maura,
plays the nun who agrees to Angela's selfless
scam, only because she doesn't want to be separated from her lover. But Angela's self-induced
stigmata bring the convent unexpected fame, as
well as new enemies who could destroy their relationship. Word spreads fast of the "miracle,"
causing the old prioress to be ousted from her
job, and a call for an Inquisition hearing. Soon
Angela and Ana—constantly cuddled together in
their bare-cell bed—are caught up in knife-edge
nunnery power games. *Extramuros* is a compulsive, offbeat art movie—it's like a lesbian version
of the Jim and Tammy Faye Bakker story, with
self-flagellation thrown in. But it's also a serious
and passionate work, with the same outspoken
femmes-against-fascism theme as *Mädchen In
Uniform*. Best of all, *Extramuros* isn't coy about
its characters' sexuality. With Carmen Maura,
Mercedes Sampietro, Aurora Bautista

Eyes That Do Not See
(see *Ojos Que No Ven*)

F2M (Female to Male)
Dir. Latta, Cayte
1992 Australia English
15 mins. video color Documentary
Dist. (U.S.): Australian Film Commission

Jasper, a 30-year-old lesbian female-to-male pre-
op transsexual, talks about growing up wanting to
be a boy, and the physical and emotional
changes involved in recreating himself as a man.

Fabian's Freeak Show
Dir. Contempo, Museo
1994 USA English
30 mins. video color Other
Dist. (U.S.): Please Louise Productions
The Freak Show is in town, and you're invited to
join ringmasters Jeffrey Winter, Charles Wurmfelt,
and Alison Hennessy queers in a night of gender-
bending, uppity-low-budget video and the tailor-
made media circus *Fabian's Freeak Show* by
Museo Contempo.
     Warning: *Fabian's Freeak Show* con-
tains campy yet rather graphic violence and even
a little taste of the sexually explicit.

Fabulous Dyketones Rock Around the Clock, The
Dir. Wolfe, Kathy
1986 USA English
3 mins. video color Other
Dist. (U.S.): Wolfe Video
The Dyketones give a new spin to the Bill Haley
classic.

Faerie Tales
Dir. Roques, Philippe
1992 USA/France English
20 mins. video color Documentary
Dist. (U.S.): Roques, Philippe
Philippe Roques takes us to the northern
Californian countryside to meet men who identify
as faeries. "It wasn't difficult coming out as a
gay," says one Berkeley teacher in *Faerie Tales*,
"But it took a lot of guts to come out as a faerie."

Faeriefilm
Dir. Salandra, Eugene
1993 USA English
7 mins. 16mm color Experimental
Dist. (U.S.): Salandra, Eugene
Eugene Salandra's delightful documentary about
the Faerie movement—the twist is, it's animated.

Fairest of Them All
Dir. Stalman, Jason
Prod. Beatie, Lisa and Keri Batien
1995 Great Britain English
5 mins. 16mm color Other
Dist. (U.K.): Channel 4 Television
A short animation film about the backstage
bitchiness of drag performers.

Ⓐ Ⓑ Ⓒ Ⓓ Ⓔ Ⓕ Ⓖ Ⓗ Ⓘ Ⓙ Ⓚ Ⓛ Ⓜ Ⓝ Ⓞ Ⓟ Ⓠ Ⓡ Ⓢ Ⓣ Ⓤ Ⓥ Ⓦ Ⓧ Ⓨ Ⓩ

Fairies, The
Dir. Rubnitz, Tom
1989 USA English
10 mins. video color Other
Dist. (U.S.): Video Data Bank
Rubnitz's latest tape, *The Fairies*, is a sophisti-
cated return to innocence that was a big hit at
this year's Berlin Film Festival. Part of the *Tom
Rubnitz Marathon (A Dozen Tapes, Wigs
Included).*

Fairy Who Didn't Want to Be a Fairy Anymore, The
Dir. Lynd, Laurie
1992 Canada English
17 mins. 16mm color Narrative
Dist. (U.S.): Canadian Filmmakers Distribution
Centre
Dist. (U.K.): British Film Institute
A mini–musical comedy about the pros and cons
of wing removal.

Falling Through the Cracks
Dir. Hollibaugh, Amber
1991 USA English
10 mins. video color Documentary
Dist. (U.S.): Hollibaugh, Amber
In *Falling Through the Cracks*, Margie Rivera
shares her experience as a woman with AIDS.

Family Affair, A
Dir. Kelly, Alison
1993 USA English
7 mins. 16mm color Other
Dist. (U.S.): Kelly, Alison
Alison Kelly's *A Family Affair* tells a sweet story
of young lesbian love and coming out to parents.

Family Values
Dir. Stuart, David
1989 USA English
58 mins. video color Documentary
Dist. (U.S.): Hands On Productions
Family Values documents the tremendous
response from the lesbian community in providing invaluable support and love during the AIDS
crisis in San Francisco.

Fanci's Persuasion
Dir. Herman-Wurmfeld, Charles
Prod. Wurmfeld, Eden H.
1994 USA English
80 mins. 16mm color Narrative
Dist. (U.S.): Persuasion Productions
The night before Fanci's wedding to luscious girl-

friend Loretta, a spell settles upon San
Francisco. Power outages course through the city
and Fanci's family and friends are swept into a
dream world where magic takes precedent over
reality.
Things start to fall apart, beginning
with the happy couple who disagree over the
guest list. Just one block away, Olive and Theo,
two of Fanci's closest friends, are planning a
mystical wedding ceremony while her archconser-
vative parents Irving and Irene (played by Justin
Bond) are refusing to attend the wedding.
Olive and Theo have a falling out and
do battle in the realm of magic. Their occult
shenanigans cause everyone to go to pieces,
including Fanci's mother, who finds herself on a
journey through the city's sexual underground. At
her bachelorette party, Fanci's reprieve from all
the wackiness is only momentary when she finds
herself inflicted by a series of nightmarish visions
which catapult her naked and screaming through
the streets of San Francisco. Can the girl get a
grip on herself to make it to her own wedding?
Tensions build and everything comes to a spectacular conclusion at the much awaited wedding
ceremony.

Fantasy Island
Dir. Wood, Brian
1991 Great Britain English
7 mins. 16mm color Other
Dist. (U.K.): Wood, Brian
Fantasy Island creatively uses plasticine animation and, yes, Ethel Merman to portray the homophobia in Britain's Isle of Man, where until
recently homosexuality was completely illegal.

Farewell My Concubine
Dir. Kaige, Chen
1993 China/Hong Kong Cantonese
154 mins. 35mm color Narrative
Dist. (U.S.): Swank Motion Pictures
Hot on the size-13 heels of *M. Butterfly* comes
Farewell My Concubine, an even riskier tale of
gender-fuck and queer desire set in the all-male
Beijing Opera. Based on the bestseller by Hong
Kong writer Lilian Lee, the two-and-a-half-hour
opus unravels the twisted romance between two
male opera stars and a prostitute, drowning in
the raptures of history.
It is 1925 when young Cheng Dieyi is
palmed off to a sadistic Beijing Opera academy
by his mother. While at the school, the boy falls
in love with the rough-and-tumble Duan Xiaolou.
As adults, the pair become opera stars best

known for their performance of *Farewell My Concubine*, the story of a consort who commits suicide for her vanquished king. The problem, though, is that Cheng (played by Canto-pop diva Leslie Cheung) actually wants to be the idealized concubine, a role he delivers in high drag. He is devastated when Duan (Zhang Fengyi) marries Juxian (Chinese starlet Gong Li), a young prostitute. As the film's unholy trinity are hurled through fifty years of the stormiest moments in Chinese history, they are thrust constantly from the margins to the center of power and back, always at the mercies of historical and economic winds.

Rather than deliver improbably "positive" role models, director Chen Kaige (whose masterful *Yellow Earth* marked the arrival of China's "new wave") serves up unrepentant sex workers and drag queens whose complex desires don't fit the binary conventions of straight and gay. Sympathy drains from one character to another in the blink of an eye. Chen's fluid camera is constantly traveling, and although it shies away from the physical dimensions of the men's relationship, the film strives for a more emotional understanding of desire, one that doesn't spin on a Euro-American butch/femme tip. (L.C.)

Farewell, The
(see *Avskedet*)

Farewell to Charms
Dir. Pontiac, Carla
1979 Australia English
13 mins. 16mm color Experimental
Dist. (U.S.): Sydney Filmmakers Cooperative
The story of Emma, a reformed lipstick addict, her old school chum Cecily, and Stretch, the bionic bike dyke, this experimental drama questions the goals of love and romance as a woman's ultimate fulfillment.

Fast Trip, Long Drop
Dir. Bordowitz, Gregg
1993 USA English
54 mins. 16mm color Documentary
Dist. (U.S.): Drift Releasing
In the spring of 1988, video-maker/activist Gregg Bordowitz tested HIV-antibody positive, quit drinking and doing drugs, and came out to his parents as a gay man. This imaginative, autobiographical documentary began as an inquiry into these events and the cultural climate surrounding them. Then, during the writing period, a good friend was diagnosed with breast cancer, and Bordowitz's grandparents were killed in an auto-

mobile accident. The cumulative impact of all these events challenged his sense of identity, the way he understood his own diagnosis, and the relationship between illness and history.

Anything but solemn, this chronicle of AIDS activism, personal testimony, and representational concerns is a kaleidoscopic blast of visual stimulation, intellectual irreverence, and emotional confrontation. Painful and difficult subjects are treated with humor and compassion. The artist's Jewish cultural heritage is mined for ways to cope with loss and despair. The culture of television is scrutinized and skewered. Images from the archives of AIDS activist media explore the development of community responses to government inaction under the Reagan/Bush administrations and bring us to the current state of the AIDS crisis. Everything is questioned: the government, the media, the medical establishment, institutionalized AIDS politics, even activism itself—as well as we, the viewers.

Bordowitz embraces all of this within a personal vision that is playful, passionate, angry, smart, and sassy (with some klezmer music thrown in to top it off). Ultimately he has given us a courageous work of art.

Fasten Your Seatbelts
(see *Out On Four: Episodes 1 & 2*)

Fat Chance
Dir. Golden, Anne
Prod. Lock Up Your Daughters
1994 Canada English
7 mins. video color Other
Dist. (U.S.): Golden, Anne
Question: What's a fat girl to say when her big body is missing from even her own fantasy? Answer: "Now there's more of me to fuck."

Fatboy Chronicles, The (Part One : Rene, Rene, Qu' est-ce-que c' est?)
Dir. Broussard, Rene
1995 USA English
24 mins. video color Experimental
Dist. (U.S.): Broussard, Rene
Rene, Rene refers to the artist's great unrequited love for Rene, a cherubic young boy with whom the artist has been obsessively in love with since the first grade. Aside from sharing the same name, the two boys' lives and sexual preferences couldn't have been more different. The video also looks at the origins of Broussard's attraction to fat boys and to the act of flagellation, while

(A)
(B)
(C)
(D)
(E)
(F)
(G)
(H)
(I)
(J)
(K)
(L)
(M)
(N)
(O)
(P)
(Q)
(R)
(S)
(T)
(U)
(V)
(W)
(X)
(Y)
(Z)

focussing on issues of abuse and molestation, which will play a key role throughout the video series of "The Fatboy Chronicles."

Fated to Be Queer
Dir. Bautista, Pablo

1992 USA

29 mins. video color Experimental

Dist. (U.S.): Bautista, Pablo

Fated to Be Queer is a moving documentary that illuminates issues and concerns for the Filipino American Gay community. Four men discuss topics including cultural homophobia, racism, images of gay men of color, and the sexual politics between rice queens and sticky rice.

Fear of Disclosure
Dir. Zwickler, Phil, and David Wojnarowicz

1989 USA English

5 mins. 16mm b&w Documentary

Dist. (U.S.): Zwickler, Phil

Fear of Disclosure is about the difficulty of revealing that you're HIV positive to a potential lover; in the background, Pyramid Club go-go boys size up each other's mortality.

Fearless: The Hunterwali Story
Dir. Wadia, Riyad Vinci

1993 India English/Hindi

62 mins. 35mm color Documentary

Dist. (U.S.): JBH Wadia/ Wadia Movietone

From 1935 to 1959, Fearless Nadia was the whipcracking, pistol-packing, singing, dancing, daredevil queen of the Indian screen. Riyad Wadia's spectacular biography of India's legendary stunt actress captures the unique persona of the Australian-born femme-firecracker who thrilled audiences with her daring portrayals of fearless, rough-and-ready heroines. From her first starring role as Hunterwali (The Lady with the Whip), through such hits as *Diamond Queen*, *Lady Robinhood*, and *Jungle Goddess*, Nadia dominated the Indian box office.

The first true feminist of Indian cinema, Nadia's physical prowess and selfless fearlessness made her an idol for the oppressed peasantry of pre-Independence India (as she preached tolerance and secularism) and challenged the male chauvanism of the day. Not a lesbian herself, but certainly a strong feminist, Nadia's exploits should be immensely enjoyable to lesbian and gay audiences for her charm, charisma, and, of course, camp value.

"She was a big, butch Zorro-type who socked men in the jaw and leapt around with a whip."—*Variety*

Feed Them to the Cannibals
Dir. Reid, Fiona Cunningham

1993 Australia/Great Britain English

67 mins. 16mm color Documentary

Dist. (U.K.): Dangerous To Know

Aside from San Francisco, perhaps the only place better to celebrate lesbian and gay pride is Sydney, Australia, where each February hundreds of thousands of lesbians and gays arrive for Mardi Gras. *Feed Them to the Cannibals* is the colorful story of a year in lesbian and gay life in Sydney, both backstage and on the streets. It offers a concise history of the Australian gay movement (and is especially interesting about the earlier divisions between men and women), and culminates in the largest open-air gay event in the Southern Hemisphere. Along the way, we also get to enjoy the sights of the pre–Mardi Gras Sleaze Ball, which leaves Sydney's straights speechless, or envious, or both.

Feeling of Power #6769, The
Dir. Beck, Robert

1990 USA English

9 mins. video color Experimental

Dist. (U.S.): Kitchen, The

The Feeling of Power #6769 is affirmation in another tempo, combining television appropriation, the ever-popular street demo footage, and imaginative electronic special effects with a dynamite original guitar soundtrack. *The Feeling of Power* more or less insists that the gay and lesbian community do its own information gathering, and that we partake in a little countersurveillance of our own.

Fell
Dir. Franchini, Frankie

1993 USA English

5 mins. video color Narrative

Dist. (U.S.): Franchini, Frankie

A short video about falling in love.

Female Impersonator, The
Dir. Chaplin, Charlie

1916 USA English

10 mins. 16mm b&w Narrative

Dist. (U.S.): Olson, Jenni

Fired from a film shoot, Charlie Chaplin returns to the set dressed as a woman. The men on the set flirt with her and, in a disturbing conclusion, Charlie reveals his masquerade. This film is silent.

Female Misbehavior
Dir. Treut, Monika

1983-92 USA/Germany English
80 mins. 16mm color Documentary
Dist. (U.S.): First Run Features
Female Misbehavior consists of four shorts made
by German director Monika Treut over the last ten
years, and running from ten to thirty minutes
each. The subjects include performance porn,
transexuality, bondage, and Camille Paglia. The
film is an exploration of sexual deviation up
against mainstream feminism and orthodox
female heterosexuality.

     Dr. Paglia is a portrait of the queru-
lous author of *Sexual Personae* who has been
called things from "academic Rottweiler" to
"antifeminist feminist." With the composure of a
speed freak, she whips herself into a confessional
tirade.

     Annie is the vehicle for porn star/per-
formance artist Annie Sprinkle. Born Ellen
Steinberg from New York, she presents herself as
a classic schleppe in the premakeover stage.
Before our very eyes, Annie Sprinkle emerges as
the colorful butterfly from the nondescript larva.
Making up her face in the mirror, she tells us she
likes to explore all of her different personalities,
especially the ones that make her feel sexy. We
see her playing comically on stage with her boobs
like a vintage Betty Boop cartoon character. The
act continues as she invites the audience to take
a flashlight and look at her cervix.

     Max profiles transsexual Native
American Max (born Anita) Valerio, who lives in
San Francisco. Unlike Camille and Annie, Max is
not pushing an act, but is promoting our understanding of what it's like for a longtime lesbian to
change her body and attitudes on the way toward
becoming a heterosexual man. On camera, we
meet Max, who for all intents and purposes looks
just like an older teenage boy.

     The fourth item in this collection,
Bondage, is a bit boring. We hear from a New
York tit torturer in S/M drag about the pleasures
of being an exhibitionist. The woman goes into
extensive detail about the ropes and hooks that
she can string throughout her apartment to serve
as a spiderweb in which to truss her victims.
Stroking her whip, she confides it isn't so much
an instrument of pain as it is a way of waking up
sensations. Since the fantasies she speaks about
are never enacted on screen, this film segment
wears thin after the first five or ten minutes.

     Female Misbehaviour is bound to be
controversial on many levels, and it's supposed to
be. Treut's portraits of modern sexual outlaws are

fascinating, amusing, and rendered with wit and
noncondescending intellect. (R.T.)

Ferdous (Paradise)
Dir. Mann, Shakila
1990 Great Britain English
8 mins. video color Experimental
Dist. (U.S.): Frameline
Dist. (U.K.): Mann, Shakila
Portrays two lesbian lovers and offers a sensual
exposure of the proscriptions of the Koran
against "deviant" sexuality, which specifies that
lesbians or homosexuals must "be confined until
their death."

Fertile La Toyah Jackson Video Magazine
Dir. Castro, Rick
1993 USA English
53 mins. video color Other
Dist. (U.S.): Pywackett Productions
Bizarre fin-de-siècle fun with Dick and Jane:
Vaginal Creme Davis hosts her first hour-long
video 'zine. Vaginal and *Taste of Latex* publisher
pal play Valley Girl twins! Santa Monica hookers
reveal their fashion secrets! See Vaginal out-
Leeza Leeza Gibbons!

Fiction and Other Truths:
A Film about Jane Rule
Dir. Weissman, Aerlyn and Fernie Lynne
Prod. Fraticalli, Rina
1995 Canada English
57 mins. 16mm color Documentary
Dist. (U.S.): Great North Releasing
An insightful film that delves into lesbian history,
examining the life of famous lesbian novelist and
activist Jane Rule. Her first published novel,
Desert of the Heart sent shock waves through the
literary community, but nevertheless went on to
become a best-seller and a highly successful film
that remains a favorite among lesbian audiences.
A committed political activist and intellectual,
Jane found herself fleeing the rabid McCarthyism
of the fifties with her lifelong companion Helen
Sonthoff. Settling in Canada, she continued to
foster public awareness and debate around issues
of sexuality, representation, and censorship.

     Winner of the 1995 San Francisco
International Lesbian & Gay Film Festival
Audience Award for Best Documentary.

Fighting Chance
Dir. Fung, Richard
1990 Canada English
31 mins. video color Documentary

Ⓐ
Ⓑ
Ⓒ
Ⓓ
Ⓔ
Ⓕ
Ⓖ
Ⓗ
Ⓘ
Ⓙ
Ⓚ
Ⓛ
Ⓜ
Ⓝ
Ⓞ
Ⓟ
Ⓠ
Ⓡ
Ⓢ
Ⓣ
Ⓤ
Ⓥ
Ⓦ
Ⓧ
Ⓨ
Ⓩ

Dist. (U.S.): Video Data Bank
A documentary look at four Asian men living with HIV infection.

Fighting for Our Lives: Facing AIDS in San Francisco
Dir. Seidler, Ellen, and Patrick DuNah
1987 USA English
29 mins. video color Documentary
Dist. (U.S.): Seidler, Ellen
A history of AIDS in San Francisco that traces its effects on gay and other communities. Discusses how political and medical issues converged and surveys support groups that emerged.

Fighting in Southwest Louisiana
Dir. Friedman, Peter, and Jean-Francois Brunet
1991 France French
27 mins. video color Documentary
Dist. (U.S.): Filmmaker's Library
Lesbians and gays from around the world have created a variety of housing situations that reflect their lifestyles, as well as their social and political status. *Fighting in Southwest Louisana* is a portrait of Danny Cooper, an openly gay mailman living with his lover in a Victorian house in Vinton, Louisiana.
Red Ribbon Award Winner: 1992 American Film and Video Festival.

film, a
Dir. Nicoletta, Daniel
1977 USA English
25 mins. S8mm color/b&w Experimental
Dist. (U.S.): Nicoletta, Daniel
An autobiographical film about my destiny, my love of San Francisco, and life here; it is an effort to explore and translate into film my various perceptions, emotions, and experiences.

Film for Two
Dir. Mignatti, Victor
1981 USA English
30 mins. 16mm color Narrative
Dist. (U.S.): n/a
Angst and more angst as two men struggle to sustain their relationship. A beautifully photographed portrayal of young love in New York City. Gold medal winner at the 1981 Chicago Film Festival.

Fin Amour
Dir. Fry, Katherine
Prod. Cole-Baker, Alex
1995 New Zealand English

13 mins. 16mm opt. color Narrative
Dist. (U.S.): Chocolate Fish Productions
Fin Amour is a medieval love story of two women. Maria is a mystic seeking spiritual love and Beatriz is a female troubadour who plays the game of courtly love. Inevitably there is conflict.

Final Solutions
Dir. Tartaglia, Jerry
1990 USA English
10 mins. 16mm color Experimental
Dist. (U.S.): Canyon Cinema
The third installment of Jerry Tartaglia's AIDS trilogy, *Final Solutions* looks at the end solution offered by consumer culture to the epidemic: management by promotion of death-terror.

Finding Our Way Together
Dir. Dworkin, Mark
1989 USA English
28 mins. video color Documentary
Dist. (U.S.): American Red Cross
Finding Our Way Together from the state of Washington presents a wide variety of formal and informal support systems for people with AIDS.

Fingered!
Dir. Raymond, James
1992 USA English
12 mins. video color Narrative
Dist. (U.S.): Frameline
A woman looking for sex without commitment learns that some things are worth committing to.

Firewords
Dir. Henaut, Dorothy Todd
1986 Canada English
90 mins. 16mm color Documentary
Dist. (U.S.): National Film Board of Canada
Louky Bersianik, Jovette Marchessault, and Nicole Brossard are three respected yet controversial Quebec writers. *Firewords* offers an intimate glimpse at their struggles and at their successes in creating a distinctive women's literature. Rooted in Quebec, with its unique vitality, these three writers have achieved recognition at home, in North America, and in Europe. They have confirmed that fresh approaches are still possible. Their voices, individually and collectively, leap over barriers of culture and politics, bringing feminist questioning to the heart of everyday life. In examining personal and global issues from a female perspective, they have touched on human relationships, work, justice, poverty, loneliness, and the future.

Fireworks
Dir. Anger, Kenneth
1947 USA English
15 mins. 16mm b&w Experimental
Dist. (U.S.): Canyon Cinema
Dist. (U.K.): British Film Institute
A startling homoerotic fantasy Anger filmed in his
Hollywood home at age 17.

Fireworks Revisited
Dir. Zalcock, Bev
1994 Great Britain English
9 mins. 16mm color Experimental
Dist. (U.K.): Cinenova
Bev Zalcock's *Fireworks Revisited* takes a girlie
angle on Kenneth Anger's homoerotic classic,
Fireworks (with a bit of Scorpio Rising thrown in
for good measure).

First Base
Dir. Siler, Megan
1991 USA English
13 mins. 16mm color Narrative
Dist. (U.S.): Frameline
Dist. (U.K.): Cinenova
A coming of age comedy about two young girls
masquerading as women. One tries for her first
kiss from a boy but soon realizes that it's better
with her girlfriend.

First Comes Love
Dir. Friedrich, Su
1991 USA English
22 mins. 16mm b&w Experimental
Dist. (U.S.): Women Make Movies
This contemplative short provokes a flow of
ambivalent and intensely personal meditations on
love and the ritualized institution of marriage.

5
Dir. Boyle, Bernie
1977 USA English
15 mins. S8mm color Other
Dist. (U.S.): n/a
1) I am a homosexual 2) A fractured fairy tale 3)
A to Z (almost)—a gay alphabet 4) Emergency
Ward 5) Doctor's love money or Is surgery a sexual crime. Plus, reptiles by Iolo.

Five Minutes, Ms. Lenska
Dir. Gaspar, Tomas
1979 USA English
2 mins. S8mm color Other
Dist. (U.S.): n/a
A drag spoof on Rula Lenska.

Five Naked Surfers
Dir. Tiffenbach, Joe
1985 USA No Dialogue
20 mins. 16mm color Other
Dist. (U.S.): n/a
Five Naked Surfers captures a day at the beach
with a group of surfer boys who don't surf—or
anything else—with clothes on. The film is silent.

Five Ways to Kill Yourself
Dir. Van Sant, Gus
1987 USA English
3 mins. 16mm color Other
Dist. (U.S.): Frameline
Early dry humor from Gus Van Sant.

Flames of Passion
Dir. Kwietniowski, Richard
1989 Great Britain English
18 mins. 16mm b&w Narrative
Dist. (U.S.): Frameline
Dist. (U.K.): British Film Institute
Flames of Passion is a very English eighteen-
minute melodrama by Richard Kwietniowski (no
stranger to San Francisco audiences through his
previous festival gems, *Alfalfa* and *Ballad of
Reading Gaol*). *Flames of Passion* takes its title
from the movie Celia Johnson and Trevor Howard
walk out of in the classic British tearjerker *Brief
Encounter*. This witty pocket-size remake follows
a dishy doctor aboard a train bound for strange
romance. With Richard Seymour, and Don Greig
    Winner of the 1990 San Francisco
International Lesbian & Gay Film Festival
Audience Award for Best Short Film.

Flaming Creatures
Dir. Smith, Jack
1963 USA English
45 mins. 16mm b&w Experimental
Dist. (U.S.): Filmmaker's Cooperative
Dist. (U.K.): ICA Projects
Smith's films, along with the films of Kenneth
Anger, Gregory Markopoulos, and later Andy
Warhol, are the avant-garde precursors of con-
temporary gay cinema. *Flaming Creatures* is his
most famous and controversial.

Flaming Ears
(see *Rote Ohren Fetzen Durch Asche*)

Flesh and Paper
Dir. Parmar, Pratibha
1990 Great Britain English
26 mins. 16mm/video color Documentary
Dist. (U.S.): Women Make Movies

Ⓐ
Ⓑ
Ⓒ
Ⓓ
Ⓔ
Ⓕ
Ⓖ
Ⓗ
Ⓘ
Ⓙ
Ⓚ
Ⓛ
Ⓜ
Ⓝ
Ⓞ
Ⓟ
Ⓠ
Ⓡ
Ⓢ
Ⓣ
Ⓤ
Ⓥ
Ⓦ
Ⓧ
Ⓨ
Ⓩ

A sensual tapestry of the life and work of Indian lesbian poet Suniti Namjoshi.

Flesh on Glass
Dir. Turner, Ann
1981 Australia English
40 mins. 16mm color Narrative
Dist. (U.S.): Australian Film Commission
This beautifully produced and acted film tells a story of Catholicism, guilt, and their impact on one woman's obsessive love for her brother's wife.

Flip Side, The
Dir. Corzine, Georgina
1993 USA English
4 mins. video color Experimental
Dist. (U.S.): Corzine, Georgina
A trio of poetry videos.

Florence and Robin
Dir. Finnis, Nick
1994 Great Britain English
51 mins. video color Documentary
Dist. (U.K.): Recorded Delivery Productions,Ltd.
The British-produced Florence and Robin offers a portrait of an American lesbian couple and their quest for a child through artificial insemination. Florence and Robin talk frankly about trying to become parents, finding a donor, deciding which of them would carry the child—and the impact of this process on their relationship. This thoroughly engaging video was partly filmed in San Francisco.

Florida Enchantment, A
Dir. Drew, Sidney
Prod. Vitagraph
1914 USA English
63 mins. 16mm b&w Narrative
Dist. (U.S.): Frameline
Frustrated by her fiancé's affairs with hotel maids, a New York heiress pops one of the magic seeds that change women into men and men into women. But after shaving "her" morning mustache, she forgets vengeance under newfound pleasure in embracing other women at the Ft. Lauderdale resort. Such is the first of many sexual reversals in the astonishing silent feature A Florida Enchantment from 1914, the first full year of U.S. feature-length filmmaking. While its camera style is simple, its way of toying with gender-specific body gestures remains amazingly witty to contemporary audiences today.

Flower Market, The
Dir. Waters, Jack
1993 USA English
15 mins. video color Experimental
Dist. (U.S.): Naked Eyed Cinema
The Flower Market is a funny and languid short about budding eroticism.

Flowing Hearts: Thailand Fights AIDS
Dir. Goss, John
1992 USA/Thailand English
32 mins. video color Documentary
Dist. (U.S.): Video Data Bank
Flowing Hearts: Thailand Fights AIDS is a document of grassroots education, focusing on performances by The White Line Dance Troupe (which uses Thai and modern dance to enact AIDS awareness) and interviews with Thai gay/AIDS activists.

Fly That Friendly Sky
Dir. Bautista, Pablo
1992 USA English
4 mins. video color Other
Dist. (U.S.): Bautista, Pablo
A humorous look at flying, fantasy, and safer-sex.

Foetal Gay's Nightmare, A
Dir. Layumans, Rune
1991 Phillippines English
5 mins. video color Experimental
Dist. (U.S.): Jurgen Bruning Filmproduktion
A Foetal Gay's Nightmare is an intensely personal and experimental exploration of the shrouded pleasures of gay sex that also addresses fears and hesitations about being gay.

Fontvella's Box
Dir. Hayn, Stefan
1992 Germany English
17 mins. 16mm color Other
Dist. (U.S.): Hayn, Stefan
Fontvella's Box weaves its hilariously bizarre tale of a drag queen and her special fashion-producing furry box.

Food for Thought
Dir. Perkins, T.K.
1977 USA English
6 mins. S8mm color Documentary
Dist. (U.S.): n/a
A Shot in the Dark production. What started out as a simple documentary became an exercise in hit/run cinema. Murphy's Law prevails.

Foolish Things
Dir. Wells, Peter
1982 New Zealand English
11 mins. 16mm color Experimental

Dist. (U.S.): New Zealand Film Commission
A man undresses teasingly behind a scrim. Another drives city streets at night pondering the trauma of relationships. An abstract film full of humor and playful irony.

For a Lost Soldier
Dir. Kerbosch, Roeland
1992 Netherlands Dutch
90 mins. 35mm color Narrative
Dist. (U.S.): Strand Releasing
Dist. (U.K.): Dangerous To Know
For a Lost Soldier was voted Best Feature at the 1993 Turin Gay and Lesbian Film Festival. It's a lush, moody, and romantic movie, based on the best-selling Dutch autobiography by Rudi van Dantzig. A chain of events leads contemporary choreographer Jeroen (played by *The Fourth Man's* Jeroen Krabbe) to recall his first erotic friendships. Sent away as a boy during World War II to a small fishing village, young Jeroen develops a strong friendship with another new boy, Jan. In the games and stories that mark the beginning of his sexuality, Jeroen always plays the spectator. Then comes Liberation, and the arrival of the Allies. Jeroen finds a new friend in the handsome Canadian soldier Walt (Andrew Kelley). *For a Lost Soldier* is a rich period piece, portraying the optimism and hope of a newly-liberated village alongside the warmth of a liberating relationship between the boy and the soldier, neither of whom even speak the same language. Surprisingly subtle, Roeland Kerbosch's artful film describes the bold, joyful affection that this unlikely duo nevertheless share.

Forbidden Love
Dir. Weïssman, Aerlyn, and Lynne Fernie
1992 Canada English
85 mins. 16mm color Documentary
Dist. (U.S.): Women Make Movies
Dist. (U.K.): Dangerous To Know
Compelling, often hilarious, and always rebellious, the nine women interviewed in *Forbidden Love* paint a portrait of lesbian sexuality and survival in Canada during the 1950s and 1960s, when lesbian love was "the love that dared not speak its name." Against a fascinating backdrop of lesbian pulp-novel covers, tabloid headlines, archival photographs, and film clips, these women recount stories about their first loves and their search for the beer parlors and bars where openly gay women were tolerated in Vancouver, Toronto, and Montreal. With the irreverence and candor of true survivors, they describe the

butch/femme subcultures they found in these bars and the harassment and intolerance they encountered as they sought to live and love in their clandestine world.

Their histories are interwoven with a fictional love story inspired by the then-popular lesbian paperback novels. An interview with novelist Ann Bannon and the reminiscences of the women who read these books brings to life the contrast between the way lesbians were fictionalized and their actual experiences. As it proudly shows a community once consigned to the twilight world of silence and exile, *Forbidden Love* brings lesbian history out of the closet and onto the screen.

Forbidden Love
(see *Zapovezena Laska*)

Forms and Motifs
Dir. Hetherman, Margaret
1994 USA English
40 mins. 16mm color Narrative
Dist. (U.S.): Hetherman, Margaret
Margaret Hetherman's award-winning film *Forms and Motifs* is inspired by Kalman Egyed's collection of exquisite beadwork and embroidered designs. A young woman, Cece, is not satisfied with the direction her life is taking when she discovers her grandfather's portfolio of designs. She decides that these patterns need to come to life and enlists the help of her surrogate family, three lively drag queens. Their goal? To create a most glamorous piece! It becomes a reality, but can they make it on the runway? All the designs in this delightful film were authentically revived.

Forsaken
Dir. Mosvold, Frank
1994 USA English
12 mins. 16mm color Narrative
Dist. (U.S.): Mosvold, Frank
A boy is forced to choose between love and religious faith.

Fortune and Men's Eyes
Dir. Hart, Harvey
1971 Canada/USA English
102 mins. 35mm color Narrative
Dist. (U.S.): Frameline Archive
John Herbert's famous stage play about the horrors of prison life, transformed into a sexually explicit movie about "a country club for sado-masochistic homosexuals," according to Vito Russo in *The Celluloid Closet*.

It's a tough, tragic drama involving

Ⓐ
Ⓑ
Ⓒ
Ⓓ
Ⓔ
Ⓕ
Ⓖ
Ⓗ
Ⓘ
Ⓙ
Ⓚ
Ⓛ
Ⓜ
Ⓝ
Ⓞ
Ⓟ
Ⓠ
Ⓡ
Ⓢ
Ⓣ
Ⓤ
Ⓥ
Ⓦ
Ⓧ
Ⓨ
Ⓩ

violence, sex roles, and epic bitchiness. The film was made under difficult conditions: the actors suffered in subzero temperatures on location in a real, disused Quebec prison, and first director Jules Schwerin was replaced by Harvey Hart. "Lester Persky, the producer, wanted only a kind of sex fantasy," says Schwerin, "He wanted a great deal of nudity and was interested only in the exploitation element."

The movie is saved from its exploitative tendencies by the performance of Michael Greer, fresh from *The Gay Deceivers*. Greer stars as the prison's resident outrageous drag queen, a role he had also occupied in more than 400 performances of the Sal Mineo stage production.

Forward, Bound
Dir. Humphrey, Daniel
1993 USA English
30 mins. 16mm b&w Narrative
Dist. (U.S.): Humphrey, Daniel
Daniel Humphrey's *Forward, Bound* is the intensely serious, near-wordless biography of a man beset by bad memories.

Framed Youth: The Revenge of the Teenage Perverts
Dir. Cole, Jeff, Jimi Somerville, Trill Burton, Pom Martin, Nicola Field, Rose Collis, and Toby Kettle
1983 Great Britain English
50 mins. video color Documentary
Dist. (U.S.): Frameline
Dist. (U.K.): Albany Video
Cheeky British lesbian and gay teenagers hit London's streets with video cameras and microphones to confront normals' views on homosexuality. The results are both humorous and revealing. Produced by the teenagers themselves, *Framed Youth* features a segment by Bronski Beat's Jimmy Somerville.

Framing Lesbian Fashion
Dir. Everett, Karen
1992 USA English
60 mins. video color Documentary
Dist. (U.S.): Frameline
Dist. (U.K.): Cinenova
Karen Everett's *Framing Lesbian Fashion* looks at the evolution of lesbian attire and identity—butch/femme, flannel, androgyny, cross-dressing and drag, queer flourescents, S/M and leather, lipstick, and more. Featuring interviews with Sally Gearhart, JoAnn Loulan, Arlene Stein, Kitty Tsui and others, *Framing Lesbian Fashion* incor-

porates archival photos and personal stories to document the sociology and history of lesbian fashion.

Frankenstein Created Woman
Dir. Fisher, Terence
Prod. Nelson-Keys, Anthony
1967 Great Britain English
92 mins. 35mm color Narrative
Dist. (U.S.): n/a
A Hammer horror film more transphobic than positively queer, in which Peter Cushing implants the soul of a recently dead man into a buxom female body. The poor guy can't handle the prospect of a penis-free existence and runs around stabbing people. The film has its effective moments, though, in representing the rage of nonconsensual embodiment. (S.S.)

Frankfurter
Dir. Keane, Tina
1994 Great Britain English
4 mins. 16mm color Other
Dist. (U.K.): Cinenova
Austrian filmmaker A. Hans Scheirl tells a story about something she once did with a hot dog.

Frankie and Jocie
Dir. Taylor, Jocelyn
1994 U.S.A. English
20 mins. video color Documentary
Dist. (U.S.): Third World Newsreel
A gay black woman and her straight brother discuss sexuality, desire, violence, self-hate, and notions of family.

Frankie Goes Downtown
Dir. Soffa, Fred
1993 USA English
8 mins. 16mm b&w Other
Dist. (U.S.): Soffa, Fred
Frankie rehearses his come-on lines and clothing options before going in search of urban love.

Frankly, Shirley
Dir. Moores, Margaret
1987 Canada English
11 mins. video color Narrative
Dist. (U.S.): V-Tape
Frankly, Shirley portrays the less than successful reunion of two ex-lovers.

Frau und Geschlecht (Basic Instincts)
Dir. Fockele, Jorg
1993 Germany German
6 mins. 16mm color Experimental
Dist. (U.S.): HFF Munchen

Hungry pussy striking back.

Free Love
Dir. Bonauro, Tom
1991 USA English
7 mins. video color Other
Dist. (U.S.): Morgan Creek Records
San Francisco band Voice Farm and Oblong Rhonda get themselves some of that. This time the extended version.

Freebird
Dir. Silver, Suzie
1993 USA English
8 mins. video b&w/color Experimental
Dist. (U.S.): Video Data Bank
In *Freebird*, Suzie Silver takes center stage with her multiple personas who rock through the ages, claiming their moments of fame.

French Bitch
Dir. Rosen, Andre
1993 USA English
5 mins. video color Other
Dist. (U.S.): Pussy Tourette
Another great music video from Pussy.

French Twist
(see *Gazon Maudit*)

Frenzy [excerpt]
Dir. Reiter, Jill
1993 USA English
11 mins. video color Narrative
Dist. (U.S.): Reiter, Jill
An excerpt from the soon to be finished first feature film from Jill Reiter starring Kathleen Hanna of Bikini Kill in a new wave/punk rock kitchy queer girl love story.

Fresa y Chocolate
(Strawberry and Chocolate)
Dir. Alea, Tomas Gutierrez,
and Juan Carlos Tabio
1993 Cuba Spanish
110 mins. 35mm color Narrative
Dist. (U.S.): Swank Motion Pictures
When Cuban writer Senal Paz won the 1990 Juan Rulfo Prize for *El lobo, el bosque y el hombre nuevo* (*The Wolf, the Woods and the New Man*), Cuba was entering the "Special Period," the official euphemism for life after Soviet subsidies.

With the economic crisis resonating from the dinner table to the movie screen, the Cuban film industry that had been financing thirty to forty films annually only four years ago, now struggles to make three or four. So the odds would seem to be against a feature adaptation of Paz's critical tale of Cuban intolerance and government repression of homosexuals.

Fresa y Chocolate (*Strawberry and Chocolate*) was not only made, it swept all the top awards at the 1993 New Latin American Film Festival in Havana, won critical and popular acclaim at festivals from Berlin to Telluride, and was nominated for the Best Foreign Film Oscar in 1995.

Paz and director Tomas Gutierrez Alea (Juan Carlos Tabio directed during Alea's hospitalization and shares codirector credit) insist theirs is not a "gay film" or critical of Cuban revolutionary ideals. On the contrary, it's message of tolerance and inclusion reflect the "clarified" party line on homosexuality. Taking place in 1979, before the Mariel boatlift, the movie charts the unlikely friendship of Diego, a flamboyant gay artist, and David, a rigid political science student and Communist party stalwart. Diego wants sex. David wants to be a good revolutionary and uses the friendship to spy on the evidently subversive and "antisocial" gay man. When he realizes how profoundly Diego is committed to Cuba and its culture, hard-line dogma and personal prejudices melt in the film's climactic embrace.

Jorge Perrugoria's initially campy turn as Diego grows more complex as he's forced to choose between who he is and the country he loves. Vladimir Cruz's David stands in for the Cuban Everyman, yet reveals the humanity behind the communist compañero. Both actors make impressive feature film debuts.

Cuba's legacy of forced labor camps for homosexuals (known as UMAPs), and official persecution of gays as "human scum" was exposed internationally in Nestor Almendros's 1983 documentary *Improper Conduct*. Ten years later, *Fresa y Chocolate* is being praised as a historic breakthrough. Despite entrenched prejudices, Cubans almost rioted for seats at initial screenings, fearing the film would be yanked by government censors. The day it was released, a crowd of over 200 refused to disperse until a final screening was added at 2:30 a.m. The film's popularity continued to grow unabated. Many Cubans in exile, however, condemn the film as cynical propaganda and a shallow take on the truth.

"*Strawberry and Chocolate* has caught the interest and provoked admiration

Ⓐ
Ⓑ
Ⓒ
Ⓓ
Ⓔ
Ⓕ
Ⓖ
Ⓗ
Ⓘ
Ⓙ
Ⓚ
Ⓛ
Ⓜ
Ⓝ
Ⓞ
Ⓟ
Ⓠ
Ⓡ
Ⓢ
Ⓣ
Ⓤ
Ⓥ
Ⓦ
Ⓧ
Ⓨ
Ⓩ

among those who do not know or who wish to ignore the rules for survival of the average Cuban in Cuba," wrote Sergio Giral, former director of the Cuban Film Institute, in the *Miami Herald*. Having defected in 1992, the openly gay filmmaker condemns the film as "too little too late for those of us who know the truth and are still waiting for our 'UMAP's List.'"

With Cuba more reliant than ever on international goodwill and hard currency, Diego and David's platonic hug is seen by those who have suffered for their sexual identity as an attempt to give the revolution a kinder, gentler face. In a country where gay and lesbian Cubans can still lose their jobs and be thrown out of the party, the film doesn't reflect any substantive change as much as a political PR coup.

How truthful is this film, they argue, when most young gay and lesbian Cubans are shocked to learn that Castro himself spoke in March 1994, in the pages of *Vanity Fair*, about "rectification," allowing that the revolution perhaps went too far in the treatment of homosexuals?

Paz, Alea, and Tabio have all come under fire since the film's release as apologists for the regime that created or encouraged the intolerance the film attacks.

Paz dismisses the criticism as coming from those whose vision of Cuba, revolution, and the power of film are as unyeilding and limiting as the policies and prejudices his film examines. (E.G.)

Fresh Kill
Dir. Cheang, Shu Lea
1994 USA English
80 mins. 35mm color Narrative
Dist. (U.S.): Strand Releasing
Kill is Dutch for "stream," and Shu Lea Cheang's audacious directorial debut is a lethal comedy swimming through a torrent of toxic multinational treachery. *Fresh Kill* tells the story of two young lesbian parents (Sarita Choudhury and Erin McMurtry) caught up in a global exchange of industrial waste via contaminated sushi. The place is New York and the time is now. Raw fish lips are the rage on trendy menus across Manhattan. A ghost barge, bearing nuclear refuse, circles the planet in search of a willing port. Household pets start to glow ominously and then disappear altogether. The sky opens up and snows soap flakes. People start speaking in dangerous dialects. The crisis escalates when a multinational corporation is implicated and the

couple's infant daughter mysteriously vanishes. After uncovering censored information, a group of young New Yorkers makes an unlikely alliance with activists in the developing world and strikes back.

A riveting and densely packed film, *Fresh Kill* evokes the furious rhythms of channel surfing with its rapid-fire editing style. Cheang and screenwriter Jessica Hagedorn (author of the award-winning novel *Dogeaters*) conjure a trippy, extraliterary dimension, where Jorge Luis Borges' search for his "Dreamtiger" intersects with lesbian-erotic flights into cyberspace. Language, meaning, and communication collide around a contemporary "Tower of Babel," as characters wrestle control of the flow of garbage and information from corporate gods. Intervention, or "breaking in," is key to the way Cheang has structured the film. Long, formalistic shots are interrupted by commercial break-ins. Cyber activists from Africa break in on a multinational satellite dish. Different characters will show up in the most unlikely places, breaking in on the narrative. Abandoning static shots, Cheang concerns herself with movement. Her use of cinematic space is less about a rooted territorial reference than a fluid way of exploring routes.

The interrelationships between *Fresh Kill's* characters, and the language they speak in, challenges cinematic representations of "reality." The characters speak in poetic and elegant constructs that don't sound like "real" movie dialogue, yet remain faithful to urban vernacular. The characters' provocative genealogies problematize ideas about race, which has traditionally been represented as a naturalized identity. A black woman is the mother of a white woman who, in turn, is the mother of a black child, and a Native American man and South Asian woman, both Indians, are father and daughter. On another level, the range of complexity Cheang portrays is true to American urban culture and begins to articulate unexpressed ideas about kinship and family. But while *Fresh Kill* may have the style and nerve of an "urban" movie, it transgresses that specificity, placing the local on a continuum with the global. (L.C.)

Fried Green Tomatoes
Dir. Avnet, Jon
1992 USA English
130 mins. 35mm color Narrative
Dist. (U.S.): Swank Motion Pictures
Please see under *Basic Instinct* for Judith Halberstam's entry.

Friend of Dorothy, A
Dir. O'Connell, Raoul
1994 USA English
25 mins. 16mm color Narrative
Dist. (U.S.): Strand Releasing
A shy sophomore suffers a crush on his seemingly unattainable roommate.
      Winner of the 1994 San Francisco International Lesbian & Gay Film Festival Audience Award for Best Short Film.

Friendly Witness
Dir. Sonbert, Warren
1989 USA English
31 mins. 16mm color/b&w Experimental
Dist. (U.S.): Canyon Cinema
San Francisco–based Warren Sonbert presents his first sound film in twenty years. Set to girl-group golden oldies, *Friendly Witness* is possibly the most extraordinary and cleverest music video ever made. Sonbert has segued the best bits from his lifetime of travels, teasing scraps of stories; old hippies, soldiers, and even camels boogie to "Please Mr. Postman" and "Will You Still Love Me Tomorrow?" In the final, more sombre part, music by Gluck paves the way for a darkening tone.

Friends Forever
(see *Venner for Altid*)

Frisk
Dir. Verow, Todd
Prod. Hu, Marcus
1995 USA English
90 mins. 16mm opt. color Narrative
Dist. (U.S.): Strand Releasing
More queer psychokilling on parade, in this case unabashedly explicit. An adaptation of Dennis Cooper's infamous novel of the same name, *Frisk* is director Todd Verow's descent into savagery and insanity, the story of a man named Dennis (Michael Gunther) who may or may not be a serial killer. In any event, the obsessive, brooding Dennis fantasizes about sexual torture and murder. The movie is a surreal collage of these harrowing dream-fucks come to life, set to a rollicking, hard-rock score. The picture's rough-hewn style and sexy, nerve-wracking set pieces are impressive; less so are its oblique structure and is he or isn't he? evasiveness. One of the most challenging queer films of the new new wave, it showcases the amazing talents of a bevy of edgy actors, notably Alexis Arquette *(Grief)*, Parker Posey *(Party Girl)*, and Jim Lyons *(Postcards from America)*. (E.P.)

From Bejing to Brooklyn
Dir. Webb, Kelly
Prod. Sandler, Arlene, Anie Stanley, and Kelly Webb
1994 USA English
17 mins. video color Other
Dist. (U.S.): Wet Spot Cinema
From Beijing to Brooklyn pits militant antiporn feminist Bernice-Be-Good against a harem of proud sex workers who battle it out with their pussy powered kung-fu.

From Dental Dams to Latex Gloves
Dir. Fisher, Lisa
1994 USA English
2 mins. video color Other
Dist. (U.S.): Fisher, Lisa
A quick and easy lesbian safe-sex message.

Fruta, La
Dir. Chang, Roly Barrero
1991 USA/Mexico English
3 mins. video color Experimental
Dist. (U.S.): Ferrera-Balanquet, Raul/Latino Midwest Video Collective
La Fruta is a sublime, cheeky moment of eroticism.

Fuck Film
Dir. Kadet
Prod. Private Eye Productions
1995 USA English
5 mins. video color Other
Dist. (U.S.): Private Eye Productions
A video about fucking film; choose your method.

Fuji
Dir. Bardsley, Gil
1995 Canada English
10 mins. 16mm color Narrative
Dist. (U.S.): Bardsley, Gil
The story of a gay friendship between a Mexican drag queen and his closest friend.

Fun Down There
Dir. Stigliano, Roger
1988 USA English
89 mins. 16mm color Narrative
Dist. (U.S.): Frameline
Dist. (U.K.): Metro Tartan
Roger Stigliano's first feature is a fresh, comic, coming-of-age drama about Buddy, a young man from upstate New York, who arrives in New York City and falls into love affairs with two men at the same time. The film follows Buddy over the course of a week: from home where, anxious to

Ⓐ
Ⓑ
Ⓒ
Ⓓ
Ⓔ
🄵
Ⓖ
Ⓗ
Ⓘ
Ⓙ
Ⓚ
Ⓛ
Ⓜ
Ⓝ
Ⓞ
Ⓟ
Ⓠ
Ⓡ
Ⓢ
Ⓣ
Ⓤ
Ⓥ
Ⓦ
Ⓧ
Ⓨ
Ⓩ

leave, he quarrels with his sister, to New York City, where he meets Joe, and then Angelo. Joe and Angelo initiate Buddy into sex and city life, while demonstrating their own complete ignorance of life outside New York. One of Stigliano's greater achievements in making *Fun Down There* is not the explicit representatioon of sexual acts, but his realistic incorporation of sexual acts into everyday life. A refreshing performance by Michael Waite as Buddy along with the use of real time and dead-pan humor give *Fun Down There* much of its charm.

Fun with a Sausage
Dir. Wilhite, Ingrid
1984 USA English
12 mins. video color Narrative
Dist. (U.S.): Wilhite, Ingrid
A lesbian classic.

Funeral Parade of Roses
Dir. Matsumoto, Toshio
Prod. Kudo, Mitsuru
1969 Japan Japanese
105 mins. 35mm b&w Narrative
Dist. (U.S.): Pacific Film Archive
Scandalous when it first appeared, *Funeral Parade of Roses* is still a sensational depiction of the gay demimonde as it existed in the Tokyo of the late '60s. Eddie, the wiggy protagonist, is a young roustabout who works at the Genet, a gay bar managed by the much desired Gonda. Dressed in miniskirts and false eyelashes, Eddie is rivaled for the affections of Gonda only by Leda, his ferocious transvestite mistress. It's cross-dressers in a cold war gone hot. The first Japanese film to deal unabashedly with gay culture (the original press materials say "seven gay boys appear on stage, all performed by real gay boys") *Funeral Parade of Roses* is also a modern parody of the Oedipus legend. But here the Oedipal story is totally inverted—Eddie must eliminate his obstructive mother for the wild embrace of his father. The fatalism of the story doesn't deter our amazement at the performance director Toshio Matsumoto has elicited from his flamboyant but nonprofessional cast, particularly the two leads. Peter, who plays Eddie, is a famous female impersonator known for his emancipated woman, while Osamu Ogasawara, enlisted to play Leda, does a virulent portrayal of the kimonoed siren. By enacting its love triangle in drag, *Funeral Parade of Roses* redresses the Oedipal myth—an essential bit of anarchy.

G.I. Sports

Dir. unknown
1985 USA English
20 mins. 16mm b&w Documentary
Dist. (U.S.): n/a
Military men exercising.

Gab
Dir. Moriyasu, Ann Akiko
1988 USA English
11 mins. 16mm color Narrative
Dist. (U.S.): Moriyasu, Ann Akiko
A group of people gather at a wake for a mutual friend, Gab.

Gabriella on the Half Shell
Dir. Troche, Rose
1994 USA English
10 mins. video color Narrative
Dist. (U.S.): KVPI
From the director of *Go Fish*, the latest in the continuing adventures of Gabriella.

Gangtime
Dir. McAlpin, Loring
1993 USA English
23 mins. video color Documentary
Dist. (U.S.): GANG c/o McAlpin, Loring
From New York, *Gangtime* tells the stories of our generation—coming out, cheap sex, first dates—with terrific, snappy style.

Ganze Leben, Das (The Whole of Life)
Dir. Moll, Bruno
1983 Switzerland German
112 mins. 16mm color Experimental
Dist. (U.S.): Pro Helvetia
Barbara, a fifty-year-old lesbian whose lifespan has taken her through correction homes, mental hospitals, prisons and bouts of prostitution, approached filmmaker Bruno Moll suggesting that he make a film of her life. Moll agreed and engaged an actress, Serena Wey, to interpret episodes in Barbara's past. Barbara has in mind a Hollywood-style bio starring an actress on the order of Susan Hayward dramatically telling her story of a life ruined by bourgeois standards. The result is a semidocumentary mixing black-and-white segments of Barbara and Serena discussing the project with color scenes depicting little stories from the 1950s, the heyday of bourgeois existence.

Although she initially disapproves of the young actress—"She's too feminine," complains Barbara, "most people are bisexual, but I'm 100% lesbian!"—the two women eventually develop a rapport, culminating in a funny, sweet scene in which Barbara shows Serena how to make a pickup in a lesbian bar.

Garbage Can Man
Dir. Smolen, Wayne
1977 USA English
3 mins. S8mm color Experimental
Dist. (U.S.): Mears, Ric
Shows what can happen spontaneously with an open field, two people, a camera, and a free afternoon.

Garden, The
Dir. Jarman, Derek
1990 Great Britain English
92 mins. 35mm color Experimental
Dist. (U.S.): International Film Circuit
Dist. (U.K.): British Film Institute
Viewers who embrace the elliptical, "experimental," style of rock music videos will welcome *The Garden*, British filmmaker Derek Jarman's ninth feature—a challenging, ultimately very moving look at the link between homosexuality and religion. Set in the garden and surrounding headlands of his home in rural England, it takes us on a shrewd, often puzzling journey that works on at least two levels. First as a sardonic retelling of the Passion story that alternates a gay couple with Christ, then as a surreal barrage of images and sounds that are humorous, shocking, and seemingly unrelated. It isn't often that one film includes both a campy version of "Think Pink" (from the 1957 musical *Funny Face*) and a bizarre scene of gay lovers being tarred and feathered with molasses and cotton batting.

Is it important—or even possible—to understand every reference and image in *The Garden*? You won't need to penetrate all of Jarman's private obsessions to be moved by the heartbreaking elegy he reads near the film's end. While it's clear that Jarman is making a connection between the Christ story, gay oppression, and his personal battle with AIDS, stylistically he is demanding that we look through his enigmatic eyes for 92 minutes. The result is a visually dense, nearly hypnotic work of art that further solidifies Jarman's reputation as England's premiere gay filmmaker.

Gay Day, A
Dir. Hammer, Barbara
1973 USA English
3 mins. 16mm color Experimental
Dist. (U.S.): Canyon Cinema
One of the legendary Barbara Hammer's earliest films, *A Gay Day* is a satire about lesbian

monogamy, shot in red filter—with a dirge for a soundtrack.

Gay Deceivers, The
Dir. Kessler, Bruce
1969 USA English
105 mins. 35mm color Narrative
Dist. (U.S.): Olson, Jenni
Yes, Virginia, there were other gay-themed films of the '60s besides *Boys in the Band*—and *The Gay Deceivers* is the best of them. The plot's simple: two straight all-American boys play sissy to dodge the draft; they move into a swishy all-gay L.A. apartment complex, and a comedy of misunderstanding ensues. *The Gay Deceivers* is like "Love, American Style" on drugs; it's lurid, weird, and unintentionally funny.

What makes the movie really treasurable, however, is Michael Greer (who went on to feature as another queen in *Fortune in Men's Eyes*); his swishes and turns were such a hit with audiences that the distributor switched ad campaigns after a week's release, billing him as the star.

Gay Freedom Day Parade 1976
Dir. Hansen, Bob
1976 USA English
6 mins. S8mm color Documentary
Dist. (U.S.): n/a
A home movie–style documentary of the 1976 Gay Freedom Day Festivities.

Gay Is Out
Prod. Horses, Inc.
1981 USA English
18 mins. video color Documentary
Dist. (U.S.): n/a
A critique of gay clichés and rigid community stereotypes.

Gay Lives and Culture Wars
Dir. Velasquez, Elaine
Prod. Bernstein, Barbara, and Elaine Velazquez
1995 USA English
28 mins. video color Documentary
Dist. (U.S.): Democracy Media
Gay Lives and Culture Wars was created to battle the antigay propaganda being produced by the religious right. This challenging video focuses on gay youth and their families as they confront Oregon's controversial antigay measures of 1994.

Gay Olympics '82
Dir. Amathonte, Genita
1983 USA English

Ⓐ Ⓑ Ⓒ Ⓓ Ⓔ Ⓕ Ⓖ Ⓗ Ⓘ Ⓙ Ⓚ Ⓛ Ⓜ Ⓝ Ⓞ Ⓟ Ⓠ Ⓡ Ⓢ Ⓣ Ⓤ Ⓥ Ⓦ Ⓧ Ⓨ Ⓩ

10 mins. video color Documentary
Dist. (U.S.): n/a
An effective treatment of the emotion, beauty, and grace of the first Gay Olympics.

Gay Rock 'n' Roll Years, The
Dir. Brown, Shauna
Prod. Beavan, Clare
1991 Great Britain English
60 mins. video color Documentary
Dist. (U.S.): Fulcrum Productions
The Gay Rock 'N' Roll Years is a giddy zip through the '50s onward, using archive clips and pop music. (It's also a spoof of a British TV series called "The Rock 'n' Roll Years," which uses vintage footage and hits-of-the-year to shine a light on days gone by.) All the great stuff is here—Tom Robinson, Sandie Shaw, the Pet Shop Boys, Kylie Minogue—as well as some especially scary '70s disco fashions. The music is cut to queer moments in British history: from the campaign for law reform to Clause 28; from Dirk Bogarde to chanting lesbians invading a prime-time TV news broadcast.

Gay San Francisco
Dir. Raymond, Jonathan
1965-70 USA English
60 mins. 16mm color Documentary
Dist. (U.S.): Muckerman, Ed
Shot between 1965 and 1970, Gay San Francisco is a rediscovered work that includes scenes filmed at Aquatic Park, Land's End, the Tenderloin, Polk and Market Streets, and at lesbian and gay gatherings. After making the rounds to a variety of gay bars, we move to Twin Peaks (the "Swish Alps") for a BYOB gay party. Our lesbian gathering is more subdued, sitting in a circle, petting cats; this gathering quickly changes its mood when a young woman takes off her blouse while doing the jerk. Intercut with these scenes are interviews with three couples—gay men, lesbians and transvestites. They discuss everything from orgies and jealousy to police harassment and job security for cross-dressers. The highlight of the film is a visit to a Halloween drag show at On the Levee. David Kelshey is at the organ, and on stage is a parade of some of San Francisco's finest drag.

Gay Tape: Butch and Femme
Dir. Dougherty, Cecilia
1985 USA English
29 mins. video color Documentary
Dist. (U.S.): Dougherty, Cecilia
A candid, insightful look at lesbian butch and femme role models, the women that exhibit these characteristics, and their places in society.

Gay TV
Dir. Speck, Wieland
1989 Germany German
12 mins. video color Other
Dist. (U.S.): Speck, Wieland
In this sexy and informative takeoff on television news, viewers learn how to use a condom.

Gay USA
Dir. Bressan, Arthur
1977 USA English
78 mins. 35mm color Narrative
Dist. (U.S.): Frameline
Before the better-known *Word is Out*, Bressan produced his hands-across-gay-America panorama, *Gay USA*. Arthur Bressan on *Gay USA*: "When the Anita Bryant debacle happened I was hurled into making a political gay documentary. Suppose someone were to film every gay demo on June 27, 1977, from all the cities? It would be like *Triumph of the Will*, only I would call it *Triumph of the Fag, Triumph of the Dyke* . . . My naive dream at that point was that if we all saw ourselves in our numbers we would never buy into the guilty trip again. Not from Anita Bryant or from Mayor Koch or from Cardinal Cook. Not even from AIDS."

Gay Youth
Dir. Walton, Pam
1992 USA English
40 mins. video color Documentary
Dist. (U.S.): Filmmaker's Library
Dist. (U.K.): Cinenova
A stirring tape about two teens: Bobby Griffith, who killed himself at the age of 20, and Gina Gutierrez, a 17-year-old high school senior who has received acceptance and support for her sexual identity. One story is about death, the other about life; director Pam Walton shows what can make the difference.

Gazon Maudit (French Twist)
Dir. Balasko, Josiane
Prod. Berri, Claude
1994 France English
105 mins. 35mm color Narrative
Dist. (U.S.): Swank Motion Pictures
In *French Twist* (a.k.a. *Gazon Maudit*, French slang for "dyke"), Marijo, a butch lesbian (played by director/screenwriter Josiane Balasko), befriends Loli (Victoria Abril), a housewife whose husband (Alain Chabat) is cheating on her. When

Loli decides Marijo can give her the tenderness her spouse cannot, she kicks him out of her bed and invited Marijo in.

Though this scenario may sound like a recipe for stereotyping, Balasko instead crafts the best lesbian comedy of the year. With its deft delineation of the shifting power dynamic of a three-way homo/hetero relationship, *French Twist* is also the season's most sophisticated lesbian film—if one can apply this label at all, given the equal focus on heterosexual concerns. (D.M.)

Genderfuck
Dir. Gilerman, Svetlana
1993 Australia English
4 mins. video color Other
Dist. (U.S.): Gilerman, Svetlana
Genderfuck argues for the need for people to accept both their masculinty and femininity. If you have ever felt that you don't fit into the societal expectations of male or female, you might consider yourself transgendered.

Gentlemen
Dir. Farringdon, David
1988 Great Britain English
14 mins. video color Narrative
Dist. (U.S.): n/a
Gentlemen is an ode to the public toilet—"Jarman meets Orton."

Gently Down the Stream
Dir. Friedrich, Su
1983 USA English
14 mins. 16mm color Experimental
Dist. (U.S.): Women Make Movies
Dist. (U.K.): Cinenova
Gently Down the Stream uses material from a succession of dreams taken from eight years of journals to exorcise the mysterious ritualistic power of repeating images.

Geography of the Imagination
Dir. Andrews, Jan
1993 USA English
15 mins. 16mm b&w Experimental
Dist. (U.S.): Andrews, Jan
An evocative experimental short.

Gerbroken Spiegels (Broken Mirrors)
Dir. Gorris, Marleen
Prod. Heilningen, Matthjis Van
1984 Netherlands Dutch
110 mins. 35mm color Narrative
Dist. (U.S.): First Run Features
Marleen Gorris's first feature *A Question of*

Silence has become somewhat of a classic in feminist circles. With her new film we believe Gorris will be recognized as a premier filmmaker. Most of the action of *Broken Mirrors* takes place in a brothel called Happy House, run by Ellen, the Madam. Working there are Dora, an Academy of Art graduate; Irma, a good natured naive girl; Francine, a hard successful Hooker; Jackie, an elegant and indifferent english vamp; Tessa, a colored girl from Surinam; and the vulnerable and remote Linda. Diane, who has a baby girl and who is married to a heroin addict, is a newcomer in the business. Running parallel to the story of the women in the sex club is the fate of Bea. She is an ordinary housewife kidnapped by a man and locked in a cellar. Although Bea and the prostitutes have little in common, it becomes clear how their destinies are intertwined, merging into a surprising conclusion.

Winner of the 1985 San Francisco International Lesbian & Gay Film Festival Audience Award for Best Feature.

Gertrude Stein and a Companion
Dir. Cirker, Ira
Prod. Walzog, Mary
1986 USA English
87 mins. video color Narrative
Dist. (U.S.): Tapestry Productions
Gertrude and Alice get fine treatment in this literate and stylish portrait of their lives. The script, adapted by Win Wells from Stein's and Toklas's writings, is top-notch, as are performances by Jan Miner as Gertrude and Broadway standout Marian Seldes as Alice.

It is the afternoon of July 27, 1946, and Gertrude Stein is dead. Now "alone" in their famous salon, a place usually alive with gatherings of the avant-garde from the literary and art worlds, Alice sets out to write to Picasso with the news of Gertrude's death. In her attempt to tell how it happened, she begins to relive the events of their lives together.

In a style not unlike Stein's free verse, scenes from their public and private life are interwoven with Alice's recollections. Director Ira Cirker sucessfully marries theatrical and video techniques to render this compelling portrait of Gertrude's and Alice's tempestuous forty-year relationship. An interesting counterpoint to the recently released *Waiting for the Moon*, this video offers a fresh look at two of literature's most interesting figures.

Ⓐ
Ⓑ
Ⓒ
Ⓓ
Ⓔ
Ⓕ
Ⓖ
Ⓗ
Ⓘ
Ⓙ
Ⓚ
Ⓛ
Ⓜ
Ⓝ
Ⓞ
Ⓟ
Ⓠ
Ⓡ
Ⓢ
Ⓣ
Ⓤ
Ⓥ
Ⓦ
Ⓧ
Ⓨ
Ⓩ

Gertrude Stein: When This You See, Remember Me
Dir. Adato, Perry Miller
1970 USA English
89 mins. 16mm color Documentary
Dist. (U.S.): American Federation of Arts
Dist. (U.K.): British Film Institute
The Autobiography of Alice B. Toklas provides the text for this documentary overview of the life of Gertrude Stein, complemented by film clips, newspaper clippings, and footage of her paintings and her entourage of friends.

Get It Girl: Lesbians Talk about Safe Sex
Dir. Gant, Ella
1994 USA English
45 mins. video color Documentary
Dist. (U.S.): Gant, Ella
A down-and-dirty sextalk home movie.

Get Over It
Dir. Katsapetses, Nicholas
Prod. Hu, Marcus
1995 USA English
90 mins. 16mm b&w Narrative
Dist. (U.S.): Strand Releasing
Get Over It is an insightful caustic comedy about a group of handsome but emotionally selfish young gay men and their highly dysfunctional sexual entanglements. When Steven (Tony Morgan) is unceremoniously dumped by his boyfriend Derek (Nicholas Katsapetses), his best friend Pam (Deborah Cordell) in a well-intentioned but misguided attempt to coax him out of depression, invites all their friends up from L.A. The group is made up of supposedly straight Spencer (Christian Canterbury) who has read somewhere that to be fully in touch with his sexuality, a man must exercise his sphincter muscle to its full extent; his exasperated wife; Christine and Sarah, a lesbian couple who are joined at the clit and who never argue; and Robert, who brings his beautiful but bratty eighteen-year-old boyfriend Michael. Constantly swapping partners, the boys can't seem to stop arguing among themselves. Quickly fed up, the women ditch them and drive back to L.A. leaving the boys to untangle their own mess. Meanwhile, Steven is left feeling even more down in the dumps.

Ghost Body
Dir. Cutrone, Christopher
1993 USA English
20 mins. video color Experimental
Dist. (U.S.): Cutrone, Christopher

A compelling, quixotic account of the ambivalences of interracial desire.

Girl Power (Part 1)
Dir. Benning, Sadie
1993 USA English
15 mins. video color Experimental
Dist. (U.S.): Video Data Bank
Dist. (U.K.): London Video Access
In her latest Pixel Vision *Girl Power*, festival favorite Sadie Benning remembers her childhood fantasies, where oral fixations intersect with pop culture.

Girl's Best Friend, A
Dir. Clark, Kathy
1988 USA English
10 mins. video color Documentary
Dist. (U.S.): Clark, Kathy
A Girl's Best Friend is a touching personal story of a woman losing a friend to AIDS.

Girls Will Be Boys
Dir. Tomboy, Texas
1993 USA English
6 mins. video color Other
Dist. (U.S.): Frameline
A drag king date where they skip dinner and a movie. Released in the U.S. as part of *She's Safe*, a feature-length package of lesbian safe-sex videos.

Give AIDS the Freeze
Dir. Joritz, Cathy
1991 Germany English
2 mins. 35mm b&w Other
Dist. (U.S.): Joritz, Cathy
A scratch AIDS public service announcement.
Winner of the 1991 San Francisco International Lesbian & Gay Film Festival Audience Award for Best Short Film.

Give Me Body
Dir. Bautista, Pablo
1991 USA English
9 mins. video color Experimental
Dist. (U.S.): Bautista, Pablo
Give Me Body questions the construction of brawn, beauty and objectivity from a gay Asian-American perspective.

Glad To Be Gay, Right?
Dir. Reeder, Andre
1993 Netherlands Dutch
48 mins. video color Other
Dist. (U.S.): Reeder, Andre
Made for Dutch TV, and clearly influenced by the

style of British TV's Out, *Glad To Be Gay, Right?* shows the difference of having a black director; three out of these five gripping coming-out stories are told by people of color.

Glasses Break

Dir. Buchanan, Justine
1991 Great Britain English
18 mins. 16mm color Narrative
Dist. (U.S.): Women Make Movies
Offers a bittersweet recollection of a love affair.

Glen or Glenda? (I Changed My Sex)

Dir. Wood, Ed
1953 USA English
67 mins. 16mm b&w Narrative
Dist. (U.S.): Wade Williams Distribution
Dist. (U.K.): Mass Productions
This brilliantly bad movie by Ed Wood defines postmodern transgender aesthetic sensibilities. Seriously. Boldly innovative in its use of found footage, the film requires voice-over narration to render intelligible its jarring visual discontinuities, making it a theory-head's wet dream that mocks the distinction between high art and garbage. The film's impassioned defense of sexual diversity makes it fun for all kinds of viewers. (S.S.)

Glitterbug

Dir. Jarman, Derek
1994 Great Britain No Dialogue
52 mins. 35mm color Experimental
Dist. (U.K.): Basilisk
Derek Jarman's last film is a luminous, lyrical history of the maker's life between 1970 and 1986, set to new music by Brian Eno. Jarman once again reinvents himself and his style in *Glitterbug*. Using rare and unseen moments from his archive of Super 8 footage, he structures the film in short, chronological sequences. *Glitterbug* opens in his studio by the Thames, where Jarman made his first film. There is also a sequence at the second Alternative Miss World contest (a very '70s event), as well as behind-the-scenes shots from the making of *Sebastiane* and *Jubilee*. *Glitterbug* catches up with the '80s in shots of dancer Michael Clarke, and Tilda Swinton in an uncanny precursor of *Orlando's* garden scene.
   Glitterbug is entirely wordless. Brian Eno's moving score lends the film a beautiful pace, while Jarman's exquisite images engrave themselves on the eye.

Gloria's Point of View

Dir. Walters, Jamie
1984 USA English
4 mins. video color Other
Dist. (U.S.): n/a
A reasonable opinion of our times, this is our strongest political statement this year.

Go Fish

Dir. Troche, Rose
Prod. Kalin, Tom, and Christine Vachon
1994 USA English
85 mins. 35mm b&w Narrative
Dist. (U.S.): Samuel Goldwyn Company
Go Fish serves up bundles of gossip, drama, and sex as it tracks the lives of an extraordinary group of lesbian friends. Kia (T. Wendy McMillan), a professor, is involved with Evy (Migdalia Melendez), a divorcee who's not out to her mother, yet. Kia decides to set up her roommate Max (Guinevere Turner) with an ex-student of hers, Ely (V. S. Brodie), who's just ending a long-distance relationship. And then there's the perpetually horny Daria (Anastasia Sharp).
   Many years in the making, this debut feature from writer/director Rose Troche and cowriter Guinevere Turner was one of Frameline's 1992 Completion Fund grant recipients. Coexecutive-produced by Tom Kalin (*Swoon*) and 1994 Frameline Award–winner Christine Vachon, *Go Fish* has the charm and audacity of such debut independent features as *She's Gotta Have It* and *Slacker*.
   A three-star review from the prestigious *Screen International* compares *Go Fish* to 1991's *Poison*, suggesting that *Go Fish* signals "the belated advent of lesbian cinema," and it brightly pegs the film's key audience as, simply: "lesbians everywhere."

Goat Named Tension, A

Dir. Goodnight, Kate
1992 USA English
6 mins. 16mm b&w Experimental
Dist. (U.S.): Chicago Filmmakers
Dist. (U.K.): Cinenova
An absolutely charming, sensual, and elaborate experimental pun.

Goblin Market

Dir. Smith, Jo
1993 USA English
9 mins. video color Other
Dist. (U.S.): Smith, Jo
Dist. (U.K.): Cinenova
Drawn from Christina Rossetti's notoriously lesbo-erotic poem, this is a lush and sexy period piece.

Ⓐ Ⓑ Ⓒ Ⓓ Ⓔ Ⓕ Ⓖ Ⓗ Ⓘ Ⓙ Ⓚ Ⓛ Ⓜ Ⓝ Ⓞ Ⓟ Ⓠ Ⓡ Ⓢ Ⓣ Ⓤ Ⓥ Ⓦ Ⓧ Ⓨ Ⓩ

Godzilla Voice
Prod. CNA/Art Available
1984 USA English
14 mins. video color Documentary
Dist. (U.S.): n/a
Pure theater, serious video, this bawdy, original presentation leaves no stone unturned. Turning the gay experience inside out.

Golden Gate Bridge Blockade, The
Prod. Nadel, Arl Spencer
1989 USA English
6 mins. video color Documentary
Dist. (U.S.): Nadel, Arl Spencer
The Golden Gate Bridge Blockade was taped when a camera crew found themselves caught in a blockade staged by Stop AIDS Now Or Else.

Golden Positions, The
Dir. Broughton, James
1970 USA English
32 mins. 16mm color/b&w Experimental
Dist. (U.S.): Canyon Cinema
The Golden Positions refines the format of Broughton's landmark film, *The Bed* (1968). It begins with a navel in close-up. "Let us contemplate," Broughton says as the camera zooms back to frame the entire naked male form. *San Francisco Chronicle* critic John Wasserman said of the film: "A lovely, poetic, humorous and crystal investigation of mankind standing, sitting, and lying down."

Good Dyke Gone Mad, A
Dir. Pearl, Heather
1993 USA English
11 mins. video color Narrative
Dist. (U.S.): Pearl, Heather
Heather Pearl's hilarious, low-budget, high-energy portrait of *A Good Dyke Gone Mad* features Diane DiMassa and her alter ego, Hothead Paisan (featuring music by Joan Jett and L7).

Gracious Flab, Gracious Bone
Dir. Leder, Evie
1993 USA English
14 mins. video color Documentary
Dist. (U.S.): Leder, Evie
Poet, novelist, and fat-activist Susan Stinson shares her thoughts and her art.

Grapefruit
Dir. Dougherty, Cecilia
1989 USA English
40 mins. video color Experimental
Dist. (U.S.): Video Data Bank

Cecilia Dougherty's *Grapefruit* could just as easily screen in the Fun for Boys and Girls sampler. John and Yoko—a.k.a. Susie Bright and Shelley Cook—replay the whole glorious Beatles story in lesbian drag. Miles more inspiring than the Paul McCartney concert, Grapefruit is a wry lesbian retake on popular culture.

Great Dykes of Holland, The
Dir. Taylor, Jennifer Maytorena
1993 USA English
6 mins. video color Other
Dist. (U.S.): Taylor, Jennifer Maytorena
Dutch girls lip synch to a Disney ditty and visit the Folsom St. Fair.

Greek Love and Sapphic Sophistication
(see *Out On Tuesday, Program 3*)

Green on Thursdays
Dir. Bushala, Dean, and Deidre Heaslip
1993 USA English
80 mins. video color Documentary
Dist. (U.S.): First Run Features
An important documentary about antigay violence in America, *Green on Thursdays* also has a snappy, modern, no-voice-over style.

Greetings from Out Here
Dir. Spiro, Ellen
1993 USA English
58 mins. video color Documentary
Dist. (U.S.): Video Data Bank
Videomaker Ellen Spiro captures the people, places, politics, and queer roadside signs of the South. In a series of vivid moving picture postcards, Spiro visits landmarks, events, and just plain characters, including the Gay Rodeo, Mardi Gras, Gay Pride in Atlanta, Rhythmfest women's music festival, the Short Mountain Radical Faerie sanctuary, Dollywood, and Miss Miller's Eternal Love and Care Pet Cemetery. Interviews with gay men and lesbians along the way convey the range of Southern lives—from Iris, a black lesbian living in a bus in the Ozarks to Rita, a retired military officer, now a drag queen in New Orleans. With strength and insight, the interviews in *Greetings from Out Here* addresses the politics of being out in the South, the impact of AIDS in the rural South, and the relation between the gay and civil rights movements.

Greetings from Washington D.C.
Dir. Winer, Lucy
Prod. Epstein, Robert, Frances Reid, Greta Schiller, and Lucy Winer
1981 USA English

30 mins. 16mm color Documentary
Dist. (U.S.): Women Make Movies
Greetings from Washington D.C. is a 30-minute color documentary film about the National March on Washington for Lesbian and Gay Rights.

On October 14, 1979, approximately 125,000 lesbians and gay men from across America marched on the national capital. Frances Reid, Robert Epstein, Lucy Winer, and Greta Schiller, four independent filmmakers from San Francisco and New York, decided to doument the event so that the gay community would not have to depend only on the commercial media for coverage of the event.

Historically, this was the first national gay rights demonstration. With this in mind, the filmmakers decided to focus on the geographical diversity of the people participating, as well as overall documentation of the day. After deciding to pool resources and equipment, the filmmakers set out to record this historic event, with the help of a $2,000 donation and the contribution of their own time and labor. Working with an all-volunteer crew of twenty-five lesbians and gay men, most of whom were professional filmmakers, they divided into four roving camera crews. Each crew interviewed a wide variety of people at the gathering site in the morning, along the march route, and finally at the rally in front of the Washington Monument. Throughout the day they continued to document the overall event, as well as shooting "Movie Snapshots."

These snapshots were set up with stationary cameras in postcard settings. With backgrounds that clearly establish them in Washington, D.C., lesbians and gay men came before the cameras to make their statements to the world, to their parents, to their friends at home. Everyone and anyone was invited in front of the camera to deliver any message they wished. It is these statements, some funny, some poignant, some profound, that open and close the film. They, more than anything else, capture the humor, the struggles, the depth, the strength, and the diversity of gay people in this country.

Most of the funding for *Greetings from Washington D.C.* was raised from small individual donations and grassroots fundraisers within the gay and lesbian community. Contributions ranged from $1 to $2000, with the total budget of the film set at $30,000. Many people donated their time, labor, and services to help complete the project.

Greta's Girls
Dir. Schiller, Greta
1976 USA English
15 mins. 16mm b&w Documentary
Dist. (U.S.): Jezebel Productions
A look at the relationship of an interracial lesbian couple.

Grey Hideaway
Dir. Aldighieri, Merril, and Joe Tripician
Prod. Jacobs, Raymond, and the Gay Men's Health Crisis
1986 USA English
6 mins. video color Other
Dist. (U.S.): Gay Men's Health Crisis
A gay male erotic music video which is part of a longer work, *Chance of a Lifetime*, to be shown later this evening. This segment depicts group sex against a background of gray metal grid, bodies standing out like living sculpture in an industrial environment.

Grid-Lock: Women and the Politics of AIDS
Dir. Wichterich, Beth
1992 USA English
28 mins. video color Documentary
Dist. (U.S.): Wichterich, Beth
This powerful examination of women and the AIDS crisis offers a searing indictment of government health agencies and presents a plea for research, diagnosis, and caregiving services for women with HIV/AIDS.

Grief
Dir. Glatzer, Richard
1993 USA English   ·
85 mins. 16mm color Narrative
Dist. (U.S.): Strand Releasing
Dist. (U.K.): Dangerous To Know
Grief is a bittersweet comedy set behind the scenes on a bad daytime TV drama, starring *Last Exit to Brooklyn*'s Alexis Arquette, *Swoon*'s Craig Chester, and Illeana Douglas from *Alive*. It's a low-budget, big-laugh *Soapdish*-y riff.

The TV show is in trouble. Jo, the ebullient, chain-smoking producer, is leaving to become a Hungarian housewife; the men in suits upstairs are squeezing the budget; the photocopier keeps breaking down; and, worst of all, someone is leaving nighttime cum stains on the office sofa. Clearly, the courtroom drama's bizarre on-screen confessions—involving lesbian trapeze artists and schizophrenic housewives—are but nothing compared to the backstage antics.

Ⓐ Ⓑ Ⓒ Ⓓ Ⓔ Ⓕ Ⓖ Ⓗ Ⓘ Ⓙ Ⓚ Ⓛ Ⓜ Ⓝ Ⓞ Ⓟ Ⓠ Ⓡ Ⓢ Ⓣ Ⓤ Ⓥ Ⓦ Ⓧ Ⓨ Ⓩ

Melancholy Bill (Craig Chester) and patronizing Paula (Nicholas Nicklebly's Lucy Gutteridge) are prime candidates to replace Jo, but it's a tough choice. Besides, Bill is still recovering from the year-old loss of his boyfriend, and he's caught up in a foolish crush on Alexis Arquette.

Grief delivers something we've been lacking for a long time: smart, uncomplicated old-fashioned comedy—decked out in '90s style. Director Richard Glatzer used to produce "Divorce Court," so the film has a true sense of the absurdity of cheap television. All the performances are shamefully good; Kent Fuhr is a standout as Jo, the Eve Ardenesque TV producer, combination den mother and dragon lady. And on top of all this, Glatzer throws in some amusing courtroom cameos, including Mary Woronov and Paul Bartel.

Winner of the 1993 San Francisco International Lesbian & Gay Film Festival Audience Award for Best Feature.

Growing Up and I'm Fine
Dir. Bolton, James
1990 USA
11 mins. 16mm color Narrative
Dist. (U.S.): Growing Up Productions
Two homeless boys, one of them sick with AIDS, develop a close friendship on the streets of L.A.

Guadalcanal Interlude
Dir. unknown
1944 USA English
8 mins. 16mm b&w Documentary
Dist. (U.S.): National Archives
Soldiers on R&R at Guadalcanal are entertained by an outrageous Army drag troupe. A gem from the National Archives, Washington, D.C.

Guess Who's Coming to Dinner
Dir. Kwietniowski, Richard
1991 Great Britain English
25 mins. video color Other
Dist. (U.K.): Maya Vision
A gay dinner party where all the guests have one thing in common—working with food. Waiters, chefs, caterers, and food writers swap stories as they eat their way through a beautiful four-course meal.

Guess Who's Coming to Visit
Dir. Biskup, Marianne
1993 USA English
9 mins. video color Narrative
Dist. (U.S.): Biskup, Marianne

In Marianne Biskup's Guess Who's Coming to Visit, after de-dyking the house before Mom comes, the strain of the closet finally proves too much when Mom unexpectedly returns.

Hail the New Puritan
Dir. Atlas, Charles
1986 Great Britain English
85 mins. video color DocumentaryDist. (U.S.): Electronic Arts Intermix
Michael Clark, the sexy, internationally acclaimed twenty-three-year-old "rock star" of the British dance world is the subject of Hail the New Puritan, produced by Charles Atlas for Channel 4 in Great Britain.

Atlas employs a fictional/documentary style to present a wild chronicle of a day in Clark's life. Clever shooting and editing accentuate the superb dancing of Clark's company and the unabashed sexuality that infuses the punk star's work.

Hail the New Puritan begins with a skillfully executed dream sequence and follows Clark from waking through returning home at dawn the following morning. During this very active day Clark charms his way through an interview with a dance critic, works out with his company, performs in a surreal skit with members of the post-punk band The Fall, travels to a cemetery to participate in the filming of an underground featurette, has an erotic encounter in a mirrored bedroom, leads the action at a nightclub and finally heads home, where he dances to exhaustion to Elvis Presley's "Are You Lonesome Tonight."

At the heart of Hail the New Puritan are ten principal dance sequences that Atlas weaves into a colorful time capsule of the punk scene of 1980s London.

Haircut
Dir. Hammer, Barbara
1977 USA No Dialogue
6 mins. 16mm color Experimental
Dist. (U.S.): Hammer, Barbara
Silent. A lesbian feels more lesbian the shorter her hair gets.

Half a Million Strong
Prod. Jabaily, Barbara
1988 USA English
29 mins. video color Documentary
Dist. (U.S.): Jabaily, Barbara/KBDI-TV
Barbara Jabaily's Half a Million Strong documents the 1987 March on Washington for Lesbian and Gay Rights.

Hallowed
Dir. Stevens, Ylonda
1994 USA English
8 mins. 16mm color Other
Dist. (U.S.): Stevens, Ylonda
A lesbian remembers her gay male friend lost to AIDS.

Halloweenie
Dir. Daughton, Bill
1986 USA English
13 mins. 16mm color Other
Dist. (U.S.): Cinema Guild
A six-foot penis at the Halloween Parade, Greenwich Village.

Happy Gordons, The
Dir. Crickard, Paula
Prod. Hyndman, Marilyn
1994 Northern Ireland English
26 mins. video color Documentary
Dist. (U.K.): Cinenova
This exciting new documentary takes a unique look at an Irish community once hidden by religious and traditional prejudices. Being gay in Ireland was once a crime, now Irish laws give gays and lesbians complete equality with heterosexuals. *The Happy Gordons* explores the reasons for this sudden change of heart. Three gay Irish emigrants living in New York recount their stories of why they left Ireland and why emigration is such a big part of the Irish culture. Humorous and innovative. *The Happy Gordons* uses theater and music, exciting footage of Gay Pride marches in Dublin and Belfast, the St. Patrick's Day demo in New York, and lots of interesting interviews to keep those who watch it totally absorbed. For anyone who has an interest in the diversity of Irish culture, this must be the most compelling documentary to come from Northern Ireland, ever.

Hard Reign's Gonna Fall, A
Dir. Lance, Dean
1990 USA English
7 mins. video color Other
Dist. (U.S.): Video Data Bank
A Hard Reign's Gonna Fall turns Bob Dylan's song into a semianimated activist aria.

Hard to Swallow
Dir. Coray, Tony and Jim Hankle
1991 USA English
6 mins. video color Experimental
Dist. (U.S.): Coray, Tony

Hard to Swallow approaches the subject of death with a reluctant sense of inevitability and fluid beauty.

Harlequin Exterminator
Dir. Balletbò-Coll, Marta
1991 Spain English
12 mins. 16mm color Narrative
Dist. (U.S.): Frameline
A clever, romantic comedy of obsession.

Harold and Hiroshi
Dir. Askinazi, Ed
1989 USA English
38 mins. 16mm color Narrative
Dist. (U.S.): Askinazi, Edward
Ed Askinazi's *Harold and Hiroshi* is set at a New England University on the eve of the Pearl Harbor bombing, which brought the United States into World War II. Harold is a Jewish boy from New York. Hiroshi is his Japanese exchange student roommate. Together they share their cultures and develop subtle erotic interest . . . until December 7, 1941, hits, and everything changes.

Hatachi No Binetsu
(Slight Fever of a 20-Year-Old)
Dir. Hasiguch, Ryosuke
1993 Japan Japanese
114 mins. 16mm color Narrative
Dist. (U.S.): PIA Corp.
An audacious teen movie from Japan, concentrating on a bored middle-class quartet: two hustlers, Tatsuro and Shin, and their two female best friends. Tatsuro is the better hustler. He spends his days skipping school or coolly entertaining clients; but when Shin declares his love for him, Tatsuro has to enter the real world *Slight Fever of a 20-Year-Old* is a raw, honest movie about the loves and loneliness of Tokyo late teens.

Haut und Haar (Skin and Hair)
Dir. Otterbach, Carolin
1994 Germany No dialogue
5 mins. 16mm color Experimental
Dist. (U.S.): Otterbach, Carolin
A beautiful body portrait.

Haven
Dir. Mead, Wrik
1992 Canada English
4 mins. video color Experimental
Dist. (U.S.): Canadian Filmmakers Distribution Centre
Animated magazine cut-outs of two men having sex lead into appropriated gay porn images,

Ⓐ Ⓑ Ⓒ Ⓓ Ⓔ Ⓕ Ⓖ Ⓗ Ⓘ Ⓙ Ⓚ Ⓛ Ⓜ Ⓝ Ⓞ Ⓟ Ⓠ Ⓡ Ⓢ Ⓣ Ⓤ Ⓥ Ⓦ Ⓧ Ⓨ Ⓩ

blurred to the point where they become abstract colour and motion. All this is set to pastoral sounds, sex noises, and a reporter's voice-over about the Royal Canadian Mounted Police "fruit box" experiments—official, and ludicrous, attempts to expose closeted gay men.

Hazel's Photos
Dir. Bartoni, Doreen M.
1988 USA English
6 mins. 16mm color Other
Dist. (U.S.): Bartoni, Doreen
Comments of contemporary women as they look at found photos and reimagine the lives of their peers at the turn of the century.

He Would Have Loved Me to Death
Dir. Taylor, Mark
1993 USA English
10 mins. 16mm color Experimental
Dist. (U.S.): Taylor, Mark
A beautiful, abstract black-and-white vision—joke?—of the fear and expectations of love.

He's Like
Dir. Goss, John C.
1986 USA English
26 mins. video color Experimental
Dist. (U.S.): Video Data Bank
He's Like is about what four men understand about the men in their lives. Director John Goss examines masculinity and male self-image through a collection of quasi-documentary stories.

He-She Pee
Dir. Surkis, Alisa
1994 USA English
7 mins. video color Other
Dist. (U.S.): Surkis, Alisa
A look at restroom confusion.

Heart Exposed, The
(see *Couer Decouvert, La*)

Heart of Seduction, The
Dir. Blumen, Rebecca A.
1991 USA English
6 mins. 16mm b&w Experimental
Dist. (U.S.): Blumen, Rebecca
The Heart of Seduction approaches the subject of death with a reluctant sense of inevitability and fluid beauty.

Heatwave
Dir. Stephens, Kathy
Prod. Suleyman, Erol

1994 Great Britain English
15 mins. 16mm color Narrative
Dist. (U.S.): Stephens, Kathy
Set in the long, hot, English summer of 1976, Sally is obsessed with the girl next door, nineteen-year-old sophisticated Louise.

Heaven, Earth and Hell
Dir. Harris, Thomas Allen
1993 USA English
25 mins. video color Experimental
Dist. (U.S.): Third World Newsreel
African-American artist Thomas Allen Harris uses the metaphor of the trickster, in his beautifully rendered *Heaven, Earth and Hell*, to search among the deceptions of race, history, and love. Harris describes a transformative journey, recounting his yearning for acceptance and the choices made to construct himself out of blackness.

Heaven's a Drag
(see *To Die For*)

Heavenly Creatures
Dir. Jackson, Peter
1994 New Zealand English
100 mins. 35mm color Narrative
Dist. (U.S.): Swank Motion Pictures
Ever since this crime that Miramax says "shocked a nation" occurred in Christchurch, New Zealand, the Parker-Hulme Affair, as it's called, has given writers a thrill in retelling. Since the story broke in 1954, it's been through as many interpretations as the United States' own case of homophilic, cold-blooded teen crime, the 1924 Leopold and Loeb case.

In both cases, after the reporters had their fun with it, other interpreters stepped in: Leopold and Loeb got hanged by Hitchcock's *Rope* (1948) and pathologized in *Compulsion* (1959); Parker and Hulme got a novel titled *Obsession* (T. Gurr/H. H. Cox, 1958). Later, Leopold/Loeb got a postmodern retouch with *Swoon*—and Parker/Hulme got redeemed as a pair of lost lesbian herstory in a play called *Daughters of Heaven*.

When Peter Jackson—whose directorial credits include the sci-fi comedy *Bad Taste*, the puppet feature *Meet the Feebles*, and the blood-gorged *Dead Alive*—adds his bag of horror tricks to the mix, he places the story in another genre altogether. With an arsenal of facial close-ups, an endless stock of large, movable nonhuman objects, and a derby's worth of tracking shots, Jackson turns the girls' matricide crime into eerie entertainment while also giving them redeeming psychological treatment. It's horror with a social agenda.

Heavenly Creatures enters the girls' fantasy world and budding sexual world from their point of view—we see their idols, their clay figures, their stories, good times, desires, as eccentric, not horrific. We see the parents, however, as aberrant. In one characteristically humorous horror shot, the psychologist's mouth fills the entire screen as he delivers the judgment on Pauline to her parents by elongating the unspeakable word: "Ho-mo-sex-u-al." We are horrified: but—pleasingly—at the man of authority, not the girl he's labeling; horrified at homophobia, not two girls in lust.

In a film that combines carefully calibrated horror-craft tricks with intelligence, Peter Jackson combines solid social defense and a scarifying good time. (S.G.)

Hell Without Limits
(see Lugar Sin Limites, El)

Hello-Goodbye
Dir. Waggoner, David
1977 USA English
3 mins. S8mm color Experimental
Dist. (U.S.): n/a
Illustrated music.

Helms = Death
Dir. Maxwell, Peter Edward
1991 USA No Dialogue
1 mins. 16mm b&w Other
Dist. (U.S.): Maxwell, Peter Edward
Peter Maxwell's abrasive, angry, and silent celluloid graffiti.

Henry and June
Dir. Kaufman, Philip
1990 USA English
140 mins. 35mm color/b&w Narrative
Dist. (U.S.): Swank Motion Pictures
Based on Anais Nin's accounts of her stormy relationship with writer Henry Miller and his wife June, this film would have been more appropriately titled Anais and June.

Maria de Medeiros stars as Anais—evolving from wide-eyed innocent to wide-eyed sophisticate, her ardor for June is the most powerful element of the film. Uma Thurman plays June as a sultry big blonde who knows what she wants. She wants Anais. Fred Ward's Henry is 1930s macho straight out of a gangster movie—this guy knows how to smoke a cigarette.

As they play out their sexual and emotional claims on one another, Anais's passion for June evolves to become the central force of the triangle. Their seduction begins in a movie theater as they watch the goodnight kiss scene from the 1931 German lesbian film Mädchen In Uniform. June whispers to Anais, "You're like the teacher, and I'm the little girl." This tension is what makes the film work. It's a very long film, and the love scene betwen June and Anais that we wait for is ultimately disappointing, but it's a wait of considerable pleasure.

We're all accustomed to sitting through boring heterosexual plots, waiting for the lesbian subplots to resurface (Candice Bergen's lesbian character in Sidney Lumet's 1966 film, The Group, is a prime example; clocking in at over two hours' running time, Bergen's brief appearance at the beginning—before she runs off to Europe—baits you for the length of the film, until she returns for an equally brief appearance in the final ten minutes). Henry and June presents lesbianism as a resurfacing element throughout; it propels the narrative in a very positive way; and although lesbianism is ultimately presented as a phase that Nin passes through within the film, there's tons of incidental lesbian content in the meantime: The clip from Mädchen In Uniform, a scene in a lesbian bar, references to June's other lesbian lover, etc.

The film presents Nin's lesbianism as a complex issue (though not complex enough, it's true, to resist being interpreted as merely a convenient erotic variation to spice up a film for straight people). The primary difference in this film's attitude toward lesbianism (as compared to classic mainstream portrayals of lesbian desire such as Personal Best or Lianna) is that director Philip Kaufman plays out more potential motivations for such desire. The film plays both sides of the lesbian sex issues fence (unconsciously, I presume). At one point, in a hot moment in bed with her husband, Anais tells him she would like to "fuck June like a man." At another point, when she takes her husband to a brothel to watch two prostitutes have sex, she tells one of the women to "stop pretending you're a man." It seems doubtful that Philip Kaufman would actually have his finger on the pulse of the lesbian sexual agenda, and yet he seems to have hit the mark with this dialogue.

A moody soundtrack, sensuous cinematography and art direction, and a backdrop of magicians and low-life characters vividly evoke Paris in the '30s. Although the minor characters

Ⓐ Ⓑ Ⓒ Ⓓ Ⓔ Ⓕ Ⓖ Ⓗ Ⓘ Ⓙ Ⓚ Ⓛ Ⓜ Ⓝ Ⓞ Ⓟ Ⓠ Ⓡ Ⓢ Ⓣ Ⓤ Ⓥ Ⓦ Ⓧ Ⓨ Ⓩ

are poorly developed (and the major characters are only developed through their erotic relations to one another), the film holds together overall (though maybe the heterosexuals will be bored by it). And Uma Thurman's June will go down (as it were) in lesbian cinema history as the latest and brightest in a long line of neurotic, pathetic, manipulative, alchoholic dyke characters whom we love quite as madly as we hate. (J.O.)

Her Appetite
Dir. Fullman, Katrina
1994 USA English
9 mins. video color Experimental
Dist. (U.S.): Fullman, Katrina
A luscious mélange of bodies and edibles.

Her Giveaway
Prod. Smith, Mona M.
1989 USA English
15 mins. video color Documentary
Dist. (U.S.): Women Make Movies
Her Giveaway is one Native American lesbian's experience of overcoming drug addiction and discovering that she has AIDS; part education and prevention video, this production by the Minnesota American Indian AIDS Task Force is engaging and hopeful. There ought to be more videos like this.

Her Sweetness Lingers
Dir. Mootoo, Shani
1994 Canada English
12 mins. video color Experimental
Dist. (U.S.): Video Out
Shani Mootoo combines elegant poetry with stunning imagery and we get a glimpse at the beginnings of a romantic affair set to the tune of "Me & Mrs Jones."

Here Be Dragons
Dir. Winter, Stephen
1993 USA English
14 mins. 16mm color Narrative
Dist. (U.S.): Stephen Winter Filmworks
An African-American New York couple battle with infidelity and other demons in Stephen Winter's *Here Be Dragons.*

Hermes Bird
Dir. Broughton, James
1979 USA English
11 mins. 16mm color Experimental
Dist. (U.S.): Canyon Cinema
In the delightful and clever *Hermes Bird* we hear a Broughton poem as we watch a penis grow erect.

Hero of My Own Life
Dir. Chapnick, Debby
Prod. Musselman, David, and The Glines
1986 USA English
31 mins. video color Documentary
Dist. (U.S.): BAMC
A personal portrait of David Summers, musical comedy performer, cabaret singer, and person with AIDS. How he has dealt with both his homosexuality and diagnosis, problems with his family, and the continuing supportive relationship he maintains with his lover. An opportunity to view public and private aspects of a man involved in the community.

Heroes
Dir. Canalli, John
1987 USA English
28 mins. video color Documentary
Dist. (U.S.): Canalli, John
Among the heartening reactions to AIDS has been the flowering of support services for those with AIDS. *Heroes* documents several San Francisco AIDS care groups and individuals including Shanti, the Metaphysical Alliance, Project Inform, a woman who massages people who have AIDS, and a man who conducts art classes for them. The tape features inspirational and informative interviews with people who have survived AIDS for more than five years and concludes with some potent thoughts about the true nature of heroism.

Hey Bud
Dir. Zando, Julie
1987 USA English
11 mins. video color Experimental
Dist. (U.S.): Video Data Bank
Hey Bud revolves around the suicide of Bud Dwyer—a government official who committed suicide before a television audience—intercut with scenes of the artist and her girlfriend playing dress-up. *Hey Bud* peeks in on the relative powers of exhibitionism and voyeurism, and asks how women can reappropriate them.

Hi Mom!
Dir. Hinton, Lee
1993 USA English
9 mins. video color Other
Dist. (U.S.): n/a
Hi Mom! celebrates the 1992 Lesbian and Gay Freedom Day parade with a peek at last year's participants saying a candid hello to their mothers.

Hidden Pleasures
(see *Placeros Ocultos, Los*)

His Red Snow White Apple Lips
Dir. Yahnke, John
1991 USA English
7 mins. video color Experimental
Dist. (U.S.): Yahnke, John
John Yahnke's *His Red Snow White Apple Lips* conjures the work of Kenneth Anger.

History of the World According to a Lesbian, The
Dir. Hammer, Barbara
1988 USA English
16 mins. video color Experimental
Dist. (U.S.): Frameline
From the Platonic Cave to Post-Punk, the tape traces the invisible and visible references to women who love women from prehistory to contemporary times with the sarcastic sounds of the '50s lesbian quartet from Seattle, The Sluts from Hell.
> Released by Frameline in the U.S. as part of a package of four of her short videos, entitled, *Barbara Hammer Program #2*.

History of Violence, A
Dir. Acosta, Danny
1991 USA English
7 mins. 16mm color Narrative
Dist. (U.S.): Frameline
Danny Acosta's disturbing, accomplished, and controversial *A History of Violence*.

History of Western Sexuality, The
Dir. Kllc, Aaron
1994 USA English
11 mins. 16mm color Narrative
Dist. (U.S.): Kllc, Aaron
A very funny story about a straight woman who sets out to procure a man for her bisexual boyfriend.

History Will Accuse Me
Dir. George, Carl
1993 USA English
20 mins. video color Documentary
Dist. (U.S.): Cinephile Productions
A personal account of a stay in Havana.

Holding
Dir. Beeson, Constance
1971 USA English
13 mins. 16mm color Other
Dist. (U.S.): Canyon Cinema

In *Holding*, the love of two women for each other is communicated through physical contact, fantasy, and nature.

Hollywood and Homophobia
Dir. Beavan, Clare
Prod. Brown, Shauna
1992 Great Britain English
20 mins. video color Documentary
Dist. (U.K.): Fulcrum Productions
Hollywood and Homophobia is an energetic argument between *Basic Instinct's* makers and opponents (including a trip to the Oscars).

Holy Mary
Dir. Tartaglia, Jerry
1991 USA English
5 mins. 16mm color Other
Dist. (U.S.): Canyon Cinema
Jerry Tartaglia's irreverent papal fashion short.

"Home Movie"
Dir. unknown
1960 USA No Dialogue
10 mins. 16mm color Other
Dist. (U.S.): Stevenson, Jack
An aggressive Avon lady jumps a client in this 1960s technicolor porn fragment.

Home Movie
Dir. Oxenberg, Jan
1971 USA English
10 mins. 16mm color Experimental
Dist. (U.S.): Frameline
Dist. (U.K.): Cinenova
Home Movie (with camerawork by Donna Deitch, among others) deals with Jan Oxenberg's growing up and coming out.
> As early as 1975, Jan Oxenberg began to drastically change lesbian film history. With *Home Movie* and *A Comedy in Six Unnatural Acts*, she proved that it was possible to reflect on the lesbian image in a self-conscious way, informed by a wonderful sense of humor and by a many-sided stylistic knowledge of the medium.

Home Stories
Dir. Mueller, Matthias
1991 Germany English
6 mins. 16mm color Experimental
Dist. (U.S.): Canyon Cinema
A brilliant cinematic montage (a distillation of the position of women in the Hollywood melodrama and thriller). Winner 1991 German Film Critics Award.

Home Sweet Home

Ⓐ Ⓑ Ⓒ Ⓓ Ⓔ Ⓕ Ⓖ Ⓗ Ⓘ Ⓙ Ⓚ Ⓛ Ⓜ Ⓝ Ⓞ Ⓟ Ⓠ Ⓡ Ⓢ Ⓣ Ⓤ Ⓥ Ⓦ Ⓧ Ⓨ Ⓩ

Dir. Haber, Ron

1991 Great Britain English
17 mins. video color Documentary
Dist. (U.K.): Maya Vision
Lesbians and gays from around the world have created a variety of housing situations that reflect their lifestyles, as well as their social and political status. In *Home Sweet Home*, produced for this year's Out series on London's Channel Four, lesbians and gay men discuss the different strategies they've adopted in order to integrate their housing needs with their various lifestyles.

Home You Go
Dir. Cullen, Colette

1993 Great Britain English
12 mins. 16mm color Narrative
Dist. (U.K.): L.C.P.D.T. Film and Video Dept.
A little lesbian weekend fantasy.

Homicidal
Dir. Castle, William

1961 USA English
87 mins. 16mm b&w Narrative
Dist. (U.S.): Kit Parker Films
Homicidal is a shamelessly exploitative and wonderfully intriguing adventure in 1960s gender psychology starring the remarkable Jean Arless (whose actual gender is never revealed, but we're pretty sure she's a woman who does good male drag).

    The film starts with a girl happily seated at her dollhouse. She's interrupted by a young boy, who steals her doll (but, is he a boy?). Flash forward to a marriage, a murder, a lonely mansion, and a mute, wheelchair-bound woman from Denmark. Lured in yet? Director William Castle, a master of horror film marketing—*Homicidal* features a "Fright Break" near the end to give the timid time to scram—was in top form with this spooky movie. Dismissed as a mere Psycho ripoff in its day, *Homicidal* turns out to be something else again, offering an eerie commentary on what makes boys boys and girls girls.

Homophobia is Known to Cause Nightmares
Dir. Handelman, Michelle

1993 USA English
7 mins. 16mm b&w Experimental
Dist. (U.S.): M & M Productions
An experimental short by Michelle Handelman.

Homosexual Desire in Minnesota
[excerpt]

Dir. Hubbard, Jim

1985 USA English
25 mins. S8mm color Experimental
Dist. (U.S.): Hubbard, Jim
Excerpts of Hubbard's *Homosexual Desire in Minnesota* are alternately "bluesy and exuberant" in rendering the nature of the gay movement in the early 1980s.

Homosexuality: What Science Understands
Dir. Mach, Henry
Prod. Harrison, James

1987 USA English
54 mins. video color Documentary
Dist. (U.S.): Harrison, James
The first part of this worthwhile tape, produced by Intelligence In Media, refutes past notions of the "pathological" homosexual. Surprise, homosexuals are just like everyone else, which means they (we) occasionally need therapy. Positive ways to counsel lesbians and gays are suggested in the second half. A tape of interest to the general public, teachers, and counseling professionals alike, *Homosexuality: What Science Understands* offers a rational and low-key discussion of its topic.

Homoteens
Dir. Jubela, Joan

1993 USA English
60 mins. video color Documentary
Dist. (U.S.): Frameline
In *Homoteens*, five young gays and lesbians in New York City have produced their own vivid autobiographical portraits with the help of video maker Joan Jubela. Each portrait is unique, and each of these homoteens has a style all their own. Monique talks about her girlfriends and about being a Latina dyke in New York City. Peter, who is white and middle-class, tapes the story of his long-distance relationship with his closeted boyfriend, Richard. An anonymous 15-year-old talks about being hassled in school and shows his scrapbooks of gay and black American history. 17-year-old community organizer Henry Diaz offers a look at the organization that helped him come out, Youth Force. And Nicky, a 19-year-old Afro-Caribbean-American lesbian, tells us about her girlfriend, growing up as a Jehovah's Witness and being institutionalized for being a lesbian.

    Winner of the 1993 San Francisco International Lesbian & Gay Film Festival Audience Award for Best Video.

Honored by the Moon
Prod. Smith, Mona M.
1989 USA English
23 mins. video color Documentary
Dist. (U.S.): Women Make Movies
Honored by the Moon was almost entirely produced at a conference for American Indian gays, lesbians, their friends, and supporters; it tells personal stories of what it means to be lesbian and gay—from a Native American perspective.

Horror Vacui—Die Angst Vor Der Leere (Horror Vacui—The Fear of Emptiness)
Dir. Von Praunheim, Rosa
1984 Germany German
85 mins. 16mm color Narrative
Dist. (U.S.): Exportfilm Bischoff & Co.
Rosa von Praunheim, virtuoso of camp shadows and glitter politics (and auteur of the midnightly *City of Lost Souls* shown in the 1983 festival) has reinvented the Expressionistic soul of Berlin as a backdrop to the terrifying and entertaining adventures of a young gay student, Frank, seduced by the contemporary superstitions of authority: industry, religion, magic, science, art and romance. Heedless of the warnings of his self-assured and worldly lover—fearing meaninglessness more than insecurity or even death—Frank falls spellbound, first by a posturing professor who has cunningly combined the worst (and most attractive) of determinist philosophies; then by the hypnotic, hedonistic Madame, the gargantuan, alluring mistress of the cult of Optimal Optimism. With a little bit of help from a fascinating assortment of enemies, Frank must escape the *Cabinet of Caligari* maze and the gilded, gaudy, crudely sophisticated Magic Cabaret. There are times when being assured of one's sexual identity—when all else has been taken away—comes in handy.
Starring Lotti Huber, Friedrich Steinhauser, Volkert Milster, Thomas Vogt and Ingrid van Bergen. Photographed by Elfi Mikesch.

Hot and Cold
Dir. Staley, Samantha
1995 USA English
11 mins. 16mm b&w Experimental
Dist. (U.S.): Staley, Samantha
A silent film showing the struggle of a woman trying to overcome an abusive relationship.

Hotheads
Dir. Livingston, Jennie
1993 USA English

6 mins. video color Documentary
Dist. (U.S.): Off White Productions, Inc.
Comedian Reno and cartoonist Diane DiMassa (creator of *Hothead Paisan*) talk about combating homophobia.

Hours and Times, The
Dir. Munch, Christopher
1991 USA English
58 mins. 35mm color Narrative
Dist. (U.S.): Strand Releasing
Dist. (U.K.): ICA Projects
In the mid-sixties, on the upcurve of the Beatles' rise and fall, producer Brian Epstein escorted John Lennon to Barcelona for a weekend of recuperation. Christopher Munch's haunting *The Hours and Times* takes off from there. Epstein's infatuation leads to a strange episode usually missing from the official John Lennon biographies, set against the bare backdrop of a humid Spanish hotel room. It's a brilliant achievement: halfway through, you suddenly suspend all disbelief and become completely drawn into every detail of the drama.
Awarded prizes at the Sundance and Berlin Festivals. Even Siskel and Ebert reviewed the film:
ROGER EBERT: Gene, I think that you're a little overwrought in calling it a tragic love story. Have you ever spent a weekend with somebody that you wanted to sleep with and they didn't want to sleep with you? I mean, that's not tragedy that's just life.
GENE SISKEL: Oh, but Roger, let me explain why that's tragedy.
ROGER: Why is that tragedy?
GENE: Why is that tragedy? If you really love someone, okay . . .
ROGER: Yeah.
GENE: . . . and they won't love you back?
ROGER: I've heard of the concept of having a crush on somebody and not getting anywhere with them, and that's just the way it goes!

House of Pain
Dir. Hoolboom, Mike
1995 Canada English
80 mins. 16mm b&w Narrative
Dist. (U.S.): Canadian Filmmakers Distribution Centre
From the director of the Caligari-esque *Kanada*, *House of Pain* is a wordless psychodrama in four parts: Precious, Scum, Kisses, and Shiteater.
"Provocative and engaging, *House of Pain* is an exploration of the temple we call the

body. Conjuring both adoration and aversion, it is not an easy viewing experience, nor is it for the faint of heart."

—Liz Czach,
Toronto International Film Festival

Household
Dir. Smolen, Wayne
1977 USA English
3 mins. S8mm color Experimental
Dist. (U.S.): Mears, Ric
An experiment in using visuals and sound to give the feeling of an indescribable mood that I often have.

Housewife and the Plumber, The [Pout #3 excerpt]
Dir. Pout Collective
1993 Great Britain English
60 mins. video color Other
Dist. (U.K.): Dangerous To Know
See what happens when the lady plumber comes to fix the sink! In "Pout #3," the hilarious antics of the irreverent British Pout Collective focus on safe-sex in this third wild episode of their made-for-home-video series.

How Deep Is Your Love
Dir. Kraus, Al
1985 USA English
4 mins. video color Other
Dist. (U.S.): n/a
We won't say where it came from, but we know where it's going.

How He Goes
Dir. Hildebran, Gretchen
1994 USA English
14 mins. 16mm color Narrative
Dist. (U.S.): Hildebran, Gretchen
A small-town boy is secretly sleeping with a closeted member of his underground rock band in Gretchen Hildebran's plaintive How He Goes. Meanwhile their band is on the verge of breaking up. Unable to come out in this oppressive environment our young hero hits the road.

How Many Lesbians Does It Take to Change a Lightbulb?
Dir. Glazier, Alison and Eve Arbogast
1994 USA English
14 mins. video color Other
Dist. (U.S.): Glazier, Alison
San Francisco comics Suzy Berger, Amy Boyd, Mimi=Freed and Karen Ripley entertain and amuse us.

How to Kill Her
Dir. Simo, Ana Marie
Prod. Troyano, Ela
1990 USA English
15 mins. 16mm b&w Narrative
Dist. (U.S.): Women Make Movies
How to Kill Her uses a beautiful combination of film noir spoofing and Puerto Rican jazz, and the result is an acute, if perverse, insight into the reality of unrequited affection.

How to Seduce a Preppy
Dir. X, Rick
1985 USA English
30 mins. video color Other
Dist. (U.S.): City Heights Closet Case Show
Manhatten cable homosex impressario Rick X demonstrates with lascivious delight the subtle maneuvers that bring victory in How to Seduce a Preppy.

How to Turn Heads
Dir. Tupper, Krista
Prod. Tupper, Krista, and Allen Braude
1994 Canada English
6 mins. 16mm color Other
Dist. (U.S.): Tupper, Krista
A tongue-in-cheek response to the "recruitment of children to the homosexual 'lifestyle.'"

Human Still Life [Rough Cut]
Dir. Canalli, John
Prod. Ego Video
1984 USA English
11 mins. video color Other
Dist. (U.S.): n/a
A personal perspective of creative block, artistic process, and a basic how-not-to guide with a sense of humor. Sensitively filmed, intriguing and sensual.

Hunting Season, The
Dir. Moreira, Rita
1992 Brazil Portugese
30 mins. video color Documentary
Dist. (U.S.): Rita Moreira Producoes
The Hunting Season shows the deadly truth of what lies behind homophobic language: Brazil's lesbian and gay population—"deers"—are being keenly slaughtered in a ghastly series of hate crimes. Intercutting images from Hollywood movies (The Deer Hunter and Cruising) director Rita Moreira stops people on the streets of Saõ Paulo for a quick health check on the state of the nation—"They should be killed" is the most com-

mon reply. *The Hunting Season* then goes behind the scenes to illustrate both the bureaucratic incapacity and individual acts of courage that the spate of violence has exposed.

Hustle with My Muscle
Dir. Rubnitz, Tom
1986 USA English
3 mins. video color Other
Dist. (U.S.): Video Data Bank
Part of the *Tom Rubnitz Marathon (A Dozen Tapes, Wigs Included)*.

Hustler White
Dir. LaBruce, Bruce, and Rick Castro
Prod. Bruning, Jurgen, and Bruce LaBruce
1995 USA English
80 mins. 35mm color Narrative
US Dist: Strand Releasing
UK Dist: Dangerous To Know
Fag superstar Bruce LaBruce and photographer Rick Castro present their wild tale of Santa Monica Boulevard street hustlers. Tony Ward, the Joe Dallesandro of the '90s, stars as Monti, a clumsy stud on the street.

Hyena's Breakfast, The
Dir. Mikesch, Elfi
1983 Germany German
25 mins. 16mm color Experimental
Dist. (U.S.): Mikesch, Elfi
The Hyena's Breakfast starts with sensual images of a woman running through the streets. A man speaks to her over the phone, insisting that she return to him. But Maria's attention is drawn to her own visions of suffering and death, which are Catholic imagery. After experiencing the purification of self-chastisement, she can laugh about herself, forget the man, and open the door to a woman.

Hysterio Passio
Dir. Lee, Quentin
1994 USA English
2 mins. 16mm color Other
Dist. (U.S.): Lee, Quentin
A hyper-short flick about two gay Asian men and a phantasmatic vagina.

I
Dir. Mendias, Joel Roman
1995 USA English
15 mins. 16mm color Other
Dist. (U.S.): Mendias, Joel Roman
Haunted by memory, obsessed with a recurring and enigmatic dream, a man sits at his desk . . . and writes.

I Am a Man
Dir. Devakul, M. L. Bhandevanop
1988 Thailand Thai
115 mins. 35mm color Narrative
Dist. (U.S.): Thai Motion Picture Producers Association
This Thai adaptation of Mart Crowley's play *The Boys in the Band* has a sort of psychotronic low-tech look that's a cross between a 1968 episode of "Hawaii Five-O" and a Herschell Gordon Lewis epic. Other than that, it's pretty faithful to the original in plot and action. The queens of Crowley's play are expressionistically interpreted here as drag queens (the birthday girl even sports a tiara!) and the cowboy as a young macho dancer. The best scene is still the same: as the Michael character decorates the birthday cake and the others dance to Charlie Parker, the straight friend (and a hunky young country boy) suddenly walk in.
With Likit Ekmongkol, Dr. Seri Vongsemontha, Chalit Fiengarom, Sinjai Hongthal.

I Am My Own Woman
(see *Ich Bin Meine Eigene Frau*)

I Am Your Sister
Dir. Russo, Catherine
1991 USA English
59 mins. video color Documentary
Dist. (U.S.): Third World Newsreel
Political statements and outstanding poetry by lesbian women of color recited at the Audre Lorde Conference in Boston in October 1990. The statements are about black cultural politics and the poetry is movingly read by women reflecting a heritage of oral traditions. This audio-visual piece about the conference is a valuable historical document.

I Became a Lesbian and So Can You
Dir. Donahue, Elizabeth
1994 USA English
12 mins. video color Other
Dist. (U.S.): Donahue, Elizabeth
Just your basic infomercial extolling the virtues of lesbianism.

I Changed My Sex [trailer]
Dir. Wood Jr., Ed
1953 USA English
10 mins. 16mm b&w Other
Dist. (U.S.): Olson, Jenni
A fascinating trailer from Ed Wood Jr.'s 1953 low-budget exploitation feature (also known as *Glen or Glenda*).

Ⓐ Ⓑ Ⓒ Ⓓ Ⓔ Ⓕ Ⓖ Ⓗ **Ⓘ** Ⓙ Ⓚ Ⓛ Ⓜ Ⓝ Ⓞ Ⓟ Ⓠ Ⓡ Ⓢ Ⓣ Ⓤ Ⓥ Ⓦ Ⓧ Ⓨ Ⓩ

I Didn't Know What Time It Was
Dir. Ehorn, Scott
1994 USA English
4 mins. 16mm color Other
Dist. (U.S.): Ehorn, Scott
An exquisitely lyrical montage.

I Don't Want to Be a Man!
(see *Ich Mochte Kein Mann Sein!*)

I Don't Want to Be e Boy
Dir. Behrens, Alec
Prod. Behrens and Muijser
1994 Netherlands English
30 mins. video color Documentary
Dist. (U.S.): Behrens, Alec
I Don't Want to Be a Boy is a candid documentary of transsexual prostitutes working in New York City's Meat Market District. This film dares to show us just how dangerous these streets are and the courage it takes to survive them.

I Dream of Dorothy
Dir. McDowell, Peter
1991 USA English
7 mins. video color Narrative
Dist. (U.S.): McDowell, Peter
In a nod to *The Wizard of Oz*, a closeted gay boy finds himself transported to San Francisco.

I Got that Way from Kissing Girls
Dir. Butler, Julie
1990 USA English
6 mins. 16mm b&w Other
Dist. (U.S.): Frameline
I Got that Way from Kissing Girls is an extended set of romantic couples, set to Patsy Cline.

I Like Dreaming
Dir. Lofton, Charles
1994 USA English
6 mins. video color Experimental
Dist. (U.S.): Lofton, Charles
Charles Lofton's engaging rumination on the pleasures of subway cruising.

I Like Girls for Friends
Dir. Zando, Julie
1987 USA English
3 mins. video color Experimental
Dist. (U.S.): Video Data Bank
In *I Like Girls for Friends* the audience is seduced by the female narrator, while at the same time repelled by her need for love and approval.

I Need a Man Like You . . .
Dir. Paakspuu, Kalli, and Daria Stermak
1986 Canada English
24 mins. 16mm color Other
Dist. (U.S.): Women Make Movies
A timely and playful lampooning of some of the most resistant sex stereotypes around today, *I Need a Man Like You . . .* delivers a colorful and zany lineup of Toronto's finest Queen Street Performers.

I Never Danced the Way Girls Were Supposed To
Dir. Suggs, Dawn
1992 USA English
10 mins. video color Experimental
Dist. (U.S.): Third World Newsreel
Lisa and Jackie ponder some details of lesbian identity in Dawn Suggs's witty look at "just another day in your average black lesbian household."

I Object
Dir. House of Color
1991 USA English
5 mins. video color Experimental
Dist. (U.S.): Electronic Arts Intermix
House of Color's *I Object* uses fast editing to ask questions about who is excluded from conventional images of beauty and eroticism.

I Remember Running
Dir. Gosney, Kristin
1994 USA English
3 mins. video color Experimental
Dist. (U.S.): Gosney, Kristin
One woman's tale of her history of domestic violence.

I Shot Andy Warhol
Dir. Harron, Mary
Prod. Kalin, Tom, and Christine Vachon
1995 USA English
100 mins. 35mm color Narrative
US Dist: Samuel Goldwyn Company
UK Dist:
Lili Taylor's gruff, streetwise, and slightly unbalanced portrayal of Valerie Solanas should earn her some kind of Academy Award. In Mary Harron's recreation of Andy Warhol's Factory milieu of the '70s, one gets a sense of the bitchy, competing for coolness clique that somehow resembles the New York queer film scene of the '90s. Although Taylor's Solanas seems far cooler and hipper (very '90s dyke) than we had always pictured her (strident, plain-looking lesbian-femi-

nist), she's an irresistible hero.

I Shot My W.O.D.
Dir. Miller, Tanya, and Julie Wyman
1995 USA English
9 mins. video color Other
Dist. (U.S.): Wyman, Julie
Two desperately single dykes take to the streets on Christmas Eve to shop for that glittering and elusive Woman Of their Dreams (W.O.D.).

I, The Worst of All
Dir. Bemberg, Maria Luisa
1990 Argentina Spanish
109 mins. 35mm color Narrative
Dist. (U.S.): First Run Features
Based on the book *The Traps of Faith* by Nobel Prize–winning poet Octavio Paz, Maria Luisa Bemberg's exquisite film tells the remarkable story of 17th-century Mexican poet Sister Juana Ines de la Cruz (Assumpta Serna), one of the greatest poets of the Spanish language. Born with an intense passion to write and possessing an incredible intellect, Juana enters the convent in order to avoid marriage and to continue her writing. As the Inquisition rages around her and the politics of the church becomes more and more repressive, Juana begins to attract much attention for her free-thinking, controversial plays and poems. A new and liberal-thinking viceroy takes power and his beautiful, educated wife, Maria (Dominique Sanda) takes an interest in Juana. The two are immediately taken with each other and begin an intimate relationship that is at first intellectual, but soon becomes much more. Juana begins to write many tortured love poems to Maria that amuse her husband, but anger the woman-hating archbishop. Maria uses her husband's power and influence to protect Juana, but the viceroy is eventually sent back to Spain with his wife and Juana is left alone to battle against the Machiavellian plots of the Catholic church.

A powerful indictment of religious and political tyranny, *I, The Worst of All* is widely considered to be Maria Luisa Bemberg's most brilliant film. One of Argentina's most important woman directors, Bemberg made her first film at the age of 59 and championed the rights of women in all of her works. Bemberg died of cancer in 1995.

I Want What I Want
Dir. Dexter, John
1972 Great Britain English
97 mins. 35mm color Narrative

Dist. (U.S.): Orion Classics
Dist. (U.K.): British Film Institute
In this sympathetic transsexual portait Anne Heywood reads so easily as female in her role as "Roy" that the queerest moments are probably unintentional. As "Wendy," Heywood comes off poofy, but the character has tons of femme pride and packs a copy of *The Second Sex* (like Simone said, one is not born a woman; rather, one becomes one). Cheesy yet effective attempted suicide scene ties with a twist into the issue of genital surgery. (S.S.)

I Was I Am
Dir. Hammer, Barbara
1973 USA English
8 mins. 16mm b&w Experimental
Dist. (U.S.): Hammer, Barbara
Transformation of heterosexual princess to a bike dyke in Hammer's first 16mm film.

I Will Not Think about Death Anymore
Dir. Buncel, Irene
1993 Canada English
19 mins. 16mm color Experimental
Dist. (U.S.): Pearl Films
Irene Buncel's *I Will Not Think about Death Anymore* introduces us to a Canadian Jewish lesbian who has recently lost a friend to AIDS and cannot sleep because she is obsessed with death. That night she meets a leather dyke named Death at the grocery store. Death takes her on an unforgettable motorcycle ride in the Canadian countryside, where her fears about dying, both as a Jew and as a queer, are eloquently examined.

I'll Show You
Dir. Jones, Stephen
1992 Australia English
3 mins. video color Narrative
Dist. (U.S.): Jones, Stephen
I'll Show You is Stephen Jones's witty combating of stereotyping of gay men and lesbians; a comic skit about labels.

I'm Gonna Eat Worms
Dir. Eingang, Al
1993 USA English
 mins. video color Other
Dist. (U.S.): San Francisco AIDS Foundation/ Prevention Dept.
Al Eingang's low-budget raunch tour-de-force.

I'm Still Alive:
A Person With AIDS Tells His Story
Dir. Aue, Michael

Ⓐ Ⓑ Ⓒ Ⓓ Ⓔ Ⓕ Ⓖ Ⓗ Ⓘ Ⓙ Ⓚ Ⓛ Ⓜ Ⓝ Ⓞ Ⓟ Ⓠ Ⓡ Ⓢ Ⓣ Ⓤ Ⓥ Ⓦ Ⓧ Ⓨ Ⓩ

1987 Germany German
58 mins. video color Documentary
Dist. (U.S.): EBS Productions
San Franciscan Peter Sieglar is the subject of *I'm Still Alive*. Sieglar was born in Germany. He returned there in 1986 to reveal to his family that he had AIDS. The trip home helped to crystallize his thoughts on AIDS, homosexuality, and the meaning of his life, all of which he generously shares with director Micheal Aue (and us). A very sweet and hopeful tape, *I'm Still Alive* is a testament to the wisdom and resilience of the human spirit.

I'm You, You're Me
Dir. Saalfield, Catherine, and Debra Levine
1993 USA English
26 mins. video color Documentary
Dist. (U.S.): Women Make Movies
Dist. (U.K.): Cinenova
A powerful profile of women prisoners in New York dealing with HIV/AIDS.

I've Heard the Mermaids Singing
Dir. Rozema, Patricia
1987 Canada English
81 mins. 35mm color/b&w Narrative
Dist. (U.S.): Swank Motion Pictures
Dist. (U.K.): British Film Institute
In this debut feature film, writer/director Patricia Rozema presents the story of Polly (Sheila McCarthy), a charmingly inept amateur photographer who takes a part-time receptionist job in an art gallery where she develops a crush on the curator, Gabrielle (Paule Baillargeon). Polly recognizes her infatuation with Gabrielle when Gabrielle's lover, Mary (Ann-Marie McDonald) comes into town.

As Polly speaks directly to the camera/audience, her story is illustrated through flashbacks and fantasy sequences. Director Rozema employs different film and video stock to convey Polly's story: grainy black-and-white for Polly's fantasies; freeze frames for Polly's photos; videotape for Polly's present narration; and full color for life. This structure produces a unique sensitivity to Polly's point of view as a character, and makes for an extremely original and enjoyable film.

This modern lesbian classic won the Prix de Jeunesse at the Cannes Film Festival in 1987. (J.O.)

I've Never
Dir. Jennings, Pamela
1992 USA English

6 mins. video b&w Experimental
Dist. (U.S.): Video Data Bank
A video dealing with interracial relationships. Part of *Those Fluttering Objects of Desire*, released in the U.S. on a twenty-minute compilation with *Vanilla Sex*, *Brown Sugar Licks Snow White*, and *What's the Difference between a Yam and a Sweet Potato?*

Ice Palace, The
(see Is-Slottet)

Ich Bin Meine Eigene Frau
(I Am My Own Woman)
Dir. von Praunheim, Rosa
1992 Germany German
91 mins. 35mm/16mm color Documentary
Dist. (U.S.): Cinevista
Charlotte von Mahlsdorf has led an exemplary life as an eccentric personality. Rosa von Praunheim—gay independent post-Fassbinder German filmmaker—brings this iconoclastic subject to the screen with a fascinating bio-profile of von Mahlsdorf, notorious transvestite art collector/curator and winner of the Federal Order of Merit Cross, one of the highest decorations granted by the former Federal Republic of Germany.

What's most interesting about von Praunheim's film treatment of Charlotte is the absolute equivalence given to her achievements as a longtime sexual pervert, Nazi resister, gay liberator, and conservative-looking housekeeper with a genius for restoring palaces, manors, and antique mass-produced Victoriana. Charlotte is not a simple character: she's complex and colorful, with a repertoire of bawdy stories and gruesome World War II recollections; at the same time she is a historical gay figure who's made a huge difference simply by following her own queer proclivities with boundless bravery and enthusiasm.

Charlotte, née Lothar Berfelde, defines herself as a woman trapped in a man's body. When she was a young boy, her grand-uncle said that Lothar should have been a girl living at the turn of the last century, while a transvestite lesbian aunt allowed young Lothar to roam around her Prussian farmhouse in girl's attire.

Now a 60-something lady who loves to don Victorian lingerie and display her ever-youthful butt, Charlotte speaks fondly of her mostly deceased ex-lovers. She's always had a penchant for older men, and time has outrun most of them.

There was a time, after the Wall went

up, when gay East Berliners were barred from meeting one another in public; gay bars were closed and gays were prohibited from placing "contact ads" in newspapers or magazines. That's when Charlotte met one of her great loves in response to a number scrawled on the wall of a public latrine.

Never a stranger to the threat and reality of fascism, she experienced brutality at the hands of the Nazis and literally killed her Nazi father in his sleep. Young Lothar spent time in a psychiatric hospital and a reformatory before being released due to events ushered in by the Second World War. Given the circumstances of Charlotte's life and her pivotal role as the Mother of Gay German Liberation, it's no coincidence that she appeared in Heiner Carow's *Coming Out*, the first out gay East German film—which happened to open the same day the Berlin Wall came down.

In an interview in the December, 1992 issue of *Artforum*, director von Praunheim speaks about what drew him to the idea of making a film about Charlotte: "Perhaps she can be compared to Quentin Crisp: a queen, a transvestite, who fought for her identity with a great deal of charm, gentility, courage and endurance. It's really gratifying when unusual people, types who are usually only laughed at, looked down on by the middle class, who are funny and unique, can be made accessible to large audiences through a careful, caring mediation, like the one I try to provide through my films." (R.T.)

Ich Lebe Gern, Ich Sterbe Gern
(Living And Dying)
Dir. Acklin, Claudia
1990 Switzerland/Germany
80 mins. video color Documentary
Dist. (U.S.): Frameline
"My name is André Ratti; I am 50 years old; I am a homosexual and I've got AIDS." When André Ratti on July 2, 1984 dropped this bombshell at a press conference organized for "AIDS-Help Switzerland," it prompted a tremendous reaction. A man who, through his TV show "MTW," had weekly visited the good Swiss citizen, dared to tackle the two biggest taboos of his society – sexuality and death.

Living and Dying examines the life of a complex, difficult man who refused to make things easy for the people around him by bowing to their conceptions of sexuality and illness. He was a homosexual who craved sex and had little need for the romantic relationships sought by so many of his peers. He inspected his AIDS without sentiment or sorrow and never allowed it to interfere with his popular "issues and discussion" TV talk show. Expressing his opinions over the Swiss airwaves was as much heaven as he ever needed.

Director Claudia Acklin has gathered an engaging collection of Ratti's coworkers and friends to share their memories, successfully mixing them with clips from Ratti's show and interviews conducted over the years of his illness. While *Living and Dying* should capture both your heart and mind, it's not likely to make you cry. That's probably just what this spirited man would have wanted.

Ich Mochte Kein Mann Sein!
(I Don't Want to Be a Man!)
Dir. Lubitsch, Ernst
1919 Germany German
50 mins. 35mm b&w Narrative
Dist. (U.S.): George Eastman House
This silent female-to-male cross-dressing classic from Ernst Lubitsch will be presented with live musical accompaniment by Dennis James on the mighty Castro Wurlitzer.

Ossi likes to drink, smoke, play poker, and do a lot of things that aren't becoming to a respectable young lady. When her male guardian, Dr. Kersten, lays down the law, she decides to adopt a new wardrobe and assume the identity of a fashionable young man. But when "gentleman" Ossi ends up in the back of a cab with a drunken Dr. Kersten she learns that life as a man isn't as easy as it looks! Comic in tone, the film explores the privileges and problems of gender and features some charming twists of homo- and lesbo-erotic humor.

Ich und Frau Berger (Me & Mrs. Berger)
Dir. Kull, Heidi
1991 Germany German
4 mins. video color Other
Dist. (U.S.): Frameline
This quirky music video portrays an animated intergenerational love affair.

If Every Girl Had a Diary
Dir. Benning, Sadie
1990 USA English
6 mins. video b&w Experimental
Dist. (U.S.): Video Data Bank
If Every Girl Had a Diary is a fragmented collection of impressions that develops into a video diary.

Ⓐ Ⓑ Ⓒ Ⓓ Ⓔ Ⓕ Ⓖ Ⓗ Ⓘ Ⓙ Ⓚ Ⓛ Ⓜ Ⓝ Ⓞ Ⓟ Ⓠ Ⓡ Ⓢ Ⓣ Ⓤ Ⓥ Ⓦ Ⓧ Ⓨ Ⓩ

If Only
Dir. Daschbach, John
1994 USA English
6 mins. 16mm color Narrative
Dist. (U.S.): Daschbach, John
Two boys yearn for each other at their high school dance.

If She Grows Up Gay
Dir. Sloe Goodman, Karen
1982 USA English
23 mins. 16mm color Documentary
Dist. (U.S.): Frameline
A young, black, working-class lesbian mother talks about raising her daughter in New York City.

If They'd Asked for a Lion Tamer
Dir. Oremland, Paul
1986 Great Britain English
40 mins. video color Documentary
Dist. (U.K.): Kinesis Films
The loony British "biopic" of drag sensation David Dale.

Ifé
Dir. Keller,Len
1993 USA English
5 mins. 16mm b&w Narrative
Dist. (U.S.): Frameline
Dist. (U.K.): Dangerous To Know
Len Keller's *Ifé* follows one day in the life of a black French lesbian in San Francisco.

Il Etait une Fois dans L'est
(Once Upon a Time in the East)
Dir. Brassard, Andre
Prod. Lamy, Pierre
1974 Canada French
100 mins. 16mm color Narrative
Dist. (U.S.): n/a
A transvestite nightclub is the center of activity for a wildly diverse group of people, all marginal members of society, doing the best they can in an oppressive world. An old woman wins one million trading stamps, while another readies a country-western nightclub act. An aging "Duchess" returns home, a young girl contemplates an abortion, a young man prepares for the drag of his life as Cleopatra—all of these people know and rely on each other for good or ill.
    This French-Canadian entry in the Cannes Film Festival explores life on the outskirts of conventional society with honesty, humor, and empathy. *Once Upon a Time in the East* is the first feature directed by André Brassard, the most sought-after stage director in Canada.

Illegal Acts
Dir. Mossanen, Moze
1982 Canada English
21 mins. 16mm color Experimental
Dist. (U.S.): Mossanen, Moze
A brilliantly photographed and eye-opening visit to a chicken processing plant is at the center of this disturbing film, a clever comment on the gay struggle.

Illegal Tender
Dir. Bettell, Paul
1986 Great Britain English
15 mins. video/16mm color Experimental
Dist. (U.S.): Frameline
A gorgeous montage of homo desire.

Illuminado las Aguas
Dir. Ferrera-Balanquet, Raul
1992 USA/Mexico English
4 mins. video color Experimental
Dist. (U.S.): Ferrera-Balanquet, Raul/Latino Midwest Video Collective
Illuminado las Aguas is a mood held between lovers and dancers.

Images
Dir. unknown
1983 USA English
9 mins. video color Other
Dist. (U.S.): n/a
Witchcraft and ritual hold their place in this isolated but compelling piece.

Imagining October
Dir. Jarman, Derek
1984 Great Britain English
27 mins. 16mm color Experimental
Dist. (U.K.): Basilisk
With *Imagining October*—generally regarded as his best short film—Derek Jarman for the first time engages with the politics that were to become central to his subsequent film work.

Immaculate Conception
Dir. Foley, Kim
1985 USA English
13 mins. video color Documentary
Dist. (U.S.): n/a
A well-crafted, sensible look at the option of artificial insemination for lesbians and gay men.

Improper Conduct
(see *Mauvaise Conduite*)

In a Glass Cage
(see *Tras El Cristal*)

In a Man's World
Dir. Lefkowitz, Karen
1993 USA English
4 mins. video color Experimental
Dist. (U.S.): Lefkowitz, Karen
Offers a clever monologue on the absence of images for women's sex.

In Loving Memory
Dir. Knight, Leone
1992 Australia English
6 mins. video b&w Experimental
Dist. (U.K.): Cinenova
Takes on the taboo subjects of fetishism and S/M.

In My Father's Bed
Dir. Freeman, Marilyn
1993 USA English
70 mins. video color Other
Dist. (U.S.): Downs, Randa
Lesbian playwright/performer Randa Downs presents a powerful display of healing and courage in this one-woman show. With honesty, sensitivity, and even humor, *In My Father's Bed* recounts her survival of father/daughter incest.
Through her masterfully constructed characters (therapists, sister, mother, father) and direct monologues, Downs creates an emotional journey for her audience that is deeply affecting, bold, and cathartic. Confronting her memories, fears, shame and anger, Downs reclaims her childhood and shares her process of recovery. The sparsely staged performance is captured gracefully and unobtrusively by director Marilyn Freeman.
"Downs makes the guilt and boundless anger she has felt come alive. Through her simple, honest writing and good theatrical sense, her story is healing and engrossing."
—*Boston Globe*

In Plain View
Dir. Olivier, Felix
1992 France/USA English
25 mins. 16mm color Narrative
Dist. (U.S.): Chicago Filmmakers
In New York, day after day, an old writer watches the tumultuous lives of his neighbors, Pierre and his bisexual Brazilian lover, Ulysses. Felix Olivier's *In Plain View* is a refreshingly—and furiously—serious film about loneliness and the passage of time.

In Search of Margo-Go
Dir. Reiter, Jill
1995 USA English
11 mins. video color Narrative
Dist. (U.S.): Reiter, Jill
A Nu-Wave/Punque Rock kitchy queer girl love story.

In the Cards
Dir. Sheahan, Karen
1994 USA English
7 mins. 16mm color Narrative
Dist. (U.S.): Sheahan, Karen
A lesbian confronts her inner fool during a Tarot reading.

In View of Her Fatal Inclination, Lilo Wanders Gives Up the Ghost
Dir. Fockele, Jorg
1994 Germany German
3 mins. 35mm color Other
Dist. (U.S.): HFF Munchen
A stunning drag queen meets an unhappy ending.

(In)Visible Women
Dir. Spiro, Ellen, and Marina Alvarez
1991 USA English/Spanish subtitles
26 mins. video color Documentary
Dist. (U.S.): Video Data Bank
Focuses on the heroic and empowered responses of Latina women who are HIV positive. Like the best documents of activists and educational work, *(In)Visible Women* exactly captures human panic, frustration, inspiration, and action; it's one of the most inspiring tapes in the festival.
Winner of the 1992 San Francisco International Lesbian & Gay Film Festival Audience Award for Best Video.

Incredibly True Adventures of Two Girls in Love, The
Dir. Maggenti, Maria
Prod. Hall, Dolly
1995 USA English
93 mins. 35mm color Narrative
Dist. (U.S.): Fine Line Features
Maria Maggenti's debut feature film tells the touching and comic story of first love between two girls in their senior year of high school. From the wrong side of the tracks, cute and out tomboy Randy (Laurel Hollomon) lives with her two lesbian aunts and works after school as a gas station attendant. Middle-class Evie (Nicole Parker) is the prettiest, smartest, and most popular girl at

Ⓐ Ⓑ Ⓒ Ⓓ Ⓔ Ⓕ Ⓖ Ⓗ ❶ Ⓙ Ⓚ Ⓛ Ⓜ Ⓝ Ⓞ Ⓟ Ⓠ Ⓡ Ⓢ Ⓣ Ⓤ Ⓥ Ⓦ Ⓧ Ⓨ Ⓩ

school. Convinced there is something wrong with her Range Rover, Evie stops by the gas station one day. Instantly taken with one another, the two girls embark on a friendship which develops into a tender but hilarious romance. When Evie's mother leaves on a weekend business trip, the two girls decide to celebrate their newfound love in Evie's mansionlike house. This results in a series of comic misadventures in which everyone becomes involved, including the jealous husband of Randy's former fling.

Inevitable Love
Dir. Mach, Henry
1986 USA English
85 mins. video color Narrative
Dist. (U.S.): Atkol

Inevitable Love is an erotic, explicit story of two supposedly straight male friends and wrestling partners who go their separate ways, have a number of gay sexual experiences, and end up reunited, passionately, inevitably in love.

The settings are familiar to erotic film fans—an army barracks, a gymnasium, a restroom, the grubby dressing room where factory workers hang out, the front seat of a car—but the action is different. Some is very quiet and sensual involving feathers and whipped cream. Some is more raunchy and some is just fun, including a strip poker game. It's all related to the story of Hal, who runs off to grad school, and Gary, who joins the army.

Gary makes love with his army buddies, with Casey Donovan in the car, and with coworkers, all the while writing letters to Hal, wanting to come out to him but never being able to. Gary's life takes a romantic route as he becomes involved with a respected—and very sensual—gay activist and writer.

The producers call *Inevitable Love* a healthy sex video because they've chosen to portray a wider spectrum of sex—intercourse with condoms for one—than can be currently be called absolutely safe. Still, this is an important new step in erotic filmmaking and a film that shows how easily we can modify our behavior.

Infidel
Dir. Saalfield, Catherine
1989 USA English
45 mins. 16mm color Experimental
Dist. (U.S.): Kitchen, The

Simply stated, Arroe is a black fashion model, a lesbian, who deals with issues of racism in an industry that is intolerant of variation from either the passive Anglo ideal, or that of the exoticized, primitivized woman of color. There is nothing simple about Catherine Saalfield's *Infidel*, however, as the film uncovers and repositions layers of myth about female beauty, the function of racism in standardizing our ideals, and the necessity of female self-consciousness in a scheme that demands both conformity and uniqueness. Partly autobiographical, partly extracted from collective experience, this jumpy, tightly crafted narrative reconstructs the process behind the formulation of self-image.

Innings
Dir. Beavan, Clare
Prod. Brown, Shauna
1991 Great Britain English
3 mins. video color Other
Dist. (U.K.): Fulcrum Productions

Innings is a musical response to celebrity outing made for British television's "Saturday Night Out," but withdrawn before broadcast.

Inside Monkey Zetterland
Dir. Levy, Jefery
Prod. Cohen, Tani
1992 USA English
92 mins. 35mm color Narrative
Dist. (U.S.): I.R.S. Releasing

While zealots of all kinds battle it out on the political fronts, Jefery Levy's *Inside Monkey Zetterland* is a film in which zealotry is passé. It's a film in which gayness, as Vito Russo had hoped it one day would be, is both incidental and non-pathological and, well, playful—yet boring. It's about a playwright and his mom and her lesbian daughter and her pregnant (not-by-her) girlfriend, and the family's maybe-gay terrorist tenants and psychopathic celebrity-chasing neighbors, a film with all the right celebrities (Sandra Bernhard, Ricki Lake, Lance Loud, Rupert Everett) in all the wrong roles. Grace Zetterland (Arquette), the foxy lesbian whose girlfriend gets pregnant, inhabits a subplot of earnest, futile protest: She's spotted with a group of picketers in front of her Mom-the-daytime-TV-star's studio chanting "Gays and dykes can act." But this film—which is full of gays, or people who have played gays, or people who fans would like to think are gay—doesn't necessarily give witness to that point. Freedom, apparently, doesn't come without pain. (S.G.)

Interior Decorator from Hell
Dir. Roth, Sonja
1988 USA English
16 mins. 16mm color Narrative

Dist. (U.S.): Rotman, Keith
A bleak Dana, longing for Richard, engages an unusual interior decorating service, resulting in a comedic twist of fate.

International Sweethearts of Rhythm
Dir. Schiller, Greta, and Andrea Weiss
1986 USA English
30 mins. 16mm color Documentary
Dist. (U.S.): Frameline
Dist. (U.K.): British Film Institute
The International Sweethearts of Rhythm was an all-women, mostly black musical group that breathed refreshing life into the big band sound of the 1930s and 1940s. Faced with almost insurmountable sexism and racism as they toured the country, the band was a surprising, though somewhat underground, success. This captivating film includes interviews with band members—all who have clear, and very entertaining, memories of a special time in their lives. The interviews are mixed with amazing footage from the era. Codirectors Greta Schiller and Andrea Weiss also gave us the classic gay march documentary, *Greetings from Washington D.C.*

Interview with the Vampire
Dir. Jordan, Neil
1994 USA English
120 mins. 35mm color Narrative
Dist. (U.S.): Swank Motion Pictures
Neil Jordan (*The Crying Game, The Company of Wolves*) was the ideal choice to translate Anne Rice's purple supernaturalism to the screen with its more subversive elements intact. After so many sympathetic but asexual portraits of gay partnership in mainstream cinema (e.g., *Philadelphia*), *Interview*'s perverse turnabout is quite satisfying—it gives us nothing but pure, sweaty lust. Never mind the fact that a vampire's kiss isn't quite the same as an actual fuck; the feeling, at last, was there, as big and robust as $50 million could make it. Blond-tressed Tom Cruise (no one's dream Lestat, but surprisingly credible) carries on a bickering noctural union through the ages with sulky Brad Pitt. Their chemistry, however, is nothing compared to that between Pitt and Antonio Banderas, as the ruler of a Parisian vampire clan. When these two hovered millemeters short of a smooch for several long seconds, an overexcited audience's scream could be heard 'round the world. Swanky, gaga homoerotic fun. (D.H.)

Intrepidissima
Dir. Balletbò-Coll, Marta
1992 Spain Catalan
7 mins. 35mm color Narrative
Dist. (U.S.): Frameline
Dist. (U.K.): British Film Institute
Intrepidissima is a cathartic triumph for every little tomboy forced to go shopping for dresses, from the director of the 1992 hit, *Harlequin Exterminator*.
Winner of the 1993 San Francisco International Lesbian & Gay Film Festival Audience Award for Best Short Film.

Intro to Cultural Skit-Zo-Frenia
Dir. Ajalon, Jamika
1993 USA English
10 mins. video color Experimental
Dist. (U.S.): Third World Newsreel
A savvy sideswipe at attitudes towards lesbian/gay people of color (particularly those of black or mixed-racial heritage).

Invocation of My Demon Brother
Dir. Anger, Kenneth
1969 USA English
11 mins. 16mm color Experimental
Dist. (U.S.): Canyon Cinema
The Shadowing forth of Lord Lucifer, as the Powers gather at a midnight mass.
"A film that no number of viewings will ever exhaust, a film that will always remain a source of mysterious energy as only great works of art do . . ."   —Jonas Mekas, *Village Voice*
"Anger's purest visual achievement . . . a conjuration of pagan forces that comes off the screen in a surge of spiritual and mystical power. It has weirdly compelling imagery, with a soundtrack by Mick Jagger on a Moog Synthesizer that has the insistent hallucinatory power of voodoo."
—Richard Whitehall, *L.A. Free Press*

Iowa City Women's Rugby
Dir. Gohman, Goo
1984 USA English
8 mins. video color Other
Dist. (U.S.): Gohman, Goo
Goo Gohman sheds light on girl jocks in Iowa City Women's Rugby.

Iro Kaze (Colour Wind)
Dir. Oki, Hiroyuki
1991 Japan No Dialogue
10 mins. S8mm color Experimental
Dist. (U.S.): Image Forum, Tokyo
In *Colour Wind*, Oki develops his technical sophistication and his openness to new forms

Ⓐ Ⓑ Ⓒ Ⓓ Ⓔ Ⓕ Ⓖ Ⓗ Ⓞ Ⓙ Ⓚ Ⓛ Ⓜ Ⓝ Ⓞ Ⓟ Ⓠ Ⓡ Ⓢ Ⓣ Ⓤ Ⓥ Ⓦ Ⓧ Ⓨ Ⓩ

and themes. Although the film is silent, the mood represents a panorama of gay feelings and sentiments, which makes for a thrilling and wonderful viewing experience.

Irome (Colour Eyes)
Dir. Oki, Hiroyuki
1992 Japan No Dialogue
8 mins. 16mm color Experimental
Dist. (U.S.): Image Forum, Tokyo

Colour Eyes is a swooning collage of lovers and love objects. It is Oki's most recent work and probably his most erotic.

Is Mary Wings Coming?
Dir. Charman, Karen
1993 Australia English
10 mins. video color Narrative
Dist. (U.S.): Charman, Karen

A teacher-student romance transcends the academic jargon of desire in Karen Charman's *Is Mary Wings Coming?*

Is That All There Is to the Greenhouse Effect?
Dir. Paik, Esther Koohan
1990 USA English
6 mins. video color Other
Dist. (U.S.): Paik, Esther Koohan

Miss Connie Champagne poignantly and gorgeously asks *Is That All There Is to the Greenhouse Effect?*

Is-Slottet (Ice Palace, The)
Dir. Blom, Per
Prod. Svendsrud, Gunnar
1987 Norway Norwegian
78 mins. 35mm color Narrative
Dist. (U.S.): Norsk Films A/S

The Ice Palace is the story of two girls age 11, Siss and Unn. Unn is a recent arrival in the little rural community; her mother is dead and she has never seen her father. She lives with her aunt. As a stranger, Unn is excluded from the circle of friends at school. Siss on the other hand has both friends and parents.

The two girls become increasingly attracted to each other, in a relationship full of budding expectations and silent longing for warmth and tenderness. One evening when they meet they are for the first time hurled into confronting their intense feelings. The following day, Unn cannot face another encounter with Siss and sets off alone, out into the cold, unfrequented landscape. Eventually she disappears inside the frozen waterfall—the ice palace.

Siss never sees Unn again. She, too, is alone now, and she struggles through a long winter, fighting the frost that has taken a firm hold of her soul.

The Ice Palace is, like the novel it is based on, a story about budding emotions, about children on the threshold of the adult world, about the dark land within us where our impulses conflict with dreams.

Tarjei Vesaas (1897–1970), author of the novel, is one of Norway's best-known authors. He wrote 20 novels, in addition to numerous collections of short stories, poems, and plays. Several of his works have have been adapted for the screen. Translated into several languages, his novel *The Ice Palace* is one of Norwegian literature's most widely read books. The novel was published in 1963 and was awarded the Nordic Council's Prize for Literature.

It Wasn't Love
Dir. Benning, Sadie
1992 USA English
20 mins. video b&w Experimental
Dist. (U.S.): Video Data Bank
Dist. (U.K.): London Video Access

It Wasn't Love is a sexy genderfuck tale of lesbian lust on the road.

It's a Lezzie Life: A Dyke-U-Mentary
Dir. Wilhite, Ingrid
1988 USA English
30 mins. video color Narrative
Dist. (U.S.): Wilhite, Ingrid

It's a Lezzie Life is a sitcom set in a certain freewheelin' West Coast city.

It's a Mitzvah
Dir. Jacobson, Fran
1994 Great Britain English
5 mins. 16mm color Experimental
Dist. (U.K.): London Film Makers Co-op

Two nice Jewish girls think about commitment.

It's a Queer World
Dir. Farthing, Cheryl
1993 Great Britain English
40 mins. video color Other
Dist. (U.K.): Alfalfa Entertainments, Ltd.

How queer can TV be? *It's a Queer World* is a global survey of the tastiest bits from contemporary lesbian and gay TV shows. Highlights of this fast-moving collage include clips from Berlin's "Lasbisch TV," the Dutch version of "Out On Tuesday," and a very weird kids program: "The Thea and Theo Show." It's hosted by Lily Savage,

England's first lady of drag.

It's That Age
Dir. Kot, Hagar
1990 Israel Hebrew
40 mins. 16mm Narrative
Dist. (U.S.): Kot, Hagar
From Tel Aviv, the first Israeli lesbian love story, *It's That Age*. Daniella is a bratty, confused teen who keeps singing "The Man I Love" to herself; instead of a man, she finds Michal, a 32-year-old sculptress who lives in a seductive, overblown studio apartment. They embark on an intense and moody affair, bound to end in tears—but affecting along the way.

It's the Look I'm After
Prod. Baron Infinity Mind, O.D.C.
1981 USA English
20 mins. video color Other
Dist. (U.S.): n/a
This original edit, produced for the festival, is one of several versions of the video maker's video diary produced in East Asia during 1980–1981.

Jack and Jill
Dir. unknown
1983 USA English
 mins. video color Other
Dist. (U.S.): n/a
Our own well constructed parody of talk shows and talk show hosts.

Jackie and the Beanstalk
Dir. Steinman, Connie Boy
1990 USA English
20 mins. 16mm color Narrative
Dist. (U.S.): Connie Boy Productions
It's more a low-budget, lesbian *Land of the Giants* than a fairytale remake—resourceful, silly, and pretty minty.

Jane Show, The
Dir. Mossanen, Moze
1992 Canada English
10 mins. video color Other
Dist. (U.S.): Mossanen, Moze
The Jane Show is a "traditional" broadcast production that features Toronto drag queen/performance artist Skye Gilbert in an interview with herself.

Jean Genet
Dir. Boun Seillem, Antoine
Prod. Societe Temoins
1983 France French
52 mins. 16mm color Documentary
Dist. (U.S.): Societe Temoins
Until this film, Jean Genet had never accepted an onscreen interview. An engaging speaker, Genet talks freely of his love for the darkness of prison and the light of Greece, of his commitment to the Black Panthers and the Palestinians, and in the cell of a penal colony for children, the birth of his writing career, which he says has given him the strongest emotions of his life. Born in 1910 in Paris, Genet wrote his first novel while serving one of many prison sentences. His work includes *The Maids* and *The Balcony* and the novels *Querelle*, *The Funeral Rites*, and *Our Lady of the Flowers*.

Jeanne & Hauviette
Dir. Foley, Elizabeth
1993 USA English
13 mins. 16mm color Narrative
Dist. (U.S.): Foley, Elizabeth
In this lush period piece, Joan of Arc's lover Hauviette recalls their last day together.

Jeffrey
Dir. Ashley, Christopher
1995 USA English
100 mins. 35mm color Narrative
Dist. (U.S.): Orion Classics
Presented as a surprise sneak preview in the 1995 festival, this adaptation of Paul Rudnick's hit stage-play is a good old-fashioned AIDS-era gay romantic comedy starring Steven Weber in the title role; with Patrick Stewart and Bryan Batt costarring, and featuring cameos by Sigourney Weaver and Olympia Dukakis.

Jellyfish Kiss [trailer]
Dir. Harp, Thom
1994 USA English
2 mins. video color Narrative
Dist. (U.S.): Blind Eye Films
A sexy trailer for *Jellyfish Kiss*, a new local lesbian feature.

Jesus Died for Somebody's Sins (But Not Mine)
(see *Out On Tuesday, Program 2*)

Jewel's Darl
Dir. Wells, Peter
Prod. Maynard, John, and Bridget Ikin
1985 New Zealand English
28 mins. 16mm color Narrative
Dist. (U.S.): New Zealand Film Commission
The adventures of Mandy, a man in drag, and Jewel, a transsexual and the love of his life. They

Ⓐ Ⓑ Ⓒ Ⓓ Ⓔ Ⓕ Ⓖ Ⓗ Ⓘ Ⓙ Ⓚ Ⓛ Ⓜ Ⓝ Ⓞ Ⓟ Ⓠ Ⓡ Ⓢ Ⓣ Ⓤ Ⓥ Ⓦ Ⓧ Ⓨ Ⓩ

are both trapped on the fringes of an unsympathetic, mocking society that refuses to try to understand their unusual relationship. Richard Hanna and Georgina Beyer give brilliant, very moving performances in a cleverly told and beautifully photographed film directed by Peter Wells, one of New Zealand's most distinctive new directors.

Joan Sees Stars
Dir. Braderman, Joan
1993 USA English
58 mins. video color Other
Dist. (U.S.): Video Data Bank
It's been a long time since Joan Braderman introduced us to the pleasures of shouting at the screen in *Joan Does Dynasty*. Now she's back, with a tribute to Liz, Oprah, and the demented mind of a mad old movie queen.

Through the miracle of video art, Braderman literally walks over our favorite icons (Liz in *Cleopatra*! Liz in *Suddenly Last Summer*!) in her breathless two-part blabfest, *Joan Sees Stars*. Her premise is that VCRs were invented for the age of AIDS and chronic fatigue syndrome: "Certain movie stars began to dominate my mental life . . . images were my medicine . . . everyone can afford a TV, but no one can afford welfare."

Dedicated to local performer Leland Moss, *Joan Sees Stars* is a refreshingly old-fashioned, postmodern shot of perfectly-cooked pop culture cuisine.

Joaquin
Dir. Raoul, Serge
1981 USA English
28 mins. 16mm color Documentary
Dist. (U.S.): n/a
Joaquin La Habana is an intelligent, insightful drag performer. This film documents several stages of his life and work.

Jodie Promo
Prod. Olson, Jenni
1995 USA English
30 mins. 35mm color Other
Dist. (U.S.): Olson, Jenni
From *Freaky Friday* to *Nell*, Jodie Foster has been one of the most versatile actresses of her generation. As a tomboy role model, as a budding adolescent, and as one of the strongest women actresses of the '80s she's also one of our hottest heartthrobs. Featuring some of the brightest highlights of her distinguished career, this compilation of coming attractions serves up a trailer

tribute to one of the biggest screen heroes of the '90s.

Joe-Joe
Dir. Dougherty, Cecilia, and Leslie Singer
1993 USA English
52 mins. video color Narrative
Dist. (U.S.): Frameline
An irreverent and dynamic featurette starring Cecilia Dougherty and Leslie Singer as gay British playwright Joe Orton. Bizarrely hilarious dialogues between Joe and Joe in their daily lives as working-class dykes in the Mission district are intercut with campy musical interludes and sex scenes. Making the most of the unique visual capabilities of pixel vision, *Joe-Joe*'s hovering camera is combined with a great soundtrack and classy cameos by Kevin Killian, Amy Scholder, Sadie Benning, and Angela Hans Scheirl.

Joggernaught
Dir. Mobley, Doug
1993 USA English
50 mins. video color Other
Dist. (U.S.): Mobley, Doug
Somewhere between the style of George Kuchar and a low-budget, sexed-up "Seinfeld." Mobley's diarylike adventures are deceptively ordinary but full of razor wit and sharp detail. Spend an imaginative hour with Doug and his daily obsessions: car trouble and straight teenagers.

Johanna D'arc of Mongolia
Dir. Ottinger, Ulrike
1989 Germany German
165 mins. 35mm color Narrative
Dist. (U.S.): Women Make Movies
In this lesbian *Lawrence of Arabia*, director/writer Ulrike Ottinger has created an ethnographic farce which crisscrosses Europe, Asia, and time itself. Constructed in two parts, this challenging road movie lets us travel on the exotic Trans-Siberian before we are swept away to the dramatic Mongolian steppes. No experienced traveler has seen the world until they have been on the historic Trans-Siberian. The original train was a miniature museum and magnificent hotel on wheels, with luxurious cuisine and spacious compartments in which the passengers could gather and amuse themselves. In this film, the famous railway is an elegant backdrop for a surreal meeting of an unusual group of international passengers. They are the sophisticated Lady Windermere (Delphine Seyrig); American musical star Fanny Ziegfeld (Gillian Scallisis); a prim German schoolteacher (Irm Hermann); a beauti-

ful, young Spanish adventuress (Ines Sastre); and a trio of klezmer musicians. They trade songs with Yiddish actor, Micky Katz, a Russian officer, and his young "attaché" (Christoph Eichhorn) who resents giving up his ballet lessons for assignment to Siberia. The ladies transfer to the Trans-Mongolian train and are abducted by a troop of wild Mongolian women who lead them to their nomadic tents in the sweeping grasslands. Camels, wild horses, Buddhist priests, and a shaman provide a bit of culture shock for the group. The encounter, however, proves to be one the Mongolians won't easily forget.

John Lindquist:
Photographer of the Dance
Dir. Brodsky, Bob, and Toni Treadway
1981 USA English
28 mins. 16mm color Documentary
Dist. (U.S.): Brodsky & Treadway
A beautiful film (shot originally on Super-8, and also available in 35mm) which incorporates interviews with Mr. Lindquist and others with many of Mr. Lindquist's photos. Included are rare pictures of Ted Shawn, Ruth St. Denis, Agnes De Mille, Martha Graham, and many more.

John Sex: The True Story
Dir. Rubnitz, Tom
1983 USA English
4 mins. video color Other
Dist. (U.S.): Video Data Bank
John Sex includes everything you (n)ever wanted to know about the hair-do of the '80s. Part of the Tom Rubnitz Marathon (A Dozen Tapes, Wigs Included).

Johnny
Dir. Al Brask, Ulrik
1988 Denmark Danish
8 mins. video color Other
Dist. (U.S.): Art Com Media Distribution
A modern interpretation of Slavology. Part of the Nordic Selections package from Art Com.

Jollies
Dir. Benning, Sadie
1990 USA English
11 mins. video b&w Experimental
Dist. (U.S.): Video Data Bank
Dist. (U.K.): London Video Access
Using a plastic Fisher-Price Pixel camera, teenage videographer Sadie Benning explores growing up lesbian in a working-class Milwaukee neighborhood.

Jomasay
Dir. Layumas, Rune
1991 Philippines English
5 mins. video color Experimental
Dist. (U.S.): Jurgen Bruning Filmproduktion
Jomasay is an intensely personal and experimental exploration of the shrouded pleasures of gay sex, that also addresses fears and hesitations about being gay.

Jonathan and David
Dir. Church, John
1994 USA English
11 mins. video color Narrative
Dist. (U.S.): Church, John
A modern erotic interpretation of the biblical relationship between Jonathan and David.

Journey, The
(see Reise, Eine)

Journey to Avebury
Dir. Jarman, Derek
1971 Great Britain English
10 mins. 16mm color Experimental
Dist. (U.K.): Basilisk
Journey to Avebury beautifully reflects Derek Jarman's fascination with ancient history, paganism, and Celtic traditions.

Joy of Apples, The
Dir. Phung, Dennis
1980 USA English
3 mins. 16mm color Other
Dist. (U.S.): n/a
Two apples meet and make love.

Joystick Blues
Dir. Ginsburg, Lisa
1990 USA English
5 mins. video color Other
Dist. (U.S.): Frameline
Joystick Blues is a dildo-drama which tells a true crime-of-nature story.

Judy's Do
Dir. Craig, Scott
1992 USA English
5 mins. video color Narrative
Dist. (U.S.): Craig, Scott
Enjoy the simple charms of the street-hustling hair-queens in the hilarious Judy's Do.

Juggling Gender
Dir. Gold, Tami
1992 USA English
27 mins. video color Documentary

Ⓐ Ⓑ Ⓒ Ⓓ Ⓔ Ⓕ Ⓖ Ⓗ Ⓘ Ⓙ Ⓚ Ⓛ Ⓜ Ⓝ Ⓞ Ⓟ Ⓠ Ⓡ Ⓢ Ⓣ Ⓤ Ⓥ Ⓦ Ⓧ Ⓨ Ⓩ

Dist. (U.S.): Women Make Movies

Juggling Gender features a lesbian performance artist talking about growing up, coming out, lesbian-feminism, and having a beard.

Jumping the Gun
Dir. Schneider, Jane
1993 Australia English
10 mins. 16mm color Narrative
Dist. (U.S.): First Run Features
Dist. (U.K.): British Film Institute

On the morning after a one-night stand, a woman fantasizes life together with her sleeping trick from honeymoon to breakup.

Jungfrauenmaschine, Die
(The Virgin Machine)
Dir. Treut, Monika
1988 West Germany German
85 mins. 16mm color Narrative
Dist. (U.S.): First Run Features
Dist. (U.K.): Out On a Limb

At first glance this new film by Monika Treut recounts a very simple story, that of a young woman who sets out to find happiness, as did Parsifal, the simple fool.

Unhappy in Germany, and pursued by her former lover Heinz, Dorothy Muller decides to continue her investigation of romantic love in America, following the footsteps of her mother, who immigrated to the U.S. many years before. In the mythical dreamland of California, Dorothy by chance meets several very remarkable women. Susie Sexpert initiates Dorothy into the practical arsenal of the American pragmatics of love. Dominique, a Hungarian from Uruguay, presents herself as a humorous, sisterly friend. And finally, Shelley Mars portrays the sly lesbian sex therapist with whom Dorothy falls romantically, naively in love.

This dream romance quickly dissipates and Dorothy finds something else: a narcissistic, self-ironic relationship with herself; robbed of her dreams, but still curious enough for us to know this is not the end of her adventure.

With the expert camera work of Elfi Mikesch, Monika Treut employs a unique experimental form allowing us to enter the protagonist's world so that we may see and hear the world through Dorothy's eyes and ears. The direction and camera style also reflect the film's two locales; Germany, where Dorothy experiences paranoia, and California, the wonderland where Dorothy reacts with amazement at the strange land and people.

Jungle Boy, The
Dir. Greyson, John
1985 Canada English
15 mins. video color Experimental
Dist. (U.S.): Video Data Bank

This tape is based on the 1985 washroom bust in St. Catherine's, Ontario, where one of the thirty-two men arrested committed suicide. Greyson combines narrative drama with appropriated scenes from the movie of the same name.

Just Another Girl
Dir. Ross, Rock
1982 USA English
4 mins. 16mm color/b&w Experimental
Dist. (U.S.): Ross, Rock

This enthusiastic time-lapse montage of men and women in drag was made for a time capsule.

Just Because of Who We Are
Prod. Dickerson, Tony, Abigail Norman, Robin Omata, Lydia Pilcher, Akua Dean, Kafi Afua, and Dareshi Kyi
1986 USA English
28 mins. video color Documentary
Dist. (U.S.): Women Make Movies
Dist. (U.K.): Cinenova

Just Because of Who We Are is an exhilarating tape about lesbian women whose love and savvy empower them against homophobia and sexism. The gritty lesbians in *Just Because* overcome violence, familial rejection, arrest, and attempts at hospitalization to "cure" them of lesbianism. *Just Because* goes beyond merely recounting the well-documented problems lesbians face to show strategies the women successfully employed against those who tried to abridge their civil rights.

Just for Fun
Dir. Oiye, David
1993 Canada English
23 mins. 16mm color Narrative
Dist. (U.S.): Direct Cinema

A realistic story taking place in a high school, depicting the power of peer pressure prevalent among the perpetrators of gay-bashing, 80 percent of whom are under the age of 18.

Just Friends
Dir. Williams, Heather
1983 Australia English
5 mins. 16mm color Narrative
Dist. (U.S.): Australian Film Commission
The painful breakup of an affair.

Kachapati: Spray the Wall
Dir. Wright, Georgia B.
1993 USA English
1 mins. video color Experimental
Dist. (U.S.): Wright, Georgia B.
An exquisitely simple representation of female ejaculation.

Kahala
Dir. Harding, Karen, and Sara Banks
1979 USA English
17 mins. video color Narrative
Dist. (U.S.): n/a
A drama.

Kain and Abel
Dir. Brynntrup, Michael
1994 Germany German
10 mins. 16mm color Experimental
Dist. (U.S.): Brynntrup, Michael
Shows how God sows the seeds of discord and divides mankind into good and evil.

Kamikaze Hearts
Dir. Bashore, Juliet
Prod. Legler, Heinz, Sharon Hennessey,
and Bob Rivkin
1986 USA English
88 mins. 16mm color Narrative
Dist. (U.S.): Legler/Bashore Productions
Dist. (U.K.): Metro Tartan
"When I first met her I thought she was sleazy, she needed to make a living, she was fucking on camera—I thought she was just another dumb porno slut. But I was wrong." —Tigr Mennett

So begins *Kamikaze Hearts*—it's a raw story about an impossible relationship between a young woman, Tigr (Tigr Mennett), who becomes obsessed with a beautiful porn star, Sharon Mitchell. From their first meeting Tigr is mesmerized by "Mitch"—by her joie de vivre and flamboyant sensuality. Tigr's life is changed forever when she is drawn underground into Mitch's world, a world of strip joint rock and roll, mainlined cocaine, and high-paying commercial sex. Filmed on location in San Francisco, notorious home of the XXX film industry, where North Beach provides an existential backdrop to Tigr's dark odyssey.

Stylistically, *Kamikaze Hearts* is best described as a dramatic documentary. But this is not a "docudrama" in the made-for-TV-movie sense, with actors portraying "real people" in "real situations." Tigr calls it a docudrama, an intensely personal narrative with real people playing themselves in scenes from their lives. Additionally, a documentary camera crew followed Tigr and Mitch through the production of Gerald Greystone's ill-fated sex opera version of Bizet's *Carmen*. Into the fabric of this eccentric footage, director Juliet Bashore and editor John Knoop have woven a bizarre drama by turns absurd, ironic, ridiculous, and simultaneously brutal, disturbing, even tragic.

Kamikaze Hearts resists easy classification. The film draws freely from both documentary and dramatic conventions. It is complicated, stirring, and controversial.

Kanada
Dir. Hoolboom, Mike
1993 Canada English
65 mins. 16mm color Narrative
Dist. (U.S.): Cinema Esperanca International
Kanada is the film that doesn't answer the question: How can I miss you so much when I can't stand to be with you? In this futuristic patriarchal nightmare, nobody fits together, but everyone is intimate. *Kanada* takes place in a future of civil war, French-Canadian separatism, and lesbian drama as usual.

In his Caligariesque headquarters, a megalomaniac plans to end the world with a televised war, just after he kisses his boyfriend. A skeleton narrates the latest news: all rectums will be sewn shut. We are relieved when two marvelously human lesbians take control of the screen.

The couple, a highly politicized hooker and her more middle-class lover languish in priviliged sighing. In a moment of respite, the couple make love. "Sometimes the rest of your life lasts an afternoon." The present, for these women, is all there is.

Kathy
Dir. Dougherty, Cecilia
1988 USA English
12 mins. video color Experimental
Dist. (U.S.): Dougherty, Cecilia
Cecilia bakes a pie while someone's in the bedroom with Susie. With Susie Bright and Honey Lee Cottrell

Kazetachi No Gogo (Afternoon Breezes)
Dir. Yazaki, Hitoshi
1980 Japan Japanese
105 mins. 16mm b&w Narrative
Dist. (U.S.): Shu Kei's Creative Workshop
This beautifully bleak account of a Tokyo daycare worker's obsession with her roommate cap-

Ⓐ Ⓑ Ⓒ Ⓓ Ⓔ Ⓕ Ⓖ Ⓗ Ⓘ Ⓙ Ⓚ Ⓛ Ⓜ Ⓝ Ⓞ Ⓟ Ⓠ Ⓡ Ⓢ Ⓣ Ⓤ Ⓥ Ⓦ Ⓧ Ⓨ Ⓩ

tures the bittersweet pain of unrequited love. Natsuko's coworker Etsuko asks her how she feels about men. "Not for me," she says, "I won't degrade myself."

Based on an actual newspaper story, *Afternoon Breezes* presents Natsuko's repressed lesbianism (she vomits every time she feels attracted to a woman) as a crush which evolves into obsession. Natsuko's roommate Mitsu has a boyfriend, Hideo, who occasionally stays overnight with her. Natsuko breaks up their relationship by sleeping with Hideo (and she becomes pregnant). Mitsu discovers what Natsuko has done and kicks her out. Utterly desolate, Natsuko descends into a deep depression. She follows Mitsu through the streets, subways, and bars of Tokyo, stands outside Mitsu's apartment watching her window, takes Mitsu's garbage home with her and rolls around in it on the floor. In an ambiguous ending, while Mitsu is away Natsuko goes to her apartment.

The film is relentlessly melancholic, with lots of ponderous long-takes of Natsuko hanging around, pining over Mitsu, obssessing, and being depressed. These real-time sequences are complemented with a remarkably complex use of sound (editing from quiet to rain to crickets, ringing bells, squeaky doors, dripping faucet, screaming kids). Conveying meaning through a wonderfully simple use of action and objects, the film has surprisingly little dialogue.

"*Afternoon Breezes* offers the cinema's most incredible and moving account of lesbian obsession since *The Bitter Tears of Petra von Kant*." —Tony Rayns. (J.O.)

Keep Your Laws Off My Body
Dir. Saalfield, Catherine, and Zoe Leonard
1990 USA English
13 mins. video color Other
Dist. (U.S.): Kitchen, The
Dist. (U.K.): Cinenova
Catherine Saalfield and Zoe Leonard's *Keep Your Laws Off My Body* is a high-contrast critique of the issue of "body law." A quiet, roving camera documents scenes from the lesbian bedroom—taking, touching, making love—which are intercut with street shots of police lines, demonstrators in confrontation with them, some to the point of arrest.

Keeping the Faith
Dir. Koocher, Nina
1986 USA English

30 mins. 16mm color Narrative
Dist. (U.S.): n/a
Two female college friends meet after several years and deal with the quite different paths each has taken since graduation.

Ken Death Gets Out of Jail
Dir. Van Sant, Gus
1987 USA English
3 mins. 16mm color Other
Dist. (U.S.): Frameline
A youth who's just come out of jail tells us about it.

Kenneth Anger's Hollywood Babylon (BBC Arena)
Dir. Finch, Nigel
Prod. Wall, Anthony
1991 Great Britain English
60 mins. video color Documentary
Dist. (U.K.): BBC TV
Directed by Nigel Finch (who also made *The Lost Language of Cranes*, and went on to make *Stonewall*), *Hollywood Babylon* is part portrait of an artist as a tongue man, part death-styles of the rich and famous. Finch's film is even more irreverent than Anger's best-selling tell-alls. Along the way: Lupe Velez's violent suicide, Fatty Arbuckle's disgrace, human ashtray James Dean, Marianne Faithfull in person, and the man who embalmed Marilyn Monroe.

Khush
Dir. Parmar, Pratibha
1991 Great Britain English
24 mins. 16mm color Documentary
Dist. (U.S.): Women Make Movies
Dist. (U.K.): Cinenova
Khush is an Urdu word meaning ecstatic pleasure as well as happy and gay. It has been appropriated by South Asian lesbians and gays around the world as a definition for themselves. Pratibha Parmar shot her film in Britain and India, interspersing real-life experiences with dreamlike fantasies, Indian film clips, and dance performance. In India homosexuality is illegal. The lives of western South Asian lesbians and gay men are riddled with racism and rejection. Parmar: "As an Asian lesbian filmmaker it is crucial to me that the joy, desire, and passion embodied in our lives through music, dance images, and political activism are represented in all their unexplored contradictions, exciting wholeness, and mysterious and erotic fantasy."

Winner of the audience award for Best Short Documentary in the 1991 San Francisco Festival.

Kiev Blue
Dir. MacDonald, Heather
1992 USA Russian
28 mins. video color Documentary
Dist. (U.S.): Filmmaker's Library
A warm and engaging portrait of nine gay men and lesbians in Kiev who tell their stories about growing up, coming out, and trying to create a community. In Russian with English voice-over.

Killer Babe
Dir. Wright, Annie
1994 Netherlands Dutch
7 mins. video color Other
Dist. (U.S.): Wright, Annie
An edgy Barbie doll enactment of the story of lesbian serial killer Aileen Wuornos.

Killing of Sister George, The
Dir. Aldrich, Robert
1968 Great Britain English
138 mins. 35mm color Narrative
Dist. (U.S.): n/a
Dist. (U.K.): British Film Institute
This notorious film, containing the first lesbian "love scene," realized all of a 1968 lesbian's worst fears: that she be seen as a sick, depraved, unhappy, and doomed creature. Released on the eve of the modern Gay Liberation Movement, one can speculate that this film fueled the lesbian community's rage and demand for civil rights. The rampant homophobia of the 1960s was all too apparent in the film and the media's reviews and treatment of it. While three other mild-mannered lesbian-theme films opened in 1968, the devastating *Sister George* was the one that received extensive media attention, called a "film devoted to showing the nitty-gritty of gay life . . . an outcast, but still very human group . . ." Too, it was no accident that Robert Aldrich, the director of *Whatever Happened to Baby Jane* and *The Big Knife*, was chosen to direct this horror-show lesbian film. June Buckridge (Beryl Reid) who plays Sister George on a TV soap, is the stereotypically obvious and obnoxious butch. She is outrageous, sadistic, and dominating towards Childie (Susannah York), her passive, live-in girlfriend, whom she ritualistically punishes for breaking the rules. Into this picture of domestic bliss comes chic TV exec Mercy Croft (Coral Browne), the smooth, professional dyke who passes in a straight world. Billed as a black comedy, the story has its funny moments and is told with wit and snappy dialogue. Sister George's wild drunken episode with two nuns in a taxi is hilarious, as are George's rousing send-ups of the TV writers and brass.

Kim
Dir. Gajilan, Arlyn
1987 USA English
27 mins. video color Documentary
Dist. (U.S.): Frameline
Kim is the candid personal testimony of a young Puerto Rican lesbian's coming out and coming of age in New York City. An intensely personal story unfolds as Kim takes us through the bar scene, the life of an exotic dancer, and the finding of feminism, which plays an important role in Kim's developing perspective on sexuality, love, and her relationship with her mother.

Kindling Point, The
Dir. Rice, Teri
1993 USA English
45 mins. video color Other
Dist. (U.S.): Teri Rice/Egocentric Productions
Teri Rice's lyrically constructed triptych of scenes proceeds gradually from bondage, whipping, and wax to its titular finale, *The Kindling Point*.

Kipling Meets the Cowboy
Dir. Greyson, John
1985 Canada English
22 mins. video color Experimental
Dist. (U.S.): Video Data Bank
Kipling Meets the Cowboy gently tosses cowboy porn and the Western classic *Red River* starring Montgomery Clift and John Wayne into a tale of Rudyard Kipling's escapades on the lecture circuit.

Kiss
Dir. Newby, Chris
1992 Great Britain English
6 mins. 35mm color Experimental
Dist. (U.K.): British Film Institute
An examination of a peculiar physical phenomenon.

Kiss of the Spider Woman
Dir. Babenco, Hector
1985 USA/Brazil English
119 mins. 35mm color/b&w Narrative
Dist. (U.S.): New Yorker Films
Dist. (U.K.): British Film Institute
Manuel Puig's novel (which was also adapted for the stage, and later the Broadway musical stage) becomes an epic art-pic weepie. William Hurt is the queen who narrates Maria Montez–like camp film sagas (given fantasy embodiment by Sonia

A
B
C
D
E
F
G
H
I
J
K
L
M
N
O
P
Q
R
S
T
U
V
W
X
Y
Z

Braga) to pass the time in his South American jail; Raul Julia is the macho political prisoner who makes his nelly cellmate's heart flutter. Rumor had it that the actors were initially cast in each other's roles. In any case, Hurt won an Oscar for what is essentially a case of technically impressive miscasting. A big hit at the time, with enduring critical support. But does the world really need another self-sacrificing, puppy-eyed gay man on screen whose (straight) object of desire finally takes pity and gives 'im a mercy bonk? It's just the same old Tragic Outcast syndrome in a new prestige package. (D.H.)

Kiss on the Cliff, The
Dir. Waterer, Reid
1994 USA English
21 mins. 16mm color Narrative
Dist. (U.S.): Waterer, Reid
This pensive tale of missed opportunities has two teenage boys in love with one another.

Kiss, The
Dir. Jortner, Michael
1994 USA English
5 mins. 16mm color Narrative
Dist. (U.S.): Jortner, Michael
A sweet San Francisco story of chance and romance.

Konsequenz, Die (Consequence, The)
Dir. Petersen, Wolfgang
1977 Germany German
100 mins. 16mm b&w Narrative
Dist. (U.S.): Frameline Archive
Remember when gay movies were all about gay subjects? Remember when they appeared only once a year, and they were usually made in Europe? For those people who recall that excitement of discovery, we present a rare revival screening of one of the best '70s gay dramas.

Thomas (Ernst Hannawald), the cherubic son of a prison warden, secretly seduces Martin (Jurgen Prochnow), one of his father's inmates. After Martin is released, the two try to build a life together, but they are thwarted at every turn. Thomas's father sends Thomas to a boy's reformatory, where—in an amazing scene—Martin arrives disguised as a new teacher . . .

The Consequence describes the persistence of pure love and the intolerance of a repressive society. Seen today, it still contains many surprises, and its sympathy with the gay lovers is refreshingly loyal. Bizarrely enough, *The Consequence* was directed by Wolfgang Petersen, whose later credits include *The Boat* (Prochnow

starred as the Captain), *The Neverending Story*, and *In the Line of Fire*.

Kore
Dir. Trang, Tran T. Kim
1994 USA English
17 mins. video color Experimental
Dist. (U.S.): Third World Newsreel
Kim-Trang's *Koré* addresses sexual politics on a variety of levels.

Koukei Dori (Landscape Catching)
Dir. Oki, Hiroyuki
1992 USA No Dialogue
5 mins. S8mm color Experimental
Dist. (U.S.): Image Forum, Tokyo
Hiroyuki Oki continues to develop his technical sophistication and his openness to new forms and themes, culminating in a sensuality that is apparent in this, one of his latest two films.

Krokodillen in Amsterdam (Crocodiles in Amsterdam)
Dir. Apon, Annette
1989 Netherlands Dutch
88 mins. 35mm color Narrative
Dist. (U.S.): Women Make Movies
At last, the European answer to *Desperately Seeking Susan*. Gino is a flighty blonde with a poodle hair-do who's as happy in a fox fur as black leather biker gear. Nina is a sulky activist who dreams of the ultimate terrorist act. Together they share a passion for the color blue and hatch a plot to rob Gino's rich uncle. It's a cute, girl-meets-girl movie with moments of inspired, lunatic humor. They first bump into each other on the sidewalk outside Gino's house-she's locked herself out. Nina show her how to break in, and Gino's first expression of gratitude is "Would you like a bath—with bubbles?" Instead, Nina settles for dinner in a swank restaurant, and hints at her plan for robbery. Nina needs the money to fund her history-making act of sabotage; Gino wants the money to buy a house. Naturally, they team up. Aside from being a brilliant hiss-and-boo girls' adventure movie, *Crocodiles* by-the-by features flashy editing and an evocative atmosphere of nighttime Amsterdam. (It was made by Annette Apon, whose first feature film was based on Virginia Woolf's *The Waves*.) It's also a shock—after *A Woman Like Eve* and a couple of heavy-handed lesbian-themed films from the Netherlands—to come across an adroit, energetic comedy which knows what it's doing and does it with style.

Although *Crocodiles* never explicitly addresses lesbianism (Nina is characterised as misguidedly but incorrigibly heterosexual), it has lots of fun playing the field.

With Joan Nederlof and Yolanda Entius

Kuro Tokage (Black Lizard, The)
Dir. Fukasaku,Kinji
1968 Japan Japanese
86 mins. 35mm color Narrative
Dist. (U.S.): Cinevista
Black Lizard is the nickname of the heroine of this classic Japanese film, the story of a mysterious jewel thief played by Akihiro Maruyama, a female impersonator. Visually stunning, *Black Lizard* is best known for its screenplay adaptation by Yukio Mishima, one of Japan's most prolific and respected gay writers of classics *Confessions of a Mask* and *The Sailor Who Fell from Grace with the Sea*, appears in the film as one of the *Black Lizard's* eerie human statues. The film was released two years before Mishima committed suicide by ceremonial seppuku at age 45.

Kustom Kar Kommandos
Dir. Anger, Kenneth
1965 USA English
4 mins. 16mm color Experimental
Dist. (U.S.): Canyon Cinema
Dist. (U.K.): British Film Institute
To the soundtrack of "Dream Lover" a young man strokes his customized car with a powder puff.

"*Kustom Kar Kommandos* was originally to be an eight-part, 30-minute film which Anger describes as 'an oneiric vision of a contemporary American (and specifically Californian) teenage phenomenon, the world of hot-rod and customized cars.' Anger made the episode presently shown as *Kustom Kar Kommandos* to raise funds to finish the film, but was unable to do so and the project was abandoned."

—Marilyn Singer,
The American Federation of Arts

L Is for the Way You Look
Dir. Carlomusto, Jean
1991 USA English
102 mins. video color Other
Dist. (U.S.): Women Make Movies
A fun-filled exploration of lesbian history, incorporating discussion of events, images, gossip, and role models.

L'Amico Fried's Glamorous Friends
Dir. Jacoby, Roger
1976 USA English
12 mins. 16mm color Experimental
Dist. (U.S.): Canyon Cinema
L'Amico Fried's Glamorous Friends is a delightful silent romp around sexual clichés and performance—with an angelic ending.

L'Hiver approche
(Winter Is Approaching)
Dir. Bensoussan, George
1975 France French
14 mins. 35mm color Experimental
Dist. (U.S.): Unifrance Film
An intense look at Paris, a nocturnal Paris, dark and mysterious, as a young man walks the streets looking for his desire.

L'Ingenue
Dir. Wilhite, Ingrid
1984 USA English
12 mins. video color Narrative
Dist. (U.S.): Wilhite, Ingrid
A humorous look at a day in the life of a baby dyke.

L'Usure (By Attrition)
Dir. Crepeau, Jeanne
1986 Canada French
8 mins. 16mm color Narrative
Dist. (U.S.): Women Make Movies
No point in going further! The problem is clear: The closeness that once linked these two girls has been worn thin by routine, by force of habit, by attrition. On a deserted street they meet to confide in each other, to dissolve the malaise that has estranged them, and to learn how to kiss again.

L-Shaped Room, The
Dir. Forbes, Bryan
1962 Great Britain English
124 mins. 16mm b&w Narrative
Dist. (U.S.): Films Incorporated
The L-Shaped Room stars Leslie Caron as a young pregnant woman who moves into a seamy London rooming house where she encounters Johnny (Brock Peters), who is painfully in love with Caron's ex-lover (Tom Bell), and a lesbian tenant, an ex-vaudevillian, beautifully played by Cicely Courtenidge. The lesbian and gay characters, not found in the novel upon which the film is based, were creations of the director, based on people he knew when he toured in British theater.

Ⓐ Ⓑ Ⓒ Ⓓ Ⓔ Ⓕ Ⓖ Ⓗ Ⓘ Ⓙ Ⓚ **Ⓛ** Ⓜ Ⓝ Ⓞ Ⓟ Ⓠ Ⓡ Ⓢ Ⓣ Ⓤ Ⓥ Ⓦ Ⓧ Ⓨ Ⓩ

La Couer decouvert
(Heart Exposed, The)
Dir. Laforce, Jean-Yves
1986 Canada French
106 mins. video color Narrative
Dist. (U.S.): Canadian Broadcasting Corporation
(Montreal)

Jean-Marc is a 39-year-old French teacher who has recently ended a 7-year relationship. He is disillusioned and uncertain about his future but knows he isn't ready for a new relationship. At a Montreal bar he meets Mathieu, a handsome 24-year-old aspiring actor. They head for a café and while having coffee, Jean-Marc suddenly excuses himself and disappears into the Montreal summer night, leaving Mathieu alone and confused. Jean-Marc's reluctance to begin a new relationship is only the first problem in this thought-provoking drama from Canada. After they begin to date, Jean-Marc becomes concerned with their age difference and finds himself unable to handle the anxiety it creates. It's at this point that he learns that Mathieu has a five-year-old son, Sebastien, from a marriage that ended when Mathieu finally accepted his homosexuality and admitted it to his understanding wife. The conflicts for Jean-Marc multiply as he finds that his closest friends, a very lively group of lesbians, aren't all that taken with his new lover and that Mathieu feels overly scrutinized by the women. As the story progresses and Sebastien becomes an integral part of the lovers' lives, Jean-Marc finds he has some questions to answer. Does he want to help raise a child? Does he need the problems a child could mean to their relationship? Does he love Mathieu? Does Mathieu really love him? Well-written and completely sympathetic to all its characters, *The Heart Exposed* also succeeds in recreating the look of a classic film romance.

Winner of the 1989 San Francisco International Lesbian & Gay Film Festival Audience Award for Best Feature.

Laberinto de Pasiones
(Labyrinth of Passions)
Dir. Almodovar, Pedro
1982 Spain Spanish
90 mins. 35mm color Narrative
Dist. (U.S.): Cinevista

Labyrinth of Passions narrates several love stories. The majority of them end happily while the rest end unhappily but with a certain ray of hope. The couple around whom the story revolves and

who simultaneously provoke intense passions of all types is composed of Sexilia (a young egomaniac, member of a violent, feminist musical group—Las Ex—and daughter of a brilliant gynecologist) and Raza Niro, the heir to an overthrown Arabian emperor who is more interested in cosmetics and men than in international politics. In the background of it all, Madrid, the most evolved city in the Western world: full of violence, persecutions, changes of images, obesity that doesn't feel ashamed of itself, remedies for people with dry lips and weak fingernails, a future full of uncertainty, and a past whose mark is indelible. And on top of all this love and love's difficulties.

Labor More Than Once
Dir. Merzky, Liz
1983 USA English
52 mins. video color Documentary
Dist. (U.S.): Women Make Movies

Marianne MacQueen is a lesbian who has lost the custody of her son to the new wife of her ex-husband. Ms. MacQueen comes up against homophobia in the courts and in society as she battles to regain the rights to her son. *Labor More Than Once* is a remarkable story of one mother's determination and honesty versus a system dead set against her.

Labyrinth of Passions
(see *Laberinto de Pasiones*)

Lady
Dir. Sachs, Ira
1993 USA English
28 mins. 16mm b&w Other
Dist. (U.S.): Frameline

In Ira Sachs's wonderfully twisted faux-documentary *Lady*, Dominique Dibbel (of the Five Lesbian Brothers) stars as a lesbian playing a gay man playing a '70s TV star, or something like that. This is the loopiest genderfuck of the year.

Lady in Waiting, The
Dir. Taylor, Christian
1993 USA English
30 mins. 16mm color Narrative
Dist. (U.S.): Taylor, Christian

Christian Taylor's Academy Award-nominated short story *The Lady in Waiting* is set in the late '70s. A prim and proper English woman is sent to New York to deliver a letter to her employer's mistress; she doesn't count on being stuck—during a blackout—in a high-rise with black drag queen Rodney Hudson.

Ladyboys
Dir. Marre, Jeremy
1992 Great Britain English
60 mins. video color Documentary
Dist. (U.S.): Harcourt Films
Made for Channel Four TV, *Ladyboys* follows two teenage Thai boys in their quest to escape rural poverty by becoming successful "katoi," or female impersonators.

Land Beyond Tomorrow
Dir. Farrel, Nicci
1993 USA English
4 mins. video color Experimental
Dist. (U.S.): Ritschel-Cederbaum, Sherry
In 1991 Nicci Farrel decided to follow her dreams to make videos; a week later she was diagnosed with cancer. Her first video, *Land Beyond Tomorrow*, is an experimental interpretation of a vision she received after a two-year battle with chemotherapy, radiation, and a near-death experience from a bone marrow transplant.

Landscape Catching
(see *Koukei Dori*)

Language of Boys, The
Dir. Christopher, Mark
1990 USA English
5 mins. video color Other
Dist. (U.S.): Christopher, Mark
Boys—in the flesh, and from "Johnny Quest."

Lasbisch TV
Dir. Lasbisch TV Collective
1992 Germany German
20 mins. video color Other
Dist. (U.S.): Lasbisch TV
A collectively produced monthly lesbian cable show from Berlin, *Lasbisch TV* covers a variety of international items.

Last Call at Maud's
Dir. Poirier, Paris
Prod. Kiss, Karen
1993 USA English
77 mins. 16mm color/b&w Documentary
Dist. (U.S.): Frameline
Until its closing in September 1989, Maud's was the longest-lasting lesbian-owned lesbian bar in the world. Like many, I took Maud's for granted, assuming it would always be around as a some-time alternative to the dance and cruise clubs which had begun to spring up in the mid and late '80s. And like many I was sad to see it go.
Thanks to the director Paris Poirier

and her lover, producer Karen Kiss, we now have a film all about the venerable institution and its role as a lesbian watering hole throughout the late '60s, '70s and '80s. This film will be a special treat for those regulars who formed the core social group: the softball team, the yearly Pussies talent line-up, the bartenders, the friends of owner Rikki Streicher, and other associated Maudies. For those like myself, who were more peripheral customers, it's great fun to share the memories with those who kept the place going and who kept Maud's open for three generations' worth of lesbian shenanigans.

Last Call at Maud's features interviews at the bar with lesbian luminaries such as Judy Grahn, Sally Gearhart, Del Martin, Phyllis Lyon, JoAnn Loulan, Mary Wings, Pat Norman, Susan Fahey, and of course, Rikki Streicher.

The history of Maud's parallels the evolving herstory of the lesbian community and the gay rights movement overall. As the longest-lasting lesbian bar, it was witness to and staging ground for all sorts of cultural changes. No matter how isolated or new in town, women could find other lesbians at the bar. Coming out, followed by paying a first visit to a queer bar, has been a veritable rite of passage in the gay community. Throughout time, in different cities and countries, and whether one drinks or not, queer bars have always served as beacons for gay people in search of one another. And it was a bar, after all, the Stonewall, which kicked off the public mobilization by queers for gay rights.

Cole Valley is just a hop from Haight-Ashbury, and Maud's was there to witness the influx of the long-haired hippie dykes of the time. It was there when Harvey Milk was killed. It was there through the beginning of the AIDS crisis. And it was there for the dykes on bikes after many Freedom Day parades. When Maud's opened in 1966, women were prohibited by law from dancing with each other in public. Female bartending was also against the law at that time.

Paris Poirier has done a marvelous job with *Last Call at Maud's*. Without the intrusion of narration, she lets the women and the artifacts make their own statements. She's included archival footage from patrons' personal collections of photographs, home videos, and memorabilia. We see photos from San Francisco's mixed gay bars like The Black Cat, and early dyke bars like Tommy's, Mona's and Chi Chi's—all precursors of Maud's. We see headlines from the newspapers describing underground gay bars as "resorts for sexual perverts." We hear about

Ⓐ Ⓑ ⓒ Ⓓ Ⓔ Ⓕ Ⓖ Ⓗ Ⓘ Ⓙ Ⓚ **Ⓛ** Ⓜ Ⓝ Ⓞ Ⓟ Ⓠ Ⓡ Ⓢ Ⓣ Ⓤ Ⓥ Ⓦ Ⓧ Ⓨ Ⓩ

police raids and gay patrons finding their names listed in the morning newspapers. There were even raids at Maud's and alarms that would go off, warning the girls to stop dancing together. Rikki Streicher tells us that when she opened the bar in 1966 it was called Maud's Study. She says, "People would talk to each other on the phone and say, 'Well do you want to go to the library tonight?' That's how careful one had to be back then."

There are a lot of bar stories in the film, but one of my favorites was related by Hydie Downard, a Maudie since the late '60s: "So, Janis Joplin came into the bar and I thought this was my big chance. So I Put 'Another Piece Of My Heart' on the jukebox and sang my heart out onto my beer bottle like a microphone. I mean, I really tried my best. And I think, okay, now she's going to say something. Then this note comes down the bar and it says, 'It took me ten years in the street to get that song and you blew it in ten minutes.'" (R.T.)

Last Island, The
Dir. Gorris, Marleen
1990 Netherlands English
101 mins. 35mm color Narrative
Dist. (U.S.): First Floor Features
Full of drama, suspense, and graphic violence, *The Last Island* is a feminist *Lord of the Flies* for the '90s. As insightful and disturbing as her previous features (*Broken Mirrors* and *A Question of Silence*), here Marleen Gorris shows the underbelly of patriarchy and the desperation of the human condition as two women, five men, and a dog struggle to survive after their plane crashes on a deserted island. Two of the men are gay and one of the women seems to be a lesbian (although this is never explicitly stated).

A feminist film every man should see, this uncompromising indictment of male power and privilege is a masterpiece of politically engaged filmmaking. An apocalyptic allegory on the human condition. *The Last Island* takes on the thorniest ethical and moral issues of our time—reproductive rights, control of the body, mercy killing, the hypocrisy and tyranny of the Catholic church in relation to women and in relation to homosexuality, etc.

Last of England, The
Dir. Jarman, Derek
Prod. Mackay, James, and Don Boyd
1987 Great Britain English
87 mins. 35mm color Experimental

Dist. (U.S.): International Film Circuit
Dist. (U.K.): Sales Company, The
"Relentlessly narcissistic, repetitive, head-ache inducing . . . mindbendingly self-indulgent." Derek Jarman's latest film has been swamped with a tide of homophobic hate from critics; its controversy has disguised its modest intentions and sensitive address. Behind the poison-pen pans there's a uniquely critical movie struggling to be seen.

The Last of England is a nonnarrative collage on Britain today. It has twice the energy and bite of *My Beautiful Laundrette*, and none of the story. Jarman divides his movie into three strands, starting with seductive black-and-white shots of himself at home in London, trying to sum up his feelings about being gay and being an outsider in Britain today. This is undercut with a home movie scrapbook of his wartime childhood, a homosexual *Hope and Glory*, in which the sentimental colors—his mother's blue-and-white print dress, the red chrysanthemums—contrast with his acid hindsight.

In the film's most controversial section, Jarman arranges a series of angry tableaux: Tilda Swinton tears her wedding dress, dockside, in an amazing parody of the Royal Wedding: a soldier and his lover fuck on top of the Union Jack. It's like an issue of *The Face* redesigned by Kenneth Anger.

Undoubtedly, *The Last of England* is a difficult movie if you're not prepared for its innovative structure, but what's exciting is the meeting between Jarman's two personas: the shocking surrealist who made *Sebastiane* and *Jubilee*, and the newly despairing don't-get-mad-get-even didacticist. If there's ever an ad for the contradictions and attractions of late '80s Britain, this is it.

Last Paintings of Derek Jarman, The
Dir. Jordan, Mark, and John Piper
Prod. Granada Television
1994 Great Britain English
30 mins. video color Documentary
Dist. (U.K.): Granada TV
On the edge of blindness and short of breath, Derek Jarman creates his final seventeen paintings shortly before his death.

Last Song, The
Dir. Akarasainee, Pisan
1986 Thailand Thai
90 mins. 35mm color Narrative
Dist. (U.S.): Thai Motion Picture Producers Association

From the *Bangkok Post* comes this notice: *"The Last Song* was a hit. Director-producer Pisan Akarasainee thinks that the gay theme alone was not solely responsible for the movie's popularity—the lesbian theme helped too." And indeed it does in this story of a hunky country boy Boonthern (which means "long stem" in Thai), who comes to the big city to seek his fortune. He shortly finds himself being supprted by a high-class female impersonator (played by Thai cabaret star Somying Daorai), head-over-her-six-inch-heels in love with him. Boon seems to enjoy things well enough with Somying, but, alas, feels he must do the "natural" thing and fall in love with a young girl, Orn, who, unfortunately for him, is a lesbian. But not for long if her domineering mother has anything to say about it. Mom won't let up until her daughter gives up her lovely butch girlfriend, Praew.

An incredible tug of hearts develops as Praew tries to keep Orn, Orn tries to straighten out but lapses, Somying fights to keep Boon and Boon chases Orn while also trying to start a singing career. The machinations of these four are witnessed by a veritable gaggle of drag queens, who flutter, shriek, and squeal with all the joie de vivre of their Western counterparts.

The Last Song is made a smidge funnier because of occasional sub-titling faux pas ("There he goes again, over-pandering his new boyfriend") and a few spots where the titles don't seem to coincide with the picture on the screen. These problems aside, it is an intriguing glimpse at Thai gay life. It ends with apparently requisite sad endings for the les/gay characters who don't straighten out, but they return (even the dead ones) in the sequel to get their revenge.

"Garish item."—*Variety*

Last Stop, The
Dir. Dinwiddy, Ross, and Mark Adams
1994 UK English
25 mins. 16mm b&w Narrative
Dist. (U.S.):
Dist. (U.K.): Basilisk
An authentically sexy story about an unexpected weekend adventure.

Last Supper, The
Dir. Roberts, Cynthia
Prod. Klymkiw, Greg
1994 Canada English
96 mins. 16mm color Narrative
Dist. (U.S.): Klymkiw, Greg
A terminally ill man bids the world an elaborate

farewell in this poetic adaptation of Hillar Liijota's play, originally presented on stage by Toronto's DNA Theatre. Chris (Ken McDougall), a dancer, shares a final night of food, wine, and reminiscence with his lover Val (Jack Nicholsen), after which his physician (Daniel MacIvor), who will assist him in ending his life, explains to Val the ritual Chris has devised. Chris performs a "dance" in his bed—he asks Val, a photographer, to document it—then the death scenario, which culminates in two lethal injections, is set into motion.

Though *The Last Supper* takes place in a single room and its individual sequences unfold in an approximation of real time, director Cynthia Roberts's nicely conceived camera movements and Rembrandt-like lighting maintain visual interest. McDougall, who died shortly after filming, is particularly strong as the ailing Chris, who steers his lover (and himself) through a traumatic moment with grace and thoroughly appropriate touches of gloomy wit. In death Chris proves not only how much he loves Val, but life itself.

The Last Supper won the "Gay Teddy Bear" Audience Award for Best Feature at the 1995 Berlin Film Festival.

Late Bloomers
Dir. Dyer, Julia, and Gretchen Dyer
1995 USA English
104 mins. 35mm color Narrative
US Dist
UK Dist
A charming tale of unexpected romance between the gym teacher and the receptionist at a suburban high school. Well written, nicely acted, and thoughtfully directed this feature should appeal to straight audiences as much as it does to pro-marriage gays and lesbians. Carly and Dinah fall in love as the world around them falls apart. Fired from their jobs, they get married as the ultimate gesture of how their love deserves to be accepted by the world. Not a greatly sophisticated drama, but a good quality message movie.

Latex—Step Out Smartly
Dir. Boudreau, Charline
1992 Canada English
1 mins. video color Other
Dist. (U.S.): Frameline
Released in the U.S. as part of *She's Safe*, a feature-length package of lesbian safe-sex videos.

Laundromat
Dir. Mears, Ric

Ⓐ Ⓑ Ⓒ Ⓓ Ⓔ Ⓕ Ⓖ Ⓗ Ⓘ Ⓙ Ⓚ **Ⓛ** Ⓜ Ⓝ Ⓞ Ⓟ Ⓠ Ⓡ Ⓢ Ⓣ Ⓤ Ⓥ Ⓦ Ⓧ Ⓨ Ⓩ

1977 USA English
1 mins. S8mm color Narrative
Dist. (U.S.): Mears, Ric
A "typical American housewife" comes clean at the laundromat—my first film made for class at San Francisco State.

Laura, Ingrid, and Rebecca
Dir. Roques, Philippe
1990 USA English
7 mins. video color Documentary
Dist. (U.S.): Roques, Philippe
Three lesbian activists from ACT UP speak candidly about their experiences with group politics. They manage to integrate anger and action, AIDS activism and pro-choice work, making it clear that men's and women's health body issues are not gender exclusive.

Lavender Tortoise, The
Dir. Woodard, Ken
1991 USA English
15 mins. video color Documentary
Dist. (U.S.): Chicago Filmmakers
Join Ggreg Taylor and his merry band of fags and dykes as they make their way to America's ultimate fantasy world—Disneyland. Stops on the way in the City of Angels include the Max Factor museum, Rodeo Drive, and the pool at the Coral Sands.

Law of Desire, The
(see Ley del Deseo, La)

Lawless
Dir. Tartaglia, Jerry
1977 USA English
10 mins. 16mm color Experimental
Dist. (U.S.): Canyon Cinema
Lawless features gay theatrics with Warhol superstar Ondine and Margaret Gormley.

Lawn Butch
Dir. Ritschel-Cederbaum, Sherry
1991 USA English
1 mins. video color Other
Dist. (U.S.): Ritschel-Cederbaum, Sherry
A great new product commercial.

Le Jupon rouge (Manuela's Loves)
Dir. Lefebvre, Genevieve
1987 France French
90 mins. 35mm color Narrative
Dist. (U.S.): International Home Cinema
Comparable to such European lesbian favorites as Novembermoon and Another Way, Manuela's Loves adds a French twist to the typical lesbian

drama—a ménage à trois, to be exact. Shifting attractions are played out between three women of different ages in this overlooked French feature. The eldest, Bacha (legendary Italian actress Alida Valli) is an Amnesty International human rights activist and concentration camp survivor. Her younger fashion designer friend Manuela (Marie-Christine Barrault) is her primary emotional support. When Manuela meets the beautiful young Claude (Guillemette Grobon), the two begin a relationship that incites Bacha's intense jealousy. Manuela is torn between her love for Bacha and her desire for Claude.

"A women's film in the best sense, Manuela's Loves is an emotionally gripping drama . . . among the year's best debut features." —Variety

"Manuela's Loves is a romantic story told with delicacy and a classical sense of cinema. Beautifully shot and impeccably acted in the great tradition of European cinema."
—Kay Armatage,
Toronto International Film Festival

Le Poisson d' amour
Dir. Gauthier, Paula
1994 USA English
11 mins. 16mm color Narrative
Dist. (U.S.): Gauthier, Paula
An exploration of the public/private dualities of a lesbian love affair.

Leather Boys, The
Dir. Furie, Sidney J.
Prod. Stross, Raymond
1964 Great Britain English
107 mins. 16mm b&w Narrative
Dist. (U.S.): Kit Parker Films
An implied homoerotic tension between Pete (Dudley Sutton) and Reggie (Colin Campbell) is the primary theme of this British drama. Gradually this tension becomes identified as the probable reason for Reggie's lack of sexual interest in his new wife, Dot (Rita Tushingham). Director Furie presents a very subdued treatment of the issue until the last half hour of the film when Dot accuses Pete and Reggie of being "queer." Denying her charge, they agree that they are just good friends. After a few melodramatic twists, Pete and Reggie decide to sail off to America together and are about to get on a ship when, stopping in a waterfront bar, Reggie realizes that Pete really is gay. Reggie abandons Pete and walks off alone.

In contrast to the drugs, girls, and

rock 'n' roll ambience that American biker pics are associated with, *The Leather Boys* is rather staid in its drama. The 'sensational' biker backdrop is distinctly British, and really the film is a serious drama focusing on the lives of its young working-class protagonists (who happen to be very interested in motorcycles). (J.O.)

Legend of Fong Sai-Yuk, The
Dir. Yuen, Corey
1993 Hong Kong Cantonese
106 mins. 35mm color Narrative
Dist. (U.S.): Rim Film Distributors
In *Legend*, the fighter Fong Sai-Yuk (Jet Li) learns his skills from his mother (Josephine Siao). Mrs. Fong is a resilient woman who submits to her husband's cruel abuse but is protective of her son. When her son competes for the hand of a woman in marriage, he is defeated by her mother, Mrs. Lu. To regain her family honor, Mrs Fong dons men's clothes and passing herself off as Fong Sai-Yuk's brother, Fong Dai-Yuk, challenges Mrs Lu.

In the course of their spectacular kung fu match, the two women fall in love with each other. Mrs. Lu confides to Fong Sai-Yuk that while her husband is a good man, she has never felt passion for him the way she does for Fong Dai-Yuk. In the film's bittersweet romantic conclusion, Mrs. Lu declares to Mrs. Fong, "maybe in another life, there will be room for our love."

Les Amities particulieres
(This Special Friendship)
Dir. Delannoy, Jean
1964 France French
99 mins. 16mm color Narrative
Dist. (U.S.): Frameline Archive
Based on Roger Peyrefitte's *This Special Friendship* is the story of homosexual love up against the authoritarianism of the Catholic Church. The innocent and affectionate love of two schoolboys, naturally and openly portrayed, contrasts with the repressed and guilt-ridden homosexuality of the school priests. After repeated attempts to stop the boys' encounters, a priest lies to the younger boy to get him to leave the school and end the forbidden relationship. Tragically, the boy commits suicide by jumping from a speeding train. Despite the typical 1960s resolution of gay love in cinema, the homosexual love, though destroyed, is glorified, and the Church is challenged for its condemnation of homosexuality.

Lesbian Avengers Eat Fire Too
Dir. Baus, Janet, and Su Friedrich
1993 USA English
55 mins. video color Documentary
Dist. (U.S.): Wolfe Video
Looks at the first year of the all-out, all-lesbian direct-action girl gang.

Lesbian Bed Death: Myth or Epidemic.
An Investigative Report.
Dir. Foiles, Stacey
Prod. Ardioto, Saundra
1995 USA English
11 mins. video color Other
Dist. (U.S.): Foiles, Stacey
A hilarious send-up of that all-too-common lesbian malady.

Lesbian Impress Card, The
Dir. Wilhite, Ingrid
1990 USA English
1 mins. video color Other
Dist. (U.S.): Wilhite, Ingrid
The Lesbian Impress Card—don't leave the festival without it.

Lesbians
Dir. Walton, Pam
1986 USA English
5 mins. 16mm color Documentary
Dist. (U.S.): Walton, Pam
This "talking heads" documentary short makes its points quickly and concisely by introducing the viewer to a small group of lesbians discussing their lives.

Lesbians Who Date Men
Dir. Nolan, Monica
1994 USA English
15 mins. video color Documentary
Dist. (U.S.): Nolan, Monica
Monica Nolan's fast-paced survey scans the range of public opinions, pro and con, on *Lesbians Who Date Men*.

Let Me Die, Again
Dir. Knight, Leone
Prod. McMurchy, Megan
1995 Australia English
15 mins. 35mm color Other
Dist. (U.S.): McMurchy, Megan/Suitcase Films
Paul Capsis plays a suicidal diva in this lush, musical melodrama that looks at the queerness in opera and the operatic in queer lives. Our diva is crushed when her true love sees her in all her

Ⓐ Ⓑ Ⓒ Ⓓ Ⓔ Ⓕ Ⓖ Ⓗ Ⓘ Ⓙ Ⓚ Ⓛ Ⓜ Ⓝ Ⓞ Ⓟ Ⓠ Ⓡ Ⓢ Ⓣ Ⓤ Ⓥ Ⓦ Ⓧ Ⓨ Ⓩ

nakedness and rejects her.

Let's Play Prisoners
Dir. Zando, Julie
1988 USA English
22 mins. video b&w Experimental
Dist. (U.S.): Video Data Bank
Let's Play Prisoners is about how power is exchanged between females. It presents three restagings of a short story in which a young girl is manipulative and cruel towards her girlfriend, whose adoration verges on masochism.

Buffalo-based videomaker Julie Zando has become known for exploring difficult subjects—female masochism, erotic obsession, and victimization. Not feminist fairy tales, her tapes look frankly at relations of power and submission between women, as lovers, friends, and mothers/daughters, as she probes the connections between dependency and love, power and control.

Let's Pretend
(see *Out On Tuesday, Program 4*)

Letter to My Grandma
Dir. Howe, Alyssa Cymene
1995 USA English
6 mins. video color Narrative
Dist. (U.S.): Howe, Alyssa Cymene
A narrative reflection on the fifty-five-year history of the filmmaker's grandmother and her female partner.

Ley del Deseo, La (Law of Desire)
Dir. Almodovar, Pedro
Prod. Almodovar, Agustin
1987 Spain Spanish
100 mins. 35mm color Narrative
Dist. (U.S.): Cinevista
Dist. (U.K.): Metro Tartan
The hit of this year's Berlin Film Festival, *Law of Desire* has been creating a stir all over the world. Critics have been shocked by its sexual explicitness in this age of safe-sex but have also been overwhelmed by director Pedro Almodovar's wild sense of humor and equally wild sense of the outrageous. When both Vito Russo and Pauline Kael rave about a film you can be sure of something special. The story is part fantasy, part murder mystery and part erotic comedy. It's about Antonio, who loves Pablo, who loves Juan. It's also about Pablo's sister Tina (played by Carmen Maura, who nearly steals the film) who was his brother before undergoing a sex change. The four characters become involved in a tale of sexual intrigue and danger that leads to murder and amnesia. Pedro Almodovar has been called the Spanish John Waters and directed last year's hit *What Have I Done to Deserve This?* which featured Carmen Maura as the slum mother. She has been compared to both Anna Magnani and Bette Midler and seems destined for international stardom.

Winner of the 1987 San Francisco International Lesbian & Gay Film Festival Audience Award for Best Feature.

Lianna
Dir. Sayles, John
1983 USA English
110 mins. 35mm color Narrative
Dist. (U.S.): Swank Motion Pictures
Dist. (U.K.): British Film Institute
John Sayles's lesbian coming-out drama offers a sensitive, if slightly dated portrayal of an academic housewife's sexual awakening. *Lianna* has its share of flaws (as do most lesbian coming-out films of the '80s), but Linda Griffiths's portrayal of the titular lesbian shines through. And Rex Reed called it "100 times better than *Personal Best*." (J. O.)

Lick
Dir. B., Hima, and Eliza O. Barrios
1995 USA English
10 mins. video color Other
Dist. (U.S.): B., Hima
Lick brings to life the revenge fantasies of a jilted lover.

Lick Bush in '92
Dir. Gomez, Gabriel
1993 USA English
89 mins. video color Documentary
Dist. (U.S.): Gomez, Gabriel
A fascinating documentation of Chicago drag queen (and favorite local hero) Joan Jett Black's campaign shenanigans on the road to the presidency in 1992.

Lie Down with Dogs
Dir. White, Wally
Prod. Pierson, John
1994 USA English
84 mins. 35mm color Narrative
Dist. (U.S.): Swank Motion Pictures
Tommie (Wally White) is fed up with the daily grind of New York, where he earns a living passing out flyers in Times Square and inhabits a tiny apartment. On an utter whim, he decides to escape to fabulous boy-filled Provincetown where

he begins searching for the ideal houseboy gig, the only kind of job that seems to be available in this gay summer paradise. During his frustrating job hunt, he meets Guy (Bash Halow), a tireless party animal who doesn't let the small things—jobs, friendships, his conscience—get in the way of a good time. He also becomes sexually involved with Tom (Randy Becker), a good-for-nothing but incredibly hot moocher who survives P-Town by bumming everything from cheeseburgers to cigarettes. Emotionally unfulfilled but sexually gratified Tommie can't seem to get away. Meanwhile Tommie keeps running into seemingly unattainable hunk-o-rama Ben (Darren Dryden), whom he dismisses as just another mindless stuck-up pretty boy . . . until they finally connect on the bike trail.

An outrageous comedy about the foibles of twenty-something gay boys, *Lie Down with Dogs* features the high-energy music of one of the music industry's top producers, Jellybean Benitez.

Liebe, Eifersucht und Rache (Love, Jealousy and Revenge)
Dir. Brynntrup, Michael
1992 Germany German
7 mins. 16mm color Experimental
Dist. (U.S.): Chicago Filmmakers
Michael Brynntrup's hilarious and hot *Love, Jealousy and Revenge* is a comedy about subtitling and crossed lines.

Lieve Jongens (Dear Boys)
Dir. De Lussanet, Paul
Prod. Van Heijningen, Matthijs
1980 Netherlands Dutch
90 mins. 35mm color Narrative
Dist. (U.S.): Netherlands Ministry of Culture
An astute, wickedly funny satire on certain aspects of gay male behavior, *Dear Boys* was a somewhat controversial entry when shown at the festival in 1981. Some viewers complained that Paul de Lussanet's film completely lacked sympathy for its comic, sex-obsessed characters, while others praised it for cleverly and subtly exaggerating S/M, pornography youth & beauty obsessions, sentiment, and just about everything else.

Dear Boys is the story of Wolf, a wealthy and talkative novelist suffering from writer's block. He arranges for his much younger lover Tiger to seduce another beautiful young man. Wolf then begins an elaborate seduction of his own of the new boy, accomplished through a series of erotic, comic sex fantasies that Wolf tells the boy and that we see on the screen. There is nothing sacred in these fantasies that explore Catholic guilt, S/M, sexual possession, sexual jealousy, and the trauma of romantic love.

As the story unfolds there is great pleasure in seeing Wolf, one of the most outrageous gay characters ever put to film, struggle desperately to hold onto the two lovers he so shamelessly manipulates. *Dear Boys* is based on a novel by Gerald Reve, Holland's most successful gay writer.

Life in the Kitchen
Dir. Smith, Sally
1989 New Zealand English
8 mins. 16mm color/b&w Narrative
Dist. (U.S.): New Zealand Film Commission
Life in the Kitchen is a moody and lively study in fantasy. Our solitary protagonist experiences a sweet and imaginative mind trip peopled with friendly food fetishists. She also enjoys a side dish of body painting.

Life on Earth as I Know It
Dir. Furneaux-Cook, Lesley
1989 Australia English
9 mins. 16mm Narrative
Dist. (U.S.): Women Make Movies
A short story about love, loneliness, and meteorology. Lois is depressed and despairs of finding a meaningful relationship in the big city. When she moves into an all-women household on the wrong side of town, there's stormy weather ahead.

Life on Earth is smart and stylish—a new benchmark for lesbian filmmaking that manages to be both humorous and lyrical about coming out.

Lifetime Commitment: A Portrait of Karen Thompson
Dir. Zeldes, Kiki
1987 USA English
32 mins. video color Documentary
Dist. (U.S.): Women Make Movies
In 1983, Sharon Kowalski was critically injured and disabled in a car accident. Since that accident, her lover, Karen Thompson, has been fighting a full-time legal battle against Sharon's family and the courts of Minnesota for the right to see Sharon, care for her, and resume their partnership in love, which Sharon has communicated she too wishes to continue. Her specific case is made poignant and relevant for all people whose

Ⓐ
Ⓑ
Ⓒ
Ⓓ
Ⓔ
Ⓕ
Ⓖ
Ⓗ
Ⓘ
Ⓙ
Ⓚ
Ⓛ
Ⓜ
Ⓝ
Ⓞ
Ⓟ
Ⓠ
Ⓡ
Ⓢ
Ⓣ
Ⓤ
Ⓥ
Ⓦ
Ⓧ
Ⓨ
Ⓩ

rights may be jeopardized by systems of law and morality that deny the validity—and the reality—of lesbian and gay partnerships.

Lift Off
Dir. Unknown
1983 USA English
30 mins. video color Other
Dist. (U.S.): n/a
Aptly named, it is found footage of every sort combined in an eclectic and very effective way.

Like a Dog
Dir. Amazon Broadcasting Company
1984 USA English
12 mins. video color Other
Dist. (U.S.): n/a
Humorous grassroots video.

Like Mother, Like Son
Dir. Kennerley, Annette
1994 Great Britain English
5 mins. 16mm color Other
Dist. (U.K.): Cinenova
Annette Kennerley's five-year-old son talks about dressing up in women's clothing in the eye-opening *Like Mother, Like Son.*

Lillian's Dilemma
Prod. Vitagraph
1914 USA English
20 mins. 35mm b&w Narrative
Dist. (U.S.): Library of Congress
Produced by the Vitagraph Studios in 1914, *Lillian's Dilemma* is a sort of proto-screwball comedy of cross-dressing—the dilemma arising from Lillian's disguise as a man to infiltrate her brother's school and the loss of her woman's dress to a curious schoolboy.

Lily & Lulu Go to the March
Dir. Marnell, Lily, and Luciana Moreira
1994 USA English
11 mins. video color Other
Dist. (U.S.): Marnell, Lily
The trials and treats of coupledom as Lily and Lulu get sexy, get ready, and go to the March.

Limités
Dir. Torrealba, José
Prod. Torrealba Productions
1994 Canada English
47 mins. video color Documentary
Dist. (U.S.): Robin, Jean
In José Torrealba's *Limités*, Peruvian photographer Carlos Quiroz unveils the artistic process behind capturing the male nude. Inundated with

doe-eyed and hung French-Canadian models, *Limités* visits Quiroz's private photo sessions, allowing you to witness the intimate relationship established between camera and subject, a relationship in which the distinctions separating the artistic and the commercial are constantly changing and forever blurred. Lounging naked around the studio, even the models themselves—some of whom could very well be straight—offer surprisingly intelligent insights into how and why they do what they do. Encompassing the vast range of nude photography, Quiroz's work, in being so erotically charged, is, in his words, "an invitation to masturbate, to become an accomplice with the model to reach orgasm." In doing so, the simple act of looking becomes a sexual act in and of itself. After this film, you may never flip through another blue magazine in quite the same way again.

Limitless
Dir. Johns, Jennifer
1991 USA English
5 mins. 16mm color Experimental
Dist. (U.S.): Frameline
Limitless captures a pair of bodybuilders, a man and a woman, in a sensual montage.

Limitless Place, A
(see *Lugar Sin Limites, El*)

Linda/Les and Annie
Dir. Sprinkle, Annie
1989 USA English
28 mins. video color Documentary
Dist. (U.S.): Sprinkle, Annie
Dist. (U.K.): London Video Access
In the "first female-to-male transsexual love affair in herstory," Annie and Les explore and explain the context and functions of Les's dual genitalia.

Lipotaktis (Deserter)
Dir. Korras, Giorgas, and Christos Voupouras
1988 Greece Greek
121 mins. 35mm color Narrative
Dist. (U.S.): Greek Film Centre
Christos in an intense, infatuated Athenian who follows army runaway Manolis to his small Greek hometown, hoping to entice him away from an oppressive circle of family and friends. It's probably a hopeless cause. *Deserter* is a downbeat, slow, and sad-eyed drama—the kind of film that divides audiences (as it has done already in Berlin and London). Sophisticated San Franciscans may have no sympathy for the story

of a closeted middle-class man's doomed pursuit of a surly straight village lad, yet—in context—*Deserter* is a marvel.

Simply put, Christos is the first compassionate gay portrayal in Greek cinema (remember the transvestite-hooker-killer-queer "hero" of *Angel?*). Double credit, then, to directorial duo Giorgas Korras and Christos Voupouras for not grabbing an off-the-rack coming out confessional. Instead, they've sewn up one of gay cinema's most difficult themes—loneliness and frustration.

It's easy to think of homo melancholy as ugly, invented, and unwanted, and in the hand of Hollywood that might be true. But this is the gay version. *Deserter* takes time to dwell on the real details of infatuation (hours of waiting for looks and smiles), and effortlessly captures the other difficulties between men of different backgrounds. It's a classic: one of the first movies about gayness and alienation that is neither judgmental nor remote.

Liquor, Guns and Ammo
Dir. Karpinski, Barbara
1994 Australia English
7 mins. video color Experimental
Dist. (U.S.): Karpinski, Barbara
A femme's story for her Daddy.

Little Bit of Lippy, A
Dir. Bernard, Chris
1992 Great Britain English
75 mins. video color Other
Dist. (U.K.): BBC TV
From British television, a film about British transvestism. *A Little Bit of Lippy* is a fruity, cross-dressing comedy set in the north of England. Marian (Alison Swann) and Rick (Danny Cunningham) are a working-class couple whose marriage has gone stale. In search of some sexual oomph, Marian surprises Rick one night in her scanties. Problem is, he's gotten to the make-up box before her. Directed by Chris Bernard (maker of *Letter to Brezhnev*), *A Little Bit of Lippy* is a terrific, stylish blend of surreal cinematography (including a hilarious visual spoof of Brian de Palma's *Dressed to Kill*) and absurdist Mike Leigh–style observation (when Marian consults a famous drag queen for advice on what to do with her cross-dressing hubby, he announces, "Underpants or ladies' briefs—what's the difference? It's what's inside that counts."

Live to Tell:

The First Gay Prom in America
Dir. Lang, Charley
1995 USA English
27 mins. 16mm color Documentary
Dist. (U.S.): Lang, Charley
Live to Tell documents a historic event, the first gay prom in America, put on by the students of the EAGLES Center, a grassroots, alternative high school in West Hollywood. Watch as these courageous kids tackle societal oppression and their own personal struggles to put on this life-affirming event.

Living and Dying
(see *Ich Lebe Gern, Ich Sterbe Gern*)

Living End, The
Dir. Araki, Gregg
1991 USA English
85 mins. 16mm color Narrative
Dist. (U.S.): October Films
Two fatalistic L.A. boys—one's an impulsive, on-the-edge psycho cutie; the other listens to the Smiths a lot, and likes Godard movies—discover they're HIV positive and set about on an unplanned, unhinged serio-comic spree of violence and abandon. *The Living End* has been described as a homo *Thelma & Louise*, which is true enough—but it's also far more than that. Director Gregg Araki has taken on the issues and energy of gay youth in 1992, and turned them into a mad, anarchic and unsettlingly powerful experience. (It's mostly set on the road," explains Araki, "It's like a Hope/Crosby movie . . . in which Crosby fucks Hope.")

Living with AIDS
Dir. DiFeliciantonio, Tina
1986 USA English
25 mins. 16mm color Documentary
Dist. (U.S.): DiFeliciantonio, Tina/Naked Eye Productions
The compelling story of Todd, a young San Franciscan with AIDS, and the people who provided him with practical and emotional support during the last months of his life.

Living with AIDS: Women and AIDS
Dir. Juhasz, Alexandra
1988 USA English
28 mins. video color Documentary
Dist. (U.S.): Gay Men's Health Crisis
AIDS education and political action on behalf of heterosexual women and lesbians, with an emphasis on women of color.

Ⓐ Ⓑ Ⓒ Ⓓ Ⓔ Ⓕ Ⓖ Ⓗ Ⓘ Ⓙ Ⓚ **Ⓛ** Ⓜ Ⓝ Ⓞ Ⓟ Ⓠ Ⓡ Ⓢ Ⓣ Ⓤ Ⓥ Ⓦ Ⓧ Ⓨ Ⓩ

Loads
Dir. McDowell, Curt
1980 USA English
22 mins. 16mm b&w Experimental
Dist. (U.S.): Canyon Cinema

I was obsessed with straight men and wanted them to know what it was like to be made love to by another man. I've always thought of straight men as virgins—they haven't experienced sex with a man yet. *Loads* was filmed with that in mind, to give them a virginal look. When I saw a hot man from my window, I'd follow him, and when we'd reach a streetcorner I'd announce: "I'm a filmmaker; I'd like to film you." If they asked: "Doing what?" I'd say: "Jerk off." I wanted to see them reach an orgasm, with a woman, without a woman, with a woman in mind, or with me. None of them chose to do it with a woman, they preferred to look at magazines or at me. I got more bold with each person. I always filmed each guy without a crew. That created some awkward situations filmwise; if I wanted to have sex with them, I'd put the camera on a tripod, or I'd ask them to film me. There isn't anything they did that they didn't know they were doing. They are sort of aware of their attractiveness.

There were seven vignettes in total and although I decided not to release them, I couldn't stop pulling them out of the drawer and watching them on the editing machine. By 1980 I figured that if I was so fascinated by them, maybe other people would be too. I had a ball making the soundtrack, since the episodes were originally shot silent. I recorded myself jerking off, fantasizing about and remembering these six guys. (I eliminated one of them because he didn't fit with the mood of the others.) I realised that if I lied my dick would go soft; I used a stiff prick as my barometer for whether I was telling the truth about what I liked about these guys.

London Story, The
Dir. Potter, Sally
1986 Great Britain English
15 mins. 35mm color Experimental
Dist. (U.S.): Women Make Movies
Dist. (U.K.): Cinenova

This lively accessible spy spoof by Sally Potter revolves around the unlikely alliance of three eccentric characters and their mission to uncover government foreign policy duplicity. Beautifully and humorously set-choreographed against London's most famed locales in Technicolor.

Long Time Comin'
Dir. Brand, Dionne
1993 Canada English
53 mins. 16mm color Documentary
Dist. (U.S.): Women Make Movies

Faith Nolan is one of Canada's most outspoken lesbian feminist musicians. Grace Channer, her close friend and fellow activist, is a visual artist who conveys her political concerns through her paintings and sculptures. An empowering portrait of these two Canadian black lesbian feminist artists, *Long Time Comin'* addresses issues of racism, sexism, and reclaiming identity. In this deft portrait of their friendship and lives, filmmaker Dionne Brand creates a loving testament to the power of women's activism.

Long Weekend (O'Despair), The
Dir. Araki, Gregg
1989 USA English
93 mins. 16mm color Narrative
Dist. (U.S.): Strand Releasing

The grainiest gay movie of the year is also the funniest. After his love-or-loathe first feature *Three Bewildered People in the Night*, director-writer-producer Gregg Araki looks bound to win over everyone with *The Long Weekend*. For openers, there's double the drama and humor: His new film follows *Six Bewildered People*, but it's a breezier adventure. College friends Michael, Rachel and Sara—and their bemused lovers—team up again five years later for one long holiday weekend. Over three days they change their ideas and their partners even faster than L.A. nightclubs change names. It's twentysomething set by the light of a shopping mall, where all the characters are too doped-up or simply can't stop talking. If anyone can get wit or meaning out of them, it's Araki. *The Long Weekend* is what gay cinema ought to be—droll, detached, and undetermined.

Note: *The Long Weekend* also chaperones this year's major theme in gay-male movies: bixexual melancholy. This is about modern youngsters who can't decide whether they crave relationships with the same sex, the opposite sex, or with their complete collection of The Smiths singles. None of *Weekend's* protagonists know what they want, but if Frameline installed armrest electronic pollsters, we would be sure to tell them.

Longtime Companion
Dir. Rene, Norman
1990 USA English
99 mins. 35mm color Narrative

Dist. (U.S.): The Samuel Goldwyn Co.
Touted as "the first motion picture drama to focus on AIDS" (actually, Arthur Bressan's 1986 film *Buddies* was the first) the film covers nine years in the lives of a group of gay men living in New York City, from the onset of the AIDS crisis in 1981 to the present.

From the film's press kit: Writer Craig Lucas articulates his vision of the film, "The film's about the culture of our lives. I wasn't out to educate anyone. I set out to tell, like a witness, what I'd experienced." Director Norman Rene adds, "It was essential that the people we encounter are human and identifiable, so that the film is not about New Yorkers and gays, but about people with whom audiences could identify." [New Yorkers and gays are not human and identifiable?]

Ralph Novak film critic for *People* magazine: "It's too bad this film about the effects of AIDS on the New York gay community is so insular it all but blares out, 'Straight people, stay away!'. . . The effect of this sexual ethnocentrism is likely to distance straight audiences from the emotional upheaval the men go through. More's the pity, for the film's essence has to do with love more than sexual preference."

Vito Russo in *The Advocate*: "It is the first major movie to deal with gay men and AIDS; it doesn't try to explain gay life to a mainstream audience; and it contains more affection and intimacy between men than virtually any other film in recent memory." Profits from the film were shared with various AIDS organizations, including the Gay Men's Health Crisis in New York City. (J.O.)

Look
Dir. Copi, Susannah
1992 USA No Dialogue
5 mins. 16mm b&w Experimental
Dist. (U.S.): Frameline
Two girls cruise each other at a party.

Looking for a Space
(see *Buscando un Espacio: Los Homosexuales en Cuba*)

Looking for Langston
Dir. Julien, Isaac
1988 Great Britain English
40 mins. 16mm b&w Experimental
Dist. (U.K.): British Film Institute
The first time I saw Isaac Julien's *Looking for Langston* I sat utterly mesmerized by the film's complex poetic vison: for the first time in cine-ma, black homoerotic desire was given voice and concrete image. Saturated by film and literary portraits of homosexual life in which white men eternally occupied center stage, black gay communities across the country welcomed *Looking for Langston* with a collective sigh—of released frustration and nervous excitement, and ultimately profound visceral satisfaction at finally seeing some of our inner dreams and communal sensibilities captured so evocatively on screen.

What was especially delicious was the exceptional level of thought Julien's film displayed in addressing the politics of race and sexuality within the historical framework of the Harlem Renaissance. Almost from the first frame it was evident that Julien's "meditation" as he aptly described his experimental work, was not engaged in merely fabricating new, simplified "positive" images to challenge the distortions and silences of the past. Rather, the film's singular accomplishment was in illuminating the intrinsic hybridity—the multidimensionality—of African-American experience and cultural politics: race was not the be-all and end-all of black identity. Equally critical in understanding, articulating, and debating black identity politics were matters of sexuality, color consciousness within black society, class identification, and privilege. Black history as a consequence could thus be viewed from fresh perspectives, illuminating unconsciously overlooked and oftentimes deliberately suppressed information and experience that shape how blacks and nonblacks alike comprehend "the black experience." (M.R.)

Lord and Master
Dir. Boyd, Troy
1992 USA English
7 mins. video color Experimental
Dist. (U.K.): BBC TV
Lord and Master is not afraid to use S/M to raise questions about race.

Loredana
Dir. Milstead, J. D. Salome
1994 USA English
7 mins. 16mm b&w Experimental
Dist. (U.S.): Milstead, J. D. Salome
Another stunning evocation from one of San Francisco's most talented experimental filmmakers.

Lorenza
Dir. Stahlberg, Michael
1992 Germany German
20 mins. 35mm color Documentary

Ⓐ Ⓑ Ⓒ Ⓓ Ⓔ Ⓕ Ⓖ Ⓗ Ⓘ Ⓙ Ⓚ Ⓛ Ⓜ Ⓝ Ⓞ Ⓟ Ⓠ Ⓡ Ⓢ Ⓣ Ⓤ Ⓥ Ⓦ Ⓧ Ⓨ Ⓩ

Dist. (U.S.): Stahlberg, Michael/Hocschule fur Fernsetter und Film

A beautiful, eye-opening portrait of a campy, talented Chilean-German gay artist. Lorenza lost both his arms in an accident at age 9: "I came to be an exhibitionist by my handicap. People stare at me whether or not I dress flamboyantly."

Loss of Heat
Dir. Deville, Noski

1994 Great Britain English

20 mins. 16mm color Experimental

Dist. (U.S.): Women Make Movies

An expressive fictional portrayal of a pair of lesbian couples, one in Spain, the other in London, dealing with epilepsy.

Lost Heart, The
Dir. Vogelmann, Hilou

1993 Germany German

25 mins. 16mm color Narrative

Dist. (U.S.): Vogelmann, Hilou

A surprising fantasy/parable of repressed lesbian desire.

Lost Language of Cranes, The
Dir. Finch, Nigel

1992 Great Britain English

87 mins. 16mm color Narrative

Dist. (U.K.): BBC TV

Owen and Rose seem like a standard married middle-aged couple—except that Owen spends his Sundays sneaking off to a gay porno theater. Owen's closeted life falls apart when his happy, well-adjusted son Philip decides to come out as gay.

The Lost Language of Cranes is a BBC adaptation of David Leavitt's late-'80s novel, given a handsome Great Performances gloss by director Nigel Finch. Cranes, the movie, is a careful, classy, and painful melodrama of melancholy and miscommunication.

The main change is from the original story's New York Jewish setting to nondenominational suburban London; it works superbly. The mediocrity of England is the perfect metaphor for the claustrophobia all the characters feel. The film also captures the novel's wry humor, and was partly shot in real gay London locations—except for the porno theater scenes, which had to be invented (gay porn is illegal in Britain).

Lost Love
Dir. Zheutlin, Cathy

1982 USA English

12 mins. 16mm color Narrative

Dist. (U.S.): Frameline

A fanciful fantasy on the theme of lesbian heartbreak. Is there life after the end of a relationship?

Lost Lucy Episode, The
Dir. Wineland, Thom

1990 USA English

22 mins. video color Other

Dist. (U.S.): Wineland, Thom

Lucy insists Ethel help her discover their past lives with the aid of Dr. Shirley's New Age guidebook and a questionable dose of sleeping pills.

Lost Sleep
Dir. Black, Julie X.

1995 USA English

3 mins. 16mm color Narrative

Dist. (U.S.): Black, Julie X.

Two women experience Lost Sleep in a soft, soft bed.

Lot in Sodom
Dir. Webber, Melville, and James Watson

1933 USA English

20 mins. 16mm b&w Experimental

Dist. (U.S.): Em Gee Film Library

Inspired by German expressionism, Lot in Sodom is an early and important film in the history of American avant-garde cinema. The story of the Sodomites is told with pointed psychological confrontations, geometrical decors, and multiple superimposition of the same image echoing across the screen. The overlapping multiplies the sensual landscape of human flesh and gives a choreographic grace to the erotic movements of the Sodomites.

Louise Nevelson Takes a Bath
Dir. Walters, Jamie

1983 USA English

4 mins. video color Documentary

Dist. (U.S.): n/a

An in-depth overview of a world-famous sculptress and personality.

Love and Human Remains
Dir. Arcand, Denys
Prod. Frappier, Roger, Pierre Latour, Max Fils, and Atlantis Films

1993 Canada English

99 mins. 35mm color Narrative

Dist. (U.S.): Sony Pictures Classics/New Yorker

The combination of film director Denys Arcand and volatile gay playwright Brad Fraser may seem a bit odd, but Arcand's Love and Human

Remains is equal parts comedy, thriller, and human drama.

Fraser's award-winning play received critical accolades and has played to packed houses both in the States and in Canada. Unlike other stage adaptations, *Love and Human Remains*, which was written for the screen by Fraser himself, is adamantly cinematic. Strangely poignant and viciously funny, Arcand's vision of Fraser's controversial work studies the co-dependent relationships between a gay man and his friends.

Starring Thomas Gibson (bisexual Beecham in *Tales of the City*), as a twenty-something waiter/actor who was once a child TV star, *Love and Human Remains* intermingles the friends in his life; his straight best friend, a dead-on, lookalike for Rob Lowe; his roommate who is juggling two affairs, one with a beautiful but perky girl and a married man; and a prostitute who has an uncanny ability to have psychic visions about a serial killer stalking the streets of Toronto. Thrown into the mix are ex-lovers and a young man who has developed a crush for the aspiring actor.

Darkly romantic and comic, Arcand's first foray into the English language is fiercely un-American in its depiction of mature relationships between various genders and sexual identities, while still examining the undercurrents of a damaged generation.

Love and Lashes
Dir. Rowley, Adam
1993 Great Britain English
14 mins. video color Other
Dist. (U.K.): Rowley, Patrick
Enjoy the droll shenanigans of two British drag queens in *Love and Lashes*.

Love and Marriage
Dir. Ardill, Susan
1991 Great Britain English
40 mins. video color Documentary
Dist. (U.K.): Maya Vision
A documentary that looks at marriage in the lesbian and gay community. Produced for Britain's 1991 Out series on Channel Four, *Love and Marriage* is a discussion of the issues raised by the push for domestic partnership laws in Britain, the U.S. and Denmark. The spirited dialogue asks the questions: Would such laws be a truly radical initiative, or a complete sellout to the notion of equality with heterosexuals? Are lesbian and gay couples lucky to be free of the burden of marriage? What hidden legal pitfalls are being created for lesbians and gays with a "second class" of marriage?

Love Beneath a Neon Sky
Dir. Rey, Christina
1993 USA English
3 mins. video color Experimental
Dist. (U.S.): Fearless Productions Inc.
An evocative early short from the maker of *Change the Frame*.

Love Crisis
Dir. Amazon Broadcasting Company
1984 USA English
3 mins. video color Other
Dist. (U.S.): n/a
Humorous grassroots video.

Love, Jealousy and Revenge
(see *Liebe, Eifersucht und Rache*)

Love Like Any Other, A
Dir. Stempel, Hans, and Martin Ripkens
1982 Germany German
90 mins. 16mm color Narrative
A Love Like Any Other, the first feature film by Frankfurt film critics Hans Stempel and Martin Ripkens, is the story of a young gay couple in Berlin. Wieland, a teacher, and Wolf, a bookseller, live a quiet, amiable, and affectionate life together, keenly aware of social responsibility and domestic decorum. The danger that emerges as a threat to their marriage is their need to conform to the norms of a middle-class, heterosexual lifestyle. Wolf's dream of opening an antiquarian bookstore is shattered by Wieland's refusal to give up the security of his civil service career. Wieland sympathizes with a group demanding "squatters' rights" but withdraws his support when reprimanded by the director of his school. The couple seem willing to compromise in every situation, including their love relationship, which is more conservative than either of them realize. While they do allow themselves sexual adventures with other men—and they speak proudly of their promiscuity—they are in no way prepared to involve themselves with other people. Their relationship with a young artist ends when he exposes their outwardly emancipated life together as being, ultimately, a mere variant of middle-class, possession-related living.

Love Machine, The
Dir. Snee, Patrick
1994 USA English
20 mins. 16mm color Narrative

Ⓐ Ⓑ Ⓒ Ⓓ Ⓔ Ⓕ Ⓖ Ⓗ Ⓘ Ⓙ Ⓚ Ⓛ Ⓜ Ⓝ Ⓞ Ⓟ Ⓠ Ⓡ Ⓢ Ⓣ Ⓤ Ⓥ Ⓦ Ⓧ Ⓨ Ⓩ

Dist. (U.S.): Snee, Patrick
A comedy about codependency and cheap tricks.

Love Makes a Family
Dir. Leech, Maria, Dan Veltri,
and Remco Kobus
1992 USA English
30 mins. video color Documentary
Dist. (U.S.): Veltri, Dan
A Bay Area–made portrait of three families, demonstrating different ways that lesbians and gays are becoming parents today. Open-captioned for the hearing impaired.

Love on the Line
Dir. Beckman, K. O.
Prod. Doff, Jonathan
1985 USA English
1 mins. video color Narrative
Dist. (U.S.): Sirus
A short, sexy piece about man, woman, and telephone that is a delightful turn-on with snappy music by "Blue" Gene Tyranny.

Love Strikes Hard
Dir. Seidler, Ellen
1994 USA English
5 mins. video color Other
Dist. (U.S.): Seidler, Ellen
A music video about lesbian love and lust.

Love that Dare Not Speak Its Name, The
Dir. Maxwell, Isabel
1982 Great Britain English
27 mins. 16mm color Documentary
Dist. (U.S.): n/a
This film looks with honesty and sensitivity at the lifestyles of five homosexual women and seeks to lift the veil of fear and explode some of the myths surrounding lesbianism.

Love Triangle
Dir. Wolfe, Kathy
1985 USA English
3 mins. video color Other
Dist. (U.S.): Wolfe Video
A Gayle Marie music video.

Love/Sex
Dir. Decent, Dean R.
1985 USA English
8 mins. video color Other
Dist. (U.S.): Decent, Dean R.
Dean Decent studies the organic relationship between Love/Sex.

Loverville

Dir. Zachary, Bohdan
1992 USA English
6 mins. video color Other
Dist. (U.S.): Zachary, Bohdan
Loverville offers a misanthropic commentary on Valentine's Day and gay male coupledom.

Loverville 2: The Honeymoon
Dir. Zachary, Bohdan
1993 USA English
10 mins. 16mm color Other
Dist. (U.S.): Zachary, Bohdan
Starts with the return of Scott Capurro's annoying ex-roommates. The dexterous duo take a celebration trip to Paris, where a garçon comes between them and their romance. Thanks to the miracle of modern special effects, *Loverville 2* was shot entirely in director Bohdan Zachary's kitchen in San Francisco.

Lucifer Rising
Dir. Anger, Kenneth
1980 USA English
30 mins. 16mm color Experimental
Dist. (U.S.): Canyon Cinema
Dist. (U.K.): British Film Institute
"*Lucifer Rising* . . . is perhaps Anger's most ambitious work to date; its subject—Lucifer, the fallen angel—has possessed and inspired Anger for a decade. Christian theology views Lucifer as the personification of evil; Anger's task was to depict him as a bringer of light, God's beautiful but rebellious favorite. Edited in a number of forms during the past ten years, Anger's *Lucifer Rising* has consistently displayed magnificent landscape and seascape cinematography as well as memorable performances by Marianne Faithfull, Anger himself (as the Magus), and prominent members of London's cultural scene. For the expanded edition, however, Anger has recut the entire work and added a haunting music track recorded behind the walls of Tracy Prison by his original Lucifer, Bobby Beausoleil, now serving a life sentence there.
"Anger has called *Lucifer Rising* 'visual music,' it awakens ideas and feelings almost without the aid of characters or story. The viewer, like Lucifer, awakens mysteriously, magically to a new vision of the world in which everything is miraculous and strange."
—American Federation of the Arts

Ludwig
Dir. Visconti, Luchino
1973 Italy/France/Germany Italian

173246 mins. 35mm color Narrative
Dist. (U.K.): British Film Institute
Continuing a late *Damned/Death in Venice*/etc. vein of aristocratic homosexual angst, Visconti settled on what seemed a perfect vehicle for his slightly dotty, grand talent: the 19th-century gay "mad king" who built enormous fantasy castles and nearly bankrupted Bavaria. The film was brutally reedited by distributors, then released to dismal response. Yet in its intended, four-hour form (restored by collaborators after the director's death), Ludwig still has a glassy, undecided quality, as if Visconti had grown suddenly embarrassed by his identification with the subject. Even the all-male orgy scene seems lethargic. Being crazy, whimsical, very rich, and readily supplied with boy-toys must have been more fun than you'd guess at here. Oft-dissed Visconti protege Helmut Berger isn't bad as the monarch; Romy Schneider livens things up as a merry royal relative. Slow, handsome, of interest mostly to devotees. (D.H.)

Lugar Sin Limites, El
(A Limitless Place/Hell Without Limits)
Dir. Ripstein, Arturo
1977 Mexico Spanish
110 mins. 35mm color Narrative
Dist. (U.S.): Azteca Films
La Manuela is a drag queen living with his daughter in the whorehouse they own on the edge of a dying town in rural Mexico. Both are drawn to, yet fearful of, Pancho, a brutal man who has never been able to accept the attraction he feels for La Manuela. When Pancho's violent behavior surfaces (and it does so regularly) and he begins to torment the young daughter, demanding that she strip in the brothel's saloon, La Manuela comes to her rescue, boldly seducing the raging Pancho with a dance that leads to a passionate kiss. *Hell Without Limits* is a moving story of sexual oppression in the Third World that rises above simple melodrama, largely thanks to the creation of its strong central character, La Manuela. By the film's final scenes he has grown from a flighty, effeminate cliché into the moral core of the film. He is far more honest about himself than any of the other characters and emerges, after a series of agonizing confrontations, as a truly heroic figure. Director Arturo Ripstein began his film career in 1963 when he worked as Luis Buñuel's assistant on *The Exterminating Angel* and *Simon of the Desert*. *Hell Without Limits* is his ninth film as director.

Luminous Procuress
Dir. Arnold, Steven
1971 USA English
87 mins. 16mm color Narrative
Dist. (U.S.): n/a
A major avant-garde success in the early 1970s, this film by Steven Arnold was shot in San Francisco and features the legendary comedy/drag group The Cockettes. We follow two naive young men in their journey through an elaborate bordello comprised of a strange combination of cloisters and chambers, jungle grottos and ivied forests, banquet halls and temples—all of it located in an undefinable area of time and space. Bizarre and erotic, *Luminous Procuress* was greeted with rave reviews by even mainstream critics when it was released in 1971. Molly Haskell in the *Village Voice* called it "a West coast *Satyricon*" while the *L.A. Times* said it is a "strangely compelling, highly imaginative work of unabashed hedonism."

Luna Tune
Dir. Clement, Carol
1978 USA English
2 mins. 16mm color Other
Dist. (U.S.): Women Make Movies
Lesa Gidlow reads her poetry, accompanied by sand animation in *Luna Tune*.

Lune
Dir. Eltringham, Billie
1993 Great Britain English
28 mins. 16mm color Narrative
Dist. (U.S.): Bournemouth Film School (Barbara Hawkins)
A precocious girl with a serious crush pursues an older woman in the charming seaside romance, *Lune*.

Luppies
(see *Out On Tuesday, Program 1*)

Luscious Brite
Dir. Fischer, Karl E.
1982 USA English
2 mins. 16mm color Other
Dist. (U.S.): n/a
An on-target parody of an all-too-familiar television commercial.

Lush Life
Dir. Conroy, Dennis, and David E. Johnston
1994 USA English
7 mins. video color Experimental
Dist. (U.S.): Conroy, Dennis

Ⓐ Ⓑ Ⓒ Ⓓ Ⓔ Ⓕ Ⓖ Ⓗ Ⓘ Ⓙ Ⓚ **Ⓛ** Ⓜ Ⓝ Ⓞ Ⓟ Ⓠ Ⓡ Ⓢ Ⓣ Ⓤ Ⓥ Ⓦ Ⓧ Ⓨ Ⓩ

Voyeurism, sado-masochistic fantasy, and masturbatory hallucinations.

M. Butterfly
Dir. Cronenberg, David
1993 USA English
100 mins. 35mm color Narrative
Dist. (U.S.): Swank Motion Pictures
Although *M. Butterfly* doesn't exactly have wings, it takes up where *The Crying Game* and *Orlando* left off in the gender-envelope. Like the ever-winking *Orlando*, John Lone's purposely unfeminine Butterfly puts the audience in a conspiratorial position against the hapless white male protagonist. And as there was in *The Crying Game*, there is, of course, the hoax, but this surprise shifts the audience position from sympathy for the "devil" to sympathy for the diva. (S.G.)

M-A-S-S
Dir. Pavlow, Bruce
1981 USA English
29 mins. video color Narrative
Dist. (U.S.): n/a
M-A-S-S poses as a postmodern TV mystery. A gay sensibility lurks behind the screen.

Ma Vie
Dir. Langlois, Denis
1992 Canada English
21 mins. 16mm color Narrative
Dist. (U.S.): Cinema Libre
Denis Langlois describes his protagonist's life from 1968 to 2038 (Chapter 1: his confused mom's violent reaction to his hippieish coming out; Chapter 5: the appeal of stripped pine and casual sex; Chapter 13: postmodernism).

Macho Dancer
Dir. Brocka, Lino
1987 Philippines Filipino
133 mins. 35mm color Narrative
Dist. (U.S.): Strand Releasing
In the landscape of Lino Brocka's *Macho Dancer*, sexual agency is inseparable from economic necessity. The film follows the travails of Pol (Allan Paole), a young man from the provinces who migrates to Manila after his American GI sugar daddy leaves and cuts off his family's sole source of income. After finding work as a go-go boy and male prostitute, Pol meets his mentor, Noel (Daniel Fernando). Their camaraderie lapses into shower dances and porn videos as Pol becomes enmeshed in Noel's search for his sister, who has been abducted to work in a brothel. When Noel is killed, Pol avenges his friend's murder and eventually returns to the countryside alone.

Using the conventions of equatorial melodrama, Brocka has tried to infuse the story with a harsh materialist read on the nature of human relations and love. But ultimately it's hampered by his inability to subvert the conventions of the melodrama. The audience is implicated in the voyeurism of sex tourists but never asked to interrogate their own position in relation to what's unfolding on screen. (L.C.)

Macumba
Dir. Mikesch, Elfi
1981 Germany German
88 mins. 16mm color Experimental
Dist. (U.S.): Frameline
Macumba is a smart allegory about phallocentrically structured language and thinking. It seeks to show, in an anarchistic and creative way, the expression of pleasure and the eroticism of women.

Isabel is lying on the roof terrace of a Berlin house, recalling an indefinable desire that she calls "Macumba," a desire that is somehow connected to a passion for destruction. Vincent is on the roof as well. His point of view, his movement, the ground under his feet— everything is unstable, which he enjoys. In the midst of the demolition of their house Isabel and her friends encounter Max Taurus, a private detective. He has no idea that he has entered a dead end. Only after rejecting his "square way of thinking" can Isabel follow her own fantasies and wishes. She starts to write several stories, ready to abandon them once she becomes bored. The story of Frank Tannenzauber whose nihilistic narcissism initially fascinates but soon repels her, leads her to denounce the virtues of violence. Isabel is intrigued by Franciska who is feeling powerful and wants to leave, longing for "something else." Isabel allows Franciska to seduce her. Franciska stays. Or was it just a dream? "And we imagined a love beyond hope," Isabel says.

Mad about the Boy
Dir. Umen, Alix, and Lisel Banker
1994 USA English
8 mins. video b&w Other
Dist. (U.S.): Video Data Bank
A pixel vision montage about the lesbian saga of being mistaken for a boy.

Mad, Mad World of Stella Slick, The
Dir. unknown
1982 USA English

3 mins. 16mm color Experimental
Dist. (U.S.): n/a
Splintered chaotic imagery and the best of popular music.

Madagascar Skin
Dir. Newby, Chris
Prod. Baines, Julie
1995 Great Britain English
93 mins. 35mm color Narrative
Dist. (U.K.): British Film Institute
The thing about Chris Newby's *Madagascar Skin*. The thing that sharpens its style and sharp, often local, humor with substance. The thing is, in a way, we've all been there. Although surrounded by pumped and primped muscle queens at a gay British disco, Harry is very much alone. His face stained by a large red birthmark in the shape of the island of Madagascar, Harry manages to insinuate himself into a backroom threesome only to be rejected once the lights come on. Despondent and suicidial, he drives to the coast and breaks down on a rocky beach, his car covered in kelp. One day, he discovers an upturned bucket on the beach and under it, the badly bruised and comatose head of Flint, who's been buried up to his neck in the sand for the tide to claim. Harry rescues this burly tattooed man and the two begin a strangely domestic life in an appropriated seaside cottage.

Interest leads to affection which swells into desire. Director Newby (*Anchoress*, and the shorts *Relax* and *Kiss*) places an indordinate emphasis on forging an aesthetic beauty out of slimy, weatherbeaten life. His camera draws out pale blue and black warmth in the most overcast gray. *Madagascar Skin* is a film that unfolds in small, daily gestures and exchanges, but it shuns conventional cinematic "reality" for the trippier fields of passion. It suggests the ways we can imagine a love informed by class affinities, and desire that transgresses the commercial dictates of bio-consumerism and corporal fascism. (L.C.)

Madame Simone
Dir. Allard, Martin
1992 Canada English
12 mins. video color Narrative
Dist. (U.S.): Allard, Martin
From Sydney's Mardi Gras to New York Wigstock: *Madame Simone* is a short portrait of a beyond-grunge drag queen. M. Simone hears voices inside her head—compelling her to travel all the way from Canada to Wigstock to unleash her

high-scream, six-arm, Lt. Uhura–style outfit.

Madame X—Eine Absolute Herrscherin (Madame X—An Absolute Ruler)
Dir. Ottinger, Ulrike
1977 Germany German
141 mins. 16mm color Experimental
Dist. (U.S.): Exportfilm Bischoff & Co.
The bizarre and imaginative story of Madame X, the cruel, uncrowned ruler of the China Seas, who sends an appeal to all women to exchange their everyday safe, but boring existences for a world of uncertainty and danger, but also for a world full of love and adventure.

Made for TV
Dir. Rubnitz, Tom
1984 USA English
15 mins. video color Other
Dist. (U.S.): Video Data Bank
Made for TV features a tour de farce performance by Ann Magnuson in about 50 zillion roles (her Lena Lovich is a scream!). Part of the *Tom Rubnitz Marathon (A Dozen Tapes, Wigs Included)*.

Madonna and Child
Dir. Davies, Terence
1980 Great Britain English
30 mins. 16mm b&w Narrative
Dist. (U.S.): Frameline
Dist. (U.K.): British Film Institute
The second in a trilogy of films that present the portrait, from childhood to the grave, of Robert Tucker, a lower-middle-class Liverpool homosexual, tormented by the conflicts of religion, guilt, and frustration over his masochistic homosexuality, childhood nightmares, and compulsive social respectability. In these harsh black-and-white movies Davies's impressionistic style appears to pay homage to the Japanese master Yasujiro Ozu, with shots that linger over quiet, empty rooms. Released as part of a package of three films by Terence Davies, *The Terence Davies Trilogy*.

Madonna In Me
Dir. Leder, Evie
1993 USA English
4 mins. video color Experimental
Dist. (U.S.): Leder, Evie
A personal exploration of Madonna videos, and sex.

Mädchen In Uniform (1931)
Dir. Sagan, Leontine
1931 Germany German

Ⓐ Ⓑ Ⓒ Ⓓ Ⓔ Ⓕ Ⓖ Ⓗ Ⓘ Ⓙ Ⓚ Ⓛ Ⓜ Ⓝ Ⓞ Ⓟ Ⓠ Ⓡ Ⓢ Ⓣ Ⓤ Ⓥ Ⓦ Ⓧ Ⓨ Ⓩ

90 mins. 16mm b&w Narrative
Dist. (U.S.): Films Incorporated
An enduring lesbian classic, *Mädchen In Uniform* was an immediate popular and critical success when it was released in 1931. In Germany it was generally considered the best film of the year, while in New York, the *World Telegram* called it "the year's ten best programs rolled into one." The reviewer for the *New York Herald Tribune*, echoing the prevalent critical assumption at the time, summed up the film's theme as: "the drama of the need for tenderness and sympathy as opposed to the harshness of a tyranical system of boarding school domination."

While educational tyranny is certainly in the foreground of Mädchen's narrative, film historians, until recent years, have been unable to see the film as an antifascist, specifiaclly anti-Nazi metaphor. What seems today to be so clearly a story of lesbian love has for years been shrouded in safe, suspiciously guarded interpretation. A young girl at a German boarding school falls wildly, hopelessly in love with her beautiful young teacher, a woman who wants desperately to respond to another woman. Their story is brilliantly portrayed. The struggle against sexual repression that forms the core of the film can no longer be ignored. Director Leontine Sagan is well known for her unusual, avant-garde montage style and superb use of sound.

Mädchen In Uniform (1957)
Dir. von Radvanyi, Geza
1957 Germany German
91 mins. 35mm color Narrative
Dist. (U.S.): Altermedia
The classic story of the infatuation of a schoolgirl for her tender teacher was first filmed in 1931. This 1957 version, starring Lilli Palmer and Romy Schneider, is much more lavish, in color, and influenced as much by Hollywood as by pre-war Germany. The setting is still a turn-of-the-century girls' boarding school in Germany, and the theme remains the struggle for love in an authoritarian system, but the luminous presence of Palmer (Fraulein von Bernberg) and Schneider (Manuela) and the openness and emotion of their performances give this newer version great impact.

This version of *Mädchen In Uniform* was released in the United States very briefly in 1965, and has remained unseen here since then.

Magic Cottage
Dir. Orr, Joe

1993 Great Britain English
30 mins. video color Narrative
Dist. (U.K.): Orr, Joe
A hilarious, provocative spoof on *Night of the Living Dead.*

Maidens
Dir. Thornley, Jeni
1978 Australia English
33 mins. 16mm color Documentary
Dist. (U.S.): Sydney Filmmakers Cooperative
A film of poetic intensity, colliding images, and lucid personal narration. *Maidens* is a compilation documentary of four generations of the filmmaker's maternal family (from 1906–1977) using images drawn from old family photos to slides, home movies, and excerpts from historical Ausralian womens films.

Making of "Monsters," The
Dir. Greyson, John
1990 Canada English
35 mins. 16mm color Experimental
Dist. (U.S.): Canadian Film Centre
With musical numbers like "I Hate Straights" and a catfish playing the role of Bertold Brecht, *The Making of "Monsters"* explores the culture of antigay violence in North America.

Making of "The Lost Language of Cranes," The
Dir. Skeet, Brian
1992 Great Britain English
10 mins. video color Documentary
Dist. (U.K.): BBC TV
A BBC adaptation of David Leavitt's famous late-'80s gay novel. Brian Skeet's crisp film about the movie's production—made for BBC's nightly arts series, "The Late Show"—concentrates on the translation from Leavitt's New York Jewish setting to nondenominational suburban London.
Skeet's film also offers a sideways look at how things are done at the BBC.

Mala Noche
Dir. Van Sant, Gus
1985 USA English
78 mins. 35mm color/b&w Narrative
Dist. (U.S.): n/a
Filmed on the streets of Portland, Oregon, *Mala Noche* is a stunning, ultra-realistic look at a younger gay man's unrequited love for a 16-year-old illegal alien from Mexico. Walt, who is openly and happily gay, lives and works among the transients, winos, and migrant workers that make up Portland's skid row. When he meets Johnny he

develops a hopelessly doomed passion that he seems to know is pointless and unrealistic but can't seem to shake.

Director Gus Van Sant has created a beautiful, highly stylized black-and-white film that features a charming, understated performance by Tim Streeter as Walt. The anguish he feels over his obsessive attachment to a non-English-speaking, frightened teenager is at once pathetic and completely understandable—the characters and milieu are that well defined.

Mala Noche has been compared to *Stranger Than Paradise* and it does have a similar low-key realistic tone, but Van Sant's visual style is infinitely more interesting. It suits perfectly his original, matter-of-fact depiction of Walt, one of the most believable, likable gay characters seen in years.

Mala Noche's gritty, reckless-seeming style—and its story of passionate delinquency—prefigures the pleasures of *My Own Private Idaho* and *Drugstore Cowboy*.

Malaysian Series, Part 1-6
Dir. Nurudin, Azian
1987 USA English
15 mins. video color Experimental
Dist. (U.S.): Frameline
Azian Nurudin gets things cracking with a whip and a TV in *Malaysian Series, Part 1*. The series continues with a succession of performances, whipping and beating various objects.

Male Escorts of San Francisco: Raphael, the Call Bear [excerpt]
Dir. Link, Matthew
1992 USA English
10 mins. video color Documentary
Dist. (U.S.): Link, Matthew
An interview with San Francisco's first bear-for-hire.

Male Escorts of San Francisco, The
Dir. Link, Matthew
1992 USA English
42 mins. video color Documentary
Dist. (U.S.): Link, Matthew
Matthew Link interviews six different men in his thoughtful, unsensational tape, *The Male Escorts of San Francisco*. It answers almost all the questions you might ever have, and offers a different take on America's favorite city.

Male Gayze, The
Dir. Waters, Jack
1990 USA English

11 mins. video color Experimental
Dist. (U.S.): Naked Eyed Cinema
A dancer relates a salutary anecdote about losing a competition in Europe and being courted by one of the judges—who turns out to be fixed on exploiting his image. "If there's a distinction between pornography and erotica," says the narrator, "then pornography always produces a victim." The voice-over is paired with what seems like home movie footage; in the mismatch, it raises provocative questions about power and relationships. What are the ramifications of the "twisted" affair between this black man and the Afrophile choreographer?

Man I Love, The
Dir. Comstock, William
1994 USA English
3 mins. video color Other
Dist. (U.S.): Comstock, William
A beautiful found footage montage reflection on love.

Man Like Eva, A
(see *Mann Wie Eva, Ein*)

Man of No Importance, A
Dir. Krishnamma, Suri
1995 Great Britain English
100 mins. 35mm color Narrative
Dist. (U.S.): Sony Picture Classics
Lovingly acted and crafted, this *Masterpiece Theatre*-style seriocomedy recalls seminal Brit liberal-humanist dramas like *A Taste of Honey*, and is set in the same repressive early 1960s milieu. Albert Finney plays Alfie, a bus conductor whose en-route "performances" endear him to daily patrons, even as they embarrass the hunky driver (Rufus Sewell) he secretly pines for. When Alfie tries to stage Oscar Wilde's Salome on the local church stage, and casts an unwed young mother (Tara Fitzgerald) in the title role, all prudish hell breaks loose. The film is witty and touching by turns. Yet you might wonder why at this late date we're still making/watching films about pitiable, twinkle-eyed homosexuals who sacrifice everything for others—and neither expect nor get much happiness for themselves. It's that old catch-22: Gays seem most lovable (or at least least threatening) when rendered essentially sexless. (D.H.)

Man of the Year
Dir. Shafer, Dirk
Prod. Keener, Matt
1994 USA English

Ⓐ Ⓑ Ⓒ Ⓓ Ⓔ Ⓕ Ⓖ Ⓗ Ⓘ Ⓙ Ⓚ Ⓛ Ⓜ Ⓝ Ⓞ Ⓟ Ⓠ Ⓡ Ⓢ Ⓣ Ⓤ Ⓥ Ⓦ Ⓧ Ⓨ Ⓩ

87 mins. 35mm color/b&w Narrative
Dist. (U.S.): Artisan Productions
This debut autobiographical feature from Dirk Shafer combines fiction and documentary to portray his story, about how he became 1992's *Playgirl* "Man of the Year."

Maneaters
Dir. Zen, Michael
1984 USA English
90 mins. 16mm color Narrative
Dist. (U.S.): n/a
Continuing the legend of Falconhead, director Michael Zen returns once again to the man-eating mirror that devours the bodies and souls of young narcissistic men. What could have been a routine porno film, is actually a highly stylized and beautifully photographed work of eroticism that avoids the clichés and slipshod technical values of the average gay adult film.

Mano Destra
Dir. Ueblemann, Cleo
1986 Germany German
53 mins. 16mm b&w Experimental
Dist. (U.S.): London Film Makers Co-op
Dist. (U.K.): London Film Makers Co-op
Cleo Ueblemann's *Mano Destra* is a relentless physiological experience of cinematic bondage and sensory manipulation. A European lesbian cult classic, this is S/M cinema.

Manuel Y Clemente
(Manuel and Clemente)
Dir. Romero, Javier Palmero
1985 Spain Spanish
93 mins. 35mm color Narrative
Dist. (U.S.): Spanish Ministry of Culture
Manuel and Clemente, lovers and employees of a church-owned insurance company, dream of being successful in life and are drawn to El palmar de Troya where there is a dubious yet prosperous trade in religious icons and relics. Manuel and Clemente see their chance; posing as a "prophet," Clemente initially is a great success as a visionary. When the insurance company learns what the pair is up to in their spare time, they are dismissed and must survive solely on the alms Clemente collects for his visions. Winning support from a group of millionaires, the resourceful couple manages to purchase the land they use for their apparitions, cutting out the competition. Still lacking the support of the Church, they manage to convince an old Vietnamese bishop to inaugurate them as priests,

then as bishops. When the pope dies in Rome, Clement appoints himself to the office of the Holy Father. The pair's dreams have all come true.

Manuela's Loves
(see *Le Jupon Rouge*)

Mara
Dir. Linders, Angela
1985 Netherlands Danish
58 mins. 16mm color Narrative
Dist. (U.S.): Netherlands Ministry of Culture
Looking for her Portuguese lover, Mara has traveled to Lisbon where, in search of Luisa, she ultimately finds herself. In a kaleidoscope of memory, fantasy, and reality, Mara wanders through the breathtaking landscape of coastal Portugal reflecting on their past love.

With a style remniscent of Maya Deren and Stan Brakhage, director Angela Linders brings the viewer into Mara's psychological turmoil of trying to relive the past.

Marching for Freedom
Dir. Landy, Craig
1993 USA English
78 mins. video color Documentary
Dist. (U.S.): Project 1993 Productions
The definitive you-are-there experience of the March on Washington, D.C.

Marcial's Version
(see *Version de Marcial, La*)

Margaret and Adele
Dir. Gundlach, Daniel, Jerry Freeman, and Judith Freeman
1981 USA English
30 mins. 16mm b&w Documentary
Dist. (U.S.): Gundlach, Daniel
A captivating film that shows the relationship between a very unique Jewish mother and her developmentally-disabled daughter during the last days of the mother's life. The moody still photography used in much of the film gives it a quiet, almost somber look, which contrasts eerily with a soundtrack consisting largely of Adele's story-telling and Margaret's enthusiastic piano playing.

Margaret Atwood and the Problem with Canada
Dir. MacIvor, Daniel
1993 Canada English
6 mins. video color Other
Dist. (U.S.): Da Da Kamera

Daniel MacIvor's amazingly hilarious diatribe/portrait of a beer-drinking, chain-smoking queen who saw Margaret Atwood in a restaurant and proceeds to tell us all about *Margaret Atwood and the Problem with Canada.*

Mark Called
Dir. Lux, Billy
1993 USA English
4 mins. 16mm color Narrative
Dist. (U.S.): Lux, Billy
Mark Called is a road-poem romp through the rodeo, country fairs, and tourist attractions, with steamy promises at journey's end.

Mark of Lilith, The
Dir. Fionda, Bruna, Polly Gladwin, and Isiling Mack-Nataf
1986 Great Britain English
32 mins. 16mm color Narrative
Dist. (U.S.): Women Make Movies
Dist. (U.K.): Cinenova
Lilia, a white bisexual vampire, meets up with a black lesbian researcher, whose perspectives jolt her out of a blindness caused by patriarchal society.

Marta: Portrait of a Teen Activist
Dir. Ebert, Matt
1992 USA English
10 mins. video color Other
Dist. (U.S.): Ebert, Matt
A spoof on queer activists.

Mason's Life
Dir. Lowy, Peter
1979 USA English
13 mins. 16mm b&w Narrative
Dist. (U.S.): Lowy, Peter
A Kingsley Amis story with a gay twist. Honorable Mention: American Photographic Society

Massillon
Dir. Jones, William
1992 USA English
70 mins. 16mm color Experimental
Dist. (U.S.): Drift Distribution
Describing his hometown of Massillon, Ohio William Jones writes in his program notes, "I lived in Massillon for eighteen years of my life; I returned for a while to find beauty in this place, but also to rid myself of its influence."

"Ohio is the birthplace of psychos," Jones exclaims in a 1992 interview for *The Advocate.* "I know people who went to school with Jeffrey Dahmer. I have a considerable amount of pride about being from Ohio." He hesitates and adds ponderously, "I don't know if that comes across in the film."

Massillon is a remarkably sensual film, evoking a feel of the Midwest in essence—seasons change, wind blows, birds chirp, cars pass by, cows stand in a field—you are there. Divided into three parts (Ohio, The Law, and California), *Massillon* ranges through the personal to the political and back again. The film's gentle editing is complemented by the reassuring intonation of Jones's voice-over as he describes his childhood, his researching of state sodomy laws, and the etymology of the language of sexuality.

"The original inspiration was actually when I recorded this fundamendalist radio preacher in July of 1986," he explains. "I was 23 years old, and living in Ohio at the time." The radio preacher's tirade about the Supreme Court's upholding of the Georgia state sodomy law in the Hardwick decision, serves as the soundtrack at the center of the film.

In the first part of the film, road signs, construction sites, churches, fields, and highway overpasses fill the screen as Jones relates anecdotes of growing up gay in a small town in Ohio. In the last part of the film, the arid landscapes of his new home in Santa Clarita, California, are accompanied by his voice-over analysis of theories of homosexuality. A very dense concluding quotation from Diderot ties the film's strands of personal sexual politics into a brilliant knot of childhood memories, etymological meanings, and historical analysis.

Jones continues, "The film begins in a way that leads the spectator into a voyeuristic position. But that voyeurism isn't indulged, it's frustrated—one never gets to see the things that are described. This was a way of luring the spectator into a place where all sorts of things could be explained and our assumptions about sexuality could be examined on the most fundamental level."

Challenging some of the most firmly entrenched conventions of filmmaking, Massillon has no human actors and consists almost entirely of long, static, landscape shots.

Massillon's methodical pace, thoughtful compositions, and sensual concern with sound and image place it clearly within a particular tradition of experimental filmmaking. "Of all the filmmakers I list as influences, and that I admire, lesbians are sort of prominent in this list," Jones notes. "For experimental, or

Ⓐ
Ⓑ
Ⓒ
Ⓓ
Ⓔ
Ⓕ
Ⓖ
Ⓗ
Ⓘ
Ⓙ
Ⓚ
Ⓛ
Ⓜ
Ⓝ
Ⓞ
Ⓟ
Ⓠ
Ⓡ
Ⓢ
Ⓣ
Ⓤ
Ⓥ
Ⓦ
Ⓧ
Ⓨ
Ⓩ

challenging, cinema lesbians are really ahead of gay men, or have been in the last ten or twenty years. I made my film hoping to utilize some of the great strengths of films by great filmmakers—who happen to be lesbian." Explaining his affinity for lesbian films, Jones adds, "Inasmuch as they are informed by a certain kind of feminism, they are necessarily distrustful of a certain kind of spectacle which unfortunately continues to characterize a lot of gay men's film." One might compare Jones's film to works by Chantal Akerman, Su Friedrich, or Ulrike Ottinger; all filmmakers he mentions as influences on his own work.

Identifying as a gay filmmaker, Jones is articulate about balancing his passion for film as a medium and having a gay political consciousness. "I hope that the two could be combined in some way that's rigourous and thoughtful. I made the only film my conscience would let me make and I'd like to think that I could continue to make that kind of film. And it happens that gay subjects are the nearest and dearest to my heart." (J.O.)

Matsumae-Kun No Senritsu (Melody For Buddy Matsumae)
Dir. Oki, Hiroyuki
1992 Japan No Dialogue
50 mins. 16mm color Experimental
Dist. (U.S.): Image Forum, Tokyo
The last film in Oki's Matsumae trilogy—*Melody for Buddy Matsumae*—chronicles ten days spent in a seaside town: five of them with a visiting boyfriend, and five more after his departure.

Matter of Life and Death, A
(see *Out On Tuesday, Program 1*)

Maurice
Dir. Ivory, James
1987 Great Britain English
140 mins. 35mm color Narrative
Dist. (U.S.): October Films
Dist. (U.K.): British Film Institute
It was a fairly brave move on director James Ivory and producer Ismail Merchant's part to follow up their hit *A Room with a View* with this less popularly viable E.M. Forster adaptation. James Wilby plays the pedigreed protagonist whose public life in 1910s England constantly struggles against his private sexual inclinations. In the end, he abandons all in favor of love with a lower-class worker. Mounted with the duo's usual period decorousness and typically well acted (by a cast

including Hugh Grant, Rupert Graves, Denholm Elliott, Billie Whitelaw, and Ben Kingsley), *Maurice* suffers nonetheless from faithfulness to its source material. While the gay theme may have been close to Forster's heart (close enough for him to hide the manuscript until after death), it did not occasion his finest literary hour. Earnest, admirable, but rather plodding, just like the book. (D.H.)

Mauvaise Conduite (Improper Conduct)
Dir. Almendros, Nestor, and Orlando Jiminez Leal
Prod. les Film du Losange
1984 France French
115 mins. 35mm color Documentary
Dist. (U.S.): Cinevista
Improper Conduct breaks an uncomfortable and unnecessary silence by exposing the oppression of gays that has accompanied Castro's Cuban Revolution, now 25 years old. By documenting victims (artists and homosexuals scattered around the world) *Improper Conduct* creates a uniquely challenging film experience. One that asks the politically sophisticated as well as naive to recognize the ugly truth: The persecution of homosexuals exist even when other forms of persecution have been condemned.

Winner of the 1984 San Francisco International Lesbian & Gay Film Festival Audience Award for Best Documentary.

Maya
Dir. Benedek, Catherine
1992 USA English
10 mins. 16mm b&w Narrative
Dist. (U.S.): Frameline
Maya's mother wants her to get married. But she falls for a woman in her Afro-Caribbean dance class.

Maybe I Can Give You Sex ? Part One
Dir. Bruning, Jurgen, and Rune Layumas
1992 Philippines/Germany
30 mins. video color Documentary
Dist. (U.S.): Jurgen Bruning Filmproduktion
Confronting the issues of racism, sexism, and neocolonialism, *Maybe I Can Give You Sex?* is a two-part collaboration between Rune Layumas in Manila and Jurgen Bruning in Berlin. These tapes look at the construction of male gender roles in the Philippines and examines the lives of macho dancers, bar boys, and their customers.

Maybe I Can Give You Sex ? Part Two
Dir. Layumas, Rune, and Jurgen Bruning

1992 Germany/Philippines
19 mins. video color Documentary
Dist. (U.S.): Jurgen Bruning Filmproduktion
See description above.

Mayhem
Dir. Child, Abigail
1987 USA English
20 mins. 16mm color Experimental
Dist. (U.S.): Canyon Cinema
An homage to film noir with soap opera thrillers and Mexican comic books generating the action. The film links the screen, the bedroom, and the streets to create a mosaic of the way modern culture sends mixed signals about sexuality to men and women.

Me and Mrs. Jones
Dir. Zoller, Claudia
1994 Germany German
16 mins. video color Other
Dist. (U.S.): Zoller, Claudia
A glimpse at the beginnings of a romantic affair, set to the tune of "Me & Mrs. Jones."

Me and Rubyfruit
Dir. Benning, Sadie
1989 USA English
4 mins. video b&w Experimental
Dist. (U.S.): Video Data Bank
Dist. (U.K.): London Video Access
In *Me and Rubyfruit*, Benning offers a wonderfully personal take on *Rubyfruit Jungle*.

Me & Mrs. Berger
(see *Ich und Frau Berger*)

Me Show, The
Dir. Canalli, John
1983 USA English
15 mins. video color Other
Dist. (U.S.): n/a
A theatrical presentation on the definitive statement on self-indulgent and mutual admiration societies.

Media Blackmale
Dir. Bruno, Wendell
1992 Canada English
5 mins. video color Documentary
Dist. (U.S.): Bruno, Wendell
An angry, eloquent (and anti-Mapplethorpe?) tape.

Meet Johnny Eagle
Prod. Baron Infinity Mind, O.D.C.
1981 Canada English

5 mins. video color Documentary
Dist. (U.S.): n/a
Originally produced for John Anderson's "The Gina Show" on Cable 10, Vancouver.

Meeting of Two Queens, The
Dir. Barriga, Cecelia
1991 Spain English
14 mins. video color Other
Dist. (U.S.): Women Make Movies
A brilliant cinematic montage (Garbo and Dietrich together at last).

Melody for Buddy Matsumae
(see *Matsumae-Kun No Senritsu*)

Memento Mori
Dir. Hubbard, Jim
1994 USA English
20 mins. 16mm/Scope color Experimental
Dist. (U.S.): Pig's Eye Productions
A self-processed meditation on death, and the personal and cultural rituals that surround it.

Memory Pictures
Dir. Parmar, Pratibha
1989 Great Britain English
24 mins. video color Documentary
Dist. (U.S.): Frameline
Memory Pictures is a British documentary which uses as its central figure a gay Indian man, Sunil Gupta, whose family migrated from Delhi to Canada in the late 1960s. Gupta uses his work to share his life in an interracial relationship. By the way of pictures and the story he tells, we meet his parents and the man with whom he lives. The omnipresent storyteller guides us through Gupta's life as an outsider who faces issues of being different. A lovely musical score and beautiful still photography make *Memory Pictures* unforgettable.

Memsahib Rita
Dir. Parmar, Pratibha
1994 Great Britain English
20 mins. 16mm color Narrative
Dist. (U.K.): British Film Institute
Pratibha Parmar's first narrative film is the story of Shanti, a streetwise East End girl, who is regularly harassed by local National Front boys until one evening when the mysterious Memsahib Rita appears. Memsahib Rita is an elusive mother figure who brings together the best aspects of an Asian movie star and a Hollywood femme fatale. She comes to Shanti's defense on the anniversary of her mother's death.

Ⓐ
Ⓑ
Ⓒ
Ⓓ
Ⓔ
Ⓕ
Ⓖ
Ⓗ
Ⓘ
Ⓙ
Ⓚ
Ⓛ
Ⓜ
Ⓝ
Ⓞ
Ⓟ
Ⓠ
Ⓡ
Ⓢ
Ⓣ
Ⓤ
Ⓥ
Ⓦ
Ⓧ
Ⓨ
Ⓩ

Men Behind Bars
Dir. Cvitanich, Jim, and Mark Abramson
Prod. MEN Video
1986 USA English
120 mins. video color Other
Dist. (U.S.): Bijou Video
The video of the annual stage extravaganza produced by San Francisco bartenders with lots of familiar faces and bods. Besides a full orchestra, there is a star-studded cast of local talent including Tom Ammiano, Suzy Berger, Sharon McKnight, Rita Rockett, Jose Sarria, Danny Williams, and Gail Wilson. Comedy skits, singing, dancing, you name it, it's all here.

Men In Love
Dir. Huestis, Marc
1989 USA English
90 mins. video color Narrative
Dist. (U.S.): Catamas, Scott
Men In Love begins in San Francisco at a memorial service for Victor Charpier, a beloved teacher who has just died from AIDS. Among the many left in his wake is Steve, a young man in his late twenties who was one of Victor's primary caretakers in the final months. Victor has requested that Steven scatter his ashes on Maui in Hawaii, so Steven travels there. On the island he meets an extraordinary community of people who are striving to lead their lives in a balanced and harmonious way. Far away from his own urban world, Steven is able to step back and take a look at the crucial issues in his life. He falls in love with Peter, a native Hawaiian. Steven is slowly transformed by his experiences on Maui. With Peter, Steven finds ways he can practice safe sex and be fulfilled. Through the practice of Tantra yoga, he also learns how to be in touch with his own feelings and to increase his awareness of others, as well as the world around him.
 Men In Love was later transferred to film and released in cities throughout the United States.

Men Like Me
Dir. Shaw, Sylvie
1994 Australia English
25 mins. 16mm color Documentary
Dist. (U.S.): Mead, Rebecca
From Australia comes *Men Like Me*, a documentary that makes creative use of computer video technology to break down the stereotyped concept of gender. This film is both humorous and educational in its examination of the social and physical transformation from female-to-male of the filmmaker's friend, Dale.

Men Maniacs
Dir. Hick, Jochen
1995 Germany German
86 mins. 16mm color Documentary
Dist. (U.S.): Hick, Jochen
Jochen Hick's engaging new documentary takes an up-close look at the circuit of leatherman contests, making pit stops in Chicago, New York, and San Francisco. Hick's camera captures contestants as they excitedly prepare to compete. Through revealing interviews with not only contestants but S/M porn actors, uniform fetishists, and long-term slaves, the film gives us an unprecedented behind-the-scenes glimpse into this close knit community of sexual radicals.
 Special attention is paid to Amsterdam-based "Tom of Hamburg," a former "International Mr. Leather" title holder, S/M porn star, and porn producer. His current battle with AIDS is poignantly addressed by the filmmaker. The startling physical transformation we see in Tom is jolting. Yet one is inspired by the openness and courage of this important member of the leather community. We are also treated to several entertaining and informative interviews with San Francisco's own Mr. Marcus.
 Hick's camera also follows the many men who cruise these events looking for sexual and play partners. They speak with a frankness and humor about their obsessions with boot licking, domination, and submission. We are made privy to the rituals of encounter and seduction in the halls and elevators of the hotels where the men stay for the duration of these leather events. *Men Maniacs* not only brings us backstage but shows us the erotically charged contests with plenty of fantasy, flesh, and flogging.

Meridad Proscrita
Dir. Ferrara-Balanquet, Raul, and Enrique Novelo Cascante
1990 Mexico/USA Spanish
8 mins. video b&w Experimental
Dist. (U.S.): Frameline
Meridad Proscrita is a sad, sepia love story set in Mexico, shot in a scratchy, Gus Van Sant style—one of the most moving films in this year's festival.

Mermaids, Fish & Other Non-Bipeds
Dir. Rinkenberger, Ginger
1995 USA English
15 mins. video color Narrative
Dist. (U.S.): Rinkenberger, Ginger

A girl falls for her wheel-chair bound roommate.

Messiah at the City
Dir. Kounin, Dennis
1979 USA English
16 mins. video color Documentary
Dist. (U.S.): n/a
Disco-funk. The band Messiah, fronted by L.Z. and Jerry Kirby (who worked with Sylvester) play at The City nightclub. Camera by Berne Boyle.

Meteor and Shadow (Meteore et Ombre)
Dir. Spetsiotis, Takis
1985 Greece Greek
101 mins. 35mm color Narrative
Dist. (U.S.): Greek Film Centre
In *Meteor and Shadow* Greek director/writer Takis Spetsiotis has avoided the clichés of the typical film biography. Instead he has fashioned a fascinating portrait of the poet Napoleon Lapathiotis (1888–1944) that both celebrates his life and stylishly depicts his tragic fall and eventual suicide. A romantic, charming leftist homosexual, Lapathiotis created a scandal in Athens when he refused to follow the rules of conservative Greek society. Turn-of-the-century Athens is conveyed rather than reconstructed in a bold departure from traditional period films and Spetsiotis makes great use of the junkies, gays, and avant-garde singers that surrounded Lapathiotis during his life as a poet. An unusual, striking film that won awards for best actor, set design, costume design, and make-up at the prestigious Thessaloniki Film Festival in 1985. Takis Spetsiotis was born in 1954 and studied film and English in Athens and London before beginning his filmmaking career with the short films *Lisa and the Other* and *Beauty*. In 1982 he created a half hour television film called "Napoleon Lapathiotis" that served as the inspiration for the feature-length *Meteor and Shadow*.

Mi Pollo Loco
Dir. Durham, Andrew
Prod. Martinez, Rico
1995 USA English
35 mins. video color Narrative
Dist. (U.S.): Vargas, Victor
An over-the-top drag spoof of *Mi Vida Loca*, with drag queens sporting nine-inch nails and hot cholo boys from the 'hood.

Midnight Dancers
Dir. Chionglo, Mel
1994 Philippines Filipino
118 mins. 35mm color Narrative
Dist. (U.S.): First Run Features
Dist. (U.K.): Dangerous To Know
Forced by economic hardship to leave his studies, Sonny returns home to find his two older brothers both working as "macho dancers" in a Manila gay bar. The film follows the three brothers as they embark on various relationships and (mis)adventures. The oldest has a wife and child but is also involved with an older rich man. He has been plying the trade for years and at 23 he is already fast becoming a has-been. The second brother, Dennis, lives a life on the streets and on the edge in which everything is a hustle, from dancing to car stealing. Against the admonishment of their mother, Sonny joins his brothers in the sex trade. Faced with the harsh reality of poverty, she can do nothing but accept their efforts to support the family. While working at the bar Sonny becomes romantically involved with a transvestite. Their relationship provides the love and stability he needs to survive in the pits of the Manila sex industry. Meanwhile, Dennis's exploits are beginning to bring danger to himself and his family. Currently banned in the Philippines, the film is a searing indictment of the abhorrent conditions of crime and poverty against which these three young men and their close-knit family battle for survival.

Midnight Life and Death
Dir. Wam, Svend, and Peter Vennerod
1980 Norway Norwegian
90 mins. 35mm color Narrative
Dist. (U.S.): Mephisto Films
Jacob, a doctor, meets and falls immediately in love with John, a young medical student. In a candle-lit bedroom they consummate their affair. At first, Jacob's wife, Jennifer, is shocked and hurt by the relationship, but gradually finds herself deeply involved with both men and drawn to an expanded understanding of romantic/sexual possibilities. With the music of ABBA in the background Jacob, John, and Jennifer embark on a touching, often very funny triangle. A relationship that finds the three roaming the snowy Norwegian landscape, at an outrageous Christmas dinner in the country, and at a loud, colorful Oslo disco. Eventually they come face-to-face with contemporary homophobia—in the form of an eerie black American-made van.

Mephisto Films is a Norwegian production company launched by Svend Wam and Peter Vennerod in 1976. Their first feature film, *The Silent Majority*, a major hit in Norway, was shown at the Cannes Film Festival. After several

Ⓐ Ⓑ Ⓒ Ⓓ Ⓔ Ⓕ Ⓖ Ⓗ Ⓘ Ⓙ Ⓚ Ⓛ Ⓜ Ⓝ Ⓞ Ⓟ Ⓠ Ⓡ Ⓢ Ⓣ Ⓤ Ⓥ Ⓦ Ⓧ Ⓨ Ⓩ

more productions they filmed *Life and Death* in Oslo in 1980. *Life and Death* has been screened at both the Berlin and Chicago Festivals.

Midwestern Skidmarks
Dir. Duesing, James, and Christopher Lewis
1986 USA English
46 mins. video color Other
Dist. (U.S.): Duesing, James
Midwestern Skidmarks is a variety show that takes the viewer on a roller-coaster ride through haywire narratives, wacked-out video effect humor, spiraling video artists/performance artist collaboration, and modified dirt hot rods. The line of irreverent narrative fragments runs from empty-headed high school reunions at convenience stores to the thrust toward consumer rapture.

Miguel
Dir. Kehr, Walter
Prod. Janowski, Markus
1995 USA/Germany English
18 mins. 35mm color Documentary
Dist. (U.S.): Kehr, Walter
A look at Club Fuck, and the tattoo and piercing culture of Los Angeles.

Million Eyes of Su-Muru, The
Dir. Shonteff, Londsay
1967 Great Britain English
86 mins. 16mm/Scope color Narrative
Dist. (U.S.): Olson, Jenni
In this world of international espionage where loving men is against the law, the stunning Su-Muru (Shirley Eaton) is globally known as the most diabolical, bizarre, and sadistic woman who ever lived. Her all-female, man-hating Amazon cult kidnaps a CIA agent (Frankie Avalon) as part of their plot for the destruction of all mankind. Klaus Kinski steps in with possibly the strangest role of his career, as the creepy homosexual president of Sinonesia who gets turned to stone. It's a little bit James Bond (lots of buxom blondes and typically stupid dialogue), a little bit *Black Lizard* (Su-Muru turns all the men into statues), and a little bit bad '60s Kung Fu movie (it was shot in Hong Kong at Shaw Bros. Studios).

Minders, The
Dir. Read, Melanie
1985 New Zealand English
50 mins. video color Narrative
Dist. (U.S.): Women Make Movies
The Minders is a lush fantasy about a celestial utopia ruled by women.

Minor Disturbances
Dir. Ashley, Carol
1992 USA English
17 mins. 16mm color Narrative
Dist. (U.S.): Frameline
In *Minor Disturbances* a disenchanted housewife, her lesbian lover, and her jealous husband form a triangle of household melodrama portrayed against a collage of 1950s educational films.

Minoru and Me
Dir. Nakata, Toichi
1992 Great Britain Japanese & English
45 mins. video color Documentary
Dist. (U.S.): Nakata, Toichi
British-based filmmaker Toichi Nakata invited his Japanese pal Minoru to visit him in London. Minoru—who has cerebral palsy—tells Toichi he has a confession to make. *Minoru and Me* is the (real life) video result. It's a horribly honest drama: Toichi becomes obsessed with portraying Minoru as disabled and dependent; Minoru becomes increasingly disgusted and unable to state what he's traveled so far to say. In their arguments and silences, there's a lot to learn about disability, about coming out, and about the role of the filmmaker.

Miracle on Sunset Boulevard
Dir. Huestis, Marc
1977 USA English
15 mins. S8mm b&w Narrative
Dist. (U.S.): Outsider Enterprises
Norma Desmond meets the great Goddess. Yes, miracles happen; one of them being that I made it through this film of one alive, Thank Goddess!! A remake you're not likely to see any other place but here. With much affection to Silvana, my nova, and to Delores, Our Lady of Perpetual Health.

Mirror, Mirror
Dir. Fleming, Edward
1978 Denmark Danish
107 mins. 35mm color Narrative
Dist. (U.S.): Danish Film Institute
Edward Fleming has mixed riotous, bitchy comedy with traces of melancholy in this story of a group of middle-class drag queens, played spectacularly by some of Denmark's best known actors. Without sensationalism, *Mirror, Mirror* creates a subtle, affectionate empathy between the audience and the lives on the screen, clearly members of an oppressed minority. Bent, out of work, shoplifts little gifts for his friends. His

mother spends her days dreaming of imagined past glories as an international ballet star. Their relationship is at the center of this richly textured film that is both amusing and compassionate.

Mirto
Dir. Marzi, Giampaolo
Prod. CFP Milano
1994 Italy Italian
12 mins. 16mm color Narrative
Dist. (U.S.): Marzi, Giampaolo
Andrea, while washing his Levi 501s, discovers a new life.

Miss Otis
Dir. Drinkrow, Lars, and Uren Jurgen
1993 Great Britain English
13 mins. 16mm color Narrative
Dist. (U.K.): Drinkrow, Lars and Uren, Jurgen
Plays out a classic film noir with a twist—in brilliant color.

Miss Ruby's House
Dir. Collins, Lisa
Prod. Berman, Shari, and Diane Lloyd
1993 USA English
18 mins. 16mm color Narrative
Dist. (U.S.): Collins, Lisa
When a Brooklyn babysitter, the neighborhood matriarch, is killed by a stray bullet, the reminiscences of five women (all played by Lisa Collins) entwine, weaving the tale of their lives.

Mister Reagan
Dir. Amazon Broadcasting Company
1984 USA English
4 mins. video color Other
Dist. (U.S.): n/a
Another humorous grassroots video from the Amazon Broadcasting Company.

Mister Sisters, The
Dir. Wilhite, Ingrid
1994 USA English
12 mins. video color Narrative
Dist. (U.S.): Wilhite, Ingrid
Two dykes ponder the possibilities of being gay men.

Moffie Called Simon, A
Dir. Greyson, John
1986 Canada English
15 mins. 16mm b&w Documentary
Dist. (U.S.): Frameline
The case of Simon Nkodi, jailed black gay activist and student leader in South Africa. The film examines the connection between the gay and antiapartheid movements.

Mondays
Dir. Redding, Judith
1992 USA English
3 mins. video color Experimental
Dist. (U.S.): Redding, Judith
The sensual *Mondays* offers laundry as a metaphor for life.

Mondo Diviso, Il (The Split World)
Dir. Cipelletti, Claudio
Prod. CFP-Milano
1994 Italy Italian
12 mins. 16mm color Narrative
Dist. (U.S.): Cipelletti, Claudio
A young man begins to explore his sexuality.

Monsters in the Closet
Dir. Reeves, Jennifer Todd
1993 USA English
15 mins. 16mm color Experimental
Dist. (U.S.): Reeves, Jennifer Todd
A brilliant experimental reflection on coming out as a lesbian.

Montreal Main
Dir. Vitale, Frank
Prod. Vitale, Frank, and Allan "Bozo" Moyle
1974 Canada English
90 mins. 16mm color Narrative
Dist. (U.S.): Vitale, Frank
Montreal Main is a film that clashes two very different worlds in a setting as realistic as the corner bar. Frank is the inarticulate, self-proclaimed artist; the faded tail of the youth comet of the '60s. Johnny is thirteen and is just ready to emerge from the swaddlings of the suburbs. They meet in a strange moment of mutual need, only to be separated by all those forces which keep society neat, clean-cut, and in its place.

More Love
Dir. Shimada, Koshi
Prod. Togoh, Ken
1984 Japan Japanese
60 mins. 35mm color Narrative
Dist. (U.S.): n/a
The rice-paper closet door slides back confidently at last. Supported in a beautifully filmed and melodramatic (often somber) framework, *More Love* is a startling and welcome breakthrough for Japan's first generically gay film. Though male-bonding is built into Japanese culture, the openly gay lifestyle is a recent and threatening phenomenon, and the film's handling of one young man's

Ⓐ Ⓑ Ⓒ Ⓓ Ⓔ Ⓕ Ⓖ Ⓗ Ⓘ Ⓙ Ⓚ Ⓛ Ⓜ Ⓝ Ⓞ Ⓟ Ⓠ Ⓡ Ⓢ Ⓣ Ⓤ Ⓥ Ⓦ Ⓧ Ⓨ Ⓩ

tragedy identifies the ecumenism of homosexuality in that country today. This young man's coming out topples his mother's precarious sanity. Further stumbling blocks to living "happily gay ever after" bring the story to a sad denouement. One is real (his un-confessed father, a Catholic priest cast as a villainous, hypocritical dispenser of guilt), and the other imagined (the panic headlines concerning AIDS). Despite the ending, and the censorship of full frontal nudity, there is more sensuality in this film, per frame, than in most other gay cinema; and emotional, explicitly sexual acts defy the viewer's belief that anything is left unseen. Though confined within a self-repressive society, the film expresses an unabashed physical affection between men that cannot be denied.

More Than a Paycheck
Dir. Leban, Lexi
1994 USA English
10 mins. 16mm color Experimental
Dist. (U.S.): Leban, Lexi
A woman reflects on her girlfriend in this captivating experimental short.

Moscow Does Not Believe in Queers
Dir. Greyson, John
1986 Canada English
27 mins. video color Documentary
Dist. (U.S.): Video Data Bank
Based on the experience of attending the 1986 Moscow Youth Festival as an "out" gay delegate, this tape is an eccentric diary of those ten days. Reconstructions of adventures in Moscow's gay subculture are cut with lurid Rock Hudson headlines and scenes from his Cold War classic *Ice Station Zebra*.

Mother Show, The
Dir. Rubnitz, Tom
1992 USA English
4 mins. video color Experimental
Dist. (U.S.): Kitchen, The
The Mother Show stars Frieda and is as strange and silly as you'd expect from director Tom Rubnitz.

Mother's Hands
Dir. Smith, Vejan
1992 USA English
10 mins. video color Experimental
Dist. (U.S.): Third World Newsreel
Mother's Hands that cook, clean, and care are also the hands that abuse in this powerful tape from Vejan Smith.

Mothers
Dir. Weissman, David
1989 USA English
9 mins. 16mm color Narrative
Dist. (U.S.): Weissman, David
Two very different groups of mothers and their babies collide in a San Francisco park.

Mouse Klub Konfidential
Dir. Baker, Jim
1978 USA English
9 mins. S8mm color Experimental
Dist. (U.S.): n/a
An erotic and controversial film equating Disney with fascism.

Mr. W's Little Game
Dir. Shores, Lynn
1934 USA English
10 mins. 16mm b&w Other
Dist. (U.S.): Rohauer Collection, The
The fabulously clever New York drama critic Alexander Woolcott teaches an intriguing little word game to his table companion at a restaurant.

Mr. Wonderful
Dir. Marlise, Malkames
1992 USA English
7 mins. video color Other
Dist. (U.S.): Malkames, Marlise
A cheerful cut-up penis carnival.

Mud Luverz
Dir. Pearl, Heather, and Nance Paternoster
Prod. Pearl, Heather, Nance Paternoster,
and Amy Simpson
1994 USA English
25 mins. video color Narrative
Dist. (U.S.): Pearl, Heather
Hectic urban life impels a San Francisco dyke to escape the city.

Muerte de Mikel, La (The Death of Mikel)
Dir. Uribe, Imanol
1984 Spain Spanish
89 mins. 35mm color Narrative
Dist. (U.S.): Spanish Ministry of Culture
Mikel is dead. Beginning with his funeral, the film then spins out the circumstances of his life and death, set against a background that embodies a range of emotions and tensions: tradition and independence; tolerance and rejection; joining and isolation. This area is the Basque country, itself a contradiction, with its scenic beauty and its history of bloodshed.

Mikel is a young married man involved in the classic dual battle with his homosexuality, the struggle with himself and with society. The object of his desire is a man who has with great pains been able to bridge the male-female roles—the transvestite cabaret star Fama (played by himself).

Yet in Basque country it is impossible to stay removed from the political climate. With terrorism virtually endemic, its hand also touches Mikel, as well as the reality of the severe measures of control undertaken by the police. He is a member of a radical, but legal, political group, where again the conflict between party and personal loyalty arises.

The sum total is that it is just too much. Mikel finds that he cannot cope. His death produces the expected irony, that he resolves nothing for himself, and everything for his family and party.

Mujeria: Olmeca Rap
Dir. de la Riva, T. Osa Hidalgo
1991 USA English & Spanish
3 mins. video color Other
Dist. (U.S.): Women Make Movies
A Chicana-lesbian animated musical montage that imagines the Olmeca culture and the 3000-year-old monolithic heads as female characters. Released as *Mujeira*, and packaged together with another short video by Teresa "Osa" Hidalgo de la Riva, *Primitive and Proud*.

Mulberry Bush, The
Dir. Sandler, Arlene
1994 USA English
5 mins. video color Experimental
Dist. (U.S.): Sensory Circus, Inc.
Starring Viva Kneival "the female Jeff Stryker" and a host of Fisher Price toys in one big Jill-Off.

Muscle
Dir. Hisayasu, Sato
1993 Japan Japanese
60 mins. 35mm color Narrative
Dist. (U.S.): Strand Releasing
Dist. (U.K.): Dangerous To Know
Muscle starts with a fleshy montage of Asian muscle men, and a torrid sex scene that ends with one lover cutting off the other's arm—and that's just in the first three minutes! While *Muscle* is one of the hottest, most exciting discoveries of the year, be warned: it is certainly not for the faint-hearted.

In Tokyo, a writer for a physique magazine falls into an obsessive, operatic S/M affair with a dangerously charismatic bodybuilder. After disarming his lover, the writer wanders urban backstreets, looking for his one-armed master.

Muscle's pleasures don't lie in its plot (of which there's not much, anyway), but in its passionate perversity. The film is full of cinematic jokes, and is breathtaking to look at. Its real achievement is to invent an alternative erotic dream world; in that sense, *Muscle* is very much in the tradition of *Ai No Corrida* and *The Fourth Man*.

My Addiction
Dir. Gilbert , Sky
1993 Canada English
60 mins. 16mm color Narrative
Dist. (U.S.): Canadian Filmmakers Distribution Centre
Andy Warhol and Paul Morrissey are alive and well and living in the director and cast of *My Addiction*.

"I love Dick. I want to wash his socks. I want to watch him move. I want him to be unable to think about me because it's too much . . ." Married man Matt is so in love with wild hustler Dick that, one night, he leaves his wife and plants himself in Dick's apartment. Dick's hooker roommate Marvette warns Matt that Dick will kill him when he returns, but Matt's not going anywhere, he's addicted to Dick.

Canadian director Sky Gilbert is best known to Bay Area audiences for his Theatre Rhinoceros productions *My Night with Tennessee* and *Drag Queens in Outer Space*. But *My Addiction* is unlike anything you've seen before. It's a genuine discovery, a haunting, low-tech, two-room drama about neuroses, sex, and compulsive behavior. Doesn't sound funny? Wrong: *My Addiction* is one of the drollest films we've seen in a long time.

My Beautiful Laundrette
Dir. Frears, Stephen
1985 Great Britain English
97 mins. 35mm color Narrative
Dist. (U.S.): Swank Motion Pictures
Dist. (U.K.): British Film Institute
Made as a British telefilm, *My Beautiful Laundrette* hit theater screens like an intoxicating gulp of fresh air, spiralling director Frears, screenwriter Hanif Kureishi, and actor Daniel Day Lewis to new career planes. A young South Londoner on the make, Omar (Gordon Warnecke) treads a risky line between the upward mobility of his Pakistani-immigrant relatives and the dole-

Ⓐ Ⓑ Ⓒ Ⓓ Ⓔ Ⓕ Ⓖ Ⓗ Ⓘ Ⓙ Ⓚ Ⓛ Ⓜ Ⓝ Ⓞ Ⓟ Ⓠ Ⓡ Ⓢ Ⓣ Ⓤ Ⓥ Ⓦ Ⓧ Ⓨ Ⓩ

queue punkdom of childhood pal Johnny's (Lewis) friends. Prankish, witty, stylish, the movie works on many levels as a critique of Thatcher-era race/class divisions. But for gay audiences, it's the sizzling (and matter-of-factly treated) sexual chemistry between Omar and Johnny that caps a contemporary classic. (D.H.)

My Beautiful Lorgnette
(see *Out On Tuesday, Program 1*)

My Brother's Keeper
1995 USA English
100 mins. 35mm color Narrative
Dist. (U.S.): n/a
John Lithgow—making amends for his similar double-duty in Brian DePalma's dismal *Raising Cain*—portrays identical twins in a small East Coast town. When the beloved schoolteacher sib is diagnosed with AIDS, the stage is set for hostile community response à la Ryan White. This TV drama distinguishes itself by choosing another direction entirely: Spurred by one housewife/mother's spontaneous gesture of solidarity, the local populace takes the high road and refuses paranoid "controversy" to further trouble already fretful lives. Conventionally crafted, but admirable as right-minded agitprop for the masses. Ellen Burstyn, Veronica Cartwright, and Annette O'Toole are also featured. (D.H.)

My Courbet . . . Or, A Beaver's Tale
Dir. Patten, Mary
1992 USA English
9 mins. video color Documentary
Dist. (U.S.): Patten, Mary
My Courbet . . . Or, A Beaver's Tale offers a quick overview of such famous lesbian artists as Romaine Brooks, Frida Kahlo, Della Grace, and Millie Wilson.

My Dinner at Dan's
Dir. Carlton, Wendy Jo
1993 USA English
6 mins. video color Other
Dist. (U.S.): Carlton, Wendy Jo
Wendy Jo Carlton's fun little interview with her bisexual pal.

My Failure to Assimilate
Dir. Dougherty, Cecilia
1995 USA English
20 mins. video color Experimental
Dist. (U.S.): Dougherty, Cecilia
Cecilia Dougherty's latest video exploration into the conflict between identity and assimilation.

My Father is Coming
Dir. Treut, Monika
1991 USA / Germany English and German
82 mins. 35mm color Narrative
Dist. (U.S.): Tara Releasing
Dist. (U.K.): Out On a Limb
My Father is Coming recounts the quirky assimilation of a German girl into New York's East Village culture. It's the story of Vicky, a waitress and frustrated actress, who despite a German accent, a series of disastrous auditions, and a checkered love life, still dreams of starring roles and a fulfilling sexual relationship. Vicky's life is complicated by the visit of her Bavarian father, who thinks his daughter is enjoying a successful career and marriage in New York. But Vicky's attempts to hide the truth and her deceptions soon take second stage to her father's New York adventures. She slips into an affair with Lisa, her lesbian Puerto Rican friend, and meets a handsome stranger with an unusual secret.

In some ways *My Father is Coming* is a tale of cultures clashing and the immigrant experience, but in many others it is about sex and the body. For both Vicky and her father, New York becomes an escape from the intellectual traditions of the fatherland into a world where appetites and sensory experiences take precedence.

My Grandma's Lady Cabaret
Dir. Myers, Elizabeth
1992 Great Britain English
10 mins. 16mm color Narrative
Dist. (U.K.): University of Bristol
A young dyke visiting her grandma learns a wonderful family secret.

My Hustler
Dir. Warhol, Andy
1965 USA English
67 mins. 16mm color Narrative
Dist. (U.S.): Museum of Modern Art
A quote from Andy Warhol describes one of his best-known films in deceptively simple terms: "*My Hustler* was shot by me, and Charles Wein directed the actors while we were shooting. It's about an aging queen trying to hold on to a young hustler and his two rivals, another hustler and a girl, the actors were doing what they did in real life, they followed their own professions on the screen." *My Hustler* has alternately been held in esteem as a classic of gay cinema and dismissed as boring. The critical literature surrounding *My Hustler*, while extensive, is often compromised by

factual errors. For over fifteen years it was impossible to assess any claim made about this film or to dispel the myths that surrounded Warhol's career as a filmmaker. Until the late '80s, when the Whitney Museum and the Museum of Modern Art began their efforts to restore and exhibit Warhol's body of work, the films he personally directed were virtually inaccessible.

Andy Warhol withdrew these films from circulation in 1972. He was attempting to secure financing for major motion pictures, and perhaps justifiably thought that these earlier films would undermine his credibility in Hollywood. He never managed to make the commercial crossover. Although Warhol himself didn't seem to realize it, his work was so radical and threatening that "Warhol films" could never have been Hollywood products without losing precisely those qualities that had made them compelling in the first place.

Andy Warhol's Hollywood ambitions were not as unlikely as they may seem today. Warhol was consistently producing films (one every two weeks at the peak of his output) on a model more industrial than artisanal, and he had managed to make some money at it. *My Hustler* and *Chelsea Girls* in particular were financial successes. Perhaps this could only have happened in the '60s, when economically vulnerable Hollywood studios lost touch with their audiences, and when the underground cinema reached curious and disaffected spectators with works of aesthetic and moral courage.

Considering the legal battles around the underground cinema in the '60s, one of Warhol's more courageous decisions was his choice of subject matter. His cinema serves as a document of the hip, mostly gay, "flaming creatures" who made their impression on the world in the mid-'60s. In the hopes of achieving fame (or at least infamy), many brilliant, and ultimately tragic, young people flocked to Warhol and appeared in his films. They did "what they did in real life," only to the greatest possible effect. The Superstars, as some of them would come to be called, enacted their dramas of self-presentation under very special circumstances.

Up to 1965, the date of *My Hustler*, Warhol's narrative films generally consisted of two long takes, each lasting 33 minutes, the length of a 1,200-foot reel of 16mm film. Whether actors recited Ronald Tavel's antidramatic, "ridiculous" scripts or were left to improvise, they had to deal with a relentlessly turning camera that stopped only when a reel was over.

The pressure to fill up this period of time in an amusing way brought out resourceful, even cruel, performances. *My Hustler* employs this form of narrative filmmaking—like many of Warhol's artistic strategies, perfect in its stupidity—although the film, with three shots in its first reel and one in its second, breaks slightly with the Warholian convention.

Shot on Fire Island over a Labor Day weekend, *My Hustler* united some of Warhol's most gifted improvisers. Ed Hood, the "aging queen" who dominates the conversation in the first reel, has called "Dial-a-Hustler" and sent for Paul America, the title character. Ed's rivals, Joe Campbell (the Sugar Plum Fairy of Lou Reed's song, "Walk on the Wild Side") and Geneviève Charbon (Edie Sedgwick's roommate, cast expressly to make her jealous) evaluate the merits of this butch young stud and cut each other down in caustic repartee.

During the bitchy dialogue, Warhol executes a number of rather shaky pans and zooms. The effect of these moves, made by the man who facetiously called the static camera his "contribution" to the art of film, is devastating. Warhol's cinematography rarely adhered to the standards of professionalism that applied to narrative (or for that matter, to avant-garde) cinema. Nevertheless, there was an uncanny sense of justice in his camera work. A highly sophisticated intelligence governed the choice of what was shown and what remained off-screen. In *My Hustler*, the camera makes its way from Ed in his beach house to Paul on the beach, a reverse angle achieved in one long take. With a simple gesture, Warhol reveals Mr. America in the distance while suggesting his inaccessibility. The perspective of the microphone doesn't change, and voices off-screen describe an object of desire oblivious to the gaze of the camera and to the gazes of the other characters.

The second reel plays out in a single static shot of Joe Campbell and Paul America grooming themselves for over a half an hour in a bathroom of the beach house. The cramped space and the monotonous action sustain a remarkable degree of suspense. There is a fragile interplay of aggression and innuendo, as the two men rehearse their postures of masculinity. Each character is deliberately ambiguous about his sexuality in order not to lose the upper hand in a subtle game of seduction. The stakes of the game have already been made clear in a line Joe delivered to Ed: "The more of a man he is, the more you'll want him." After Paul emerges from the shower, the towel he has wrapped around him briefly drops, and both he and Joe struggle to maintain their composure in the erotically charged atmosphere.

To complicate matters further, Joe has claimed that he has already had sex with Paul, much to Ed's consternation. Paul doesn't admit to this encounter of the previous night, nor does he at first admit to being a hustler, but he needs some advice from Joe, who is an old hand. The john, Ed, is something of a cheapskate, and Joe tells Paul that he can do better. Joe will show him the ropes, for a price. Paul begins to see the prospect of financial gain in the hustling racket, but ignores Joe's come-on. In discussing the appeal of his profession with Paul, Joe makes his most pointed remark, an aphorism that could well sum up the film as a whole: "Everybody's out hustling for something, and there are a lot of people waiting to be hustled."

Just as Joe makes his most blatant pass at Paul by giving him a very friendly massage, the seduction is interrupted. One by one, three characters enter the foreground at the edge of the frame. Each makes his or her respective offer for the services of Paul America. The third offer comes from the heretofore unseen Dorothy Dean, who applies lipstick and talks to Paul in her Mae West voice. She tells him the truth he will have to face eventually, "You are very pretty, but you're not exactly literate, and that would help in old age." She utters the last line in the film, a question that is never answered, "Why be tied down to these old faggots?"

The refusal of a romantic ending— nothing, not even a deal, is consummated—may strike those applying the standards of a mainstream "queer cinema" as an expression of self-hatred, or at least a failure of nerve. But the narrative elements that would justify this sort of ending, characters with easily understood psychological motivations overcoming obstacles to fulfill their desires, would be quite out of place in a Warhol film. The characters of My Hustler "follow . . . their own professions on the screen," but their psychology (at least by conventional standards) remains opaque. These characters succeed in expressing cunning and naked self-interest, but their schemes are so convoluted, their pronouncements are so venomous, that something as sensible as overcoming obstacles isn't ever seriously considered.

The characters of My Hustler speak in the language of domination. This language makes explicit what the title of the film invokes

from the very beginning; My: possession, or a claim of ownership; Hustler: one who engages in sex as work, or one who uses others to attain his own ends. The film in its most superficial aspects is a crude sex comedy, but it really succeeds at something far more ambitious: capturing a sense of the instrumentality of human relationships in a class society. The characters in the film express the everyday violence of the society in which they operate, pre-liberation gay America, a place and time which are, to some extent, still with us. Ed Hood describes his own situation, but he makes a comment that has wider implications when he says, "Our animosity has certain historical reasons."

In contrast to the films of most of his contemporaries, Warhol's work stands as a refusal of the conception of cinema as a free play of the imagination. He was, and may remain, the most rigorously antiromantic gay filmmaker. (Perhaps only the Fassbinder of Fox and His Friends challenges him in this respect.) The literal-mindedness that distinguished Warhol as a filmmaker, and infuriated a portion of his audience, prevented him from offering a fantasy of escape or a contrived sense of closure. What was at stake in Warhol's refusal is suggested by a line from Mark Rappaport's film Imposters, delivered by Ronald Tavel's associate in the Theatre of the Ridiculous, Charles Ludlam: "All bourgeois dreams end the same way. Marry royalty and escape." Paul America receives propositions (if not proposals) from suitors of a higher social station, but he doesn't respond. He is not transported away from oppression—as the working class lover will be at the end of E.M. Forster's Maurice—nor is there any hope of such a salvation. Andy Warhol couldn't imagine a gay film with a happy ending, but as My Hustler demonstrates, what could have been construed as his lack of imagination was actually his greatest asset as an artist and social critic. (W.J.)

My Idol
Dir. Tang, Sikay
1994 USA English
4 mins. video color Experimental
Dist. (U.S.): Tang, Sikay
A fantasy montage of unavailable lesbian intimacy stolen from Chinese porno movies.

My Mother's Secret
Dir. Spadola, Meema
1992 USA English
18 mins. video color Documentary

Dist. (U.S.): Spadola, Meema

In this intense low-budget homemade piece, children of lesbian mothers say frankly and honestly how they feel about their moms.

My Name Is Edwina Carerra
Dir. Bryant, Cliff
1986 USA English
10 mins. 16mm b&w Narrative
Dist. (U.S.): Chicago Filmmakers
Edwina and her two gay roommates square off.

My New Friend
Dir. Van Sant, Gus
1985 USA English
3 mins. 16mm color Other
Dist. (U.S.): Frameline
Another darkly funny chapter in the filmmaker's pursuit of the unattainable straight male. Gus meets a headbanger, takes him for an espresso, a ride, and a swim—and then loses him. Van Sant once again turns his ironic deadpan camera on himself in this short but revealing film.

My New Lover
Dir. Topping, John
1992 USA English
10 mins. video color Other
Dist. (U.S.): Topping, John
A riotous tale of a man so desperate for the perfect lover that he creates his own.

My Own Private Idaho
Dir. Van Sant, Gus
1991 USA English
105 mins. 35mm color Narrative
Dist. (U.S.): Films Incorporated
Dist. (U.K.): British Film Institute
The quest to excavate and claim queer images in film has long been hampered by an obvious obstacle: Until recently, lesbians and gay men have been largely invisible in the dominant cinema, or, if represented at all, cloaked in such elaborate subterfuge that meaning had to be dredged from the shadows, scavenged unabashedly from the celluloid scrapheap of coded glances, clandestine smiles.

Now, since the taboo surrounding queer sexuality on film has loosened, more and more same-sexers are caught in flagrante delicto, kissing, at least, if not actually making love. While certainly a heartening developement, and a halting one, there is also something amiss in movieland.

Of films that show explicit queer sex (pornography aside), many are adopting a trajectory as conventional as that of the most stringently heterosexual fare: meet, flirt, demur, kiss, and, at the penultimate moment, take to the sheets. In the blush of the newfound liberation, there appears to be a rush to frame lesbian and gay passion with the same sentimental dictates that inform most mainstream movies.

Happily, there are exceptions to the formula, most often from film and video makers working in opposition to the standards of narrative cinema. In Super 81/2 and Joe-Joe, for example, hilariously raunchy nuggets from directors Bruce LaBruce and Cecilia Dougherty/Leslie Singer, respectively, fucking is more spontaneous than rarefied, an insouciant pastime valuable in itself, not merely as a punctuation mark to a tale of domesticated—albeit lavender-tinged—love.

Other contemporary filmmakers are honoring the erotic thrill of secrecy and sin by crafting melodramas as juicy and twisted as such classics of homo repression as Reflections in a Golden Eye and Walk on the Wild Side. Still others are charting the visceral sting of denial, the hollow pain of unrequited love that somehow feels even more excruciating when reflected from the shimmering canvas of our collective dream reel. Sure, an overt onscreen lip-lock between two men or women can be a big bang, but so too can be a gesture rebuffed, a touch withheld. Sometimes, a plunge into desperation can be the queerest kick of all.

A pair of movies from 1991, Salmonberries and My Own Private Idaho, demonstrate the heightened anguish of squelched desire as well as any that have come before or since. Companion pieces in the study of dislocation and its consequences, the films also forge a link with the past by suggesting there is something unseemly, at once repellent and wildly alluring, in lusting after one's own gender. That the thwarted lover in each film is played by a celebrity of hugely iconic structure—River Phoenix for his precocious brilliance and early death, k.d. lang for her renown as an enigmatic, butch heartthrob—only adds to the shared mood of meloncholy. Phoenix and lang denied? Could it be? Rarely does the blur between fantasy and its converse seem so poignant.

In Percy Adlion's Salmonberries, lang is Kotzubue, an Alaskan pipeline worker of uncertain heritage who falls for a German émigré, Roswitha (Rosel Zech), the librarian in a remote town. Roswitha first sees Kotzubue as a bad natured boy, until Kotzubue (literally) strips between the library stacks and courts the older woman with a gift of freshly caught fish. Roswitha reciprocates by showing off her collection of salmonberries, eerily displayed in glass jars lining the walls of her bedroom. Roswitha's response is tempered with ambivalence, however, even when she impulsively escorts Kotzubue to Germany on a pilgrimage into her past.

The sequence of jagged, off-kilter fade-outs in which Kotzubue attempts to seduce Roswitha in a Berlin hotel room is a classic of yearning dashed; every woozy dip of the camera signals another of Kotzbue's agonized, one-sided swoons. Later, when Kotzebue snowmobiles across the blank Alaskan tundra with Roswitha in tow, the soundtrack swelling with lang's ballad, "Barefoot," the movie fairly reeks of tortured resignation. *Salmonberries*, though freighted with murky pretensions, is a masterpiece of longing laid bare, a virtual case study in vulnerability and its bittersweet repercussions.

My Own Private Idaho, Gus Van Sant's deliriously unhinged story about street hustlers in the Pacific Northwest, is a less hyperbolic exploration of the same emotional landscape. One of the pleasures of the film is watching best friends Mike (Phoenix) and Scott (Keanu Reeves) cavort through Idaho, to Seattle, to Portland and back again, a pair of cool cats gay-coded in leather and grunge. Scott, ostensibly straight, is nonetheless exceedingly tender with Mike, a narcoleptic prone to sudden slumber at inopportune moments. For his part, Mike is crazy in love with Scott, and while his simmering amour remains inarticulated for most of the movie, *My Own Private Idaho* exudes a sweet romanticism even as it sets up the class gulf between the friends as an impossible divide. Eventually, Mike does profess his craving for Scott in one of the most beautifully nuanced depictions of naked desire ever captured on film. The scene transpires around a campfire as Scott and Mike move from benign conversation to the charged terrain of what they mean to one another. The give and take is hushed, poetic, almost unbearably raw, culminating in Mike's murmured plea, "I really want to kiss you, man." Their ensuing hug, a fumbling lurch, is nothing short of heartbreaking.

Mike, like Kotzebue, will not find what he's looking for, a truth both wrenching and strangely validating, especially emerging as it does from a milieu—the movies—usually wedded to the imperative of the upbeat ending. For Mike and Kotzebue, love, intimacy, and lust fully met are distant dreams, more accessible in sleep,

perhaps, than in waking. Disappointment is not solely the province of lesbians and gay men, of course, yet to pretend it's less than a central feature of queer experience is to deny outsider status. Better to embrace marginality and its possibilities, harrowing and otherwise, for informing a cinema that resonates with more than just the facile palliative of happily-ever-after. (E.P.)

My Polish Waiter
Dir. Terracino
1994 USA English
12 mins. 16mm b&w Narrative
Dist. (U.S.): Terracino
Timith carries a torch for Balki, a silent and inscrutable Polish waiter, and learns that the words "good," "better," and "blintzes" truly are the vocabulary of love.

My Sister, My Love
Dir. Arthur, Karen
1978 USA English
102 mins. 35mm color Narrative
Dist. (U.S.): n/a
Also known as *The Mafu Cage*, this little-seen feature is a fascinating addition to the homoerotic "strange sisters" thriller genre. Lee Grant is the starched astronomer who has her hands full at home maintaining control over wild-child sib Carol Kane; they'd both been raised under unusual circumstances by an African primatologist father, leaving younger Carol unequipped to deal with normal society. A la *The Fox*, introduction of a male romantic rival (James Olson) in this incestuous cloister proves most unfortunate. Over-the-top, natch, but also strikingly designed and acted, with some truly creepy-sexy scenes. (D.H.)

My Skin is a Map
Dir. Grandell, Steven
1993 USA English
6 mins. video b&w Other
Dist. (U.S.): Grandell, Steven
Tim Miller talks about his experiences as a gay man in this pixel vision and 16mm performance montage.

My Sorrow Means Nothing to You
Dir. Hengst, Clifford
1990 USA English
4 mins. video color Other
Dist. (U.S.): Hengst, Clifford
Clifford Hengst with some help from a friend lets it all out. A lip synch to black comedienne Lady Reed.

My Sweet Peony
Dir. Lee, Karin
1994 Canada Cantonese and English
30 mins. 16mm color/b&w Narrative
Dist. (U.S.): Moving Images Distribution
Portrays the parable of Zamma, a Chinese-Canadian woman who works as a guide in a Classical Chinese Garden. She is faced with three suitors: a white man and a white woman who fetishize her Asian identity and an older Chinese-Canadian lesbian with whom she gradually develops a friendship.

Myra Breckenridge
Dir. Sarne, Michael
1970 USA English
94 mins. 35mm color Narrative
Dist. (U.S.): Films Incorporated
Great period costumes and sets, a cameo by Mae West, and ironic use of film clips from the Golden Age of Hollywood provide plenty of queer viewing pleasure in this adaptation of Gore Vidal's transsexual fable, though this 1970 vintage movie aged more like vinegar than fine wine—not exactly bad but difficult to savor for 94 minutes. (S.S.)

N'oublie pas que tu vas mourir (Don't Forget You're Going To Die)
Dir. Beauvois, Xavier
1995 France French
118 mins. 35mm color Narrative
Dist. (U.S.): Leonor Films
Don't Forget You're Going To Die? How could we? A young bourgeois man with a promising bourgeois future has been drafted. He doesn't want to go. He invents every possible excuse not to be inducted, but he is. On his first night in the barracks, he fakes a suicide, winds up in the hospital, and learns he is HIV positive. Storm clouds roll in and he decides to live his life to the fullest, befriending an Arab ruffneck who introduces him to the fleeting pleasures of dope, bisexual hustling, brothel threesomes, and drug running. Realizing his biological clock is ticking away, he runs away to Italy, falls in love with a young flawless Franco-Italian woman, leaves her to get high in a moving train, and eventually winds up in Bosnia as a soldier for the Serbian army. I didn't make this up. Director Xavier Beauvois, who stars as the young seropositive brat, did. His insipid and misogynist romanticism obscures any possibility of real drama in this artless and corny movie. (L.C.)

Nagua (Drifting)
Dir. Guttman, Amos
1983 Israel Hebrew
80 mins. 35mm color Narrative
Dist. (U.S.): Interpictures
Israel's first gay identified film is a low-key, off-beat story of a young filmmaker stalled on his way down, leveled at a turning point when the realities of failure and the promise of dreams collide. Robi (Sagalle, macho popular star in Lemon Popsicle, Israel's American Graffiti) detaches himself from the comings and goings on of Tel Aviv's tightly closeted gay circles to test his emotional independence. But it's a shaky break with a married ex-lover, an ex-girlfriend, and a gabby granny bugging him. With the collapse of a single-minded purpose and no sense of "community" gay or otherwise, to fall back on, Robi begins to drift, nagua (a little nuts), until it all starts to come together again.

Naomi's Legacy
Dir. Levy, Wendy
1994 USA English
26 mins. video color Other
Dist. (U.S.): Crazy Hearts Films
Wendy Levy's beautifully layered fictional rendering of a Jewish lesbian girlhood incorporates old photographs and home movie footage to reconstruct Naomi's Legacy.

Narcissus
Dir. Lunger, Jeff
1978 USA English
3 mins. 16mm color Experimental
Dist. (U.S.): Lunger, Jeff
A silent, optically printed retelling of the Greek myth.

Naughty Boys
Dir. De Kuyper, Eric
1983 Netherlands Dutch
107 mins. 16mm b&w Narrative
Dist. (U.S.): Netherlands Ministry of Culture
Suddenly, the party is over, even if the partygoers don't wish to acknowledge the fact. After the ball is over life goes on, even the morning after the night before. Six men, wearing evening dress, are determined to prolong their weekend away from it all, in a world that no longer exists. They all want to belong, but none of them succeeds. The differences between them all are too great, so they begin to resemble each other. They speak English to each other, but they all have accents. They use an international language to create a link. From

Ⓐ Ⓑ Ⓒ Ⓓ Ⓔ Ⓕ Ⓖ Ⓗ Ⓘ Ⓙ Ⓚ Ⓛ Ⓜ Ⓝ Ⓞ Ⓟ Ⓠ Ⓡ Ⓢ Ⓣ Ⓤ Ⓥ Ⓦ Ⓧ Ⓨ Ⓩ

time to time they revert to their native tongues, or they speak another language (French, Italian, German, Dutch) as if by mistake. They talk about women; they wait for girlfriends to return but without much faith. The telephone is their only connection to the outside world we never see. In the void left after the party, there is an occasional revival. The party always goes on. Suddenly dejection and sadness make way for an outburst of lively music and dance. Daisy storms in suddenly, only to disappear again almost at once. In a remote room, a piano is playing, accompanying a woman who sings as a ghostly reminder of the party.

Neapolitans, The
Dir. Corsicato, Pappi
1992 Italy Italian
83 mins. 35mm color Narrative
Dist. (U.S.): First Look Pictures
Slim on gay content but high on gay style, it relates a trio of modern stories set in three different parts of southern Italy's seductive city. In the first tale, Aurora (Iaia Forts) sees her smug, nouveau riche world crumble when her shady, never-seen husband sleeps with his secretary. In the closing comic story, Libera (also played by Forte) has a similar problem with her lazy husband's infidelity, but she hatches a plan to exact revenge and profit. Carmela's tale is the one that holds most interest for gay audiences. Handsome Sebastiano arrives home from reform school; Carmela doesn't mind that her son is gay, but she can't cope with his questions about his long-gone father. Amid plans for a neighborhood wedding (and Sebastiano's seduction of a local salesman), the truth comes out.

Negative Man
Dir. Joritz, Cathy
1985 USA English
3 mins. 16mm color Experimental
Dist. (U.S.): Joritz, Cathy
A scratch film which foregrounds the superficial self-importance of male authority figures.

Neighborhood Voices
Dir. Kerr, Barbara T.
1986 USA English
29 mins. video color Documentary
Dist. (U.S.): n/a
Stories of gay Greenwich Village in the 1950s and 1960s told by people who were there at the time. Included are interviews by stand-up comic Tom Ammiano and poets Audre Lorde and Joan Nestle.

New Pupil, The
Dir. Cahn, Edward
1940 USA English
10 mins. 16mm b&w Narrative
Dist. (U.S.): Olson, Jenni
The "Our Gang" kids present a schoolyard force full of same-sex affection and a classic drag scene with Alfalfa and Spanky.

New Year, A
Dir. Benning, Sadie
1989 USA English
4 mins. video b&w Experimental
Dist. (U.S.): Video Data Bank
Dist. (U.K.): London Video Access
A New Year is Benning's first video, made at age 15.

New York Loft
Dir. Hammer, Barbara
1983 USA English
9 mins. 16mm color/b&w Experimental
Dist. (U.S.): Canyon Cinema
"Both New York Loft and Doll House convey a strong sense of resourcefulness, this 'making something' out of interiors, specifically domestic spaces. And domestic they are, in an avant-garde sort of way. The filmmaker gives plentiful evidence of arranging things, moving them, adjusting, placing, and replacing. The lens is seen as Barbara films into a round mirror. How different are the visions of this woman-with-a-movie-camera from Vertov of sixty years ago! Each extols the camera-eye, but Hammer replaces Vertov's sociopolitical kino-truths with adventures in domestic space."
—Claudia Gorbman, Jump Cut

Nexus
Dir. Bond, Rose
1984 USA No Dialogue
7 mins. 16mm color Experimental
Dist. (U.S.): Chicago Filmmakers
Out of a kinetic weave of India ink line-spirals and waveforms emerges the dark silhouette of a nude woman walking on a tropical beach, a metaphor for the journey of self-discovery to follow. Painted directly on 35mm film, Rose Bond's imagery moves freely between abstraction and representation, connecting art and nature through symbols of femininity derived from ancient matriarchal cultures. Nexus is a joyous and profound dance of life set to the rhythms of African marimba music by Sukutai.

Nexus

Dir. Johns, Jennifer
1992 USA No Dialogue
6 mins. 16mm color Experimental
Dist. (U.S.): Frameline
Uses a spiraling editing structure and mirrored images to express connections between women.

Nice Girls Don't Do It
Dir. Daymond, Kathy
1990 Canada English
13 mins. 16mm color Other
Dist. (U.S.): Chicago Filmmakers
Dist. (U.K.): Cinenova
A posthysterical demonstration of female ejaculation, providing factual information and instruction, as well as subjective reactions to this newly recognized pleasure.

Nico-Icon
Dir. Ofteringer, Susanne
1995 Germany German
70 mins. 35mm color/b&w Documentary
Dist. (U.S.): Roxie Releasing
She was Andy Warhol's moon goddess; her drawled vocals characterized the sound of the band Velvet Underground. Her beauty and reticence has fascinated Lou Reed, Jackson Browne, Jim Morrison, Iggy Pop, and many others. The name that appears on her birth certificate is Christa Paffgen. Christa the girl became the gamine model, the cover girl with a fringe who appeared on the pages of the magazine Twen and, briefly, in Fellini's La Dolce Vita. Her career moved from New York's underground to Philippe Garrel's subculture. Like many of her generation, she believed in the drug heroin and survived the consumption of it for many years, to become a contemporary icon of another kind: Her fans saw her as the embodiment of gloom and the death wish. When she died on Ibiza in 1988, the cause of death was a bicycle accident; her body, which had stood up to so much, could not cope with the withdrawal symptoms.
     This film follows the various stages in her restless life from Lubbenau to Berlin, Paris, New York, and Manchester.

Night Visions
Dir. Bociurkiw, Marusia
1989 Canada English
60 mins. 16mm color Narrative
Dist. (U.S.): Winds Of Change Productions
Night Visions is an hour-long drama dealing with issues of lesbianism and race within the context of an urban community of women fighting for its

survival. The story draws from actual events, legal battles, custody cases, and actions that have occurred in Canada during the last decade. These struggles are humanized through the simultaneous depiction of passionate relationships among these women—political, sexual, humorous, serious—existing amid the political turmoil of the community. A Native single mother (Nea) is fighting a child custody battle, pitted against the Children's Aid and her white ex-husband. A lesbian photographer (Morgan) has her erotic photographs seized by the police. The two women meet through a mutual friend (Helena), a feminist activist who encourages them to find common cause. But cultural difference and racism intervene; contact with Morgan and her friends complicates Nea's life to the point of crisis; the narratives end separately. "Hope lies in what we do amongst ourselves, the messages we send to one another in the night," says Nea to Helena. "You have your struggle, and I have mine." In a "night" of state repression and systemic racism and homophobia, the vision of community and common cause appears and disappears like a dream.

Night with Derek, A
Dir. Kwietniowski, Richard
Prod. Kwietniowski, Richard, and Peter Murphy
1995 Great Britain English
25 mins. video color Documentary
Dist. (U.K.): Alfalfa Entertainments, Ltd.
A broad range of Derek Jarman's aquaintances celebrate his dizzying love of life a year after his death. Clancy Chassay, the young actor who debuted in Derek's film Wittgenstein, provides a mischievous potted biography for Jarman beginners, and also reveals for the first time his Famous Last Words.

Nighthawks
Dir. Peck, Ron, and Paul Hallam
1978 Great Britain English
113 mins. 35mm color Narrative
Dist. (U.K.): British Film Institute
Jim, a gay teacher in a London comprehensive school, lives the classic double life: straight days in school, gay nights in bars and discos. With each new pick-up the same tension and uncertainty arises: Is there anything more to gay life than the one-night stand? At school he find himself overworked and forced to hide his true experiences and feelings. After the traditional year-end school dance and a drunken staff party, Jim finally pours out something of himself to a friend-

ly female teacher. It is a step toward openness and enables Jim to face the inevitable explosion triggered by his curious 14-year-old students.

Writers/directors Ron Peck and Paul Hallam began work on *Nighthawks* in 1975, creating the first feature film to come out of a gay community. Conceived as a "panoramic view of gay life in London," they soon realized it couldn't cover everything, and that what was needed was "hundreds of gay films, not half a dozen, to make homosexuality visible in the cinema."

Nightshift
Dir. Gonzalex, A.P.
1982 USA English
6 mins. 16mm b&w Other
Dist. (U.S.): n/a
A moody, artfully edited black-and-white look at one of San Francisco's less popular neighborhoods.

Nightwork
Dir. Schneider, Jane
1993 Australia English
11 mins. 16mm color Narrative
Dist. (U.S.): Australian Film, Television & Radio School
A clever look at a pair of dykes on bikes who are nearly pulled apart by obsessive jealousy.

976
Dir. Weissman, David
1987 USA English
3 mins. 16mm color Other
Dist. (U.S.): Frameline
A spiritually titillating alternative to phone sex.

Nineteen Nineteen
Dir. Brody, Hugh
1984 Great Britain English
99 mins. 35mm color Narrative
Dist. (U.K.): British Film Institute
Maria Schell (Sophie) and Paul Scofield (Alexander) turn in magnificent performances as former patients of Freud who meet for the first time in Vienna in 1970. Sophie convinces a wary Alexander to meet after she sees him interviewed on TV about his experience with Freud. In their one-day encounter, in a reluctant Alexander's cluttered apartment, the two sit down to talk.

Sophie is now a divorced New Yorker of nearly 70, Alexander is a lonely widower; both still harbor resentment of Freud's treatment of their youthful "problems." Their personal narratives, shown in flashback, are poignant; Freud is an unseen but vivid presence in the therapy scences. Stellar casting includes Colin Firth (*Another Country*) as the aristocratic young Alex, who cannot equate sex and self-respect. Clare Higgins is the headstrong Sophie, who defies her father with a lesbian affair and is sent to Freud to be "cured."

A memorable portrayal of loss, anger, regret, and eventual acceptance by Schell and Scofield, both triumphant in roles worthy in every way of their talent.

1999—Nen No Natsu Yasumi (Summer Vacation: 1999)
Dir. Kaneko, Shusuke
1988 Japan Japanese
90 mins. 35mm color Narrative
Dist. (U.S.): New Yorker Films
One of the most visually exciting films in recent memory, *Summer Vacation: 1999* features a hypnotizing narrative that is both deceptively simple and full of unexplainable mystery. Set in a boys' school in a remote, beautiful area of Japan, *Summer Vacation* tells the story of four teenage students who spend their summer vacation at school—unsupervised and untouched by the outside world. As the story begins, Yu has decided to take his own life—he is in love with the exquisitely beautiful Kazuhike, who is also loved by another of the boys, Naeto. Kazuhike ignores Yu's love letters and the depressed Yu decides to jump from a cliff into a tranquil lake at the school's edge. Just as the shock of the suicide begins to subside, in walks a new student who looks and sounds exactly like the dead boy, Yu.

Summer Vacation: 1999 looks at teenage homosexual love with a refreshing and compassionate honesty. These four boys may be suffering terribly as they try to understand the power of their newly discovered romantic emotions, but they are victims of their passions and not their sexuality. To underscore his interest in the mystery of sexual attraction, director Shusuke Kaneko has cast girls to play the parts of all four boys, later dubbing their voices with those of four young actors.

1970's Porn Trailers
Dir. unknown
1972 USA English
12 mins. 16mm color Other
Dist. (U.S.): Stevenson, Jack
Four rare trailers for seventies classics like *Get That Sailor* ("Servicemen who bend over backwards to please . . . the ultimate in sexual realism!").

94 Arcana Drive
Dir. Mangaard, Annette
1993 Canada English
18 mins. 16mm color Narrative
Dist. (U.S.): Canadian Film Centre
A punchy short about an unusual kind of marital problem.

Nitrate Kisses
Dir. Hammer, Barbara
1992 USA English
77 mins. 16mm color/b&w Documentary
Dist. (U.S.): Strand Releasing

Taking the updraft on the current wave of lesbian archivism, Barbara Hammer does in film what Lillian Faderman did in her book *Odd Girls and Twilight Lovers*. She presents a narrative history of queer life (including an extensive gay male section) from the '20s to the voices of people beginning to speak for themselves against the backdrop of queer cultural history.

In this nonlinear film, Hammer makes a point of showing how history comes from fragments which are left to us to interpret. She holds to the theory that this approach comes closer to the truth of life, which is experienced in disjointed images, symbols, and processes that only verge on being meaningful after we assign meaning to them. She knows how nonnarrative film makes most people uncomfortable, and this film seems more than her others to take her audience into consideration. She is, after all, working on creating a collective, rather than a personal, vision of queer cultural history.

The impulse to archive begins with a quotation from Adrienne Rich, who warns us that whatever is left out, ignored, or censored about a people will become not merely unspoken, but unspeakable. Hammer underscores her project as an attempt to uncover hidden history with a view toward a future that will give credence to queers and which will exhibit a strong lesbian visibility. Artifacts live longer than the people who create them, and works of art, like films, continue to have a life of their own through time.

Hammer interweaves images from the past and the present in a viable way. Traveling to Willa Cather's final resting place, we see a monument erected to her, and hear a tour guide speaking about the house where she wrote and lived. Not once is her lesbianism mentioned. Before her death, Cather and her female lover burned all of her letters. She didn't want anything of her personal life to be revealed. And so, except for the work of the lesbian decoders, Cather would have remained invisible as a lesbian role model. Since not all lesbians are writers or artists, lesbian visibility is often perpetuated through oral history and a shared secret iconography. Hammer shows us the icons, and the people in her film speak about the preliberation days and the decoys involved in living "in the life."

Since sexuality is a major defining characteristic of a lesbian identity, Hammer doesn't shirk in presenting this reality. Unlike other cultural documentaries, Hammer displays graphic sex in her film. The sex she shows is not run-of-the-mill titillation. Her first sex partners are old lesbians, quite wrinkled and beyond the prime. They tongue-kiss, caress, and then go full boogie with cunnilingus and manual penetration. It's something we don't often see on screen. In fact, I don't think I've ever seen it on screen.

While searching through archives for her film, Hammer came across a large number of outtakes from the 35mm nitrate film, *Lot in Sodom* (1933), which now has the distinction of being the first queer film made in America. Most of the men in it were filmed seductively, either naked or in posing straps, or in very effeminate drag. Hammer uses lots of footage from this film, and she intercuts it with present-day erotic scenes of lovemaking between a black/white young male couple. While the narrator explains the Hollywood Film Code 1934–1961, which prohibited same-sex eroticism and outlawed miscegenation, we see the white guy putting a condom over his partner's erect cock.

Nitrate Kisses continues unveiling transgressions with political bravado. There is a quotation from Pat Califia about denied eroticism. We hear a woman with a heavy German accent speaking about lesbians held in World War II concentration camps. The few accounts we have, she says, come from straight women who have written about the two types of lesbianism in the camps. There was the "disgusting" kind: physical sex between those who were seen as criminals, prostitutes, asocial perverts. And then there was the idealistic kind between Jewish women and political types, which was seen to be "orderly," platonic. Essentially, there are no accounts by lesbians themselves of life in the camps, and so it remains as a hidden history. On screen, between shots of rubble and steel gratings, we see two dykes making love, one with a leather harness strap on, penetrating her companion. A voice speaks about how fluid sexual categories are and how no specific sexual identity

Ⓐ Ⓑ Ⓒ Ⓓ Ⓔ Ⓕ Ⓖ Ⓗ Ⓘ Ⓙ Ⓚ Ⓛ Ⓜ **Ⓝ** Ⓞ Ⓟ Ⓠ Ⓡ Ⓢ Ⓣ Ⓤ Ⓥ Ⓦ Ⓧ Ⓨ Ⓩ

should be denied.

The film ends with a reflection of Barbara Hammer, with her camera in hand, looking through a window and waving at two punk lesbians who've just been having sex. The last words are from a speech given at the Lesbian Herstory Archives about how lesbians have shared a long history of discrimination by the various medial establishments which have used arguments of "biology" to prove that we're less than human. "Never again," is the message. (R.T.)

No Fairy Tale
Dir. Morgana, Aimee
1993 USA English
1 mins. video color Other
Dist. (U.S.): Morgana, Aimee
A safe-sex public service announcement.

No Glove, No Love
Dir. Peterson, Inka, and Anja Schulz
1991 Germany No Dialogue
2 mins. video color Other
Dist. (U.S.): Art Com Media Distribution
A very hot public service announcement from Germany.

No Help Needed
Dir. unknown
1940 USA English
6 mins. 16mm b&w Other
Dist. (U.S.): Olson, Jenni
This rare fragment of 1940s porn features two portrayals of women fooling around with each other (no help needed).

No Money, No Honey
Dir. O'Shea, John
1992 USA English
4 mins. video color Other
Dist. (U.S.): O'Shea, John
A music video with Vaginal Creme Davis.

No More Nice Girls
Dir. Braderman, Joan
1989 USA English
44 mins. video color Documentary
Dist. (U.S.): Women Make Movies
No More Nice Girls traces and recollects a feminist history by visually layering the personal and political histories of women who were active in the '70s feminist art movements.

No Need to Repent
Dir. Alter, Ann
1989 USA English

27 mins. 16mm color Documentary
Dist. (U.S.): Women Make Movies
No Need to Repent is a documentary portrait of the Rev. Jan Griesinger, whose solid Midwestern upbringing has produced a church woman of unusual conviction and persistence of vision. The film is a loving profile of a stong woman. It also manages to chronicle the kind of grassroots movement-building familiar to a generation of feminist activists.

No No Nooky T.V.
Dir. Hammer, Barbara
1987 USA English
12 mins. 16mm/video color Experimental
Dist. (U.S.): Frameline
No No Nooky T.V. confronts the feminist controversy around sexuality with electronic language, pixels, and electronic interface.

Released by Frameline in the U.S. as part of a package of four of her short videos, entitled Barbara Hammer Program #2. Also released in the U.S. along with four of her other short films as a feature-length package, Lesbian Humor: The Films of Barbara Hammer, Volume I.

No Ordinary Love
Dir. Witkins, Doug
Prod. Kabillio, Eli
1995 USA English
104 mins. 16mm color Narrative
Dist. (U.S.): Rapid Film Group
Dist. (U.K.): Capella
A comedy-drama about the tangled lives and loves of six not entirely likable L.A. friends who are left to pick up the pieces after the death of Tom (Dan Frank), their darkly charismatic and manipulative leader. Despite the emotional and sexual abuse they suffered at the hands of Tom, both Wendy (Ericka Klein) and Kevin (Smith Forte) still carry a torch for him and are disconsolate with grief over his demise. The solace they find in each other eventually leads to more than either can handle. Then there's Andy (Robert Pecora) who seems to have nothing better to do than to walk around in his skimpy underwear all day. For reasons unknown, he is unhappy with Ben (Mark S. Larson) the seemingly harmless new housemate. Meanwhile Ben goes on snooping expeditions through the house and performs inexplicable chores in the basement. When his motives come to light and Tom's twisted mind games come back to haunt them, everyone does battle for a cut of the stakes in this sexy stylish film riddled with blink-and-you'll-miss-them plot

twists and turns. But you'll no doubt be distracted by the dilemma of 18-year-old Vince (Koing Kuoch) who has a crush on his hunky cholo neighbor (Tymme Reitz).

No Porque Fidel Castro Lo Diga (Not Because Fidel Castro Says So)
Dir. Sanchez, Graciela
1988 Cuba Spanish
10 mins. video color Documentary
Dist. (U.S.): Frameline
Details public reaction to Cuba's small but growing gay and lesbian community.

No Regret (Non, Je ne regrette rien)
Dir. Riggs, Marlon
1992 USA English
30 mins. video color Documentary
Dist. (U.S.): Frameline
Through music, poetry, and, at times, chilling self-disclosure, five seropositive black gay men speak of their individual confrontation with AIDS. Each man tells a singular and at the same time familiar story of self-transformation—from panic, resignation, and silence to the discovery of the redemptive, healing power in being vocal and visible.

No Sad Songs
Dir. Sheehan, Nick
1985 Canada English
61 mins. 16mm color Documentary
Dist. (U.S.): Salzgeber & Co.
Amid the hysteria, the misleading medical revelations, and the avalanche of contradictory information, along comes No Sad Songs, a sane and brilliantly made film about AIDS from Canada.

Calmly and lucidly, 37-year-old Jim Black talks about the disease that is killing him. His face is emaciated but his mood is serene, his sense of humor unchanged. He tells of his life and the immense tenderness he feels for his best friend, Kevin, and of his brother's family and their rejection. He speaks of the death he is facing with courage. The case of Catherine Hunt is equally moving. Her brother is an AIDS patient and for her, family love is the most precious thing on earth. Their stories are creatively juxtaposed with a series of performances by Canadian musicians and performance artists including David Roche delivering a devastating monologue dressed as a fireman.

The documentary portions of No Sad Songs are narrated by Kate Reid, a Canadian character actress for featured roles in Atlantic City and countless other films, as well as a starring role as Mrs. Willy Loman in Death of a Salesman opposite Dustin Hoffman. Director/producer Nick Sheehan has worked as a writer in Toronto's independent film community and is currently developing a feature-length comedy-drama called Star Baby.

No Saintly Girl
Dir. Whitaker, Claire
1993 USA English
32 mins. video color Documentary
Dist. (U.S.): Whitaker, Claire
Claire Whitaker's lively memoir of the Catholic girls' boarding school of her youth and of her coming to terms with her sexual identity.

No Skin Off My Ass
Dir. LaBruce, Bruce
1990 Canada/Germany English
75 mins. 16mm b&w Narrative
Dist. (U.S.): Strand Releasing
Dist. (U.K.): Dangerous To Know
Bruca LaBruce, Toronto's underground homo filmmaker extraordinaire, plays a punk hairdresser who picks up a cute young skinhead in the park and locks him up in his apartment in this cheap and dirty, sweet and charming, unabashedly erotic, and refreshingly unpretentious movie. Shot in gritty black-and-white, with a visual style that goes from ragged to lyrical, it is one of the most directly sensual and sexual gay films around, one with the point of view that "being a fag is a definite plus." Or, as the skinhead's militant, filmmaking dyke sister says: "The whole world's a fag." She delights in humiliating him by filming him in front of her half-naked girlfriends (the opus she's working on is called Girls of the S.L.A.). Most of No Skin Off My Ass takes place in the intimacy of the relationship between the romantic, seductive LaBruce and the initially reluctant, not very talkative skinhead, played by dreamy Klaus Von Bücker. There's lots of action in the tub, plus a touch of leather here and a dab of peanut butter there. It's a perfect Friday night late-show flick and while it may look like it cost $4.98 to make, the admission price is right: $3 a head, skin or not.

Nobody's People
Dir. Whiteley, Sara
1992 USA English
7 mins. video color Documentary
Dist. (U.S.): Whiteley, Sara
Portrait of an outlaw: Christian porno-

Ⓐ Ⓑ Ⓒ Ⓓ Ⓔ Ⓕ Ⓖ Ⓗ Ⓘ Ⓙ Ⓚ Ⓛ Ⓜ Ⓝ Ⓞ Ⓟ Ⓠ Ⓡ Ⓢ Ⓣ Ⓤ Ⓥ Ⓦ Ⓧ Ⓨ Ⓩ

grapher/author Red Jordan Arobateau.

Nocturne
Dir. Chamberlain, Joy
1990 Great Britain English
58 mins. 16mm color Narrative
Dist. (U.K.): Maya Vision
Marguerite, a 45-year-old upper-class woman, returns to the family mansion to attend her mother's funeral. Flashback sequences reveal her emotionally impoverished childhood as the mature Marguerite roams the relic-filled rooms. Meanwhile, down the road, two lesbian lovers are thumbing a ride. Picked up by a man in a sedan, they smirk as he warns them against hitchhiking, alluding to grisly crimes committed in the area. "Go on, tell us about what happened," goads Theresa, while her girlfriend fondles her from the backseat. More surprises await us from the somewhat sociopathic couple. The driver stops to take a leak and they make off with the car. They arrive at Marguerite's house, breaking in through the french doors where she is playing the piano. It's intrigue at first sight, as Marguerite, dressed for defense, enjoys her first wet T-shirt experience.

What follows will take even the seasoned dyke by surprise. Marguerite accompanies the couple to the nursery and dresses them in her old children's clothes. Frocked in smocks, they trot off to dinner, grossing out the housekeeper who knows lines will be crossed at the supper table (and they are).

Nocturne is reminiscent of Harold Pinter's screenplay for *The Servant.* We're not sure who's controlling who. The threesome provoke and tease each other in ways that would put *Tom Jones* to shame. Further flashbacks open closet doors in Marguerite's past, and we're invited into a complex psychological reality that releases possibilities and passions for the heroine.

At last, a film that describes a lesbian landscape full of contradiction, innuendo, and hauntings from a lesbian-positive point of view. Made for British TV, *Nocturne* has a tightly constructed (hour-long) plot, as well as characters we sympathize with, or love to hate, even when they turn on us.

None of the Above
Dir. Fowler-Smith, Penny
1993 Australia English
13 mins. 35mm color Experimental
Dist. (U.S.): Australian Film, Television & Radio School

A glamorous Technicolor cogender fetish extravaganza.

Normal Life
Dir. Normals, The
1993 Brazil Portugese
6 mins. video color Documentary
Dist. (U.S.): MIX Brasil
Highlights the presence of gays and lesbians within Brazilian society.

Norman, Is That You?
Dir. Schlatter, George
1976 USA English
92 mins. 16mm color Narrative
Dist. (U.S.): Swank Motion Pictures
It would be easy to dismiss *Norman, Is That You?* as an extended one-note pro-gay fag joke, but that would do it a disservice. While it does wallow in stereotypical character types (straight, gay, white, black, etc.), director George Schlatter's 1976 film combines what were obviously the best of intentions (what was that about the road to hell?) with a plot that could only have started life as some well-meaning Broadway comedy. Besides, who can resist Hollywood's idea of what homosexuals were wearing in the mid-'70s? It's about a black man whose parents discover that he's gay while visiting one weekend to tell him that they are getting a divorce. He's a combination of two black gay stereotypes: the Mandinka buck (an incredibly durable and pervasive representation of black masculinity and sexuality) and the deracinated WASP wanna-be (the epitome of aggressive assimilation, he's sociopolitically and culturally white). The white lover (Dennis Dugan) is a flamboyant queen (funny and nonthreatening to the dominant culture's notions of masculinity). "Sanford & Son's" Redd Foxx plays the homophobic father with Neanderthal abandon, while Pearl Bailey plays the mother as the archetypical sassy, wise-cracking black woman. Basically, everyone comes off as a buffoon.

North of Vortex
Dir. Giannaris, Constantine
1991 Great Britain English
55 mins. 16mm b&w Narrative
Dist. (U.K.): Maya Vision
A sensual change of pace: a studied black-and-white road movie about a bisexual poet, two hitchhikers, and the American landscape.

Giannaris was named Best Gay Filmmaker of the Year (1992) by the British magazine *Gay Times.*

Not Angels but Angels
Dir. Grodecki, Wiktor
1994 Czech Republic Czech
80 mins. 35mm color Documentary
Dist. (U.S.): Salzgeber & Co.
A profound and moving documentary about
teenage boy prostitutes in Prague. Astonishingly
frank and refreshingly unsentimental, *Not Angels
but Angels* is graced with a gang of wry and self-
aware interviewees.

Not Because Fidel Castro Says So
(see *No Porque Fidel Castro Lo Diga*)

Not Like That: Diary of a Butch-A-Phobe
Dir. Bradley, Maureen
1994 Canada English
14 mins. video color Other
Dist. (U.S.): Video Out
Maureen Bradley examines the causes for her
own internalized fear of looking or acting butch.

Nous etions un seul homme
(We Were One Man)
Dir. Vallois, Philippe
1979 France French
90 mins. 16mm color Narrative
Dist. (U.S.): Frameline
A modern gay classic, *We Were One Man* takes
place in France in 1943 and is the story of Guy,
a French farmer about to be married, and Rolf, a
wounded German soldier. One day Guy finds
Rolf, takes him home, nurses him to health and
tries to prevent his return to the army. Gradually
the men discover a mutual atraction that leads to
an intense relationship and a lyrical, highly erotic
love scene.

Rolf is a soldier who doubts the value
of his committment to the Nazi cause. Guy
blocks out memories of his recent incarceration
in a mental hospital and suffers from hallucinations. Their relationship serves as a catalyst for
both men as they explore long-repressed feelings.
We Were One Man had its U.S. pre-
miere at the Chicago International Film Festival
in 1980, where it was awarded the prestigious
Silver Hugo. Written, produced, edited, and
directed by France's premiere gay director,
Philippe Vallois, who went on to direct the great
body-building murder mystery spoof, *Rainbow
Serpent*.

Novembermund (Novembermoon)
Dir. Grote, Alexandra Von
1984 Germany German

106 mins. 35mm color Narrative
Dist. (U.S.): Osburg, Barbara
Dist. (U.K.): British Film Institute
Novembermoon portrays one part of Franco-
German history which has not yet been the subject of a feature film. The film deals with the
German Occupation and the French collaboration
with the German army. It is the story of a
woman's apparent collaboration in an attempt to
save the life of the woman she loves. November
Messing, a German Jewess, emigrates to Paris
with her father in 1933. After German troops
enter and occupy France in 1940, November is
allowed to flee the free zone. However, someone
informs the Gestapo and she is arrested. The persecution of French and German Jews is not easily
dealt with. Anti-Semitism was already strong in
France even before the war and many French collaborated actively and passively with the fascists.
Novembermoon is a film that reaches beyond the
horrors of World War II. It is a film against every
kind of violence and the persecution of minorities.

Now Playing
Dir. MacLean, David
1988 Canada English
22 mins. video color Narrative
Dist. (U.S.): V-Tape
In *Now Playing*, the denizens of a former porno
theater return to their old haunt to reminisce.

Now That It's Morning
Dir. Bartlett, Neil
1992 Great Britain English
11 mins. 35mm color Narrative
Dist. (U.K.): Film Four International
Now That It's Morning is a meltingly sad love
story set in 1962, photographed by Nina Kellgren
(who shot *Looking for Langston*) and directed by
Neil Bartlett, new star of the British gay arts
scene.

Nuclear Family
Dir. Canalli, John, and Marty Monroe
1980 USA English
10 mins. S8mm color Narrative
Dist. (U.S.): n/a
A look at the typical American family of the
nuclear age.

Nude Descending
Dir. Kijak, Stephen
1992 USA English
14 mins. 16mm color Experimental
Dist. (U.S.): Kijak, Stephen
A photograph, a painting, and a letter shape the

memory of a surreal one-night stand.

Nude Inn
Dir. Fontaine, Richard
1969 USA English
20 mins. 16mm color Other
Dist. (U.S.): Fontaine, Richard
From Richard Fontaine (best known for his AMG posing pouch pictures like *The Days of the Greek Gods*), *Nude Inn* is an all-singing, all-dancing, and almost all-nude version of television's "Laugh-In," featuring Fontaine's favorite drag star, Miss Glory Holden.

Nudes (A Sketchbook)
Dir. McDowell, Curt
1975 USA English
30 mins. 16mm b&w Other
Dist. (U.S.): Canyon Cinema
Though it includes studies of both male and female subjects, Curt McDowell's *Nudes* is fundamentally a male homosexual catalog of sexual (often graphic) interpretations of the personalities of friends, lovers, and relatives. Highly romantic, this collection of cinematic drawings is thought by many to be the fimmaker's most accomplished work.

Nuit Sauvage, La (Savage Nights)
Dir. Collard, Cyril
1993 France French
126 mins. 35mm color Narrative
Dist. (U.S.): Swank Motion Pictures
There's never been a film maudit like this one: Writer/director/star Cyril Collard died just as this first feature created a sensation at Cannes, with its over-the-top, clearly autobiographical portrait of HIV-positive sexual compulsiveness. His protagonist postures around Paris looking chic and doomed, engaging in anonymous encounters while richocheting between literally/figuratively "unsafe" liaisons with a "straight" soccer player (Carlos Lopez) and underage girl (Romane Bohringer). They love each other! They hate each other! They kiss! They slap! Etc. Dazzlingly cinematic, the film nonetheless grows repetitious in the extreme. Is it a daring, "outlaw" statement of reckless desire? Or an exasperating vanity project about self-absorbed characters only their models could love? Whatever your reaction is, it won't be neutral. (D.H.)

Nun, The
(see *Religieuse, La*)

Obelisk, The
Dir. Garey, Melinda
1989 USA English
22 mins. 16mm color Narrative
Dist. (U.S.): Garey, Melinda
"There are worse things than silliness," says one of the two sailors in *The Obelisk*, based on an E.M. Forster short story. Probably, but this'll do—a strangely out-of-synch summer's day tale with a loopy punchline.

Occupied Territories
Dir. Baum, Jennifer
1993 Canada English
35 mins. 16mm color Documentary
Dist. (U.S.): Baum, Jennifer
Occupied Territories is about a Jewish woman living in New York, her roommate, and her two gay male friends who are involved in an interracial relationship. The film offers challenging impressions of the power relations within the woman's milieu of diverse friendships. What does it mean to own your own space as a Jew? As a queer? As a person of color? What does it mean to occupy your own territory?

Odd Girl Out
Dir. Carland, Tammy Rae
1994 USA English
17 mins. video color Experimental
Dist. (U.S.): Franklin Media Distribution
A video diary that traces both the erotic and class roots of the artist's coming-out process. Tammy Rae Carland has created an excellent pixel vision scrapbook of her adolescence.

Odds and Ends
(A New-Age Amazon Fable)
Dir. Parkerson, Michelle
1993 USA English
28 mins. video color Narrative
Dist. (U.S.): American Film Institute
Michelle Parkerson's long-awaited African-American lesbian sci-fi drama.

Of Man; For Dad
Dir. Shat, Scott
1988 USA English
6 mins. video color Experimental
Dist. (U.S.): n/a
Family home movies and queer bestiality collide.

Off the Rails
Dir. Hawthorne, Stephen
1991 Great Britain English
48 mins. video color Documentary
Dist. (U.K.): BBC TV
The flip-side to "America's Funniest Home

Videos." In a new move for access television, the BBC developed a series called "Video Diaries," in which various "ordinary" people were given a camera and allowed to develop their own highly personal documentaries. *Off the Rails* lets 18-year-old Stephen Hawthorne revisit his strictly religious provincial parents, as well as chronicle a few weeks in the life of his relationship with urban boyfriend Bertie.

Ohrenwurm, Der
Dir. Fritsch, Herbert
Prod. Balzli, Res
1986 Switzerland German
12 mins. 16mm color Narrative
Dist. (U.S.): Balzli, Res
The pleasure of digging around in one's ears.

Ojos que No Ven (Eyes that Do Not See)
Dir. Gutierrez-Gomez, José, and José Vergelin
1987 USA English
52 mins. video color Documentary
Dist. (U.S.): Latino AIDS Project
A series of educational "telenovelas" for the Hispanic community. Tape shows AIDS as it affects a cross-section of the community, from the streetwise to the affluent.

Okoge
Dir. Nakajima, Takehiro
1992 Japan Japanese
120 mins. 35mm color Narrative
Dist. (U.S.): Cinevista
Okoge in Japanese means rice that is stuck to the bottom of the rice-pot and is colloquially used to refer to "fag-hags." This is the hilarious story of one such lovely young girl and her relationship with a strapping young man and his corporate-closeted married lover. She often lets the two men use her flat for their trysts, to the chagrin of her inquistive neighbors. The closeted lover's wife eventually finds out about this secret meeting place, leading to a series of very campy and highly enjoyable scenarios.

Olivia (Pit of Loneliness)
Dir. Audry, Jacqueline
1951 France French
88 mins. 35mm color Narrative
Dist. (U.S.): JEF/Film Classic Exchange
Dist. (U.K.): Cinenova
Like the more well-known *Mädchen In Uniform*, this story of a young girl's love for her teacher was written and directed by women. Although it ends tragically, the film's lesbian characters are sympathetically portrayed. *Olivia* is a beautifully

photographed melodrama, and the only film of the 1950s to deal openly with lesbianism.

Released in the United States in 1954 as *Pit of Loneliness*, this rarely seen French lesbian boarding school drama was censored for American audiences. In *The Celluloid Closet* Vito Russo reprints the following censor's notation on the film: "Eliminate in Reel 5D: Scene of Miss Julie holding Olivia in close embrace and kissing her on the mouth. Reason: Immoral, would tend to corrupt morals." The film's advertising campaign sensationalized the "immoral" lesbian angle as only Hollywood can, promising viewers a look at "The secret of a woman's love-starved soul in the daring drama of an unnatural love."

The film's stars are French leading lady Simone Simon and Edwige Feuillere, the noted actress, stage director, and member of La Comedie Francaise, who received excellent notices for her performance. The script by Colette is remarkable for the unblinking, if sometimes furtive, passion of Miss Julie and *Olivia*, which, unusual for films or books of the period, grows out of a genuine attraction to each other rather than a failed heterosexual romance or other such disaster.

Olivia was directed by Jacqueline Audry, whose film credits include *Gigi* (1949) and *Mitzou* (1956). Audry, known for "sensitive observations of the sentiments of women," lives up to her reputation in *Olivia*. Although the film ends with the tragedy and condemnation of deviancy requisite of 1950s films about homosexuality, throughout most of the film Audry succeeds in creating a generally credible (and oftentimes steamy) relationship between the protagonists.

Olympia
Dir. Perzely, Mark
1995 USA English
6 mins. 16mm color Documentary
Dist. (U.S.): Perzely, Mark
A whirlwind view of the 1994 Gay Games.

On a Queer Day [work in progress]
Dir. McDowell, Peter
1995 USA English
10 mins. video color Experimental
Dist. (U.S.): McDowell, Peter
Two tourist couples are captivated by queer San Francisco.

On Becoming
Dir. Rizzo, Teresa

1993 Australia English
26 mins. video color Documentary
Dist. (U.S.): Rizzo, Teresa
On Becoming explores notions of gender identity and gender as performance, and paves the way for the body of the future.

On Guard
Dir. Lambert, Susan
Prod. Duncan, Digby
1984 Australia English
51 mins. 16mm color Narrative
Dist. (U.S.): Women Make Movies
Dist. (U.K.): Cinenova
Winner of the Best First Feature Award when shown at the San Francisco International Film Festival in 1984, *On Guard* is director Susan Lambert's story of a group of women who attack a segment of the medical/scientific establishment in Australia that they feel is potentially harmful to women's bodies and self-determination. There's more than one righteous dyke and lots of personal drama in the outfit. The assignment: mess up the computer memory banks in the genetics institute. The risks: loss of jobs, life, commitment, kids, cooperation, and love. The complication: One of the would-be saboteurs has been keeping a diary of their plans, and has lost it. The reality: a dual-paced thriller-adventure laced with conspiracy and caring.

On the Safe Side
Dir. Turnley, Bill
Prod. Chalgren, Jim
1985 USA English
28 mins. video color Documentary
Dist. (U.S.): Minnesota AIDS Project
A production of the Minnesota AIDS Project designed to encourage discussion of safe sex among gay men. It goes beyond the familiar lists of sexual practices to reach a more personal level of awareness by showing Midwestern men talking about how they are dealing with the challenges of the present health crisis.

Once Upon a Time in the East
(see *Il Etait une Fois dans L'est*)

One and the Other Time
Dir. Turner, Sarah
1990 Great Britain English
5 mins. 16mm b&w Experimental
Dist. (U.K.): Cinenova
A calm evocation of an abusive lover.

One Fool
Dir. Wolfe, Kathy
1985 USA English
3 mins. video color Other
Dist. (U.S.): Wolfe Video
A Karen Shoemaker music video.

One Foot on a Banana Peel, the Other Foot in the Grave
Dir. Botas, Juan, and Lucas Platt
1993 USA English
83 mins. 16mm color Documentary
Dist. (U.S.): Clinica Estetico
One Foot on a Banana Peel, the Other Foot in the Grave is about an AIDS clinic in Greenwich Village where several men sit together for hours in the clinic's Dolly Madison Room where they receive their intravenous medication. Artist Juan Botas started bringing his video camera with him to document the stories of the men he met in the room. When Botas died, the project was finished by his producers and codirector, Lucas Platt.

It's much like watching somebody's well-edited home movies. You are at once hovering between captivation and boredom, between indifference and voyeurism, and between annoyance and pathos.

Your tolerance of this documentary will depend on where you are on the AIDS-In-Your-Life continuum. If you're in the Larry-Kramer-I've-Cornered-the-Market-on-AIDS-Related-Emotions range, this will irk you endlessly. If you're in the Good-Feeling-Homo-Who-Cried-for-Four-Days-after-*Philadelphia* range, this will rip your heart right out. If you're somewhere in the middle, you might want to catch this simply for the experience. You might also want to wonder about filmmakers' and audiences' unyielding dependence on heroism and bravado when it comes to portraying AIDS on screen. (J.C.)

100 Days before the Command
(see *Sto Dnej Do Prikaza*)

100 Seconds with Sasha
Dir. Gelke, Hans, and Uta Stork
1993 USA English
2 mins. video color Other
Dist. (U.S.): Gelke, Hans
A collage portrait of Sasha, a male-to-female transsexual living in a San Francisco South of Market hotel.

103 Degrees
Dir. Marcolina, Kirk
1993 USA English

5 mins. 16mm b&w Documentary
Dist. (U.S.): Marcolina, Kirk
A raw documentary about an HIV-positive, 17-year-old ex-hustler.

One Nation Under God
Dir. Maniaci, Teodoro, and Francine Rzeznick
1993 USA English
83 mins. 16mm color Documentary
Dist. (U.S.): First Run Features
Dist. (U.K.): Films Transit
This riveting documentary offers the most dynamic historical overview of gays and lesbians in modern American society since *Before Stonewall*. Focusing on the contemporary religious Right Wing proliferation of curative therapies for homosexuality, *One Nation Under God* offers historical context as well as a political analysis of a frighteningly large movement. Extensive archival footage conveys the history of attempts to cure, discourage, and stigmatize homosexuality through medical and psychiatric pathologies. Archival interview footage of the scary, straight-faced authorities of the '50s and '60s are contrasted with today's experts on "reparative therapy." Featuring interviews with individuals currently involved with the ex-gay movement, the film's highlight is its interview with the ex-ex-gays, Gary and Michael, cofounders of the ex-gay organization, Exodus International. Gary and Michael, who fell in love with each other and denounced the movement, speak candidly, with warmth and humor, about their own personal, spiritual, and political growth.
     Winner of the 1993 San Francisco International Lesbian & Gay Film Festival Audience Award for Best Documentary.

One Sings
Dir. Canalli, John
1985 USA English
20 mins. video color Narrative
Dist. (U.S.): n/a
Two parallel stories, one presented in a formal, dramatic style, the other in subscript form, that reveal the coinciding aftereffects of love gone wrong and the coping mechanisms we use to move on.

Only a Test
Dir. unknown
1983 USA English
5 mins. video color Other
Dist. (U.S.): n/a
So artistic, it's autistic. This piece covers the world in a well composed static shot.

Only the Brave
Dir. Kokkinos, Ana
1994 Australia English
59 mins. 16mm color Narrative
Dist. (U.S.): First Run Features
Dist. (U.K.): Dangerous To Know
This hard-edged voyage through a few days in the life of a tough teenage girl is one of the most powerful lesbian features we've ever seen.
     Alex (Elena Mandalis) and her best friend Vicki (Dora Kaskanis) are both Greek Australian; they hang out with a gang of girls who party heavily and like to set things on fire. Longing to escape the harsh chaos of her surroundings and to find the mother who abandoned her when she was a child, Alex plans to go to Sydney with Vicki. Amid the travails and dismal drama of her high school, Alex comes to realize her emerging attraction to Vicki and to her teacher.
     Very much a film of the '90s, Ana Kokkinos's sobering portrayal of disillusioned youth has the jarring punch and tragic catharsis of such classic social dramas as *Over the Edge* and *Rebel without a Cause*.
     Winner of the 1994 San Francisco International Lesbian & Gay Film Festival Audience Award for Best Feature.

Optic Nerve
Dir. Hammer, Barbara
1985 USA English
16 mins. 16mm color/b&w Experimental
Dist. (U.S.): Canyon Cinema
Dist. (U.K.): London Filmmaker's Co-op
Optic Nerve returns to a more personal film representation, one that works on an intellectual and emotional level to explore aging and family. Sound score by Helen Thorington.
     Released by Facets Multimedia in the U.S. along with five of her other short films as a feature-length package, *Optical Nerves: The Films of Barbara Hammer, Volume IV*.

Oranges Are Not the Only Fruit
Dir. Kidron, Beeban
1989 Great Britain English
165 mins. 16mm color Narrative
Dist. (U.K.): BBC TV
Oranges is the best lesbian coming-of-age film yet. Originally planned as a three-parter for British television, this complex story takes us through the hazardous journey of a heroic young girl's escape from a religious upbringing. The film opens with the mother, the young Jess, and her

Ⓐ Ⓑ Ⓒ Ⓓ Ⓔ Ⓕ Ⓖ Ⓗ Ⓘ Ⓙ Ⓚ Ⓛ Ⓜ Ⓝ Ⓞ Ⓟ Ⓠ Ⓡ Ⓢ Ⓣ Ⓤ Ⓥ Ⓦ Ⓧ Ⓨ Ⓩ

white dog sitting atop a gravestone. Mum is alluding to her fall from grace while living in Paris as a young girl, and her rebirth as a Christian. "She'd never heard of mixed feelings," Jess tells us in voice-over. The screenplay, adapted by Jeanette Winterson from her own novel of the same title, is droll and endearing, frightening and funny—even while describing the perverted pedagogy of Christian cultists. It's a strange beginning of a life. Young Jess, ever observant and precocious, tells schoolmates that there are no toilets in hell. Later, she trots off to assist the "Society of the Last," her mother's odd evangelical group in a musical mission. they hold forth on the beach, but heathens throw sand into Miss Jewbury's accordion; she loses her F sharp. (*Oranges* has some of the best examples I've ever seen of older women characters who are nuanced, nurturing, and know how to survive). Part One ends as the looney Christians go off the deep end. The plots in Part Two not only gel, but thicken into a horrifying climax. Now teenage Jess meets the winsome Melanie, who works at a fish stall. They are immediately stuck on each other and, over a fish carcass, the schoolgirl crush is off and running.

Jess is a great kisser on Saturday night and Sunday morning finds her locking eyes with Melanie singing "He Touched Me" at service. But the word is out among the faithful; Jess and Melanie are damned if not doomed. In saving them from the evils of lust, the Christians reveal themselves as true torturers. The heroic Jess triumphs over her situation and finally gains enough distance from her past to create a future for herself.

This landmark lesbian film is certainly the best—if not the only—initiation story that is positive and mature in characterization and plot, helped by the playful and quirky score of Rachall Portman.

Winner of the 1990 San Francisco International Lesbian & Gay Film Festival Audience Award for Best Feature.

Order, The
Dir. Manfredini, Nilo
Prod. Horses, Inc.
1980 USA English
5 mins. S8mm color Experimental
Dist. (U.S.): n/a
The Order is the first Super-8 film produced by Horses, Inc.; it is 5 minutes in length, in color, with sound. *The Order* was shot 1:1, which means that it was filmed as one complete take,

and is totally unedited. The film has been described as "a great parody with an on-target punchline" (Dennis Harvey, *The Michigan Daily*). *The Order's* highly stylized content startlingly juxtaposes images of fantasy with practicality. The film is both comedic and satiric, prodding the audience to question its own reactions of laughter at the situation portrayed. The success of this first Super-8 filmmaking attempt is indicated by awards received by Horses in connection with *The Order* this year: The film was named a winner at both the 10th Annual Ann Arbor Super-8 Film Festival, and the 1980 Los Angeles International Film Exposition.

Orgasm of Hot Blood
Dir. Dumas, Chris
1994 USA English
13 mins. 16mm color Narrative
Dist. (U.S.): Dumas, Chris
A classy revenge story.

Orientations
Dir. Fung, Richard
1984 USA English
57 mins. video color Documentary
Dist. (U.S.): Third World Newsreel
A documentary by and about lesbian and gay Asians that opens with a ritualistic dance symbolizing the invisibility and bondage of Asian homosexuals in a white heterosexual society. The three main topics covered by this work are coming out, the racist encounter and the importance of the lesbian and gay community.

Orlando
Dir. Potter, Sally
1993 Great Britain/Russia/France/Italy English
93 mins. 35mm color/b&w Narrative
Dist. (U.S.): New Yorker Films
When the mythic Jesus entertained the masses, he used a lot of fish stories to get his points across. Sally Potter, whose critical reputation lately has just about reached that biblical proportion, uses women in much the same way. Her film *Orlando* is a stately adventure in historical cross-dressing that speaks in parable about the problems of ownership.

Earnest, gallant, coy—and infused with two-line witticisms that border on sloganeering—this film carries on Derek Jarman's tradition of turning American activists into Anglophiles. Potter's film transfers Virginia Woolf's flamboyant vision into amazingly adequate entertainment. This version is a simple one: Boys meets girl. Boy becomes girl. Girl meets man. Girl becomes pregnant. And book becomes film. Although *Orlando* the film spans four centuries, two continents, and as many sexes, the ageless protagonist Orlando him/herself keeps it anchored in one easy coming-of-age story. Orlando grows from audacity to compassion to womanhood. And Potter (whose other films include difficult post-structuralist themes) learns how to use a spoon-ful of narrative to help the postmodern medicine (sexism, imperialism, film, and the male bias of history) go down.

The resulting film is a visual pageant, but the elegant choreography and outsized cos-tumes offer a stark contrast to the situation this film speaks to—specifically England's demise. Nearing the year 2000, the country has down-sized its imperialist role in the world.

Orlando himself suffers the privilege shakedown in the film. He was born to be wild (i.e., male) in the 16th century and invested with a home by his admiring mentor, Queen Elizabeth I, played by writer, sometime actor, and gay-celeb Quentin Crisp, in the 17th. But by the 18th cen-tury, he started losing things: love, his male privi-lege, and, finally, his home. It takes until the 20th-century close for Orlando to come to terms with the loss—as s/he sits beneath the oak tree and the angel-winged Jimmy Somerville coos, "At last, at last, free of the past, neither a woman nor a man," overhead.

While Woolf's book let Orlando keep the house, Potter's version makes Orlando's per-sonal liberation contingent on the act of willingly giving the property up: between Woolf's time and Potter's, imperialism/colonialism—the brutal assumption that foreign "others" needed England to own them—had, well, lost its charm. Potter's Orlando replaces nostalgia for the "owning" days with a celebration of their demise. She doesn't just turn Orlando into a woman, she makes a woman of England—and she makes that woman "liberated in the late 20th-century model."

The body politic rests on one particu-lar body: Tilda Swinton's, the woman who plays Orlando. Celebrated for her peach-fuzz androgy-ny, when she suits up as a man for her Far East journey, she looks anything but: her blond, curled horse-hair wig is adjusted too frequently; she seems to fidget in her outergarments. The result-ing historical drag show—a woman dressed like a man, out East doing diplomacy—is a jarring physical picture that makes a sarcastic comment on "official" history: men wrote it as if only men lived it.

But back in England, it's Swinton's

resolute, violet-to-hazel-to-green-eyed stare that transcends gender. Whether s/he is a biological man or a woman, she fixes that stare on the object of her choice without apology. Every glance at a woman, in the beginning, has an ele-ment of homosexual irony. Every glance at a man, in the end, has the weight of history behind it—we know that this is definitely not a glance of the passive, simple so-called girlish variety. When Swinton fixes her eyes on the audience (she addresses the camera directly more than a few times in the film), she brings us in on the joke.

Self-consciousness is clearly one of Potter's strong suits—a quality that seems to erupt from her critique of the medium itself. Part of Orlando-the-woman's liberation in the end is turning over a video camera to her child, who's playing in the tall grass. She doesn't own the house. And she doesn't even have control over the child's point of view. She manages to let go. If Potter's film is as much about capturing the right to tell a story as Woolf's book was about the project of writing itself, Potter captures that right only to eventually free it. (S.G.)

Orpheus, The Day Before
Dir. Minerba, Giovanni
1994 Italy Italian
12 mins. 16mm color Narrative
Dist. (U.S.): Minerba, Giovanni
A contemporary rendering of the ancient Orpheus.

Ostia
Dir. Cole, Julian
1987 Great Britain English
26 mins. 16mm color Experimental
Dist. (U.S.): Frameline
The reconstruction of the events leading to the murder of Pier Paolo Pasolini, the inevitability of which he himself had perhaps foreseen.

Other Families
Dir. Chvatal, Dorothy
1993 USA English
49 mins. video color Documentary
Dist. (U.S.): Fanlight Productions
Deals with artificial insemination and spends some time with seven adults who were raised by lesbian mothers.

Other Families
Dir. Jones, William
1992 USA English
15 mins. video color Documentary
Dist. (U.S.): Drift Distribution
From the maker of *Massillon*, a concise analysis

Ⓐ Ⓑ Ⓒ Ⓓ Ⓔ Ⓕ Ⓖ Ⓗ Ⓘ Ⓙ Ⓚ Ⓛ Ⓜ Ⓝ Ⓞ Ⓟ Ⓠ Ⓡ Ⓢ Ⓣ Ⓤ Ⓥ Ⓦ Ⓧ Ⓨ Ⓩ

of the notion of the family in American culture.

Other Half, The
Dir. Gili, Jonathan
Prod. Mirzoeff, Edward
1984 Great Britain English
30 mins. video color Documentary
Dist. (U.K.): BBC TV
A British documentary focusing on the affectionate, solid relationship between Sir Angus Wildon, a well-known English novelist and his lover of 32 years, Tony Garrett. Their inspiring story is told through a combination of day-to-day and interview footage. *The Other Half* is one episode of a six-part BBC series on contemporary relationships.

Other Woman, The
Dir. unknown
1983 USA English
29 mins. video color Narrative
Dist. (U.S.): n/a
An aspiring actress and her maid get drunk and critique the men in their lives and we find out they have more in common than expected.

Other Woman, The
Dir. Slane, Andrea
1991 USA English
13 mins. video color Experimental
Dist. (U.S.): Slane, Andrea
Andrea Slane's *The Other Woman* delves into the ambiguous—sadomasochistic?—relationships between three women.

Our Gay Brothers
Dir. Snider, Greta
1993 USA English
7 mins. 16mm color/b&w Experimental
Dist. (U.S.): Drift Distribution
What do gay men think about women's bodies? It's a subject that both men and women would often rather not talk about. Against an image-track of sensually resonant found footage, Greta Snider's gay friends speak honestly, if somewhat disturbingly, on this mostly uncharted area of the lesbian and gay community psyche.

Our House: Lesbians and Gays in the Hood
Dir. Not Channel Zero /
Black Planet Productions
1992 USA English
30 mins. video color Documentary
Dist. (U.S.): Third World Newsreel
An affirming, thoughtful inspection of identity issues for lesbian and gay African Americans (and everyone else).

Our Lady of L.A.
Dir. Forrest, Kathleen, Cheri Gaulke,
and Sue Mayberry
1986 USA English
29 mins. video color Documentary
Dist. (U.S.): Gaulke, Cheri
Produced by members of The Woman's Building in Los Angeles, *Our Lady of L.A.* is a captivating look at worship of the Earth Goddess there. Women of various races describe her influence on their lives and their city.

Our Mom's a Dyke
Dir. Olavarria, Juliette
1995 USA English
23 mins. video color Documentary
Dist. (U.S.): Olavarria, Juliette
Three daughters reflect back on their lives since their mother came out to them eleven years ago in Juliette Olavarria's video *Our Mom's a Dyke*. They very touchingly share with us the love they have for their mother while honestly telling us about the difficulties they have had with others and with themselves in coming to accept their mother's sexuality.

Our Trip
Dir. Hammer, Barbara
1980 USA English
4 mins. 16mm color Experimental
Dist. (U.S.): Canyon Cinema
"Feminist filmmaker and performance artist Barbara Hammer has celebrated her recent trip to Peru with her friend Corky Wick through a diaristic animation of photographs they took during their travels. Landscapes and portraits are given growing patterns of framing and texture with magic markers and tempera paint, expressing the richly evocative folk art of the Incan people they saw as we hear their native music resonate on the soundtrack." —Anthony Reveaux
Released in the U.S. along with four of her other short films as a feature-length package, *Lesbian Humor: The Films of Barbara Hammer, Volume I.*

Out for a Change: Addressing Homophobia in Women's Sports
Dir. Mosbacher, Dee
1995 USA English
28 mins. video color Documentary
Dist. (U.S.): Woman Vision Productions
This probing documentary on homophobia in

women's sports interviews many of the top names in women's sports, including Martina Navratilova.

Out for Laughs
Dir. Carr, Shan
1992 USA English
30 mins. video color Other
Dist. (U.S.): Carr, Shan
Out for Laughs is a queer "Laugh-In"; see your favorite local queer comics show their stuff in the brilliant half-hour TV variety show.

Out in Africa
(see *Out On Four: Episodes 1 & 2*)

Out in Africa
Dir. Symons, Johnny
1994 USA English
20 mins. video color Documentary
Dist. (U.S.): Symons, Johnny
A series of interviews with gay men in Zimbabwe and South Africa. Symons shot the tape while backpacking through Africa; he captures a unique picture of gay life there.

Out in Comedy
Dir. Leech, Marla
1994 USA English
21 mins. video color Other
Dist. (U.S.): Leech, Marla
A look at queer stand-up comedians.

Out in South Africa
Dir. Hammer, Barbara
1994 USA English
51 mins. video color Documentary
Dist. (U.S.): Women Make Movies
Barbara Hammer was invited to have a retrospective of her films and videos at South Africa's first-ever lesbian and gay film festival, and lucky for us she took her camcorder with her. You'll want to join her as she takes us on a never-before-seen tour of South Africa's gay life postapartheid. Barbara made it an integral part of her trip to go into the townships to teach a video class to some very eager students, who then took this knowledge back to their respective communities. There are many compelling interviews and visits to the townships, most especially to a "shebeen" (a gay bar that is held in a home) that help to make this a powerful documentary.

Out in Suburbia
Dir. Walton, Pam
1988 USA English
28 mins. video color Documentary
Dist. (U.S.): Filmmaker's Library

Out in Suburbia looks at women living and loving in the 'burbs.
Winner of the 1989 San Francisco International Lesbian & Gay Film Festival Audience Award for Best Documentary.

Out of Many . . . One, Part III
Dir. Perica, Lou
1983 USA English
6 mins. S8mm color Other
Dist. (U.S.): n/a
Part of the 1983 Super-8 Gay Festival.

Out of Our Time
Dir. Pacilio, Casi
1988 USA English
70 mins. 16mm color Narrative
Dist. (U.S.): Back Porch Productions
An exciting first feature by two new young talents on the independent film scene, *Out of Our Time* juxtaposes two circles of women—one a literary/artistic society of women in Chicago circa 1930, the other a contemporary group of feminists. The two circles are linked by Valerie Ward and Jacquelyn Matthews, granddaughter and grandmother respectively, both of whom, in their own eras, grapple with the frustrations of not fulfilling themselves as writers, and share a dream of being published. Jacquelyn is a writer for a prominent 1930s fashion magazine who wants to have her novel published. Val is a typesetter for a small urban feminist newspaper, insecure about publishing and reading her poetry. The film skillfully interweaves the stories of these two eras, showing us the parallels in the choices, issues, and struggles that both contemporary and women of the past encounter. The 1930s period scenes convincingly recreate a sense of aristocratic bohemia, of women fighting for an artistic identity in a world where using a male pseudonym was the most accessible venue to being published. The contemporary scenes are humorous, witty, and realistic as bonds of friendship are shown to be at the core of one's identity and at the same time a threat to it.

Out of the Shadows
Prod. Washington D.C. Media Project
1990 USA English
21 mins. video color Documentary
Dist. (U.S.): Unity
Out of the Shadows is narrated by Essex Hemphill, whose poetry resounds through *Tongues Untied*. Reminiscent of early gay coming-out stories, *Out of the Shadows* introduces an attorney, a community organizer, an older man

Ⓐ Ⓑ Ⓒ Ⓓ Ⓔ Ⓕ Ⓖ Ⓗ Ⓘ Ⓙ Ⓚ Ⓛ Ⓜ Ⓝ Ⓞ Ⓟ Ⓠ Ⓡ Ⓢ Ⓣ Ⓤ Ⓥ Ⓦ Ⓧ Ⓨ Ⓩ

from an earlier generation of gays, and three transvestites and transsexuals who all share the same issues of coming to terms with being black and gay.

Out On Four: Episodes 1 & 2
Dir. Woodward, Phil
Prod. Hird, Christopher
1989 Great Britain English
100 mins. video color Documentary
Dist. (U.K.): Channel 4 Television

On St. Valentine's Day, 1989, Britain's Channel Four launched Out On Tuesday, a daring and innovative eight-week series of one-hour programs dealing with topics of interest to lesbians and gay men.

This progam presents two of the episodes from the series, which will be presented in its entirety during the festival. This program features *Crimes of Passion*, Clare Beavan's racy investigation of dyke detectives, a must for fans of alternative best-sellers Mary Wings, Katherine Forrest, and Ruth Rendell. Discover the way to tell if your sex scene is well written, and how *She Came in a Flash*, was nearly *She Came Too Often*. Also featured is *Out in Africa*, Melanie Chait's fascinating film on how two prominent political activists in South Africa are combining the struggle against apartheid with the struggle for gay rights. Simon Nkoli and Ivan Toms, currently serving the maximum prison sentence for refusing the draft, made no secret of their sexuality, forcing fellow activists to reevaluate their own prejudices against gays. As a result, the African National Congress has become the first liberation movement to acknowledge the importance of lesbian and gay rights, rather than dismissing demands with the usual "we'll deal with that after the revolution."

Hosted by groovy lesbian comedy duo Parker and Klein, this next edition of the series looks at lesbian and gay foster parents and presents a short film by Mark Finch about cult cinema entitled *Fasten Your Seatbelts*.

Out On Four: Episodes 3 & 4
Dir. Woodward, Phil
Prod. Hird, Christopher
1989 Great Britain English
100 mins. video color Documentary
Dist. (U.K.): Channel 4 Television

Directed by Connie Giannaris, maker of the Communards' videos, *Disco's Revenge* examines the history of gay disco music from Britain's adoption of Tamla Motown, through the soul of Sylvester and Summer, the high energy of Evelyn Thomas, Divine, and Miguel Brown, through its appropriation by Frankie Goes to Hollywood and Bronski Beat to the recent gay Latinization of House and its distinctive dance trends of "voguing." The informed talking heads include Neil Tennant of the Pet Ship Boys, producer and Heaven DJ Ian Levine, and Chicago house star Frankie Knuckles. Giannaris's conscious, crafted use of visual seduction provides an appropriate approach to gay disco history. As Frankie Knuckles remembers the worst excess of *Saturday Night Fever* he turns knowingly to the camera, adjusts his sun-specs, and delivers a suitably camp farewell, "All that polyester, I couldn't stand it." The program concludes with Richard Kwietniowski's short film *Alfalfa*, a gay romp through the alphabet. The next episode of the series is hosted by Julian Clary, who introduces an analysis of the appeal of programs like "Dynasy" and "Golden Girls" to gay audiences. The program also includes a report from Newcastle on the lesbian/gay scene in England's northernmost city.

Out On Four: Episodes 5 & 6
Dir. Woodward, Phil
Prod. Hird, Christopher
1989 Great Britain English
100 mins. video color Documentary
Dist. (U.K.): Channel 4 Television

Featured in this installment is *After Stonewall*, a look back at the twenty years since the fateful day that a police raid on a bar in New York's Greenwich Village sparked off the modern Gay Rights Movement. The program also talks to some of the most vocal participants from the lively seventies about the sense of purpose that motivated them at the time and, in many cases, about their anger and disappointment in what they see as apathy amongst the British gay community towards Clause 28.

The next program takes a hard look at the clause which illegalizes "promotion" of homosexuality, interviewing author of the clause, conservative MP David Wilshire and challenging Saatchi & Saatchi to develop an ad campaign to "sell homosexuality to the public. Also included is a lively report from Hollywood on how gay roles are seen as a bad career move for movie actors. Interviewer John Lyttle follows the passionate bits from *My Beautiful Laundrette* and *Desert Hearts* with such crucial questions as "Who thought up the champagne-sex scene?" and "Is Helen Shaver a good kisser?" He also asks Harvey

Fierstein if he'd ever consider playing a straight role ("W-e-ll . . . I've always wanted to do Eleanor of Aquitaine . . ."). Plus a penetrating ten-minute look at gay men, lust, and safe-sex campaigns.

Out on the Road with 2 Nice Girls [trailer]
Dir. Rzeznick, Francine, and Zinka Benton
1993 USA English
3 mins. video color Documentary
Dist. (U.S.): Rzeznik, Francine
Out on the Road gives a tease of a trailer for a feature-length tour documentary on 2 Nice Girls.

Out On Tuesday, Program 1
Dir. Kwietniowski, Richard
Prod. Ardill, Susan, and Clare Beavan
1990 Great Britain English
100 mins. video color Documentary
Dist. (U.K.): Channel 4 Television
Right Wing, Right Off, Right Hons, Right? probes those gays who still vote Tory, or at least crave Conservatism in some form. Out-gay Tory ex-MP Matthew Parris argues the case for Margaret Thatcher's "sexual tolerance"! In *Luppies*, upwardly-mobile dykes outline their aspirations with unladylike ambition. *My Beautiful Lorgnette* affectionately quizzes the phenomenon of the opera queen. The second part includes *Walk On Bi*—a catalog of the confusions and options created by self-declared bisexuals—and a report on Amnesty International's attitude to adopting gays as Prisoners of Conscience. Plus *A Matter of Life and Death* asks what it's like for gay men who have buried so many friends; one interviewee describes the film as a bold break-out from the "tyranny" of positive thinking: "I've said that AIDS was the best thing that's ever happened to me," he says, "But that was last year." Presenter: Communards' Richard Coles.

Out On Tuesday, Program 2
Dir. Kwietniowski, Richard
Prod. Ardill, Susan, and Clare Beavan
1990 Great Britain English
100 mins. video color Documentary
Dist. (U.K.): Channel 4 Television
Sex 121 and the Gulag scarily shows how AIDS is being spread through the Soviet states because of inadequate blood testing and the complete absence of disposable needles; meanwhile, Melanie Chait's interviewees speak keenly of—at last—lesbian and gay freedom. Plus from the maker of last year's *Disco's Revenge*, a piercing peek at punk rock's gay roots: *Jesus Died for Somebody's Sins (But Not Mine)*. And photographer Sunil Gupta profiles British gay Asian artist Alan Desouza. Part Two includes Melanie Chait's second special report on sex and Eastern Europe: *Polskiseks*. The new Solidarity government in tandem with the traditional Catholic Church is seeking to ban abortion; Bea Campbell polls the opinions of Polish gay men and women. Also in this episode, a one-to-one with New Yorker Sarah Schulman, author of *After Delores*.

Out On Tuesday, Program 3
Dir. Kwietniowski, Richard
Prod. Ardill, Susan, and Clare Beavan
1990 Great Britain English
100 mins. video color Documentary
Dist. (U.K.): Channel 4 Television
Flesh and Paper is a lyrical look at Indian poet Suniti Namjoshi, directed by Pratibha Parmar. Namjoshi is a wry writer who works lesbian themes into a complex picture of Indian culure. Simon Callow presents *White Flannel*, a witty tour of the homosexual novelists and characters who've inspired so many British costume drama queers, like *Maurice* and the boys of *Brideshead Revisited*. In part two: a "Rough Trade Guide" to the EC capitals (*A Song for Europe*) and a travelogue—sort of—on the nation most celebrated by gay historians and travel agents (*Greek Love and Sapphic Sophistication*). Plus a profile of the almost implausibly outspoken Irish senator David Norris, who successfully overturned Eire's antigay laws in European Court.

Out On Tuesday, Program 4
Dir. Kwietniowski, Richard
Prod. Ardill, Susan, and Clare Beavan
1990 Great Britain English
100 mins. video color Documentary
Dist. (U.K.): Channel 4 Television
First, *Women Like Us*, a fifty-minute essay on older lesbians. The women—whose ages range from 50-80—come from different cultures, classes, and backgrounds but all discuss first love, romance, the social pressures that led them to marry, and their late-in-life coming out. An excellent history of the changing image of lesbians and lesbianism from the 1920s to today. More dyke demographics in Part Two. Many lesbian mothers have become pregnant through donor insemination, a scheme which offers frozen sperm to prospective mothers and guarantees the donor's anonymity. However, a proposed amendment to a new piece of British legislation wants to limit D.I. treatment to married or stable straight couples, and to allow children to trace their fathers at 18. *Let's Pretend* talks to lesbian

Ⓐ Ⓑ Ⓒ Ⓓ Ⓔ Ⓕ Ⓖ Ⓗ Ⓘ Ⓙ Ⓚ Ⓛ Ⓜ Ⓝ Ⓞ Ⓟ Ⓠ Ⓡ Ⓢ Ⓣ Ⓤ Ⓥ Ⓦ Ⓧ Ⓨ Ⓩ

mothers and tackles the threat to drive self-insemination underground. Also: *School for Scandal*, an exposé of the worst of British newspapers.

Out: Stories of Lesbian and Gay Youth
Dir. Adkin, David
1993 Canada English
79 mins. 16mm color Documentary
Dist. (U.S.): Filmmaker's Library
Out is a spirited overview of the lives and struggles of lesbian and gay youth in Canada. In this groundbreaking film, director David Adkin covers a broad range of concerns as he breaks the silences, smashes the stereotypes, and boldly brings out a new generation of outspoken, articulate, and proud lesbian and gay young people.
The film's rich cross-section of interviews reflects a diversity of economic backgrounds, religious, ethnic, and cultural heritages. Frank interviews with parents, along with discussions of homophobia, coming out, and finding community make the film a great primer for young people, gay and straight.

"OUT" Takes
Dir. Goss, John
1989 USA English
13 mins. video color Other
Dist. (U.S.): Video Data Bank
John Goss outlines gay sensibility, homophobia, and gender roles on broadcast TV in a montage of scenes from a popular Japanese TV show, "Pee Wee's Playhouse," and Rex Reed's *At the Movies*.

Outcasts
Dir. Grode, Leigh B.
1991 Netherlands English
25 mins. 16mm color/b&w Documentary
Dist. (U.S.): Frameline
Docudrama about the search for the fate of lesbians in Nazi concentration camps. Fictional scenes of a lesbian love story are well balanced with Grode's personal account of her search and the stories she found.

Outlaw
Dir. Lebow, Alisa S.
1994 USA English
27 mins. video color Documentary
Dist. (U.S.): Women Make Movies
Labor and transgender activist Leslie Feinberg shares with us her experiences as a woman who has spent much of her life passing as a man and fighting for transgender rights.

Outlaw Poverty, Not Prostitutes
Dir. Leigh, Carol, a.k.a. Scarlot Harlot
1990 USA English
21 mins. video color Documentary
Dist. (U.S.): Reality Productions
Outlaw Poverty, Not Prostitutes is a documentary by and about prostitutes at the World Whore's Summit. In listening to the women's experiences you definitely get that "tip of the iceberg" feeling. The women speak from the heart, and with a keen understanding of just where is the bottom line of sexual politics.

Outsiders, The
Dir. Kan-Ping Yu
1986 Taiwan Chinese
90 mins. 35mm color Narrative
Dist. (U.S.): Oriental Films Ltd.
In this well-shot and well-paced suspense story, Ahching, a young student thrown out of his house for being gay, takes up with other abandoned gays in a park in central Taipei. Several of the cute young boys are given shelter and guidance by a fiftyish photographer, Yiang, and his feisty female landlord, Lee Manhua. Ah-ching becomes passionately involved with Wang Kei-Lung, recently returned to Taiwan under mysterious circumstances, ten years after killing his lover, whom Ah-ching resembles.
The Outsiders (literally "the bastard children" in Chinese) is the first film with a homosexual theme to be licenced by the government of Taiwan. Based on a popular 1983 novel by Shiang Yeong, it received a multitheater premiere in Taiwan and opened to good reviews.
Director Yu Kan-Ping portrays principal characters Yiang and Lee Man-Hua as caring providers to the boys and a true sense of family develops among this group of social misfits. Their rise to success after Yiang quits his photography business to open the Blue Angel, a bar and disco that figures in the suspenseful conclusion, seems a just reward.
The Outsiders offers a revealing look at gay life in Taiwan and the boys (and one girl who plays a nelly boy because, supposedly, not one femme could be found in all of Taiwan) are adorable.

Over Our Dead Bodies
Dir. Marshall, Stuart
1991 Great Britain English
84 mins. 16mm color Documentary
Dist. (U.K.): Maya Vision
Over Our Dead Bodies is a documentary look at the renaissance in lesbian/gay activism, or as it is

more popularly called by its proponents, queer activism. It starts with the beginnings of ACT UP in New York, which came out of the lesbian and gay community's anger and frustration with the U.S. political and medical establishment's inadequate, incompetent response to the AIDS epidemic. Next it looks at the birth of Queer Nation (USA) and Outrage (UK) and their relationship to the new lesbian and gay politics, and the AIDS activist movement.

This film makes a strong connection between past and present political movements while examining the connection between AIDS and queer activism, and their common investment in direct-action politics. While *Over Our Dead Bodies* details the actual successes of AIDS activism, it also depicts the terrible toll the epidemic has had on the gay and lesbian community, and the need to learn how to successfully integrate grief with political activism. It explores the constructive expression of anger and frustration by the new breed of activist, the burn-out and exhaustion associated with queer activism, and the reclamation of the word "queer" as a self-empowering, self-identifying term.

Oy Gay
Dir. Haber, Rosalind
1992 Great Britain English
29 mins. video color Documentary
Dist. (U.K.): Maya Vision
Oy Gay was made for British TV's *Out* series. It is a concise account of the political and cultural concerns of gay and lesbian Jews in Great Britain. *Oy Gay* rings with messages of tolerance and survival.

P.A.N.I.C. in Griffith Park
Dir. Garlington, Lee
Prod. Praiser, Ian, and David Reid
1987 USA English
70 mins. video color Narrative
Dist. (U.S.): Reid, David
P.A.N.I.C. in Griffith Park is a videotape of a popular Los Angeles play about late 1980s life, had the so-called LaRouche Initiative of 1986, Proposition 64, been approved by California voters. The authorities lack enough facilities to hold and test all those of suspected of being seropositive for the AIDS virus, so L.A.'s Griffith Park becomes a temporary concentration camp. Four gay men and a drug-abusing rock and roller are rounded up and must deal with life under the rules of Proposition 64.

The concentration camp atmosphere lends itself to self-reflection on the part of the incarcerated, particularly those who remember Griffith Park in more carefree days. The grim reality of post–Larouche California and the cynical way in which AIDS is used as a pretext for executing a malicious social agenda are offset by the humanity and humor of the camp members. Micheal Alden gives a fine performance as the idealistic Craig, who craftily attempts to force the hand of the hypocritical camp authorities.

P.A.N.I.C. in Griffith Park was initially produced as a fundraiser for the "No on 64" campaign. Writer David Reid has cleverly woven his immediate goal of informing voters about the danger of the LaRouche Initiative into a potent and dramatic exploration of the rights of homosexuals and people with AIDS.

P.A.R.A.N.O.R.M.A.L.
Dir. Pereira, Leda, and Ruth Slinger
1994 Brazil Portugese
5 mins. video color Documentary
Dist. (U.S.): MIX Brasil
An in-your-face personal account of a lesbian paraplegic.

P(l)ain Truth
Dir. Pohjola, Ilppo
1993 Finland English
15 mins. 35mm color Experimental
Dist. (U.S.): Zeitgeist Films
A "symbolic documentary" based on the experience of Rudi, a female-to-male transsexual. Like nothing you've ever seen, this stunning vision of self-transformation is both painful and cathartic. From the director of *Daddy and the Muscle Academy.*

P4W: Prison for Women
Dir. Dale, Holly, and Janis Cole
1981 Canada English
81 mins. 16mm color Documentary
Dist. (U.S.): n/a
Dist. (U.K.): British Film Institute
A documentary of unusual impact, *Prison for Women* is the first feature by Canadians Janis Cole and Holly Dale. They have gone into the only federal penitentiary for women in Canada and have come out with a heart-wrenching film showing the desperate plight of the inmates. The stories of five of the women are told in their own words. The lives they reveal are bleak and empty. Worst of all, few of them see any hope for their futures. Almost no opportunity is offered for rehabilitation; the only job training available is in cosmetology. Some of the few bright spots in the

Ⓐ
Ⓑ
Ⓒ
Ⓓ
Ⓔ
Ⓕ
Ⓖ
Ⓗ
Ⓘ
Ⓙ
Ⓚ
Ⓛ
Ⓜ
Ⓝ
Ⓞ
Ⓟ
Ⓠ
Ⓡ
Ⓢ
Ⓣ
Ⓤ
Ⓥ
Ⓦ
Ⓧ
Ⓨ
Ⓩ

film are the segments dealing with Janise and Debby, two women who met in prison and fell in love. Their happiness when they are together is infectious. Ironically, after being brought together by imprisonment, it is freedom that may cause these two lovers to lose each other. Debby is scheduled for release in 489 days. Janise has 20 more years to go. The helplessness these two feel as they discuss their separation is typical of all of the prisoners. Unable to direct their own lives, to be with their loved ones, to even walk down a street, these women are truly forlorn. The loss and the anger that they feel as a result is seen in every face in the film, and is heard in every story.

Package, The
Dir. Symons, Johnny, and Luna Hananel
1993 USA English
5 mins. video color Other
Dist. (U.S.): San Francisco AIDS Foundation/ Prevention Dept.
A safe-sex short.

Palace
Dir. Dutton, Syd, and Scott Runyon
1972 USA English
20 mins. 16mm color Documentary
Dist. (U.S.): n/a
A short documentary on the 1970s San Francisco drag troupe, the Cockettes. Founded on New Year's Eve 1969–1970, the Cockettes performed their midnight shows at the Palace Theater, a Chinese language movie house in North Beach. Their productions were a combination of musical comedy, agit-prop theater, and drag show; theatrical pageants of costume and improvisation.

Pandora's Box
Dir. Beauchamp, Annie
Prod. Coombs, Steven, and Bernard Purcell
1994 Australia English
8 mins. 35mm color Narrative
Dist. (U.S.): Australian Film, Television & Radio School
A visual tour de force that turns an ordinary travel case into Cocteau's wardrobe.

Paper Cranes
Dir. Reed, Peter
1991 USA English
18 mins. 16mm color Narrative
Dist. (U.S.): Concrete Foundation, A
Set in three periods (1950, 1970, and 1990), *Paper Cranes* investigates aspects of male bonding while examining the cultural notions of honorable death.

Parachute
Dir. Eckhard, Sabine
1986 Germany German
13 mins. 35mm b&w Narrative
Dist. (U.S.): n/a
A woman receives anonymous letters accompanied by a series of photographs to do with herself that confuse, worry, but also increasingly fascinate her.

Parade 1983
Prod. Media Manetta Productions
1983 USA English
5 mins. video color Documentary
Dist. (U.S.): n/a
A powerful encapsulation of our lives, our opinions, ourselves. Sensitively conceived, excellent original score.

Paradise Framed
Dir. Ruven, Paul
1994 Netherlands Dutch
58 mins. 35mm color Other
Dist. (U.S.): Rabarts, Marten
Part of a film triptych on AIDS supported by the Red Hot Organization in London, this haunting film symbolically explores the pain of loss and the search for community. With lush and startling imagery, director Paul Ruven takes us on a vision quest for liberation from the daily prison wrought by our emotional and psychic repressions.

Parallel Sons
Dir. Young, John G.
Prod. Spione, James, and Nancy Larsen
1995 USA English
93 mins. 35mm color Narrative
Dist. (U.S.): Young, John G.
Set in a sleepy upstate New York town, where a cup of coffee is still thirty-five cents and cross burning is a mundane weekend pastime, *Parallel Sons* follows the chance meeting of Seth (Gabriel Mick), an aspiring young white artist, and Knowledge (Lawrence Mason), an African-American correctional-facility escapee. Despite the brutal circumstances of their introduction— the wounded Knowledge attempts to rob the diner where Seth works nights—their lives become irreversibly entangled when Seth hides Knowledge in the woods, safe from the racist sheriff, and nurses him back to health. But Seth's act of kindness goes beyond compassion, for Seth's personal world is fueled by the romanticized notion of what it is to be young and black from the inner city. His art is heavily influenced

by graffiti. He can lip synch to rap without missing a beat. He wears gangsta clothes and his hair in dreads, albeit blond. Knowledge becomes more than a patient as they both tentatively discover a far deeper commonality drawing them closer together. When a sudden accident drives them further away from the law, they embark on a desperate journey in search of freedom.

Strung taut with dramatic and sexual tension, *Parallel Sons* proves first-time feature director John G. Young a skilled master of cinematic storytelling. Speaking to anyone who has longed to escape from where they came but fears where they might go, *Parallel Sons* is more about kindness, compassion, and the need to be loved than it is about the differences that make one man white and the other black.

Winner of the 1995 San Francisco International Lesbian & Gay Film Festival Audience Award for Best Feature.

Parents Come Out
Dir. Tat, Rob
Prod. Cooper, Aaron, and Pat Blumenthal
1985 USA English
28 mins. video color Documentary
Dist. (U.S.): Cooper, Aaron
An insightful documentary of eight women and men who have lesbian daughters or gay sons. These are the stories of parents who questioned, learned, and pushed themselves beyond the simplistic explanations and prejudices of a homophobic society to reach a better understanding and accceptance of their children.

Paris is Burning
Dir. Livingston, Jennie
1990 USA English
70 mins. 16mm color Documentary
Dist. (U.S.): Swank Motion Pictures
Dist. (U.K.): Dangerous To Know
They call themselves the Children. They are messengers, welfare recipients, salespeople, and prostitutes. By night they are Krystle and Blake Carrington. As black and hispanic gay men, the Children inhabit two worlds—an everyday world of discrimination and poverty, and the world of "Realness," where through costume and competition, dance and inspired performance, they imitate and transcend the powerful fantasy media that excludes them. "It's like going through the Looking Glass," says one. "It's how being gay should be."

Paris is Burning becomes firm friends with a number of the Children as they meet along the piers, where they exchange news and sex and practice voguing. Each of the Children belongs to the House that suits him best (the House of Chanel, the House of Saint Laurent, the House of Ninja, and others). Monthly fashion balls—the dramatic pivot of the film's disco-beat action and of the subculture itself—take place in Harlem or Brooklyn. Members of rival Houses talk about competing for trophies and cash prizes in categories such as High Fashion Eveningwear, Face, Model's Body, and most curious and serious of all, "Realness." In the Realness category, drag queens try to pass for real women, butch queens for real men—that is, heterosexual men. (There are also subcompetition categories like Executive Realness and Schoolboy Realness.) As one of the judges explains, "If you can pass the trained eye and not give away the fact that you're gay, that's when it's Real." What is a "real" woman, what is a "real" man? *Paris is Burning* is a giddy celebration of this subculture, these contradictions. And if you're not interested in these questions, there's always the superglamorous costumes.

Winner of the 1990 San Francisco International Lesbian & Gay Film Festival Audience Award for Best Documentary.

Paris Was a Woman
Dir. Schiller, Greta
Prod. Schiller, Greta, Andrea Weiss,
and Frances Berrigan
1995 USA/Great Britain English
75 mins. 16mm color/b&w Documentary
Dist. (U.S.): Jezebel Productions
Written by Andrea Weiss and directed by Greta Schiller (the same team that brought us *Before Stonewall, International Sweethearts of Rhythm*, and *Tiny and Ruby: Hell Divin' Women*), *Paris Was a Woman* tells the story of the extraordinary community of lesbian artists, writers, photographers, and editors who were drawn to the city of Paris between the two World Wars. This in-depth exploration features home movies and rare archival footage of Colette, Janet Flanner, Gertude Stein, Sylvia Beach, and other luminaries of the time.

Parisian Blinds
Dir. Hammer, Barbara
1984 USA No Dialogue
6 mins. 16mm color/b&w Experimental
Dist. (U.S.): Canyon Cinema
This silent short is an abstract study that questions the perceptions of tourists by repeating the route of an excursion boat in Paris.

Ⓐ Ⓑ Ⓒ Ⓓ Ⓔ Ⓕ Ⓖ Ⓗ Ⓘ Ⓙ Ⓚ Ⓛ Ⓜ Ⓝ Ⓞ Ⓟ Ⓠ Ⓡ Ⓢ Ⓣ Ⓤ Ⓥ Ⓦ Ⓧ Ⓨ Ⓩ

Released by Facets Multimedia in the U.S. along with five of her other short films as a feature-length package, *Optical Nerves: The Films of Barbara Hammer, Volume IV.*

Parting Glances
Dir. Sherwood, Bill
1986 USA English
90 mins. 35mm color Narrative
Dist. (U.S.): October Films
Dist. (U.K.): British Film Institute
Bill Sherwood's romantic seriocomedy made a charming gay addition to the mid '80s Amerindie production boom. Charting 24 hours before two handsome young NYC lovers part (one leaving for a job abroad), the film has a sweet tenor somewhat compromised by the fact that its yuppie protagonists are far less interesting than one subsidary role: Steve Buscemi's marvelous, antic PWA/artist best-friend. Sherwood himself died of AIDS in 1990 at the age of 38. (D.H.)

Party
Dir. Sessoms, Charles
1993 USA English
26 mins. video color Narrative
Dist. (U.S.): AIDS Films
A short salutory drama about how a condom comes between two lovers.

Party Favor, The
Dir. Udelson, Lisa
Prod. IKON Creative Pictures/ N.K. Tannenbaum
1995 USA English
21 mins. 35mm color Narrative
Dist. (U.S.): IKON Creative Pictures
A hilarious comedy that puts an unexpected twist on a typical suburban bridal shower. A lesbian couple who are trying to have a baby attend this traditional heterosexual ritual, and leave with a very special party favor.
Winner of the 1995 San Francisco International Lesbian & Gay Film Festival Audience Award for Best Short Film.

Paso Doble
Dir. Lambert, Lothar
1983 Germany German
90 mins. 16mm color Narrative
Dist. (U.S.): Igelfilm GmbH
"Papa's in love with him." "With a foreigner?!" Lothar Lambert's *Paso Doble* is the answer to whether a long-underground filmmaker (*Fucking City, Fraulein Berlin*) can make his way to the light without losing his integrity, cast members, or wacky sexful sense of humor. It's an ordinary, nuclear Berliner family . . . except that the hausfrau (the bounteous Ulrike S.) can't get her macho hubby (the wonderfully stolid Albert Heins) to dancing class to learn the Paso Doble in preparation for their vacation to Spain, to take off his toupee, nor out of his disgusting habit of jacking off in bed. Their teenagers, Tanya and Christian, feel the lack of sexual knowhow and muscles, respectively. German inhibitions are loosened by the hot Spanish sun. On their return, Mama takes off with a Persian poetry-intoning masseur, while Papa Erich brings home another kind of Spanish son—hunky, young, mute, supple, sexy, and gay. The erotic energies in *Paso Doble* are transformed into wit and unexpected sensual beauty as the family "problem" turns out to be its solution and its salvation.

Pasolini, un delitto Italiano (Pasolini, an Italian Crime)
Dir. Giordana, Marco Tullio
Prod. Cecchi Gori, Vittorio
1995 Italy/France Italian
100 mins. 35mm color Narrative
Dist. (U.S.): Cecchi Gori Group
This Italian docu-drama on the events following the assassination of Communist poet, activist, and filmmaker Pier Paolo Pasolini attempts to unveil the reasons why the truth around his death remains, officially, cloaked in secrecy and ambiguity. Director Marco Tullio Giordana follows the teenager who, after allegedly being propositioned by Pasolini, bludgeoned him to death, then ran him over with the director's own Alfa Romeo. Giordana begins to dig into the layers of Italian society that were threatened by Pasolini's lyrical and incisive politics, suggesting a broad and insidious conspiracy of Church, organized crime, and government. But while it touches on some of Pasolini's more incisive attacks on the system, it falls into the very narrative lies that Pasolini spent his whole life critiquing. Giordana is more interested in Pasolini as a flat, symbolic icon than in how his work and his life meshed organically to threaten the powerbrokers of the Western world by challenging his audiences to forsake passive specatorship and think critically about history and ideology. This JFK–like epic leaves us with a pointless and objective ambivalence; one that, at best, pushes us to shrug our shoulders. (L.C.)

Passage a L'Acte
Dir. Arnold, Martin
1993 Austria English

12 mins. 16mm b&w Experimental
Dist. (U.S.): Sixpack Films
Martin Arnold rereads a moment from the film *To Kill a Mockingbird*, mocking the unity of the American family.

Passing
Dir. Whitely, Sara
1991 USA English
3 mins. 16mm b&w Experimental
Dist. (U.S.): Frameline
In *Passing*, a woman is transformed from her everyday self to a masculine, and then a feminine extreme.

Passion: A Letter in 16mm
Dir. Rozema, Paticia B.
1985 Canada English
28 mins. 16mm color Narrative
Dist. (U.S.): Filmmaker's Cooperative
A stylish, complex depiction of a woman's one-sided, unsatisfying love affair with a strong performance by Linda Griffiths (who went on to star in John Sayles's *Lianna*) as the miserable but insightful woman.

Passion of Remembrance, The
Dir. Sankofa Black Film Workshop
1986 Great Britain English
80 mins. 16mm color Experimental
Dist. (U.S.): Third World Newsreel
Dist. (U.K.): Sankofa
Produced by the Sankofa Black Workshop, a film cooperative formed in 1983 by black, feminist, and gay filmmakers, *The Passion of Remembrance* is a work about racism, sexism, homosexuality, and the generation gap, and their effects on a black British family. The film has two story lines: one features a black man and woman in a desert landscape, discussing the plight of blacks in the U.K. He is aggressive, she shows restraint. The second shows life for the Baptiste family through its personal histories from the '50s to the '80s. Issues of race and sexuality arise, fragments of identities surface and suggest the diversity of a black family's experience in Britain. Writer/directors Maureen Blackwood and Isaac Julien also use footage from the inner-city riots that swept Britain in 1981 and shots of gay demonstrations to portray the government's harsh attitude toward its minorities. Although its scope exceeds its technical expertise, *The Passion of Remembrance* reflects a new generation of filmmakers' response to social issues, and has been praised for directing itself mainly to Britain's black community rather than preaching at whites.

Paul Cadmus: Enfant Terrible at 80
Dir. Sutherland, David
1984 USA English
64 mins. 16mm color Documentary
Dist. (U.S.): n/a
When a morally indignant admiral threw Paul Cadmus's painting of rowdy sailors out of a WPA exhibition in 1934, it was only the first scandal in the artist's unusual career. In this intimate film portrait, Cadmus, now 80, draws from the nude, demonstrates his mastery of ancient painting techniques, and candidly recounts his past as a prominent American scene painter and controversial social satirist.

Pauline's Birthday, or The Beast of Notre Dame
Dir. Matthies, Fritz
Prod. Bendixen, Heinz
1977 Germany German
84 mins. 16mm color Documentary
Dist. (U.S.): n/a
A documentary about a small gay S/M theater in the basement of the MC-Club in Hamburg, *Pauline's Birthday* records the improvisational rehearsals of a group of elderly men and hustler-type boys, orchestrated by the club's owner-genius, Pauline (a.k.a. Harry Pauly). The rehearsal scenes are interspersed with brief interviews with the individuals involved and the result is an insightful depiction of an underground gay community. The older men seem to be the most self-accepting, offering hope for the street boys who have been drawn into their world. "I don't want to hide . . . I don't want to riot," says one of the older men, "I feel perfectly free, it is my fate, this is just how I am." Gradually, as we watch them rehearse, a sense of caring emerges, the men for each other and us for them. An unscripted jolting death of one of the play's leading actors occurs during the play's premiere, and *Pauline's Birthday* unintentionally becomes a poignant meditation on aspects of gay life.

Peach
Dir. Parker, Christine
1993 New Zealand English
16 mins. 35mm color Narrative
Dist. (U.S.): First Run Features
Dist. (U.K.): British Film Institute
"Taste it while it's ripe, or let it rot." A young Maori woman is seduced (and abandoned) by her white trash boyfriend's coworker—a butch and sexy tow-truck driver.

Ⓐ
Ⓑ
Ⓒ
Ⓓ
Ⓔ
Ⓕ
Ⓖ
Ⓗ
Ⓘ
Ⓙ
Ⓚ
Ⓛ
Ⓜ
Ⓝ
Ⓞ
Ⓟ
Ⓠ
Ⓡ
Ⓢ
Ⓣ
Ⓤ
Ⓥ
Ⓦ
Ⓧ
Ⓨ
Ⓩ

Pearl Diver
Dir. Hammer, Barbara
1984 USA English
6 mins. 16mm color Experimental
Dist. (U.S.): Canyon Cinema
Pearl Diver is about the frustration of communication between two women who try to tell each other "I love you" underwater making humorous a very wet situation. Filmed in Super-8 in Baja, California, and rephotographed in 16mm to emphasize the quality of light underwater and the dual nature of living in both air and water, reflective of the female experience of living in a man's world.

Pearl Harbor & the Explosions
Dir. Leighton, Geoff
1979 USA English
16 mins. video color Other
Dist. (U.S.): n/a
Music, music, music.

Peccatum Mutum (The Silent Sin)
Dir. Silver, Suzie, and Lawrence Steger
1988 USA English
35 mins. video color Experimental
Dist. (U.S.): Video Data Bank
This expressionistic tape "exists somewhere in a dark, hazy past, " and explores relationships among cloistered nuns. *Peccatum Mutum* is a poetic and sardonic attack on the denial of desires of the flesh in favor of the spirituality Catholicism imposes on nuns. Set in a convent, this film tells the story of insatiable lesbian desire.

Pedagogue
Dir. Marshall, Stuart
1988 Great Britain English
10 mins. video color Other
Dist. (U.S.): Video Data Bank
A teacher (Neil Bartlett) interviews for a job in *Pedagogue*, Stuart Marshall's send-up of Clause 28–related British homohysteria.

Performance Art in Atlanta
Dir. Maurer, Michael
1984 USA English
3 mins. video color Documentary
Dist. (U.S.): n/a
A great selection of performance poetry from the deep South.

Performance Notes:
A Bar is a Bar is a Bar
Dir. Rorex, LeeAnn
1994 USA English
18 mins. video color Other
Dist. (U.S.): FortGod HellCat Productions
A hilarious monologue about New York City and lesbian bars.

Peril or Pleasure?
Feminist-Produced Pornography
Dir. Torrice, Andrea
1989 USA English
28 mins. video color Documentary
Dist. (U.S.): Torrice Productions
Peril or Pleasure? Feminist-Produced Pornography raises important questions about erotica, porn, and censorship, which remain unresolved among feminists after several years of debate. Producer Andrea Torrice presents the pros and cons through interviews with women active on both sides of the issue. On the one hand are aspects of pornography as ritual, and as exploration and celebration of sexuality, while questions about exploitation, "sexual terrorism," and sex misinformation linger.

Perilous Liaisons
Dir. Boudreau, Charline
1991 Canada No Dialogue
10 mins. video color Other
Dist. (U.S.): Boudreau, Charlene
Fetishized lesbian erotic imagery in sequential silent tableaux.

Perils of Pedagogy, The
Dir. Greyson, John
1984 Canada English
5 mins. video color Experimental
Dist. (U.S.): Video Data Bank
A meditation on the unconscious collaboration between the dominant mainstream cultural values and the supposedly alternative gay ghetto, focusing on the limited role options available to young gay men, caught between two worlds. The actor and director are trying to produce a music video of *To Sir With Love* slowed down to sound like Perry Como, but their relationship and the dominant culture intervene and interrupt.

Personal Best
Dir. Towne, Robert
1982 USA English
124 mins. 35mm color Narrative
Dist. (U.S.): Swank Motion Pictures
Like it or not, *Personal Best* was a landmark film. Robert Towne's 1982 Hollywood feature delves into the world of women's sports as a setting for a

lesbian relationship between two women athletes: Chris Cahill (Mariel Hemingway) and Tory Skinner (Patrice Donnelly), who meet at the 1976 Olympic Track Trials and become friends and then lovers and then friends.

The lesbianism of Hemingway's character is treated as a phase (she goes off with a male water-polo player in the end); while Donnelly's character (who is at least portrayed as a "real" lesbian) gets to utter some really great lesbian lines, such as, in response to Hemingway's reluctance to define the true nature of their relationship: "We may be friends, but we also happen to fuck each other every once in a while." And, on meeting Hemingway's new boyfriend: "He's pretty cute, for a guy."

A memorable love scene, consisting of tickling and nervous giggling and Mariel Hemingway saying, "This isn't so bad, I kind of like this." (J.O.)

Personal Best: Gay Body Culture
Dir. Kwietniowski, Richard
1991 Great Britain English
20 mins. video color Documentary
Dist. (U.K.): Alfalfa Entertainments, Ltd.
A look at the lesbian and gay pursuit of health and happiness through the world of sports and fitness training. *Personal Best: Gay Body Culture*, produced for Channel Four's 1991 Out series, takes a look at the appeal of sports and exercise for the participants as well as the spectators. Meet a lesbian football player and visit a nude gay swim club as this intriguing tape explores the allure of the gym, the myth of the "perfect" body, and the relationship between sports and sexuality.

Personally Yours
Dir. Robinson, Jeff
1995 USA English
8 mins. 16mm color Narrative
Dist. (U.S.): Robinson, Jeff
A young man's hopeless search for the love of his life through the personals.

Pervola, Sporen in de Sneeuw (Pervola, Tracks in the Snow)
Dir. Seunke, Orlow
Prod. Musch, Jan, and Tijs Tinbergen
1985 Netherlands Dutch
95 mins. 35mm color Narrative
Dist. (U.S.): Netherlands Ministry of Culture
A perfectly realized adult fairy tale, *Tracks in the Snow* should be the film that establishes Dutch director Orlow Seunke as a major new filmmaking

talent. His only previous feature, *A Taste of Water*, won a Golden Lion at the 1982 Venice Film Festival and Tracks in the Snow is an even more original, haunting work.

Simon and Hein are two feuding brothers, one gay and bohemian, one heartless and materialistic, who are obliged to bury their father where his will dictates—in Pervola, a frigid, unmapped wasteland to the north, where nature and civil turmoil pose logistical obstacles. Their journey is laced, as is the entire film, with an unusual combination of the outrageous (white-robed gypsies on skis, a goofy drunken guide, a pack of marauding wolves) and the poignant. Seunke's vision of an extrvagant, surreal frozen landscape is so complete that the language the actors speak is made-up mock-Finnish that was developed by the screenwriters and actors as the film was being made.

The blending of theater and life that occurs in this film has been compared to the work of Ingmar Bergman, though its unusual story and startling imagery signal the arrival of a unique vision, one that includes gay sensibilities in a fantasy tale of family love.

Peter Fucking Wayne Fucking Peter
Dir. Yung, Wayne
1994 Canada English
5 mins. video color Other
Dist. (U.S.): Video Out
Employs accordion accompaniment and explicit male/male sex to discuss the politics of fucking.

Philadelphia
Dir. Demme, Jonathan
1994 USA English
119 mins. 35mm color Narrative
Dist. (U.S.): Films Incorporated
Philadelphia didn't make me cry, until the last ten minutes.

Crying at movies has a pretty bad rap. It's okay to laugh noisily or scream with fear, but if you issue a sniffle you're a pariah. Only a few weeks ago, the *New York Times* ran a semihumorous item on the odd spectacle of men bawling at movies. Somehow we are meant to be ashamed of being lachrymose in the dark.

But we all need to weep, and the catastrophe of AIDS is certainly something to sob about. Since AIDS appeared, it's hard for me to see any movie about loss, or death, or suffering, or illness, and not to find metaphors for AIDS. *Shadowlands, Fearless, Remains of the Day*—you name it, and I've invented an allegory.

A B C D E F G H I J K L M N O P Q R S T U V W X Y Z

Now, with *Philadelphia*, here's a Hollywood movie that really is about the subject, and it doesn't let you cry.

Some people might want to be made angry by a film about AIDS, of course, and that has great validity. But if I was honest, I'd have to say I just want to wail. *Philadelphia* teases people like me. By omitting standard TV movie scenes, Jonathan Demme keeps you on orange alert, ready-revved for a cathartic moment to dampen your ducts.

In the last ten minutes, it comes. Tom Hanks's screen family is saying goodnight to him as he lies in his hospital bed. His straight brother starts to hug him, and suddenly finds himself strangled by unexpected sobs. The brother can't speak. It's an amazing moment, spurring audiences everywhere to plangency and lament.

My other reaction was a little more academic, a snippy quibble with *Philadelphia's* publicity campaign which claims it as the first Hollywood movie about AIDS. While *Philadelphia* deserves credit for many things, its achievements need to be put in perspective.

First of all, let's deal with the hype. *Philadelphia* is not Hollywood's first AIDS foray. This suspicious honor belongs to a slew of mischievous money-makers from the mid '80s onward—what I like to dub the Hollywood Subtext Set. Among these are body horror stories like *The Fly*, *Lifeforce* and *Fright Night* (the initial revulsion reaction), as well as fantasy melodramas like the bizarre Joel Schumacher companion pieces *Flatliners* and *Dying Young*.

The Subtext Set is quite different from the movies I find unintentionally allegorical. *The Fly* and *Dying Young* intentionally play around with the idea of AIDS, without actually naming the disease. I mean, Julia Roberts nursing cancer-stricken Campbell Scott, fresh off the set from *Longtime Companion*. Hello?

Pitched against the Subtext Set, *Philadelphia* comes off looking really good. But let us not ignore network television, which has been pumping out old-fashioned, talky tales ever since Aidan Quinn 'essed up to puritanical pop Ben Gazzara in 1986's *An Early Frost*.

AIDS is TV's knee-jerk tearjerker. The epidemic narrative has been to late-'80s TV what the coming-out story line was to the early '80s, culminating in HBO's *And the Band Played On*. *Philadelphia* also needs to be measured against these goggle-box gargantuans. In all the Hanks hype, everyone seems to be forgetting that far more people spend an evening with Dan Rather

than with a date at the local cineplex. Even if *Philadelphia* becomes 1994's *Jurassic Park*, most Americans will still be more familiar with AIDS from "Oprah" and "One Life To Live."

In Europe, the AIDS-themed TV drama is a major industry; in England alone, Claire Bloom, Miranda Richardson and most recently Helen Mirren have all played the wives of HIV positive hubbies. All of these fictions are designed to make us mourn, but in offering multiple identification figures (the mother, the father, the doctor, the researcher) they rarely succeed in this ambition.

It's quite tempting to let *Philadelphia's* publicists get away with their giddy self-congratulation, just to see what Hollywood's next move will be. We're told that if *Philadelphia* does boffo box office, then watch out for more AIDS-themed films. I can't wait: Sharon Stone as a monogamous lesbian mom with tumbling T-cells, struggling to get PWA benefits? Tom Cruise as a burnt-out ACT-UPer who falls for the communications director at Burroughs-Wellcome (played by Will Smith)?

The wish to embrace *Philadelphia* is understandable. For most Americans, Hollywood is still the locus of all social signification. If it's not enacted by a major movie star, it doesn't exist. In the argument for equal time, *Philadelphia* takes us all one step further in the right direction.

But abroad, Hollywood is taken a little more irreverently. Lesbians and gay men, too, have good reason to be a little cynical. Queer filmmakers have been chronicling the epidemic since it began. From *Parting Glances* onward, independent gay-made movies have combined integrity with melancholy, and they've managed very well without Tom Hanks, thank you.

One of the best independent movies is Arthur Bressan's last film, *Buddies*, made in 1986, by which time 11,000 people had died from AIDS in this country. (For the record, that figure in 1994 is over 204,000.) *Buddies* is a love story between a dying activist and his initially naive caregiver. Bressan uses a limited budget to advantage; every prop becomes a symbol, minimalism becomes moving. The result is *eau de Douglas Sirk*.

Philadelphia reminded me of *Buddies* in its incessant close-ups; unlike Demme's signature use of this cinematic standby, Bressan and other low-budget pioneers have to use close-ups out of necessity. *Philadelphia* is also the first big-budget or mainstream movie to be at least half as smart as the gay ones that have preceded it.

Ultimately, I liked Demme's dry-start drama for the same reason I like Arthur Bressan's micromelodrama: when you're allowed to cry, you cry honestly.

Ten North American gay-made movies about AIDS: *Parting Glances* dir. Bill Sherwood 1985; *Buddies* dir. Arthur Bressan 1986; *Common Threads* dirs. Rob Epstein & Jeffrey Friedman 1988; *Men in Love* dir. Marc Huestis 1989; *Together Alone* dir. P.J. Castellaneta 1990; *Tongues Untied* dir. Marlon Riggs 1990; *Longtime Companion* dir. Norman Rene 1990; *Voices from the Front* dirs. Testing The Limits 1991; *The Living End* dir. Gregg Araki 1992; *Zero Patience* dir. John Greyson 1993. (M.F.)

Pictures for Barbara
Dir. Hammer, Barbara
1981 USA English
10 mins. 16mm color Experimental
Dist. (U.S.): Canyon Cinema
A new friend. A new film. Transcontinental: Oakland to Plainfield, Vermont. Transpersonal: my house to yours. The fall leaves turned as our spirits transformed. Won't you come visit me?

"Two Barbaras (one of whom is Hammer on the West Coast, and a friend named Barbara on the East Coast) exchange letters and Polaroid pictures. About women's strength, spirituality and the violence of the external world."
—Judy Whitaker, Chicago Filmmakers

Pink Narcissus
Dir. Bidgood, Jim
1971 USA English
70 mins. 35mm color Narrative
Dist. (U.S.): Strand Releasing
Dist. (U.K.): Dangerous To Know
Even if you've never seen the glorious *Pink Narcissus* you've probably dreamt about it. A young man excapes from the real world in a sequence of pink satin fantasies—he's a slave chosen by the emperor, a bullfighter, a wood nymph, a harem boy. *Pink Narcissus* has no story to speak of, but it feels compulsively pacey. Loved for its imaginative eroticism in 1971, it was also derided for campy content ("as many spangles, feathers and gilded costumes as in Ziegfield Follies," protested Parker Tyler, a boy who should know). Eighteen years on, in a brand new print, you can begin to see—between the Walter Mitty premise and the Beauty School Drop-Out decor—a passionate intelligence and

the spirit of Genet. *Pink Narcissus* may appear narcissistic (and so what?) but it's also cheekily about narcissism. While Hollywood was grappling with the gloss of gay life—how many nelly queens make a good party?—in *Boys in the Band*, *Pink Narcissus* set about scraping at the nitty-gritty. It's all here: caballeros and bike boys; striptease and tearoom sex. *Pink Narcissus* delves beyond the surface of gay fantasy and finds that there's an expansive two-way mirror underneath.

Described by Parker Tyler as a major cult film made with the "heart and will of someone devoted to prick worship and the hermetic myth of an all male fantasy world," *Pink Narcissus* proved to be the hit of the 1984 New York Gay Film Festival, playing to sold-out crowds. This legendary erotic art film stands as a landmark at the juncture of the gay underground tradition and the porno industry. Seven years in the making, this dreamy surrealist film has been praised for its untarnished poetry and entrancing performance by teenage male beauty Bobby Kendall. Controversy surrounding the original production caused the director Jim Bidgood to go uncredited until 1984.

Pink Pimpernel, The
Dir. Greyson, John
1989 Canada English
32 mins. video color Other
Dist. (U.S.): Video Data Bank
More pointed interviews—and a comic remake of *The Scarlet Pimpernel*—in *The Pink Pimpernel*. Someone is making drug runs to the U.S. for treatments not available in Canada. Who's really beneath the blush-colored masks? Community activists explain the problems of procuring treatment for PWAs and then go on to lasso other issues, while back in the narrative, Toronto's gay community worries about the safety of Sir Percy. Greyson throws a third ball into the game—a series of safe sex-erotic interludes in the style of other gay artists (A Safer *Querelle*, A Safer Genet). Greyson's work has always been smart and funny; *Pink Pimpernel* and *The World is Sick* (sic) are even better. These new tapes are what more AIDS media ought to be like: passionate, playful, complex, and sharp.

Pink, The
Dir. Fry, Katherine
1993 New Zealand English
8 mins. 16mm color Narrative
Dist. (U.S.): Fry, Katherine

Ⓐ Ⓑ Ⓒ Ⓓ Ⓔ Ⓕ Ⓖ Ⓗ Ⓘ Ⓙ Ⓚ Ⓛ Ⓜ Ⓝ Ⓞ Ⓟ Ⓠ Ⓡ Ⓢ Ⓣ Ⓤ Ⓥ Ⓦ Ⓧ Ⓨ Ⓩ

Dist. (U.K.): Dangerous To Know

A fairy-tale proto-lesbian princess turns her beau into a frog.

Pink Triangles

Prod. Cambridge Documentary Films, Inc.

1981 USA English

35 mins. 16mm color/b&w Documentary

Dist. (U.S.): Cambridge Documentary Films

Pink Triangles is a fascinating, informative film in which both the roots and the current manifestations of homophobia are explored. Historical documents and interviews with people who know about prejudice first-hand are mixed, showing how lesbians and gay men experience discrimination and oppression. The historical perspective of homophobia is revealed, along with its links to other forms of oppression (against women, blacks, radicals, and Jews) and the reasons why this particular prejudice is felt so strongly. The treatment of gays in ancient and medieval times, in the Nazi death camps, and during the witch hunts of the McCarthy years are all shown. These past atrocities are linked to the present through TV interviews and paid political announcements from today's moral majority.

Pink Triangles shows how society looks for scapegoats in times of trouble, and how the past can be repeated. The best way to avoid this is to continue educating our society and ourselves. *Pink Triangles* is an important part of this effort.

Pink Triangles

Dir. unknown

1983 USA English

8 mins. video color Documentary

Dist. (U.S.): n/a

A gay pride rally and a Klan event are scheduled on the same day in Chicago. The result is a quick, action-packed tape full of temper and tension.

Pink Ulysses

Dir. de Kuyper, Eric

1990 Netherlands Dutch

98 mins. 16mm color/b&w Experimental

Dist. (U.S.): Strand Releasing

If *Pink Narcissus* were remade for the '90s, here's what it would look like: sexier, more self-conscious, a riper kind of camp. Director Eric de Kuyper previously made an impression on San Francisco audiences with *Casta Diva, Naughty Boys*, and *A Strange Love Affair*—all movies in which the stories are drowned beneath operatic tableaux of irresistible, unattainable men. *Pink*

Ulysses is a step in the direction of a tangy and intoxicating new gay style. Eric de Kuyper is a bit like Homer's Penelope, who wove by day and undid the same work each night. *Pink Ulysses* is a patchwork of ideas and heavenly bodies, gingerly held together by the thread of Ulysses's twenty-year-long return from Troy. There's the narrative—some nonsense about Penelope fancying her son more than her long-gone Homeric hubby—which is shot in the style of those Italian Steve Reeves pictures, all saturated color and anachronistic historical detail (Penelope carries a patent leather clutchbag). The other part of the film works like footnotes like explore fantasies: an extended black-and-white jerk-off scene involving a boy and his mirror, a long anecdote about a husband and his inebriate wife, and pop-video inserts to a giddy mix of music, from Zarah Leander to Stravinsky's "Rites of Spring."

Give *Ulysses* all your attention—not just for the loin-clothed beefcake and caustic camp, but for the sleepy, slow passages and intellectual pirouettes. Whichever way you look at it, *Pink Ulysses* is clearly going to be one of the year's cultiest gay movies.

Place Called Lovely, A

Dir. Benning, Sadie

1991 USA English

14 mins. video b&w Experimental

Dist. (U.S.): Video Data Bank

Dist. (U.K.): London Video Access

Sadie Benning shows us her raw and disturbing impressions of a violent world in *A Place Called Lovely*.

Place in the Sun, A

Dir. Giannaris, Constantine

Prod. Collins, Christopher

1994 Great Britain English

45 mins. 16mm b&w Narrative

Dist. (U.K.): Maya Vision

The collapse of Eurocommunism makes for strange bedfellows in the latest from Constantine Giannaris (*Caught Looking, North of Vortex*). Ilias (Stavros Zalmas), a bored and blasé thirty-five-year-old Athenian, falls in love with Panagiotis (Panagiotis Tsetsos), a muscular, eighteen-year-old economic refugee from Albania. These two have nothing in common, sexually or otherwise, but that doesn't stop them from embarking on an emotionally lopsided, ill-fated relationship.

Giannaris's Genet-tinged narrative, related as much through carefully wrought imagery as dialogue, is heavy on atmosphere and the palpable sensation of desire. Taken literally, *A Place in the Sun*'s scenario is a queer activist's horror—the beautiful Panagiotis isn't above bilking and bashing gays, and Ilias willingly becomes an accessory after the fact to a capital crime—though anyone who's ever been caught up in passion's wild throes is likely to empathize with Ilias's romantic and moral dilemmas.

Place of Rage, A
Dir. Parmar, Pratibha
1991 Great Britain English
52 mins. 16mm color Documentary
Dist. (U.S.): Women Make Movies
A dynamic celebration of African-American women and their achievements, featuring interviews with Angela Davis, June Jordan and Alice Walker. Within the context of civil rights, black power, and feminist movements, the trio reassesses how women such as Rosa Parks and Fannie Lou Hamer revolutionized American society. Angela Davis recounts her involvement with the Black Panthers and the Communist party. Archival footage is interwoven with June Jordan's poetry, linking issues of homophobia, racism, U.S. imperialism, and liberation struggles worldwide. The insights of Alice Walker and filmmaker Trinh T. Minh-ha further enrich this engrossing portrait of black feminism. A stirring chapter in African-American history.

Placeros Ocultos, Los (Hidden Pleasures)
Dir. De la Iglesia, Eloy
1978 Spain Spanish
97 mins. 35mm color Narrative
Dist. (U.S.): Strand Releasing
Made prior to *The Deputy* which played in our 1983 festival, Eloy de la Iglesia's *Hidden Pleasures* covers similar territory. Here, Eduardo, a handsome, fortyish, gay bank president plays a waiting game with Miguel, a young student he notices on the streets. As he becomes more and more obsessed with the boy, Eduardo follows Miguel to where he lives and sends him a job offer to come and work at the bank. Soon, Miguel is also doing private work at the banker's apartment typing (with two fingers) Eduardo's unfinished novel. All of this in an effort to get closer to any possible sexual encounter with Miguel.

After Miguel's friends begin to talk about this close friendship, Eduardo decides that he must reveal his true feelings to the boy. Accepting of his sexuality, Miguel introduces his girlfriend to Eduardo and a platonic ménage à trois develops. However, a powerful conflict waits

in the wings in the form of less tolerant forces—vindictiveness, greed, and ignorance.

One of the first militant Spanish gay films from the post-Franco era, *Hidden Pleasures* is a timeless work of courage, honesty, and commitment.

Plague, A
Dir. Wilson, Emjay
1985 USA English
2 mins. video color Experimental
Dist. (U.S.): Wilson, Emjay
An experimental video poem about AIDS and loss.

Plague on You, A
Prod. Lesbian and Gay Media Group
1985 Great Britain English
28 mins. video color Documentary
Dist. (U.K.): Albany Video
A Plague on You is a sharp and defiant critique of the British establishment's representation of AIDS by a London-based lesbian and gay media collective. An ambitious work, it attempts to separate the real from the unreal in the presentation of AIDS in England.

Plastic Rap
Dir. Rubnitz, Tom
1983 USA English
5 mins. video color Other
Dist. (U.S.): Video Data Bank
Part of the *Tom Rubnitz Marathon (A Dozen Tapes, Wigs Included)*.

Playing Poseidon [work in progress]
Dir. Rubio, R.X.
Prod. Conroy, Dennis
1995 USA English
10 mins. video color Experimental
Dist. (U.S.): Rubio, R.X.
A nostalgic Super-8 memory piece on sexual innocence, family, friendship, and the impact of the movies.

Playing the Part
Dir. McCabe, Mitch
1994 USA English
38 mins. 16mm color Documentary
Dist. (U.S.): First Run Features
An angst-ridden yet humorous look at the conflicts that arise when the filmmaker attempts to tell her parents that she is a lesbian. Her openly gay college life in Boston is at great odds with that of her well-to-do parents in Grosse Pointe, Michigan. We watch as she attends society balls,

Ⓐ Ⓑ Ⓒ Ⓓ Ⓔ Ⓕ Ⓖ Ⓗ Ⓘ Ⓙ Ⓚ Ⓛ Ⓜ Ⓝ Ⓞ Ⓟ Ⓠ Ⓡ Ⓢ Ⓣ Ⓤ Ⓥ Ⓦ Ⓧ Ⓨ Ⓩ

puts up with her nagging mother, and visits with her father's plastic surgery patients, trying to spill the beans about her sexuality the whole time.

Please Decompose Slowly
Dir. Moret, Alfonzo
1992 USA English
20 mins. video color Experimental
Dist. (U.S.): Moret, Alfonzo
A lyrical autobiographical questioning of culture, identity, and sexuality.

Pleasure
Dir. Mossop, Rowley
1987 USA English
11 mins. video color Other
Dist. (U.S.): V-Tape
Television is the key to *Pleasure* by Rowley Mossop.

Pleasure Beach
Dir. Bressan, Arthur J., Jr.
Prod. Lawrence, Richard
1982 USA English
78 mins. 16mm color Narrative
Dist. (U.S.): Rod & Reel Films
Arthur Bressan Jr., director of the critically acclaimed *Abuse*, has created a film that many gay men have longed for—a humorous, skillfully photographed and edited, interesting, and exceptionally erotic X-rated film. Set in the sunny world of the southern California coast, *Pleasure Beach* concerns two lifeguards and their sexually explicit adventures. With a driving, well-planned rhythm and equally good performances, the film zips along with never a dull moment.

Pleasure Garden, The
Dir. Broughton, James
1953 USA English
38 mins. 16mm b&w Experimental
Dist. (U.S.): Canyon Cinema
A joyous musical fantasy celebrating Love in the Park and the victory of the pleasure principle over all prudes and killjoys. *The Pleasure Garden* was made in London with a professional cast and shot in the ruined gardens of the Crystal Palace.

"In Chaplin, Rene Clair, Buster Keaton, Jacques Tati we enjoy on a big scale the fruits of the poetic turned comic. Broughton is of their kind, except that he holds more strongly to feeling, makes short cuts they daren't, sees and sings out of himself, and never dilutes a joke or a movement. *The Pleasure Garden* thus combines the pleasure of Keystone with the love lyric. It springs like the lark, and mingles oddity, grace,

satire, and laughter without a dead moment."
—*Sight and Sound*
"It's on the side of the angels. It's a great testimony for Love."
—Allen Ginsberg

PMS (Positioning My Sexuality)
Dir. Colyer, Vince
1992 Canada English
12 mins. 16mm color Other
Dist. (U.S.): n/a
A droll and creative catalog of role models available for gay men.

Poetry for an Englishman
Dir. Daley, Martin
1987 Australia English
25 mins. 16mm color Narrative
Dist. (U.S.): South Pacific Films
Janie knows her brother has a secret, and she wants that secret more than anything else in the world. *Poetry for an Englishman*, set on a remote stretch of the Australian coast, is a woman's reminiscence of a summer in her childhood. A time when, from afar, she witnessed events she would never forget and couldn't understand . . . perhaps she understood better than anybody.

Poison
Dir. Haynes, Todd
1991 USA English
85 mins. 35mm color/b&w Narrative
Dist. (U.S.): Zeitgeist Films
This first feature by the director of the notorious, legally-suppressed *Karen Carpenter Story* also mixes camp with surprisingly poignant elements. It interweaves three stories, each told in distinct filmic styles. One is a mock-documentary about a suburban child who's killed his father; another uses '50s sci-fi conventions as a metaphor for AIDS hysteria. The most memorable, and controversial, adapts Jean Genet's writings in a tense, erotic, dreamlike story of a young thief's prison life. At the time of its release, *Poison* became another locus in the Far Right campaign against "government-funded pornography," along with Mapplethorpe exhibits and the de-funded "NEA Four" performance artists. Of course, it's no more "obscene" than most other R-rated art flicks. But Haynes's mixed messages do disturb many viewers. Uneven but always intriguing, *Poison* is quasi-experimental cinema poking its head aboveground to offer satire, poetry, and provocation in equal measure. (D.H.)

Poisoned Blood
Dir. Fleras, Jomar
1991 Philippines English
32 mins. video color Documentary
Dist. (U.S.): Jurgen Bruning Filmproduktion
Poisoned Blood is a Filipino video documentary by Jomar Fleras that tackles issues such as Spanish and American colonial rule, folk Catholicism, U.S. military bases, prostitution, homosexuality, poverty, and government and private AIDS-prevention efforts.

Political Funerals
Dir. Wentzy, James
1995 USA English
29 mins. video color Documentary
Dist. (U.S.): AIDS Community Television
A forceful and moving documentary that courageously documents a bold new movement within AIDS activism that rejects the notion that one should die of AIDS quietly and peacefully.

Politics of Disco, The
Dir. Chiu, Terry
1993 USA English
14 mins. 16mm color Narrative
Dist. (U.S.): Chiu, Terry
A serious drama spanning the gay male generation gap.

Polskiseks
(see *Out On Tuesday, Program 2*)

Poodle-Poo-Poo Miracle Mask, The
Dir. Huestis, Marc
1977 USA English
1 mins. S8mm color Narrative
Dist. (U.S.): Outsider Enterprises
Featuring Tede Matthews getting the ultimate beauty treatment.

Pool Days
Dir. Sloan, Brian
1993 USA English
27 mins. 16mm color Narrative
Dist. (U.S.): Strand Releasing
Dist. (U.K.): Dangerous To Know
"One Life to Live"'s Josh Weinstein signs on a new attendant and finds himself the object of desire for both the health club's amorous aerobics instructor and a male club member. Which way to turn? What's a boy to do?
　　　　Released in the U.S. as part of *Boys Life*, a feature-length package of three gay shorts.

Pools
Dir. Hammer, Barbara, and Barbara Klutinis
1981 USA English
8 mins. 16mm color/b&w Experimental
Dist. (U.S.): Canyon Cinema
My aesthetics in comaking *Pools* with Barbara Klutinis was to bring an experiential and physiological sense of the body to the members of the audience watching the film in terms of the locations, the swimming pools designed by the first woman architect to graduate from the School of Beaux Arts in Paris, Julia Morgan.
　　　　Released by Facets Multimedia in the U.S. along with four of her other short films as a feature-length package, *Perceptual Landscapes: The Films of Barbara Hammer, Volume III.*

Porcaria
Dir. Paulo, Filipe
Prod. Kary, C. Grace
1995 Canada English
35 mins. 16mm b&w Narrative
Dist. (U.S.): Canadian Filmmakers Distribution Centre
Almodovarish *Porcaria* (loosely translated as "piggery") is a salacious sex farce set in Toronto's Little Portugal. Amalia, a bank clerk, finds herself competing with a young gay lodger for the sexual attentions of her beefy unemployed husband. Seemingly defeated, she turns to Steinar, the Icelandic telephone repairman for some much needed release.

Portrait of a Marriage
Dir. Whittaker, Stephen
1990 Great Britain English
220 mins. 16mm color Narrative
Dist. (U.K.): BBC TV
Portrait of a Marriage is the story of the tempestuous relationship of Vita Sackville-West and Violet Trefusis-Keppel. After five years of marriage Vita's husband, Harold Nicholson, confesses his homosexuality. Ironically, at the same time Vita's childhood friend, Violet, tells her that she has always loved her. This is the beginning of the women's passionate and moody relationship. Disguised as a married couple, they stay in hotels, spending an exciting and romantic time in France. Vita feels homesick for her children and guilty for betraying Harold but, back home, postpones telling him the truth. When Violet marries Deny Trefusis—under the condition that they have no sex—Vita becomes jealous, afraid she'll lost Violet. They meet again and decide to spend their lives together. Both tell their husbands. As

Ⓐ
Ⓑ
Ⓒ
Ⓓ
Ⓔ
Ⓕ
Ⓖ
Ⓗ
Ⓘ
Ⓙ
Ⓚ
Ⓛ
Ⓜ
Ⓝ
Ⓞ
Ⓟ
Ⓠ
Ⓡ
Ⓢ
Ⓣ
Ⓤ
Ⓥ
Ⓦ
Ⓧ
Ⓨ
Ⓩ

the women are on their way to the South of France, the men decide to follow and bring them back home.

Vita is portrayed as very ambivalent; incapable of hurting Harold because of her tender, sweet nature and incapable of forgetting Violet because she is passionately in love with her. Since this reflects the point of view of Vita's son, Nigel Nicholson (he wrote the book that the film is based on), it is understandable that he was happy his parents found one another again.

Portrait of Jason
Dir. Clark, Shirley
1967 USA English
106 mins. 16mm b&w Documentary
Dist. (U.S.): Museum Of Modern Art
Interview with black male prostitute, Jason Holliday.

Positive (Positiv)
Dir. von Praunheim, Rosa
1990 Germany English
90 mins. 16mm Documentary
Dist. (U.S.): First Run Features
Positive follows *Silence=Death* as the second part of Rosa von Praunheim's trilogy about AIDS and activism (the third, *Asses on Fire*, is still being made). He brings his European perspective to the ravages, anger, and achievements of AIDS-torn New York. The principal speaker is Phil Zwickler, who decided after the death of his lover not to keep his grief to himself but to act publicly, actively, and radically as part of a national movement against ignorance, illness, and underfunding. Von Praunheim also talks to Larry Kramer, Michael Callen, Larry Mass—and even manages to rope in Ronald Reagan.

Possession
Dir. Nix, Laura
1994 USA English
5 mins. video color Experimental
Dist. (U.S.): Nix, Laura
An autobiographical exploration of my relationship with a Victorian armchair.

Postcards from America
Dir. McClean, Steve
Prod. Vachon, Christine
1994 USA English
93 mins. 35mm color Narrative
Dist. (U.S.): Strand Releasing
Dist. (U.K.): Dangerous To Know
Postcards is inspired by the poetic and autobiographical writings of David Wojnarowicz, specifically his books *Close to the Knives* and *Memories that Smell Like Gasoline*. The film weaves together three fictional stories from the life of a young gay outsider. A violent suburban childhood spent with an abusive father in New Jersey in the early 1960s is seen from a queer child's perspective; it leads to his years as a teenage hustler on the streets of New York, and eventually to his adult fascination with anonymous sex, the American desert and the open road. The film deals with the conflict between the young David and his family, and later, between David and society at large; in representations which are suppressed in the dominant culture—those American taboos of sex and desire, death and AIDS. "McLean has found himself a brilliant cast of unknowns, and it is to his great credit that he can balance such naturalistic scenes that seem to owe much to the spirit of Cassavetes with the more stylized and eliptical moments. For the film draws its strength from the way it jumbles together the different segments from David's life and makes connections between them. Certainly McLean has created an extraordinarily textured film full of moments that will blaze in the audiences memory. The cinematography that evokes the sunglazed landscapes and the twilight interiors alike as burnished fragments, the soundtrack's snatches of plaintive pop songs that spin their own melancholy tales, along with Stephen Endelman's ethereal score haunt the mind long after the last reel. It may make for a bleak portrayal , for despite the sparks of comedy and the moments of tenderness, the film unwinds towards a terrible mourning. But McLean's distinctive vision sends the message home to the heart like no other.

Potluck and the Passion, The
Dir. Dunye, Cheryl
1993 USA English
22 mins. video color Narrative
Dist. (U.S.): Frameline
Sparks fly when a black lesbian couple invite their different sets of friends over for a potluck in Cheryl Dunye's *The Potluck and the Passion* (which was assisted by Frameline's Film and Video Completion Fund).

Pout
Dir. POUT video collective
1992 Great Britain English
10 mins. video color Other
Dist. (U.K.): Dangerous To Know
Pout is a wonderfully raw and sexy "queervideomag" brought to us by a London video collective.

Pouvoir Intime

Dir. Simoneau, Yves
Prod. Bonin, Claude
1986 Canada French
87 mins. 35mm color Narrative
Dist. (U.S.): Simcom International
Martial, a burly security guard (Robert Gravel) and his lover Janvier (Jacques Lussier), a blond waiter, get caught up in a bungled Brinks-style caper planned by a gang of small-time, lovable thugs. The group is led by Theo, a 50-year-old ex-con, and his accomplices include his 17-year-old son, Robin. An unforeseen twist of events changes everything, and Martial is unexpectedly trapped inside the truck with all the loot. The truck is taken to a warehouse used for storing old theater sets and the thieves try in vain to persuade Martial to leave his armored refuge. Convinced that that is his only chance for survival, Martial refuses to leave the truck, and all the characters settle down to an interminable wait in this strange baroque setting. Director Yves Simoneau keeps this tautly-paced thriller on track with the aid of some of Quebec's finest acting and technical talents. A wonderfully satisfying ending in which, for the first time in film history, the queer gets off with the loot.

Prague

Dir. Snee, Patrick
Prod. Snee, Patrick, and Judith Zissman
1995 USA English
9 mins. 16mm b&w Narrative
Dist. (U.S.): Snee, Patrick
Donald expresses his distress about Michael's leaving in a series of letters he sends to Michael's new address before Michael has even left.

Prayer Before Birth, A

Dir. Duckworth, Jacqui
1992 Great Britain English
20 mins. 16mm color Experimental
Dist. (U.S.): Women Make Movies
Dist. (U.K.): Cinenova
An experimental rendering of a young black lesbian's struggle with multiple sclerosis.

Premonition of Absurd Perversion in Sexual Personae Part 1

Dir. Maybury, John
1993 Great Britain English
60 mins. video color Experimental
Dist. (U.K.): Limelight
Another cutting-edge visual experiment from British artist John Maybury, *Premonition of Absurd Perversion in Sexual Personae Part One* serves up a provocative video tribute to the male body, a steamy Kenneth Anger for the video age.

A wholly self-financed work made possible from years of award-winning music video production for artists such as Sinead O'Connor and the Smiths, *Premonition* presents Maybury's trademark avant-garde, high-tech style focused on the male body politic. Forming a diptych with *Remembrance of Things Fast*, subtitled *True Stories*, *Visual Lies*, *Premonition* is another engaging yet highly challenging work that subverts spectatorial assumptions with queer abandonment.

Preservation of the Song

Dir. Martin, Carter
1995 USA English
32 mins. 16mm color Narrative
Dist. (U.S.): Martin, Carter
A dramatic story about two gay activists in an interracial relationship. The film introduces us to the conflicts arising from cultural differences, varying activism styles, and the emotions of being AIDS caregivers.

Prick Up Your Ears

Dir. Frears, Stephen
1987 Great Britain English
110 mins. 35mm color Narrative
Dist. (U.S.): The Samuel Goldwyn Co.
Dist. (U.K.): British Film Institute
Written by Alan Bennett, Stephen Frears's immediate followup to *My Beautiful Laundrette* chronicles the disasterous partnership between young, scruffy, sexy gay playwright-on-the-rise Joe Orton (Gary Oldman) and his eventually unneeded, very needy mentor Kenneth Halliwell (Alfred Molina). As an agent, Vanessa Redgrave narrates their flashback progress to Orton's 1967 murder at the height of his fame. The brilliantly performed film captures the repressive British '50s and swinging '60s in quicksilver mood shifts. But in the end, enjoyment depends on your taste for seeing two gifted, impossible personalities mutually self-destruct. (D.H.)

Pride and Prejudice

Dir. Engleman, Dorothy
1992 USA English
30 mins. video color Documentary
Dist. (U.S.): Engleman, Dorothy
Pride and Prejudice is a primer about homophobia, the closet, and coming out today—nicely spliced together with visual jokes and in-the-know references.

(A) (B) (C) (D) (E) (F) (G) (H) (I) (J) (K) (L) (M) (N) (O) (P) (Q) (R) (S) (T) (U) (V) (W) (X) (Y) (Z)

Priest
Dir. Bird, Antonia
1994 Great Britain English
110 mins. 35mm color Narrative
Dist. (U.S.): Swank Motion Pictures
Antonia Bird's well-made, allegory-packed, ser-
mon-filled, new social melodrama is a philosophical fencing match made for people who still
have some faith left. *Priest* is a study in class
contrasts and moral ones—good priest versus bad
priest; the so-called sin of homosexuality versus
the universally damned sin of incest—that offers
high melodrama but gets bogged down in the
theological details.

    The old priest (Father Matthew
Thomas, played by Tom Wilkinson) is giving ser-
mons the young one (Father Greg Pilkington,
played by Linus Roache) says sound like "political speeches for the Labour party." Meanwhile
Father Greg is giving "by the bootstraps" messages to his impoverished audience that Father
Tom finds "offensive." While the old priest is
singing and drinking in a karaoke bar, grooving
with Peruvian flutes in new school Catholic mass,
and getting it on in a loving but discreet relationship with the beautiful housekeeper, the young
one is gritting his teeth, chomping at the bit to
do the Lord's work. But in this working-class
area, it turns out, there are far too many demons
to exorcise at once: not the least of which are
troubling young Father Greg himself. He has the
forbidden gay desire: "I turn to him [Jesus, as
seen on the cross] for help, and I see a naked
man, utterly desirable," he confesses to another
priest, by way of explaining the bind he's in.
(S.G.)

Primas
Dir. Robles, Augie
1995 USA English
7 mins. video color Narrative
Dist. (U.S.): Brava! For Women in the Arts
Two young female cousins awaken passion in
each other.

Primitive and Proud
Dir. de la Riva, T. Osa Hidalgo
1992 USA English & Spanish
15 mins. video color Other
Dist. (U.S.): Women Make Movies
Released as *Mujeira*, together with *Mujeira:
Olmeca Rap.*

Prince In Hell
(see *Prinz In Holleland*)

Prince of Peace
Dir. Scheugl, Hans
1993 Austria German
8 mins. 16mm color Experimental
Dist. (U.S.): Sixpack Films
Intelligent and avant garde, *Prince of Peace* is
the *Koyaanisqatsi* of toilet shorts.

Prinz In Holleland (Prince In Hell)
Dir. Stock, Michael
1993 Germany German
96 mins. 16mm color Narrative
Dist. (U.S.): Stock, Michael
Prince in Hell is a hard-hitting parable about post
reunification Berlin; a hardcore drama about
junkies and prostitution wrapped in the trappings
of fairytale metaphors. A youthful, disenchanted
queer trio fuck each other, then fuck each other
over. Amidst the vanishing countercultural niches
of Berlin, P.C. Stefan tries to prevent his
boyfriend Jockel from the downward spiral of
heroin addiction. Jockel finds more sympathy in
the arms of the mischievous Micha, and the two
tour the landscape of drinking, demos, drag bars,
and the threat of Nazi street violence. A first feature by director Michael Stock, *Prince in Hell*
updates Fassbinder for a '90s audience. It has
the sheen of an anarchist's dream—drug-taking,
unsafe sex, S/M, vomiting—but beneath the
nihilism is a surprisingly romantic heart.
Nevertheless, a warning is necessary: This film
contains graphic scenes which may be upsetting
to some viewers.

Prisonnieres
Dir. Silvera, Charlotte
1988 France French
100 mins. 35mm color Narrative
Dist. (U.S.): World Marketing Film
Seven women, chained together at a Paris station, find their lives entwined just as firmly when
they arrive at Rennes women's prison.
Prisonnieres propels its inmates through a series
of sometimes somber, soap opera–style set
pieces. In the atmosphere of barely suppressed
violence, some cope by compliant submission,
others by outright rebellion. But unanticipated
loyalties and friendships also emerge; young,
armed robber Sabine finds herself drawn to the
quiet, older Lucie. Of all women's prison movies,
Prisonnieres gets closest to the pace and pacts of
cell block subculture. The lesbian content consists of one unbelievable love affair, its stilted
passion resulting in a suicide attempt, a major
flaw in an otherwise humanistic movie. With

Agnes Soral, Annie Girardot, and Bernadette Lanfont

Private Pleasures
Prod. Fatale Video
1985 USA English
30 mins. video color Narrative
Dist. (U.S.): Fatale Video
Another lesbian porn video from Fatale.

Projections (Pet Shop Boys compilation)
Dir. Jarman, Derek
1989 Great Britain English
46 mins. video color Other
Dist. (U.K.): Basilisk
In the U.S. Derek Jarman is considered primarily a gay filmmaker; few on this side of the Atlantic know of the strong ties he had to pop music, working throughout his career with an incredible range and number of artists—everyone from Alice Cooper to Adam Ant, Throbbing Gristle to Marianne Faithfull!

Projections is a compilation of visually striking shorts, never before seen in the U.S., created by Derek Jarman to serve as background to the Pet Shop Boys' 1989 tour. Shown together and set to Pet Shop Boys pop ballads, *Projections* presents Jarman at his most carefree and whimsical, combining found-footage holidays and factories with the playful antics of the Pet Shop Boys, friends of the director, and even Jarman himself.

The result is the reverse of a film soundtrack: lyrical streams of images accompany the progression of the songs and augment their emotional content. By eschewing standard music video convention of narrative, lip-synch, and beat-driven editing, Jarman allows himself to riff off the Boys' songs with greater creative reign. The sequence for "Paninaro" takes off from the language of song's title to an imaginary picture-postcard Italy filled with pouting young hustlers and knife-wielding girl-on-girl action. "It's a Sin" explores a well-oiled Bacchic orgy—it's Greek mystery cult meets homo kitch.

Projections also features *Studio Bankside*, Jarman's first ever film, and *A Garden in Luxor*, both used at a benefit concert with the Pet Shop Boys in Manchester, 1992.

Proof
Dir. Moorhouse, Jocelyn
1992 Australia English
91 mins. 35mm color Narrative
Dist. (U.S.): Films Incorporated
Writer/director Jocelyn Moorhouse has created an utterly original, memorable story in this first theatrical feature. It's a romantic triangle of sorts, with intricate chesslike moves between a bitter, withdrawn blind man (*Priscilla: Queen of the Desert*'s Hugo Weaving), his perversely antagonistic female housekeeper (Genevieve Picot), and the sexy restaurant dishwasher (Russell Crowe, from *The Sum of Us*) he befriends. Like Harold Pinter, Moorhouse can manipulate her characters with shocking, witty, sometimes pitiless bravado. What's unexpected is the enormous depth of feeling at the film's center. Though these people are too emotionally blocked to admit any such feelings out loud, *Proof* is—among other things—a film about pained, hesitant guy-guy courtship. You don't need a compass to guess where things between Weaving and Crowe might head after the final fade. (D.H.)

Proportion
Dir. Waggoner, David
Prod. Poof Productions
1977 USA English
3 mins. S8mm color Narrative
Dist. (U.S.): n/a
Another fanciful film on loan to us from Poof Productions.

Proust's Favorite Fantasy
Dir. Kwietniowski, Richard, and Roger Clark
1991 Great Britain English
2 mins. 16mm color Other
Dist. (U.S.): Frameline
Dist. (U.K.): Alfalfa Entertainments, Ltd.
A hotel room, a gendarme, and a chicken.

PSA
Dir. Rappaport, Ann
1986 USA English
2 mins. video color Other
Dist. (U.S.): n/a
A brief cute lavender animated public service announcement for Christ Chapel Metropolitan Community Church of Santa Ana, California.

Psychosynthesis
Dir. Hammer, Barbara
1975 USA English
8 mins. 16mm color Experimental
Dist. (U.S.): Canyon Cinema
The subpersonalities of me, my baby, athlete, witch, and artist are synthesized in this film of impositions, intensities, and color layers coming quietly together through the healing powers of natural touchstone.

Ⓐ Ⓑ Ⓒ Ⓓ Ⓔ Ⓕ Ⓖ Ⓗ Ⓘ Ⓙ Ⓚ Ⓛ Ⓜ Ⓝ Ⓞ Ⓟ Ⓠ Ⓡ Ⓢ Ⓣ Ⓤ Ⓥ Ⓦ Ⓧ Ⓨ Ⓩ

Psyclones on Heat
Dir. Walters, Boyd
1988 Great Britain English
22 mins. 16mm color Documentary
Dist. (U.K.): Walters, Boyd
Psyclones is the first in a trilogy of films reflecting the changing attitudes and styles of gay men in the 1980s. This film covers the early '80s, "The Age of Innocence."

Pubic Beard
Dir. Stanley, Anie
1992 USA English
3 mins. S8mm color Experimental
Dist. (U.S.): Stanley, Anie
Pubic Beard's title says it all.

Public
Dir. Dong, Arthur
1970 USA English
5 mins. 16mm color Narrative
Dist. (U.S.): DeepFocus Productions
Based on a poem by the filmmaker; an animated fable about a five-year-old boy who confronts sexual oppression and the politics of war. First Prize, California High School Film Festival

Public Opinion
Dir. Dvoracek, Ted
1993 USA English
24 mins. 16mm color Narrative
Dist. (U.S.): Dvoracek, Ted
A stylized, serious piece about a priest, an actor, and a bathhouse.

Puce Moment
Dir. Anger, Kenneth
1949 USA English
7 mins. 16mm color Experimental
Dist. (U.S.): Canyon Cinema
Dist. (U.K.): British Film Institute
"A lavishly colored evocation of the Hollywood now gone, as shown through an afternoon in the milieu of a 1920's film star.
"*Puce Moment* is a fragment from an abandoned film project entitled *Puce Woman.* The soundtrack used here is the second one; the first was the overture to Verdi's I Villi. The film reflects Anger's concerns with the myths and decline of Hollywood, as well as with the ritual of dressing, with the movement from the interior to the exterior, and with color and sound synchronization . . ." —Marilyn Singer,
The American Federation of Arts

Pull Your Finger Out: Lesbians Rock
Dir. Hindley, Emma
Prod. Margetts, Juliet
1994 Great Britain English
13 mins. video color Documentary
Dist. (U.K.): Polari Productions Ltd.
Covers the ever-growing dyke rock scene and takes a look at English bands Sister George and Atomic Kandy.

Puppet Characters
Dir. Gray, Donna
1979 USA English
2 mins. 16mm color Other
Dist. (U.S.): Gray, Donna
An amazing look at the creation of stuffed doll toys.

Put Your Lips Around Yes
Dir. Lindell, John
1992 USA English
4 mins. video color Other
Dist. (U.S.): Drift Distribution
Word Power.

Q.C. Girls, The
Dir. Smartt, William
1989 USA English
11 mins. video color Documentary
Dist. (U.S.): n/a
William Smartt's *The Q.C. Girls* is probably the most ragged video you'll see at this year's festival—it's raw and overwhelmingly intense. Smartt takes his camera to McMinnville, Tennessee, where everyone cruises the strip on a Saturday night in their cars. He befriends several sassy dykes, who stay alive through giving as good as they get from local bigots.

Que He Hecho Yo Para Merecer Esto? (What Have I Done to Deserve This?)
Dir. Almodovar, Pedro
Prod. Hachuel, Herve
1984 Spain Spanish
106 mins. 35mm color Narrative
Dist. (U.S.): Cinevista
Gloria works as a charwoman and does not have a minute to herself. Her own home alone would give her enough work to keep her busy all day long. She shares the small apartment with her chauvinist taxi-driver husband, her mother-in-law, her two sons, and a lizard. She is not a happy woman. Like many housewives, she has not enjoyed the same opportunities as those of Caroline of Monaco.
Her husband is even still in love with

a German woman he worked for fifteen years ago. Her twelve-year-old son has an attraction to his friends' fathers. His brother, age fourteen, is a smack dealer. So Gloria goes through her days cleaning, washing, ironing, cooking, taking the kids to the doctor, trying to get uppers, suffering cold turkey, never having an orgasm, unable to afford the hairdresser, and never being chased by Madrid's ten most sexy men. Gloria is reaching the breaking point.

Eventually everyone leaves (her husband in an outrageous incident of domestic violence), and at last she is alone.

An endearing, witty, and surprisingly feminist tale from one of the world's finest new film talents.

Queen Christina
Dir. Mamoulian, Rouben
1933 USA English
100 mins. 35mm b&w Narrative
Dist. (U.S.): Swank Motion Pictures

In MGM's 1933 historical drama *Queen Christina*, the one and only Greta Garbo gives the drag performance of her career. Swaggering about castle and countryside in male attire, the Swedish queen is as butch as they come and then some.

Based on the real-life story of the 17th-century Queen Christina of Sweden, the film makes a bit of a sexual orientation adjustment (the real queen was a lesbian, Garbo's queen is portrayed as straight). However, just underneath the heterosexual act is a clear queer appeal and it's easy to imagine the queen as a dyke and her male love interest as a queen.

Her apparent love interest through the first half of the film is the Countess Ebba Sparre (Elizabeth Young). And an early scene in the film features one of the nicest girl-girl kisses in Hollywood history.

When the queen meets Antonio (John Gilbert) in a country tavern/inn (where she is traveling in male disguise), they end up having to share a room together. In a very provocative sequence of misgendered identities the queen is propositioned by a barmaid, she then reveals to Antonio that she is a woman, and, on waking in bed together the following morning the couple are seen by a servant who raises his eyebrows at the two "men."

When pressed by her valet to marry ("But your majesty, you cannot die an old maid"), the queen replies, "I have no intention to. I shall die a bachelor."

Indeed, Garbo herself died a bachelor and at this point her own lesbianism is common knowledge. The behind-the-scenes history of this film (according to Mercedes D'Acosta in her autobiography) has it that Garbo and D'Acosta had been lovers. According to D'Acosta, she and Garbo had developed the film together, and D'Acosta was fired as screenwriter from the project because she was making it too clear that the queen was a lesbian. This seems to come through quite clearly in the beginning of the film, and changes somewhat strangely when the queen has a fight with the countess somewhere in the second reel. The queen thereafter toys with the affections of a court ambassador (whom she's obviously not interested in) until she meets Antonio. When she gives up her throne to be with Antonio (in real life she gave it up to be with Ebba Sparre) the film makes its ultimate break with reality.

In *The Celluloid Closet*, Vito Russo cites the following excerpt from a *New York Herald Tribune* review of a 1933 biography on Christina which makes reference to the anticipated release of the film: "The one persistent love of Christina's life was for the Countess Ebba Sparre, a beautiful Swedish noble-woman who lost most of her interest in Christina when Christina ceased to rule Sweden, the evidence is overwhelming, but will Miss Garbo play such a Christina?"

No such Christina here, unfortunately. A small consolation—Antonio dies and Christina goes off alone in the end. (J.O.)

Queen is Dead, The
Dir. Jarman, Derek, John Maybury, and Richard Heslop
1986 Great Britain English
15 mins. 35mm color Other
Dist. (U.K.): Basilisk

Three songs by The Smiths: "The Queen is Dead," "There is a Light That Never Goes Out," and "Panic."

Queen, The
Dir. Simon, Frank
1968 USA English
68 mins. 16mm b&w Documentary
Dist. (U.S.): First Run Features
Dist. (U.K.): British Film Institute

This notorious documentary chronicles the "Miss All-America Camp Beauty Pageant" as drag artistes around the country compete for the crown at Manhattan's Town Hall. Billed as a *Paris Is Burning* precursor for its early '90s rerelease,

Ⓐ Ⓑ Ⓒ Ⓓ Ⓔ Ⓕ Ⓖ Ⓗ Ⓘ Ⓙ Ⓚ Ⓛ Ⓜ Ⓝ Ⓞ Ⓟ Ⓠ Ⓡ Ⓢ Ⓣ Ⓤ Ⓥ Ⓦ Ⓧ Ⓨ Ⓩ

The Queen is actually something trickier—long on local color and cinema verité neutrality, short on insight. We don't get to know individual contestants to any great depth, and aspects of the event itself seem suspicious: Why are so many media people present? Why does the audience seem to consist of slumming uptown straight couples? (Otherwise the hall looks fairly empty.) Judges purportedly included Andy Warhol, Edie Sedgwick (a dead ringer for contestant Richard, or vice versa), George Plimpton, and Terry Southern, yet we never see them. Nor do we get to see finished versions of the giddy production numbers glimpsed in rehearsal. Real drama intrudes only at the end, when a couple of losing queens vent fire at the selection process. Were the festivities created primarily as a media stunt? If so, how accurately can they reflect drag culture of the era? One may leave *The Queen* with a lot of nagging questions. But it does offer a window onto one aspect of pre-Stonewall gay life, as well as some memorable bits. Dig that ensemble go-go dance to "It's a Grand Old Flag." (D.H.)

Queens of Columbus: Performance Art & Art of Illusion
Dir. Baumann, Thomas
1992 USA English
28 mins. video color Documentary
Dist. (U.S.): n/a
Everything you ever wanted to know about drag queens (old school). Queens of Columbus is unapologetic, tightly-focused, and very engaging.

queer
Dir. Rauch, David
1994 USA English
10 mins. video color Documentary
Dist. (U.S.): Rauch, David
One of the first gay works made entirely on digital video.

Queer Across Canada
Dir. Bradley, Maureen
1993 Canada English
10 mins. video color Other
Dist. (U.S.): V-Tape
Maureen Bradley's punchy cross-country dictionary of sexual identities.

Queer Carpentry Seminar
Dir. Fair, Andy, and Tom Hill
1993 USA English
5 mins. video color Other
Dist. (U.S.): Hill, Tom/Queer Action Figures
Chock-full of pierced, tattooed types hard at work

constructing something.

Queer Christmas
Dir. Arnesen, Heidi
1995 USA English
7 mins. video color Narrative
Dist. (U.S.): Arnesen, Heidi
Queers buying X-mas trees.

Queer Love Poem, A
Dir. Parnes, Uzi
1991 USA English
11 mins. video color Experimental
Dist. (U.S.): n/a
Uzi Parnes's A Queer Love Poem focuses on the body of the boy who got away.

Queer Son
Dir. Seitchik, Vickie
1993 USA English
49 mins. video color Documentary
Dist. (U.S.): Frameline
An inspiring and affecting film about PFLAG and parents of lesbian and gay children; each of the film's diverse interviewees speaks entertainingly and compassionately.

Queers Among Queers: A Bay Area Perspective
Prod. White, C.B.
1994 USA English
30 mins. video color Documentary
Dist. (U.S.): Eidetix
The locally produced Queers Among Queers offers up an articulate series of interviews with bi community activists.

Queers Are Not Enough
Prod. Anderson, Kris, and Justine Pimlott
1992 Canada English
27 mins. video color Documentary
Dist. (U.S.): Chicago Filmmakers
This vigorous overview of the 1990 Gay Games critiques issues around assimilation, diversity, cooptation, and representation.

Querelle
Dir. Fassbinder, Rainer Werner
Prod. Dieter Schidor
1983 Germany German
107 mins. 35mm color Narrative
Dist. (U.S.): Films Incorporated
Dist. (U.K.): British Film Institute
Producer Dieter Schidor originally took the task of filming Genet's sadist-and-sailors dockside drama to Bernardo Bertolucci (who could only,

according to Schidor, "present it as cock poetry"), then Werner Schroeter (who would turn it into "faggot poetry"), and finally Fassbinder ("I thought he might make it gay kitchen trash"). Hardly trash, the result is instead one of the most overdetermined gay films of all time: starring salty Jeanne Moreau, blank-face Brad Davis, and a surreal *Barbarella*-style seaport.

Racing Colours
Dir. Iadereste, Stephen
1977 USA English
3 mins. S8mm color Experimental
Dist. (U.S.): n/a
My first experience in film painting during which you may cheer for your favorite color.

Rage & Desire
Dir. Gabriel, Ruppert
1991 Great Britain English
17 mins. 16mm color Documentary
Dist. (U.S.): Frameline
Dist. (U.K.): Zone Prods.
A memorial to black gay photographer Rotimi Fani-Koyode. Ruppert Gabriel's elegant, personal film also raises powerful questions about race, sexuality, and identity.

Raid on a Peruvian Lesbian Bar
Dir. unknown
1991 Peru Spanish
8 mins. video color Documentary
Dist. (U.S.): International Gay & Lesbian Human Rights Commission
Extraordinary, disturbing footage of a raid on a Peruvian lesbian bar; it's lifted from a TV news report, and it is not presented here as an activist work, but as a piece of journalism that inspires one to activism.

Rainbow Serpent, The
Dir. Vallois, Philippe
Prod. Vassaire, Daniel
1983 France French
90 mins. 35mm color Narrative
Dist. (U.S.): Frameline
The Rainbow Serpent is a fully developed tale of suspense set in the world of bodybuilding that reminded one critic of "Diva rewritten by Dali with rock replacing opera." A rookie cop investigating a bodybuilder suspected of murder is drawn into the erotic world of gyms and body worship. An S/M relationship develops between the men as *The Rainbow Serpent* tells its unusual tail of homoeroticism between heterosexual men. It is both a comic stylization of a French

police movie that even includes fantasy musical production numbers and a startling depiction of sexual ambiguities.

Rainer Werner Fassbinder: The Last Works
Dir. Gremm, Wolf
1982 Germany German
60 mins. 16mm color Documentary
Dist. (U.S.): Regina Ziegler Filmproduktion
Shot in Berlin during Fassbinder's last working days, *The Last Works* is a personal documentary directed by Wolf Gremm, who also directed Fassbinder in his last acting role in *Kamikaze 1989*. While working on *Kamikaze* and his last directorial effort, *Querelle* (both shot in Berlin), Fassbinder stayed as the guest of Gremm and his producer and wife, Regina Ziegler. The film includes scenes of Gremm directing Fassbinder in *Kamikaze* and clips from the film. There are also intimate closeups of Fassbinder shooting *Querelle*. The film reveals the late director's physical decline and his heavy dependency on alcohol and drugs during working hours as well as his passion for every detail in the production of his films.

Raising Nicholas
Dir. Pearlstein, Ferne
1991 USA English
4 mins. 16mm b&w Other
Dist. (U.S.): Chicago Filmmakers
An artful dialogue by Ferne Pearlstein between an adopted Honduran boy and his gay male parents.

Rambles
Dir. Press, Richard
Prod. Noschese, Poynton, and Richard Press
1994 USA English
11 mins. 16mm b&w Narrative
Dist. (U.S.): Press, Richard
Confronted with the inevitability of the aging process, a gay man seeks refuge in anonymous sexual encounters in New York's Central Park.

Random Access
Dir. Struck, Andreas
Prod. Brydon, Simon
1995 Great Britain English
11 mins. 35mm color Narrative
Dist. (U.K.): Struck, Andreas
A fairy tale in which two guy's lives take on new meaning after they encounter the Madonna.

Rapture

Ⓐ Ⓑ Ⓒ Ⓓ Ⓔ Ⓕ Ⓖ Ⓗ Ⓘ Ⓙ Ⓚ Ⓛ Ⓜ Ⓝ Ⓞ Ⓟ Ⓠ Ⓡ Ⓢ Ⓣ Ⓤ Ⓥ Ⓦ Ⓧ Ⓨ Ⓩ

Dir. Whitely, Sara
1992 USA English
8 mins. 16mm color Documentary
Dist. (U.S.): Frameline
Dist. (U.K.): Dangerous To Know
In Sara Whitely's portrait of ritual ball dancing, balls and bells attached by temporary piercings tear the skin of the dancers as they dance into an ecstatic state of *Rapture*.

Rasen No Sobyo
(Rough Sketch of a Spiral)
Dir. Kojima, Yasushi
1990 Japan Japanese
103 mins. 16mm color Documentary
Dist. (U.S.): Herald Ace
The first gay Japanese documentary, *Rough Sketch of a Spiral* takes an intimate look at the personal lives of gay men in Osaka. The star is 25-year-old Yoshiichi Yano, who has written a play he hopes will open the public's eyes to the status of gays in contemporary Japan, a society with deep-rooted prejudices against homosexuality. With abundant humor and nonchalant candor, director Yasushi Kojima follows the day-to-day efforts of Yano to produce his play, while introducing us to Yano's friends and actors in the play, including a stunning drag queen and a charming 60-year-old man who claims to be gay but a virgin. Much of the film focuses on scenes of Yano and his lover (23-year-old Takaski, who says of his life with Yano, "Together, it's nothing special but apart . . . we gasp," as he lets out a sigh that perfectly captures the joy and angst of first love). From courtship to the traumas of infidelity, Takashi and Yano open up before the camera honestly and without a trace of timidity. Their scenes together are a reassuring reminder of the universal nature of romantic relationships while the final scenes, of the play, show Yano's success as a fledgling playwright.

Ravissement, La
Dir. Boudreau, Charline
1992 Canada English
4 mins. video color Narrative
Dist. (U.S.): Frameline
Released in the U.S. as part of *She's Safe*, a feature-length package of lesbian safe-sex videos.

Raw Meet
Dir. Allyn, Jerri
1986 USA English
3 mins. video color Documentary
Dist. (U.S.): Allyn, Jerri

In Jerri Allyn's humorous *Raw Meet*, the artist boxes with trainer Zebra Davis while recounting incidences of sexual harrassment.

Ray
Dir. McClain, Allen
1977 USA English
6 mins. S8mm color Narrative
Dist. (U.S.): n/a
"The war is over. Let's not talk about the war." This film depicts one man for whom the war is not over.

Ray Navarro Memorial Tape
Dir. Saalfield, Catherine, and Gregg Bordowitz
1990 USA English
30 mins. video color Documentary
Dist. (U.S.): Saalfield, Catherine
Ray Navarro was a key video maker and AIDS activist who died while making a work about Latino gay male assimilation into white gay culture; *Ray Navarro Memorial Tape* is a tribute to him and his activism.

Ray's Male Heterosexual Dance Hall
Dir. Gordon, Bryan
1988 USA English
23 mins. 35mm color Narrative
Dist. (U.S.): Fox/Lorber
Ray's Male Heterosexual Dance Hall tells the offbeat story of Sam Logan and his search for a job—a really good one.
      Winner of the 1989 San Francisco International Lesbian & Gay Film Festival Audience Award for Best Short Film.

Razor Head
Dir. Chomont, Tom
1984 USA English
4 mins. 16mm color Experimental
Dist. (U.S.): Filmmaker's Cooperative
In the silent *Razor Head*, the ritual of erotic shaving is the basis for an S/M variation on getting a haircut.

Re Generation
Dir. Gaffney, Stuart
1995 USA English
6 mins. video color Other
Dist. (U.S.): Gaffney, Stuart
Re Generation explores two men's feelings about contracting HIV. Part One is the fictional story of a youth who rejects the label for a new generation of young gay men getting AIDS; the voice-over narration is accompanied by abstract visuals and

extreme body close-ups. Part Two is an interview with Frank Sears, who recalls the 1981 incident when he believes he contracted HIV; his story contrasts sharply with Part One.

Recent Sorrows
Dir. Barrish, Jerry R.
Prod. Edery, Simon
1984 USA English
80 mins. 16mm color Narrative
Dist. (U.S.): Barrish Films
Recent Sorrows is a native San Franciscan's look at the dissolution of two love affairs, one straight, one gay, that run parallel until they run headlong into murder. Tim is an aging Lothario in love, clinging to the romanticism of his wounded relationship with Kate. Vic is alone with his magic tricks, fighting the rejections of his inconsistent lover; Neal, with weapons that will destroy them all. Barrish—whose *Dan's Motel* emerged as a favorite at the 1982 New Directors Series in New York, sets a laid-back pace, open-minded and designed for provocative conversation that lets the nature of his characters' lives override the oversimplification of sexual preference.

Red Light, Green Light
—Meeting Strangers
Dir. Unknown
1965 USA English
20 mins. 16mm color Documentary
Dist. (U.S.): Olson, Jenni
Ever wonder where society gets the idea that lesbians and gays are sick predatory creatures? *Red Light, Green Light* provides the answer. It's a children's educational film from the '60s that teaches kids that meeting a homosexual is worse than falling into a ditch or getting hit by a speeding car.

Reference
Dir. Prokpiuk, Cesary
1993 Australia English
3 mins. video color Other
Dist. (U.S.): Prokpiuk, Cesary
Reference takes a dim view of anonymous sex.

Reflections
Dir. Ellsworth, Robert
1993 USA English
18 mins. 16mm color Narrative
Dist. (U.S.): Ellsworth, Robert
Adds a twist of queerness and buckets of (non-consensual) sex and violence to the haunted house genre.

Reflections in a Golden Eye
Dir. Huston, John
1967 USA English
109 mins. 16mm/35mm color Narrative
Dist. (U.S.): Kit Parker Films
Homosexual urges haunt Marlon Brando in John Huston's CinemaScope rendition of Carson McCullers's novella. Military man Brando is married to Elizabeth Taylor, the quintessence of '60s womanhood, but he finds handsome Private Williams (Robert Forster) more enticing. Brando's love goes unrequited—Williams has a reverent obsession for Taylor, who's two-timing her husband with Brian Keith—though Huston does allow Brando to fondle with loving intensity a Baby Ruth wrapper the good private drops on the sidewalk. Zorro David plays the ultraqueeny Filipino houseboy of Brando and Taylor's neighbors, Keith and Julie Harris. Though David turns in a vigorous performance, it unfortunately represents the psychologically traumatized Brando's entire conception of homosexual possibility—the resulting repression of his desire leads inevitably to murder. (D.M.)

Reframing AIDS
Dir. Parmar, Pratibha
1987 Great Britain English
30 mins. video color Documentary
Dist. (U.K.): Albany Video
A compelling tape by an Asian woman who lives in Britain. Analyzes AIDS in terms of race, gender, sexual orientation, and social standing. Stylistically mature and thoughtful presentation.

Regarde Moi
Dir. Aubert, Elisabeth
Prod. Moaligou, Yann
1993 France French
9 mins. 35mm color Narrative
Dist. (U.S.): Aubert, Elisabeth
A few glances and an ambiguous dialogue between two women lead us to Pigalle, where quietly we transgress the boundaries of a forbidden world.

Reise, Eine (The Journey)
Dir. Grossman, Gerda
1992 Germany German
12 mins. 16mm color Experimental
Dist. (U.S.): Sixpack Films
The beautiful tale of a pair of obsessive lovers.

Relax
Dir. Newby, Christopher
1990 Great Britain English

Ⓐ
Ⓑ
Ⓒ
Ⓓ
Ⓔ
Ⓕ
Ⓖ
Ⓗ
Ⓘ
Ⓙ
Ⓚ
Ⓛ
Ⓜ
Ⓝ
Ⓞ
Ⓟ
Ⓠ
Ⓡ
Ⓢ
Ⓣ
Ⓤ
Ⓥ
Ⓦ
Ⓧ
Ⓨ
Ⓩ

20 mins. 16mm color Narrative
Dist. (U.S.): Frameline
Dist. (U.K.): British Film Institute
An imaginative and intense short in which a young gay man explores his feelings, leading up to the result of an HIV test. Released in the U.S. as part of a feature-length package of gay short films, *Boys Shorts: The New Queer Cinema*.

Religieuse, La (The Nun)
Dir. Rivette, Jacques
1966 France French
100 mins. 35mm color Narrative
Dist. (U.S.): Interama, Inc.
Directed by French filmmaker Jacques Rivette, this widely acclaimed drama, based on Diderot's 1796 novel, caused a scandal in the sixties for being too anti-Catholic. Two different convents, under the guidance of three different abbesses, are the sites of corruption, abuse of power, and uninhibited sexual behavior. The story centers around a young aristocratic woman, Suzanna, sent to a convent because her mother needs to be rid of the disgrace of having an illegitimate child. The first abbess understands Suzanna's doubts about her vocation and offers her the love her mother denied. But the abbess soon dies and her successor treats Suzanna with cruelty and sadism, especially after she decides to revoke her vows. Eventually she is transferred to another convent. Here the abbess welcomes her with, "how beautiful she is!" Suzanna rejects her advances and escapes with the help of her confessor. When she realizes that in the profane world, men want to possess her sexually as well, she commits suicide. For once it is not the lesbian character who dies. The asexual main character serves to reveal the excesses of the clerical world, and while the film is not free from misogyny, it is a powerful work that is neither exploitative nor sensational.

Remembrance
Dir. Tartaglia, Jerry
1990 USA English
5 mins. 16mm color Experimental
Dist. (U.S.): Canyon Cinema
"Growing up as I did, watching movies," says filmmaker Jerry Tartaglia on the soundtrack of *Remembrance*, ". . . I naturally assumed that life was glamorous, friends were charming and witty, and, style being everything, of course, that parties were elegant and sophisticated." Repeated scenes from *All About Eve* and his own home movies only prove him partly wrong.

Remembrance of Things Fast
Dir. Maybury, John
1993 Great Britain English
60 mins. 16mm color Experimental
Dist. (U.K.): Limelight
Remembrance of Things Fast investigates some of the seedier rest-stops along the information superhighway. Award-winning British music video director and artist John Maybury—sadly, one of the U.K.'s best-kept secrets—places Tilda Swinton, Rupert Everett, and porn star Aiden Brady in a hyper-real videoscape amid menacing dominatrices and transgender aristocrats. Fluid and nonlinear, Maybury's work defies narrative conventions and explores the outer limits of experimental video.

Disturbing, challenging, at times painfully beautiful, *Remembrance* represents both the culmination of Maybury's work and the cutting edge of video production today; many of the state-of-the art editing techniques were invented as the work was shot. Swinton and Everett appear as viewers have never seen them before—less actors than objects, their images distorted, pulsating, and visually deconstructed to expose the "true stories and visual lies" of queer existence in the postmodern age. Testing the limits of global television and the clichés of the three-minute attention span, *Remembrance of Things Fast* provides an exhilarating and subversive commentary on our technophilic culture of images.

Remnants
Dir. Shirley, Nolan
Prod. Wineland, Thom
1994 USA English
7 mins. video color Experimental
Dist. (U.S.): Queer Shock Productions
The story of four friends, a new relationship, and a bashing.

Requiem
Dir. Zraggen, Tim
1987 USA English
6 mins. video color Experimental
Dist. (U.S.): Video Free America
Video maker Tim Zraggen's stylized memorial to a friend (music by Eric Holsinger).

Reservaat (Reservation)
Dir. Van Gool, Clara
1988 Netherlands No Dialogue
9 mins. 16mm/35mm b&w Experimental
Dist. (U.K.): Cinenova

A sensual study of two women dancing tango in a park.

Resonance
Dir. Cummins, Steven and Simon Hunt
1990 Australia English
12 mins. 35mm color Experimental
Dist. (U.S.): Frameline
Dist. (U.K.): Dangerous To Know
A sublime short about queer-bashing in the back streets of Sydney. Released in the U.S. as part of a feature-length package of gay short films, *Boys Shorts: The New Queer Cinema*.

Revenge of the Wicked Witch
Dir. Plendl, Mat
1993 USA English
16 mins. video color Narrative
Dist. (U.S.): Plendl, Mat
The world's most misunderstood witch goes to Vegas.

Revolutions Happen Like Refrains in a Song
Dir. Deocampo, Nick
1987 Philippines Filipino
85 mins. S8mm color Other
Dist. (U.S.): n/a
Grand Prize winner at the 9th International Super-8 and Video Festival in Brussels, *Revolutions Happen Like Refrains in a Song* is the third film of Nick Deocampo's trilogy about the links between poverty and prostitution in the Philippines. The film traces the revolution that deposed Ferdinand Marcos and updates the lives of the people in his two earlier films, Oliver (1983), the story of a young gay who supports his family with his drag act at a Manila bar, and *Children of the Regime* (1985), about children forced by poverty into prostitution.

Deocampo is a filmmaker who sees his homosexuality as his "manner of perception, as a form of consciousness." From its images of the revolution, to Oliver's erotic "Spider" routine—a metaphor for the web of poverty in which the protagonist finds himself caught—to footage surreptitiously shot in Manila's child-sex dens, *Revolutions* is an uncompromising view of the Philippines.

Deocampo has only one purpose in filming his country, "to speak out the truth in our people's lives." Film becomes a "radical intrument" in his hands and the "truth" in 1987 was that Oliver was still supporting his family by working at a Manila gay bar and children were still selling their bodies in order to survive. Deocampo reveals this, then wonders aloud, "Will it take another revolution to change people's lives?"

Rhythm Divine: The Story of Disco, The
Dir. Oremland, Paul
1991 Great Britain English
55 mins. video color Documentary
Dist. (U.S.): NBD Picture Ltd.
"Drag up and wear wigs" suggests the hostess of a trendy New York club, unsuccessfully trying to explain the main principles of disco in Paul Oremland's ravey, completist history, *The Rhythm Divine*. In three parts, *The Rhythm Divine* tracks disco's development from Motown to Philadelphia, Funk, HiNRG, Space, Euro Electro Beat, Techno, House, and beyond, and laces its story with the music of cornerstones like Sylvester, Divine, Donna Summer, and Jimmy Somerville. Also interviewed: Miquel Brown, Nile Rogers, Neil Tennant, Giorgio Morodor, and Sinitta. Made for England's Channel Four, *The Rhythm Divine* is probably the most amusing piece of modern history you'll ever see.

Ride, The
Dir. Smolen, Wayne
1977 USA English
3 mins. S8mm color Experimental
Dist. (U.S.): Mears, Ric
A film that is very much me. A ride on the Santa Cruz roller coaster.

Right Stuff, The
Dir. Canalli, John
1986 USA English
20 mins. video color Experimental
Dist. (U.S.): Canalli, John
One of the locally produced segments of the weekly Gay Cable Network program shown on San Francisco Viacom Cable Channel 6 cohosted by Doris Fish and roommate Tippy. Included is a performance by comedian Danny Williams and a commercial by José Sarria. Camp humor and drag for days.

Right to Fight, The
Dir. Franken Medienwerkstatt
1988 Germany German
60 mins. video color Documentary
Dist. (U.S.): EBS Productions
Ultimately optimistic, this program shows what is possible when people with AIDS refuse to be victims and take charge of their lives. A sequel to *I'm Still Alive*, the tape visits Peter Sieglar back

Ⓐ Ⓑ Ⓒ Ⓓ Ⓔ Ⓕ Ⓖ Ⓗ Ⓘ Ⓙ Ⓚ Ⓛ Ⓜ Ⓝ Ⓞ Ⓟ Ⓠ Ⓡ Ⓢ Ⓣ Ⓤ Ⓥ Ⓦ Ⓧ Ⓨ Ⓩ

at home 2 years after his diagnosis. He is now actively involved in AIDS education and is surrounded by a community eager to lend its support. *The Right to Fight* offers new ideas and direction as it shows the ways San Franciscans have learned to cope emotionally, physically, and financially with this devastating public crisis.

Right Wing, Right Off, Right Hons, Right?

(see *Out On Tuesday, Program 1*)

Rights and Reactions
Dir. Zwickler, Phil
1987 USA English
58 mins. video color Documentary
Dist. (U.S.): Tapestry Productions
Rights and Reactions chronicles the recent and successful fight for a gay rights ordinance in New York. The passage of Intro 2 was the culmination of a fifteen-year effort by homosexual rights activists. "Separation of Church and State" takes a beating as Protestants, Jews, and Catholics line up on both sides to stake their moral ground in front of the New York City legislature. Tempers flare, contept citations abound, and Harvey Fierstein makes an appearance. A dramatic and excellent tape that indicates why the bill might have been needed.

rising
Dir. Gee, Daven
1994 USA English
16 mins. 16mm b&w Experimental
Dist. (U.S.): Gee, Daven
A witty, seductive nightmare about American family life.

Risk Group
Dir. Nikishin, A.
1988 USSR Russian
60 mins. video color Documentary
Dist. (U.S.): American Film Institute
A Russian AIDS documentary.

Risk: Lesbians and AIDS
Dir. Baus, Janet
Prod. Dyke TV
1995 USA English
15 mins. video color Documentary
Dist. (U.S.): Baus, Janet
Both the government and the medical establishment do not consider woman-to-woman transmission of HIV to be important, but then they don't really care whether we live or die. So why do lesbians let themselves be lulled into believing they are not at risk? *Risk: Lesbians and AIDS* breaks

through the misconceptions and gives us the facts we need to know about AIDS.

Rispondetemi
Dir. Pool, Lea
1992 Canada French
15 mins. 35mm color Narrative
Dist. (U.S.): Cinemaginaire
Lea Pool's *Rispondetemi* is a searing descent into the past of a woman lying between life and death.

Rites of Passage
Dir. Heijnis, Gerda
1992 Netherlands no dialogue
22 mins. 16mm color Experimental
Dist. (U.S.): Dutch Film and TV Academy
Operatic, industrial, and idyllic, this allegory of a cross-dressing girl and her mother offers an exquisite portrayal of lost and regained gender identity.

Robert Having His Nipple Pierced
Dir. Daley, Sandy
1970 USA English
33 mins. 16mm color Documentary
Dist. (U.S.): Daley, Sandy
The year is 1970. Robert Mapplethorpe is having his nipple pierced. You are there. Robert's boyfriend comforts him while Robert's roommate, Patti Smith, gives a drugged-up voice-over babelogue about her bizarre childhood, her tits, her transvestite brother, shaving her pubic hair, Bob Dylan, and whatever else happens across her wonderful little mind. (J.O.)

Robert Mapplethorpe (BBC Arena)
Dir. Finch, Nigel
Prod. Wall, Anthony
1988 Great Britain English
60 mins. video color Documentary
Dist. (U.K.): BBC TV
Made for BBC's Arena, this profile of controversial photographer Mapplethorpe traces his development from Brooklyn art school bad boy to Manhattan celebrity darling. Like Mapplethorpe's work itself, the documentary was the target for censorship when broadcast in Britain, and some of Mapplethorpe's work was removed from the film. "The policy is that you can show penises, but not erect ones," director Nigel Finch told London's *Time Out* magazine. "We wanted to use one of Mapplethorpe's dick photos which was in between. So we sat with the BBC lawyers trying to work out what was and wasn't an erection. The definition we finally came up with was a 'vertically self-sustaining member.'"

Rock Hudson's Home Movies
Dir. Rappaport, Mark
1992 USA English
58 mins. video color Other
Dist. (U.S.): Video Data Bank
Dist. (U.K.): Multimedia Home Entertainment
In Mark Rappaport's new tape Rock Hudson's Home Movies, Rock, played by a Rock-alike, journeys through an array of cleverly-edited clips and 'fesses up to the homosexual connotations. This new Rock is more militant than the old, and he never fails to point out a '90s way of looking at his pre-'60s persona. The result is a dizzying, smart-ass, high-wire comedy about Hollywood and homosexuality.

Rocking the Cradle
Dir. Marcolina, Kirk
Prod. Cohen, Polly
1994 USA English
26 mins. 16mm color Documentary
Dist. (U.S.): Marcolina, Kirk
A filmmaker struggles to address his mother's fears of gay parenting.

Roger: The Death of Wayne
Dir. Justice, Wayne
1979 USA English
5 mins. S8mm color Narrative
Dist. (U.S.): n/a
A conflict between personalities and sexualities of a young man who was run over by a bus and came back to life and was killed in a bowling accident.

Roman Springs on Mrs. Stone, The
Dir. Harrison, Ray
Prod. Gay Girls Riding Club
1963 USA English
22 mins. 16mm/video b&w Narrative
Dist. (U.S.): Tremaglio Productions
A real blast of the Italian gigolo syndrome, a young hustler and the aging heiress, there's more to this than three coins in the fountain! The second production from the Los Angeles–based Gay Girls Riding Club. Like their other films, The Roman Springs on Mrs. Stone was shot on Sundays, and was shown at the Los Angeles gay bar, The Brownstone.

Room 303
Dir. Speck, Wieland
1991 Germany No Dialogue
16 mins. 16mm color Experimental
Dist. (U.S.): Frameline

A wordless account from a dying man's bedside. Released as part of Among Men, a feature-length package of five short films by Wieland Speck.

Rosebud
Dir. Farthing, Cheryl
1992 Great Britain No Dialogue
14 mins. 16mm color Narrative
Dist. (U.S.): Women Make Movies
Dist. (U.K.): British Film Institute
The hottest lesbian coming out story you've ever seen. There's tons of voyeurism, cruising, and girls making out in this shiny, sexy color fantasy.

Rote Ohren Fetzen Durch Asche (Flaming Ears)
Dir. Scheirl, Angela Hans, Dietmar Schipek, and Ursula Purrer
1992 Austria German
84 mins. 16mm color Experimental
Dist. (U.S.): Women Make Movies
Dist. (U.K.): Cinenova
In a blast of color and sound this new Austrian feature portrays a futuristic tale of urban lesbian angst. In the year 2700, amid the caustic ruble of the town of Asche, a peculiar gang of lesbian characters live out a squalid and violent existence. A fragmented and bizarre drama of lust, jealousy, and revenge develops between the film's three protagonists: Spy (a brooding cartoonist), Volley (Spy's ruthless antagonist), and Nun (a necrophiliac nun in a red plastic outfit). The film's technical innovations in Super-8 cinematography (blown up to 16mm), sound, editing, set and costume design are as remarkable as the story being told. Co-directed by a trio of Austrian filmmakers, Flaming Ears stakes out a new lesbian aesthetic for the '90s.

Rough Outrageous
Dir. Hickson, Michelle
1992 Great Britain English
4 mins. video color Other
Dist. (U.K.): Hickson, Michelle
A spunky music video celebration of the dykes of London's activist group. Outrage, by the Lesbian C&W group, The Well Oiled Sisters.

Rough Sketch of a Spiral
(see Rasen No Sobyo)

Rove
Dir. Patierno, Mary
1991 USA No Dialogue
3 mins. 16mm b&w Experimental
Dist. (U.S.): Patierno, Mary

Ⓐ Ⓑ Ⓒ Ⓓ Ⓔ Ⓕ Ⓖ Ⓗ Ⓘ Ⓙ Ⓚ Ⓛ Ⓜ Ⓝ Ⓞ Ⓟ Ⓠ Ⓡ Ⓢ Ⓣ Ⓤ Ⓥ Ⓦ Ⓧ Ⓨ Ⓩ

The filmmaker's camera travels over her lover's body: "Freedom of movement over a wide area."

Roy Cohn/Jack Smith
Dir. Godmilow, Jill
Prod. Hope, Ted, James Schamus, and Marianne Weems
1993 USA English
90 mins. 16mm color Documentary
Dist. (U.S.): Strand Releasing

In one of his final, bravura performances, Ron Vawter—a founding member of the experimental Wooster Group—reinvents the essence of two very different white gay men, both of whom died of AIDS: Roy Cohn, the closeted, high-rolling lawyer who rallied to Joseph McCarthy's side during the Communist witch hunts, and Jack Smith, the erstwhile filmmaker (*Flaming Creatures*) and flamboyant godfather of camp. The lives of these two men, worlds apart, are brilliantly woven together in a collage of live performance, taped rehearsals, and behind-the-scenes glimpses of actor and audience.

Vawter, who starred in several stage productions and films—most recently as a homophobic attorney in *Philadelphia*—died of AIDS less than seven months after this film was made. Jill Godmilow expertly captures his legacy on film, his uncanny ability to move within a character and find the ticking parts. For the Roy Cohn role, Gary Indiana reimagines the text of a speech that Cohn gave to the American Society for the Protection of the Family; it's a masterful evocation of the man who could excoriate gays and Jane Fonda between loving paeans to his domineering mother. Jack Smith wrote the performance piece recreated here. Bedecked in seraglio drag, Vawter's Smith draws us into a private harem, where kitsch winks slyly at the "Sodom and Gomorrah" of Cohn's antigay rants.

RSVP
Dir. Lynd, Laurie
1991 Canada English
23 mins. 16mm color Narrative
Dist. (U.S.): Frameline
Dist. (U.K.): British Film Institute

Laurie Lynd's acclaimed and powerful *RSVP*. Jessye Norman's performance of *Le Spectre de la Rose* (from Berlioz's *Les Nuit D'Ete*) ties together a near-wordless tour-de-force about the impact of one man's death on those who loved him. Be prepared to weep. Released in the U.S. as part of a feature-length package of gay short films, *Boys Shorts: The New Queer Cinema*.

Rules of the Road
Dir. Friedrich, Su
1993 USA English
31 mins. 16mm b&w Experimental
Dist. (U.S.): Women Make Movies

An Oldsmobile station wagon serves as a touchstone to a love affair in Su Friedrich's witty and resonant *Rules of the Road*.

Running Gay
Dir. Chowdhry, Maya
1991 Great Britain English
20 mins. video color Documentary
Dist. (U.K.): Sheffield Film Co-op

A look at the lesbian and gay pursuit of health and happiness through the world of sports and fitness training. *Running Gay*, produced by Britain's Sheffield Film Co-op, discusses the problems lesbians and gays face in the sport world, including the pressure of being an "out" athlete.

S.S.
Dir. Haeberli, Eric
1993 USA English
4 mins. video color Other
Dist. (U.S.): Haeberli, Eric

A grotesque mess of brain-banging and Barbie Dolls.

Sacred Lies, Civil Truths
Dir. Saalfield, Catherine, and Cyrille Phipps
1993 USA English
58 mins. video color Documentary
Dist. (U.S.): Black Planet Productions

A sharp overview of the strategies and historical workings of the religious right's war against the civil rights movement.

Safe
Dir. Haynes, Todd
Prods. Vachon, Christine, and Lauren Zalaznick
1995 USA English
90 mins. 35mm color Narrative
Dist [U.S.]

Safe tells the story of Carol White, a Los Angeles housewife whose affluent environment turns against her in the form of an inexplicable illness. What begins as sudden allergic reactions to everyday chemicals, fragrances and fumes turns increasingly violent, transforming the laminated safety of Carol's existence into a terror of everyday life. When she is diagnosed with an immunity disorder called "Twentieth Century Disease," and sets off to New Mexico in search of treatment,

Carol's journey turns inward. And, in the crisis of identity that results, *Safe* reveals the ways in which disease infests our basic sense of who we are.

Safe Is Desire [excerpt]
Dir. Sundahl, Debi
Prod. Fatale Video
1993 USA English
10 mins. video color Narrative
Dist. (U.S.): Fatale Video
An excerpt from Fatale's first feature-length lesbian safe-sex video.

Safe Place, A
Dir. Guttman, Amos
1977 Israel Hebrew
29 mins. 16mm b&w Narrative
Dist. (U.S.): Frameline
A Safe Place, Guttman's first short film, shares a high school boy's struggle with his emerging gay identity as he encounters underground sex in a cinema hall.

Safe Sex is Fun
Dir. Broggi, Paolo, and Hans Gelke
1994 USA English
5 mins. video color Other
Dist. (U.S.): Broggi, Paolo
A fun safe-sex video.

Safe Sex Is Hot Sex
Dir. Bradley, Maureen
1992 Canada English
3 mins. video color Other
Dist. (U.S.): Frameline
Released in the U.S. as part of *She's Safe*, a lesbian safe-sex video package.

Safe Sex: The Manual
Dir. Lawson, Greg
1993 Netherlands English?
2 mins. 35mm color Other
Dist. (U.S.): Lawson, Greg
An extremely animated lesson in the art of application.

Safe Soap
Dir. Golden, Anne
1992 Canada English
1 mins. video color Other
Dist. (U.S.): Frameline
Released in the U.S. as part of *She's Safe*, a lesbian safe-sex video package.

Safer Sister
Dir. Perez, Maria
1992 USA English

1 mins. video color Other
Dist. (U.S.): Frameline
Released in the U.S. as part of *She's Safe*, a lesbian safe-sex video package.

Safety In Numbers
Dir. Slade, Eric
1993 USA English
5 mins. video color Other
Dist. (U.S.): San Francisco AIDS Foundation/ Prevention Dept.
Safe sex video—what happens when friends get together?

Saint Genet (BBC Arena)
Dir. Williams, Nigel, and Charles Chabot
Prod. Finch, Nigel, and Anthony Wall
1985 Great Britain English
60 mins. video color Documentary
Dist. (U.K.): BBC TV
An electric confrontation with French writer, ex-con, and outlaw hero Jean Genet, who granted the BBC an exclusive interview just days before his death. The real pleasure of this film is not the biographical detail, but the antagonism between subject and interrogator. At first the young interviewer asks nervous questions in imprecise French ("Did you say 'I' amour'?" asks Genet. "I thought you said 'la morte'"); finally, Genet becomes impatient and turns tables on the man and his crew ("I dreamed the technicians of this little film revolted"). It's the end of television.

Saint Mulekicker
Dir. Hunter, Simeon
1992 USA English
5 mins. 16mm color Documentary
Dist. (U.S.): n/a
Saint Mulekicker is a raw short about S/M, scarification, and L.A. performance artist Ron Athey.

Sally Forth
Dir. Petersen, Inka
1990 Germany German
20 mins. video color Documentary
Dist. (U.S.): Petersen, Inka
Sally Forth draws a charming portrait of a lesbian bicycle courier and political activist.

Salmonberries
Dir. Adlon, Percy
1991 Germany English/German
94 mins. 35mm color Narrative
Dist. (U.S.): Roxie Releasing
Please see under *My Own Private Idaho* for Elizabeth Pincus's essay.

Ⓐ
Ⓑ
Ⓒ
Ⓓ
Ⓔ
Ⓕ
Ⓖ
Ⓗ
Ⓘ
Ⓙ
Ⓚ
Ⓛ
Ⓜ
Ⓝ
Ⓞ
Ⓟ
Ⓠ
Ⓡ
Ⓢ
Ⓣ
Ⓤ
Ⓥ
Ⓦ
Ⓧ
Ⓨ
Ⓩ

Salome
Dir. Rambova, Natasha and Charles Bryant
1922 USA English
22 mins. 16mm b&w Narrative
Dist. (U.S.): Em Gee Film Library
Based on a work by Oscar Wilde, *Salome* was not well received by censors or critics when it was presented by Alla Nazimova in 1922. Starring a reputedly all-gay cast, this highly stylized silent film horrified censors, who deleted several sequences, including a gay relationship between two Syrian soldiers. Artist Aubrey Beardsley inspired the sets and costumes which were executed by Natasha Rambova.

Salt Mines, The
Dir. Aikin, Susan, and Carlos Aparico
1990 USA Spanish
47 mins. video color Documentary
Dist. (U.S.): Third World Newsreel
Lesbians and gays from around the world have created a variety of housing situations that reflect their lifestyles, as well as their social and political status. Alongside the Hudson River with a magnificent view of the towers of lower Manhattan is a secluded area where the sanitation department stores its out-of-service trucks. Here a community of homeless transvestite prostitutes has gathered. The place is called the Salt Mines, the street name for an adjacent shed covering a huge gray mountain of road salt, used to melt snow from the streets.

Salut Victor!
Dir. Poirier, Anne Claire
1988 Canada French
83 mins. 16mm color Narrative
Dist. (U.S.): Frameline
In *Salut Victor!* Canadian filmmaker Anne Claire Poirier has created an intimate chamber piece around two older gay men whose divergent life experiences could never have anticipated their late-in-life friendship. For Philippe, a quiet distinguished gentleman, old age means frail health, loneliness, and loss of freedom. Resigned to the infirmities of age, he moves to a comfortably situated home for the elderly; there, amid anonymous surroundings, he prepares to sit out his final years, waiting for the end. This solitary vigil is almost immediately disrupted by another resident—Victor, a handsome lion of a man whose spirit is undaunted by a withering of the flesh. For him, the wheelchair liberates, the male nurses delight, and an occasional surreptitious nip of cognac revitalizes. His gregarious, often irreverent familiarity ruffles Philippe's dignified reserve. Yet gradually he warms to Victor's generous charm and a tender friendship evolves, reviving laughter, dreams, and secrets confided. Based on Edward O. Phillips's book, *Matthew and Chauncy*, *Salut Victor!* draws a sensitive and revealing portrait of friendship. While infused with a sense of humor and fantasy, this simply-told tale is all the more poignant for the realities it addresses—the physical and emotional effects of age, the euphoria of past loves, the pain of difficult choices, loneliness, and ultimately, loss. As played by Jacques Godin and Jean-Louis Roux, friendship is cherished as much for its mystery as for its delight!

San Fernando Valley
Dir. Price, David A.
1993 USA English
32 mins. video color Narrative
Dist. (U.S.): Price, David A.
A clever short story about two gay men working on a bad daytime TV show, "San Fernando Valley." Is this what goes on behind the scenes at "Melrose Place"?

San Francisco Gay Freedom Day Parade 1980
Dir. Esteves, Roberto
1980 USA English
8 mins. video color Documentary
Dist. (U.S.): Esteves, Roberto
A short look at the 1980 Gay Day parade.

Sandra's Garden
Dir. Dickson, Bonnie
1991 Canada English
34 mins. video color Documentary
Dist. (U.S.): Women Make Movies
The National Film Board of Canada's award-winning Sandra's Garden, directed by Bonnie Dickson, tells a lesbian's brave story of surviving incest.

Sano y Sanitario
Dir. Derrios, Javier
1991 Cuba No Dialogue
10 mins. 35mm color Narrative
Dist. (U.S.): Soberon, Edgar
Sano y Sanitario is an erotically charged short set in a men's restroom—a Cuban *Un Chant d'amour*.

Sappho
Dir. Hammer, Barbara
1978 USA English

7 mins. 16mm color Experimental
Dist. (U.S.): Canyon Cinema
Using the 6th-century B.C. lyricist's poetry, a group of women unwrap the papyrus gauze of the lesbian goddess and bring her to life. Made by Barbara and six students, at the Women's Building in Los Angeles.

Sari Red
Dir. Parmar, Pratibha
1988 Great Britain English
12 mins. video color Experimental
Dist. (U.S.): Women Make Movies
Sari Red is Parmar's visual poem made in memory of Kalbinder Kaur Hayre, a young Indian woman killed in a 1985 racist attack in England. A meditation on the threat of violence in the lives of Asian women, *Sari Red* draws on the resonant meanings of red blood spilt in violence and the red sari, which symbolizes sensuality and intimacy between Asian women.

Satdee Night
Dir. Armstrong, Gillian
1982 Australia English
10 mins. 16mm color Narrative
Dist. (U.S.): n/a
An early short film from the director of *My Brilliant Career* and *Starstruck*.

Savage Nights
(see *Nuit Sauvage, La*)

Scars
Dir. Boschman, Lorna
1987 Canada English
11 mins. video color Documentary
Dist. (U.S.): Women In Focus
An exploration of self-scarring.

Scattered Remains
Dir. Broughton, James, and Joel Singer
1988 USA English
14 mins. 16mm color Experimental
Dist. (U.S.): Canyon Cinema
Scattered Remains is a multifaceted exploration of moral questions. Broughton metamorphoses from scene to scene as he is heard in a variety of voices and seen in magic visualizaion by comaker Joel Singer.

Scattering Stars
(see *Sternenschauer*)

Scene from Frankie and Johnny, A
Dir. Jortner, Michael
1995 USA English

7 mins. video color Narrative
Dist. (U.S.): Jortner, Michael
Based on Terrence McNally's screenplay, two people, one afraid, one confident, decide whether they will love each other or not.

School for Scandal
(see *Out On Tuesday, Program 4*)

Schweigen=Tod (Silence=Death)
Dir. von Praunheim, Rosa
1990 Germany English
60 mins. 16mm color Documentary
Dist. (U.S.): First Run Features
Rosa von Praunheim is probably the world's most restless gay filmmaker. When Praunheim announces a new film, you know to expect an anarchic attitude and a surprising subject. He's notorious for outraging the gay community with his warts-and-all approach and giddy mix of frivolity with fist-in-the-face fury. Last time he tackled AIDS was in 1985, with his musical melodrama, *A Virus Knows No Morals*. Now he's settled down. In *Silence=Death* he lets his interviewees carry the anger and outrage. It's the first of three films on AIDS activism. Praunheim platforms New York's artists against AIDS. He and journalist Phil Zwickler talk to Keith Haring and survivors David Wojnarowicz, Allen Ginsberg, Paul Smith, and Rafael Gamba.

Phil Zwickler: "I worked on another of the Festival films, *Silence=Death*, with Rosa von Praunheim. We included monologues by David Wojnarowicz as a community's indictment of the daily, malignant neglect by a murderous government—scorching testaments that kick ass! Wojnarowicz is the voice of our time, in this angry, confused epidemic. His work in writing, painting, and photography also celebrates the angry response as necessary and good. ("And I am caring this rage like a blood-filled egg . . .") These are the types of things I want to see. I won't accept the way things are. And neither do these filmmakers. I love them and celebrate their vision and expression."

Scorpio Rising
Dir. Anger, Kenneth
1963 USA English
29 mins. 16mm color Experimental
Dist. (U.S.): Canyon Cinema
Dist. (U.K.): British Film Institute
A "high" view of the Myth of the American Motorcyclist. The machine as totem, from toy to terror. Thanatos in chrome and black leather. Part I—Boys & Bolts. Part II—Image Maker. Part

Ⓐ
Ⓑ
Ⓒ
Ⓓ
Ⓔ
Ⓕ
Ⓖ
Ⓗ
Ⓘ
Ⓙ
Ⓚ
Ⓛ
Ⓜ
Ⓝ
Ⓞ
Ⓟ
Ⓠ
Ⓡ
Ⓢ
Ⓣ
Ⓤ
Ⓥ
Ⓦ
Ⓧ
Ⓨ
Ⓩ

III—Walpurgis Party. Part IV—Rebel Rouser.

> ". . . a masterpiece in the specific sense that it is composed of clarities of the fire and water workings of your earlier films into a ritual of order, depth and complexity."
> —Stan Brakhage

Screamers
Dir. Fairfield, Paula
Prod. Pandora Pictures Inc.
1994 Canada English
30 mins. 16mm color Narrative
Dist. (U.S.): Pandora Pictures Inc.
Set against a backdrop of knife-throwing and inflatable breast implants, *Screamers* is a film about screaming: wanting to scream, not wanting to scream, wanting to be heard—breaking the sound barrier.

Scrubbers
Dir. Zetterling, Mai
1982 Great Britain English
93 mins. 35mm color Narrative
Dist. (U.S.): Orion Classics
Scrubbers was made to cash in on the controversy and commercial success of the 1979 movie *Scum*, itself based on a banned BBC play about reform school violence. But *Scrubbers* takes its same-sex liaisons more seriously than *Scum* did. Ex-Scandinavian movie-star-turned-director Mai Zetterling makes prison life both harsh (beware: some scenes are not for the squeamish) and kind of tender (a lesbian limerick writer screams poetic obscenities from her cell). Like *Prisonnieres*, *Scrubbers* uses an ensemble to explore the prison formula, but Zetterling puts the smart money on Eva, a lesbian orphan who busts herself back inside to rejoin her faithless lover. Some scenes have an honest, dreamy quality. "I love you, Eva, I fuckin' love you," yells her lover, and the humorous, tender message booms out over the quadrangle, where prisoners pass notes and joints from window to window. Scrubbers even suggests that, for some, lesbianism is a choice: "Give us a lick, not a prick." Pulpy, poetic, and political.

> *Scrubbers* comes closest to a recognizable reality that evokes the serious desperation of women behind bars. What do you do if your lover is shut up in one prison, and you're locked in another? Break out, commit a worse crime and, if you're lucky, get jailed close to her. That's what Carol does, and ends up only a cell block away from her beloved. Unfortunately, her beloved has shacked up with someone else.

Worse, Carol is seen as a snitch by Annetta, her coescapee who's also been caught. Annetta's anger knows no bounds and lines are quickly drawn among the inmates. Eddie, a stone butch we will all recognize, offers her protection to Carol for a not unattractive price, and the game between stoolies, patsies, goodies, and butches is on. After getting used to the accents, you'll be kept on the edge of your seat by *Scrubbers*' characters and predicaments. Their love affairs are intensely emotional and believable. Their desperation is high voltage. We're locked up with these women as we hear their tragic histories and see their resultant high security situations. And the constant screaming, singing, and yelling voices that bounce off the cement block will make you feel like you're there. With Amanda York, Chrissie Cotterill, and Kate Ingram.

Sea of Time
Dir. Gaulke, Cheri
1993 USA English
12 mins. video color Other
Dist. (U.S.): Gaulke, Cheri
A lesbian couple reflects on the spiritual relationship between the death of their close gay male friend and the forthcoming birth of their child.

Seams
Dir. Ainouz, Karim
1993 Brazil/USA Portugese
30 mins. 16mm color Experimental
Dist. (U.S.): Frameline
In Portugese, "veado" means "deer," but also "faggot" or "queer," as Karim Ainouz points out in his beautiful, suggestive film Seams. It's a lyrical visit with his five Brazilian great aunts, each of whom relates stories about romance, marriage, suffering, and survival in a man's world; from this anecdotal evidence, Ainouz assembles a subtle, salutory story about the machinery of machismo.

Searanch: The True Story
Dir. Hanlon, Terri
1988 USA English
3 mins. video color Other
Dist. (U.S.): Hanlon, Terri
Searanch is a mediocre California resort colony—but then, lesbian heartbreak can happen anywhere.

Search, The
Dir. Morgan, Benjamin Jeremiah
1993 USA English
3 mins. video color Other
Dist. (U.S.): Morgan, Benjamin Jeremiah

A lesbian searches for a resolution between her religion and sexuality.

Searching for Contact
Dir. Dabek, Nina
1992 USA English
7 mins. 16mm color Documentary
Dist. (U.S.): Dabek, Nina
In *Searching for Contact*, Nina Dabek muses on Yiddish, a relationship to history, and the need for continuity with a heritage.

Sebastiane
Dir. Jarman, Derek, and Paul Humfress
1977 Great Britain Latin
90 mins. 35mm color Experimental
Dist. (U.K.): British Film Institute
Long the subject of fascination among gay men (Yukio Mishima had his first orgasm while looking at a print depicting his martyrdom), St. Sebastiane was an obscure Roman mystic who might barely be remembered today were it not for the homoerotic rumors which have persistently clung to him. In *Sebastiane*, directors Derek Jarman and Paul Humfress bring all the implied into the foreground, creating the frankly homosexual world of their St. Sebastiane. In the process they have pulled off an amazing trick. They have made a beautiful film which evokes a realistic feeling of another place and time, explores the dual nature of spirituality and sexuality, and also depicts an ultimate homosexual fantasy.

Handsome nude men seen relaxing together, practicing for battle, and having sex might be enough to make this film the cult favorite that it is, but this is no mere porn movie. Every element, including the excellent photography, editing, Latin dialogue (with subtitles), and music by Brian Eno combine to lift the viewer into the world of *Sebastiane* and into the tug-of-war between the soul and flesh which is at the heart of this story.

Sech Wie Pech & Schwefel (Birds of a Feather)
Dir. Kremfresch
1990 Germany German
50 mins. 16mm color Narrative
Dist. (U.S.): Nagel, Marga
Crisp and colorful, this peppy new featurette portrays the sundry escapades of the German lesbian revue group, Kremfresch. As a slapstick lesbian allegory, *Birds of a Feather* works with and against conventions of silent film style to create an iconoclastic lesbian camp.

This "pretend family" of lesbians (a doctor, a superhero, an alcoholic, a creampuff-fiend, and a femme beauty queen in lingerie and hair rollers) are low on privacy and big on togetherness. They watch TV together, sleep together (in one bed), bathe together, and cruise together. In pursuit of romance and employment they encounter a vast array of women, including a butch sea captain, an East German border guard, and a bare-chested Amazon on horseback.

With a smart visual style, an enchanting musical soundtrack, and fine performances, Kremfresch brings forward a new aesthetic in the German lesbian cinema.

Second Awakening of Christa Klages, The
Dir. Von Trotta, Margarethe
1977 Germany German
88 mins. 16mm color Narrative
Dist. (U.S.): n/a
Von Trotta's first solo feature containing thematic microcosms of her later, better funded films: women discovering independent action; sexuality as a natural outgrowth of friendship; and the motives of violence in a hostile world. Christa (Tina Engel) is introduced in the process of taking a teller (Katharina Thalback) hostage in a bank robbery, naively planned to fund a day-care nursery. She's on the run from then on but it's a flight to discovery, aided by a lesbian relationship with an old school friend and the painful recognition of new values.

Second Generation Once Removed
Dir. Saxena, Gita
1990 USA English
19 mins. video color Experimental
Dist. (U.S.): V-Tape
The divorce of her German mother from her Indian father creates difficulty for a woman learning to accept her Indian heritage. "In India, in love you don't fall, you rise," her father tells her. Now she starts playing with the image to suit herself and her experience.

Secrets
Dir. Cullen, Colette, and Sarah Myland
1993 Great Britain English
6 mins. 16mm color Other
Dist. (U.K.): L.C.P.D.T. Film and Video Dept.
Feminine protection products are spoofed.

Seduction: The Cruel Woman
(see *Verführung: Die Grausame Frau*)

See Saw

Ⓐ Ⓑ Ⓒ Ⓓ Ⓔ Ⓕ Ⓖ Ⓗ Ⓘ Ⓙ Ⓚ Ⓛ Ⓜ Ⓝ Ⓞ Ⓟ Ⓠ Ⓡ Ⓢ Ⓣ Ⓤ Ⓥ Ⓦ Ⓧ Ⓨ Ⓩ

Dir. Porter, Andrew

1993 Australia English

2 mins. video color Other

Dist. (U.S.): Porter, Andrew

From Australia, *See Saw* has fun with a glory hole gag.

Self Defense

Dir. Donovan, Paul

Prod. Donovan, Michael

1983 Canada English

90 mins. 35mm color Narrative

Dist. (U.S.): n/a

One of the most controversial gay-related movies ever made, *Self Defense* has been called "a gay version of Friday the 13th" by Vito Russo and was bitterly criticized for its excessive violence at a forum following its screening at New York's gay film festival. It has also been praised as an exciting suspense thriller that revolves around a sympathetic—if somewhat patronizing—characterization of a gay man. If nothing else, *Self Defense* is a very interesting example of mainstream filmmakers, including gay characters in a film genre that usually excludes them.

The story is simple. During a police strike in Halifax, Nova Scotia, a group of rightwing fascists invade a gay bar and methodically execute everyone in it except Daniel, a timid young man who manages to escape. He is followed by the murderers to the apartment of a stranger who lets him in and then refuses to turn him over to the thugs. What follows is similar to Peckinpah's *Straw Dogs* in its suspense and violence as the residents of the apartment building fight off the murderers who try just about everything to get to Daniel.

Self Defense is undeniably exciting, gripping from its first horrifying scenes and certain to elicit a strong response from its festival audience.

Separate Skin

Dir. Fishel, Deirdre

1987 USA English

26 mins. 16mm color Narrative

Dist. (U.S.): n/a

Dist. (U.K.): Cinenova

Separate Skin is about Emily, a young woman who is the child of Holocaust survivors, who struggles with her childhood fears and fantasies of love. Her relationships, with a man and then with a woman, fail to relieve her anxiety, but instead force her to confront the pain in her past and to make peace with her own life.

Sergeant Matlovich Versus the U.S. Air Force

Dir. Leaf, Paul

1978 USA English

100 mins. 16mm color Narrative

Dist. (U.S.): Kit Parker Films

Brad Dourif challenges the military's ban on gays in this NBC made-for-TV movie. Well-meaning if a bit dull, *Sergeant Matlovich* is a time capsule that walks a typically '70s fine line, trying to "educate" the masses about gays without alienating them. Rue McClanahan does a nice turn as Matlovich's mother and Marc Singer plays his loyal straight friend. Note: the real-life Matlovich wasn't thrilled with the film. He thought Dourif too "wimpy" and was particularly irked that the TV version of a suicide attempt had him "rescued" by the heterosexual Singer. (D.M.)

Sergei Eisenstein

Dir. Katanyan, Vassili

1958 USSR Russian

50 mins. 16mm b&w Documentary

Dist. (U.S.): Em Gee Film Library

A look at the life and work of the pioneering Soviet filmmaker, who happened to be gay.

Serial Clubber Killer

Dir. Leite, Duda, and Gisela Mathias

1994 Brazil Portugese

10 mins. video color Documentary

Dist. (U.S.): MIX Brasil

An exposé of Saõ Paulo's gay club scene.

Serving in Silence: The Margarethe Cammermeyer Story

Dir. Korty, John

1994 USA English

100 mins. 35mm color Narrative

Dist. (U.S.): n/a

Barbra Streisand executive-produced this fine telefilm about the much-awarded Army medical officer who bravely combated her discharge for admitted lesbianism. Judy Davis (a tad over the top, but we love her anyway) is the artist-lover; their smooch fired up a predictable war of words over broadcast "permissiveness." It's not exactly deep and wet, but it ain't no mere peck on the cheek, either. Intelligent and forceful, the movie methodically makes a case for the absurdity of institutionalized prejudice at the highest levels. (D.H.)

Seth's Aunts

Dir. Dabek, Nina

1992 USA English
3 mins. 16mm color Documentary
Dist. (U.S.): Frameline
A three-minute treat; a story of a young boy who cannot tell the difference between Nina, his Jewish-lesbian aunt, and her lover Penny.

7 Steps to Sticky Heaven
Dir. Nguyen, Hoang Tan
1995 USA English
24 mins. video color Experimental
Dist. (U.S.): Nguyen, Hoang Tan
In *7 Steps to Sticky Heaven* you'll hear the voice of the director as he interviews Asian men about being "sticky" (Asian men who date other Asian men). Nguyen adds spice to his recipe with interesting time sequencing alterations, subtitles, and homemade porn.

Seven Women
Dir. Ford, John
1965 USA English
87 mins. 35mm color Narrative
Dist. (U.S.): Swank Motion Pictures
Set in China in the summer of 1935, *Seven Women* renders invisible the qualifications of missionaries for the work they ought to do. The all-women mission is threatened from within as well as from outside. Everything appears calm as missionary head Agatha Andrews, in her high-necked dress with keys clinking at her side, methodically performs her duties. But (n)e(u)rotic tension is brewing and Ms. Andrews soon turns out to be a closeted dyke suffering from the repression she advocates. One of the women, Florrie, a jolly soul, is pregnant but fears she is too old to give birth without problems. The arrival of Dr. Cartwright is a fantastic coupe de theatre. Donkeys and workers accompany a perfectly cross-dressed Anne Bancroft in cowboy drag. Dr. Cartwright is extravagant, cynical, and profane. The youngest girl at the mission, who happens to be the object of Ms. Andrews's latent sexual desire, becomes the doctor's best mate. In the film's second half the mission is attacked by Mongolian robbers, who renowned director John Ford, in his last film, depicts in a shockingly racist manner. The women manage to cope with extremely dangerous situations. Dr. Cartwright inspires them to great bravery but in the end she is forced to surrender to a feminine role.

17 Rooms or, What Lesbians Do in Bed
Dir. Sheldon, Caroline
1985 Great Britain English
9 mins. video color Experimental

Dist. (U.S.): Women Make Movies
Dist. (U.K.): Cinenova
A landmark lesbian short.

76 Trombones
Dir. Dougherty, Cecilia
1987 USA English
3 mins. video color Experimental
Dist. (U.S.): Dougherty, Cecilia
An early video from the maker of such '90s festival favorites as *Coalminer's Granddaughter* and *Joe-Joe*.

Sewing on Breast
Dir. Stanley, Anie
1991 USA English
2 mins. 8mm color Experimental
Dist. (U.S.): Stanley, Anie
Sewing on Breast goes under the skin to explore the truthfulness of flesh.

Sex 121 and the Gulag
(see *Out On Tuesday, Program 2*)

Sex and the Sandinistas
Dir. Broadbent, Lucinda
1991 Great Britain English
25 mins. video color Documentary
Dist. (U.S.): Women Make Movies
Filmed by a Nicaraguan crew, *Sex and the Sandinistas* was made in close collaboration with the lesbian and gay movement in Managua. Without assuming any prior knowledge of Nicaraguan history, the film brings to life the extraordinary and valuable experience of lesbians and gays coming out in the whirlwind of a Latin American revolution.

Sex Bowl
Dir. Baby Maniac
1994 USA English
6 mins. video color Other
Dist. (U.S.): Women Make Movies
A video of multiple orgasm in the ghetto by Baby Maniac (a.k.a. Shu Lea Cheang and Jane Castle).

Sex Change—Shock! Horror! Probe! (BBC Arena)
Dir. Jackson, Jane
Prod. Clarke, Kristiene
1989 Great Britain English
50 mins. video color Documentary
Dist. (U.K.): BBC TV
Made for Channel Four television, *Sex Change* is quite unlike any other documentary—or fictional exposé—of transsexualism. Written and produced

Ⓐ Ⓑ Ⓒ Ⓓ Ⓔ Ⓕ Ⓖ Ⓗ Ⓘ Ⓙ Ⓚ Ⓛ Ⓜ Ⓝ Ⓞ Ⓟ Ⓠ Ⓡ Ⓢ Ⓣ Ⓤ Ⓥ Ⓦ Ⓧ Ⓨ Ⓩ

by Kristiene Clarke (who also produced *Armistead Maupin: A Man I Dreamt Up*), herself a transsexual, *Sex Change* deals with the post-op life. A handful of transsexuals describe their politics and positions today.

Sex Elvis Boy
Dir. Cole, Jeff
1993 Great Britain English
8 mins. video color Experimental
Dist. (U.K.): Dangerous To Know
Inspired by adventures in public places, *Sex Elvis Boy* takes us to London's Hampstead Heath.

Sex Fish
Dir. Maniac, E. T. Baby
1993 USA English
6 mins. video color Other
Dist. (U.S.): Women Make Movies
A truly sexy and shiny collaboration by Ela Troyano, Shu Lea Cheang and Jane Castle.

Sex Is
Dir. Huestis, Marc
1993 USA English
80 mins. 16mm color Documentary
Dist. (U.S.): Outsider Enterprises
Dist. (U.K.): Multimedia Home Entertainment
A 30-minute video sneak preview of San Francisco filmmaker Marc Huestis's erotic documentary was presented at the 1991 festival.
Sex Is was completed, transferred to film, and released in 1993 and went on to win the Audience Award at the Berlin International Film Festival. According to *Variety*, *Sex Is* was the fifth-highest-grossing documentary in the U.S. in 1993–1994.
Whether innocence was lost in the bathhouse, the confessional, or on the Senate floor—where cotton-stuffed politicians started feeling comfortable talking about sodomy—local filmmaker Marc Huestis, in his documentary film *Sex Is* . . . shows us where to find it. The case, as Huestis makes it, is that gay sex is, was, and ever shall be. Amen. His film outlines a generalized Body Gaysexual and fills the form with talking heads who are black, white, Latino, Asian, religious, pornographic, celibate, unashamed, shy, pained, and/or financially comfortable. Splicing porn clips between interviews—which travel from sex, drugs, rock 'n' roll to early childhood memories—*Sex Is* . . . has both ripe poetry and tears, reasons to party and reasons to protest. (S.G.)

Sex Is Sex
Dir. Bergen, Brian, and Jennifer Milici

1995 USA English
51 mins. video color Documentary
Dist. (U.S.): Bergen, Brian
Topically arranged excerpts from candid discussions with male prostitutes in New York City.

Sex, Lies, Religion
Dir. Kennerly, Annette
1993 Great Britain English
5 mins. 16mm color Other
Dist. (U.K.): Cinenova
An erotic encounter between three women in a cemetery.

Sex of the Stars (Le sexe des etoiles)
Dir. Baillargeon, Paule
1993 Canada French
100 mins. 35mm color Narrative
Dist. (U.S.): First Run Features
This transgender twist on *Kramer vs. Kramer* is a bittersweet delight about a girl and her father. Marie-Pierre (Denis Mercier), formerly Pierre, happens to be a transsexual. Returning to the daughter she had left behind in Montreal, Marie-Pierre attempts to reconcile her daughter's need for a father with her own need to be true to her gender.
Looking uncannily like a young k.d. lang, Marianne Mercier gives an outstanding performance as Camille, a twelve-year-old girl facing the fears and insecurities of puberty. In her friendship with Lucky (Tobie Pelletier), a slightly older boy at school, she learns some of life's gritty realities. When Lucky discovers the truth about Camille's father he reveals his own secret—he's a street hustler.
Along the lines of William Hurt's Molina in *Kiss of the Spider Woman*, Denis Mercier's Marie-Pierre is painted as a charismatic and pathetic figure. And just as Hurt won an Oscar for Molina, Mercier won a Genie (the Canadian equivalent of the Oscars) for his Marie-Pierre.
Director Paule Baillargeon is probably best known by American audiences for her role as the Curator in Patricia Rozema's *I've Heard the Mermaids Singing*. *Sex of the Stars* is her second feature film as a director. In her sensitive and unique approach to a timely subject, Baillargeon exemplifies the innovation and style of contemporary Canadian cinema.

Sex Wars
Dir. Farthing, Cheryl, and Penny Ashbrook
1993 Great Britain English
30 mins. video color Documentary

Dist. (U.K.): Alfalfa Entertainments, Ltd.
What do gay men think about lesbians? What do lesbians think about gay men? *Sex Wars* is a provocative installment from Channel Four's Out TV series.

Sexlock
Dir. Cowan, Jeff
Prod. Cowan, Jeff, and HiC Luttmers
1995 USA English
3 mins. video color Other
Dist. (U.S.): Cowan, Jeff
A commercial spoof for the hormonally challenged!

Sexual I.D.
Dir. unknown
1983 USA English
4 mins. video color Other
Dist. (U.S.): n/a
The funniest short, in the most naive style. In memory of Butchy, a hustler who loved his work.

Shadows
Prod. Fatale Video
1985 USA English
30 mins. video color Narrative
Dist. (U.S.): Fatale Video
Another lesbian porn video from Fatale.

Shaman Psalm
Dir. Broughton, James, and Joel Singer
1981 USA English
7 mins. 16mm b&w Experimental
Dist. (U.S.): Canyon Cinema
Gay men everywhere are invited to become "champions of the hug" and "warriors of the kiss" in this unfaltering sensitive film by poet James Broughton and Joel Singer.

Shame
Dir. McBride, Steve
1995 Great Britain English
17 mins. 16mm color Narrative
Dist. (U.K.): Dangerous To Know
The tale of an unscrupulous reporter's attempt to out two famous gay boys.

Shared Lives
Dir. Seidler, Tamsin Orion
1994 U.S.A. English
10 mins. video color Documentary
Dist. (U.S.): Seidler, Tamsin Orion
Three lesbians who have lesbian mothers discuss the emotional and psychological intricacies of their relationships.

Shasta Woman
Dir. Mason, Crystal
1992 USA English
36 mins. video color Documentary
Dist. (U.S.): Frameline
Norma Jean Croy was charged with conspiracy to commit murder, and since 1978 she has been serving a life sentence for a crime she and her brother Hooty never committed. Hooty received the death penalty, appealed, and was released. Norma Jean was denied parole three times and has no future appeal date set. Produced by Bo and directed by Crystal Mason, *Shasta Woman* is a story of courage, injustice, and racism.

She Begins
Dir. Gunnarsdottir, Hrafnhidur
1989 USA/Iceland English
9 mins. video color Experimental
Dist. (U.S.): n/a
She Begins is an experimental meditation on femininity, hairstyles and gender.

She Can Probably Fix It
Dir. Storm, Harriet
1993 USA English
6 mins. video color Other
Dist. (U.S.): Storm, Harriet
A fortuitous highway encounter with the cutest girl in North America in Harriet Storm's *She Can Probably Fix It*.

She Don't Fade
Dir. Dunye, Cheryl
1991 USA English
23 mins. video color Narrative
Dist. (U.S.): Third World Newsreel
Dist. (U.K.): Dangerous To Know
A self-reflexive look at the sexuality, love life, and friendships of a young black lesbian.

She Even Chewed Tobacco!
Prod. Freedman, Estelle, and Liz Stevens
1983 USA English
40 mins. video b&w Documentary
Dist. (U.S.): Women Make Movies
This forty-minute slide-tape show is full of wonderful stories and images of women who passed as men in early San Francisco. They dressed as men, worked for men's wages, and many courted and married the women they loved. A rare work of lesbian herstory. Original research by Allan Berube.

She Makes Love With Her
Dir. Shmueli, Nili

Ⓐ
Ⓑ
Ⓒ
Ⓓ
Ⓔ
Ⓕ
Ⓖ
Ⓗ
Ⓘ
Ⓙ
Ⓚ
Ⓛ
Ⓜ
Ⓝ
Ⓞ
Ⓟ
Ⓠ
Ⓡ
Ⓢ
Ⓣ
Ⓤ
Ⓥ
Ⓦ
Ⓧ
Ⓨ
Ⓩ

1992 Israel Hebrew
15 mins. video color Documentary
Dist. (U.S.): Shmaeli, Nili
Yonit and Limor share the meaning of emerging lesbian identity in Israel.

She Must Be Seeing Things
Dir. McLaughlin, Sheila
1987 USA English
90 mins. 16mm color Narrative
Dist. (U.S.): First Run Features
She Must Be Seeing Things, Sheila McLaughlin's first feature, is both very personal and nearly universal in its understanding of the dynamics of intimate relationships. Funny, touching, and very real, the story of Agatha, a lawyer, and Jo, her filmmaker girlfriend, is a deft exploration of jealousy's effect on a lesbian relationship.

Throughout the film Jo and Agatha's professional lives pose a striking contrast to the intimacy of their life together. The tension of their sexual attraction for each other and the details of that intimacy become a framework for the film's more explicit narrative. At the same time, the strength of their feelings comes to constitute a parallel drama—one that starts a dialogue with the current debates over women's sexuality in the '80s as well as with current theories on the nature of voyeurism in contemporary cinema.

Sheila McLaughlin comes from the world of downtown New York theater, where she performed in the 1970s with Richard Foreman's "Ontological Hysterical Theatre" company. Her first short film, *Inside Out*, screened at the Berlin Film Festival in 1978. Her most recent film, *Committed*, based on the life of Frances Farmer, was codirected wth Lynne Tillman. McLaughlin played Justin, the dazzling blonde seductreess in the hit of the 1985 festival, *Seduction: The Cruel Woman*.

Sheila Dabney (Agatha) and Lois Weaver (Jo) are both Obie Award–winning actresses and McLaughlin has gathered a crew for *She Must Be Seeing Things* of equal stature. Director of Photography Mark Daniels shot Yvonne Rainer's *The Man Who Envied Women*, while well-known German filmmaker Heinz Emigholz shot the integral period film-within-the-film segments. Acclaimed composer John Zorn makes his movie debut with his score, the sound-editing was done by Margie Crimmins, who worked on the Oscar-winning *Witness to War*, and the art director was Leigh Kyle, who did the art direction on Lizzie Borden's *Working Girls*.

She Shoots, She Scores
Dir. Arbogast, Eve
Prod. Glazier, Alison
1995 USA English
7 mins. video color Documentary
Dist. (U.S.): Glazier, Alison
Experience the thrill of women's ice hockey.

She Thrills Me
Dir. Bradley, Maureen
1993 Canada English
15 mins. video color Documentary
Dist. (U.S.): Video Out
Women talk about sex—what they want, what they like, what they do.

She's a Talker
Dir. Goldberg, Neil
1993 USA English
2 mins. video color Experimental
Dist. (U.S.): Goldberg, Neil
A demented survey of queer cat owners.

She's Real: A Document of Queer Rock
Dir. Thane, Lucy
Prod. Thane , Lucy, and Abby Moser
1995 USA/UK English
20 mins. video color Documentary
Dist. (U.S.): Thane, Lucy
A look at the dyke rock scene in San Francisco, New York, and London.

Shell
Dir. Lee, Karen
1987 USA English
7 mins. 16mm b&w Narrative
Dist. (U.S.): Lee, Karen
A stylized black-and-white film about a woman troubled by her mother's reaction to her lesbianism.

Shipwrecked
Dir. Waggoner, David
1977 USA English
5 mins. S8mm color Narrative
Dist. (U.S.): n/a
Starring in order of appearance, Kenny Price and J.J. Hecker. Deals with Everyman's journey to self-discovery.

Shirley Temple and Me
Dir. Hammer, Barbara
1993 USA English
3 mins. video color Experimental
Dist. (U.S.): Hammer, Barbara
Shirley Temple and Me is a clever excerpt from

Barbara Hammer's forthcoming autobiographical feature.

Shisheng Huamei (Silent Thrush, The)
Dir. Cheng, Sheng-fu
1992 Taiwan Hokkien and Mandarin
100 mins. 35mm color Narrative
Dist. (U.S.): Anthex Film Co.
On the surface, *The Silent Thrush* is a fascinating mixture of exoticism and eroticism. It tells the story of Yuh (Li Yu-shan), a young girl who joins a Taiwanese opera company. Chia-feng, the company's star and Yuh's childhood idol, soon falls in love with her, provoking the intense jealousy of Ai-ching, the star's longtime lover. Their melodrama of lesbian love is played out amidst the troupe's day-to-day problems.

Shit Fit
Dir. Kelly, Joe
Prod. Paul, Craig
1994 USA English
2 mins. video color Other
Dist. (U.S.): Kelly, Joe
A degenerate drag queen humiliation trip to hell (not for the queasy).

Shot Through My Head
Dir. Kadet
Prod. Kadet/Helyx
1995 USA English
6 mins. video color Experimental
Dist. (U.S.): Private Eye Productions
Parallels the loss of a lover with that of a brother, driven by the resurrecting function of memory.

Show Me
Dir. Araki, Gregg, and Jaie Laplante
1994 USA English
3 mins. video color Other
Dist. (U.S.): Desperate Pictures
Gregg Araki's Soundgarden video, made for Red Hot's *No Alternative* album but never released.

Shriek, The
Dir. Huestis, Marc
1977 USA English
8 mins. S8mm color Documentary
Dist. (U.S.): Outsider Enterprises
A critical look at 1970s Castro clone culture. A film that is very different from anything I've done in terms of style, imagery, editing, and content. Inspired by the film Edvard Munch and dedicated to the thousands of silent crys that often haunt Castro Street.

Sightings

Dir. Keller, H. Len
1995 USA English
15 mins. 16mm color Narrative
Dist. (U.S.): Keller, H. Len
Delves into the desires of two beautiful black lesbians who catch each other's eye at the laundromat, but can't quite seem to connect.

Significant (Br)other
Dir. Lofton, Charles
1993 USA English
5 mins. video color Experimental
Dist. (U.S.): Lofton, Charles
Images of the black male body that are both objectifying and affirming.

Silence . . . Broken
Dir. Simmons, Aishah Shahidah
1993 USA English
8 mins. video color Experimental
Dist. (U.S.): Simmons, Aishah Shahidah
Silence . . . Broken incorporates poetry and experimental structure to speak out against racism, sexism, and homophobia.

Silence = Death
(see *Schweigen=Tod*)

Silence of the Lambs, The
Dir. Demme, Jonathan
1991 USA English
118 mins. 35mm color Narrative
Dist. (U.S.): Swank Motion Pictures
Please see under *Basic Instinct* for Judith Halberstam's essay.

Silencis (Silent Moments)
Dir. Xavier, Daniel
1983 Spain Spanish
14 mins. 16mm b&w Narrative
Dist. (U.S.): n/a
Silent Moments is a short film with a long tale. A gem of voyeurism in camerawork, acting, and idea all designed around a Spanish army officer (Adolph Myer) and his inability to accept his attraction to his gay son (Carles Artigas). The freedom he witnesses from his hiding places finally inspires him to strip from full dress uniform to nakedness to join the male members of his family (including the last appearance of Ocana, the painter, as mother). The reluctant discovery and disrobing are the barings of a macho soul in torment under the violent military, religious, and moral dictatorship. The rest is sensuality and silence.

Silent Pioneers

Ⓐ Ⓑ Ⓒ Ⓓ Ⓔ Ⓕ Ⓖ Ⓗ Ⓘ Ⓙ Ⓚ Ⓛ Ⓜ Ⓝ Ⓞ Ⓟ Ⓠ Ⓡ Ⓢ Ⓣ Ⓤ Ⓥ Ⓦ Ⓧ Ⓨ Ⓩ

Dir. Winer, Lucy
Prod. Snyder, Patricia
1985 USA English
42 mins. 16mm color Documentary
Dist. (U.S.): Filmmaker's Library
Contrary to popular myth, gay men and lesbians do grow old. Through profiles of eight men and women, *Silent Pioneers* tells us their stories, of how they have lived and loved, and how, despite harmful societal prejudices about gay people, they have led meaningful lives. *Silent Pioneers* is a film about struggle and silence and the emergence from both.

Silent Thrush, The
(see *Shisheng Huamei*)

Silverlake Life: The View from Here
Dir. Joslin, Tom, and Peter Friedman
1993 USA English
99 mins. 16mm color Documentary
Dist. (U.S.): Zeitgeist Films
This groundbreaking home-video documentary (blown up to 16mm film) about the lives of a gay couple facing the reality of living with AIDS won the Grand Jury Prize for Best Documentary at the 1993 Sundance Film Festival.

    Silverlake Life by Tom Joslin (completed by Peter Friedman) intimately and painfully records the death of the author. We, like Joslin's lover Mark, are left alone and bereft by Tom's death, and the film offers no succor. Unlike the recent blockbuster AIDS film *Philadelphia, Silverlake* has no feel-good solution to the AIDS crisis. While the mainstreaaming of an AIDS narrative demands that the audience be carefully drawn into the AIDS crisis through appeals to a common humanity, *Silverlake* spares its audience nothing, and in fact attempts to involve the viewer in a spiral of pain, isolation, frustration, and fatigue. When Joslin wakes up in the middle of the night, cannot go back to sleep, and turns on the camera to record his live nightmare, there is no place for the viewer to go to escape the close and suffocating intimacy of another slow and excruciating death. The voice that confronts us through the gloom of night with its fear and tension, its petty concerns and insurmountable anxieties, this is the voice of AIDS that, as David Wojnarowicz has written, "wakens you and welcomes you to your bad dream."

    On a formal level, *Silverlake Life* engages the viewer with the mood of the personal home video, but it also transgresses the "personal" precisely by making AIDS "your" problem.

There is no comfortable distance acheived in this film, no distance of the objective documentary camera; distance collapses as the bodies of the documentary subjects themselves cave in and collapse at the center of the film. Indeed, the path of the disease is marked by ever diminishing geographies of mobility. As the disease progresses, the movement of the camera becomes more limited until, at the point of Tom's death, the camera is stationary. (J.H.)

Simone
Dir. Ehm, Christine
1984 France French
90 mins. 16mm color Narrative
Dist. (U.S.): Altermedia
Simone is the first feature from 19-year-old Christine Ehm. She has created a stylish and stylized drama of a love affair between two women, the beautiful and mysterious Simone and the gamine Francoise, first seen recovering in the hospital from a suicide attempt. The two meet on the metro, when Francoise is arguing with her well-intentioned but patronizing brother. Simone intercedes, the three laugh it off, and part as abruptly as they meet. But Simone reappears, and she and Francoise begin to establish a certain domestic routine—Francoise washes dishes while Simone plays solitaire. Little else is seen of their lives, apart or together, but within this context they argue, flirt, and act out a controlled fantasy. At issue is Simone's age (at least 20 years older than Francoise) and her inaccessibility—she will divulge nothing of her personal situation. Frustrated, Francoise struggles to integrate the elegant Simone into her life on Simone's terms and make sense of their love.

    Ehm's film seems to parody many pretentious and symbolic avant-garde films of the '60s with its minimal dialogue and rituals. She uses color liberally as an indicator of mood and depth in the women's relationship. Initially they wear bright yellow boots and Francoise's apartment has yellow touches throughout. Then it changes to orange, red, burgundy, and black. The device works, adding a cohesive element to the film's fragmented structure. Both actresses are appealing in their respective roles, intrigued by each other but perhaps wary of a relationship grounded in the reality of daily life.

Simple Facts
Dir. Yanick, Paquin
1992 Canada English
13 mins. 16mm color Narrative

Dist. (U.S.): Images en Stock

In the bittersweet *Simple Facts*, a man tells us about the two people he's been thinking about all day—a woman and a man.

Simulation, A
Dir. Verabioff, Mark
1985 Canada English
2 mins. video color Other
Dist. (U.S.): n/a

The mystique and allure of a boy in photon flashback.

Singing Seas
Dir. Summerville, Mark
1988 New Zealand English
10 mins. 16mm Narrative
Dist. (U.S.): New Zealand Film Commission

Singing Seas is a campy, operatic reverie of gay tribal life on a South Pacific island, somewhere on the map between Bruce Weber and Lindsay Kemp.

Sink or Swim
Dir. Friedrich, Su
1990 USA English
48 mins. 16mm color Experimental
Dist. (U.S.): Women Make Movies

Su Friedrich's work has the rare quality of being emotionally compelling and experimental all at once. While her point of departure is usually personal experience, she elaborates on the material until the film reaches an autonomous meaning. Using the formal aspects of the cinematic material and the seductive potential of narrative, she creates involvement and distance at the same time. In terms of content, her films are about the cultural and political determination of her emotions in which her being lesbian is of crucial importance.

Sink or Swim, Su Friedrich's most recent film, is not only about her complex relationship with her father but also shows the development of a girl's notions of sexuality. Alphabetically ordered intertitles structure the narrative like chapters, helping the viewer handle the intense imagery.

Sis: The Perry Watkins Story
Dir. Cartagena, Chiqui
1994 USA English
60 mins. video color Documentary
Dist. (U.S.): Cartagena, Chiqui

Drafted in 1967, Perry Watkins served 15 years in the U.S. Army as an openly gay man. He was discharged in 1982 under the provisions that ban homosexuals from serving in the armed forces. With the help of the ACLU, Sgt. Watkins won his case after nine years in court. The U.S. Supreme Court ruled in his favor, making Watkins the first gay officer to defeat the ban against gays in the military.

Chiqui Cartagena's funny, vivid, and astute documentary is a rare, affirming experience. Cartagena asks all the right questions: Why has Watkins' precedent-making case not been embraced by the gay community? Why has the black community not celebrated his struggle and success? Thankfully, Watkins himself, a charismatic figure, is on hand to set the record straight.

Winner of the 1994 San Francisco International Lesbian & Gay Film Festival Audience Award for Best Video.

Sister Is (Not) A Mister, The
Dir. Zay, Julia
1994 USA English
9 mins. video color Experimental
Dist. (U.S.): Zay, Julia

Gender stuff.

Sister Louise's Discovery
Dir. Hetherman, Margaret
1994 USA English
10 mins. 16mm color Narrative
Dist. (U.S.): Hetherman, Margaret

A young nun must come to terms with her sister's sexuality.

Sister, My Sister
Dir. Meckler, Nancy
1995 Great Britain English
89 mins. 35mm color Narrative
Dist. (U.S.): Seventh Art Releasing

In 1932 provincial France, two domestics brutally killed their employer and her daughter. Their only claimed motivation: an argument about an iron-burnt blouse. The case inspired several dramatic treatments, including Genet's famous play *The Maids*. Adapting Wendy Kesselman's much later stage treatment *My Sister in This House*, director Nancy Meckler has crafted a brilliant psychological drama in which extreme class tension and sexual repression make this "mystery's" bloody outcome seem all too understandable. Julie Walters is grotesquely funny as Madame, the bourgeoise widow who runs her household and woeful teenage offspring (Sophie Thursfield) with the same prudish, heavy hand. Joely Richardson and Jodhi May are the young sibling-servants who eventually crack under pressure—

Ⓐ Ⓑ Ⓒ Ⓓ Ⓔ Ⓕ Ⓖ Ⓗ Ⓘ Ⓙ Ⓚ Ⓛ Ⓜ Ⓝ Ⓞ Ⓟ Ⓠ Ⓡ Ⓢ Ⓣ Ⓤ Ⓥ Ⓦ Ⓧ Ⓨ Ⓩ

but not before their us-against-the-world confederacy discovers secret, incestuous erotic release. A far cry from erstwhile "crazy homicidal lesbo" portrayals, *Sister, My Sister* evokes sympathetic passion, pathos, and rueful humor en route to its searing finale. (D.H.)

Sisters of Darkness
Dir. Almodovar, Pedro
1983 Spain Spanish
113 mins. 35mm color Narrative
Dist. (U.S.): Cinevista
Director Pedro Almodovar's third feature, *Sisters of Darkness* is an engaging, sometimes scary combination of melodrama and comedy. It centers on Yolanda Bell, a beautiful young singer who accidentally kills her boyfriend, is chased by the police, and ends up in a convent where the Mother Superior is one of her biggest fans. A drug user, Yolanda shoots heroin in the convent and begins an ambiguous relationship with the mother whose "Humble Redeemers" are dedicated to saving young girls from the dangers of sex and drugs. Pedro Almodovar is emerging as one of post-Franco Spain's most exciting filmmaking talents—a logical heir to Luis Buñuel. He was born sometime in the decade of the fifties and moved to Madrid in 1970, where he immediately became a self-described hippy. He began his film career playing hippy extras in numerous Spanish films and in the mid-'70s began working with Super-8 film. For the next few years he made countless Super-8 productions: great biblical epics, domestic melodramas, musicals, love stories, and even trailers for other films. No matter where he showed his work the response was the same: keep making movies, we want more. Finally in 1978 he shot his first short feature in 16mm (*Salome*) which was followed by *Pepi, Luci, Boom and Other Girls Like Mom, Labyrinth of Passions, Sisters of Darkness,* and *What Have I Done to Deserve This?*

Six Degrees of Separation
Dir. Schepisi, Fred
1994 USA English
111 mins. 35mm color Narrative
Dist. (U.S.): Swank Motion Pictures
Although Will Smith conducted a public ugh-fest in *Premiere* magazine to distance himself from what looks like a kiss in this film, the film itself doesn't tread lightly on matters of sexuality, class, and race. This comedy of white panic, white guilt, and white naïveté is good, biting satire. Donald Sutherland's and Stockard

Channing's flashbacks are ingeniously folded into party anecdotes to convey the white Manhattan social club's panic about race. The Adult Children of Idle Parents club at Harvard performs its spoiled-kid melodrama with the perfect touch of overacting. Channing's bon mot timing is exact, and her personal awakening believable. And Will Smith himself is spot-on. By the time Smith has finished delivering his impersonation with charm and sincerity, we're properly caught up in a confusion of race stereotypes, bad luck, art world pretense, and dinner plates. The kiss—as it supposedly didn't actually occur—doesn't even matter. (S.G.)

Six Million and One
Dir. Goralsky, Michal
1993 USA English
20 mins. video color Other
Dist. (U.S.): Goralsky, Michal
In *Six Million and One*, Michal Goralsky speaks about the paralyzing struggle a lesbian experiences when she begins to address the complexities of her Jewishness, the Holocaust, and memory.

Skin Complex
Dir. Lennhoff, Stephen
1992 Great Britain English
20 mins. video color Documentary
Dist. (U.K.): Maya Vision
Disturbing, smart, fast-paced stab at gay skinhead culture raises issues of race, racism, fascism, and fashion.

Skin Deep
Dir. Onodera, Midi
Prod. Onodera, Midi, Mehernaz Lentin, and Phillip Ing
1994 Canada English
85 mins. 35mm color Narrative
Dist. (U.S.): Films Transit
Alex Koyama is an obsessed filmmaker who can think of nothing but the exploitation film she is making about the pleasure and pain of tattooing. In response to an ad she has placed in a tattoo magazine, she receives an enticing letter from young transgendered Chris. The letter describes the sexual pleasure one can experience while being tattooed; this intrigues Alex and she hires Chris as a production assistant, but more importantly as a potential research source for her film. Instantly enamored with Alex, Chris misinterprets all the attention and falls desperately in love. Alex enjoys this new infatuation and dismisses the warnings of her neglected girlfriend,

Montana. Alex continues to provoke Chris, who is in the process of coming to terms with a sexuality that is not accepted by the mainstream. Chris's efforts at communication are misinterpreted by Alex, who sees Chris as delusional. Finally pushed to the limit by Alex's selfishness, Chris is forced to commit a desperate act in order to regain Alex's attentions.

Set amongst the downtown urban art world of Toronto, Midi Onodera's stylish thriller attempts to break down preconceived notions of sexuality and gender.

Sleepin' Round
Dir. Rogowski, Michael
1985 Australia English
22 mins. 16mm color Narrative
Dist. (U.S.): Australian Film Institute
A slick, visually magnificent story of a handsome young advertising executive's break-up with a longtime lover and his comic and realistic look for a new companion. Using a round bed placed in a church converted to a home as a central image, *Sleepin' Round* presents a poignant look at the trauma of losing a lover and the frustration of trying to start over with someone new. The hero in this Australian film begins a new, intensely romantic relationship with his milkman only to find himself repeating the same dismal patterns that led to the failure of his first relationship. Filmed in vivid color, this is one of the most original and creative short films about gay love seen in years.

Sleeping Subjects
Dir. Lee, Quentin
1993 USA English
28 mins. video color Experimental
Dist. (U.S.): Lee, Quentin
Quentin Lee's cheerfully self-reflexive melodrama (or, as Lee describes it, "a Benetton ménage à trois about a black gay man, a bisexual Chinese guy, and a Caucasian woman").

Sleepy Haven
Dir. Muller, Matthias
1993 Germany No Dialogue
15 mins. 16mm b&w Experimental
Dist. (U.S.): Muller, Matthias
Sleepy Haven is a wordless dream inspired by Joseph Conrad's words: "The sea heaved with long and lingering swells, like a chest in the sleep. Ebbing and flowing unceasingly, it was mingling millions of shades, shadows, drowned dreams and reveries." Muller's blue-tinted images of sailors and seamen melt in the mind.

Slight Fever of a 20-Year-Old
(see *Hatachi No Binetsu*)

Sluts and Goddesses Video Workshop, or How To Be a Sex Goddess in 101 Easy Ways, The
Dir. Beatty, Maria, and Annie Sprinkle
1992 USA English
52 mins. video color Documentary
Dist. (U.S.): Sprinkle, Annie
Dist. (U.K.): Cinenova
The Sluts and Goddesses Video Workshop, or How To Be a Sex Goddess in 101 Easy Ways is sure to be a bright and educational experience for all. You can learn how to have more sensual and sexual pleasure in your life. Follow along as Annie Sprinkle exhaustively catalogs the joys of sex, along with her "Transformation Facilitators," which include Divianna Ingravallo, Jocelyn Taylor, and Carol Leigh (a.k.a. Scarlet Harlot).

Smoke
Dir. D'Auria, Mark
1993 USA English
90 mins. 16mm color Narrative
Dist. (U.S.): D'Auria, Mark/Ancestor Films
Deeply moving and personal, *Smoke* uses minimal language, a stylized vision, and icons drawn from a Roman Catholic childhood to construct a dark and penetrating dream. Not since *Eraserhead* has a film evoked a world as disturbed, haunted, and weirdly erotic.

Michael is an alienated loner with a penchant for fiftysomething men, who works as a bathroom attendant in a fancy Manhattan hotel. Submerged in a self-deprecating search for a father figure, he pursues a married detective (whom we never see), and is in turn pursued by a mafia-type ex-boyfriend who bullies and intimidates him throughout the film.

Resisting his mother's wishes to attend his brother's birthday, Michael goes to church for the first time in years. There, something happens that sets off hallucinogenic flashbacks to his youth, when he and his brother suffered from high fever. In the present day Michael's life starts to take on an even more surrealistic quality.

Religious, erotic, obsessive, and inescapable, *Smoke* envelops the viewer with a frightening passion that is simultaneously empty and full of meaning, beautiful and repulsive. Like a bad seed planted within the mind of a child, Michael's life unfurls into a relentless and seduc-

Ⓐ Ⓑ Ⓒ Ⓓ Ⓔ Ⓕ Ⓖ Ⓗ Ⓘ Ⓙ Ⓚ Ⓛ Ⓜ Ⓝ Ⓞ Ⓟ Ⓠ Ⓡ Ⓢ Ⓣ Ⓤ Ⓥ Ⓦ Ⓧ Ⓨ Ⓩ

tive series of images that absorb any other reality.

Snatch
Dir. none (collective process)
1990 USA English
40 mins. video color Narrative
Dist. (U.S.): Light, Lauri
"Is what we're doing here acting out?" asks one character in *Snatch*, and while the answer may unfortunately be yes, there is pleasure, if not plot, to be found in this 40-minute video.

Lots of saturated color, and yes, saturated tampons, make *Snatch* a first. Set in a lesbian whorehouse from Hell (Hell is America), a gaggle of giggling garterbelt gargoyles let us in on their scenes and secrets. We watch them boss around their nerdy clients, women who play men with an endearing sexual awkwardness and are more victims than victimizers.

Snatch features a dozen lesbians in lingerie and the cast, in costume, turns Victoria's Secret into a screaming headline. Although they bare their bosoms with peek-a-boo provocation, these women are not above being polemical. "Prostitution is the m.o. of the patriarchal capitalistic society. We sell our souls, time, and energy, or lives—to make a fucking living," explains a title sequence, but *Snatch* comes across as being more rowdily ridiculous than revolutionary. The best parts of this video are the visual jokes, a sacrificial peace symbol and a living vagina dentata.

Snow Job: The Media Hysteria of AIDS
Dir. Hammer, Barbara
1986 USA English
8 mins. video color/b&w Experimental
Dist. (U.S.): Canyon Cinema
Deconstructs the representation of AIDS in the popular press.

Released by Frameline in the U.S. along with four of her other short works as a feature-length package, *Barbara Hammer, Program #1*.

Snow White
Dir. Tschetter, Sotera
1993 USA English
4 mins. video color Other
Dist. (U.S.): Tschetter, Sotera / Point of View Films
Singer/songwriter Barbara Cohen's colorful fairytale music video.

Solo
Dir. Tiffenbach, Joe
1985 USA English
mins. 16mm color Other
Dist. (U.S.): n/a
A silent work (no sound is needed to get the full impact of this piece), *Solo* follows a handsome young man as he strips his way through the woods and finds self-gratication among the trees.

Solos Y Soledades
Dir. Berrios, Javier Antonio
1992 Cuba Spanish
22 mins. 35mm color Narrative
Dist. (U.S.): Berrios, Javier Antonio
From Cuban director Javier Berrios comes a short, superbly choreographed story about two men who meet on a bus and find that there is no safe place to consummate their passion. *Solos Y Soledades*—in Spanish only—is short on dialogue; long on erotic looks.

Some of My Best Friends Are . . .
Dir. Nelson, Mervyn
1971 USA English
109 mins. 35mm color Narrative
Dist. (U.S.): Orion Classics
Some of My Best Friends Are . . . is a rare opportunity to experience the plight of pre-Stonewall gay culture. It is an experience both infuriating and fascinating. Set in a New York gay bar on Christmas Eve, *Some of My Best Friends Are . . .* is a Grand Hotel filled with a generation of lost souls. The oppression of gay people by the very institutions that once offered them a kind of temporary safety is the subtext of the film. Yet it remains only a subtext. The overt substance of the piece degenerates into a kind of orgy of melodramatic self-pity in which homosexuals are pathetic creatures exploited by each other, as well as by their surroundings. Originally titled *The Bar* and cast as a kind of family affair from a group of well-known New York actors, *Some of My Best Friends Are . . .* contains a group of the most ghoulish and exaggerated performances ever put on screen. Rue McClanahan ("Golden Girls") plays Lita Joyce, a bitchy fag hag. The late Candy Darling weighs in with a terrific portrait of a lonely transvestite who dreams of being a real woman. Gary Sandy ("WKRP in Cinncinnati") is the bisexual hustler who discovers Candy's secret. *Some of My Best Friends Are . . .* is not great movie-making and it will drive post-Stonewall gays crazy with its bleak and relentless self-loathing, but it's eminently worthwhile as a history lesson, as well as classic camp.

Some of These Days

Dir. Miller-Monzon, John
1994 USA English
33 mins. 16mm b&w Narrative
Dist. (U.S.): Miller-Monzon, John
Hal sings "Is you is, or, is you ain't my baby?"
Geoff packs his bags and leaves. Julian moves in
and seduces Hal's broken heart with his Calvin
Klein good looks and Grandma's chicken soup,
while stealing money and turning tricks in Hal's
big beautiful Victorian bed. In this artfully shot
short film full of shady comebacks and dramatic
profiles, everyone looks good in their underwear
and thinks everyone else is a whore. Amusingly
melancholy, *Some of These Days* is what we all
imagine our break-ups and make-ups would be if
thrown up on the big screen.

Somebody Else
Dir. Amensen, Heidi
1993 USA English
5 mins. video color Narrative
Dist. (U.S.): Arnesen, Heidi
A sad story of love.

Something for Everyone
Dir. Prince, Harold
1970 USA English
112 mins. 35mm color Narrative
Dist. (U.S.): Swank Motion Pictures
Michael York stars as an ambitious, ambisexual
servant who seduces an impoverished aristocratic
widow (Angela Lansbury) and her family in
Broadway producer-director Harold Prince's filmmaking debut. *Something* is a lighter, frothier
version of Pier Paolo Pasolini's *Teorema*, full of
stereotypes—York the evil bisexual, Anthony
Corlan as Lansbury's shame-ridden homo son—
but with an aura of decadence that gays have
found captivating over the years. Though its
many darkly humorous patches and Lansbury's
tart turn as the countess are among its pluses,
Something's pacing, which was plodding by even
'70s standards, seems even more so in the '90s.
(D.M.)

Something Special
Dir. Schneider, Paul
1986 USA English
90 mins. video color Narrative
Dist. (U.S.): n/a
Cleverly written and brilliantly cast, *Something
Special* is a Hollywood teen transgender comedy
about a girl who gets to be a boy. Try to imagine
an ABC Afterschool Special with a queer sensibility and a sophisticated sense of humor—

Something Special is super fun for boys and
girls, and for girls who want to be boys.

Milly Niceman gets her "deepest,
darkest heart's desire" when she wishes on a
magical Indian eclipse powder. She wakes in the
middle of the night to discover she's grown "a
guy's thing down there." When Mr. and Mrs.
Niceman tell her she must choose between being
a boy or a girl, she asks innocently, "Can't I be
both?"

As Muddy Waters sings "Mannish
Boy" on the soundtrack, Milly becomes Willy and
learns what it means to be a boy: his girlfriend
develops a new kind of interest in him, and so
does Willy's new pal Alfie (a differently abled boy
who refers to his wheelchair as a lunar module).
When Alfie confesses his "unnatural desires,"
Willy goes for the hetero option and decides he
wants to be a girl again. Wishing upon a star does
the trick, and Alfie and Milly go off together as
happy hets.

Although the film ultimately doesn't
allow for homosexuality as an option, it plays
extensively on homoerotic potentials, and has a
blast with traditional gender roles. Patty Duke
gives an outstanding performance as Mrs.
Niceman, and Pamela Seagall is uncannily butch
and boyish as Willy (and as Milly).

Briefly released in 1986, *Something
Special* quickly disappeared from view and has
been unseen theatrically since.

Sometimes
Dir. Olson, Jenni
1994 USA English
1 mins. video color Experimental
Dist. (U.S.): Olson, Jenni
Jenni Olson shows us just what "butch" means in
30 seconds.

Sometimes . . . A Poem
Dir. Tempest, Kim
1987 USA English
4 mins. 16mm color Other
Dist. (U.S.): n/a
An animated love poem.

Son, Are You Down There?
Dir. Johnson, Carl
1984 Great Britain English
13 mins. video color Experimental
Dist. (U.S.): n/a
Uses a nonnarrative, train of thought approach
combining past isolation and present growing
awareness of a gay sexuality.

Ⓐ Ⓑ Ⓒ Ⓓ Ⓔ Ⓕ Ⓖ Ⓗ Ⓘ Ⓙ Ⓚ Ⓛ Ⓜ Ⓝ Ⓞ Ⓟ Ⓠ Ⓡ Ⓢ Ⓣ Ⓤ Ⓥ Ⓦ Ⓧ Ⓨ Ⓩ

Song for Europe, A
(see *Out On Tuesday, Program 3*)

Song from an Angel
Dir. Weissman, David
1988 USA English
10 mins. 16mm color Other
Dist. (U.S.): Frameline
Angel of Light Rodney Price gives a farewell performance.

Song of the Goddess
Dir. Pau, Ellen
1993 Hong Kong Cantonese
9 mins. video color Experimental
Dist. (U.S.): Pau, Ellen
A powerful and poetic piece from Hong Kong featuring the famous Cantonese opera duo Yum Kim-Fai and Pak Su-Sin, lesbians who play the role of lovers with Yum in male drag.

Sonny
Dir. Contempo, Museo
Prod. Please Louise Prod.
1994 USA English
2 mins. video color Other
Dist. (U.S.): Museo Contempo
Museo Contempo's daddy/boy devotion ritual.

Sortie 234
Dir. Langlois, Michel
1988 Canada French
26 mins. 16mm color Narrative
Dist. (U.S.): ACPAV
The theme of *Sortie 234* is passion, the rabid passion of Renaud for Frank. A passion which shoots like a star and explodes. In between these two poles there is Lucille, Frank's love. Lucille whom Renaud tries to tame, Lucille who becomes the go-between in this pulsating relationship.

Source, The
Dir. Corzine, Georgina
Prod. Windle, Hope
1995 USA English
3 mins. video color Documentary
Dist. (U.S.): Corzine, Georgina
An independent documentary following women attracted to the water (a.k.a. surfing).

Souvenir
Dir. Cholodenko, Lisa
1994 USA English
13 mins. 16mm color Narrative
Dist. (U.S.): Cholodenko, Lisa

Things get supernatural when a quarreling couple check into an empty motel.

Sparkle's Tavern
Dir. McDowell, Curt
1976 USA English
100 mins. 16mm b&w Narrative
Dist. (U.S.): Canyon Cinema
Veteran underground filmmaker, Curt McDowell, turns to mom with a twist on the old "coming out" story and a unique editing style that stretches real time to incorporate more than one response to each event. Written and filmed in 1976, this just-completed family album in formal undress tickles the facts aand sexual fantasy at the same time. Less explicit but more audacious than the Gothic X-comedy *Thundercrack*, *Sparkle's Tavern* plays with the inconsistencies of sexual attitudes and conventional symbols until all self-deception is exorcised—what remains is gay for all seasons.

Sparky's Shoes
Dir. Cairns, Glen
Prod. Gundy, John, Allan Magee, and Melanie McCaig
1994 Canada English
16 mins. 16mm color Narrative
Dist. (U.S.): Canadian Film Centre
When Buddy's best friend and lover, Sparky, is hospitalized with AIDS, Buddy is faced with a crisis of identity. Eventually love and eroticism bring comfort where medicine and clinical care fail. The film explores the boundaries of love, loss, and redemption in the age of AIDS.

Speaking in Riddles
Dir. O'Faherty, Mark C.
1994 Great Britain English
23 mins. 16mm color Narrative
Dist. (U.K.): Basilisk
Speaking in Riddles describes the ensuing comic attempts at satisfying everyone's appetites.

Sphinxes Without Secrets
Dir. Beatty, Maria
1990 USA English
58 mins. video color Documentary
Dist. (U.S.): Video Data Bank
This hour-long documentary seeks to answer the questions, "What is performance art? Why do women do it? And what are the strengths of this medium for putting across a political message?" Many of the currently active women performance artists speak to these questions in *Sphinxes Without Secrets*, so the video should be of spe-

cial interest to fans of Rachel Rosenthal, Arlene Raven, Diamanda Galas, and Robbie McCauley, whose works are featured.

Many others give their opinions, including Annie Sprinkle, who does something new with her breasts. While the opinionating is less engaging than the performances (and be warned, these theatrical pieces are not shown to their best advantage on video), what is striking is the overview, shown in 30 or 40 short sequences, of the range and energy of activity. Fantastical costumes, glimpsed briefly, compelling bodywork, and the images of many women engaged in such different ways onstage, most effectively describes the importance of performance art.

Recommended for theatre buffs, East Villagers, artist-activists, and costumers.

Spikes and Heels
Dir. Ataman, Kutlug
Prod. Brooks, Philippe
1994 France English
53 mins. video color Documentary
Dist. (U.S.): Filmmaker's Library
A documentary on the Gay Games IV and the 25th anniversary of the Stonewell riot, filmed entirely in New York in June 1994. Providing a comprehensive presentation of the games and various demonstrations that took place during that week, Spikes and Heels deals with homophobia, AIDS, and gay and lesbian identity in the '90s.

Spin Cycle
Dir. Burch, Aarin
1991 USA English
28 mins. 16mm color Experimental
Dist. (U.S.): Women Make Movies
Through the process of making a film, a black lesbian examines her relationship, feelings of guilt, and breaking up, as well as political questions raised in making a lesbian film. Will it be politically correct? Will it only be shown at lesbian and gay film festivals?

Splash
Dir. Harris, Thomas Allen
1990 USA English
7 mins. 16mm color Experimental
Dist. (U.S.): Third World Newsreel
An emotionally violent (and funny) flashback to prepuberty.

Split Britches
Dir. Geller, Matthew
1988 USA English

58 mins. video color Narrative
Dist. (U.S.): n/a
Split Britches is a sterling television adaption of a theater production originally conceived and directed by Lois Weaver and written in collaboration with Peggy Shaw and Deborah Margolin. Weaver, a film actress and performer with the famed WOW theater group in New York, has fashioned a humorous and unconventional narrative based on the true story of Weaver's Aunt Emma Gay Gearhart and Emma's nieces Della Mae and Cora Jane, who from 1932 to 1949 were the sole inhabitants of the defunct Gearhart plantation in the Blue Ridge Mountains of Virginia. The three women, who lived most of their lives in the kitchen of the plantation's main house, conduct a most intricate series of interactions, through which their peculiar, deep ways of loving each other are revealed.

Sprinter, Der (Sprinter, The)
Dir. Boll, Christoph
Prod. Peter Wolgemuth, and Reinery Verlag Filmproduktion
1984 Germany German
87 mins. 35mm color Narrative
Dist. (U.S.): Reinery Verlag Filmproduktion
The Sprinter stretches the length of the gay rope—what would happen if a fellow went "straight" like his mother asked? In Boll's black comedy, Weiland gives up his disco wallflower life for the healthy world of sports. Pushed by mama, inspired to championship aspirations by a sudden fatal passion for a Valkyrian shot-putter, and manipulated by a group of real-estate speculators after the stadium, Weiland rises to undreamed of heights only to meet an ineffably sad and hilarious end.

Spy, The
(Hester Reeve Does "The Doors")
Dir. Silver, Suzie
1992 USA English
5 mins. video color Other
Dist. (U.S.): Video Data Bank
A lesbian Jesus-drag music video.

St. Louis Blues
Dir. Murphy, Dudley
1928 USA English
17 mins. 16mm b&w Narrative
Dist. (U.S.): Em Gee Film Library
Bessie Smith stars in this classic short.

Stadt der Verlorenen Seelen

Ⓐ Ⓑ Ⓒ Ⓓ Ⓔ Ⓕ Ⓖ Ⓗ Ⓘ Ⓙ Ⓚ Ⓛ Ⓜ Ⓝ Ⓞ Ⓟ Ⓠ Ⓡ Ⓢ Ⓣ Ⓤ Ⓥ Ⓦ Ⓧ Ⓨ Ⓩ

(City Of Lost Souls)
Dir. von Praunheim, Rosa
1983 Germany German
89 mins. 16mm color Narrative
Dist. (U.S.): Exportfilm Bischoff & Co.

City of Lost Souls is the latest work by cult director Rosa von Praunheim, known for his radical, controversial films that usually challenge both nongay and gay audiences. A group of Americans live in the midst of the lively artists' set in Berlin. Angie Stardust, a black dancer from Harlem who once worked in drag clubs has gone into business for herself, opening a restaurant, "The Hamburger Queen," where a mixed bunch of unusual characters hang out. Gary is a dancer who is in love with magic. Tara O'Hara, a former male nurse, is proud of his androgynous charms—charms he shows off in an enticing striptease. Joaquin La Habana performs as both a man and a woman at the same time. And then there is Judith and Tron performing a wild, erotic trapeze act and Lia, from the south, who meets an East German agent who succeeds in making her East Germany's most famous rock star. Essentially a form of cabaret, the film moves from the sentimental through the witty and erotic. The players know their job, the camera work is inventive, and the music is great.

Stafford's Story
Dir. Muska, Susan
1992 USA English
3 mins. video color Other
Dist. (U.S.): Frameline
Dist. (U.K.): Dangerous To Know

A vividly described lesbian encounter at a sex club.

Staircase
Dir. Donen, Stanley
1969 USA English
100 mins. 35mm color Narrative
Dist. (U.S.): Films Incorporated

Often deeply disturbing in its portrayal of self-hating closet queens, *Staircase* stars Rex Harrison and Richard Burton as a pair of aging homosexual hairdressers. Burton's mother is the constant absent presence (upstairs in the bedroom like Tony Perkins's mom in *Psycho*); Harrison's bitchy attacks on Burton and his continual desperate claims about his own masculinity set him up as the archetypal neurotic closet queen. A contemporary audience looking beyond the dense layer of homo-hatred that envelops the film can feel an intense sympathy for these characters who are trapped in a pre-Stonewall Cinemascope rendering of an intensely homophobic stage play. Directed by Stanley (*Singin' in the Rain*) Donen. (J.O.)

Stand By
Dir. McDowell, Curt
1984 USA English
30 mins. 16mm b&w Experimental
Dist. (U.S.): Canyon Cinema

Stand By is the latest revelation in Curt McDowell's lifelong sideways search to find out "where we came from." It's cut (like *Taboo*) in the manner of an LP album, tracking personalized images of Sex, Dad and the American Way along grooves of snapshot images extended into vignettes. Dedicated to a photo of Pop in his potent prime, the film formulates an impression of overlapping generations of popular social history with a free-wheeling mix of eroticism, humor, found footage, Snakefinger's "beatnik" party, and self-exposure.

Stand on your Man
Dir. Ardill, Susan
1991 Great Britain English
20 mins. video color Documentary
Dist. (U.K.): Maya Vision

A look at the new lesbian preoccupation with Country and Western music and style. Featuring performances by k.d. lang and Patsy Cline, plus lesbian C&W bands like the Well Oiled Sisters and the Stetson Sisters.

Standard of Living, The
Dir. Raymond, James
1993 USA English
15 mins. 16mm b&w Narrative
Dist. (U.S.): Raymond, James

A charming rendition of Dorothy Parker's *Standard of Living*; a captivating period piece about Anabelle and Midge and a very special game.

State of Mind
Dir. Black, Angie
1990 Australia English
13 mins. 16mm color/b&w Experimental
Dist. (U.K.): Black, Angie

Angie Black's *State of Mind* takes us through an experimental sexual journey as a butch babe on a motorcycle recalls a past lover.

STD Cry Cia
Dir. Thomas, Brett
1995 USA English

3 mins. 16mm color Other
Dist. (U.S.): Thomas, Brett
A person with AIDS tries to access a government
social service agency only to be trapped in voice
mail.

Steal America
Dir. Phillips, Lucy
1992 USA English
92 mins. 35mm color Narrative
Dist. (U.S.): Tara Releasing
Dist. (U.K.): Rapid Film Group
Aside from the fact that Steal America's
European tourists fall into designer cars, lovers,
usable credit cards, paying jobs, and regular per-
formance gigs as easily as Marlboro habits, Lucy
Phillips's version of international Slackerhood is
pretty much a postcard-perfect picture of San
Francisco's accidental charm. If the movie could
fit on a three-by-five card, it might read
"Greetings from North Beach" over an image of
Divianna Ingravallo casually humping a Coit
Tower telescope.
　　　　Director Phillips's cast of subculture
elite for her Breathless version of the new North
Beach features motorcycle-riding butch-femme
Bad Girl Divianna, a heavily wigged Cintra
Wilson, and steamy Flying Monkeys accordionist
Clara Bellino—all successfully exorcising the
strip of its dusty Beat ghosts. Although Phillips
takes an airbrush to the North Beach you might
know, its combination of hyperrealism and home
movie making will make you want to practice
your Italian and take up a permanent job at San
Francisco's bar, Tosca. (S.G.)

Stellium In Capricorn
Dir. Wright, Georgia B.
1994 USA English
6 mins. video color Other
Dist. (U.S.): Wright, Georgia B.
Georgia Wright's Stellium In Capricorn is a stunning portrayal of an S/M scene incorporating
piercing, bondage, and lots of kissing.

Step We Gaily
Dir. Broadbent, Lucinda
1992 Scotland English
10 mins. 16mm color Documentary
Dist. (U.K.): Out On a Limb
Lucinda Broadbent's Step We Gaily takes a look
at kilts, Ceilidh dancing, and coming out in
Scotland.

Stephen
Dir. Kinney, Robert, and Donald Kinney
1991 USA English
28 mins. video color Experimental
Dist. (U.S.): Video Data Bank
Based in part on Thornton Wilder's The Bridge of
San Luis Rey, Stephen is the final installment in
a series of three productions by San Diego–based
artists Robert and Donald Kinney. Like their earlier tapes The Maids (1990) and Talk to Me Like
the Rain (1989), this latest coproduction by the
twin brothers explores gay sexuality within a popular narrative form. It focuses on the story of
twins who are also lovers, locked in a complex
and often claustrophobic emotional and sexual
relationship. Eventually they are driven apart by
jealousy and death as the tape explores the
impact of AIDS with an almost TV-melodrama
feel.
　　　　Says Robert Kinney, "I think of my
aesthetic . . . as having been influenced by Jean
Genet and daytime television."

Steps, The
Dir. Weissman, David
1984 USA English
4 mins. 16mm b&w Narrative
Dist. (U.S.): Weissman, David
A young dreamer questions the romance of revolution.

Sternenschauer (Scattering Stars)
Dir. Muller, Matthias
1994 Germany German
2 mins. 16mm color Experimental
Dist. (U.S.): Canyon Cinema
Celestial bodies explode, stars scatter, representing the afterglow of a physical encounter.

Stick Figures
Dir. Bonder, Diane
1994 USA English
3 mins. video color Experimental
Dist. (U.S.): Frameline
Stick Figures is a stark depiction of two lesbians'
recognizable and conflicting feelings of terror and
defiance when confronted by bashers.

Sticky Moments
Dir. Henderson, John
Prod. Yardley, Toni
1990 Great Britain English
40 mins. video color Experimental
Dist. (U.K.): Channel 4 Television
A surreal Channel Four game show hosted by
glamorous campster Julian Clare (previously
known as The Joan Collins Fan Club). Pulled from
the audience, heterosexual men and women are

subjected to unusual degrees of abuse by Clare, who forces them to drink down gallons of gay innuendo. Clare gets to wear great outfits, everyone has a lot of fun, and some people even win prizes.

Still Point
Dir. Hammer, Barbara
1989 USA English
8 mins. 16mm color/b&w Experimental
Dist. (U.S.): Canyon Cinema
Still Point is experimentation on another level. Visually intricate and tightly edited, the film uses a split screen to design a dialogue about lesbian notions of domesticity, private life, and the search for a validated home life.

Still Sane
Dir. Ingratta, Brenda, and Lidia Patriasz
1985 Canada
60 mins. video color Documentary
Dist. (U.S.): GIV
This film tells the extremely moving story behind an exhibition of sculptures that reflect the experiences of a lesbian artist. The sculptures are impressive women's bodies expressing the inner state of a woman who has experienced certain horrors, explained on diary excerpts written on the sculptures themselves. She has been in and out of mental institutions for three years for being a lesbian. But shock therapy, medication, and sexual abuse all failed to destroy her personality. When she is allowed to leave the hospital she is without feeling until she meets other lesbians and, for the first time in her life, begins to feel pride.

Stiller, Garbo & Jag (Stiller, Garbo & Me)
Dir. Olsson, Claes, and Alvaro Pardo
1987 Finland Finnish
47 mins. 16mm color Documentary
Dist. (U.S.): Finnish Film Foundation
A documentary about the silent-film director Mauritz Stiller (1883–1928) and his dog Charly.

Sto Dnej Do Prikaza
(100 Days before the Command)
Dir. Erkenov, Hussein
1990 Russia Russian
70 mins. 35mm color Narrative
Dist. (U.S.): Salzgeber & Co.
Hussein Erkenov's barracks drama tells of five young men who do not survive their service in the Red Army. Exposed to a round of merciless daily violence, they desperately try to resist constant humiliation, but their struggle for human dignity is a hopeless one. Although it is not in any overt

way "about" homosexuality, Erkenov's film is astonishingly direct in it's homoerotic imagery. The abundant nudity includes a scene where the soldiers bathe each other with an intimacy and tenderness that is far removed from the brutality of most of their waking hours. The director has stated that the homoeroticism in his film is quite conscious and is there to represent the only beauty existing in lives filled with ugliness and inhumanity. (Amazingly, all the roles are played by real-life soldiers except for one professional actor.)

Unseen outside Russia until Erkenov formed his own sales company and took the film to the Berlin Film Festival earlier this year, *100 Days before the Command* is not only a unique entry into the world of gay-interest cinema but another courageous example of post-cold war filmmaking from a former Iron Curtain country.

Stolen Tango
Dir. Moore, David
1992 USA English
9 mins. video color Narrative
Dist. (U.S.): Moore, David
Stolen Tango by David Moore is a seductive short about spontaneous attraction set in New York.

Stone Circles
Dir. Hammer, Barbara
1983 USA English
10 mins. 16mm color/b&w Experimental
Dist. (U.S.): Canyon Cinema
A film poem on the prehistoric stone cultures of Britain.

Released by Facets Multimedia in the U.S. along with four of her other short films as a feature-length package, *Perceptual Landscapes: The Films of Barbara Hammer, Volume III.*

Stonewall
Dir. Finch, Nigel
Prod. Vachon, Christine, and Ruth Caleb
1995 USA/Great Britain English
99 mins. 35mm color Narrative
Dist. (U.S.): Strand Releasing
Dist. (U.K.): Sales Company, The
Director Nigel Finch (who died of AIDS during the film's post-production) took on a challenging task in this adaptation of Martin Duberman's *Stonewall*. His film offers a fictional account of the lives of some of the denizens of that most legendary gay bar. Unfortunately, *Stonewall's* ever-shifting race politics and naive fascination with American patriotic ideals make for some uncomfortable stretches in this attempt at recreating that

modern gay mythological moment. (J.O.)

Stop the Church
Dir. Hilferty, Robert
1990 USA English
23 mins. 16mm color Documentary
Dist. (U.S.): Frameline
A look at the preparation for ACT UP's controversial demonstration against Cardinal O'Connor at St. Patrick's Cathedral in 1989.

Storm in a Teacup
Dir. Hindley, Emma
1992 Great Britain English
44 mins. video color Documentary
Dist. (U.S.): Hindley, Emma
This history of lesbian and gay pre-'70s meeting places in London includes an introduction to "Polari", the unique British gay slang. Made for Channel Four Out series.

Storme: The Lady of the Jewel Box
Dir. Parkerson, Michelle
1987 USA English
21 mins. 16mm color Documentary
Dist. (U.S.): Women Make Movies
Directed by Michelle Parkerson, *Storme: The Lady of the Jewel Box* is the story of Storme DeLarverie, a black woman who was the emcee and a male impersonator in the legendary Jewel Box Review, America's first integrated female impersonation show. From 1939 to 1973, the show toured black theaters across America and was in Washington, D.C., during the McCarthy era—defying common sense and '50s morality.

Story So Far: A Forgotten Classic, The
Dir. Sharif, Rif, and Noski Deville
1994 Great Britain English
25 mins. 16mm b&w Narrative
Dist. (U.K.): Deville, Noski c/o Media and Communications
The Story So Far is a smart and sexy comedy with a brilliant edge of social conscience. It's a lesbian *Lavender Hill Mob* from British codirectors Noski Deville and Rif Sharif. You're in for loads of fun and excitement when a group of black dykes stumble onto a jewel robbery.

Straight Agenda, The
Dir. Binninger, John, and Jackie Turnure
1994 USA English
19 mins. video color Other
Dist. (U.S.): Binninger, John
The Straight Agenda counters the right-wing hate video *The Gay Agenda*, with Craig Chester as the Former Straight Male and Suzy Berger as the Former Straight Female.

Straight for the Money: Interviews with Queer Sex Workers
Dir. B., Hima
1994 USA English
60 mins. video color Documentary
Dist. (U.S.): B., Hima
It's estimated that up to 10 percent of women engage in some form of sex work at some point in their lives. In this unique San Francisco portrait, video maker Hima B. interviews eight lesbian and bisexual women—lap-dancers and peep-show dancers in strip clubs—who talk about their motivations, aspirations, and identities as queer women whose jobs make them "straight for the money." Bold and articulate, the women discuss the impact of sex work on their personal lives, the feminist politics of sex work, and the need for broader understanding of a greatly stigmatized and stereotyped occupation.
    This sex-positive documentary also incorporates fascinating archival footage and interviews with sexperts Annie Sprinkle, Carol Queen, and Joan Nestle.

Straight from the Heart
Dir. Mosbacher, Dee, and Frances Reid
1994 USA English
24 mins. 16mm color Documentary
Dist. (U.S.): Woman Vision Productions
This Academy Award–nominated documentary was made in an effort to reach out to a broad audience and teach them tolerance and understanding. Parents give moving accounts of their struggles with their own homophobia and how they eventually came to accept their lesbian and gay children.

Straight to the Heart
(see *A Corps Perdu*)

Strange Love Affair, A
Dir. De Kuyper, Eric, and Paul Verstraaten
1985 Netherlands Dutch
92 mins. 35mm b&w Narrative
Dist. (U.S.): Netherlands Ministry of Culture
A Strange Love Affair is the story of Michael, an American film instructor working in Holland. Michael's area of expertise is the Hollywood melodrama, and we first see him showing clips of Joan Crawford in *Johnny Guitar* and giving a lecture on love to his students. Taking a particular interest in the professor's teachings is a young, robust Dutch athlete.

Ⓐ Ⓑ Ⓒ Ⓓ Ⓔ Ⓕ Ⓖ Ⓗ Ⓘ Ⓙ Ⓚ Ⓛ Ⓜ Ⓝ Ⓞ Ⓟ Ⓠ Ⓡ Ⓢ Ⓣ Ⓤ Ⓥ Ⓦ Ⓧ Ⓨ Ⓩ

Soon the two are having romantic dinners at Michael's house listening to the soundtrack of *Now Voyager*, during which an extended volley of meaningful glances are exchanged. The relationship established, the couple ventures off to visit the student's parents where Michael finds a love he lost fifteen years ago.

Stunningly photographed in wide-screen black-and-white, *A Strange Love Affair* owes much of of its appeal to the camera work of Henri Alekan, who photographed Cocteau's *The Beauty and the Beast* and won an Academy Award nomination for his work on William Wyler's *Roman Holiday*.

Strawberry and Chocolate
(see *Fresa y Chocolate*)

Strawberry Short Cut/Pickle Surprise
Dir. Rubnitz, Tom
1989 USA English
1 mins. video color Other
Dist. (U.S.): Video Data Bank
Sister Dimension, Billy Beyond, and the Lady Bunny demonstrate a pair of quick and easy dessert recipes.

Strider's House
Dir. Derrick, Clyde
1982 USA English
10 mins. 16mm color Narrative
Dist. (U.S.): n/a
Missed opportunity and lost love. A haunting, literate, narrative film produced as a graduate film project at the University of Southern California.

Strings
Dir. Kaufman, Jennifer
1993 USA English
18 mins. 16mm color Narrative
Dist. (U.S.): Kaufman, Jennifer
Strings recounts the story of Ani, a bi musician and her gang of friends. When Ani's friend dies of AIDS she decides it's time to move away, but her girlfriend and her boyfriend don't want her to leave.

Strip Jack Naked
Dir. Peck, Ron
1991 Great Britain English
90 mins. 16mm color Documentary
Dist. (U.S.): Frameline
Dist. (U.K.): British Film Institute
Strip Jack Naked starts out as an account of the making of Ron Peck's earlier *Nighthawks* (one of

the world's first widely distributed, gay-made and gay-themed features), and ends as a compelling look back at growing up gay in London. It's a farewell note to England's last three decades—inked with humor, politics, and a penchant for posing pouches.

In 1980, *Nighthawks* was the original homo promo—a daring, radical drama; today it seems too cautious, even downbeat and a little gloomy. In an engagingly modest voice-over, Peck explains why *Nighthawks* turned out the way it did. Inevitably, it has a lot to do with the conflicting demands of the gay community, and even more to do with Ron's own story. Some of the most gripping moments come when Peck rips away the fictional tissue from *Nighthawks* and replays scenes with himself as the film's tortured hero.

With shots of London's spooky suburban streets and a montage of teen lust objects, Peck describes following a senior boy home from school—for no clear reason—only to have the lad repudiate his innocent admirer in public. It's this unusual honesty that marks *Strip Jack Naked* as not just a lucid account of the responsibilities of a gay filmmaker, but as one of the most honest and abrasive British biographies ever made.

Stripped Bare: A Look at Erotic Dancers
Dir. Manning, Caitlin
1988 USA English
60 mins. video color Documentary
Dist. (U.S.): Manning, Caitlin
Stripped Bare explores San Francisco's erotic club scene via the testimony of dancers. Women speak about working conditions, how they came to dance, and the pleasures and pressures of their profession. Lesbian dancers describe the difference between straight male and lesbian audiences. Women discuss their feelings about using their bodies to make money. Debi Sundahl, erotic dancer and operator of Blush Productions of San Francisco, details her road to entrepreneurship in the sex industry; the differences between a women-owned erotic dance palace and various male-owned clubs are discussed. Footage of dancers on the job is interspersed with interviews.

Stripped Bare raises important questions about female sexuality and sex work as a viable occupation for women. The women are allowed to speak for themselves and to draw their own conclusions about their occupation and their alternatives in life. The tape opens an important dialogue about the expression (and past suppression) of female sexuality and the ways in which women can empower themselves via their sexuality.

Subject Is AIDS, The
Dir. Getchell, Franklin
1986 USA English
18 mins. video color Documentary
Dist. (U.S.): ODN Productions
Actress Rae Dawn Chong narrates this video combining AIDS education for young people with dramatized segments of youths discussing their thoughts and fears about AIDS and its prevention.

Suburban Queen
Dir. Faber, Mindy
1985 USA English
3 mins. video color Experimental
Dist. (U.S.): Video Data Bank
Mindy Faber fantasizes her suburban mom an African warrior/goddess. Mom ain't buyin'.

Suddenly Last Summer
Dir. Beavan, Clare
1991 Great Britain English
12 mins. video color Documentary
Dist. (U.S.): Fulcrum Productions
Suddenly Last Summer, produced for BBC TV's *Saturday Night Out*, offers a lighthearted examination of "the Martina factor" in women's tennis.

Sum of Us, The
Dir. Dowling, Kevin
1994 Australia English
99 mins. 35mm color Narrative
Dist. (U.S.): The Samuel Goldwyn Co.
David Stevens's play, a hit at home and off-Broadway, became a sort of pilgrimage rite for many gays and lesbians who dragged along (eventually grateful) parents; now you can rent the tape, hand it over to the folks, and let the sensitization process take its own course. This is the rare stage work that actually improves in screen translation, maintaining intimacy while "opening up" to lovely effect. Harry (Jack Thompson) and Jeff Mitchell (Russell Crowe) are a not-so-unusual dad/son couple on the surface: working-class, sharing a house in the wake of a wife's death, sparring amiably over household chores. The big dif is that Junior is a young gay man, and Pop doesn't mind one bit. If anything, he's too supportive, embarrassing Jeff's dates with the back-slapping eagerness of a potential father-in-law. One such incident cools the ardor of a handsome young gardener (John Polson) whose own closet home life has ill-prepared him

for such openness; on the flip side, middle-aged Harry's courtship of a lonely widow (Deborah Kennedy) crashes against her own homophobia. Full of humor and feeling, this sweet-tempered comedy—which really earns its late turn toward hankie-soaking drama toward the end—sketches a depth of family understanding most gay men and women can only fantasize about. That it comes off as utterly believable pays tribute to the superb cast, canny writing, and astute direction. The lack of overt preachiness makes this possibly the best gay-positive propagandic tool mainstream cinema has yet offered. A must. (D.H.)

Summer, 1993
Dir. Beck, Robert
1994 USA English
7 mins. video color Experimental
Dist. (U.S.): Beck, Robert
Elegy for a loss.

Summer of Love—Art Against AIDS
Dir. Rubnitz, Tom
1989 USA English
1 mins. video color Other
Dist. (U.S.): Video Data Bank
A public service announcement. Part of the *Tom Rubnitz Marathon (A Dozen Tapes, Wigs Included)*.

Summer Vacation: 1999
(see *1999—Nen No Natsu Yasumi*)

Super 8 1/2
Dir. LaBruce, Bruce
1994 Canada English
85 mins. 16mm b&w Narrative
Dist. (U.S.): Strand Releasing
Dist. (U.K.): Dangerous To Know
From the legendary auteur of *No Skin Off My Ass*, Bruce LaBruce, comes another no-budget cautionary tale for our times. Bruce plays a washed-up, strung-out porno star who's rediscovered by an undergound dyke avant-garde filmmaker, Googie (Liza LaMonica). She begins to make a documentary about him entitled, simply, Bruce. Bruce thinks that this is his big comeback, a la *Sunset Boulevard*, but Googie is only exploiting the "poor, down-on-his-luck faggot" to get financial backing for her pet project, *Submit to My Finger*, her tribute to New York underground auteur R. Kern.

Bruce spends his perpetual alcoholidays in bed with his hustler boyfriend, Pierce (Klaus Von Brucker). Meanwhile, the ambitious, incestuous, sexually adventurous Friday sisters

Ⓐ Ⓑ Ⓒ Ⓓ Ⓔ Ⓕ Ⓖ Ⓗ Ⓘ Ⓙ Ⓚ Ⓛ Ⓜ Ⓝ Ⓞ Ⓟ Ⓠ Ⓡ Ⓢ Ⓣ Ⓤ Ⓥ Ⓦ Ⓧ Ⓨ Ⓩ

(Chris Teen, Dirty Pillows) catch Googie's eye in the cemetery, and she approaches them to star in her new movie.

Other characters, such as Bruce's archrival and former costar Johnny Eczema (Mikey Mike) and Pierce's hooker friend Amy Nitrate (Kate Ashley) round out this cast of sexual misfits. *Super 8 1/2* also includes cameos from real-life undergound luminaries like Vaginal Creme Davis, Ben Weasel, and Richard Kern—not to mention aboveground TV star Scott Thompson ("Kids in the Hall") as Buddy Cole.

Mixing thinly-disguised autobiography with hardcore sex scenes, *Super 8 1/2* is a pinnacle of perversity for queer cinema. Or, as they used to say about John Waters's films, Bruce LaBruce achieves a new high in low taste. Get ready, San Francisco.

Surely to God
Dir. Moores, Margaret
1989 Canada English
25 mins. video color Other
Dist. (U.S.): V-Tape
Margaret Moores's comedy in which two women try to cash in a lottery ticket stuck to a frozen chicken.

Survival House [excerpt]
Dir. Pavlow, Bruce
1979 USA English
45 mins. video color Documentary
Dist. (U.S.): n/a
An excerpt from the documentary

Survivor, The
Dir. Winkler, Robert
1993 Austria German
2 mins. 35mm color Narrative
Dist. (U.S.): Winkler, Robert
A clever condom cliffhanger.

Susana
Dir. Munoz, Susana
1980 USA/Argentina English
25 mins. video color Experimental
Dist. (U.S.): Women Make Movies
Susana interweaves cinema verité interviews of her family and lovers with snapshots, home movies, and even a Disney cartoon to render the cultural context in which female, sexual, and ethnic identity is shaped.

Swamp
Dir. Child, Abigail
1990 USA English

35 mins. video color Experimental
Dist. (U.S.): Video Data Bank
"The Swamp: America's new family entertainment!" From bookstore to theme park, *Swamp* depicts how culture threatens to sink from sight in a mire of relentless progress. Enthusiastic overacting and fancy dress parties form the basis of Abigail Child's soap opera send-up which approaches the narrative structure of a TV serial so it can then splutter apart in a dizzying, discontinuous montage. The confused heroine, played by writer Carla Harryman, runs a beleaguered bookstore, and is trying to find time to tell her fiancé that she's seeing another woman—her psychiatrist's receptionist. As plots and characters pile up, their intrigues begin to converge.

Sweet Dreams
Dir. Cottrell, Honey Lee
1979 USA English
13 mins. 16mm color Documentary
Dist. (U.S.): Multi Focus
A frank film dealing with women and masturbation, sponsored by the National Sex Forum.

Swoon
Dir. Kalin, Tom
Prod. Vachon, Christine
1991 USA English
92 mins. 35mm b&w Narrative
Dist. (U.S.): Fine Line Features
Swoon is inspired by the story of Nathan Leopold Jr. and Richard Loeb, two Jewish law students who, in 1942, kidnapped and murdered a young boy to illustrate their intellectual superiority to others. Their capture and trial led to international media coverage, and to two movie variations: Alfred Hitchcock's *Rope* and Richard Fleischer's *Compulsion*.

But the movies neglected to mention that Leopold and Loeb were more than just a criminal couple; they were also partners in bed. Swoon pursues the boys' unusual relationship from plotting to prison bars: What compelled Leopold and Loeb to kill? Did their crime have anything to do with homosexuality? If it didn't, surely their punishment did. *Swoon* is a clever, troubling fiction about history, homophobia, ecstasy, and murder.

"*Swoon* is quintessentially a film of its time. It takes on the whole enterprise of 'positive images' . . . turning the whole thing right on its head." —B. Ruby Rich, *Village Voice*

"Sword Fight"
Dir. unknown

1960 USA English
3 mins. 16mm b&w Other
Dist. (U.S.): Baldwin, Craig
Two bare-chested girls duel it out on the rocks.

Sylvia Scarlett
Dir. Cukor, George
1936 USA English
94 mins. 16mm/35mm b&w Narrative
Dist. (U.S.): Films Incorporated
Katharine Hepburn previously did a bit of cross-dressing in Dorothy Arzner's 1933 aviatrix melodrama, *Christopher Strong*. Here she goes all out as Sylvester Scarlett, boy-thief and traveling musician. Co-star Brian Aherne tells Sylvester, "There's something that gives me a queer feeling every time I look at you." Cary Grant has an odd attraction to the young Hepburn, and actress Dennie Moore pursues Hepburn quite aggressively. It's a crazy plot that veers bizarrely from comedy to tragedy. Shot through with homo subtext, the film was a huge flop at the box office in 1936 (*Variety* called it, "Dubious entertainment for the public"). And it looks very queer indeed all these years later. As with Garbo's *Queen Christina*, the latter half of the film is disappointing. But Hepburn's a bundle of boy energy, looks like a young David Bowie, and even has a girl kiss her on the lips. (J.O.)

Sync Touch
Dir. Hammer, Barbara
1981 USA English
10 mins. 16mm color Experimental
Dist. (U.S.): Canyon Cinema
A lesbian/feminist aesthetic proposing the connection between touch and sight to be the basis for a "new cinema."
        Released in the U.S. along with four of her other short films as a feature-length package, *Lesbian Humor: The Films of Barbara Hammer, Volume I*.

T.V. Tart
Dir. Hammer, Barbara
1989 USA English
11 mins. video color Experimental
Dist. (U.S.): Hammer, Barbara
Equating broadcast television and sugar desserts as empty, nonnutritive substances, *T.V. Tart* seduces the viewer's eye with electronic colors as bright as candy.

Tag Helms
Dir. Hilferty, Robert, and Robert Hoff
1989 USA English

5 mins. video color Other
Dist. (U.S.): Hoff, Robert
A short video salute to Senator Jesse Helms.

Take Me Back to Cairo
Dir. Krause, Ute
1993 Germany German
20 mins. 35mm color Narrative
Dist. (U.S.): Oberhausen Film Distribution
Take Me Back to Cairo is a women-only reverie about an inhibited middle-aged woman who wins a trip to the Oriental Baths.

Taking Back The Dolls
Dir. Singer, Leslie
1994 USA English
43 mins. video color Narrative
Dist. (U.S.): Singer, Leslie
"Scratch the surface and whaddya get? More surface." —Jennifer North, *Taking Back the Dolls*
                Leslie Singer dykes-up *The Valley of the Dolls* in this over-the-top pixel vision melodrama. Phenomenally dry humor and truly hot sex combine as we fly through the high-fashion, druggie lesbo lives of supermodel Ann Wells (Leslie Singer), her depressive Seconal-addict roommate Jennifer North (Cecilia Dougherty) and the gun-toting Neely Shannon Chen (Valerie Soe). With music by the Carpenters, Nirvana, and Suicide and appearances from Kevin Killian and Eileen Myles.

Tales of an Exhausted Woman
Dir. Winer, Lucy
1990 USA English
30 mins. video color Other
Dist. (U.S.): American Film Institute
Tales of an Exhausted Woman is a half-hour absurdist comedy about one woman's affliction with a somewhat antisocial disease—she's been tired all her life and, yes, she's slept around.

Talk to Me Like the Rain
Dir. Kinney, Robert, and Donald Kinney
1989 USA English
17 mins. video color Narrative
Dist. (U.S.): Video Data Bank
Talk to Me Like the Rain (based on a Tennessee Williams story) is a melancholy depiction of two boys circling the ruins of their relationship.

Talking Hairs
Dir. Ardill, Susan
1991 Great Britain English
10 mins. video color Documentary
Dist. (U.K.): Maya Vision

Ⓐ Ⓑ Ⓒ Ⓓ Ⓔ Ⓕ Ⓖ Ⓗ Ⓘ Ⓙ Ⓚ Ⓛ Ⓜ Ⓝ Ⓞ Ⓟ Ⓠ Ⓡ Ⓢ ❶ Ⓤ Ⓥ Ⓦ Ⓧ Ⓨ Ⓩ

Hair on our legs, arms, faces, and heads. Lesbians and gay men discuss styles, fetishes, and phobias. A fast and furious look at the hair and the hairless.

Tall Dark Stranger
Dir. Oremland, Paul
1986 Great Britain English
40 mins. video color Narrative
Dist. (U.K.): Kinesis Films
"There is no tall dark stranger," concluded Quentin Crisp in the 1970s, and Paul Oremland's response to this starts engagingly as a salty, gay *La Ronde* for the '80s, all casual sex and cross purposes. The program then settles into the classic structure of new boy on the block, or—this being London—new chicken in town.

This rather perky primer is reminiscent of Ron Peck's feature *Nighthawks* in its images of a class-ridden gay culture. Occasionally, like Peck's film, *Stranger* goes awry when it comes to dialogue; nevertheless, the visual style is always compelling and the whole affair ends with an unusual first for network TV: a party sequence with go-go boys in leather thongs and aluminum foil.

Tangled Garden, Act II, Scene II
Dir. Anderlini, Ken
1992 Canada English
13 mins. 16mm color Experimental
Dist. (U.S.): Anderlini, Ken
A beautifully shot reinterpretation of the eroticism found in Western art's classic male nude. Combining live models with the old masters, flesh and blood is oftentimes indistinguishable from the painted canvas, ultimately challenging rigid dichotomies between gay and straight.

Taste of Honey, A
Dir. Richardson, Tony
1961 Great Britain English
100 mins. 16mm b&w Narrative
Dist. (U.S.): Kit Parker Films
Rita Tushingham won the Best Actress Award at the Cannes Film Festival for her sensitive portrayal of Jo, a young girl forced to make a life of her own. Deserted by an irresponsible mother and pregnant by a black sailor, Jo sets up housekeeping with a young homosexual (Murray Melvin) she picks up at a carnival. In its intial American release, the film was supplemented by a study guide, reprinted in *Life* magazine, on the "causes and cures" of homosexuality.

Taste of Kiwi, A

Dir. Wells, Peter
1991 New Zealand English
2 mins. 16mm color Experimental
Dist. (U.S.): Wells, Peter
Soccer and sex collide—Down Under.

Tattoo
Dir. Nichols, Paul, and Berne Boyle
1979 USA English
17 mins. video color Experimental
Dist. (U.S.): n/a
Exposure.

Taxi to Cairo
Dir. Ripploh, Frank
1987 Germany German
90 mins. 35mm color Narrative
Dist. (U.S.): Cinevista
In 1981 gay audiences were stunned and delighted by a new, bold, sexy comedy from Germany, *Taxi Zum Klo*, a film that set new standards for gay cinema. Eight years later, Frank is back, and his life in anything but under control. He is still madly in love with men; he's always been short on money; and he has just been tied up and robbed by a hustler. On top of everything his mother thinks it's high time he kissed his idle ways good-bye and started thinking about holy matrimony—otherwise he could end up being cut out of her will. Frank finds Klara, an out-of-work actress who is willing to stage a marriage farce for his mother, but their scheme has just one snag: both Frank and Klara are in love with the same man, their neighbor Eugen. Suddenly jealousy is the order of the day, and Frank finds himself torn between competing with Klara for Eugen and still needing her to collect the inheritance. Goaded by Eugen, who maintains that with Frank being gay he will never be able to keep his wife, Frank snaps. He quickly engages a sex therapist to turn him into a heterosexual. His attempts to switch land him in a chaotic mess in which the neighbors, the police, and naturally his mother are all embroiled.

Taxi Zum Klo
Dir. Ripploh, Frank
1981 Germany German
92 mins. 35mm color Narrative
Dist. (U.S.): Cinevista
A landmark film. This raw, autobiographical account of a gay schoolteacher in Berlin who is fired for coming out of the closet has been one of the most banned gay films of all time.

Tearing the Veil

Dir. Bezalel, Ronit

1989 Canada English
10 mins. video color Experimental
Dist. (U.S.): Women Make Movies
The eternal question "What is a lesbian?" asked in terms of gender stereotypes.

Tell Me No Lies
Dir. Hunter, Neil

1993 Great Britain English
30 mins. 16mm color Narrative
Dist. (U.K.): Dangerous To Know
Tell Me No Lies is a jaunty, bittersweet comedy about the näiveté of some closeted English students; "I think Jane knows I'm gay," says an anxious one to his after-hours boyfriend, "She's reading Genet and she said she'd lend it to me." Better Genet than E.M. Forster.

Tell Me Why: The Epistemology of Disco
Dir. Di Stefano, John

1991 USA English
24 mins. video color Experimental
Dist. (U.S.): V-Tape
A humorous and affectionate look at the role disco music has played in the formation of gay male identity. Combining tongue-in-cheek semiotics with well-loved disco classics and extracts from Hollywood movies of the time, director John Di Stefano exhaustively celebrates gay culture from the late '60s onward.

Temps Perdus
Dir. Waggoner, David

1977 USA English
6 mins. S8mm color Narrative
Dist. (U.S.): n/a
A love story for you and me.

Tempted
Dir. Borsboom, Anne Marie

1991 Netherlands No Dialogue
10 mins. 35mm color Narrative
Dist. (U.S.): Holland Film Promotion
Dist. (U.K.): Cinenova
Tempted offers a gorgeous seduction on horseback.

Ten Cents a Dance (Parallax)
Dir. Onodera, Midi

1986 Canada English
30 mins. 16mm color Experimental
Dist. (U.S.): Women Make Movies
A striking split screen is used throughout the three scenes that make up this provocative film, which deals with communication, sexuality, and alienation. In Scene One a lesbian and a straight woman discuss their planned sexual encounter. Scene Two is an extended overhead shot of two men who meet in a bathroom stall. Scene Three depicts phone sex between a man and a woman.

Tender Fictions
Dir. Hammer, Barbara

1995 USA English
58 mins. 16mm color Experimental
Dist. (U.S.): Hammer, Barbara
Pioneer lesbian-feminist filmmaker, Barbara Hammer, constructs an autobiography before someone does it for her in this post-modern sequel to her 1992 award-winning documentary, *Nitrate Kisses*.

Childhood stories of the artist as a young lesbian and intimate tales of the lesbian as a young artist underscore the filmmaker's life of performances. With a Swiss army knife she robs an American Express Bank in Morocco, accosts a sheperd in a field on International Women's Day, and tap dances on Shirley Temple's star on Hollywood Boulevard. This child movie star was the ideal by which Hammer's ambitious mother measured her own Barbie. Hammer's grandmother, a cook for silent actress Lillian Gish, introduced the cute, loquacious child and her mother to D. W. Griffith.

Lesbian autobiography is a slender genre, so Hammer draws from general cultural studies for critique and to provide an ironic edge to the synthesized "voices of authority". Using personal archival footage of the AFL/CIO faculty strike at San Francisco State College supported by the Black Panther Party (1968), the first San Diego Women's Music Festival (1965), and the "Take Back the Night" March in San Francisco (1979), Hammer challenges a younger generation to visualize a world before they existed.

Terence Davies Trilogy, The
Dir. Davies, Terence

1984 Great Britain English
101 mins. 16mm b&w Narrative
Dist. (U.S.): Frameline
Before *Distant Voices, Still Lives*, Terence Davies spent seven years making three darker films about his working-class, Catholic upbringing in Northern England. Part One (*Children*) introduces Robert Tucker and flashbacks to scenes from his childhood—bullying at school; a violent and sick father; early sexual fantasies. Part Two (*Madonna and Child*) is a portrait of Tucker, middle-aged and trapped between public and private person-

Ⓐ Ⓑ Ⓒ Ⓓ Ⓔ Ⓕ Ⓖ Ⓗ Ⓘ Ⓙ Ⓚ Ⓛ Ⓜ Ⓝ Ⓞ Ⓟ Ⓠ Ⓡ Ⓢ Ⓣ Ⓤ Ⓥ Ⓦ Ⓧ Ⓨ Ⓩ

ae. In Part Three (*Death and Transfiguration*), Tucker revisits his life with a new and less tortured perspective. He seems to accept his sexuality, which is transfigured by the love between his mother and himself.

"Davies is an accomplished visual storyteller, conveying information with economical, resonant images enriched by the juxtapositional structure of his film. *The Terence Davies Trilogy* stands as one of the more artful efforts in the gay-as-outsider genre."
—Mark Halleck, *New York Native*

Terence Stark: Mythographer
Dir. unknown
1987 USA English
5 mins. 16mm color Documentary
Dist. (U.S.): n/a
A portrait.

Terms of Conception
Dir. Taylor, Amanda, and Lisa Fisher
1994 USA English
32 mins. video color Documentary
Dist. (U.S.): Fisher, Lisa
Terms of Conception takes a decidedly American perspective on the subject of lesbians and artificial insemination, interviewing a Minneapolis lesbian couple and their gay friend/sperm donor. In wonderfully forthright and often humorous interviews, this revealing examination answers the nitty-gritty questions of how it actually happens. Interviews with their family members put their experience in a broader context.

Terra Nullius
Dir. Pratten, Anne
1992 Australia English
21 mins. 16mm color/b&w Experimental
Dist. (U.S.): Women Make Movies
A haunting experimental drama of family abuse.

Testing the Limits Guide to Safer Sex
Dir. Testing the Limits Collective
1987 USA English
13 mins. video color Documentary
Dist. (U.S.): Third World Newsreel
Denise Ribble, R.N., of the Community Health Project, New York, delivers safe-sex information in a wry, dry, and direct manner. Sound advice for men and women, gays, and straights.

Tex-Sex
Dir. Tomboy, Texas
1994 USA English
3 mins. video color Experimental

Dist. (U.S.): Tomboy, Texas
Tex-Sex is a sexy solo shot from the Texas Tomboy himself.

Texas
Dir. Gonzalez, Mari Keiko
1994 USA English
4 mins. video color Experimental
Dist. (U.S.): Gonzalez, Mari Keiko
Texas by Mari Keiko Gonzalez, is about masturbation, unrequited love, broken guitar strings, and all those southern girls you can't seem to resist.

Thank You and Good Night
Dir. Oxenberg, Jan
1991 USA English
83 mins. 16mm color Documentary
Dist. (U.S.): Aries Releasing
As early as 1975, Jan Oxenberg began to drastically change lesbian film history. With *Home Movie* and *A Comedy in Six Unnatural Acts*, she proved that it was possible to reflect on the lesbian image in a self-conscious way, informed by a wonderful sense of humor and by a many-sided stylistic knowledge of the medium. *Thank You and Good Night* leaves no stone (or regret) unturned as Oxenberg, through the persona of an irrepressible "inner child." Scowling Jan moves between fiction and documentary worlds to chronicle her family's struggle to come to terms with their grandmother's death. She sets out to answer the unanswerable questions: "Was her life really rotten or did she make herself miserable?" "Why didn't Grandma teach my mother how to cook?" "Why do people have to die anyway?" The real story of this death and its aftermath unfold in unforgettably powerful documentary footage. Seamlessly woven around it, Scowling Jan takes us on a quest into the past of '50s memories; into hyperspace; into different versions of the afterlife; into a series of hilarious, poignant schemes and fantasies meant to soothe the sting of her helpless confrontation with the Grim Reaper. The result is a hard-hitting, unforgettable journey, part spiritual odyssey, part cosmic tantrum, that anyone who has ever dealt with loss will recognize.

Winner of the 1991 San Francisco International Lesbian & Gay Film Festival Audience Award for Best Documentary.

That Tender Touch
Dir. Vincent, Russel
1969 USA English
88 mins. 35mm color Narrative
Dist. (U.S.): Olson, Jenni

Described by *Variety* as "One more variation on the Lesbian thing." *That Tender Touch* stars minor cult figure Sue Bernard (*Playboy's* Miss December 1966 and star of the Russ Meyer classic *Faster Pussycat! Kill! Kill!*) Bea Tompkins costars as her older lesbian ex-lover, who shows up years later (check out the Mommy/Girl iconography) to cause trouble between Bernard and her new husband. In true Hollywood style, Tompkins ends up face down in the swimming pool, another narrative casualty of the homophobia of the silver screen. "*That Tender Touch* has a multitude of scenes between the two femmes," says *Variety*, "which probably will be exploited for good response in certain bookings." While that "good response" was probably supposed to come from male audiences seeking soft-core titillation, contemporary lesbian audiences will respond wildly to the camp value of this obscure and hilarious motion picture.

This 35mm archive print is complete and unedited, but in poor condition.

That's Alright Mama
Dir. Herbert, Rachel
1994 USA English
12 mins. video color Documentary
Dist. (U.S.): Herbert, Rachel
A quirky profile of a lesbian couple who are truck drivers.

That's Amore
Dir. Russo, C.J.
1995 USA English
9 mins. video color Narrative
Dist. (U.S.): Russo, C.J.
Meeting a stranger in a pizzeria begins one woman's search for love and understanding of the nature of desire. Fueled by erotic curiosity, Italian lust, a daily horoscope, and lots of pizza, *That's Amore* unfolds as a humourous self-reflective quest on what defines sexual attraction and intrigue.

That's Masculinity
Dir. Munden, Marc
Prod. Watson, Paul
1991 Great Britain English
40 mins. video color Documentary
Dist. (U.S.): n/a
Part of a 1991 BBC series dealing with men and masculinity called "From Wimps to Warriors," *That's Masculinity* is an example of how an oblique approach can frequently revive a well-worn subject. Director Marc Munden sets the tone with an aesthetic ode to the beautiful bodies

of an East End steam room. Two backward leather queens are quizzed on the meaning of masculinity ("It's leather, anything to get away from the cashmere sweater brigade . . . it's the sheer smell of men"). A black drag queen goes shopping for discount dresses and dishes heterosexuals with his campy pals. Startling by American documentary standards, *That's Masculinity* offers quiet observation, extraordinary eroticism, and a mellow kind of pride.

Theatrical Collage
Dir. Nicoletta, Daniel
1977 USA English
10 mins. S8mm color/b&w Documentary
Dist. (U.S.): Nicoletta, Daniel
A collection of San Francisco theatrical footage from over the years, including The Angels of Light, belly dancing, strippers, and various local performers.

Their First Mistake
Dir. Marshall, George
Prod. Roach, Hal
1932 USA English
21 mins. 16mm b&w Narrative
Dist. (U.S.): Olson, Jenni
Laurel and Hardy end up in bed again—this time with a baby. Ollie's wife complains that he sees too much of Stan and not enough of her. Stan has a solution: Ollie should adopt a baby for his wife to keep her occupied at home so that Ollie can go out nights with Stan. When Stan and Ollie return with the baby they discover that Ollie's wife has left and is suing him for divorce. Stan is also being sued for "the alienation of Mr. Hardy's affections."

Theo und Thea
Dir. Kramer, Pieter
1988 Netherlands Dutch
20 mins. video color Other
Dist. (U.S.): n/a
An episode of the Dutch children's show, "Theo und Thea"—queerer than "Pee Wee's Playhouse"—this hilarious program takes on the topic of homosexuality with a gay and lesbian studio audience.

Therese and Isabelle
Dir. Metzger, Radley
1968 France French
102 mins. 35mm color Narrative
Dist. (U.S.): Audubon Films
In this film based on the novel of the same name by Violette Leduc, Therese returns to the scene of

A
B
C
D
E
F
G
H
I
J
K
L
M
N
O
P
Q
R
S
T
U
V
W
X
Y
Z

her sexual awakening. She remembers her desolation after being sent away to a boarding school by her adored but newly married mother, and meeting Isabelle, a classmate, quite adjusted and unconcerned that her parents have left her at the school. An immediate and intense friendship develops between the adolescent girls. Their intensity leads to hurried caresses in the school chapel, in the bathroom, and ultimately to a brothel that the sophisticated Isabelle knows. Leduc's whispered poetic imagery of the "secret pearl" is narrated during the love scenes, conjuring images the screen does not reveal.

These Shoes Weren't Made For Walking
Dir. Lee, Paul
1995 Canada English
27 mins. 16mm color Experimental
Dist. (U.S.): Canadian Filmmakers Distribution Centre
A docudrama exploring the roles and aspirations of four generations of Chinese women in the director's family, using their shoes as a common reference and as a springboard for thoughtful and provocative contemplations about their experiences. These four women (paternal grandmother, mother, paternal aunt, sister) recount and discuss the cultural and socioeconomic forces that have shaped their lives.

Thick Lips, Thin Lips
Dir. Lee, Paul
1994 Canada English
6 mins. 16mm color Experimental
Dist. (U.S.): Frameline
Thick Lips, Thin Lips is Paul Lee's passionate exploration of the parallel between hate-motivated violence based on racism and that based on homophobia.

Thin Ice
Dir. Cunningham Reid, Fiona
1994 Great Britain English
88 mins. 35mm color Narrative
Dist. (U.K.): Dangerous to Know
Fiona Cunningham Reid's (Feed Them to the Cannibals) first dramatic feature film has Steffi, an ambitious photojournalist and amateur ice skater, all set to skate in the Gay Games when her sexual and skating partner skips out on her. This ruins her and journalist pal Greg's plans to break into the mainstream press by writing a cover story on lesbians and love on the ice at the Gay Games in New York. Under pressure from their editor, Steffi begins to search for a possible replacement.

One day on the ice she eyes the naively "hetero" Natalie who is taking lessons from the muscled lesbian Cosima, a former figure skating champion from Russia. Living a sheltered existence in the oppressive home of her older sister and her lecherous brother-in-law, Natalie is only beginning to come out of her shell and is excited by the prospect of finding new friends. Dangling the carrot of free lessons, Steffi maneuvers Natalie into becoming her practice partner, without letting on about her intentions. Not sure of her sexual inclinations, Steffi and Greg invite Natalie to meet them at a lesbian bar. To Steffi's delight Natalie shows up and they all have a grand time. As their friendship develops, so does their skating, and Natalie finally agrees to compete in the Gay Games. All seems well until Natalie discovers her skating partner's plan to put her on the cover of a national magazine. Just days before they're set to compete, Natalie pulls out.

Things We Said Today
Dir. Miller-Monzon, John
1992 USA English
34 mins. 16mm color Narrative
Dist. (U.S.): Frameline
The light-hearted Things We Said Today from NYU filmmaker John Miller-Monzon, may be the lesbian Slacker, with its depiction of an idiosyncratic young woman who drifts from job to job and between her lover and friend.

This Is Not a Condom
Dir. Kroetch, Michael
1990 USA English
15 mins. video color Experimental
Dist. (U.S.): n/a
This shadowy and chilling pixel vision piece is a response to governmental apathy regarding the AIDS epidemic.

This Is Not a Very Blank Tape, Dear
Dir. Cottis, Jane
1989 USA English
22 mins. video color Experimental
Dist. (U.S.): Video Data Bank
In This Is Not a Very Blank Tape, Dear, a young woman replies to her mother's incomprehension of what exactly a lesbian is, and explains why her sexual identity will inevitably bring them to conflict.

This Is Not an AIDS Advertisement
Dir. Julien, Isaac
1987 Great Britain English

5 mins. video color Experimental
Dist. (U.S.): Frameline
Dist. (U.K.): British Film Institute
Two men bop about London in a music video about sex, race, and identity.

This Special Friendship
(see *Les Amities Particulieres*)

Three Bewildered People in the Night
Dir. Araki, Gregg
1987 USA English
92 mins. 16mm color Narrative
Dist. (U.S.): Strand Releasing
David is a gay performance artist. Alicia is a video artist. They are the best of friends, sharing frustrations and feelings about love, sex, employment, and art over 3 a.m. cups of coffee. Into their world comes Craig, a would-be actor and photographer who is as ambivalent about his career plans as he is about his sexuality. Although he lives with Alicia he finds himself more and more attracted to David. *Three Bewildered People in the Night* is a refreshing, often wryly funny look at three people struggling to understand themselves and their needs as artists. The gay elements in the story are treated with unusual respect and affection as the dilemma is brought to a compassionate and original resolution.

Writer/producer/director Gregg Araki has done a remarkable job with a limited budget. He began work on the film in 1984 after graduating from USC and taking a Hollywood movie industry job at MGM. He hated it and, encouraged by the success of some recent American independent films, decided to go for broke. He quit his job, wrote the script for *Three Bewildered People in the Night*, and began production in Los Angeles, where all the action takes place. Judging from the reaction (the film won numerous awards, including the Bronze Leopard at the 40th Festival Internazionale del Film in Locarno, Switzerland) Araki has a bright future as an independent filmmaker.

Three Faces of Women
Dir. Castro, Rick
1994 USA English
45 mins. video color Narrative
Dist. (U.S.): Castro, Rick
Featuring Alexis Arquette and Vaginal Cream Davis as a frustrated couple seeking the advice of a sex therapist.

Thriller
Dir. Potter, Sally
1979 Great Britain English
30 mins. 16mm b&w Experimental
Dist. (U.S.): Women Make Movies
Since its release in 1980, *Thriller*, Sally Potter's reconstruction of Puccini's opera, *La Boheme* has become a classic in feminist film theory and a model deconstruction on the Hollywood film and the conventional role of women as romantic victims in fiction. As B. Ruby Rich wrote in her seminal review in the *Chicago Reader*: "*Thriller* is the first feminist murder mystery. Sally Potter has synthesized fantasy, wit and intellectual rigor into a fresh, startling work. Like Deren and Rainer, she has retained a sense of timing, of entertainment, and of audience. . . . *Thriller* becomes an exemplary sign of how illuminating a new feminist art might be."

Ties That Bind, The
Dir. Friedrich, Su
1984 USA English
16 mins. 16mm color Experimental
Dist. (U.S.): Women Make Movies
Dist. (U.K.): Cinenova
Su Friedrich's work has the rare quality of being emotionally compelling and experimental all at once. While her point of departure is usually personal experience, she elaborates on the material until the film reaches an autonomous meaning. Using the formal aspects of the cinematic material and the seductive potential of narrative, she creates involvement and distance at the same time. In terms of content, her films are about the cultural and political determination of her emotions in which her being lesbian is of crucial importance.

The *Ties That Bind* is based on Friedrich's asking her German mother about her life. Intertitles replaces the filmmaker's questions, allowing her mother to speak for herself and directly to the viewer. While the daughter/mother relationship is the basis for the film, it focuses on questions of complicity and resistance for a young German woman during World War II.

Till Death Do Us Part
Dir. Durrin, Ginny
1988 USA English
16 mins. video color Other
Dist. (U.S.): Durrin Films
A rap/theatrical film about AIDS and IV needle use. Vivid presentation of peer pressure, drug abuse, and personal responsibility.

Ⓐ
Ⓑ
Ⓒ
Ⓓ
Ⓔ
Ⓕ
Ⓖ
Ⓗ
Ⓘ
Ⓙ
Ⓚ
Ⓛ
Ⓜ
Ⓝ
Ⓞ
Ⓟ
Ⓠ
Ⓡ
Ⓢ
Ⓣ
Ⓤ
Ⓥ
Ⓦ
Ⓧ
Ⓨ
Ⓩ

Tim Miller: Loud and Queer
Dir. Harrison, L. Richard
1992 USA English
29 mins. video color Documentary
Dist. (U.S.): Video Data Bank
Tim Miller: Loud and Queer celebrates the talents of the provocative performance artist. Excerpts from his work *My Queer Body* are intercut with interviews and images spanning his 15-year career. He also conducts a workshop for gay men in which he confronts fear and loss, violence and love, art and activism.

Time is Money
Dir. Von Grote, Alexandria
1987 Germany German
13 mins. 35mm color Narrative
Dist. (U.S.): Ariadne Film
Time is Money tells the thrilling story of a mysterious woman who burglarizes the villas of certain people to teach them a very unusual as well as expensive lesson.

Time Off
Dir. Fox, Eytan
1990 Israel Hebrew
45 mins. 16mm color Narrative
Dist. (U.S.): Frameline
Time Off is the first Israeli film to deal seriously with homosexuality in the military. Set at the outbreak of the 1982 Lebanese War, it is really the sentimental education of a young soldier who breaks away from the bravado of his comrades for an afternoon in Jerusalem. A comic encounter with some American girls and a glancing try with a female soldier cannot prepare the shy lad for the discovery of his most macho lieutenant in a gay embrace.

Times of Harvey Milk, The
Dir. Epstein, Robert
Prod. Schmiechen, Richard
1984 USA English
87 mins. 16mm color Documentary
Dist. (U.S.): October Films
Dist. (U.K.): British Film Institute
Six years in the making, *The Times of Harvey Milk* has seen unparalleled success in the past year. From its first screening at the Telluride Film Festival last September to the winning of the Academy Award in April, the film has rewritten the history of gay cinema. Chronicling the rise to power of both Harvey Milk and the city's gay community, the film gives a nostalgic look at a unique period in the history of the gay rights movement and the city of San Francisco.

Winner of the 1985 San Francisco International Lesbian & Gay Film Festival Audience Award for Best Documentary.

Times Square
Dir. Moyle, Allan
Prod. Stigwood, Robert
1980 USA English
111 mins. 35mm color Narrative
Dist. (U.S.): Swank Motion Pictures
Dist. (U.K.): British Film Institute
Allan Moyle's 1980 teenage girl rock 'n' roll adventure, *Times Square* developed status as a lesbian cult film with showings at lesbian and gay film festivals in New York and San Francisco in the early- and mid-'80s and continues to be a favorite at lesbian and gay film festivals in the early '90s. Long-standing rumors about lesbian content removed from *Times Square* have provided ample fodder for lesbian readings of the teen girl buddy movie. Indeed, a look at Jacob Brackman's original unpublished script reveals many erotically-charged scenes between the protagonists, Nicky (Robin Johnson) and Pammy (Trini Alvarado). Some of these scenes were removed from the script prior to shooting, some of them were shot and then excised from the final cut of the film. A fragment of one such excised scene appears in the film's preview trailer—it is a one-second, barely perceivable, clip of Nicky and Pammy playing together in the river.

The basic plot of the film is conveyed in its publicity blurb: "In the heart of Times Square, a poor girl becomes famous, a rich girl becomes courageous, and both become friends." Pammy is the quiet and sheltered daughter of a prominent politician, Nicky is a streetwise troublemaker. Admitted to a hospital for the same psychiatric tests, the girls share a room and get to know each other. They escape from the hospital, create a home for themselves in a dockside warehouse and live their lives together against the gritty urban backdrop of Times Square. There's tons of romantic tension between the girls, and, most importantly—they love each other and they're not interested in boys. As their friendship begins, Pammy's first feelings for Nicky are expressed in a poem she writes in her journal (which Nicky steals): "Your ribs are my ladder Nicky, I'm so amazed, I'm so amazed." Pammy later recites T.S. Eliot to Nicky and proclaims to her, "Everything you do, or you say, is poetry. At least I think so."

Early in the film, Nicky gets Pammy a

252 | 253

job as an erotic dancer, "I'm brave, but you're pretty. I'm a freak of fuckin' nature," she tells Pammy as Pammy prepares to go on stage at the Cleo Club. Nicky (with her hair tied back and looking as butch as ever) positions herself at the front edge of the stage to watch, and Pammy focuses on Nicky as she begins to dance (in the original script she dances topless). In a later scene at the Cleo Club, Pammy watches Nicky perform her song "Damn Dog" (a poem Nicky had first read to Pammy on bended knee: "I can lick your face, I can bite it too, my teeth got rabies, I'm gonna give 'em to you. I'm a damn dog.").

While there's no explicit lesbian content in the film, the romantic tone of Nicky and Pammy's interactions is undeniable. The original script had several scenes and plot elements that developed this aspect of Nicky and Pammy's relationship, including a scene of their first meeting in the hospital, in which they have to undress in front of each other; two scenes where they take off their shirts and play together in their underwear in the river (the clip of which remains in the film's trailer); a wrestling scene; a scene of the first night that they sleep (sleep, not fuck) together; and a scene of Pammy dancing topless at the Cleo Club. Most of the scenes removed from the script/film are scenes involving erotic tension or physical contact between the girls.

There are many rituals remaining in the film, in complete forms or as remnants of rituals excised from the original script. The film relies heavily on ritual and symbolic meaning, and, in fact, contains an excess of overdetermined pieces of dialogue, references, ideas, and objects that signify the girls' bonding together and rebellion against society. Of the ritualistic elements removed from the film, three are especially significant as they convey the intensity of the bond between Pammy and Nicky. Early in the script, just after they escape from the hospital, they henna and cut each other's hair (with this scene removed, their hair inexplicably changes color and length in the second reel of the film). The girls also create a journal together, called the Doomsday Book, to write their poetry and songs in (the scene where Nicky burns the book at the end of the film is still intact although all reference to the book itself has been removed). Also excised is a scene, again relatively early in the script, where Nicky "pulls up her shirt and pulls down her jeans a little to show Pamela a tiny P and an N, tattooed prison-style on her abdomen. 'I got a lot of dumb ideas. But at least I make

'em up myself,' " says Nicky.

Times Square is one of the most remarkable rock 'n' roll soundtrack movies ever made (artists include Patti Smith Group, Pretenders, Talking Heads, and Roxy Music), and the soundtrack often provides romantic commentary on the developing relationship between the girls. "You Can't Hurry Love" accompanies their escape from the hospital, and when Johnny (Tim Curry) the disc jockey learns that "you two sweethearts have a favorite song" he plays it for them. The song is dyke-rocker Suzi Quatro's "Rock Hard."

In a letter to her father, which Johnny reads over the radio, Pammy proclaims, "We are having our own Renaissance." Indeed, they create their own scavenged culture in their pastiche clothing, the decor of their squat on the pier, their poetry and music, and in their own unique brand of political activism. They decry the hypocrisy and prejudice of the establishment in a live radio performance of "Sleaze Sister Voodoo" in which they proclaim: "Spic, nigger, faggot, bum/Your daughter is one."

Patti Smith's darkly codependent dirge of obsessive love, "Pissin' in a River" signals the beginning of the end for Pammy and Nicky. In the most heart-wrenching scene of the film Nicky destroys their home, burns their journal, and throws herself into the river. She emerges sobbing, "What the fuck is wrong with me?" Distraught, she storms into Johnny's radio station, "Put me on the radio, I got somethin' to say." When Johny hesitates she smashes the control booth window, shouting, "You fuckin' little straight!" She then calls out her song to Pammy on the air: "My heart/it's pumpin'/my foot/it's runnin'/my head/it's hurtin'/it's hurtin' me./I never told you/everything/I never said the stuff I should/I was chicken to tell you/I never thought I could./ Find me/help me/save me./Can you hear me?/Can you feel me out there?/Pammy! I'm callin' you Pammy! Pammy!"

While Nicky's previous song to Pammy, "Damn Dog," had a sexy edge to it, this one is a desperate cry for help as she realizes that they must go their separate ways. Later, as Nicky prepares for her concert in Times Square, Pammy makes it clear that she loves her but says, "I can't be like you." Nicky then proclaims her love for Pammy to the adoring crowd of teenage girl fans: "She was the best friend I ever had."

Although the removal of so much material from the original script gives the film a

Ⓐ
Ⓑ
Ⓒ
Ⓓ
Ⓔ
Ⓕ
Ⓖ
Ⓗ
Ⓘ
Ⓙ
Ⓚ
Ⓛ
Ⓜ
Ⓝ
Ⓞ
Ⓟ
Ⓠ
Ⓡ
Ⓢ
Ⓣ
Ⓤ
Ⓥ
Ⓦ
Ⓧ
Ⓨ
Ⓩ

fragmented feel and sometimes sloppy continuity, the bond between the girls is always clear, and always has some proto-lesbian resonance to it. As such, *Times Square* is a marvelous experience not only for lesbian youth, but for any girl who's ever had a crush on a girl or who's wanted to see girls on film without boys in the middle. (J.O.)

Tiny & Ruby: Hell Divin' Women
Dir. Schiller, Greta
1988 USA English
40 mins. 16mm color Documentary
Dist. (U.S.): Frameline
Dist. (U.K.): British Film Institute
i coulda played with pops, basie,
the duke.
i was mighty.
the sensation of the century,
out of this world,
supreme,
stellar
it was them girls—
white, light, bright, brown, tan, and yellow.
Yes suh
that's who
i grind my axe fuh.
—Cheryl Clarke
Tiny & Ruby: Hell Divin' Women profiles the legendary jazz trumpeter Tiny Davis and her lover and partner of over 40 years, drummer Ruby Lucas (a.k.a. Renee Phelan). Billed as the "female Louis Armstrong" in the 1940s, Tiny was until recently blowing her trumpet in Chicago blues clubs. *Tiny & Ruby* weaves together music, compelling archival material, live action performances, an evocative narrative by poet Cheryl Clarke, and an informal, intimate style to pay tribute to these two extraordinary women.

Tits and Ass
Dir. Kim, Ingin
1990 USA English
1 mins. 16mm b&w Experimental
Dist. (U.S.): Kim, Ingin
A succinct reflection on sexual harassment in stop-motion animation.

To Be with You
Dir. Garcia, Martha
(Eagle Creek Youth Center)
Prod. Ma, Ming-Yuen S., and Julia Meltzer
1995 USA English
1 mins. video color Narrative
Dist. (U.S.): Hourglass Productions

Street-smart dyke romance! One young Chicana lesbian finds love and fulfillment.

To Die For (Heaven's a Drag)
Dir. Litten, Peter Mackenzie
Prod. Fitzpatrick, Gary
1994 Great Britain English
102 mins. 35mm color Narrative
Dist. (U.S.): First Run Features
A gay drag performer (Ian Williams) dies of AIDS but returns to settle some unfinished business with his butch ex-lover (Thomas Arklie) in this sweet comedy about love, commitment, and remembrance. As the film begins, Mark's health is starting to fade and handsome Simon, typical of their relationship, is doing his best to ignore reality. Practicing a different form of denial is their ditzy upstairs neighbor Siobban (Dillie Keane), who's just found politics via an incongruous affair with the well-meaning but humorless Terry (Tony Slattery)—true love is amusingly elusive for everyone in this movie.

Much to Mark's chagrin, he and Simon have an open relationship—Mark spends his last evenings working on his quilt panel while Simon hits the town. But when Mark enters the spirit world, he finds he has a lot more control over Simon's extracurricular activities than he did while alive. Mark's endless pranks finally get Simon to face some long-submerged feelings.

There's a smidge of several old favorites—most obviously *Ghost, Blithe Spirit,* and *Truly, Madly, Deeply*—in Peter Mackenzie Litten's feature, which ends with the most satisfying expression of wish fulfillment related to the consequences of AIDS since the closing scene of *Longtime Companion.*

To My Women Friends
Dir. Sharandak, Natasha
1993 Germany/Russia Russian
64 mins. video color Documentary
Dist. (U.S.): Frameline
Revealing interviews with six Russian lesbians who convey the hardships and joys of being a lesbian in Russia. While Tatjana speaks hesitantly about her sexuality, believing it to be a private matter, Muchabat charmingly flirts with the filmmaker, "We'll make the movie after we have sex, okay?" This fascinating documentary touches on a range of issues including women's prisons, transsexuality, lesbian and gay community organizing, coming out and homophobia. Under Article 121—which criminalizes homosexuality—lesbians and gay men in Kiev face the threat of

imprisonment, blackmail, government harassment, and family rejection.

To Play or Die
Dir. Krom, Frank
1991 Netherlands Dutch
50 mins. 16mm color Narrative
Dist. (U.S.): Shooting Star Film Company
Dist. (U.K.): Dangerous To Know
Frank Krom's *To Play or Die* is a powerful school-set psychodrama. Kees is an introverted lad, bullied by his handsome classmates. When his parents leave town, Kees works up the courage to invite the ringleader, Charel, to his home. His plan is to take revenge, but Charel gets the upper hand. *To Play or Die* recalls the memories of loneliness and victimization familiar to any gay teen, and turns them into an intense, enigmatic psychological thriller.

To Ride a Cow
Dir. Lee, Quentin, and Deeya Loran
1993 USA English
24 mins. video color Narrative
Dist. (U.S.): Lee, Quentin
To Ride a Cow is a salty and deeply atmospheric local about a young Asian guy who won't commit to his girlfriend or to the boy he fucks when he just wants sex.

To Wong Foo, Thanks for Everything, Julie Newmar
Dir. Kidron, Beeban
1995 USA English
108 mins. 35mm color Narrative
Dist. (U.S.): Swank Motion Pictures
To Beeban Kidron, thanks for nothing, signed, your average queer moviegoer who expects to be insulted, condescended to, ignored, or trivialized in most Hollywood fare, but who hopes for a little reprieve in a movie so blatantly, buoyantly gay-themed. Sure, the fellows are fun/funny in their finery, but the entire gag rests on how testosterone-pumped Snipes, Swayze and Leguizamo are in real life. Gag, indeed. Then there's the unrelenting "little Latin boy" digs, the misogynist gibes at the womyn-born women of dusty Snydersville (real gals are so dowdy), and the totally dull show sequences. Hey gang, we're over it. Wash your faces, and show some deference to those of us with matching X chromosomes. We wrote the book on style. (E.P.)

Toc Storee
Dir. Ma, Ming-Yuen S.
1991 USA English
21 mins. video color Documentary
Dist. (U.S.): Ma, Ming-Yuen S.
In *Toc Storee*, Ma creates a multilevel narrative in which stories from Chinese and Japanese history—as well as the contemporary experiences of three Chinese and Japanese American gay men and texts by James Baldwin and Trinh Minh-ha—are juxtaposed with each other to create an open sense of tradition and resonance.

Toe Heel Polka, The
Dir. Boyle, Brian
1992 USA English
19 mins. 16mm color Narrative
Dist. (U.S.): Boyle, Brian
Dist. (U.K.): Dangerous To Know
Learning to dance and more.

Together Alone
Dir. Castellaneta, P.J.
1991 USA English
85 mins. 16mm b&w Narrative
Dist. (U.S.): Frameline
Dist. (U.K.): British Film Institute
Two young men have gone home together for the night. Bryan and Brian. One with a "y." One with an "i." They've had an intimate encounter of unprotected sex. As the film opens, Bryan wakes from a dream and soon after, so does Brian. But Bryan calls his bedmate "Bill." This starts the first of many rifts as the two embark on an 85 minute verbal odyssey. It's one of those all-night discussions where you tell a perfect stranger things you would never tell your closest friend. They recount stories from college. Reveal inner secrets. Argue and console. It's their attempt to make sense of their lives, the world around them, their attractions to other men, AIDS, and why their socks never match when they come out of the dryer. *Together Alone* is a small yet important landmark in gay film, presenting one of the most honest, realistic, and intimate conversations between two gay men to appear on screen. With beautiful black-and-white photography by David Denchant, *Together Alone* is an impressive first feature by P.J. Castellaneta.
　　Winner of the 1995 San Francisco International Lesbian & Gay Film Festival Audience Award for Best Feature.

Token of Love
Dir. Motyl, H.D.
1993 USA English
34 mins. video color Narrative
Dist. (U.S.): Chicago Filmmakers

Ⓐ Ⓑ Ⓒ Ⓓ Ⓔ Ⓕ Ⓖ Ⓗ Ⓘ Ⓙ Ⓚ Ⓛ Ⓜ Ⓝ Ⓞ Ⓟ Ⓠ Ⓡ Ⓢ ⓣ Ⓤ Ⓥ Ⓦ Ⓧ Ⓨ Ⓩ

H.D. Motyl's *Token of Love* takes the sadly familiar scene, of a gay break-up, adds a shower scene and blends it all into an eerie Twilight Zone–style drama.

Tokyo Cowboy
Dir. Garneau, Kathy
Prod. Butler, Lodi, and Richard Davis
1994 Canada English
94 mins. 35mm color Narrative
Dist. (U.S.): Once & Future Film Inc.
No Ogawa (Hiromoto Ida) is a Tokyo burger flipper who dreams of going West and becoming a cowboy. When he loses his job at the burger joint, he decides to take a chance and heads for the wilds of Canada to look up his childhood pen-pal. Instead of finding the cowgirl of his dreams, No is greeted by Kate's meddling mother, who sees him as a prospective husband for her closeted daughter. Kate, on the other hand, wants nothing to do with her redneck roots. She has returned to her small hometown with her lover, Shelly, in an effort to reignite her creative spark, but is unable to readjust to the claustrophobic small-town life because she is unable to come out to her mother. Shelly becomes frustrated with Kate and begins to spend more time with No teaching him about the cultural quirks of the Canadian frontier. Meanwhile No falls for Shelly and casts her as a barmaid in distress in his fantasy Western in which he is her rescuing cowboy hero. Eventually No discovers the true nature of Shelly and Kate's relationship, but Kate's mother convinces him that it is only a phase. In a final attempt to win Shelly's affections, he dons a special costume for the upcoming Halloween party. Who will get the girl in the rousing genderbending finale in which the lines between No's Western fantasy and his Western reality become blurred?

Tom of Finland
Dir. Opel, Robert
1979 USA English
21 mins. video color Documentary
Dist. (U.S.): n/a
An interview with the artist.

Tom's Flesh
Dir. Wagner, Jane, and Tom di Maria
1994 USA English
15 mins. 16mm color Experimental
Dist. (U.S.): Strand Releasing
Body, self, and sexuality are dissected in Jane Wagner and Tom di Maria's jarring exploration of *Tom's Flesh*.

Tomboy!
Dir. Logsdon, Dawn
1994 USA English
13 mins. video color Documentary
Dist. (U.S.): Logsdon, Dawn
Offers childhood nostalgia with a gender twist.

Tomboychik
Dir. DuBowski, Sandy
1993 USA English
15 mins. video color Documentary
Dist. (U.S.): Video Data Bank
New Yorker Sandy DuBowski dresses up dragesque with his grandmother and comes up with a moving portrait of a Jewish woman's life and her struggle with gender and patriarchy.

Tongues Untied
Dir. Riggs, Marlon
1989 USA English
55 mins. 16mm/video color/b&w Experimental
Dist. (U.S.): Frameline
Dist. (U.K.): British Film Institute
The first time I saw Marlon Riggs's film, *Tongues Untied*, I remember being gripped and overwhelmed by conflicting emotions—I was simultaneously happy, sad, angry, thrilled, and amazed at having seen my experience as a black gay man flash before me on the theater screen. I have seen the film twice since then, and although my initial sense of wonderment has lessened, and I am now able to view it more critically, it still has the power to move me emotionally as no other film has moved me.

Visibility means survival and self-affirmation. Invisibility means that you don't exist. For black gay men there has long been a dearth of artistic material that reflects our reality. There is very little literature or art and, until recently, no film at all. *Tongues Untied* was an attempt to fill that void by giving people a glimpse into the reality of black gay men in America.

The reason I experienced such conflicting emotion when I saw *Tongues Untied* was that I hadn't realized just how starved I was for some validation and affirmation of my existence until I saw this film. Like many black gay men, I have become disillusioned and frustrated by the absence of anything black in the gay media and arts. I have searched endlessly through gay newspapers, magazines, and films and never seen myself. In desperation, I turned to the writing of black lesbians like Audre Lorde, Jewelle Gomez, and June Jordan to get any acknowledgment of my existence. Except for *In the Life*, an anthology of writing by black gay men edited by the late Joseph Beam, and the poetry of men like Essex Hemphill and Alan Miller, there really wasn't much writing by black gay men available. And film images of black gay men were, and mostly still are, negligible or nonexistent.

That's why a film like *Tongues Untied* is so important to black gay men. It affords us our first opportunity to have our existence affirmed and validated. Finally, we get a chance to see the broad spectrum of our experience and the myriad reflections of our lives, and it is an incredibly powerful encounter. It made me happy because I was finally able to see, feel, and understand that I am not the only black gay man to feel the way I do. It made me sad and angry because it opened up wounds that I thought were closed or healed and caused me to experience all over again the pain of being a black gay men in the United States. I was thrilled (as well as a little amazed) that a film about black gay men had been made and that I was actually watching it in a movie theater.

I also feel that this film is important for the gay community in general. When it comes to consciousness-raising and education about minority issues in the gay community, it usually falls to people of color to do the consciousness-raising and education. This can be very tiring for us and often leads to much resentment, anger, and frustration. This film is a great consciousness-raising experience. For anyone who has ever been curious about or tried to understand what the black gay male experience is, this film will answer many of your questions (and probably leave you with several more). It is truly an enlightening and thought-provoking experience—one that everyone should have. (K.K.)

Too Little, Too Late
Dir. Dickoff, Micki
1987 USA English
49 mins. video color Documentary
Dist. (U.S.): Fanlight Productions
This award-winning documentary is the moving story of the families of AIDS patients and how they deal with the disease and its effects on their lives: What does it feel like to be the sister of an AIDS patient and have to listen to AIDS jokes? To be unable to talk about your dying son for fear of losing your job? To have your neighbors forbid their children to play with yours because your youngest child is ill with AIDS? In *Too Little, Too Late* several families share their pain and frustra-

tion—as well as the solace they derived from having been able to help their loved ones to a peaceful death. Barbara Peabody, cofounder of MAP (Mothers of AIDS Patients), is featured.

Top Pig, The
(see *Topsau, Die*)

Top Secret
Dir. Biello/Malkasian
1985 USA English
4 mins. video color Other
Dist. (U.S.): n/a
A satirical study of communication from boardroom to boudoir.

Topsau, Die (The Top Pig)
Dir. Holdschmidt, Angela
1994 Germany German
6 mins. 35mm color Other
Dist. (U.S.): Holdschmidt, Angela
What's a Top Pig to do when she wants to slim down? You'll just have to catch Angela Holdschmidt's amazing animation piece.

Tortures That Laugh
Dir. Maybury, John
1982 Great Britain English
16 mins. 16mm color/b&w Experimental
Dist. (U.K.): Basilisk
Probably the best film ever shot and edited as Super-8 and clearly demonstrates his mastery of the medium.

Total Eclipse
Dir. Holland, Agnieszka
Prod. Ramsay, Jean-Pierre
1995 USA English
110 mins. 35mm color Narrative
Dist. (U.S.): Fine Line Features
Dist. (U.K.): Capitol Films
The meeting of the minds—and the loins—of poets Paul Verlaine and Arthur Rimbaud is about as lush a subject for a movie as can be imagined. Just how director Agnieszka Holland (*Europa, Europa*) and screenwriter Christopher Hampton (*Dangerous Liaisons*) managed to screw it up so thoroughly is a mystery on par with the big canonical inquiries of poetry itself. Let's begin with Leonardo DiCaprio: as Rimbaud, the 19th-century writer, roustabout and self-styled libertine, DiCaprio is a disaster. With his flat intonation, inescapably American veneer and pretty-boy smirk, he's more reminiscent of Keanu Reeves than of a French intellectual. Not surprisingly, the brilliant David Thewlis (*Naked*) does a decent

Ⓐ Ⓑ Ⓒ Ⓓ Ⓔ Ⓕ Ⓖ Ⓗ Ⓘ Ⓙ Ⓚ Ⓛ Ⓜ Ⓝ Ⓞ Ⓟ Ⓠ Ⓡ Ⓢ Ⓣ Ⓤ Ⓥ Ⓦ Ⓧ Ⓨ Ⓩ

Verlaine, but then, it's hardly a stretch; once again, Thewlis rants idiotically and beats up his screen counterpart (the to-die-for Romane Bohringer). As for the rebel-poets together, what *Total Eclipse* lacks in grace, motivation, and coherence it makes up for in raw carnality. The fellows rut enthusiastically, which is more than can be said for the way they converse. Lacking all psychological nuance, not to mention revelation about literature and art, the film might as well be about a couple of rival lap dancers. Oh, that's another picture. . . . (E.P.)

Totally F***ed Up
Dir. Araki, Gregg
1994 USA English
85 mins. 16mm color/b&w Narrative
Dist. (U.S.): Strand Releasing
Dist. (U.K.): ICA Projects
Think of it as Jean Luc Godard doing "Saved by the Bell," or Antonioni doing "Beverly Hills 90210." Gregg Araki's *Totally F***ed Up* is a film very grounded in the L.A. thing. Woo-woo, it's alienation galore as six homoteens bursting with angst hang around a landscape of empty parking structures, deserted car washes, swimming pools, and mind-numbing billboards to whine, kvetch and agonize about drugs, sex, dating, suicide, violence, family, identity, and homosexuality. Oh, and they get to wear really fab eyewear and neat thrift-store fashions while doing it.

Intercut with titles, clips of movies, porn, videos, and television bites, it's cynicism galore as teen romance and hormones *ucks with being young, queer, and in L.A.

You can just about hear critics yelping "MTV-Influence," "Gen-X," "New Queer Cinema." Yeah yeah yeah. There's plenty of issues in the movie that speak to a young queer person, pretty textbook case that one. *Totally F***ed Up* can function as sort of a *Catcher in the Rye* or *The Breakfast Club* for the angst-filled queer teen set. But there is a sense that the angst-filled queer teen thrust of the film is taken more seriously by nonteens; it's sort of a ethnographic film for well-adjusted 30/40-something gays and lesbians (not queer, mind you) to watch and empathize and to confirm all they ever thought about queer youth. Of course, a real cynical Gen-X queer teen would be totally cynical about this *ucker of a film, too.

In the film, one of the teens says that he hates everything that homos like: "disco music, drag, Joan Crawford, Bette Midler." Like *The Living End*, his previous flick, Araki doesn't

trade in positive uplifting Maya Angelou-esque We-Shall-Overcome gayspeak. Any "message" (and I'm sure Araki cringes at that word) that one gets from the flick is more of an emotional reckoning, of purging one's nasty bits. It's kind of like a New Age Zen Punk thing, don't question it.

But, like gay/queer cinema since the Jurassic period, there's an ample amount of hunky men oofing each other liberally on screen. *uck, if you look at cave drawings by the gay Paleolithic men, there would simply be oodles of pictures of nekkid cavemen humping each other, too.

*Totally F***ed Up* is also the kind of flick that just drives those folks from the Gay Asian Pacific Alliance absolutely mad. Here's a flick from a gay Asian who's gotten a high hip-glam quotient (which seems to be quite important to them), and yet, Araki doesn't kowtow to the eternal tenet of gay Asian values, you know, strong positive stereotype-crushing Asian role model with good hair and pectoral muscles. This is not your Made-for-Rice-Queens wet (d)ream movie, either.

Liking the film or hating it will depend largely on whether you can stand the teenage characters portrayed and whether you think the dialogue is polemical, heartfelt, vital, or annoyingly whiny. *Totally F***ed Up* is one of those independent movies that is worth watching simply for the experience of it and also to see and support a young talented filmmaker as he develops a body of work that is essential to American culture.

But like it or hate it, you get a sense that the filmmaker doesn't really give a *uck. (J.C.)

Touch Me
Dir. Slater, John
1991 USA English
2 mins. video color Experimental
Dist. (U.S.): Slater, John
Touch Me is a smart scratch dub of some recent TV footage, which gets right to the nub of what men are afraid of.

Touchables, The
Dir. Freeman, Robert
1968 Great Britain English
97 mins. 35mm color Narrative
Dist. (U.S.): n/a
Keep an eye on late-night TV listings for this incredible relic from '60s Swinging London, in which four gorgeous, anarchic female model

types kidnap a pretty-boy pop star. They take him to their giant inflated plastic bubble-dome in the countryside, where go-go dancing, sex games, and torture are on the agenda. Meanwhile, gangsters pursue the M.I.A. group—most notably a muscle-bound black wrestler (dubbed Lilly White) who makes no bones about his own erotic interest in said boy pop-tart. It's all crazy with mod fashions, psychedelia, narrative illogic, and homoerotic atmosphere (so much so that a *Newsweek* review of the era sarcastically "reviewed" the film via an imaginary letter between "pansy" housemates. Har, har). (D.H.)

Tough Love, Smart Weapons
Dir. Love, Tony, and Joe Westmoreland
1993 USA English
9 mins. video color Narrative
Dist. (U.S.): Westmoreland, Joe
Bloodifies the revenge of a gay-bashing victim, and features a microcameo by RuPaul.

Toumanaka's Cave
Dir. Mongovia, Jack
1982 USA English
3 mins. 16mm color Other
Dist. (U.S.): n/a
Elaborately detailed, colorful, and humorous animation.

Tourist
Dir. Hammer, Barbara
1985 USA English
4 mins. 16mm color/b&w Experimental
Dist. (U.S.): Canyon Cinema
"The slide of the image into politics finds concrete expression in the film Tourist as the word 'spectacle' nestles in the Hollywood Hills like an Edward Ruscha painting. Psychic desires of 'tourists' permeate the architecture of seeing. The fleeting spectacle is a series of imaginative possessions, a conquest through the gaze accented by the shots fired on the video arcade game soundtrack. The tourist 'look' is as ephemeral as the animation of the collage suggesting a miniaturizing and glazing of the grandiose wonders of the world." —Kathleen Hulser, Centre Pompidou Released by Facets Multimedia in the U.S. along with five of her other short films as a feature-length package, *Optical Nerves: The Films of Barbara Hammer, Volume IV.*

Toys: Basic Technologies of Devotion
Dir. Seawright, Hilton
1994 Brazil Portugese
1 mins. video color Other

Dist. (U.S.): MIX Brasil
A short, short from Brazil's dynamic MIXBrasil program.

Tracce di Chlodo sul Muro (Tracks of Nail on the Wall)
Dir. Marzi, Gianpaolo
1994 Italy Italian
4 mins. 16mm color Narrative
Dist. (U.S.): Marzi, Gianpaolo
The crown of Davide grows until the roots. A lonely transvestite, an old mother, a fat singer, a beautiful stranger. Story of love and of "homemaking" solitudes.

Trans
Dir. Constantinou, Sophie
1994 USA English
12 mins. 16mm color Documentary
Dist. (U.S.): Constantinou, Sophie
Interviews female-to-male transsexual, Henry.

Transeltown
Dir. Paci, Myra
1992 USA English
23 mins. 16mm color Narrative
Dist. (U.S.): Paci, Myra
Myra Paci's *Transeltown* is a morbid and strangely tender tale of love in the tradition of David Lynch; it is simultaneously repulsive and seductive—like a lesbian *Eraserhead.*

Transportations
Dir. Wallis, Amanda
1990 Australia English
12 mins. 16mm b&w Experimental
Dist. (U.S.): Women Make Movies
A contemplation of lesbian desire in the bedroom and beyond.

Tras el Cristal (In a Glass Cage)
Dir. Villaronga, Agustin
Prod. Enrich, Teresa
1985 Spain Spanish
100 mins. 35mm color Narrative
Dist. (U.S.): Cinevista
Klaus, a doctor who has been instructed to carry out experiments on deported children towards the end of the Second World War, feels compelled to leave the country with his wife and daughter. But subconsciously he harbors the latent desire to perform the atrocious, murderous experiments, an impulse against which he wages a desperate war in his remote refuge near the cliffs. A few years later he has an accident that results in his being confined to an iron lung so that he can still

Ⓐ
Ⓑ
Ⓒ
Ⓓ
Ⓔ
Ⓕ
Ⓖ
Ⓗ
Ⓘ
Ⓙ
Ⓚ
Ⓛ
Ⓜ
Ⓝ
Ⓞ
Ⓟ
Ⓠ
Ⓡ
Ⓢ
🅣
Ⓤ
Ⓥ
Ⓦ
Ⓧ
Ⓨ
Ⓩ

breathe. One day a young man, Angelo, turns up to visit Klaus. It becomes clear that he knows about Klaus's inclinations, knowledge which enables him to needle and blackmail him. Gradually Angelo assumes Klaus's personality, and a curious friendship evolves. And there develops an even stranger relationship between Angelo and his victim's daughter, Rena. This unusual constellation reaches a point where the three involved are caught up in a battle of life and death. Powerful and deeply disturbing, this is a film that will provoke misunderstanding. Yet it should not. This brilliant debut by Catalan director Agustin Villaronga is an intense exploration of the relationships between power, masculinity, and sexuality. The cinematography is faultless, and the acting of David Sust (the nurse), Gunther Meisner (the doctor) and Marisa Paredes (his wife) is superb. Paredes appears in Pedro Almodovar's *Sisters of Darkness*, also screening at the festival.

Tread Softly
Dir. Drew, Di
1980 Australia English
27 mins. 35mm color Narrative
Dist. (U.S.): n/a
A love story of beauty and pain. "If only she'd given more time, a little attention . . . but you can't change people to what you want them to be. It's not love anymore, it's an obsession—tread softly."

Trevor
Dir. Rajski, Peggy
Prod. Rajski, Peggy, and Randy Stone
1995 USA English
18 mins. 35mm color Narrative
Dist. (U.S.): Rajski, Peggy
Diana Ross–obsessed 13-year-old Trevor plunges into despair when everyone in town discovers his crush on hunky basketball playing pal Pinky. This sweet short film is a tender and often hilarious rendering of gay adolescent angst.

Winner of the 1995 San Francisco International Lesbian & Gay Film Festival Audience Award for Best Short Film.

Triangle
Dir. Doucette, Robert
1989 USA English
6 mins. 16mm color Other
Dist. (U.S.): Chicago Filmmakers
Triangle is this year's only animated entry: a sad, sweeping story set against bohemian Berlin and the rise of Nazi power.

Triche, La
Dir. Bellon, Yannick
Prod. Petitdidier, Denise
1984 France French
101 mins. 16mm color Narrative
Dist. (U.S.): FACSEA
La Triche was screened at the NY Gay and Lesbian Film Festival, and impressed the *Village Voice* reviewer, who found it " a turn-on from beginning to end . . . Seldom have I seen an eye more knowing about sexual yearning, the ache, that can cramp existence for months, years." *La Triche* is about the relationship between Michel, a cultured but disillusioned police inspector, and Bernard, a young nightclub musician. Michel (the handsome cousin in *Cousin, Cousine*) has a wife and young son. He has also always been bisexual, and had many one-night stands. He meets Bernard during an investigation, and the two experience a violent mutual attraction. The affair becomes a relationship, then gets complicated when the case under investigation adds a blackmail attempt and murder. Bernard is implicated, and Michel is placed in a dangerous and awkward position. No longer primarily Bernard's lover, Michel must confront him, and is met with defiance. Throughout the film, the men's relationship is played out, sexual nuances and tension included, against the increasingly opposed roles of cop and suspect. A subtle film by writer/director Yannick Bellon, 64, who directs short films for screen and TV and has two other features to her credit.

Tricia's Wedding
Dir. Lester, Mark
1971 USA English
35 mins. 16mm color Narrative
Dist. (U.S.): Sebastian
Tricia's Wedding stars the Cockettes in their first film. Founded on New Year's Eve, 1969, the Cockettes combined a Haight-Ashbury counter-culture lifestyle with the new gender politics of Gay Liberation. Their mix of nudity, gay humor, and genderfuck drag assured them instant success in San Francisco. *Tricia's Wedding* is a thrillingly vicious satire of Patricia Nixon's wedding party; watch for the great scene with Mamie Eisenhower.

Trick or Treat
Dir. Jackson, Liz
1994 Great Britain English
30 mins. video color Documentary
Dist. (U.K.): BBC TV

For the last seven years John Bratherton, a Cambridge graduate in philosophy, has chosen to make his living through sex. While not wanting to deny the desperate circumstances under which many young men turn to prostitution, John states in no uncertain terms that his choice of profession is one made completely free of compulsion.

Tricycle Race
Dir. McClain, Allen
1977 USA English
3 mins. S8mm color Documentary
Dist. (U.S.): n/a
This year's positive image. Footage of the 1977 Tricycle Race from bar to bar, sponsored by the San Francisco's Tavern Guild.

Trojans
Dir. Giannaris, Constantine
1990 Great Britain English
33 mins. 16mm b&w Experimental
Dist. (U.K.): Giannaris, Constantine
Trojans is an exotic interpretation of the life and work of Konstantin Kavafy, the 19th-century Alexandrian poet. His work imaginatively combined motifs from Greek history with homoeroticism; filmmaker Constantine Giannaris restores Kavafy's context with his own fantastically sensual style.

Trouble in Paradise
Dir. Ford, Philip R.
1983 USA English
6 mins. S8mm color
Dist. (U.S.): n/a
Part of the 1983 Super-8 Gay Festival.

True Blue
Dir. Brownsey, Maureen
1992 USA English
7 mins. 16mm color Narrative
Dist. (U.S.): Chicago Filmmakers
A comedy about a lesbian, a pregnancy test, and a regrettable one-night stand.

Truth About Alex, The
Dir. Shapiro, Paul
1987 Canada English
48 mins. video color Narrative
Dist. (U.S.): Scholastic Productions, Inc.
Brad Stevens and Alex Prager are best friends. They are both popular high school students and key members of the football team. Brad is up for nomination to West Point, and Alex is a talented pianist who's counting on his football skills to land him a university scholarship. But their lives are turned upside down one day when Alex admits that he's gay. *The Truth About Alex* is a sensitive portrayal of how two boys' sense of decency, loyalty, and self-respect overcomes the prejudices and petty fears of the people around them.

Truth Game, The
Dir. Cole, Jeff
1990 Great Britain English
16 mins. 16mm color Narrative
Dist. (U.S.): Chicago Filmmakers
Dist. (U.K.): Cole, Jeff
Paul, 18, is gay and wants to tell his father. They go on holiday together and with the aid of a video camera play the truth game. Observing the tensions between a gay father and son, the film surveys the "forbidden space" between love and the erotic.

Truth or Dare
(see *Du Darst*)

Try to Remember
Dir. Hanszelmann, Stefan Christian
1984 Denmark Danish
17 mins. 16mm color Experimental
Dist. (U.S.): Danish Film Institute
Try to Remember is an almost wordless short about an athlete's fascination for his own past.

Turnabout
Dir. Bessie, Dan
1993 USA English
60 mins. 16mm color Documentary
Dist. (U.S.): Filmmaker's Library
They're entertainers, they're 92 years old, and they're gay. *Turnabout* is the amazing story of the Yale puppeteers—Harry Burnett, his cousin Forman Brown, and Brown's lover Roddy Brandon—who traveled through America for more than 70 years with their unique puppets and satirical songs.
     Dan Bessie's gorgeously nostalgic film journeys back to their novelty cabaret theater in Hollywood, where their puppets entertained stars like Helen Hayes and Liberace. *Turnabout* also reveals Forman Brown as the author of one of America's first serious gay novels, *Better Angel* (written under the pseudonym of Richard Meeker). Bessie's film is a classic example of documentary and historical research at its best; it's a joyful, entertaining 60 minutes for anyone interested in theater, old people, or little known aspects of the gay experience.

TV In Africa

Ⓐ
Ⓑ
Ⓒ
Ⓓ
Ⓔ
Ⓕ
Ⓖ
Ⓗ
Ⓘ
Ⓙ
Ⓚ
Ⓛ
Ⓜ
Ⓝ
Ⓞ
Ⓟ
Ⓠ
Ⓡ
Ⓢ
Ⓣ
Ⓤ
Ⓥ
Ⓦ
Ⓧ
Ⓨ
Ⓩ

Dir. Justice, Roger
1980 USA English
10 mins. S8mm Experimental
Dist. (U.S.): n/a
Parts One, Two, Three, and Four of the "Study of Motion" done in the film—translating both "TV In Africa" and "Study of Motion" into the film, *TV In Africa*.

21st Century Nuns
Dir. Stephan, Tom
1993 Great Britain English
15 mins. 16mm b&w Documentary
Dist. (U.K.): London International Film School
England's branch of The Sisters of Perpetual Indulgence is profiled.

25 Year Old Man Loses His Virginity to a Woman, A
Dir. Roth, Phillip B.
1990 USA English
22 mins. video color Documentary
Dist. (U.S.): Roth, Phillip B.
Philip B. Roth explores his latent heterosexuality with the knowledgeable assistance of Annie Sprinkle. A pro sex show-and-tell.

24 Hours a Day
Dir. Taylor, Jocelyn
1993 USA English
9 mins. video color Other
Dist. (U.S.): Taylor, Jocelyn
Two black dykes have a very neighborly phone sex encounter.

29 Effeminate Gestures
Dir. Boxwell, Tim
1989 USA English
8 mins. video color Other
Dist. (U.S.): Alive From Off Center
In *29 Effeminate Gestures*, performance artist/choreographer Joe Goode portrays an auto repairman who tunes up the more feminine side of his nature.

Twenty-Two
Dir. Bernard, Gene
1993 USA English
10 mins. 16mm color Narrative
Dist. (U.S.): Bermard, Gene
Dist. (U.K.): Dangerous To Know
People who you might never want as guests at any party.

Twice a Woman
Dir. Sluizer, George

1979 Netherlands Dutch
115 mins. 35mm color Narrative
Dist. (U.S.): Netherlands Ministry of Culture
One of only a handful of feature films about lesbians, this 1979 Dutch production has the traditional, obligatory "tragic ending"; however, it delights us with sensuous photography, a well-drawn lesbian character, and a minimum of ridiculous lines. True, it is a story of white, upper-class art and theater devotees who are enticed by the nether world of youth, seduction, fecundity, lesbianism, and the lower classes; it still manages to feed our hunger for some decent and positively portrayed lesbian sensuality and sexuality along the way. Bibi Andersson is marvelous as forty-year-old Laura—a museum curator, divorced from Anthony Perkins. She purposefuly and quite out of character (unless we consider the contradictions of our own lives) picks up young (we are never sure how young) Sylvia on the street in downtown Amsterdam. Sandra Dumas as Sylvia is a blaze of sexuality who dispenses with social niceties within her first three lines by suggesting to Andersson that they go to bed. Prepare to hold your breath with anticipation in the ensuing scene which is cut too soon.

There are some tasty surprises of irony, but alas, it cannot last. Perkins enters with his villainous scowl à la *Psycho* and shoots pregnant Sylvia with his big gun because obviously he could not keep her with his little one. Fortunately, this occurs in the last ten minutes—so relax, and enjoy till then. Director Sluizer signals to the Hitchcock cultists in the audience with two stuffed birds on the mantle in the final shot.

Twin Bracelets, The
Dir. Huang, Yu-Shan
1990 Hong Kong Mandarin
100 mins. 35mm color Narrative
Dist. (U.S.): Rim Film Distributors
The Twin Bracelets is like a lesbian version of *Raise the Red Lantern*. The incredible twist is that it takes place in the '80s. Hui-hua (Chen Te Jung) is a bright-eyed rebellious teenager of a Chinese minority tribe, growing up in a fishing village where people have no concept of human rights, women's liberation, lesbian love, or even divorce. Women are purchased as brides, and wives are only allowed to see their husbands three times a year if they cannot bear children. While our heroine is confronted with the daily oppression of the ancient traditions, she seeks love and escape in the arms of her childhood buddy, Hsiu (Liu Hsiao Hui). The beautiful

details of the Chinese minority village life and the atmospheric cinematography are truly a feast for the eye.

A remarkable film, written and directed by women, *The Twin Bracelets* is a deeply moving and tragic portrayal of one woman's struggle for independence and for the love of another woman. Desperately in love with Hsiu, Hui-hua flirts shamelessly with her, is intensely jealous of Hsiu's arranged marriage, and feigns injury to keep her near. When Hui-hua successfully escapes her arranged marriage, she pleads with Hsiu to fulfill their childhood vow, "to be sister man and wife; to live together and die together." In a sad and tender conclusion, Hui-hua releases Hsiu from her vow and their twin bracelets are separated.

Winner of the 1992 San Francisco International Lesbian & Gay Film Festival Audience Award for Best Feature.

Twin Cheeks:
Who Killed the Homecoming King?
Dir. Wild, Osker
Prod. Nice Guy Studio
1995 USA English
6 mins. video color Narrative
Dist. (U.S.): Wild, Osker
A sexually explicit gay version of "Twin Peaks."

Twinkle
Dir. Matusoka, George
1992 Japan Japanese
103 mins. 35mm color Narrative
Dist. (U.S.): Herald Ace
Shoko (Hiroko Yakushimaru), a translator with a drinking problem, and Matsuki (Etsushi Toyokawa), a handsome gay doctor, decide to come together in a marriage of convenience to satisfy their parents. All semblance of normalcy breaks down when Matsuki's student boyfriend becomes jealous, Shoko decides she wants a baby, and her parents find out about their son-in-law's homosexuality. ("Being married to him must be like trying to eat soup with a fork," says Shoko's dad, mystified.)

Twinkle is one of three Asian films in this year's festival that uses the springboard of an arranged marriage for its subsequent drama. If *Okoge* is the most earthy, and *The Wedding Banquet* is the most glossy, then *Twinkle* is like a Japanese twist on a French sex comedy-drama. It has a breezy stride, as well as a classy, upscale setting and a keen sense of visual humor. It's also a delicate, refreshing, and funny film about honesty and friendship.

Two Bad Daughters
Dir. Hammer, Barbara, and Paula Levine
1988 USA English
8 mins. video color Experimental
Dist. (U.S.): Frameline
Two Bad Daughters posits play as subversive activity, a sabotage of the patriarchal institutions of psychoanalysis and sadomasochism through video image processing, changing the subject/object relationship in psychoanalysis, and interrupting and reconstructing the paraphernalia of S/M sexual practice.

Released by Frameline in the U.S. as part of a package of four of her short videos entitled *Barbara Hammer Program #2*.

Two Georges, The (Dos Jorges, Los)
Dir. Nazario, Nelson
1993 USA Spanish
11 mins. video color Narrative
Dist. (U.S.): Appel, Lynn
Nelson Nazario's charming lesbian reworking of *Dona Flor and Her Two Husbands*.

Two In Twenty
Prod. Chiten, Laurel, Cheryl Qamar, and Rachel McCollum
1987 USA English
52 mins. video color Narrative
Dist. (U.S.): Wolfe Video
Two In Twenty introduces the melodramatic adventures of a typical group of lesbians in a typical American town . . .

Two Men and a Baby
Dir. Mohammed, Juanita
1993 USA English
10 mins. video color Documentary
Dist. (U.S.): Gay Men's Health Crisis
A spirited and sweet snapshot of two gay African Americans, their HIV positive child, and "three beautiful gay godfathers."

Two of Us
Dir. Tonge, Roger
1986 Great Britain English
60 mins. video color Narrative
Dist. (U.K.): BBC TV
In most instances of banned or censored TV tales, the outcry is often more imaginative than the acutal film. *Two of Us* is a rare rule-breaker; an atypical tale of working-class teens who cross the fine line from friendship to sex, it's both austere and sensual. Filmed in 1986 as part of a

Ⓐ Ⓑ Ⓒ Ⓓ Ⓔ Ⓕ Ⓖ Ⓗ Ⓘ Ⓙ Ⓚ Ⓛ Ⓜ Ⓝ Ⓞ Ⓟ Ⓠ Ⓡ Ⓢ ❶ Ⓤ Ⓥ Ⓦ Ⓧ Ⓨ Ⓩ

BBC school series, with transmission postponed in the light of Thatcherite concern over sex education, and then delayed further during the drawing up of Section 28, Britain's legislation which forbids local councils from "promoting homosexuality," *Two of Us* was finally aired on public TV in March 1988 at an unusually late hour, with two scenes abridged—the end (which suggests that Phil returns to Mathew) and an earlier embrace (amended by adding T-shirts and erasing a quick kiss). Fortunately, this special festival version will include the T-shirts off and the kiss in.

Two or Three Things I Know About Them
Dir. Mak, Anson
1991 Hong Kong Cantonese
39 mins. video color Experimental
Dist. (U.S.): Mak, Anson
An experimental four-part video that deals with the issues and concerns of an emerging lesbian community in Hong Kong. Reference is also made to Cantonese opera star Yum Kim-Fai, a lesbian who performs in male drag.

Two Quickies
Dir. Boyd, Amy, and Karla Carmony
1994 USA English
6 mins. video color Other
Dist. (U.S.): This Side of Butch
The sequel to a popular lesbian movie, and a rendering of "Green Acres" San Francisco–style.

Two Spirit People
**Dir. Levy, Lori, Gretchen Vogel,
and Michel Beauchemin**
1991 USA English
20 mins. video color Documentary
Dist. (U.S.): Frameline
Two Spirit People gives an overview of historical and contemporary Native American concepts of gender, sexuality, and sexual orientation.

Two Spirits
Dir. de la Riva, T. Osa Hidalgo
1993 USA English
27 mins. video color Documentary
Dist. (U.S.): de la Riva, T. Osa Hidalgo
Lesbian and gay Native Americans reflect on identity, gender, culture, and race.

Uh-Oh!
Dir. Zando, Julie
1994 USA English
38 mins. video color Experimental
Dist. (U.S.): Drift Distribution

A seductive rereading of Pauline Réage's *Story of O*. A man and woman narrate O's evolving relationship with Rene (played by New York lesbian poet Eileen Myles). O's submission is seen very differently than it is heard. The voice-over refers to a "he" and a "she," but the images depict O being whipped and chained by women in cowboy drag.

Undecided
Dir. Ehorn, Scott
1994 USA English
4 mins. 16mm color Other
Dist. (U.S.): Ehorn, Scott
Another wonderful found-footage montage from Scott Ehorn.

Under Heat
Dir. Reed, Peter
1994 USA English
90 mins. 35mm color Narrative
Dist. (U.S.): Furious Films
Peter Reed's steamy contemporary drama about the reunion of two brothers (hunky Eric Swanson and Robert Kneeper) with their mother (the redoubtable Lee Grant) is reminiscent of (and possibly an homage to) all those live television dramas and Broadway plays of the '50s and '60s. You know the ones—about generational conflicts and repressed passions in the Midwest and South, usually of a heterosexual nature—but this time the gay subtexts and sensibilities that were off-stage, off-screen and between the lines are squarely, unapologetically in your face.

In *Under Heat*, 36-year-old Dean (Swanson) comes to tell his family he has AIDS, but this is overshadowed by the neediness of his mother and older brother (not to mention the boy who cuts the grass, a Calvin Klein wet dream). In an effort to reconcile past and present issues—which include health, addiction, sexuality, and the father's suicide many years before—these characters begin a journey wherein they reveal themselves to each other. Ultimately, Dean's perspective on his own crisis evolves to the realization that death is the inescapable destiny each individual must face.

With the inevitability of Greek tragedy, but sprinkled with dollops of wit and slathered with some very ripe melodrama, *Under Heat* traces an arc extending roughly from Eugene O'Neill to William Binge, with nods to Tennessee Williams, Edward Albee, and Horton Foote, among others. Affording Lee Grant her biggest screen role in quite a spell, this is juicy fun indeed.

Undercover Me!
Dir. Rubnitz, Tom
1988 USA English
2 mins. video color Other
Dist. (U.S.): Video Data Bank
John Sex, international spy. Part of the *Tom Rubnitz Marathon (A Dozen Tapes, Wigs Included)*.

Unity
Dir. Huestis, Marc
1978 USA English
15 mins. 16mm color Narrative
Dist. (U.S.): Outsider Enterprises
Huestis's 1978 prize-winning short Unity was made in response to the Briggs attack on gays. Unity relates the story of a love affair between two men in the face of violent retribution form the Nazis.

Untitled
Dir. Boyle, Bernie
1977 USA English
6 mins. S8mm color Other
Dist. (U.S.): n/a
Some footage from two years ago, some from last week. Self-consciously gay, and crude in more ways than one.

Untitled
Dir. Kossoff, Leslie
1987 USA English
3 mins. S8mm color Experimental
Dist. (U.S.): n/a
Leslie Kossoff fashions a dizzying, hallucinatory self-portrait in *Untitled*.

Untitled
Dir. Larry
1977 USA English
25 mins. S8mm color Experimental
Dist. (U.S.): n/a
A gay hippie aesthetic montage.

Untitled
Dir. Latty, Yvonne
1984 USA English
2 mins. video color Other
Dist. (U.S.): n/a
Vague, but insightful. Reminiscent, yet detached.

. . . (Untitled)
Dir. Nicoletta, Daniel
1973 USA English
8 mins. S8mm color/b&w Experimental
Dist. (U.S.): Nicoletta, Daniel
Many, many years ago a professor found himself on a marvelous journey into the unknown, and never returned. Many years later a young girl from the Midwest followed . . . A colorized, pixelized version of *The Wizard of Oz*.

Untitled
Dir. Sanborn, John, and Mary Perillo
1989 USA English
10 mins. video color Other
Dist. (U.S.): Alive From Off Center
In *Untitled*, Bill T. Jones creates a tribute to his partner Arnie Zane, who died of AIDS in 1988.

Unzipped
Dir. Keeve, Douglas
1995 USA English
93 mins. 35mm color/b&w Documentary
Dist. (U.S.): Swank Motion Pictures
It's hard not to flip for fashion designer Isaac Mizrahi when he pauses mid-stroll, to toss his hat skyward—he's prettier than, and every bit as spunky as, Mary Tyler Moore. The moment occurs in *Unzipped*, Douglas Keeve's savvy portrait of his ex-squeexe Mizrahi, a showman touched by equal parts frenzy, eccentricity, and genius. He captures the curly headed boy-wonder as he rants, cajoles, vamps, and takes inspiration from *Nanook of the North*, Eartha Kitt, and much more. Of course, the film would not be complete without glimpses of Cindy, Kate, Naomi, et al., here shown primping for Mizrahi's 1994 New York show, a gloriuos affair that punctuates the movie with rousing good cheer and just a hint of the absurd. The cult of supermodel is fast becoming tedious, but Keeve's angle is sardonic, sweet, lighter than air. (E.P.)

Up In Arms Over Needle Exchange
Dir. Carlomusto, Jean, and Hilary Joy Kipnis
1988 USA English
28 mins. video color Documentary
Dist. (U.S.): Gay Men's Health Crisis
"For the first quarter (of 1988), the number of cases reported among intraveneous drug users is greater than the number of cases reported among gay men . . . it is a snapshot of two, three, five years ago . . . we know what's coming."
—Dr. Stephen Joseph,
New York City Health Commissioner.
Up In Arms Over Needle Exchange examines the controversy that surrounds the implementation of a needle exchange program to stem the spread of AIDS in New York City.

Ⓐ Ⓑ Ⓒ Ⓓ Ⓔ Ⓕ Ⓖ Ⓗ Ⓘ Ⓙ Ⓚ Ⓛ Ⓜ Ⓝ Ⓞ Ⓟ Ⓠ Ⓡ Ⓢ Ⓣ Ⓤ Ⓥ Ⓦ Ⓧ Ⓨ Ⓩ

Urinal

Dir. Greyson, John

1988 Canada English

100 mins. 16mm color Experimental

Dist. (U.S.): Frameline

Curiously transported to the present day, a group of dead lesbian and gay artists, including Sergei Eisenstein, Frida Kahlo, Langston Hughes, and Yukio Mishima, find themselves guests in the home of Toronto sculptors Frances Loring and Florence Wyle. They have been mysteriously summoned to Ontario to research the systematic policing of public washroom sex. These artists of wildly differing temperaments embark upon their research with flamboyance and aplomb, examining not only the subject at hand, but their own sexual identities. Each night, one of the six—joined by Wilde man Dorian Gray—delivers a riotous lecture on some aspect of the issue. Toronto artist Greyson's audacious film, which could be subtitled *If Only Heads Could Talk*, makes a shambles of filmic expectations. The lectures themselves—"A Social History of the Public Washroom" one night, "Washroom Sex Texts," the next—are mini-parodies, taking some facet of film discourse and knocking it off kilter. But in Urinal, the formal is firmly embraced by a fiery brand of political urgency. With an irreverence for historical propriety and a story structure that doesn't discriminate between burlesque, surrealist tableaux, and bitter fact, Greyson employs a mad pastiche to confound straight narrative, as he seeks a solution to gay harassment.

V Is for Violet

Dir. Verow, Todd

1989 USA English

15 mins. video color Experimental

Dist. (U.S.): Strand Releasing

V Is for Violet tunes in and out of the tale of two teens: a young faux-naïf hustler ("People are so friendly and nice—they just come up to you and give you money") and an actress named Violet who may be the same person. *V Is for Violet* cuts like a chain saw through their decades of debauchery in the same hotel room; it's catty, tongue-in-cheek, and makes a backdrop out of cute guys in white jockey shorts.

Vacancy

Dir. Katsapetses, Nicholas

1994 USA English

14 mins. 16mm color Narrative

Dist. (U.S.): Katsapetses, Nicholas

A Gus Van Sant–style short about the comic difficulties of forming long-term relationships in a small town like San Francisco.

Vanilla Sex

Dir. Dunye, Cheryl

1992 USA English

4 mins. video b&w Experimental

Dist. (U.S.): Video Data Bank

A video dealing with interracial relationships. Part of *Those Fluttering Objects of Desire*, released in the U.S. on a twenty-minute compilation with *Brown Sugar Licks Snow White, What's the Difference Between a Yam and a Sweet Potato?* and *I've Never*.

Vehlefanz

Dir. Kunja, Alexander

1992 Germany German

15 mins. 16mm color Narrative

Dist. (U.S.): Kunja, Alexander

Two young men in a small town find each other and the courage to show their love.

Venner for Altid (Friends Forever)

Dir. Henszelman, Stefan

1986 Denmark Danish

95 mins. 35mm color Narrative

Dist. (U.S.): Danish Film Institute

Friends Forever is a charming, exuberant drama about friendship and sexuality between three sixteen-year-old schoolboys; it's sexy, funny, and guiltless—a glimpse of popular gay cinema at its best.

Together with his mother, sixteen-year-old Kristian has moved to a new neighborhood, and he is about to start in a new school. Feeling insecure in his new surroundings, Kristian for this reason is drawn to two very different pupils he meets at school. One of them is Henrik, an independent boy who refuses to yield to group pressure, and the other is Patrick, who is the leader of a dominating and tyrannical gang. Kristian's desire for popularity and acceptance is so great that he eventually becomes part of Patrick's clique. When the gang's activities become too violent and criminal, Patrick and Kristian break away.

Kristian sees his growing friendship with Patrick as an experiment, a chance to become more independent and decisive. The friendship is soon put to the test when Kristian discovers that Patrick is gay and is sexually involved with the captain of a soccer team. While trying to accept his best friend's homosexuality, Kristian is also exploring his sexuality, first with a girl of his own age, and more seriously with an older woman, a Swedish soul singer called Ayoe. At school, Patrick and Kristian clash with the headmaster, who merely pays lip service to democracy and in fact prevents the pupils from having a say in anything. But when Kristian, together with his classmate Annette kindle the first sparks of revolt against the authorities, he begins to look beyond himself and realizes that there are more important things in life than his own small world.

Friends Forever is a film about the youth of the '80s. But it is more than just a young people's film, because it is about daring to look at the world with our own eyes, instead of looking as we are taught to see.

Winner of the 1988 San Francisco International Lesbian & Gay Film Festival Audience Award for Best Feature.

Vera
Dir. Toledo, Sergio
1986 Brazil Portugese
87 mins. 16mm/35mm color Narrative
Dist. (U.S.): Kino International
Vera is the story of a young woman who is convinced that she is a man. Vera does not identify herself as a lesbian (she believes she is a man in a woman's body). The film addresses issues of particular importance to f-to-m's—but also to butch lesbians—especially in relation to gender identification, transgender relationships, and internalized misogyny.

Vera grows up in an orphanage, and on being released when she is 18, takes a job at a research center where she meets Clara, with whom she falls in love. Vera's insistence that she is a man becomes gradually problematic in their relationship, leading up to a painfully intimate love scene where she refuses to remove her undershirt. The relationship between Clara and Vera is seriously jeopardized as they both struggle with Vera's gender dysphoria. An ambiguous ending (open to two very different interpretations) posits a disturbing fate for Vera. The film employs a very fluid flashback structure to show parts of Vera's life in the orphanage; although at times hard to follow, this fluidity gives a layer of surrealism to the film that contributes to its truly unique cinematic atmosphere.

"Toledo's Vera is one of the most intriguing portraits of gender construction—and deconstruction—yet seen on the screen."
—B. Ruby Rich, Village Voice

Verfuhrung: Die Grausame Frau

(Seduction: The Cruel Woman)
Dir. Mikesch, Elfi, and Monika Treut
1985 Germany German
85 mins. 35mm color Narrative
Dist. (U.S.): First Run Features
Dist. (U.K.): Dangerous To Know
Wanda, a mysterious dominatrix, opens a gallery of S/M erotica. Being cruel is her profession while inventing traps is her specialty. Justine, the innocent American, has to learn that passion is just another illusion. Mr. Mährsch, a journalist, is granted an interview only after having practical experience. Only Caren, an eccentric business-woman—and Wanda's lover—thinks she knows what life is all about. The film presents the world of masochistic lust as a performance of hidden desires. The rules are extremely severe and the game extremely cruel, but the participants know what they've agreed to. Both male and female characters function as archetypes in this closed universe that exists beyond psychosocial reality. Ironically, the images are highly stylized and rather harmless. This aesthetic distancing is compensated for by the point of view the camera takes, engaging and seducing us into a masochistic position. A position we share with the characters in the film.

Starring Mechtild Grossman, Udo Kier, Sheila McLaughlin, and Carola Regnier

Veronica Four Rose
Dir. Chait, Melanie
1983 Great Britain English
48 mins. 16mm color Documentary
Dist. (U.K.): Cinenova
A documentary about lesbians 16 to 23 years old. Aimed at straight society, Veronica Four Rose presents these women as they talk about being young and lesbian in a heterosexual world.

Version de Marcial, La
(Marcial's Version)
Dir. Bohm, Daniel
1990 Argentina Spanish
14 mins. 16mm/video b&w Narrative
Dist. (U.S.): Bohm, Daniel
Love, money, and betrayal are the elements of this seductive film noir.

Very Funny
Dir. Zachary, Bohdan
1994 USA English
16 mins. video color Other
Dist. (U.S.): Zachary, Bohdan
A spoof set behind the scenes at a comedy competition.

Ⓐ Ⓑ Ⓒ Ⓓ Ⓔ Ⓕ Ⓖ Ⓗ Ⓘ Ⓙ Ⓚ Ⓛ Ⓜ Ⓝ Ⓞ Ⓟ Ⓠ Ⓡ Ⓢ Ⓣ Ⓤ Ⓥ Ⓦ Ⓧ Ⓨ Ⓩ

Verzaubert (Enchanted)
Dir. Fockele, Jorg, Dirk Hauska, et. al.
1993 Germany German
89 mins. 16mm color Documentary
Dist. (U.S.): HFF Munchen
Edith was visited by the vice squad because she had a photo of her and another woman in swimsuits. Rudolf was found having fun with another boy and was immediately banished to a school in the north of England. Kathe was sent to a hypnotherapist by her parents. Wally was raped and sent to a home for problem children, where she was threatened with sterilization. This is life in Hamburg, Germany, during the '40s and '50s as told by the thirteen men and women interviewees in *Enchanted*. Looking back on a forgotten period in German History, they recall appalling anecdotes with calm, charm, and courage. Through the spirit of these survivors, *Enchanted* becomes more than a horror show; it's also a compelling and inspiring story about lesbian and gay heroism and endurance.

Vestida de Azul (Dressed in Blue)
Dir. Geminez-Rico, Antonio
Prod. Fernandez, Bernardo
1983 Spain Spanish
96 mins. 35mm color Documentary
Dist. (U.S.): Spanish Ministry of Culture
For those who think they've heard all they want to about drag and its Zen, along comes *Dressed in Blue* to shed new light on a topic familiar to gay audiences. Set in Madrid, this eye-opening, beautifully photographed documentary concerns six transvestites working as prostitutes and nightclub entertainers. They are good-natured and insightful as they share their life experiences, including a striking scene of silicone implant surgery and one man's visit (in drag) to his extended families' Sunday dinner.

Via Appia
Dir. Hick, Jochen
1989 Germany German
90 mins. 16mm color Narrative
Dist. (U.S.): Strand Releasing
Dist. (U.K.): Dangerous To Know
Frank is a German Lufthansa steward who travels the world, taking photos of boys he has sex with—he's a collector. One hot night in his favorite city, Rio de Janeiro, Frank picks up Mario and takes him to his hotel. The morning after, Mario is gone, leaving only a chilling epitaph, written in lipstick, on the bathroom mirror, "Welcome to the AIDS club."

Via Appia begins in Germany as Frank shows the first signs of HIV infection. A friend wants to shoot a documentary about him, so Frank convinces the film crew to go to Rio, in the hopes that he might find Mario, the alleged source of his infection. Jose, a handsome young hustler, becomes Frank's guide through bathhouses and beaches—and the *Via Appia*, a street where male prostitutes openly offer their services. From Rio to Saõ Paolo, the film takes the viewer into a world of beautiful bodies, sex, money, and murder. But it also allows us a closer look at a German man's psyche as he deals with a disease that he knows can kill him.

Although *Via Appia* plays like a documentary, it is a fiction feature by Jochen Hick, a Hamburg film student. Originally produced for German television, its controversial subject caused the student to preempt its broadcast. *Via Appia* finally did air in August of 1990.

Vice and the Badge, The
Dir. Fontaine, Richard
1965 USA English
8 mins. 16mm b&w Other
Dist. (U.S.): Fontaine, Richard
A classic male physique film from Richard Fontaine (*Days of Greek Gods*). For this posing extravaganza, the location is a gay bar on a beach (the alternate title for the film is *Beach Bar Nightmare*). It seems that one of the patrons is slipped a mickey and when he comes to, every man in the place has lost his pants! Good clean fun.

Vicki Picks a Tie
Dir. Walters, Jamie
1985 USA English
10 mins. video color Other
Dist. (U.S.): n/a
This is the third in a series emphasising a conceptual approach to the behind-the-scenes existence of American public personalities. In this case Vicki Morgan, mistress of the late Alfred Bloomingdale, is found bludgeoned to death with a baseball bat.

Victim
Dir. Dearden, Basil
1961 Great Britain English
100 mins. 35mm b&w Narrative
Dist. (U.S.): Films Incorporated
When *Victim* was made in 1961, 90 percent of all blackmail cases in the English courts were homosexual in origin. In this film Dirk Bogarde plays an upper-middle-class barrister who instead

of giving in to the blackmailer's demands, cooperates with the police to track them down, risking his marriage and his career. *Victim* marked a major turning point for the subject of homosexuality on the screen and changed the career of Dirk Bogarde forever. Bogarde had, until that time, played a matinee idol type in dozens of lightweight films. With *Victim* he took a chance that audiences would accept him in the role of a courageous homosexual and won out over conventional wisdom. *Victim* provided a major challenge to the censorship code in the United States, which stated that the word "homosexual" could not be uttered onscreen. In defiance of the code, *Victim* became the first film to do so in the context of pleading tolerance for the victims of blackmail by a gang of vicious homophobes. In the guise of a conventional thriller, *Victim* scored points for the legalization of homosexuality in England and preceded the repeal of that country's sodomy statutes by only six months. Although tame by today's standards, it was considered truly shocking in 1961. According to Dirk Bogarde, "While we were filming, we were treated as though we were attacking the Bible and the film's lawyers said they wanted to wash their hands after reading the script . . . yet it was the first film in which a man said 'I love you' to another man. I wrote that scene in. I said to them, 'either we make a film about queers or we don't.'"

Victor
Dir. Daniels, Christopher Leo
Prod. Hill, Brent
1992 USA English
30 mins. video color Experimental
Dist. (U.S.): Hill, Brent
A sublime, substantial, and sexy dream-drama about the relationship between an African-American soldier and his boyfriend; a military interrogation leads to flashbacks of his father, and a dizzying, tour-de-force finale.

Video Album 5: The Thursday People
Dir. Kuchar, George
1987 USA English
60 mins. video color Documentary
Dist. (U.S.): Video Data Bank
The acclaimed "video diary" of the people and events around the late filmmaker Curt McDowell. Originally shot on 8mm video, this carefully made tape was edited entirely in-camera. A lesson in video/film style as well as a lighthearted, intriguing look at McDowell's entourage.

Video Album: The Gaymes
Dir. Spiro, Ellen
1991 USA English
25 mins. video color Documentary
Dist. (U.S.): Spiro, Ellen
One look at the lesbian and gay pursuit of health and happiness through the world of sports and fitness training. Ellen Spiro (director of last year's festival hit, *Diana's Hair Ego*) offers *Video Album: The Gaymes*, a look at participants and highlights of the Vancouver Gay Games. A collage of images, sounds, and impressions, *Video Album* recreates an event that confirms the physical empowerment of lesbians and gays in the midst of an epidemic.

Viktor und Viktoria (Victor and Victoria)
Dir. Schuenzel, Reinhold
Prod. Ufa, Berlin
1933 Germany German
90 mins. 35mm b&w Narrative
Dist. (U.S.): Video City Theatrical Distribution
One of the most successful films of the 1930s, *Viktor und Viktoria* is a fast-paced comedy of sexual confusion that inspired the recent Blake Edwards version with Julie Andrews and Robert Preston. This story of an aging female impersonator who hires a young woman to replace him features musical numbers similar to those in the 1982 version. This is a classic, rarely seen example of German operetta film.

Village Idiot, The
Dir. Snee, Patrick
1992 USA English
26 mins. 16mm color Narrative
Dist. (U.S.): Snee, Patrick
In *The Village Idiot* Kate wants to be Marilyn McCoo . . . or else she's in love with her. This hilarious tale of girlhood and self-discovery offers pointed insights on race, sexuality, culture, and identity.

Vingarne (Wings, The)
Dir. Stiller, Mauritz
1916 Sweden Swedish
40 mins. 35mm color Narrative
Dist. (U.S.): Swedish Film Institute
Based on Herman Bang's novel *Mikael*, *Vingarne* is a silent melodrama about an artist's love for his newfound male model. Radically, the film opens with director Stiller and his cinematographer coming across a sensual staue of Icarus in the gardens in Stockholm. Then the movie proper begins, with artist Claude Zoret struck by love at

Ⓐ Ⓑ Ⓒ Ⓓ Ⓔ Ⓕ Ⓖ Ⓗ Ⓘ Ⓙ Ⓚ Ⓛ Ⓜ Ⓝ Ⓞ Ⓟ Ⓠ Ⓡ Ⓢ Ⓣ Ⓤ ⓥ Ⓦ Ⓧ Ⓨ Ⓩ

first sight for the young Mikael in a woodland; he adopts Mikael, who serves as inspiration for his latest sculpture. Inevitably Mikael gets his wings burnt when he starts courting Zoret's patron, the unscrupulous Lady Lucia; pained by Mikael's desertion, Zoret dies during a fierce storm before his staue of the naked boy.

Watching *Vingarne* 75 years after its production is an extraordinary experience. It's easy to get caught up in the fragmentary feel of the narrative, to work too hard at following the story instead of giving up to its original allusiveness. So, some tips to tap into that intended sense: First, bear in mind that both novelist Bang and director Stiller were known to be gay.

Second, it's interesting to compare *Vingarne* with Carl Dreyer's film of the same novel (also called Mikael). Many of the greatly sensual scenes from Dreyer's film are foreshadowed in the first version.

Finally, the most startling—and infuriatingly brief—thing about *Vingarne* is the framing device and the idea of a film-within-a-film. Confronted by the barest remains of his extraordinary conceit, we can only imagine what the original felt like.

Vintage: Families of Value
Dir. Harris, Thomas Allen
1995 USA English
72 mins. 16mm color Documentary
Dist. (U.S.): Chimpanzee Productions
This debut feature from Thomas Allen Harris brings to the screen the surprising stories of a number of gay, black siblings. Queer siblings Paul and Vanessa Eaddy talk about growing up with an abusive father; Anni Cammett, Adrian Jones, and Anita Jones look at sisterhood and the black family; and Harris and his own gay brother, Lyle Ashton Harris explore the ups and downs of their relationship.

Virgin Machine, The
(see *Jungfrauenmaschine, Die*)

Virgin, the Mother and the Crone, The
Dir. Smith, Jo
1994 Great Britain English
10 mins. 16mm color Experimental
Dist. (U.K.): Smith, Jo
An exploration of three iconic figures of womanhood.

Virus Kennt Keine Moral, Ein
(Virus Has No Morals, A)
Dir. von Praunheim, Rosa

1986 Germany German
82 mins. 16mm color Narrative
Dist. (U.S.): First Run Features
Shown at a benefit for the Shanti Project during the 1987 San Francisco Film Festival last spring, *A Virus Has No Morals* is a controversial film about an increasingly controversial subject— AIDS. A macabre, sometimes offensive black comedy by Rosa von Praunheim, *Virus* features wealthy transvestites, gay revolutionaries, a woman therapist who teaches death-meditation and gymnastics to people with AIDS, night nurses who throw dice to see who'll die first, and a snoopy woman reporter who dresses as a man to spy on the gay sex scene. The result is a provocation to everyone dealing with AIDS, from bathhouse owners and gay activists to clergy, press, and doctors. Von Praunheim's response to the health crisis is social satire, a cruel mockery of a tragic situation that has, as yet, no solution in sight. At the end, everyone's got AIDS, and the government sends everyone to Hell—Gayland. A lively, tough film by the 44-year-old Praunheim, former assistant to underground American filmmaker Gregory Markopoulos and one of the world's leading gay directors.

Vital Signs
Dir. Hammer, Barbara
1991 USA English
10 mins. 16mm color Experimental
Dist. (U.S.): Canyon Cinema
Barbara Hammer's Vital Signs looks at Western constructions of death.

Released by Frameline in the U.S. as part of a package of four of her short videos, entitled *Barbara Hammer Program #1*.

!Viva 16th!
Dir. Aguirre, Valentin, and Augie Robles
1994 USA English
30 mins. video color Documentary
Dist. (U.S.): Robles, Augie
A raw and chatty celebration of the San Francisco's lesbian and gay Chicano/Latino community.

Viva Eu!
Dir. Cypriano, Tania
1989 Brazil Portugese
18 mins. 16mm color Documentary
Dist. (U.S.): Third World Newsreel
Viva Eu! follows Brazilian artist Wilton Braga from São Paulo to New York and to Barcelona during the eight years he lived with AIDS.

Vivat Regina
Dir. Metcalf, Charlotte
1987 Great Britain English
26 mins. 16mm color Documentary
Dist. (U.S.): Metcalf, Charlotte
A seriously camp affair with the chorus boys from
La Cage Aux Folles, on the day the show closed
in London due, it seems, to fears about AIDS.

Vive L'Amour
Dir. Tsai, Ming-liang
1994 Taiwan Taiwanese
104 mins. 35mm color Narrative
Dist. (U.S.): Strand Releasing
Against the troubled radiance of contemporary
Taipei, Tsai Ming-liang's wicked follow-up to
Rebels of the Neon God delves even further into
the erotic spaces of unspoken and transgressive
love. Hsiao-kang, a teenager who works for a
designer crematorium, is canvassing for clients
one day when he sees a key left in an apartment
door. He steals it and returns later that night to
find the apartment uninhabited. Hsiao-kang,
sequestered from a society in the throes of economic development, uses the apartment as a
sanctuary where he can explore his own burgeon-
ing sexuality: taking long baths, attempting suicide, teetering around in high heels and frock,
and ultimately, falling in love.

Meanwhile, May, the real estate agent
who left the key in the door, picks up random sex
partners and brings them back to the apartment.
One of them is Ah-hung, a handsome macho who
sells women's clothing on the street. The empty
flat soon becomes the crossroads for these three
seemingly disparate lives. Although the three are
initially unaware of each other's presence, unlikely liaisons develop. The grace with which Tsai
handles this narrative of averted collisions underscores the eroticism of the illicit, and vaguely
comic, situations: like Hsiao-kang hiding under
the bed and masturbating to the sounds of May
and Ah-hung having sex on top.

The dialectical tensions between
modernity and masculinity are forcefully brought
to the fray. With next to no dialogue, Tsai uses a
visual language that, like the desire he portrays,
shatters the limitations of conventional representation. (L.C.)

Voguing: The Message
**Dir. Bronstein, David, Dorothy Low,
and Jack Walworth**
1989 USA English
13 mins. video color Documentary

Dist. (U.S.): Frameline
This pre-Madonna primer traces the roots of the
gay, black and Latino dance form.

Voices from the Front
Dir. Testing the Limits Collective
1991 USA English
88 mins. video color Documentary
Dist. (U.S.): Frameline
In New York City, a distraught activist confronts
the mayor with a story of a friend who languished
on a cot in an emergency room hallway for nine
days, only to die 48 hours after leaving the hospital. A woman is interviewed during a rally to stop
the closing of a hospital in Harlem, a section of
the city disproportionately affected by AIDS. In
1988, thousands of activists from across the
country hold the Food and Drug Administration
under siege, demanding speedier drug approval.
In 1990 they converge again, this time on the
National Institutes of Health, calling for a more
equitable clinical trial system and expanded
research into new drugs and treatment. *Voices
from the Front*, the first feature-length documentary to comprehensively cover the AIDS activist
movement in America, makes clear the emotional
and political effects of community activism using
the voices of those directly engaged. It's a powerful distillation of pictures and words from events
organized to change public consciousness,
expose profiteering by pharmaceutical companies, and challenge government inaction and
neglect concerning AIDS. As the late Vito Russo
says in the tape, "We're going to fundamentally
change the health care system in this country . . .
I don't think it's stoppable now."

Voices of Life
Dir. Wright, Patrick
1991 USA English
33 mins. video color Experimental
Dist. (U.S.): Wright, Patrick
A clever deconstruction of conventional AIDS
documentaries, which alerts us to how appearances can be extremely deceiving.

Voyage de l'ogre, Le
Dir. Paradis, Marc
1981 Canada French
24 mins. video color Experimental
Dist. (U.S.): Videographe, Inc.
Another early work by Canadian experimental
video maker Marc Paradis.

Vrouw Als Eva, Een
(Woman Like Eve, A)

A
B
C
D
E
F
G
H
I
J
K
L
M
N
O
P
Q
R
S
T
U
V
W
X
Y
Z

Dir. Van Brakel, Nouchka
1979 Netherlands Dutch
90 mins. 35mm color Narrative
Dist. (U.S.): n/a
Made with a largely female crew, *A Woman Like Eve* tells the story of a Dutch housewife (Monique van de Ven) who becomes thoroughly disgusted with her existence as a drudge and decides to leave her husband and two children to share her life with a young French woman (Maria Schneider). Truly touching, the film is definitely a discussion piece for viewers of both sexes. Described by *Variety* as "a sort of bisexual *Kramer vs. Kramer*," *Variety* goes on to describe Monique Van de Ven's performance as "excellent" and Maria Schneider's as, "vapid, somnolent" and "inexpressive" and adds that, "the nonverbal posturing of Schneider's lesbian clique is a bit arch."

Waiting
Dir. Guy, Steve
1991 USA English
8 mins. 16mm color Narrative
Dist. (U.S.): Guy, Steve
Based on the story by Edmund White, *Waiting* portrays a teenage boy's desire to leave his small town—and learning a life lesson in the process.

Waiting for the Moon
Dir. Godmilow, Jill
1987 USA English
87 mins. 35mm color Narrative
Dist. (U.S.): Laboratory for Icon and Idiom, Inc.
Linda Hunt and Linda Bassett give brilliant performances as Gertrude Stein and Alice B. Toklas in this rich period-piece biography. (J.O.)

Waiting 'Round Wynyard
Dir. Di Chiera, Franco
1982 Australia English
13 mins. 16mm color Other
Dist. (U.S.): n/a
A sensitive look at the first time for a young gay man.

Wake Up, Jerk Off, Etc
Dir. MacIvor, Daniel
1993 Canada English
2 mins. video color Other
Dist. (U.S.): Da Da Kamera
Another hilarious tape from Daniel MacIvor.

Walk on Bi
(see *Out On Tuesday, Program 1*)

Walk on the Wild Side (BBC Arena)

Dir. Marsh, James
1993 Great Britain English
40 mins. video color Documentary
Dist. (U.K.): BBC TV
Meet the real people behind Lou Reed's classic celebration of '60s transgenderism: Joe Dallesandro and Holly Woodlawn, who both confirm the decadent drag scene that inspired the world-famous song. "Lou was fascinated by transvestites," claims Jayne County. "He had this girlfriend at the time called Rachel and she was a transsexual. It's only natural that he would write a song about three drag queens."

Walk the Dog
Dir. Dailey, Tom
1989 USA English
5 mins. 16mm color Experimental
Dist. (U.S.): Dailey, Tom
Walk the Dog is creative choreography—if you can call getting-dressed-for-sex a kind of dancing.

Waltz, The
Dir. Connor, Kathleen, and Kim Foley
1985 USA English
1 mins. 16mm color Experimental
Dist. (U.S.): n/a
A very simple, beautiful line drawing of a woman dancing. Creative animation.

Wanderer, The
Dir. Dean, Margo
1995 USA English
10 mins. video color Other
Dist. (U.S.): Dean, Margo
A music video of the travels of a wandering dyke.

Wank Stallions
Dir. Murray, Alison
1993 Great Britain English
33 mins. video color Other
Dist. (U.S.): Murray, Alison /ARGUS
A staccato dance piece set on the beach.

Want
Dir. Davis, Brian
1984 USA English
13 mins. 16mm color Narrative
Dist. (U.S.): Frameline
A hard-edged drama about self-hatred and homosexuality.

Wanted!
Dir. Seaman, Gordon, K. Daymond, and Jill Batson
1994 Canada English

11 mins. 16mm color Other
Dist. (U.S.): Seaman, Gordon
Gordon Seaman, K. Daymond, and Jill Batson
hunt down Canada's most notorious homophobes
in *Wanted!*

War on Lesbians
Dir. Cottis, Jane
1992 USA English
35 mins. video color Other
Dist. (U.S.): Women Make Movies
Take a tour of the lesbian world in Jane Cottis's
War on Lesbians. Drawing on various pop culture
conventions and referents (film, television news,
and traditional talking head documentary), Cottis
poses as a gallery of characters and incorporates
the subject of lesbianism into every imaginable
arena in this potpourri of lesbian representations.

War Widow, The
Dir. Bogart, Paul
1976 USA English
83 mins. video color Narrative
Dist. (U.S.): Frameline Archive
Pamela Bellwood stars as Amy, the lonely wife of
a long overseas World War I soldier, in the rarely
seen PBS production of *The War Widow*, one of
the most requested titles each year at the festival. Constructed with a delicacy reminiscent of
Edith Wharton, *The War Widow* tells the story of
the love that grows between the conventional
Amy, who lives with her mother and daughter in a
stately New York suburb, and the free-spirited
Jenny (Frances Lee McCain) whose passion for
photography is equaled only by her passion for
Amy.

The romance between Amy and Jenny
begins innocently in a New York tearoom, when
Jenny befriends Amy, whose eyes she finds "so
deeply, painfully sad." The two women come to
know each other better as they work on one of
Jenny's photography projects. A vacation together
at the beach makes each realize the depth of
their relationship, something which forces Amy to
face "what I cannot even name when I am alone
and there is no one else to hear."

True to the lives of many lesbians of
the period, Amy's society does not easily allow
her to reconcile her love for Jenny with the duties
of her station. When her husband announces his
return, she is forced to make the ultimate
choice—between her family, including her young
daughter Beth, and her lover.

In his book *The Celluloid Closet*, Vito
Russo lauds *The War Widow* as a "positive evocation" of the lives of gay characters and as a piece
in which the central characters have a "sense of
history" and of their role in the struggle for sexual freedom.

Winner of the 1988 San Francisco
International Lesbian & Gay Film Festival
Audience Award for Best Video.

Warm
Dir. Mead, Wrik
1992 Canada English
5 mins. 16mm color Experimental
Dist. (U.S.): Canadian Filmmakers Distribution
Centre
Wrik Mead's dreamy *Warm* suggests the comfort
of an embrace as a pixilated naked male body
flailing against a crumbling brick ruin . . .
released from the anguish of containment by
another man's touch.

Warrior Marks [excerpt]
Dir. Parmar, Pratibha
1993 Great Britain French and various African
languages
10 mins. 16mm color Documentary
Dist. (U.S.): Women Make Movies
Made in collaboration with Pulitzer Prize–winning
writer Alice Walker, *Warrior Marks* is the first feature-length analysis of female genital mutilation.
With this groundbreaking work Parmar continues
her dedication to giving voice and image to the
often unseen and unspoken realities of women
around the globe.

Was Soll'n Wir Denn Machen Ohne Den Tod (What Shall We Do Without Death)
Dir. Mikesch, Elfi
1980 Germany German
110 mins. 16mm color Experimental
Dist. (U.S.): West Glen Films
Käthe and Traute live in a home for the elderly in
Hamburg, Germany. Their assistants do the best
they can to meet the needs of the old people
whose reality is in the past. Some feel extremely
lonely and most are tired of life and of their bodies that seem to give them nothing but trouble.
Käthe and Traute, however, are different: They
enjoy the tenderness and intimacy they share.
The rhythm of the film is drawn from their conversations with each other and with their helper,
Barbara. They speak as if they were dreaming,
not bothered by what happens outside of their
minds. Käthe speaks about memories, death, and
her intention to "move from an outerly to an
innerly directed vitality," which she calls reading

Ⓐ
Ⓑ
Ⓒ
Ⓓ
Ⓔ
Ⓕ
Ⓖ
Ⓗ
Ⓘ
Ⓙ
Ⓚ
Ⓛ
Ⓜ
Ⓝ
Ⓞ
Ⓟ
Ⓠ
Ⓡ
Ⓢ
Ⓣ
Ⓤ
Ⓥ
Ⓦ
Ⓧ
Ⓨ
Ⓩ

what has never been written. Besides this liberating detachment—this state of both euphoria and melancholy—the film is about the concerns of those who take care of the elderly. The toughest aspect of their work is dealing with the ruthless unhappiness which is expressed uninhibitedly and which can only be resolved by death. *What Shall We Do Without Death* was shot as a documentary and edited as a fiction film. Through this technique Elfi Mikesch renders an extraordinarily intense, yet warm impression of the joy and the sorrow that comes with old age.

Elfi Mikesch has made over ten films. She is also regarded as one of the world's leading cinematographers, having photographed feature films for Monika Treut (*The Virgin Machine*), Rosa von Praunheim (*Horror Vacui, A Virus Knows No Morals, Anita—Dance of Vices*) and Werner Schroeter (*The Roseking*).

Wavering Heterosexual Confronts the Pleasure Principle Head On and Is Forced to Decide, A
Dir. Soffa, Fred
1994 USA English
2 mins. 16mm color Narrative
Dist. (U.S.): Soffa, Fred
A film with a title that says it all.

Waving Fork, The
Dir. Giorgio, Grace
1993 USA English
9 mins. 16mm color Narrative
Dist. (U.S.): Giorgio, Grace
Beginning a new relationship with Alex, Jenny flashes back to memories of her mother. As her relationship with Alex evolves, things improve significantly between Jenny and her mother.

Way of the Wicked, The
Dir. Vachon, Christine
1989 USA English
15 mins. 16mm color Narrative
Dist. (U.S.): Women Make Movies
Dist. (U.K.): Cinenova
The Way of the Wicked is a caustic but liberating commentary on the repression of the female body in Catholicism. Drawn as an action film, it shows a girl who plans to bite the holy wafer right after her first communion. Two women rush out and bring her to a safe place, where they can celebrate the reappropriation of the body and the blood.

We All Have Our Reasons

Dir. Reid, Frances, and Elizabeth Stevens
Prod. Iris Films
1981 USA English
30 mins. 16mm color Other
Dist. (U.S.): n/a
A documentary on women and alcoholism.

We Are Family
Dir. Banks, Dasal
Prod. Sands, Aimee
1987 USA English
59 mins. video color Documentary
Dist. (U.S.): Filmmaker's Library
Susan Stamberg narrates WGBH's fine documentary about lesbian and gay parents that explores the legal and social implications of homosexual parenting through the lives of three families. Concerns about AIDS, child molestation, sex education, and the effects of the absence of a "traditional" family setting on foster children are sensitively addressed. A careful look at what life is really like in lesbian and gay families, *We Are Family* is ultimately about the well-being of children. It concludes that homosexuals are as capable as heterosexuals of being committed, loving parents.

We Were Marked with a Big A
Dir. Weishaupt, Joseph, and Elke Jeanron
1991 Netherlands Dutch
44 mins. video color/b&w Documentary
Dist. (U.S.): United States Holocaust Memorial Museum
This deeply moving film reminds the world of the forgotten history of gay survivors of Nazi Germany. As many as 15,000 gay men were sent to concentration camps, targeted by the Nazis as subversives. In this powerful documentary, three gay survivors share their stories. The "A"—which stood for "Arschficker"/"Assfucker"—refers to a symbol (which pre-dated the pink triangle) that gay prisoners were forced to wear.

We Were One Man
(see *Nous Etions un Seul Homme*)

We're Talking Vulva
Dir. Dempsey, Shawna, and Tracy Traeger
1990 Canada English
5 mins. 16mm color Other
Dist. (U.S.): Zeitgeist Films
Dist. (U.K.): British Film Institute
An outrageous feminist romp about the care and feeding of happy female genitalia.

We've Been Framed

Dir. Farthing, Cheryl
1991 Great Britain English
25 mins. video color Documentary
Dist. (U.K.): Alfalfa Entertainments, Ltd.
In *We've Been Framed* (made for Channel Four's
Out series), women of different ages, races, and
class backgrounds talk about the best, the worst,
and the first lesbian films they've seen.

Wedding Banquet, The
Dir. Lee, Ang
1993 Taiwan English
104 mins. 35mm color Narrative
Dist. (U.S.): Samuel Goldwyn Company
Winner of the Berlin Film Festival's top prize, *The
Wedding Banquet* is bound to be one of the year's
most talked-about movies. It's a delightful comedy about the conflict between modern sexual and
social values and old-world traditions. Director
Ang Lee has managed to take the issues of a gay-
centered situation and make them relevant to a
mainstream audience, with precisely observed
details and much heart-warming wit.

Gao Wai-Tung has a happy and very
settled life in Manhattan. Some shrewd real-
estate investments keep him busy and comfortably well off; regular workouts in the gym keep
him in good shape; best of all, his Caucasian
lover Simon cooks first-rate Chinese food. The
only trouble is Wai-Tung's elderly parents back in
Taiwan. They expect him to marry and give them
a grandchild. They're constantly enrolling him in
computer-dating clubs, to find him a suitable
bride.

It's Simon who comes up with a solution: A marriage of convenience with Wei-Wei, an
illegal immigrant badly in need of a green card.
But no one reckons on the sheer weight of
Chinese tradition when it comes to matters of
matrimony and procreation. Through a chain of
inevitable accidents, the simple ceremony escalates into a full-scale wedding banquet . . .

"This is to 1993 what *Strictly
Ballroom* was to 1992: a scintillating comedy
with a serious undertow and a masterly grasp of
emotional highs and lows."
—Tony Rayns, Berlin Film Festival, 1993

Wedding of the Year, Chuck & Vince
Dir. Wynne, Christine
1978 USA English
4 mins. S8mm color Documentary
Dist. (U.S.): Frameline Archive
The wedding of Chuck and Vince at the MCC
church, May 1978, with ushers, drag queens,
etc. in attendance.

Weekend Zombie Nurses
Dir. Linkhart, Carl
1983 USA English
3 mins. S8mm color
Dist. (U.S.): n/a
Part of the 1983 Super-8 Gay Festival.

Weggehen um Anzukommen
(Depart to Arrive)
Dir. Grote, Alexandra Von
1982 Germany German
89 mins. 35mm color Narrative
Dist. (U.S.): Frauen Film Production
This first feature from the hands of Alexandra
Von Grote charmed and disturbed festival audiences in 1982. There is "no-fault" divorce for
Regine and Anna when their relationship begins
to fly apart in sharp fragments. Bewildered by the
failure of their love, Anna (Gabrielle Osburg) can
only think of taking time out, running away.
Driving off for the balmy south of France to
soothe her wounded pride and dashed expectations, she gets unwanted flashes from the past—
the best and worst of times between the two
women—that haunt the journey, but the change
of locale and fresh experiences along the way are
not enough. The change to a positive identity
comes gradually through the realization that she
must look at her past self before she can depart
from it to arrive at the new present.
Cinematically, it's a crystal-clear and colorful
journey, paced to fit Anna's constantly altering
state of mind, ranging from swift, glossy, painful
images to blushing, cheerful, pastoral landscapes—an enjoyable journey to new places.

Weight of Oceans, The
Dir. Binninger, John
1991 USA English
7 mins. 16mm color Experimental
Dist. (U.S.): Binninger, John
A beautiful evocation of a dream before waking.

Weiner Brut
Dir. Fadler, Hans
1985 Austria German
97 mins. 35mm color Narrative
Dist. (U.S.): Fantom Film
Weiner Brut, the first Austrian gay film to come
to the U.S. is a riotous mixture of squatters,
princesses, punks, barons, clergy, and politicians. Nothing that is holy or worth damning to
Austrians is left out of this colorful panorama.

The long-since-ousted aristocracy, in

Ⓐ
Ⓑ
Ⓒ
Ⓓ
Ⓔ
Ⓕ
Ⓖ
Ⓗ
Ⓘ
Ⓙ
Ⓚ
Ⓛ
Ⓜ
Ⓝ
Ⓞ
Ⓟ
Ⓠ
Ⓡ
Ⓢ
Ⓣ
Ⓤ
Ⓥ
Ⓦ
Ⓧ
Ⓨ
Ⓩ

order to keep their drug supply flowing, is planning a revolution against the socialist government, helped by a gang of underprivileged youths. Soon they find that all the anarchist youths want are the crown jewels. The collaboration is shattered even further when the princess hears of a plot to turn the opera house into a rock palace.

  Weiner Brut runs all over the place in gorgeous costumes and piled-on wigs. It is a parody of the Austrian monarchy—a daring travesty of a country's past—in short, the entire Viennese "scene."

Welcome to the Dome
Dir. Hick, Jochen
1992 Germany English
15 mins. 16mm color Documentary
Dist. (U.S.): Hick, Jochen
Welcome to the Dome is a strong record of the spectacular ACT-UP action which took place during the German Bishop's Conference in late 1991; unlike New York ACT-UP's similar "Stop the Church" action at St. Patrick's Cathedral, this protest ended in violence.

Well Sexy Women [excerpt]
Dir. Unconscious Collective, The
1993 Great Britain English
50 mins. video color Documentary
Dist. (U.S.): Frameline
Dist. (U.K.): Pride Productions
The first British-produced lesbian safe-sex video! Released in the U.S. as part of *She's Safe*, a lesbian safe-sex video package.

Wendel
Dir. Schaub, Christoph
1987 Switzerland German
58 mins. 16mm color Narrative
Dist. (U.S.): Pro Helvetia
David has got himself pretty well organized, he's got friends, jobs—not bad. Broods a little, but who doesn't? Occasional political activity. He never really grasped why Wendel, his best friend for years, had left. Just took off. The fool. Emigrated. Back in the seventies they had shared their lives, their love, their apartment, and sometimes even the same woman. And now, what happens? Wendel comes back, out of the blue. They spend the day together.

West Coast Crones: A Glimpse at the Lives Of Nine Old Lesbians
Dir. Muir, Madeline
1991 USA English

28 mins. video color Documentary
Dist. (U.S.): Frameline
A group of lesbians ranging in age from 61 to 76 exchange their thoughts and feelings about growing old. They discuss the fears and invisibility that old age brings and the role that sexuality plays in their lives.

Westler—East of the Wall
Dir. Speck, Weiland
1985 Germany German
94 mins. 16mm color Narrative
Dist. (U.S.): Frameline
Westler is a story of love divided by the Berlin Wall. The film starts in Los Angeles, about as far West as a German tourist can go. Here Felix, the gay German, drives around in a convertible with his American friend, taking in all the sights of Hollywood. Later, the old world and the new socialist order replace capitalist glitter when Bruce visits Felix in West Berlin, and they decide to take the day trip to the East. During the trip, Felix meets Thomas, an East Berliner. Their only time together is when Felix comes to the East for a day trip, forced to return by midnight. As the trips across the border become more frequent, suspicion is aroused and one day a border guard asks Felix to step into an examination room where he is told to strip for closer inspection to see if any smuggling is going on. Frustrated, the couple plan to meet in Prague where they at least can spend a whole evening together and hopefully plan Thomas's escape to the West.

  Winner of the 1986 San Francisco International Lesbian & Gay Film Festival Audience Award for Best Feature.

What a Day, What a Life
Dir. Ward, Ken
1977 USA English
3 mins. S8mm color Narrative
Dist. (U.S.): n/a
Starring my very good friend Norman. This was my very, very first film so please excuse the jump cuts.

What Can I Do with a Male Nude?
Dir. Peck, Ron
1985 Great Britain English
23 mins. 16mm color Other
Dist. (U.S.): Frameline
Dist. (U.K.): British Film Institute
A short comedy on the taboo of the male nude. Its setting is a photographic studio and its basic situation a photographic session, in which the photographer runs his model through the gamut

of possibilities of "what might be permissable in respect of a male nude." Prompted in part by the latest piece of legislation in Great Britain agaist the nude, the film satirizes the repressions and confusion of the photographer, whose confidences to the audience constitute the soundtrack.

What Gets You Off
Dir. Massingale, Danielle, Grace Giorgio, and Julienne Yuhn
1994 USA English
7 mins. video color Documentary
Dist. (U.S.): Three Fun Girls
Three dykes wander San Francisco to interview the average queer in the street and find out: What gets you off?

What Have I Done to Deserve This?
(see *Que He Hecho Yo Para Merecer Esto?*)

What Is a Line?
Dir. Frilot, Shari
1994 USA English
7 mins. video color Narrative
Dist. (U.S.): Frilot, Shari
A gorgeuosly constructed musing from Shari Frilot.

What Really Happened to Baby Jane?
Prod. Gay Girls Riding Club
1963 USA English
35 mins. 16mm color Narrative
Dist. (U.S.): Tremaglio Productions
The third production from the Los Angeles–based Gay Girls Riding Club. When writer Ray Harrison saw *Whatever Happened to Baby Jane?* in 1963, he went home and scripted this parody of the film. Like their other films, *Baby Jane* was shot on Sundays only.

What Shall We Do Without Death
(see *Was Soll'n Wir Denn Machen Ohne Den Tod*)

What's A Nice Kid Like You . . .
Dir. Castellaneta, P.J.
1986 USA English
8 mins. 16mm b&w Narrative
Dist. (U.S.): Castellaneta, P.J.
An early short from the director of *Together Alone*.

What's in a Name
Dir. Rodriguez, Janelle
1993 USA English
6 mins. video color Other
Dist. (U.S.): Rodriguez, Janelle

What's in a Name shows that it's great to be a dyke except for the litany of verbal abuse we put up with.

What's the Difference Between a Yam and a Sweet Potato?
Dir. Dunlap, J. Evan, and Adriene Jenik
1992 USA English
4 mins. video b&w Experimental
Dist. (U.S.): Video Data Bank
A video dealing with interracial relationships. Part of *Those Fluttering Objects of Desire*, released in the U.S. on a twenty-minute compilation with *Vanilla Sex, Brown Sugar Licks Snow White*, and *I've Never*.

Whatever
Dir. Thorne, Kika
1994 Canada English
21 mins. video color Experimental
Dist. (U.S.): Thorne, Kika c/o LIFT
Structured around an interview with black poet Courtney McFarlane.

Whatever Happened to Susan Jane?
Dir. Huestis, Marc
1982 USA English
60 mins. 16mm color Narrative
Dist. (U.S.): Outsider Enterprises
Whatever Happened to Susan Jane? follows Marcie Clark, a suburban housewife dissatisfied with her bouffant and barbecue lifestyle, who leaves home in search of something new. She arrives in San Francisco, smack in the middle of its eccentric yet thriving artistic underground. Filmed on a shoestring budget of $20,000, *Whatever Happened to Susan Jane?* captures one of the most exciting periods of San Francisco's gay culture, featuring some of the city's most notable celebrities of the time: LuLu, Coco Vega, Silvana Nova, The Wasp Women, Tommy Pace, and an extraordinary performance by Ann Block as the naive Marcie Clark.

When Night is Falling
Dir. Rozema, Patricia
Prod. Tranter, Barbara
1995 Canada English
93 mins. 35mm color Narrative
Dist. (U.S.): October Films
This year's French lesbian farce Bushwhacked has a clever series of switcheroos that bring the lead characters together. A similar manipulation of events brings together the protagonists of *When Night is Falling*, the latest from Patricia Rozema (*I've Heard the Mermaids Singing*). The

Ⓐ Ⓑ Ⓒ Ⓓ Ⓔ Ⓕ Ⓖ Ⓗ Ⓘ Ⓙ Ⓚ Ⓛ Ⓜ Ⓝ Ⓞ Ⓟ Ⓠ Ⓡ Ⓢ Ⓣ Ⓤ Ⓥ Ⓦ Ⓧ Ⓨ Ⓩ

first meeting of Camille (Pascale Bussieres), a divinity college professor and Petra (Rachel Crawford), a circus performer, takes place at a laundrette, the second, when Petra returns Camille's clothing, which she'd deliberately switched for hers.

Camille is engaged to one of her male colleagues (Henry Czerny), but slowly realizes that she's a lesbian. *Night* has pacing problems early on, but the narrative coalesces about halfway through. Audacious Petra helps Camille accept her true nature and Camille provides Petra a certain stability she's been lacking prior to their acquaintance. (D.M.)

When Shirley Met Florence
Dir. Bezalel, Ronit
1994 Canada English
28 mins. video color Documentary
Dist. (U.S.): Filmmaker's Library
Ronit Bezalel documents the amazing fifty-five-year friendship between two Jewish women in Montreal. Shirley, a Polish refugee, is straight; her friend Florence is a lesbian. These two remarkable women talk about Shirley's marriage to Florence's brother, about Florence's lover Sophie, and about the traditional Yiddish music they play together.

When You Name Me
Dir. Beveridge, Scott
1993 USA English
12 mins. video color Narrative
Dist. (U.S.): Beveridge, Scott
A disturbingly graphic portrayal of a gay bashing.

Where Are We?:
Our Trip Through America
Dir. Epstein, Robert, and Jeffrey Friedman
1992 USA English
75 mins. 16mm color Documentary
Dist. (U.S.): Roxie Releasing
Oscar-winning document-arians Jeffrey Friedman and Robert Epstein (*Common Threads*) take their cameras into the American heartland with this spontaneous and ultimately profound feature. Traveling through the South "because it seemed so foreign to us," the very gay San Francisco two-some find homophobia in some expected places. But they also encounter poignance and sympathy through any number of chance encounters, ones that cross race, class, and sexual-preference boundaries. Where Are We? is subjective reporting at its most subtly telling, revealing the State of a Union as a fragile, abused, but touchingly

hopeful collection of individuals beyond ideological stereotypes. (D.H.)

Where the Cows Go
Dir. Ford, Maggie
1991 Great Britain English
15 mins. 16mm color Narrative
Dist. (U.S.): Frameline
A touching reminiscence of a woman institutionalized in her youth for kissing a girl.

Where There Was Silence
Dir. Bourne, Stephen
1988 Great Britain English
20 mins. video color/b&w Documentary
Dist. (U.K.): Albany Video
When Basil Dearden's *Victim* was released in Britain in 1961, it had an enormous impact on the lives of gay men in Great Britain. Starring Dirk Bogarde as a middle-class barrister who confronts his own homosexuality, Darden's film was the first mainstream British film to offer gay men credible representations of themselves and their situations. In *Where There Was Silence* five gay men, all portrayed by a single actor, recall the film and how it affected their lives. Inter-cut with extracts from *Victim*, these recollections vividly highlight what life was like for British gay men before homosexuality was decriminalized in 1967. As one of them comments, "In those days, to even discuss a film like *Victim* would have made me nervous and scared that the finger would be pointed and that I would be held to ridicule." Ending with reference to Clause 28 of the recent Local Government Bill, *Where There Was Sil*ence also goes on to question the future of gay and lesbian representation on film and video.

Where There's Smoke
Dir. Canon, Lynx
1986 USA English
30 mins. video color Narrative
Dist. (U.S.): Tiger Rose Distributing
A woman moves into a new apartment with help from the landlady. The premiere of a new lesbian erotic short.

White Flannel
(see *Out On Tuesday, Program 3*)

Who Is Poetessa Fishhouse?
Dir. Gallant, Alison, and Nicola Kountoupes
1994 USA English
15 mins. video color Experimental
Dist. (U.S.): Nicali Productions
The story of the famous San Francisco poet.

Whole of Life, The
(see *Ganze Leben, Das*)

Why I Masturbate
Dir. Brenin, Richard
1990 USA English
6 mins. video color Other
Dist. (U.S.): Brenin, Richard
Shot on a Fisher-Price pixel camera, Richard Brenin plays his guitar and sings of the many reasons for jerking off.

Why I Stopped Going to Foreign Films
Dir. Reinke, Steve
1991 Canada English
6 mins. video color Experimental
Dist. (U.S.): Reinke, Steve
Why I Stopped Going to Foreign Films takes brief images from gay porn and turns them into something lyrical and resonant.

Why Not Love?/Get Used to It
Dir. Barens, Edgar
1992 USA English
2 mins. 16mm b&w Other
Dist. (U.S.): Voodoo Peep Productions
Why Not Love?/Get Used to It is a series of gay-positive public service announcements.

Wicked Radiance
Dir. Nurudin, Azian
1992 USA Malay
5 mins. video color Experimental
Dist. (U.S.): Frameline
This film delves into aspects of S/M sexuality and the filmmaker's Muslim background (in Malay with no English subtitles).

Wigstock—The Movie
Dir. Rubnitz, Tom
1987 USA English
21 mins. video color Documentary
Dist. (U.S.): Video Data Bank
Wigstock—The Movie is a hilarious send-up of D.A. Pennebaker's *Monterey Pop* (a must-see for Joni Mitchell fans). The quintessential New York underground film/video artiste, Tom Rubnitz takes a bite out of the Big Apple and spits it out in a wild kaleidoscope of unequivocal camp and hallucinogenic color. John Sex, Happi Phace, The B-52's, Lypsinka, Ann Magnuson, Quentin Crisp, Michael Clark, and Lady Bunny are but a few of the stars that shine oh-so-brightly in Rubnitz's glittering oeuvre. A genre artist par excellence, Mr. Rubnitz can do in two minutes what most media makers wish they could do in two hours.

Everyone will have their favorite dishes from this choice menu. Part of the *Tom Rubnitz Marathon* (*A Dozen Tapes, Wigs Included*).

Wigstock: The Movie
Dir. Shils, Barry
Prod. Silvers, Dean
1994 USA English
82 mins. 35mm color Documentary
Dist. (U.S.): Samuel Goldwyn Company
Crystal Waters comes out in male drag and bumps and grinds against her studly backup dancers and RuPaul sashays on the runway in his gold metallic bodysuit. Once an underground happening, Wigstock has blossomed into a world-renowned event where some of the biggest names in music perform alongside drag superstars and queer idols. With an annual attendance of twenty thousand, Wigstock has been described as Woodstock without the bad hair.

With drag highly in vogue in Hollywood films, *Wigstock: The Movie* is a refreshingly real but wonderfully celebratory look at the high-polish event and the pioneers who started it all, including founder and emcee, the Lady Bunny. Director Barry Shils vibrantly captures the nonstop glamour of Wigstock, going from backstage preparations and rehearsals to the actual shimmering performances. Shils never lets up as he takes us on a whirlwind tour of one of the most fabulous and outrageous queer events in the world. With a dazzling cast of thousands including Lypsinka, Joey Arias, the Lady Bunny, Deee-Lite, Debbie Harry, and Jackie Beat, this is one extravaganza of a film you'll be pulling your hairpins out if you miss.

Wild Flowers
Dir. Smith, Robert
1989 Great Britain English
66 mins. 16mm color Narrative
Dist. (U.S.): Frameline Archive
Dist. (U.K.): Frontroom
Wild Flowers, filmed in a small working-class town on the west coast of Scotland, is British director Robert Smith's tribute to the strength of women, culled from childhood memories of families at whose head is the matriarch. The camerawork is slow and sensual, covering a clean and crisp seaside village. The accompanying musical score (original compositions in the Scottish tradition) floats without effort around and through the narrative. These elements, combined with a sharp screenplay and characters that are sometimes very charming, belie the fact that *Wild*

Ⓐ Ⓑ Ⓒ Ⓓ Ⓔ Ⓕ Ⓖ Ⓗ Ⓘ Ⓙ Ⓚ Ⓛ Ⓜ Ⓝ Ⓞ Ⓟ Ⓠ Ⓡ Ⓢ Ⓣ Ⓤ Ⓥ Ⓦ Ⓧ Ⓨ Ⓩ

Flowers gently and lovingly twists themes to their breaking point. Sadie, a young woman from Glasgow, is visiting her boyfriend's hometown. She agrees to stay and meet his family, and unwittingly uncovers his mothers' secret—an undiminished attraction to women. Sadie is drawn by the mother's wit and energy, and her interest in Angus (the boyfriend) diminishes by increments equal to her fascination with Angus's mother. Add to the story a bitter and unflinching grandmother (the true matriarch), a dependent husband and sons, a few local eccentrics, and a couple of harmless busybodies, and you have a typically good British film, poised for the kill.

Set in flashback, and often in Sadie's psychological space, there is the theme of tradition that is as binding as it is nurturing. What is the proper setting for passion? At what point in any life does passion concede to contentedness? And where within tradition is there a place for those who are, as the film puts it, "born dissatisfied"?

Wild Life
Dir. Goss, John C.
1985 USA English
40 mins. video color Documentary
Dist. (U.S.): Goss, John C.
A video portrait of two 15-year-old gay Latinos. The piece combines documentary-style interviews with fictional segments in which the young men act out their fantasized day in Los Angeles. As they talk about their lives, we see scenes of them changing into wild style clothes on the street, cruising around "Gay City," meeting their friends at the park, and "throwing attitude." They are questioned about the nature of being gay, relationships with friends and lovers, style and image, and their use of gay language.

Wild Reeds
Dir. Techine, Andre
1994 France French
110 mins. 35mm color Narrative
Dist. (U.S.): Strand Releasing
The French have always done coming-of-age stories particularly well, but Techine's drama rates with the best. Its characters are a teenage quartet struggling with adult emotions and desires: Leftist Maite is less girlfriend than beard to gay Francois, who has a brief fling with his otherwise straight boarding-school student Serge; Francois's roommate Henri, an angry exile from upheavals in Algeria, carries his own ambiguous weight of sexual baggage. Set in 1962, and as

much a commentary on contemporary political currents as timeless adolescent turmoil, *Wild Reeds* is a delicately sensual, complex, and resonant drama. (D. H.)

Wild Thing: A Poem by Sapphire
Dir. Dunye, Cheryl L.
1989 USA English
8 mins. video color Experimental
Dist. (U.S.): n/a
Wild Thing, A Poem by Sapphire, paints an abrasive, disturbing picture of a black youth involved in a world of poverty, isolation, and violence. Filled with strong language, "Wild Thing" explores the misogynist manifestations of a troubled youth's life and the violence he resorts to.

Wild Winds, The
Dir. Simpson, Steve
1991 USA English
8 mins. 16mm color Experimental
Dist. (U.S.): Simpson, Steve
Steve Simpson's genuinely scary surreal short.

Wild Woman of the Woods
Dir. Mootoo, Shani
1993 Canada English
12 mins. video color Experimental
Dist. (U.S.): Video Out
Shani Mootoo exposes the delights of South Asian lesbian goddesses in a snowy mountain wilderness in her exquisitely funny tape.

Wings, The
(see *Vingarne*)

Winter Is Approaching
(see *L'Hiver Approche*)

Withnail & I
Dir. Robinson, Bruce
1987 Great Britain English
105 mins. 35mm color Narrative
Dist. (U.S.): n/a
Writer/director Bruce Robinson's first feature is a loosely autobiographical comedy of two starving actor-roommates (Richard E. Grant, Paul McGann) adrift in drug-addled '60s "Swinging London." Desperately needing think space, they shamble off to the country cottage owned by Grant's outrageous swish uncle (Richard Griffiths), himself a onetime thespian with long-term delusions of grandeur. Hilarious carnal misunderstandings ensue; but a very touching, unexpected coda makes clear that the gay subtext between the principals has hardly been wishful thinking on the viewer's part. A gem. (D.H.)

Without Saying Goodbye
Dir. Miller, Tanya
1994 USA English
13 mins. video color Narrative
Dist. (U.S.): Miller , Tanya
Another moving evocation from Tanya Miller, maker of last year's stunning short, *Basic Necessities*.

Without You I'm Nothing
Dir. Boskovich, John
1990 USA English
94 mins. 35mm color/b&w Documentary
Dist. (U.S.): MCEG
Without You I'm Nothing showcases the talents and politics of a woman with a very powerful (and very queer) imagination. Sandra Bernhard's long-awaited film version of her hit one-woman show wheels through a brilliant series of stream-of-consciousness monologues and idiosyncratic vocal restylings of selections from such artists as Burt Bachrach, Hank Williams, Sylvester, and Prince. Issues around race, gender, class, religion, and sexual orientation serve as the raw material in Bernhard's social commentary as she samples, spoofs, and sneers her way through pop culture in front of an indifferent African-American audience at an L.A. nightclub. Funny, captivating, and finally disturbing, John Boskovich's masterful screen adaptation deftly articulates the perils of the culturally codependent relationship posited in the titular plea,"Without You I'm Nothing." (J.O.)

Wittgenstein
Dir. Jarman, Derek
1993 Great Britain English
75 mins. 35mm color Experimental
Dist. (U.S.): Zeitgeist Films
Dist. (U.K.): British Film Institute
Derek Jarman's first film since *Edward II* is a humorous portrait of one of this century's most influential philosophers. Made for Britain's Channel Four TV, *Wittgenstein* reflects Jarman's distinctive sense of style. Inventive images and vibrantly colored costumes (most of them containing the extraordinary Tilda Swinton) are filmed against a pitch-black background; it's what Jarman calls "the eradication of all that flim-flam." The result is so striking it almost hurts the eye. It won the Teddy Award at the 1993 Berlin International Lesbian and Gay Film Festival for Best Gay Feature.

Young Ludwig (Clancy Chassay) was born in Vienna in 1889. His family was wealthy, though mysteriously ill-fated. During studies at Cambridge University, Wittgenstein (played as an adult by Karl Johnson), is seen as an intensely brilliant thinker, not without his erotic impulses. He is patronized by Bertrand Russell (the sublime Michael Gough) and Russell's imperious mistress, Lady Ottoline Morell (Swinton, of course). Ludwig's search for intellectual self-development results in some rather shabby treatment of Johnny (Kevin Collins), the working-class man he loves.

Wittgenstein struggled with self-alienation throughout his years. He died of cancer in 1951. His final, mocking words were: "Tell them I've had a wonderful life." Jarman's film captures this life with energy and imagination.

Wolfgirl
Dir. Beiersdorf, Dagmar
1986 Germany German
85 mins. 16mm color Narrative
Dist. (U.S.): Altermedia
The story of a short but intense friendship between two very different women in Berlin. Mascha, in her mid-'30s, worked as a television editor for years before dropping out to make two self-financed and unexpectedly successful theatrical films. At the moment she's taking a break—she's run out of ideas. Her plight is made worse by her boyfriend Frank's unsympathetic attitude. He is a head of production, from a working-class background, an unscrupulous career man, and won't tolerate an unsuccessful woman around him. His attacks all come down to the same thing: "For God's sake emancipate yourself!"

In the midst of this exasperating mess Mascha meets the "wolf girl," Dennis, a young black rebel who works as a cleaner in a theater. The girl fascinates Mascha and she finally breaks off her long, loveless relationship with Frank so she can spend more time with Dennis. The two women move in together: Mascha because she wants to turn the simple, "wild" Dennis into a more sedate person, and Dennis because she has secret hopes of finding human warmth and shelter.

Director Dagmar Beiersdorf studied drama and media in Berlin and since 1968 has worked as an assistant director on films and television programs. She has also acted in all of the films of Lothar Lambert.

Woman Like Eve, A
(see *Vrouw Als Eva, Een*)

Ⓐ Ⓑ Ⓒ Ⓓ Ⓔ Ⓕ Ⓖ Ⓗ Ⓘ Ⓙ Ⓚ Ⓛ Ⓜ Ⓝ Ⓞ Ⓟ Ⓠ Ⓡ Ⓢ Ⓣ Ⓤ Ⓥ Ⓦ Ⓧ Ⓨ Ⓩ

Woman of the Wolf
Dir. Schiller, Greta
1994 Great Britain / USA English
26 mins. 35mm color Narrative
Dist. (U.S.): Jezebel Productions
An elegant and surprising fictional departure from the director of *Before Stonewall*. Set aboard a ship (sailing somewhere near The Twilight Zone), *Woman* is a haunting tale in the tradition of *Orlando*.

Woman One Day, A
Dir. Jones, Cleve
1977 USA English
6 mins. S8mm b&w Experimental
Dist. (U.S.): n/a
Images of a woman daydreaming about another woman. San Francisco State film student Cleve Jones (who went on to become the founder of The Names Project) abandoned his cinematic aspirations when Harvey Milk—on seeing this film—told him he had no talent as a filmmaker but would make a great political organizer.

Woman's Heart, A
Dir. Marian, Imri
1990 Israel Hebrew
12 mins. video color Documentary
Dist. (U.S.): Third Ear, The
Filmmaker Imri Marian introduces audiences to Zalman Shoshi, the most famous drag queen in Israel. The film is a painful and moving portrait of Zalman's life, sex, work, and need for love.

Woman's Place Is in the House, A
Dir. Porter, Nancy, and Mickey Lemle
1976 USA English
30 mins. 16mm color Documentary
Dist. (U.S.): n/a
A portrait of Massachusetts legislator Elaine Noble.

Women I Love
Dir. Hammer, Barbara
1976 USA English
25 mins. 16mm color Experimental
Dist. (U.S.): Canyon Cinema
A series of cameo portraits of the filmmaker's friends and lovers intercut with a playful celebration of fruits and vegetables pixilated in nature.
　　　　Released in the U.S. along with four of her other short films as a feature-length package, *Lesbian Sexuality: The Films of Barbara Hammer, Volume II*.

Women In Love: Bonding Strategies of

Black Lesbians
Dir. Rhue, Sylvia
1986 USA English
52 mins. video color Documentary
Dist. (U.S.): Multi Focus
Women In Love features black women talking about their public and private lives. Their discussion of families, lovers, and the way they move through society is as entertaining as it is informative.

Women Like That
Dir. Neild, Suzanne
1991 Great Britain English
25 mins. video color Documentary
Dist. (U.S.): Women Make Movies
Dist. (U.K.): Channel 4 Television
Women Like That follow eight of the sixteen lesbians who participated in the 1990 British TV documentary on older lesbian lives, *Women Like Us*. Here the women discuss how their lives have changed since the broadcast of the original program on British Channel Four television. *Women Like That* is an enlightening documentation of the voices and lives of a group of true pioneers.

Women Like Us
(also see *Out On Tuesday, Program 4*)
Dir. Neild, Suzanne
Prod. Neild, Suzanne, and Rosalind Pearson
1990 Great Britain English
40 mins. video color Documentary
Dist. (U.S.): Women Make Movies
Sixteen lesbians from diverse backgrounds, ranging in age from 50-to over 80-years-old tell about their lives from the 1920s to the present.

Women on Fire
Dir. Vaughn, Alexis
1994 USA English
11 mins. video color Documentary
Dist. (U.S.): Vaughn, Alexis
Dykes who empower themselves by eating fire, blowing fire, and lighting themselves on fire.

Women's Club
(see *Club des Femmes*)

Wonderland
Dir. Saville, Philip
1988 Great Britain English
103 mins. 35mm color Narrative
Dist. (U.S.): Vestron Pictures
From the creator of *Letter to Brezhnev*, a completely mad concoction of rent boys, arias, and dolphinariums. Eddie is a shy teen queen who

watches old weepies with his mum; his best pal Michael takes him to a local Liverpool drag disco hosted by a gingham-gowned Robbie Coltrane. When the boys witness a gangland murder, they head south—fast—to Brighton (Britain's Russian River) in the backseat of an aging opera star's Bentley. Things get weirder when Eddy starts skinny-dipping with a dolphin called Sooty, and Michael starts sleeping with the diva. Soon they're pursued by a saber-wielding assassin (played by pin-up Bruce Payne) and that's when Eddie's lip-synching to Marilyn's hits just isn't enough. Made at the same time as *Maurice*, *Wonderland* couldn't be further from England's usual couture-and-coiffeur gay sensibility. At each turn dottier and more complicated,*Wonderland* shows how gay films don't have to be genre copycats. Is it a thriller? A musical? A working-class comedy or same-sex *Big Blue*? One part social realism, two parts surrealism—you get the sense that author Frank Clarke either lost control or just transcribed a good bad dream. Either way, the result is mostly heavenly.

Word Is Out: Stories of Some of Our Lives
Dir. Mariposa Film Group
1978 USA English
130 mins. 16mm color Documentary
Dist. (U.S.): New Yorker Films
As impactful today as the day it was made, *Word Is Out* is a straightforward collection of interviews with 26 gay men and lesbians who share their unique, and yet somehow universal, stories of growing up and coming out. This one is required viewing for everyone. (J.O.)

Working Class Chronicle
Dir. Walsh, Jack
1985 USA English
42 mins. 16mm color Experimental
Dist. (U.S.): Canyon Cinema
Evocative and sometimes disturbing, this film is a courageous exploration of memory and the road to self-realization and acceptance. Jack Walsh's chronicle mixes film genres—narrative, documentary, experimental—as personal history and historical events collide. The period (1954–1969) is reconstructed through found footage, rephotographed home movies, optically printed materials, static copy-stand and icon photography (movie and rock 'n' roll stars), live-action camera work, voice-over narration, and reprocessed popular music of the times.

Working Class Dykes from Hell
Dir. Lawrence, Jacquie
1992 Great Britain English
20 mins. 16mm color Documentary
Dist. (U.K.): Lawrence, Jacquie
In the insightful *Working Class Dykes from Hell*, produced for Channel Four's Out series, working-class British lesbians talk about class differences in the lesbian community, organizing of political consciousness, and developing a sense of community.

World and Time Enough
Dir. Mueller, Eric
1994 USA English
90 mins. 16mm color Narrative
Dist. (U.S.): Strand Releasing
World and Time Enough is the first generation X gay comedy from America's heartland.

Mark (Matt Guidry), an HIV-positive artist, is obsessed with building a cathedral in honor of his father. Joey (Gregory G. Giles), his boyfriend, is a garbage collector who brings home favorite bits of junk to comfort himself as he searches for his birth parents. Their lives are very much like anyone else's: they flirt with other people, have gossipy friends, and mope about a lot.

First-time director Eric Mueller keeps his contemporary story buoyant with some delicate performances, and a good eye for Minneapolis scenery. Although there are some serious issues lurking behind the frames, Mueller puts drama first. *World and Time Enough* is also reminiscent of *Grief*, with less out-loud laughs, more locations, and a true sense of the eccentricities of everyday life. (Mueller says he was aiming for the tone of his favorite "Mary Tyler Moore Show," the one where Mary breaks into laughter at Chuckles the Clown's funeral.)

World and Time Enough has two qualities lacking in a lot of gay cinema nowadays: modesty and charm.

Winner of the 1995 San Francisco International Lesbian & Gay Film Festival Audience Award for Best Feature.

World Is Sick (sic), The
Dir. Greyson, John
1989 Canada English
38 mins. video color Other
Dist. (U.S.): Video Data Bank
John Greyson brings his trademark style to events at the Montreal 1989 International AIDS Conference in *The World is Sick (sic)*. Our guide is a preposterous drag reporter whose attempts to

Ⓐ Ⓑ Ⓒ Ⓓ Ⓔ Ⓕ Ⓖ Ⓗ Ⓘ Ⓙ Ⓚ Ⓛ Ⓜ Ⓝ Ⓞ Ⓟ Ⓠ Ⓡ Ⓢ Ⓣ Ⓤ Ⓥ Ⓦ Ⓧ Ⓨ Ⓩ

interview self-important scientists and corporate profiteers are constantly interrupted by, as she puts it, "those scruffy activists." It's a sublime way to slice through conference cant and offer another point of view on the event (Greyson is careful to explain that this is just one of many potential accounts of what happened). Along the way, AIDS activists from England, Mexico, Trinidad, Thailand, and South Africa are given center stage to shove the record back in our favor.

World of Light: A Portrait of May Sarton
Dir. Simpson, Maria, and Martha Wheelock
1980 USA English
30 mins. 16mm color Documentary
Dist. (U.S.): Ishtar Films
A short documentary about the life and work of lesbian writer May Sarton.

Wrecked for Life: The Trip and Magic of the Trocadero Transfer
Dir. Goss, John C.
1993 USA English
60 mins. video color Documentary
Dist. (U.S.): Goss, John C.
Gay discos were all the rage in the late '70s and early '80s, but a special kind of magic permeated San Francisco's legendary Trocadero Transfer. John Goss's *Wrecked for Life* features interviews with several habitués and employees from the Troc's glory days.

There's a nostalgic tinge, and a sense of the club's enduring spirit—one fellow carries his membership card in his wallet to this day. The group's recollections are so vivid that the Troc comes to life even though Goss has decide not to incorporate archival footage (though Jim, the daffy lighting man, does recreate a couple of his scintillating set-ups).

The interviewees regale the camera with tales of sex and drugs (before these activities became unfashionable, and then fashionable again); they also describe the tremendous feeling of community the Trocadero engendered. "In those days the community wasn't so divided," waxes "Disco Connie" Norman. Perhaps she's peering through time-warped glasses, but as the tape makes clear, the Trocadero provided an atmosphere highly conducive to collective abandon and nonstop dancing. Goss has rounded up an engaging ensemble for this evocative softshoe through a memorable moment in San Francisco gay history.

Wrong Son, The
Dir. Oliver, Bill
1993 USA English
15 mins. video color Experimental
Dist. (U.S.): Oliver,Bill
The Wrong Son by Bill Oliver examines gays in the military within the framework of an old TV game show, "To Tell TheTruth."

Yearning For Sodom, A
Dir. Raab, Kurt, Hanno Baethe, and Hans Hirschmuller
1989 Germany German
45 mins. video color Documentary
Dist. (U.S.): Hanno Baethe Video Production
Three and a half years before work began on this videotape, German actor Kurt Raab was commissioned to write a book about himself and the New German Film. The book was never completed. Instead, Raab decided to do sketches on video with Hanno Baethe. Six of the thirty-three sketches were completed before Raab learned that he was HIV positive. A short time later he was confined to bed in a Hamburg hospital, dependent on the help of others. Shot up to the time he died, *A Yearning for Sodom* presents excerpts from the video sketches, scenes from Raab's film work with Fassbinder, and interviews with Raab and his actor friend and main caregiver, Hans Hirschmuller.

Yma Sumac: Hollywood's Inca Princess
Dir. Czernetzky, Gunther
1992 Germany German
90 mins. video color Documentary
Dist. (U.S.): Rubicon Film
Originally from Peru, Yma's extraordinary eight-octave range brought her world acclaim in the '50s. Her first album—*The Voice of XtaBay*—is in a genre all of its own (file under Operatic Peruvian Folk Song with Full Orchestra). With international success, and a few more albums (culminating in the truly ghastly rock-disco medley *Miracles*), myths about Yma multiplied. Could she really sing live? Was she really from Peru? Spelt backwards, wasn't she actually Amy Camus from Teaneck, New Jersey?

Gunther Czernetzky's well-researched bio *Yma Sumac: Hollywood's Inca Princess* tackles all the myths, and gets at some even stranger truths. Czernetzky starts out in the hills of Peru (asking peasants if they've heard of Yma), and proceeds to America, where he talks to record producers and finally, the man who managed her New York gay cabaret comeback in the early

'80s. Along the way there's lots of rare footage, including Yma's famous encounter with David Letterman.

You Can Fight City Hall
Dir. Schaefer, Vivian
1984 USA English
32 mins. video color Documentary
Dist. (U.S.): n/a
You Can Fight City Hall is a disturbing, very important documentation of what lesbians and gay men are up against in the Midwest. Well-crafted.

You Can Open Your Eyes Now
Dir. Sandler, Arlene
1991 Canada English
3 mins. video color Other
Dist. (U.S.): Frameline
A quick and clever evocation of the relation between d.j. and dancer.

You Can't Die from Not Sleeping
Dir. Hirshorn, Harriet
1985 USA English
8 mins. S8mm color Experimental
Dist. (U.S.): Hirshorn, Harriet
An experimental documentary about homeless women in New York.

You & I Will Play
Dir. Caspersen, Randy
1994 USA English
5 mins. 16mm b&w Narrative
Dist. (U.S.): Caspersen, Randy
Two young men come to terms with their long-distance relationship.

You Just Love Your Children
Dir. Lunger, Jeff, and Ritch James
1978 USA English
14 mins. 16mm b&w Documentary
Dist. (U.S.): Lunger, Jeff
A short documentary profile of two gay-parented families.

You Little Devil, You
Dir. Kuhne, Kadet
1994 USA English
5 mins. video color Other
Dist. (U.S.): Planet Eye Productions
A sexy (and safe) solarized porno short.

You Say Maria, I Say Mariah
Dir. Jarvis, Ian, and David Collins
1994 Canada English
5 mins. video color Other

Dist. (U.S.): Collins, David
The truth about gay love in the '90s, with appearances by Julie Andrews and Porky Pig.

You Taste American
Dir. Greyson, John
1986 Canada English
24 mins. video color Experimental
Dist. (U.S.): Video Data Bank
Michel Foucault and Tennessee Williams have an affair.

You Thrive on Mistaken Identity
Dir. Chang, Melissa
1989 USA English
18 mins. video color Experimental
Dist. (U.S.): Mai Kiang/Artistic License Films
Combining photos, self-conscious monologues, dress-up, and drawings, Chang searches to define her identity as an Asian Pacific lesbian.

Young Physique, The :
"Duals" & "A Day At Fire Island"
Dir. unknown
1950 USA English
6 mins. 16mm b&w Other
Dist. (U.S.): Olson, Jenni
A pair of classic silent physique films starring Billy Hill and Jim Stryker.

Young Soul Rebels
Dir. Julien, Isaac
1991 Great Britain English
103 mins. 35mm color Narrative
Dist. (U.S.): Swank Motion Pictures
Dist. (U.K.): British Film Institute
During the opening scenes of Isaac Julien's new film *Young Soul Rebels*, as Parliament's "P-Funk Wants To Get Funked Up" echoed through my head, I was temporarily transported back to 1977—remembering the house/garage parties and clubs that I went to back then—and my feelings of nostalgia and deja vu continued throughout the film as the movie's soundtrack mirrored the soundtrack of my youth and coming out. For those old enough to remember 1977, Julien's latest work will definitely evoke memories of a youthful and maybe rebellious past.

A move toward more mainstream filmmaking by the director of *Looking for Langston*, *Young Soul Rebels* is Julien's first feature film. It is an exciting and culturally accurate portrait of growing up black in England in the 1970s that combines multicultural and polymorphous sexuality in the vigorous funk/soul and punk youth countercultures, and a murder mys-

Ⓐ Ⓑ Ⓒ Ⓓ Ⓔ Ⓕ Ⓖ Ⓗ Ⓘ Ⓙ Ⓚ Ⓛ Ⓜ Ⓝ Ⓞ Ⓟ Ⓠ Ⓡ Ⓢ Ⓣ Ⓤ Ⓥ Ⓦ Ⓧ **Ⓨ** Ⓩ

tery into a fresh and certainly long overdue look at a crucially influential period in recent cultural history—the rise of a black youth subculture in England.

Julien has set out to uncover the "hidden history" of this black youth subculture and to assert its overlooked importance. *Young Soul Rebels* is much more than simply a nostalgic look at bygone days. The issues it brings up are just as relevant today as they were in the late '70s—issues of race, class, gender, and sexuality.

Julien offers us a glimpse of London in 1977 that is a beleaguered but beguiling utopia—polychromatic, polymorphous, and pre-Thatcher. Julien says that the true legacy of that era is that "in 1977, on the dance floor when I was 17 or 18, I could see all different kinds of things happening that were exciting: there were transactions between black and white, gay and straight, the punk ethic, the soul boy and girl ethic of doing it yourself and not believing everything that everyone tells you to do and be. These are the things I want the audience to start remembering in *Young Soul Rebels*."

Julien is one of the four cofounders of Sankofa Film and Video, a collective of young black filmmakers who have been producing groundbreaking, radical works in film and television since 1983. His film is a deliberate change of pace from his earlier work—*Territories*, *The Passion of Remembrance* (codirected with Maureen Blackwood), *This Is Not an AIDS Advertisement*, *Looking for Langston*—which is more experimental and non-narrative in style. In search of a bigger budget and wider audience, Julien and his Sankofa partner Nadine Marsh-Edwards approached the British Film Institute in 1985, and encouraged by the newly appointed head of production, Colin McCabe, they began a story based on their own experiences growing up in the '70s and witnessing the "wonderfully hybrid space that existed then."

A key element in bringing together the diverse threads of the script was the inclusion of a murder mystery subplot. The film dramatizes a whole series of debates through the reactions to the murders. "The killer is there as a kind of representation," says Julien. "And though he is kind of stereotypical, I'm admitting to that because most mainstream genre movies are stereotypical. I wanted to talk about white desire and attraction and repulsion and that kind of phenomenon, in a [Franz] Fanonian way. I wanted to draw on the experience of and talk about what I see as a very central anxiety that white

subjects have about black sexuality."

Julien downplays the idea that some people may criticize his use of the stereotyped murderous repressed homosexual, particularly as the killer's repressed sexuality is conflated in his film with a Fanonian depiction of white desire for and envy of blackness and black masculinity. "The film also has a sense of that whole anxiety about blacks, and the policing of blacks and our sexuality, that has to do with the fear of the "other" within yourself. The fact that the killer is white is not just a problem for gay culture. It's a problem for society as a whole, and for white male anxiety."

It is indicative of Julien's work that he emphasizes ambivalence and interactions between different identities and attempts to blur the distinction between these identities. In *Young Soul Rebels*, which explores the friendship between Chris and Caz, two soul disc jockeys who have been friends since childhood, Chris, the lighter-skinned, less masculine character is straight, while Caz, the darker, more masculine character is gay, effectively exploding stereotypical and preconceived notions about both blackness and gayness.

Julien, who is actively engaged in black and gay politics, wants more plural and ambivalent representations of black masculinities. "Forget the macho black male stereotype. Soul boy fashion was quite effeminate. It's important to portray the construction of black masculinity which is something that's very vulnerable and fragile. . . . I think the question of internalized racism is an important one, but I don't think it's one that you can be totally moralistic about, and I think there's a lot of moralism about it out there. On the whole, though, the main problem with representations of interracial couples, be they gay or straight, is that the relationship is usually pathologized, and usually somebody has to pay the price of transgressing those racial boundries."

Unlike other films about interracial relationships which have a tendency to be pessimistic or negative in their views, *Young Soul Rebels* is much more generous and idealistic in its vision. "I wanted to make a film which would be very different, that would speak to my experiences in a more specific way," explains Julien. "And to try to grapple with some of these questions of ambivalence, sexual identity, racial and sexual differences, and make them slightly popularized, if you like, without being a populist."

Young Soul Rebels is truly a celebration of diversity—different races, lifestyles, and sexual orientations. It cannot simply be called a black film, or a gay film, or a black gay film, because it transcends the limitations of such reductive labels.

Summing up the rationale for this debut feature, Julien elucidates, "I see my role as being sort of interested in theoretical ideas, but translating those ideas into the visual terrain. What I tried to do is to hide or submerge very complex ideas about race and identity, and sexual difference and racial difference, in a form or genre that would be more widely understood." (K.K.)

Your Heart Is All Mine
Dir. Gotz, Elke
1992 Germany German
50 mins. 16mm color Narrative
Dist. (U.S.): Dimpfl, Susanne /DFFB
One of the most tender lesbian love stories to reach the screen at this year's festival, Your Heart Is All Mine is also one of the most quirky.

Hilde, played by sly beauty Karla Schender, is a secretary in an anonymous corporate firm. The pariah of the secretarial pool, her colleagues mutter, "All that she knows how to do to is work. When you look like this, what else can you do?"

Plenty, apparently! After meeting a baby butch in a butcher shop (a scene not recommended for vegetarians), Hilde sneaks into her new love's apartment, strips, and waits for her to come home from work. German angst and despair give way to 1950s pulp heartthrob as the butcher beds the secretary; keep your eyes open here for one of the loveliest of lovemaking scenes in the coming-out ouvre."

Zanne: So Many Women
Dir. Austin
1989 USA English
4 mins. video color Other
Dist. (U.S.): n/a
A lesbian music video.

Zapovezena Laska (Forbidden Love)
Dir. Kvasnicka, Vladislav
1990 Czechoslovakia Czech
44 mins. 35mm color Documentary
Dist. (U.S.): Czechoslovak Filmexport
A documentary look at homosexuality in Czechoslovakia, a country just beginning to understand that an estimated 750,000 of its citizens are gay and lesbian. Through incredibly honest interviews with gays, gay rights leaders—

and blatant homophobes—director Vladislav Kvasnicka has created a film that captures the innocence of an incipient social movement as well as a chilling look at the culture they're up against.

Zero Patience
Dir. Greyson, John
1993 Canada English
100 mins. 35mm color Narrative
Dist. (U.S.): Cinevista
Dist. (U.K.): Dangerous To Know
Presented as a surprise sneak preview in the 1993 festival. Targeting scientists looking for profit, journalists seeking fame through simplified storytelling, and activists who've lost sight of their own confusion in vigilant righteousness, John Greyson's Zero Patience is an AIDS musical that is to Hollywood AIDS stories like Philadelphia what Peter Duesberg is to the CDC: an annoyance. Stubbornly agnostic, beautifully sentimental, this film manages to turn almost every AIDS paradigm on its head. The primary message of the film, as its makers describe it in the liner notes to the CD, is "to expose the epidemic of blame that has accompanied the AIDS crisis." Specifically, they want to rescue "Patient Zero," the flight attendant who purportedly brought AIDS to North America, from his undeserved posthumous villainy. They succeed, using synchronized swimming, song and dance, nubile young men, talking assholes, and Fantastic Voyage-style life rafts. Over the top? Maybe, but it's a surreal medium for a surreal disease. (S.G.)

Zoe la Boxeuse (Zoe the Boxer)
Dir. Dridi, Karim
1992 France French
24 mins. 16mm color Narrative
Dist. (U.S.): KD Productions
A clever French faux-documentary which examines the story of a female boxer who became a man and murdered her manager.

Ⓐ Ⓑ Ⓒ Ⓓ Ⓔ Ⓕ Ⓖ Ⓗ Ⓘ Ⓙ Ⓚ Ⓛ Ⓜ Ⓝ Ⓞ Ⓟ Ⓠ Ⓡ Ⓢ Ⓣ Ⓤ Ⓥ Ⓦ Ⓧ Ⓨ **Ⓩ**

CLIP SHOWS
AND SPECIAL PRESENTATIONS

Over the years, clip and comment shows have become a staple of the gay and lesbian film festival circuit. Usually featuring about an hour of film or video clips with a lecture woven in between them, these programs have entertained and educated audiences about everything from the history of lesbian and gay pornography to queers and "Star Trek." Most of the following programs were featured in the San Francisco International Lesbian & Gay Film Festival. Many of them went on to play at other festivals around the globe.

All Girl Action:
The History of Lesbian Erotica
Bright, Susie
1989 USA English
90 video color/b&w Clip Show
Worley Management
In 1985 lesbians made the first erotic videos by and for women. But for the past 20 years, since the advent of X-rated film, the movie business has had a controversial affair with the lesbian sexual image.

From 1970s soft-focus Euro-trash to early lesbian feminist sapphistry, from B-grade Hollywood fantasies to *Desert Hearts*, the lesbian erotic picture has been a mixture of stereotype and authenticity, and whether male produced or not, it's been a reflection of the changing lesbian consciousness. Susie Bright, editor of *On Our Backs* magazine and *Herotica*, will show explicit and provocative clips from the past two decades oof lesbian sexuality on the screen, as well as introduce the contrasting perspectives of modern-day lesbian erotic video makers. Susie will also discuss the lesbian point of view as the audience and the subject, and our similarities and differences with gay men's and heterosexual erotic presentation. The presentation will include scenes from *Sweet Dreams*, *We Are Ourselves*, *Therese and Isabelle*, *Desert Hearts*, *Lianna*, *Personal Best*, *Liquid Sky*, *Aerobisex Girls*, *The Kink*, *Private Pleasures*, *Erotic in Nature*, *Reflections*, and *Waking Up*.

Annette Forster Lecture
Forster, Annette
1989 English
90 video color/b&w Clip Show
Forster, Annette

As a critic and programmer, Annette Forster has come to be recognized as an expert on international lesbian cinema. She programmed the lesbian section of Holland's 1986 International Gay and Lesbian Film Festival, one of the most ambitious and comprehensive festivals of lesbian/gay media ever organized. In this presentation she will look at the lesbian cinema's search for a new voice; a cinema that is "subversive and romantic at the same time—these films open up space for new forms of love." Excerpts will be screened from international lesbian cinema from the past fifteen years. Titles will include, among others, Chantal Akerman's *Je, Tu, Il, Elle*, Alexandra von Grote's *Novembermoon*, and Lea Pool's *Anne Trister*.

Barry Walters'
Fabulous World of Queer Pop Video
Walters, Barry
1992 USA English
90 video color Clip Show
Walters, Barry
Among the issues under scrutiny will be straight appropriation of queer signifiers, how closet-case performers wink at us while playing straight for hets, queer film directors who create subversive vids, disco divas hungry for the lavender dollar, sensitive dyke songwriters, bad girls, sissy boys, beefcake-a-go-go, heroic hairdos, and heinous hair-don'ts.

Beyond the Pale:
The Celluloid Closet of Yiddish Film
Sicular, Eve
1994 USA English
100 video color/b&w Clip Show
Sicular, Eve
An exploration of lesbian and gay subtext in Yiddish cinema during its heyday, from musical comedies such as *Yidl with His Fiddle* and *American Matchmaker*, to classic dramas such as *The Dybbuk* and *Overture to Glory*. Discussions of these and other gems of the Yiddish screen as well as such features as *Radio Days*, *Yentl*, *Colonel Redl*, *Crossfire*, and *Gentleman's Agreement* will be accompanied by clips from selected films and period home movies.

Bottoms Up:
Bar-Hopping Queers of the Silver Screen
Mangin, Daniel
1993 USA English
100 video color/b&w Clip Show
Strand Releasing

What happens when Hollywood's homosexuals get inside gay bars? This intriguing and compelling compilation of lesbian and gay bar scenes offers a unique perspective on the celluloid closet. Featuring clips from such old favorites as The Killing of Sister George and Advise and Consent, this amusing foray looks at cruising etiquette, dress codes, bar stools, and Hollywood's homophobic hangovers.

Camp for Boys & Girls
Olson, Jenni
1992 USA English
75 16mm color Special Presentation
Artistic License Films, Inc.
A vast collection of the campiest examples of American pop culture is offered up in this barrage of Hollywood trailers, educational film excerpts, TV clips, and commercials. You'll hear, "The shattering truth about girls behind bars!" You'll cheer for the queer superheroes! You'll see gay actors and bad television drag!!!

Coming Attractions
(Selling the Homo, Hollywood-Style)
Lumpkin, Michael
1990 USA English
90 35mm color/b&w Special Presentation
Olson, Jenni
Everyone agrees that mainstream movie trailers are mostly more entertaining than the features they're promoting, and the same is as true for Hollywood's gay-themed films as for any others. Hence this once-in-a-lifetime program: Frameline unveils an evening of movie previews and promos—the compleat lesbian and gay movie trailer catalog. It's for fans of the art and for anyone who can't be bothered to sit through a hundred-minute feature to learn what Hollywood thinks of homosexuals. Experience in synopsized form the drama of the sensational sales pitch (in trailers for The Killing of Sister George, Cruising, and The Gay Deceivers), the comedy of coyness (Making Love, Victim), and the humanity of Hollywood at its most perplexed (Some of My Best Friends Are . . .). Other rare previews include Women In Revolt, Glen or Glenda, Tea and Sympathy, Can't Stop the Music, A Taste of Honey, The Hunger, 99 Women, Norman Is That You? and Reform School Girls. To round out the cinematic experience: homo promos of a less conventional sort. Between the trailers, look for special yesteryear surprises like the never-screened TV ad for Johnson's Baby Powder (aimed at the lesbian market), an unusual application for a brand of auto shock absorber, and the infamous Charles Nelson Reilly Jell-o commercial. A night to remember!

Cross-Sexing the Narrative: Lesbian Subtext in Music Videos
Bociurkiw, Marusia
1992 Canada/USA English
90 video color/b&w Clip Show
Bociurkiw, Marusia
Provocative, subversive, funny, and informative, this unique presentation invites you to revel in the special pleasures of discovering and uncovering lesbian subtexts (and not-so-"sub" texts) in the music videos of k.d. lang, Joan Armatrading, Michelle Shocked, Annie Lennox, Salt 'n' Pepa, and many others. From Madonna's ever-popular girl kiss in "Justify My Love," to k.d. lang's rarely seen "I Wanna Sing You a Love Song" duet with Anne Murray, this wildly amusing presentation tours lesboeroticism, androgyny, cross-dressing, and vegetarianism.

Cyberstroika
Please Louise Productions
1995 USA English
video color/b&w Special Presentation
Please Louise Productions
Cyberstroika transforms the raw warehouse space of San Francisco's Southern Exposure gallery into a freestyle, digital extravaganza—a multimedia playground where sci-fi meets fantasy meets dreamscape meets wishful thinking. Cyberstroika is composed of six thematically-linked exhibits, each specially designed to create an environment and context in which to view digital video and multimedia presentations. The programming and architecture of Cyberstroika is by Please Louise Productions, creators of more than 75 video presentations in the Bay Area and beyond in the last two years.

1) The Safer Sex Visitors Center is a welcoming kiosk designed to ensure your safer passage into the future. This exhibit will feature monitors showcasing innovative safer-sex videos by Barbara Hammer, Joe Hoffman, Genessa Krasnow, Belial/Pink Eye Video, Ylonda Stevens, Zachary Longtree, and others; an interactive kiosk by the local gay BBS Outline and The Brothers Network Interactive Safe Sex Video Game; and a table of printed information (available in multiple languages) from local AIDS/HIV service agencies. Environmental design is by Museo Contempo and Bert Green/Circle Elephant. The Safer Sex Visitors Center is sponsored by Q Action: The Young Men's

Program of STOP AIDS PROJECT.

2) ZoLoft invites you to take a trip on a pirate spaceship, celebrating the techno visions of computer animation and hallucinogenic "rave" visuals. ZoLoft encourages you to explore, experiment with, and experience those alternative forms of reality afforded to us through synthetic means. Created by S. Topiary and curated with Gretchen Hildebran, this exhibit features an installation of screen-savers by Greg Jalbert, Lucia Grossberger-Morales, and Sara Frucht; ambient visual poetry by Elise Hurwitz; video eye candy by Belial/Pink Eye Video, Kadet Kuhne, Tari Abramovitch, and Kenneth Penn. ZoLoft environment design is by Amy Berk, Renee Rivera, and Carrie Cronenwett, and includes a live sound installation by Angela Williams; blacklight painting by Zanne; and a collage of video, slide, and text projections created by the ZoLoftian team.

3) The Hal 2000 Social Plan, the flip side of "technological progress," is a technophobic exhibit exploring the potential of new technology to only further the agenda(s) of the very same dominant institutions from which the individual "cyber-cowboy" seeks freedom. The hypercontrolled environment of this exhibit, mirroring the power these agencies wield in their regulation of technology and perpetuation of oppressive paradigms, is juxtaposed with postapocalyptic visions that decry these terrifying aspects of high-tech society. HAL's visual nightmare is framed by Lecram Nerak's Das Simulation, Elliot Anderson's Inforia, and original compilations by Please Louise Productions. Exhibit design is by Cary Boisvert, Matt Bass, and Andy Knipe.

4) The CyberExpo, playing on the conventions of the multimedia Expo or World's Fair, is a high-end "product fair" that explores the marketability and commercialization of queer multimedia, and suggests ways in which queer aesthetics might inform approaches to information, entertainment, products, and services. It is here that one is treated to some of the featured innovations of the Multimedia Age: interactive exhibits by Rex Bruce, Jordy Jones, Texas Tomboy, Quinn Hearne, the new alternative on-line service, Total Entertainment Network by Optigon Interactive, and the Go Girl pinball machine by Michael Brown, make use of such formats as CD-ROM, digital video, and the virtual environment.

5) The Bargain Basement is offered as an alternative to the CyberExpo. Since the vast majority of queers do not have access to the latest, most expensive state-of-the-art technology,

artists often work with what they can get their hands on. Innovative "experiments" on limited budgets and limited access are celebrated in this exhibit—for the radical ways that they reenvision the cultural landscape. Digital videos by Melinda Hess, Barbara Hammer, David Rauch, Donald Guarnieri, Muso Contempo, Kenn Sprenkel, Mona De Vestal, and the premiere of Christ by Jon Bush and Iguana Productions.

6) The Museo Contempo Now Lounge is a site-specific, future-funk environment created by Museo Contempo for the Southern Exposure's mezzanine, incorporating Museo Contempo's five years of Amiga-based video work, an environment by Scott Pimentel's Lycra Village, and live cocktail hosts to boot! It is here, in the heart of the new century habitat, where entertainment, shopping, communication, and education can be accessed through a cavalcade of digital boxes.

Days of Greek Gods, The (Physique Films Of Richard Fontaine)
Fontaine, Richard
1988 USA English
90 16mm b&w Special Presentation
Fontaine, Richard

Richard Fontaine is the spiritual father of modern gay erotica, the fountainhead from which all else has flowed. Although he didn't invent the idea of erotic gay films, he pioneered their commercial possibilities. His landmark The Days of Greek Gods (1949) is the earliest-known gay erotic film to play theatrical engagements.

Under the signature of Zenith Films, Richard used the Athletic Model Guild studios in Los Angeles for his early posing-strap shorts. He even convinced AMG's legendary physique photographer, Bob Miser, to start making 8mm films himself to sell via his popular Physique Pictorial. Both men used historic motifs in their work, Richard in films and Bob in still photography. The props and models and conceepts flowed freely from one medium to the other. Between them, they reinvented the glamorous sexual iconography of the gladiator. In the early days of posing-strap films (1950–1965) with their cachet of being "art studies" and requiring little more flexing while wearing a white nylon pouch, it was possible to solicit the services of up-and-coming actors and bodybuilders.

All of Richard Fontaine's short films are divided into three types: The posing films were about being a model; the historic films used antiquity as a means to a visual end; the story films were contemporary situations built on foundations either of bonding or of struggles for domination. An air of romanticism pervades these films, undeniable even in the least romantic situations. The motivations of the characters are timeless, universal. These films are, after all, about the search for love and acceptance.

Electric City Presents:
Red, Hot, and Bruised
Electric City
1995 USA English
100 video color/b&w Special Presentation
Electric City

San Francisco's own "Cheap TV" experts, Electric City Network, have chronicled the lives and losses of gay, lesbian, and transgender people for the last twelve years. Nominated for three Emmy Awards, Electric City has highlighted AIDS activism, the club scene, the court system, police riots, drag queens, dyke daddies, sex workers, street fairs, parades, protests, performers, poets, the quotables and notables, not to mention the unmentionables. *Red, Hot, and Bruised* is a kaleidoscope of amazing footage, fierce music, and historic photographs from Electric City; with help from Bill Longen, Chuck Roseberry, and some of the city's best photographers.

Uncut and uncensored, *Red, Hot, and Bruised* reviews history through the eyes and ears of a queer activist camera crew who were at the right place, at the right time recording everything from Fetish & Fantasy, to Let It All Hang Out Day, Coronations, and police brutality. Electric City was arrested in Sacramento for "conspiracy to film a demonstration" and were attacked by San Francisco's finest while taping the October 6, 1989, Castro Lock Down. Electric City was also in the rotunda of City Hall to film a body bag dance for the Day of Disaster.

Red, Hot, and Bruised will include special appearances from Jerome Caja's acting debut playing all Shakespeare's heroines, to Tom Ammiano, Chrystos, Lani Kaahumanu, Elvis Herselvis, Phatima, Patsy Cline, Lisi DeHaas, Crystal Mason, Rainbeau, Danny Williams, Doris Fish, Kate Bornstein, Pansy Division, Robert Bray, Bob Hawk, Miss Kitty, John Waters, Charles Busch, Susie Bright, Learch, Keith Hennessy, Vito Russo, Justin Bond, Lypsinka, Miss Uranus Contest, Joan Jett Blakk, and many more surprises. Sit back, relax, and enjoy the ride.

First Annual Gay Men's Erotic Safe Sex Video Awards, The
San Francisco AIDS Foundation
1992 USA English 100 video color/b&w Special Presentation
San Francisco AIDS Foundation

A steamy, voyeuristic, Academy Awards–style show featuring the best of the San Francisco AIDS Foundation's Gay Men's Erotic Safe Sex Video Contest. Launched in 1992, the competition invited anyone with access to a video camera—from first-timers to commercial porn producers—to create gay male erotica which highlights HIV risk-reduction techniques. The show features excerpts from the finalists and other notable entries, including *The Package*, directed by Jonny Symons and Luna Hananel, *Safety in Numbers* by Eric Slade (what happens when friends get together?), and Al Eingang's low-budget raunch tour-de-force, *I'm Gonna Eat Worms*. Plus Joe Hammond's computer-animated short *Evil Thoughts*, and *Bi Ways*, a bizarre commentary on the cult of cuteness by Paul Shimazaki and Prescott Chow. We'll be showing clips from all the contenders and—just like at the Oscars—the winners won't be known until the envelopes are opened on stage. The awards also include special commendations for Best Commercial/Professional Video and Best Instructional Video.

Presenting awards will be hot heart-throbs from Falcon Studios and comedian Mark Davis.

Flesh Histories
Kalin, Tom
1992 USA English
120 video color/b&w Special Presentation
Drift Distribution

Designed as a touring package for wide distribution, *Flesh Histories* is curated by Tom Kalin. Recent years have witnessed a resurgence of work concerning the individual's ability to control that most intimate space within which we have no choice but to live: our bodies. *Flesh Histories* is an excitingly diverse program of short films and tapes which present the contested zone of bodies in all their fleshy splendor, tracing the contours and complex overlaps within identities as they are based in gender, class, race, and sexuality.

Hard to Imagine: Illicit Homoerotic Film and Photography, 1850–1969
Waugh, Thomas
1991 Canada English

150 slides/16mm color/b&w Clip Show
Waugh, Thomas
This film clip and slide-show presentation on the hidden history of gay erotic film and photography is illustrated by rare archival film clips along with a collection of stunning explicit photographs.

Thomas Waugh is a film historian teaching at Concordia University, Montreal, whose book on gay male erotic film and photography (both illicit and aboveground) is forthcoming.

Idol Thoughts: Richard Dyer On Gay Porn
Dyer, Richard
1994 USA English
100 video color Clip Show
Dyer, Richard
What makes watching a porn video exciting is the fact that you are watching some people making a porn video, some performers doing it in front of cameras, and you. I do not believe I am alone or even especially unusual in being turned on more by the thought of the cameras, crew, and me in attendance. In this program we'll be looking at this phenomenon, focusing especially on porn star Ryan Idol.

Image of the Sad Young Man, The
Dyer, Richard
1994 USA English
100 video color/b&w Clip Show
Dyer, Richard
From Sal Mineo in *Rebel Without a Cause* to John Kerr in *Tea and Sympathy*, renowned gay historian and film critic Richard Dyer presents a history of gay movie melancholia. This special presentation is part lecture, part clip show; it's a unique opportunity to meet Richard Dyer in person.

"When I was growing up in the late '50s and '60s, I assented that the lot of queers like myself was a melancholy one. I don't remember exactly where I first picked up this idea, but I do remember seeing myself in the characters of Geoff in *A Taste of Honey* and both Reggie and Pete in *The Leather Boys*, or knowing that books with covers showing pairs of young men looking mournfully downward yet toward each other were for me.

"Now what interests me in looking at the image of the gay man as the sad young man is the way a stereotype can be complex, varied, intense, and contradictory, an image of otherness in which it is still possible to find oneself."
—Richard Dyer, *The Matter of Images*

Kids in the Hall
Rich, B. Ruby

1993 Canada English
100 video color Clip Show
Rich, B. Ruby
Kids in the Hall are a young Toronto comedy team with a penchant for drag, genderbending, and some of the most outrageous prohomo skits ever beamed over the airwaves. They are also one of network TV's best-kept secrets, although this has not stopped them from developing a loyal cult following. Would you believe Sappho Sluggers, a dyke softball team (played, of course, by the same five guys who play everyone else) with a martini-mixing guest coach? Or Running Faggot, a new folk hero for our times? Or Dracula, a gay esthete with a taste for rough trade?

Plus don't miss the foolproof test for gayness, as devised by beloved secretaries Kathy and Cathy (whose most ferocious insults, incidentally, are reserved for Tanya, the temp). Don't miss the shocking episode that reveals "Scott Thompson isn't gay anymore." All this, plus the public debut of "Celebrity," the AIDS sketch that CBS refused to run.

Killing Off the Queer Side: Psychological Suggestion in Mainstream Cinema
Mangin, Daniel
1995 USA English
100 video color/b&w Clip Show
Strand Releasing
A look at how mainstream films have reflected and reinforced the notion of homosexuality as a "phase" that a person must pass through on the way to becoming a fully functioning human being—and that those who don't are doomed and/or a threat to society. Clips include *The Fox*, *Desert Fury*, and *Rebel Without a Cause*, as well as such '90s Hong Kong films as *All's Well That Ends Well*, and *The Gigolo* and the *Whore, Part 2*.

Let's Watch Something Daddy Wants to Watch
Livingston, Jennie, and Jim Lyons
1993 USA English
90 video color/b&w Clip Show
Livingston, Jennie
In this spicy clip-and-comment show, Jennie Livingston and Jim Lyons explore sadomasochism in the movies, television, and, finally, in pornography. Within a queer context, this program examines the purpose and impact of sadomasochistic imagery in film. If we define sadomasochism as the consensual eroticizing of pain and/or surrender, or the sexual exchange of power, there is no

shortage of relevant images from television and the movies.

With clips from *Barbarella*, *Batman*, *Bugs Bunny*, and *Buñuel*, this program promises to be entertaining, erotic, campy, and provocative.

Looking Butch: A Rough Guide to Butches on Film

Halberstam, Judith, and Jenni Olson
1995 USA English
100 video color/b&w Clip Show
Olson, Jenni
Where once the cute little tomboy was more than acceptable in films like *Member of the Wedding* and *Paper Moon*, and girls refused to be girls in *Johnny Guitar* and *Calamity Jane*, now shades of femme have softened the celluloid butch. This lively and intriguing cruise through butch film history is hosted by Judith Halberstam, assistant professor of Literature at UC San Diego. The program was curated by Halberstam and film archivist Jenni Olson.

Looking for My Penis (The Eroticized Asian in Gay Video Porn)

Fung, Richard
1990 Canada/USA English
90 video color Clip Show
Fung, Richard
For centuries, there has been an influential current in Western thought that sees an inverse correlation between intelligence and sexuality. The most recent manifestations of this equation have cast the Asian man as a sexless math or computer whiz. This stereotype has proliferated on all levels of popular consciousness as well as in the non-Asian media. Asian men and women are almost completely absent as subject in mainstream cinema and on television. When they do appear, it is usually within a narrow range of roles. Given this context, it is hardly surprising that Asians are almost completely absent from mainstream, North American, gay erotic imagery. On the other hand, there is a growing specialty market for gay porn video featuring Asian men. Focusing on the work of Sum Yong Mahn, one of the few North American actors worthy of being called a gay porn star, this illustrated talk by Richard Fung examines the way in which Asian men have figured in porn, and explores the ideology beneath seemingly innocuous imagery. *Looking for My Penis* takes the point of view of the gay Asian man searching for sexual as well as

racial validation. What are the prospects?

Presenter Richard Fung is a Toronto-based writer and independent video producer. His work has dealt with issues of gender, race, sexuality, and colonialism, often with a specific focus on gay and lesbian Asians. Tapes include *Orientations* (1984), *Chinese Characters* (1986), *The Way to My Father's Village* (1988), *Safe Place* (1989), and *My Mother's Place* (1990).

Nelly Toons

Russo, Vito
1989 USA English
90 35mm color/b&w Special Presentation
n/a
Animated films have always followed the real-life conventions of live-action movies. We have only to compare the earliest gay characters on the screen with their cartoon counterparts to see that the cultural assumptions which form the basis for sissy characters is the same in both art forms. The sissy versus the bully was a plot device used over and over again in the early films of Harold Lloyd, Charlie Chaplin, Douglas Fairbanks, and Eddie Cantor. This same plot structure can be seen today on Saturday afternoon television for children. In animated films, as in early live-action films, homosexuality is not presented as a form of sexuality but simply indicated as a type of behavior. Therefore, the "gay" characters in cartoons are identified as such by so-called effeminate manners and, more often, by cross-dressing. This is particularly evident in Warner Brothers' Bugs Bunny cartoons in which Bugs is constantly in drag and marries Elmer Fudd on more than one occasion. Whenever sissified characters turned up in the world of macho men, in films featuring cowboys or pirates, for example, they are almost always the butt of cruel humor or of specific physical violence. Just as with live action films, the sissy in cartoons was ghettoized and labeled as the outsider in every situation. What remains true today is that the so-called "gay" characters in cartoons were often the only saving grace about bad films and the funniest characters in the good ones.

Out of the Closet and into the Universe: Queers and Star Trek

Jenkins, Henry
1994 USA English
90 video color/b&w Clip Show
Jenkins, Henry/Massachusetts Institute of Technology
Why can't "Star Trek" "boldly go" where so many

other network programs have been before? The Gaylaxians, an organization of gay, lesbian, and bisexual science fiction fans has waged a national letter-writing campaign to lobby for the inclusion of a queer character on "Star Trek: The Next Generation." Producer Gene Roddenberry promised to act on their request shortly before his death, but so far, the series has not followed through on that promise.

In his engaging clip-and-comment show, MIT Professor Henry Jenkins looks at the politics of the letter-writing campaign and the producers' responses. He also studies two aired episodes, "The Host" and "The Outcast," which were intended to appease the queer community.

Psycho Killers & Twisted Sisters: Gay & Lesbian Stereotypes of the Silver Screen
Mangin, Danny
1991 USA English
100 video color/b&w Clip Show
Strand Releasing
The negative characters in *The Silence of the Lambs* and *Basic Instinct* have inspired a new generation to join the fight against Hollywood's treatment of gays and lesbians over the decades. What exactly are they protesting? In a clip and commentary presentation, gay film historian Danny Mangin looks at a few of the cinema's most enduring stereotypes, including the gay man as psychopathic killer and the lesbian as "predator." The presentation starts off with a 1960s instructional film for children that warns them to stay away from "red light" people, a "they're out to get you" message reinforced in countless mainstream movies. Hollywood producers like to defend their individual films against charges of stereotyping by saying that my film doesn't paint all gays as evil. *Psycho Killers and Twisted Sisters* illustrates that the sum total of their output achieves precisely that effect. Mangin recently won an "Orchid" award from the Gay and Lesbian Alliance Against Defamation for his lesbian and gay film class at City College of San Francisco, cosponsored by Frameline.

Rain City Confidential
Ebert, Matt
1994 USA English
70 video color Special Program
Ebert, Matt
A program of new queer videos from the Pacific Northwest, curated by Matt Ebert.

Scenes from a Queer Planet
International Gay & Lesbian Human Rights Commission
1992 Peru, India, Russia, Argentina
Spanish/English/Russian
90 video color Special Presentation
International Gay & Lesbian Human Rights Commission
An engaging video-clip presentation offering an overview of the global situation for sexual and gender minorities, focusing on four countries' glaring human rights abuses against transvestites, lesbians, and gay men. Raw video footage and documentary-style clips from Peru, India, Russia and Argentina are presented along with commentary by activists from different international groups, including Shamakami, La Red, and the International Gay and Lesbian Human Rights Commission. The four countries are hot spots this year (1992) for international queer activism; each exemplify different types of repression as well as the different ways that cultures organize sexuality and sexual identity. Presented by Julie Dorf, Executive Director of the International Gay and Lesbian Human Rights Commission.

Seen Anything Good Lately
Lund, Peter, Lara Mac, and Tom di Maria
1994 USA English
90 video color Clip Show
GLAAD/SFBA
From Comedy Central's historic and hilarious "Out There" comedy special, to the most talked-about lesbian kiss of the year, the Gay and Lesbian Alliance Against Defamation/San Francisco Bay Area (GLAAD/SFBA) presents highlights from the broadcast TV year. Why spend dreary, mind-numbing hours in front of your set waiting for that fleeting queer moment when you can join our video hosts for a speedy, ninety-minute medley of the best moments? This specially edited compilation of news and talk shows, sitcoms and dramas shows how lesbian, gay, and bisexual representation is expanding. It also includes a mercifully short sampling of some of the vicious and vile videos used against us by the right wing. While GLAAD/SFBA's mission is to fight damaging and defamatory media images of the lesbian, gay, and bisexual community, tonight's show will focus mostly on positive and hilarious moments from both rare and talked-about TV shows. Best of all, there's no commercials.

Trailer Camp
Olson, Jenni
1995 USA English
75 35mm color/b&w
Special Presentation
Artistic License Films, Inc.
"By compiling the very best of camp trailers, [*Trailer Camp*] has at once alerted us to a parallel cinema of questionable taste and inculcated a kind of perverse nostalgia for a time when bad really did mean good. In many ways more satisfying than the complete features they promote—after all you get the joke in five minutes rather than 90—these trailers are a treasure trove of forgotten celluloid presented in uncut splendor.
  —Noah Cowan,
   Toronto International Film Festival

Twilight Tales
Yusba, Roberta
1985 USA English
80 slides color/b&w Special Presentation
Yusba, Roberta
Lesbian pulp novels 1950–1965, presented by Roberta Yusba. A slide show presentation that explores the first wave of popular lesbian literature and the unusual social conditions that fostered it.

Woman of Affairs, A:
Greta Garbo's Lesbian Past
Garber, Eric, and Mary Wings
1990 USA English
90 video b&w Clip Show
Wings, Mary
Garbo's lesbianism has been one of the best-kept Hollywood secrets during her life; now, after her death, it's already started to generate exciting posthumous speculation and publication. Gay and lesbian historians have long been aware of Garbo's affairs; documentation can now be revealed without threat of litigation. With clips from her best films and material from other sources, this look back at her career will attempt to begin an open and honest reevaluation of the public and private lives of one of the screen's brightest and most intriguing stars. Among the sources included, we'll be presenting segments from Garbo's lover Mercedes de Acosta's 1966 book *Here Lies the Heart*. She describes their topless vacation in Silver Lake (unexplained photos were published in *Oui* magazine), and also claims to have been the originator of *Queen Christina*, Garbo's most famous cross-dressing film. Many unrealized projects between them included Garbo as Dorian Gray in Oscar Wilde's story of the same name (with Marilyn Monroe as a young girl ruined by Dorian!). Other information includes Louise Brooks' confession to her biographer that she and Garbo spent the night together. Even her gaze, tells Brooks, "was intense and eloquent." New revelations about Garbo will not leave her in the shadowy realm of innuendo for much longer.

INDEXES

Lesbian Features

Agora
All Of Me
Anguished Love
Anne Trister
Antonia's Line
Avskedet (Farewell, The)
Ballad of Little Jo, The
Bar Girls
Basic Instinct
Belle
Berenice Abbott: A View of
the 20th Century
Berlin Affair, The
Black Widow
Blood and Roses
Blood Sisters: Leather, Dykes
and Sadomasochism
Born In Flames
Boys on the Side
Breaking the Silence
Brincando El Charco: Portrait of
a Puerto Rican
Butterfly Kiss
Caged
Calamity Jane
Change the Frame
Changer, The: A Record of
the Times
Claire of the Moon
Club des Femmes
(Women's Club)
Coal Miner's Granddaughter
Confessions of a Pretty Lady
Costa Brava
Daughters of Darkness
Desert Hearts
Desperate Remedies
Devotion
Dorian Gray Im Spiegel Der
Boulevardpresse (Dorian
Gray in the Mirror of
the Popular Press)
Dozens, The
Dracula's Daughter
East Is Red, The
Egymasra Nezve
(Another Way)
Entre Tinieblas
(Dark Habits)
Erotique
Even Cowgirls Get the Blues
Extramuros
Fanci's Persuasion
Fearless: The
Hunterwali Story
Female Misbehavior
Fiction and Other Truths: A Film
about Jane Rule
Firewords
Forbidden Love
Framing Lesbian Fashion
Fresh Kill
Fried Green Tomatoes

Ganze Leben, Das
(The Whole of Life)
Gazon Maudit (Bushwhacked)
Gerbroken Spiegels
(Broken Mirrors)
Gertrude Stein and a Companion
Gertrude Stein: When This
You See, Remember Me
Go Fish
Heavenly Creatures
Henry and June
Homicidal
Housewife and the Plumber,
The [Pout #3 excerpt]
I Am Your Sister
I, The Worst of All
I've Heard the Mermaids Singing
Ich Mochte Kein Mann
Sein! (I Don't Want To
Be A Man!)
In My Father's Bed
Incredibly True Adventures
of Two Girls in Love, The
Is-Slottet (Ice Palace, The)
Johanna D'arc of Mongolia
Jungfrauenmaschine, Die
(The Virgin Machine)
Kamikaze Hearts
Kazetachi No Gogo
(Afternoon Breezes)
Killing of Sister George, The
Krokodillen in Amsterdam
(Crocodiles in Amsterdam)
Last Call at Maud's
Last Island, The
Le Jupon Rouge
(Manuela's Loves)
Legend of Fong Sai-Yuk, The
Lesbian Avengers Eat Fire Too
Lianna
Lick Bush in '92
Macumba
Madame X—Eine Absolute
Herrscherin (Madame
X—An Absolute Ruler)
Mädchen In Uniform (1931)
Mädchen In Uniform (1957)
Mara
Million Eyes of Su-Muru, The
My Father is Coming
My Sister, My Love
Night Visions
1999 - Nen No Natsu Yasumi
(Summer Vacation: 1999)
Nocturne
Novembermund
(Novembermoon)
Olivia (Pit of Loneliness)
Only the Brave
Oranges Are Not the
Only Fruit
Orlando
Out of Our Time
P4W: Prison for Women
Paris Was a Woman
Personal Best

Place of Rage, A
Portrait of a Marriage
Prisonnieres
Queen Christina
Religieuse, La (The Nun)
Rote Ohren Fetzen Durch
Asche (Flaming Ears)
Salmonberries
Scrubbers
Second Awakening of
Christa Klages, The
Serving in Silence: The
Margarethe Cammermeyer
Story
Seven Women
She Must Be Seeing Things
Shisheng Huamei (Silent
Thrush, The)
Silence of the Lambs, The
Simone
Sister, My Sister
Skin Deep
Something Special
Sphinxes Without Secrets
Split Britches
Steal America
Still Sane
Straight for the Money:
Interviews with Queer
Sex Workers
Stripped Bare:
A Look at Erotic Dancers
Sylvia Scarlett
Thank You and Good Night
That Tender Touch
Therese and Isabelle
Thin Ice
Times Square
To My Women Friends
Tokyo Cowboy
Twice a Woman
Twin Bracelets, The
Vera
Vrouw Als Eva, Een
(Woman Like Eve, A)
Waiting for the Moon
War Widow, The
Was Soll'n Wir Denn Machen
Ohne Den Tod
(What Shall We Do
Without Death)
Weggehen um Anzukommen
(Depart to Arrive)
When Night is Falling
Wild Flowers
Wolfgirl

Gay Features

Absolutely Positive
Abuse
Adios, Roberto
Adventures of Priscilla,
Queen of the Desert, The
Affairs of Love, The (see
Cosas del Querer, Las)
Affengeil (Life Is Like

a Cucumber)
After the War You Have to
Tell Everyone about the
Dutch Gay Resistance
Fighters
Age of Dissent
Agora
AIDS Show, The
All Of Me
Amazing Grace
American Fabulous
Among Men
An Empty Bed
And the Band Played On
Angel
Angelic Conversation, The
Anguished Love
Apartment Zero
Aqueles Dois
Armistead Maupin Is a
Man I Dreamt Up
Army of Lovers: or Revolt
of the Sex Perverts
Asa Branca
(A Brazilian Dream)
Avonden, De
(Evenings, The)
Balcony, The
Behind Glass
Being at Home with Claude
Bigger Splash, A
Bike Boy
Birthday Tribute to Dame
Edna Everage, A
Blauer Dunst (Blue Smoke)
Blue
Boys from Brazil
Boys in the Band, The
Buddies
Can't Stop the Music
Cap Tourmente
Carrington
Casta Diva
Cat and the Canary, The
Chicken Hawk
Chuck Solomon: Coming
of Age
Clinic, The
Closing Numbers
Coming Out
Corps Perdu, A
(Straight to the Heart)
Cosas del Querer, Las
(Affairs of Love, The)
Creation of Adam
Crimes Against Nature
Cruising
Crying Game, The
Daddy and the Muscle Academy
Damned, The
Dead Dreams of
Monochrome Men
Death Watch
Desert of Love
Diputado, Il (Deputy, The)
Dona Herlinda Y Su Hijo

(Dona Herlinda and
Her Son)
Doom Generation, The
Drama in Blond
Eclipse
Edward II
Ein Mann Wie Eva
(Man Like Eva, A)
Empire State
Ernesto
Everlasting Secret Family, The
Farewell My Concubine
Fighting Chance
For a Lost Soldier
Fortune and Men's Eyes
Frankenstein Created Woman
Fresa y Chocolate
(Strawberry and Chocolate)
Frisk
Fun Down There
Funeral Parade of Roses
Garden, The
Gay Deceivers, The
Gay USA
Get Over It
Glen or Glenda?
(I Changed My Sex)
Hail the New Puritan
Hatachi No Binetsu
(Slight Fever of a 20-Year-Old)
Horror Vacui—Die Angst Vor Der
Leere (Horror Vacui—The Fear
of Emptiness)
Hours And Times, The
House of Pain
I Am a Man
I'm Still Alive: A Person With
AIDS Tells His Story
Ich Bin Meine Eigene Frau
(I Am My Own Woman)
Ich Lebe Gern, Ich Sterbe Gern
(Living And Dying)
Il Etait une Fois dans L'est
(Once Upon a Time in
the East)
Inevitable Love
Interview With The Vampire
Jeffrey
Kenneth Anger's
Hollywood Babylon
Kiss of the Spider Woman
Konsequenz, Die
(Consequence, The)
La Couer Decouvert
(Heart Exposed, The)
Laberinto de Pasiones
(Labyrinth of Passions)
Ladyboys
Last of England, The
Last Supper, The
Leather Boys, The
Les Amities Particulieres
(This Special Friendship)
Ley del Deseo, La
(Law of Desire)
Lie Down with Dogs

Lieve Jongens (Dear Boys)
Lipotaktis (Deserter)
Little Bit of Lippy, A
Living End, The
Longtime Companion
Lost Language of Cranes, The
Love Like Any Other, A
Ludwig
Lugar Sin Limites, El (A
Limitless Place/Hell Without
Limits)
Luminous Procuress
M. Butterfly
Macho Dancer
Madagascar Skin
Mala Noche
Man of No Importance, A
Man of the Year
Maneaters
Manuel Y Clemente
(Manuel and Clemente)
Massillon
Maurice
Men Behind Bars
Men In Love
Men Maniacs
Meteor and Shadow
(Meteore et Ombre)
Midnight Dancers
Midnight Life and Death
Mirror, Mirror
Montreal Main
More Love
Muerte de Mikel, La
(The Death of Mikel)
Muscle
My Addiction
My Beautiful Laundrette
My Brother's Keeper
My Hustler
My Own Private Idaho
Myra Breckenridge
N'oublie pas que tu vas mourir
(Don't Forget You're Going
To Die)
Nagua (Drifting)
Naughty Boys
Neapolitans, The
Nighthawks
1999 - Nen No Natsu Yasumi
(Summer Vacation: 1999)
No Ordinary Love
No Sad Songs
Norman, Is That You?
North of Vortex
Not Angels but Angels
Nous Etions un Seul Homme
(We Were One Man)
Nuit Sauvage, La
(Savage Nights)
Okoge
One Foot on a Banana Peel, the
Other Foot in the Grave
Outsiders, The
P.A.N.I.C. in Griffith Park
Paradise Framed

Parallel Sons
Paris is Burning
Parting Glances
Paso Doble
Pasolini, un delitto Italiano
   (Pasolini, an Italian Crime)
Paul Cadmus: Enfant Terrible
   at 80
Pauline's Birthday, or The
   Beast of Notre Dame
Pervola, Sporen in de Sneeuw
   (Pervola, Tracks in the Snow)
Philadelphia
Pink Narcissus
Pink Ulysses
Placeros Ocultos, Los
   (Hidden Pleasures)
Pleasure Beach
Poison
Portrait of Jason
Positive (Positiv)
Postcards from America
Pouvoir Intime
Premonition of Absurd
Perversion in Sexual
   Personae Part 1
Prick Up Your Ears
Priest
Prinz In Holleland
   (Prince In Hell)
Proof
Que He Hecho Yo Para Merecer
   Esto? (What Have I Done to
   Deserve This?)
Queen, The
Querelle
Rainbow Serpent, The
Rainer Werner Fassbinder:
   The Last Works
Rasen No Sobyo (Rough
   Sketch of a Spiral)
Recent Sorrows
Reflections in a Golden Eye
Remembrance of Things Fast
Revolutions Happen Like
Refrains in a Song
Right to Fight, The
Robert Mapplethorpe
Rock Hudson's Home Movies
Roy Cohn/Jack Smith
Saint Genet
Salut Victor!
Schweigen=Tod (Silence=Death)
Sebastiane
Self Defense
Sergeant Matlovich Versus the
   U.S. Air Force
Sex Is . . .
Sex of the Stars (Le sexe
   des Etoiles)
Silverlake Life: The View
   from Here
Sis: The Perry Watkins Story
Sisters of Darkness
Six Degrees of Separation
Smoke

Some of My Best
   Friends Are . . .
Something for Everyone
Sparkle's Tavern
Sprinter, Der (Sprinter, The)
Stadt der Verlorenen Seelen
   (City Of Lost Souls)
Staircase
Sto Dnej Do Prikaza
   (100 Days before
   the Command)
Stonewall
Strange Love Affair, A
Strip Jack Naked
Sum of Us, The
Super 8 1/2
Swoon
Taste of Honey, A
Taxi to Cairo
Taxi Zum Klo
Terence Davies Trilogy, The
Three Bewildered People
   in the Night
To Die For (Heaven's a Drag)
To Wong Foo, Thanks for
   Everything, Julie Newmar
Together Alone
Tongues Untied
Total Eclipse
Totally F***ed Up
Touchables, The
Tras el Cristal (In a Glass Cage)
Triche, La
Turnabout
Twinkle
Two of Us
Under Heat
Unzipped
Venner for Altid (Friends Forever)
Via Appia
Victim
Video Album 5:
   The Thursday People
Vintage: Families of Value
Virus Kennt Keine Moral, Ein
   (Virus Has No Morals, A)
Vive L'Amour
Wedding Banquet, The
Weiner Brut
Wendel
Westler—East of the Wall
Where Are We?: Our Trip
   Through America
Wigstock: The Movie
Wild Reeds
Withnail & I
Without You I'm Nothing
Wittgenstein
Wonderland
World and Time Enough
World of Gilbert and George, The
Wrecked for Life: The Trip and
   Magic of the Trocadero Transfer
   Young Soul Rebels
Zero Patience

Cogender Features

Absolutely Positive
Affengeil (Life Is Like
   a Cucumber)
After the War You Have to
   Tell Everyone about the
   Dutch Gay Resistance
   Fighters
Agora
All Out Comedy
Anguished Love
Balcony, The
Ballot Measure Nine
Before Stonewall
Bit of Scarlett, A
Black and White in Color
Borderline
Celluloid Closet, The
Changing Our Minds: The
   Story Of Dr. Evelyn Hooker
Coming Out under Fire
Complaint of the Empress, The
Craig's Wife
Darker Side of Black, A
Desire
Desperate Remedies
Diamanda Galas: Judgement Day
Doom Generation, The
Eagle Shooting Hero
Even Cowgirls Get the Blues
Family Values
Feed Them to the Cannibals
Florida Enchantment, A
Gay Rock 'N' Roll Years, The
Gay San Francisco
Green on Thursdays
Greetings from Out Here
Homoteens
I Want What I Want
Inside Monkey Zetterland
Joan Sees Stars
Kanada
L-Shaped Room, The
Last Island, The
Last Song, The
Long Weekend (O'Despair), The
Love and Human Remains
Love and Marriage
Marching for Freedom
Mauvaise Conduite
   (Improper Conduct)
Nico-Icon
Nineteen Nineteen
Nitrate Kisses
No Skin Off My Ass
One Nation Under God
Orientations
Out On Four: Episodes 1 & 2
Out On Four: Episodes 3 & 4
Out On Four: Episodes 5 & 6
Out On Tuesday, Program 1
Out On Tuesday, Program 2
Out On Tuesday, Program 3
Out On Tuesday, Program 4
Out: Stories of Lesbian
   and Gay Youth

Over Our Dead Bodies
Passion of Remembrance, The
Portrait of a Marriage
Rhythm Divine:
   The Story of Disco, The
Rights and Reactions
Risk Group
Sacred Lies, Civil Truths
Sisters of Darkness
Super 8 1/2
Times of Harvey Milk, The
Totally F***ed Up
Touchables, The
Urinal
Verfuhrung: Die Grausame Frau
   (Seduction: The Cruel Woman)
Verzaubert (Enchanted)
Viktor und Viktoria
   (Victor and Victoria)
Voices from the Front
We Are Family
Whatever Happened to
   Susan Jane?
Without You I'm Nothing
Word Is Out: Stories of Some
   of Our Lives
Yma Sumac: Hollywood's Inca
Princess

Bisexual Features

Corps Perdu, A
   (Straight to the Heart)
Doom Generation, The
Long Weekend (O'Despair), The
My Hustler
No Ordinary Love
North of Vortex
Straight for the Money:
   Interviews with Queer
   Sex Workers
Stripped Bare: A Look at
   Erotic Dancers
Three Bewildered People in
   the Night
Wild Flowers
Without You I'm Nothing

Transgender Features

Adventures of Priscilla,
   Queen of the Desert, The
All Of Me
Angel
Anguished Love
Ballad of Little Jo, The
Birthday Tribute to Dame
   Edna Everage, A
Boys from Brazil
Calamity Jane
Crying Game, The
Dorian Gray Im Spiegel Der
   Boulevardpresse (Dorian Gray
   in the Mirror of the Popular
   Press)
Dr. Jekyll and Sister Hyde
Drama in Blond
Eagle Shooting Hero

East Is Red, The
Ein Mann Wie Eva
   (Man Like Eva, A)
Farewell My Concubine
Florida Enchantment, A
Frankenstein Created Woman
Funeral Parade of Roses
Glen or Glenda?
   (I Changed My Sex)
Homicidal
I Want What I Want
Ich Bin Meine Eigene Frau
   (I Am My Own Woman)
Ich Mochte Kein Mann Sein!
   (I Don't Want To Be A Man!)
Kiss of the Spider Woman
Kuro Tokage (Black Lizard, The)
Ladyboys
Last Song, The
Legend of Fong Sai-Yuk, The
Lugar Sin Limites, El (A
Limitless Place/
   Hell Without Limits)
Luminous Procuress
M. Butterfly
Mirror, Mirror
Muerte de Mikel, La
   (The Death of Mikel)
Myra Breckenridge
1999 - Nen No Natsu Yasumi
   (Summer Vacation: 1999)
Orlando
Paris is Burning
Queen Christina
Queen, The
Sex of the Stars
   (Le sexe des Etoiles)
Silence of the Lambs, The
Skin Deep
Something Special
Sylvia Scarlett
To Die For (Heaven's a Drag)
To Wong Foo, Thanks for
   Everything, Julie Newmar
Vera
Vestida de Azul
   (Dressed in Blue)
Viktor und Viktoria
   (Victor and Victoria)
Whatever Happened to
   Susan Jane?
Wigstock: The Movie
   (Shils, Barry)

Lesbian Shorts

Absence of Us, The
Acting Up for Prisoners
Ad, The
After the Break
After the Game
Age 12: Love With A Little L
Ahh!
Airport
Alicia Was Fainting
All Day Always
All Fall Down

Alleged, The
Altered Habits
Alternative Conceptions
Amelia Rose Towers
Among Good Christian Peoples
Anastasia and the Queen
   of Hearts
Angel of Woolworths, The
Annie
Arlene Raven—April '79
Ash and Hatred
Assembly at Dyke High
Assumption, The
Audience
Awakening of Nancy Kaye, The
B.U.C.K.L.E.
Basic Necessities
BD Women
Because The Dawn
Bedtime Stories
Bedtime Stories
   [work in progress]
Beloved Murderer
Beneath the Surface
Bent Time
Bete Noire
Beyond Imagining: Margaret
   Anderson & the Little Review
Beyond/Body/Memory
Big Fat Slenderella
Big Time Wrestlers from
   Hollywood
Bird In The Hand
Birthday Party
Bisexual Kingdom, The
Bitter Strength: Sadistic
   Response Version
Bittersweet
Blond Fury
Blue Distance
Bodies In Trouble
Bodily Functions
   [work in progress]
Bondage
Both (Child, Abigail)
Breast Exam
Brown Sugar Licks Snow White
Bumps
Burden of Dykes
Burning, The
Bus Stops Here, The:
   Three Case Histories
But No One
Butch Patrol!
Butch Wax
Butch/Femme in Paradise
Caesura
Call Me Your Girlfriend
Can You Say Androgynous?
Can't Help Lovin Dat Man
Can't You Take a Joke?
Cancer in Two Voices
Carmelita Tropicana
Carol
Cat Nip
Cavale

Central Park
Certain Grace, A
Chameleon
Chasing the Moon
Chicks in White Satin
Chickula: Teenage Vampire
Choosing Children
Clean Fun with Sally Alley
Coconut/Cane & Cutlass
Comedy in Six Unnatural Acts, A
Common Flower, A
Complaints of a Dutiful Daughter
Complicated Flesh
Conception, The
Condomnation
Cool Gleam
Cool Hands, Warm Heart
Cosmic Demonstration of
    Sexuality, A
Count Me In
Covert Action
Cross Your Heart
Cruel
Cumulus Nimbus
Cunt Dykula
Cupid's True Love
Current Flow
Cutting the Edge of a Free Bird
Cuz' It's Boy
Damned If You Don't
Dance with a Body, A
Dandy Dust [trailer]
Danger Girl, The
Dangerous Bliss
Dangerous When Wet
Dare to Be Butch
Darkness of My Language, The
Death of a Writer in Two Parts
    (A Comedy of Sorts)
Ding Dong
Displaced View, The
Divine Bodies
Djune/Idexa
Do Not Listen
Do You Mind?
Do You Think that a Candidate
    Should Live Like This?
Doctors, Liars and Women
Doll House
Doll Shop
Domestic Bliss
Don't Look Up My Skirt
    Unless You Mean It
Don't Make Me Up
Donna e Mobile, La
Dorothy Arzner: A Profile
    (BBC The Late Show)
Double Entente
Double Exposure
Double Strength
Down on the River
Drama of the Gifted Child, The
Dream Wheel
Dreamgirls
Dreams of Passion
Du Darst (Truth or Dare)

[excerpt]
Dual of the Senses
Dumbshit
Dykes Rule
Dyketactics
Easy Garden, The
Eat This
Edges
8mm Lesbian Love Film
EileenMyles: An American Poem
Elegant Spanking, The
Emergence
Erotic in Nature
Esplada, A
Evolution Of a Sex Life
Execution: A Study of Mary
Exits
Exposure
Fabulous Dyketones Rock
    Around the Clock, The
Falling Through the Cracks
Family Affair, A
Farewell to Charms
Fat Chance
Fell
Ferdous (Paradise)
Fin Amour
Fingered!
Fireworks Revisited
First Base
Flesh and Paper (see Out
    On Tuesday, Program 3)
Flesh on Glass
Flip Side, The
Florence and Robin
Forms and Motifs
Frankfurter
Frankie and Jocie
Frankly, Shirley
Frau und Geschlecht
    (Basic Instincts)
Freak
Freebird
Frenzy [excerpt]
From Bejing to Brooklyn
From Dental Dams to
    Latex Gloves
Fuck Film
Fun with a Sausage
Gab
Gabriella on the Half Shell
Gay Day, A
Gay Tape: Butch and Femme
Gently Down the Stream
Geography of the Imagination
Get It Girl: Lesbians
    Talk about Safe Sex
Ghetto Girls
Girl Power (Part 1)
Girls Will Be Boys
Glasses Break
Goat Named Tension, A
Goblin Market
Good Dyke Gone Mad, A
Gracious Flab, Gracious Bone
Grapefruit

Great Dykes of Holland, The
Greta's Girls
Grid-Lock: Women and the
    Politics of AIDS
Guess Who's Coming to
    Visit
Haircut
Harlequin Exterminator
Haut und Haar (Skin and Hair)
Hazel's Photos
Heart of Seduction, The
Heatwave
Her Appetite
Her Giveaway
Her Sweetness Lingers
Hey Bud
History of the World
    According to a Lesbian, The
Holding
Holly Near
"Home Movie"
Home Movie
Home You Go
Hot and Cold
Hotheads
How Big Is Big?
How Many Lesbians Does It
    Take to Change a Lightbulb?
How to Kill Her
Hyena's Breakfast, The
I Became a Lesbian and
    So Can You
I Got that Way from Kissing Girls
I Like Girls for Friends
I Need a Man Like You..
I Never Danced the Way Girls
    Were Supposed To
I Remember Running
I Shot My W.O.D.
I Was I Am
I Will Not Think about
    Death Anymore
I'm You, You're Me
I've Never
Ich und Frau Berger
    (Me & Mrs. Berger)
If Every Girl Had a Diary
If She Grows Up Gay
Ifé
Images
Immaculate Conception
In a Man's World
In Loving Memory
In Search of Margo-Go
In the Best Interest of
    the Children
In the Cards
(In)Visible Women
Infidel
Inmates Within Myself
International Sweethearts
    of Rhythm
Intrepidissima
Iowa City Women's Rugby
Is Mary Wings Coming?
Is That All There Is to the

INDEXES

Greenhouse Effect?
It Wasn't Love
It's a Lezzie Life:
  A Dyke-U-Mentary
It's a Mitzvah
It's That Age
Jackie and the Beanstalk
Jeanne & Hauviette
Jellyfish Kiss [trailer]
Jodie Promo
Joe-Joe
Jollies
Joystick Blues
Juggling Gender
Jumping the Gun
Just Because of Who We Are
Just Friends
Kachapati: Spray the Wall
Kahala
Kathy
Keep Your Laws Off My Body
Keeping the Faith
Killer Babe
Kim
Kindling Point, The
L'Ingenue
L'Usure (By Attrition)
Labor More Than Once
Land Beyond Tomorrow
Lasbisch TV
Latex—Step Out Smartly
Laura, Ingrid, and Rebecca
Lawn Butch
Le Poisson D' Amour
Lesbian Bed Death: Myth or
  Epidemic. An investigative
  report.
Lesbian Impress Card, The
Lesbians
Lesbians Who Date Men
Let's Play Prisoners
Letter to My Grandma
Lick
Life in the Kitchen
Life on Earth as I Know It
Lifetime Commitment: A
  Portrait of Karen Thompson
Like a Dog
Like Mother, Like Son
Lillian's Dilemma
Lily & Lulu Go to the March
Liquor, Guns and Ammo
Living with AIDS: Women
  and AIDS
London Story, The
Long Time Comin'
Look
Loredana
Loss of Heat
Lost Heart, The
Lost Love
Lost Sleep
Love Beneath a Neon Sky
Love Crisis
Love Strikes Hard
Love that Dare Not Speak Its

Name, The
Love Triangle
Luna Tune
Lune
Mad about the Boy
Madonna In Me
Maidens
Malaysian Series, Part 1-6
Mano Destra
Mark of Lilith, The
Masturbation: 5 Women
Maya
Mayhem
Me and Mrs. Jones
Me and Rubyfruit
Meeting of Two Queens, The
Memsahib Rita
Men Like Me
Mermaids, Fish & Other
  Non-Bipeds
Millionaire
Minders, The
Minor Disturbances
Miss Ruby's House
Mister Reagan
Mister Sisters, The
Mondays
Monsters in the Closet
More Than a Paycheck
Mother's Hands
Mud Luverz
Mujeria: Olmeca Rap
Mulberry Bush, The
My Courbet . . . Or, A
  Beaver's Tale
My Dinner at Dan's
My Failure to Assimilate
My Grandma's Lady Cabaret
My Idol
My Sweet Peony
Naomi's Legacy
Negative Man
New Year, A
New York Loft
Nexus (Bond, Rose)
Nexus (Johns, Jennifer)
Nice Girls Don't Do It
Nightwork
No Glove, No Love
No Help Needed
No More Nice Girls
No Need to Repent
No No Nooky T.V.
No Saintly Girl
Nobody's People
Not Like That: Diary of a
  Butch-A-Phobe
Odd Girl Out
Odds and Ends
  (A New-Age Amazon Fable)
Off Our Chests
Olivia Records: More
  Than Music
On Guard
One and the Other Time
One Fool

One Single Life
One Woman Waiting
Optic Nerve
Other Woman, The
Other Woman, The
  (Slane, Andrea)
Our Lady of L.A.
Our Mom's a Dyke
Our Trip
Out for a Change: Addressing
  Homophobia in Women's
  Sports
Out in Suburbia
Out on the Road with 2 Nice
  Girls [trailer]
Outcasts
Outlaw
Outlaw Poverty, Not Prostitutes
P.A.R.A.N.O.R.M.A.L.
P(l)ain Truth
Pandora's Box
Parachute
Parisian Blinds
Party Favor, The
Passion: A Letter in 16mm
Peach
Pearl Diver
Peccatum Mutum (The Silent
  Sin)
Performance Notes: A Bar is a
  Bar is a Bar
Peril or Pleasure? Feminist-
  Produced Pornography
Perilous Liaisons
Pictures for Barbara
Pink, The
Place Called Lovely, A
Playing the Part
Pools
Possession
Potluck and the Passion, The
Prayer Before Birth, A
Primas
Primitive and Proud
Private Pleasures
Psychosynthesis
Pubic Beard
Pull Your Finger Out:
  Lesbians Rock
Queer Across Canada
Quickening
Raid on a Peruvian Lesbian Bar
Rapture
Ravissement, La
Raw Meet
Reencounter
Regarde Moi
Reise, Eine (The Journey)
Reservaat (Reservation)
Risk: Lesbians and AIDS
Rispondetemi
Rites of Passage
Rosebud
Rough Outrageous
Rove
Rules of the Road

Safe Is Desire [excerpt]
Safe Sex Is Hot Sex
Safe Soap
Safer Sister
Sally Forth
Sappho
Sari Red
Satdee Night
Scars
Screamers
Searanch: The True Story
Search, The
Sech Wie Pech & Schwefel
  (Birds of a Feather)
Second Generation Once
  Removed
Secrets
Separate Skin
Seth's Aunts
17 Rooms or, What Lesbians
  Do in Bed
76 Trombones
Sewing on Breast
Sex Bowl
Sex Fish
Sex, Lies, Religion
Shadows
Shared Lives
Shasta Woman
She Begins
She Can Probably Fix It
She Don't Fade
She Even Chewed Tobacco!
She Gets Mad
She Makes Love With Her
She Shoots, She Scores
She Thrills Me
She's Real: A Document of
  Queer Rock
Shell
Shirley Temple and Me
Shot Through My Head
Sightings
Silence . . . Broken
Sink or Swim
Sister Is (Not) A Mister, The
Sister Louise's Discovery
Six Million and One
Sluts and Goddesses Video
  Workshop, The, or How To Be
  a Sex Goddess in 101
  Easy Ways
Snatch
Snow Job: The Media
  Hysteria of AIDS
Snow White
Somebody Else
Sometimes
Sometimes . . . A Poem
Song of the Goddess
Sonny
Source, The
Souvenir
Spin Cycle
Spy, The (Hester Reeve
  Does "The Doors")

St. Louis Blues
Stafford's Story
Stand on Your Man
Standard of Living, The
State of Mind
Stellium In Capricorn
Step We Gaily
Stick Figures
Still Point
Stone Circles
Storme: The Lady of the
  Jewel Box
Story So Far: A Forgotten
  Classic, The
Suburban Queen
Suddenly Last Summer
Surely to God
Susana
Swamp
Sweet Dreams
"Sword Fight"
Sync Touch
T.V. Tart
Take Me Back to Cairo
Taking Back The Dolls
Tales of an Exhausted Woman
Tearing the Veil
Tempted
Ten Cents a Dance (Parallax)
Tender Fictions
Terms of Conception
Terra Nullius
Tex-Sex
Texas
That's Alright Mama
That's Amore
These Shoes Weren't Made
  For Walking
Things We Said Today
This Is Not a Very Blank
  Tape, Dear
Thriller
Ties That Bind, The
Time is Money
Tiny & Ruby: Hell Divin' Women
Tits and Ass
To Be with You
Tomboy!
Topsau, Die (The Top Pig)
Tourist
Trans
Transeltown
Transportations
Tread Softly
True Blue
24 Hours a Day
Two Bad Daughters
Two Georges, The
  (Dos Jorges, Los)
Two In Twenty
Two or Three Things I Know
  About Them
Two Quickies
Two Women
Uh-Oh!
Untitled (Kossoff, Leslie)

Untitled (Latty, Yvonne)
Vanilla Sex
Veronica Four Rose
Village Idiot, The
Virgin, the Mother and the
  Crone, The
Vital Signs
Waltz, The
Wanderer, The
War on Lesbians
Warrior Marks [excerpt]
Waving Fork, The
Way of the Wicked, The
We All Have Our Reasons
We're Talking Vulva
We've Been Framed
We've Only Just Begun
Well Sexy Women [excerpt]
West Coast Crones: A Glimpse at
  the Lives Of Nine
  Old Lesbians
What Gets You Off
What Is a Line?
What's in a Name
What's the Difference Between
  a Yam and a Sweet Potato?
When Shirley Met Florence
Where the Cows Go
Where There's Smoke
Wicked Radiance
Wild Woman of the Woods
Without Saying Goodbye
Woman of the Wolf
Woman's Place Is in the
  House, A
Women I Love
Women In Love: Bonding
  Strategies of Black Lesbians
Women Like That
Women Like Us (see Out
  On Tuesday, Program 4)
Women on Fire
Working Class Dykes from Hell
World of Light:
  A Portrait of May Sarton
You Can Open Your Eyes Now
You Can't Die from Not Sleeping
You Little Devil, You
You Thrive on Mistaken Identity
Your Heart Is All Mine
Zanne: So Many Women
Zoe la Boxeuse (Zoe the Boxer)

Gay Shorts
A
A.I.D.S.C.R.E.A.M.
Achilles
Across the Rubicon
ACT UP at the FDA
Adrian's Montag
  (Adrian's Monday)
ADS Epidemic, The
Aesthetics and/or Transportation
Affirmations
Afflicted
AIDS: A Priest's Testament

AIDS in the Barrio
AIDS Movie, The
AIDS/ARC Vigil
Al Margen del Margen
  (Beyond Outcasts)
Alfalfa
Algie the Miner
Alkali, Iowa
All You Can Eat
Alone Once Again
Alphabit Land: The Backyard
  Tour Featuring Wigstock '89
Alpsee
Always On Sunday
Ambiman
Amblyopia (Points of View)
American Shooting
  Numbers 1, 2 and 3
An All-American Story
An Individual Desires Solution
Analstahl (Anal Steel)
. . . and he'll grow up to be
  big and strong
Anders als die Anderen
  (Different from the Others)
Andy Makes a Movie
Andy the Furniture Maker
Andy Warhol
Anthem
Anxiety of Inexpression and the
  Otherness Machine
Aquavitae
Art of Mirrors, The
Assassination
Assassination of Anita
  Bryant, The
Attendant, The
Attention Cinemagoers
Auto Biography
Automating
Automolove
Automonosexual
Awkward for Years
Babi-It (At Home)
Bachvirus, Het
  (Bach Virus, The)
Baja Fantasy
Ballad of Reading Gaol
Balling Wonder Bread
Bar Time
Bar Yoga
Barely Human
Bashing
Basket Case
Battle of Tuntenhaüs, The
Be Careful What Kind of Skin
  You Pull Back, You Never
  Know What Kind of Head
  Will Appear
Be My Valentine
Bears in the Hall
Bears Will Be Bears
Beauties without a Cause
Beauty, Fame, Wealth, and Tears
Because We Must
Beefcake Cheesecake

Before the Act
Behind Every Good Man
Behind the Fence
Bel Ragazzo
Bertrand Disparu
  (Bertrand Is Missing)
Bette Walters Interviews Garbo
Betty Kaplowitz
Betty Walters Show, The
Between Two Worlds
Beyond Gravity
Bi-Ways
Bicentennial Movie, A
Biennale Apollo
Bilge Cruz
Bill and Ted's Homosexual
  Adventure
Bill Pope: Portrait of a
  Native Son
Billy Turner's Secret
Bitter Old Queens
  [work in progress]
Black Bag: Gender Bender
Black Body
Black Sheep Boy
Blicklust
Blow Job (Stirton, Tim)
Blow Job, The
Blow Job (Warhol, Andy)
Blue Hour, The
Bob Diva's
Bob Ross
Bogjavlar (Damned Queers)
Boot
Both (De La Rosa, Vic)
Bottom
Boy Next Door: A Profile
  of Boy George
Boy Who Fell In Love, The
Boy with Cat
Boys/Life
Breaking
Brenda and Glenda Show,
  The [excerpt]
Bridgette
Brinco, O (The Earring)
Broadcast Tapes of
  Dr. Peter, The
Broken Goddess
Built for Endurance
Bump and Grind It
Bust-Up
Cage, La
California New Wave
Can't Take That Way from Me
Caress
Carousel
Carrie
Castro at 18th
Castro Cowboy
Castro Station
Castro—The Video
Catalina
Caught Looking
Cell Mates
Cerebral Accident

Chaero
Chance of a Lifetime
Chance, The
Change
Changes
Chant d'amour, Un
Charming Mutt
Cheap Skates: The Hardly-
  Cardigan Affair
Chicken Elaine
Child and the Saw, The
Chinese Characters
Cholo Joto
Christopher Isherwood:
  Over There on a Visit
Chubs & Bears [work in progress]
Cities of Lust
Clearing, The
Cliche in the Afternoon
Clips from Kelly's Porn Movie
Clones In Love
Closet, The
Clue
Cold Bath
Color Box
Columnburium
Commercial for Murder
Common Loss
Communication from Weber
Complete St. Veronica, The
Conceicao
Condoms Are a Girl's Best Friend
Confirmed Bachelor
Connan the Waitress
Continuum 2
Cost of Love, The
Cross Body Ride
Crows
Crushed Lilies
Da Da Da
Dadshuttle, The
Dance Macabre
Dance, The
Dancing in Dulais
Dancing Is Illegal
Danny
Darling Child
Date With Fate
David Hockney's Diaries
David, Montgomery und Ich
David Roche Talks to You
  about Love
Day in the Life of Edmund
  White, A
Dead Boys' Club, The
Deaf Heaven
Dear Rock
Death in Venice, CA
Dedicated to Those Days
Defect [unfinished]
Defectors: My Vacation
Deflatable Man, The
Delius
Deliver Us from Evil
Denajua: I Like My Name
Derek Jarman, Know What

I Mean
Descent
Destiny/Desire/Devotion
Devotions
DHPG Mon Amour
Dialogo
Dick Tricks
Dinner with Malibu
Disappearing Act
Disco Years, The
Do You Know What I Mean
Don't Touch (Hors Limite)
Dottie Gets Spanked
Downey Street
Drag Attack
Drag in for Votes
Drag on a Fag
Drag Queen Marathon, The
Dream A40
Dream Becomes Desire
Dream Come True
Dream Machine, The
Drip: A Narcissistic Love Story
Dura Mater
Early Patterns
Easy Money [work in progress]
Ecce Homo
Elegy in the Streets
Elevator Girls in Bondage
Ernie and Rose
Erte
ESP: Vision
Etc.
Eunuchs: India's Third Gender
Evil Thoughts
Excerpts from the Far East
Exterminator II
Faerie Tales
Faeriefilm
Fairest of Them All
Fairies, The
Fairy Who Didn't Want to Be a
Fairy Anymore, The
Faith No More
Fast Trip, Long Drop
Fatboy Chronicles, The
  (Part One : Rene, Rene, Qu'
  est-ce-que c' est?)
Fated to Be Queer
Fear of Disclosure
Fighting in Southwest Louisiana
film, a
Film for Two
Finally Destroy Us
Fine Romance, A
Fireworks
5
Five Minutes, Ms. Lenska
Five Naked Surfers
Five Ways to Kill Yourself
Flames of Passion
Flaming Creatures
Flower Market, The
Fly That Friendly Sky
Foetal Gay's Nightmare, A
Fontvella's Box

Food for Thought
Foolish Things
Forsaken
45 RPM Love
Forward, Bound
Frankie Goes Downtown
Free Love
French Bitch
Friend of Dorothy, A
Friendly Witness
Fruta, La
Fuck the Pope
Fuji
G.I. Sports
Garbage Can Man
Gay Freedom Day Parade 1976
Gay Gourmet
Gay Is Out
Gay Olympics '82
Gay TV
Gentlemen
Ghost Body
Give Me Body
Glitterbug
Gloria's Point of View
Godzilla Voice
Golden Positions, The
Grey Hideaway
Growing Up and I'm Fine
Guadalcanal Interlude
Halloweenie
Hard Reign's Gonna Fall, A
Hard to Swallow
Harold and Hiroshi
Haven
He Would Have Loved Me
  to Death
He's Like
Heaven, Earth and Hell
Hello-Goodbye
Helms = Death
Here Be Dragons
Hermes Bird
Hero of My Own Life
His Red Snow White Apple Lips
History of Western Sexuality, The
History Will Accuse Me
Holy Mary
Household
How Deep Is Your Love
How He Goes
How To Cook A Plantain,
  Properly
How to Seduce a Preppy
Human Still Life [Rough Cut]
Hustle with My Muscle
Hysterio Passio
I
I Didn't Know What Time It Was
I Don't Want to Be a Boy
I Dream of Dorothy
I Like Dreaming
I Wanna Be In Your World
I Want to Be Evil
I'm Gonna Eat Worms
Ice Cream Sunday

If Only
If They'd Asked for a Lion Tamer
Illegal Acts
Illegal Tender
Illuminado las Aguas
Imagining October
In Plain View
In the Pictures
In View of Her Fatal Inclination,
  Lilo Wanders Gives
  Up the Ghost
Interior Decorator from Hell
Invocation of My Demon Brother
Iro Kaze (Colour Wind)
Irome (Colour Eyes)
It Never Was You
It's the Look I'm After
Jack and Jill
Jane Show, The
Jean Genet
Jewel's Darl
Joaquin
Joggernaught
John Sex: The True Story
Johnny
Jomasay
Jonathan and David
Journey to Avebury
Joy of Apples, The
Judy's Do
Jungle Boy, The
Just Another Girl
Just for Fun
Kain and Abel
Ken Death Gets Out of Jail
Kipling Meets the Cowboy
Kiss
Kiss on the Cliff, The
Kiss, The
Koukei Dori
  (Landscape Catching)
Kustom Kar Kommandos
L'Amico Fried's
  Glamorous Friends
L'Hiver Approche
  (Winter Is Approaching)
Lady in Waiting, The
Language of Boys, The
Last Paintings of Derek Jarman,
  The
Last Stop, The
Laundromat
Lawless
Legislation is Only the Beginning
Let Me Die, Again
Letter of Introduction, The
Liebe, Eifersucht und Rache
  (Love, Jealousy and Revenge)
Lifesaver
Lift Off
Limités
Living with AIDS
Loads
Long Ago (and Far Away)
Looking for Langston
Lord and Master

Lorenza
Lot in Sodom
Love and Lashes
Love Machine, The
Love that Dare Not Speak
    Its Name, The
Love/Sex
Loverville
Loverville 2: The Honeymoon
Lucifer Rising
Luscious Brite
Lush Life
M-A-S-S
Ma Vie
Mad, Mad World Of Stella
    Slick, The
Madame Of Many Faces
Madame Simone
Made for TV
Madonna and Child
Magic Cottage
Making of "Monsters," The
Making of "The Lost Language
    of Cranes," The
Male Escorts of San Francisco:
    Raphael, the Call Bear
    [excerpt]
Male Escorts of San Francisco,
    The
Male Gayze, The
Man I Love, The
Margaret Atwood and the
    Problem with Canada
Marilyn
Mark Called
Marta: Portrait of a Teen Activist
(Mas-ter-ba-shun)
Mason's Life
Matsumae-Kun No Senritsu
(Melody For Buddy Matsumae)
Maybe I Can Give You Sex ?
    Part One
Maybe I Can Give You Sex ?
    Part Two
Me Show, The
Media Blackmale
Meet Johnny Eagle
Memento Mori
Memory Pictures
Meridad Proscrita
Messiah at the City
Mi Pollo Loco
Midwest Mambo
Midwestern Skidmarks
Miguel
Milan Bleu
Minoru and Me
Miracle on Sunset Boulevard
Mirto
Miss Otis
Moffie Called Simon, A
Mondo Diviso, II
    (The Split World)
Moscow Does Not Believe in
    Queers
Mother Show, The

Mouse Klub Konfidential
Mr. Wonderful
Muscle Lens
My Dinner at Dan's
My First Suit
My Name Is Edwina Carerra
My New Friend
My New Lover
My Polish Waiter
My Skin is a Map
My Sorrow Means Nothing to You
Narcissus
Narcissus Lingerie—Screen
    Test of Lawanda Rose
Narco and Ecola
Nation
News from Home
Night Hogs in Leather
Night with Derek, A
Nightshift
976
1970's Porn Trailers
94 Arcana Drive
No Money, No Honey
No Regret (Non, Je ne
    regrette rien)
Nomads
Not a Sex Call
Now Playing
Now That It's Morning
Nuclear Family
Nude Descending
Nude Inn
Nudes (A Sketchbook)
Numbering Bad Fruit
Obelisk, The
Of Man; For Dad
Ohrenwurm, Der
On the Safe Side
On the Sentimental Side
100 Seconds with Sasha
103 Degrees
One In Seven
One Sings
Only a Test
Order, The
Orgasm of Hot Blood
Orpheus, The Day Before
Ostia
Ostranenie
Other Half, The
Out in Africa (Symons, Johnny)
Out in the Streets
Out Of Many . . . One, Part III
Out of the Shadows
"OUT" Takes
Ovid
Package, The
Palace
Paper Cranes
Party
Patsy Cline: A Tribute
Pavane for a Dead Princess
Pearl Harbor & the Explosions
Pedagogue
Performance Art in Atlanta

Perils of Pedagogy, The
Personally Yours
Peter Fucking Wayne
    Fucking Peter
Pink Pimpernel, The
Pink Triangles
Place in the Sun, A
Plague, A
Plague on You, A
Plastic Rap
Playing Poseidon
    [work in progress]
Please Decompose Slowly
Pleasure
Pleasure Garden, The
PMS (Positioning My Sexuality)
Poetry for an Englishman
Poisoned Blood
Political Funerals
Politics of Disco, The
Poodle-Poo-Poo Miracle Mask,
    The
Pool Days
Porcaria
Porn
Prague
Preservation of the Song
Prince of Peace
Project Last Supper
Projections
    (Pet Shop Boys compilation)
Proportion
Proust's Favorite Fantasy
Psyclones on Heat
Public
Public Opinion
Puce Moment
Purple Heart
Put Your Lips Around Yes
Queen is Dead, The
Queer Love Poem, A
Racing Colours
Rage & Desire
Raising Nicholas
Rambles
Random Access
Ray
Ray Navarro Memorial Tape
Ray's Male Heterosexual
    Dance Hall
Razor Head
Re Generation
Reference
Reflections
Relax
Remembrance
Remnants
Requiem
Resonance
Revenge of the Wicked Witch
Ride, The
Right Stuff, The
Rite of Passage
Robert Having His
    Nipple Pierced
Rocking the Cradle

Roger: The Death of Wayne
Roller Coaster to Hell
Roman Springs on Mrs.
  Stone, The
Room 303
RSVP
S.S.
Saddle Up
Safe
Safe Place, A
Safe Sex is Fun
Safe Sex: The Manual
Safety In Numbers
Saint Mulekicker
Salome
Salt Mines, The
San Fernando Valley
Sano y Sanitario
Scattered Remains
Scene from Frankie and
  Johnny, A
Scorpio Rising
Scrub Me Mama
See Saw
Sergei Eisenstein
Serial Clubber Killer
7 Steps to Sticky Heaven
Sex Elvis Boy
Sex Is Sex
Sexlock
Sexual I.D.
Shall We Dance
Shaman Psalm
Shame
Shanghai
She's a Talker
Shipwrecked
Shit Fit
Show Me
Shriek, The
Sigh of Love in Waiting
Significant (Br)other
Silencis (Silent Moments)
Simulation, A
Singing Seas
Skin Complex
Sleepin' Round
Sleeping Subjects
Sleepy Haven
So Unlike Their Reputation
Solo
Solos Y Soledades
Some of These Days
Son, Are You Down There?
Song from an Angel
Sortie 234
Sparky's Shoes
Speaking in Riddles
Splash
Stand By
Starway to the Stairs
STD Cry CIA
Stephen
Sternenschauer
  (Scattering Stars)
Steven Blenderman

(Artists in Iowa Series)
Sticky Moments
Still Life
Stiller, Garbo & Jag
  (Stiller, Garbo & Me)
Stolen Tango
Stopping Through
Strawberry Short Cut/Pickle
Surprise
Strider's House
Summer, 1993
Summer of Love—
  Art Against AIDS
Sunday Afternoon
Sunray
Survival House [excerpt]
Survivor, The
Tag Helms
Talk to Me Like the Rain
Tall Dark Stranger
Tangled Garden, Act II,
  Scene II
Taste of Kiwi, A
Tattoo
Tell Me No Lies
Tell Me Why: The
  Epistemology of Disco
Temps Perdus
Terence Stark: Mythographer
That's Masculinity
Theatrical Collage
Their First Mistake
They Are Lost to Vision
  Altogether
Thick Lips, Thin Lips
This Is Not a Condom
This Is Not an AIDS
  Advertisement
3 Short Films By
  Rachel Finkelstein
Three Faces of Women
Tim Miller: Loud and Queer
Time Off
To Play or Die
To Ride a Cow
To Tennessee with Love
Toe Heel Polka, The
Token of Love
Tom of Finland
Tom's Flesh
Top Secret
Tortures That Laugh
Touch Me
Tough Love, Smart Weapons
Toumanaka's Cave
Toys: Basic Technologies
  of Devotion
Tracce di Chiodo sul Muro
  (Tracks of Nail on the Wall)
Trevor
Triangle
Tricia's Wedding
Trick or Treat
Tricycle Race
Trojans
Trouble in Paradise

Truth About Alex, The
Truth Game, The
Try to Remember
Tugging the Worm
TV In Africa
21st Century Nuns
25 Year Old Man Loses His
  Virginity to a Woman, A
29 Effeminate Gestures
Twenty-Two
Twin Cheeks: Who Killed the
  Homecoming King?
Two Heads
Two Men and a Baby
Undecided
Undercover Me!
Unity
Untitled (Boyle, Bernie)
Untitled (Ikeda, Shuji)
Untitled (Larry)
. . . (Untitled) (Nicoletta,
  Daniel)
Untitled (Sanborn, John,
  and Mary Perillo)
V Is for Violet
Vacancy
Vehlefanz
Version de Marcial, La
  (Marcial's Version)
Vice and the Badge, The
Vicki Picks a Tie
Victor
Vingarne (Wings, The)
Virtual Cockpits of Tomorrow
Virus
Viva Eu!
Vivat Regina
Voguing: The Message
Voi Che Sapete
Voyage de l'Ogre, Le
Waiting
Waiting 'Round Wynyard
Wake Up, Jerk Off, Etc
Walk on the Wild Side
Walk the Dog
Wank Stallions
Want
Warm
Wasted Dreams
Watch Out for North Dakota
Wavering Heterosexual Confronts
  the Pleasure Principle Head
  On and Is Forced to Decide, A
We Were Marked with a Big A
Wedding of the Year,
  Chuck & Vince
Weekend Zombie Nurses
Weight of Oceans, The
What a Day, What a Life
What Can I Do with a
  Male Nude?
What Really Happened to
  Baby Jane?
What's A Nice Kid Like You . . .
Whatever
When You Name Me

Where There Was Silence
White Justice (A case of
  diminished capacity)
Why I Masturbate
Why I Stopped Going to
  Foreign Films
Why Not Love?/Get Used to It
Wigstock—The Movie
  (Rubnitz, Tom)
Wild Life
Wild Winds, The
Woman One Day, A
Woman's Heart, A
Working Class Chronicle
World Is Sick (sic), The
Wrong Son, The
Yearning For Sodom, A
You & I Will Play
You Say Maria, I Say Mariah
You Taste American
Young Physique, The: "Duals" &
  "A Day At Fire Island"

Cogender Shorts

ACT UP at the FDA
Acting Up for Prisoners
Actions Speak Louder Than
  Words
After Stonewall
After the Revolution
AIDS in the Barrio
AIDS Movie, The
AIDS/ARC Vigil
Al Margen del Margen
  (Beyond Outcasts)
aletheia
Alfalfa
All the Time
Alone Together: Young Adults
  Living With HIV
Analstahl (Anal Steel)
Anatomy of Desire
Anita Bryant: Pie-in-the-Face
Anniversary, The
At Home with the Stars
Balancing Factor
Bare
Because Reality Isn't Black
  and White [work in progress]
Because This Is About Love
Birthday Party at Repitition Cafe,
  The
Black People Get AIDS, Too
Body of Dissent: Lesbian and
  Gay Mennonites and Brethren
  Continue the Journey
Both of My Mom's Names
  Are Judy
Buscando un Espacio: Los
  Homosexuales en Cuba
  (Looking for a Space)
Camp Christmas
Cana, Em
Candlelight Vigil, A
Chinaman's Peak: Walking the
  Mountain

Civil Enough
Coming Out of the Iron Closet
Complaints
Comrades In Arms
Copenhagen: Gay Capitol of
  Denmark
Cut Sleeve
Deadly Deception
DiAna's Hair Ego: AIDS Info
  Up Front
Does Your Mother Know?
Dottie Gets Spanked
Double the Trouble,
  Twice the Fun
Double Trouble
Dr. Paglia
Drag on a Fag
East River Park
Educate Your Attitude
  (Fresh Talk)
Eggsplantsia
Eurotrash
Every Conceivable Position:
  Inside Gay Porn
Excess Is What I Came For
Fabian's Freeak Show
Fantasy Island
Feeling of Power #6769, The
Fighting for Our Lives: Facing
  AIDS in San Francisco
Finding Our Way Together
First Comes Love
Framed Youth: The Revenge of
  the Teenage Perverts
Gangtime
Gay Lives and Culture Wars
Gay Youth
Genderfuck
Girl's Best Friend, A
Give AIDS the Freeze
Glad To Be Gay, Right?
Golden Gate Bridge Blockade,
  The
Greetings from Washington D.C.
Guess Who's Coming to Dinner
Half a Million Strong
Hallowed
Happy Gordons, The
He-She Pee
Heroes
Hi Mom!
History of Western Sexuality, The
Hollywood and Homophobia
Home Stories
Home Sweet Home
Homophobia is Known
  to Cause Nightmares
Homosexuality: What Science
  Understands
Honored by the Moon
How to Turn Heads
Hunting Season, The
I Object
I'll Show You
Immaculate Conception
Innings

Intro to Cultural Skit-Zo-Frenia
It's a Queer World
Just for Fun
Khush
Kiev Blue
Kore
Lady
Lavender Tortoise, The
Limitless
Live to Tell: The First Gay Prom
  in America
Living with AIDS
Lost Lucy Episode, The
Louise Nevelson Takes a Bath
Love Makes a Family
Love on the Line
Margaret and Adele
Mothers
Mr. W's Little Game
My Mother's Secret
Neighborhood Voices
New Pupil, The
No Fairy Tale
No Porque Fidel Castro Lo Diga
  (Not Because Fidel Castro
  Says So)
None of the Above
Normal Life
Occupied Territories
Off the Rails
Ojos que No Ven
  (Eyes that Do Not See)
Olympia
On a Queer Day
  [work in progress]
Other Families
Other Families
Our Gay Brothers
Our House: Lesbians and Gays
  in the Hood
Out for Laughs
Out in Comedy
Out in South Africa
Oy Gay
Parade 1983
Parents Come Out
Passage a L'Acte
Personal Best: Gay Body Culture
Pink Triangles
Pout
Pride and Prejudice
PSA
Puppet Characters
Q.C. Girls, The
queer
Queer Carpentry Seminar
Queer Christmas
Queer Son
Queers Are Not Enough
Red Light, Green Light—
  Meeting Strangers
Reframing AIDS
rising
Running Gay
San Francisco Gay Freedom Day
  Parade 1980

Sea of Time
Seams
Searching for Contact
Sex and the Sandinistas
Sex Wars
Silent Pioneers
Snow Job: The Media
  Hysteria of AIDS
Spikes and Heels
Sticky Moments
Stop the Church
Storm in a Teacup
Straight Agenda, The
Straight from the Heart
Subject Is AIDS, The
Tag Helms
Talking About the Weather . . .
Talking Hairs
Ten Cents a Dance (Parallax)
Terms of Conception
Testing the Limits Guide to
  Safer Sex
Theo und Thea
Till Death Do Us Part
Toc Storee
Tomboychik
Too Little, Too Late
25 Year Old Man Loses His
  Virginity to a Woman, A
Two Spirit People
Two Spirits
Up In Arms Over Needle
  Exchange
Very Funny
Video Album: The Gaymes
!Viva 16th!
Voices of Life
Wanted!
Washington: October 14
We Were Marked with a Big A
Who Is Poetessa Fishhouse?
Wild Thing: A Poem by Sapphire
Woman One Day, A
You Can Fight City Hall
You Just Love Your Children
Zapovezena Laska
  (Forbidden Love)

Bisexual Shorts

Annie
Bisexual Kingdom, The
Boy Next Door: A Profile of
  Boy George
8mm Lesbian Love Film
History of Western Sexuality, The
Lesbians Who Date Men
Living with AIDS:
  Women and AIDS
Mark of Lilith, The
Minor Disturbances
My Dinner at Dan's
94 Arcana Drive
No Fairy Tale
Outlaw Poverty, Not Prostitutes
Porcaria
Queers Among Queers:

A Bay Area Perspective
Safe Sex Is Hot Sex
Simple Facts
Sleeping Subjects
Sortie 234
Strings
To Ride a Cow
25 Year Old Man Loses His
  Virginity to a Woman, A
Two Georges, The
  (Dos Jorges, Los)

Transgender Shorts

Across the Rubicon
Afflicted
Algie the Miner
Alphabit Land: The Backyard
  Tour Featuring Wigstock '89
Always On Sunday
Aquavitae
Beauties without a Cause
Bette Walters Interviews Garbo
Betty Walters Show, The
Brenda and Glenda Show, The
  [excerpt]
Butch Wax
Can You Say Androgynous?
Can't Help Lovin Dat Man
Changes
Cheap Skates: The Hardly-
  Cardigan Affair
Commercial for Murder
Conceicao
Cuz' It's Boy
Danger Girl, The
Dare to Be Butch
Denajua: I Like My Name
Dinner with Malibu
Drag Attack
Drag Queen Marathon, The
Dream Come True
Dreamgirls
Dual of the Senses
Elevator Girls in Bondage
Eunuchs: India's Third Gender
Fairest of Them All
Female Impersonator, The
Five Minutes, Ms. Lenska
Flaming Creatures
Forms and Motifs
Fuji
Genderfuck
Girls Will Be Boys
Guadalcanal Interlude
I Changed My Sex [trailer]
I Don't Want to Be e Boy
In View of Her Fatal Inclination,
  Lilo Wanders Gives Up
  the Ghost
It's a Queer World
Jane Show, The
Jewel's Darl
Joaquin
Judy's Do
Lady
Lady in Waiting, The

Laundromat
Let Me Die, Again
Like Mother, Like Son
Lillian's Dilemma
Linda /Les and Annie
Love and Lashes
Mad about the Boy
Men Like Me
Mi Pollo Loco
Miracle on Sunset Boulevard
Miss Otis
Mister Sisters, The
Mothers
New Pupil, The
94 Arcana Drive
Not Like That: Diary of a
  Butch-A-Phobe
On Becoming
100 Seconds with Sasha
Out of the Shadows
Outlaw
P(l)ain Truth
Palace
Poodle-Poo-Poo Miracle Mask,
  The
Queens of Columbus:
Performance Art & Art of Illusion
Right Stuff, The
Rites of Passage
Roman Springs on Mrs. Stone,
  The
Salt Mines, The
Sex Change—Shock! Horror!
  Probe! (BBC Arena)
She Even Chewed Tobacco!
Shit Fit
Sister Is (Not) A Mister, The
Sometimes
Song of the Goddess
Stafford's Story
Storme: The Lady of the
  Jewel Box
Tex-Sex
Three Faces of Women
Tomboy!
Tomboychik
Tracce di Chlodo sul Muro
  (Tracks of Nail on the Wall)
Trans
Tricia's Wedding
Two Spirit People
Vivat Regina
Walk on the Wild Side
What Really Happened to
  Baby Jane?
Wigstock—The Movie
  (Rubnitz, Tom)
Woman's Heart, A
World Is Sick (sic), The
Zoe la Boxeuse (Zoe the Boxer)

SUBJECT INDEX

Activism

Absolutely Positive
ACT UP at the FDA
Acting Up for Prisoners
After the Revolution
Age of Dissent
AIDS/ARC Vigil
Army of Lovers: or Revolt of
  the Sex Perverts
Ballot Measure Nine
Battle of Tuntenhaüs, The
Before Stonewall
Bogjavlar (Damned Queers)
Born In Flames
Bright Eyes
Broadcast Tapes of Dr. Peter,
  The
Candlelight Vigil, A
Coming Out of the Iron Closet
Condomnation
Dancing in Dulais
Deadly Deception
DHPG Mon Amour
Diana's Hair Ego: AIDS
  Info Up Front
Drag in for Votes
Dykes Rule
Eat This
Elegy in the Streets
Feeling of Power #6769, The
Final Solutions
Framed Youth: The Revenge
  of the Teenage Perverts
Fuck the Pope
Gay USA
Golden Gate Bridge
  Blockade, The
Greetings from Out Here
Greetings from Washington D.C.
Half a Million Strong
Happy Gordons, The
Hard Reign's Gonna Fall, A
Helms = Death
History Will Accuse Me
Homosexual Desire in Minnesota
I'm You, You're Me
Illegal Acts
(In)Visible Women
Keep Your Laws Off My Body
Killer Babe
Laura, Ingrid, and Rebecca
Lavender Tortoise, The
Lesbian Avengers Eat Fire Too
Lick Bush in '92
Live to Tell: The First Gay Prom
  in America
Marching for Freedom
Marta: Portrait of a Teen Activist
Moffie Called Simon, A
My Skin is a Map
No Need to Repent
No Regret
  (Non, Je ne regrette rien)
On Guard

One Nation Under God
Out in South Africa
Out On Four: Episodes 1 & 2
Out On Tuesday, Program 3
Outlaw Poverty, Not Prostitutes
Over Our Dead Bodies
Pink Pimpernel, The
Pink Triangles
Political Funerals
Positive (Positiv)
Preservation of the Song
Queers Among Queers:
  A Bay Area Perspective
Queers Are Not Enough
Ray Navarro Memorial Tape
Right to Fight, The
Rights and Reactions
Risk: Lesbians and AIDS
Sacred Lies, Civil Truths
Sex and the Sandinistas
Spikes and Heels
Stop the Church
Tag Helms
Testing the Limits Guide to
  Safer Sex
Tim Miller: Loud and Queer
Times of Harvey Milk, The
21st Century Nuns
Unity
Up In Arms Over Needle
  Exchange
Urinal
Voices from the Front
Welcome to the Dome
Women on Fire
World Is Sick (sic), The
You Can Fight City Hall

Aging/Elders

Alkali, Iowa
An Empty Bed
Antonia's Line
Castro Cowboy
Cerebral Accident
Christopher Isherwood:
  Over There on a Visit
Common Flower, A
Complaints of a Dutiful Daughter
Comrades In Arms
Day in the Life of Edmund
  White, A
Doll House
Ernie and Rose
Fiction and Other Truths:
  A Film about Jane Rule
Fried Green Tomatoes
Ich Bin Meine Eigene Frau
  (I Am My Own Woman)
Ich und Frau Berger
  (Me & Mrs. Berger)
In Plain View
Interview With The Vampire
Le Jupon Rouge
  (Manuela's Loves)
Letter to My Grandma
Madonna and Child

Maidens
Man of No Importance, A
Miss Ruby's House
Mr. W's Little Game
My Grandma's Lady Cabaret
Neighborhood Voices
Nitrate Kisses
Optic Nerve
Out On Tuesday, Program 4
Pools
Psychosynthesis
Rambles
Salut Victor!
Silent Pioneers
Staircase
Storm in a Teacup
Tender Fictions
Thank You and Good Night
Tomboychik
Turnabout
Vital Signs
Waiting for the Moon
Was Soll'n Wir Denn Machen
  Ohne Den Tod (What Shall We
  Do Without Death)
West Coast Crones: A Glimpse at
  the Lives Of Nine Old
  Lesbians
When Shirley Met Florence
Where the Cows Go
Wild Flowers
Women Like That
Women Like Us (see Out
  On Tuesday, Program 4)

AIDS and Health

A.I.D.S.C.R.E.A.M.
Absolutely Positive
ACT UP at the FDA
Acting Up for Prisoners
ADS Epidemic, The
AIDS: A Priest's Testament
AIDS in the Barrio
AIDS Movie, The
AIDS Show, The
AIDS/ARC Vigil
Al Margen del Margen
  (Beyond Outcasts)
Alone Together: Young Adults
  Living With HIV
Amazing Grace
Anatomy of Desire
And the Band Played On
Awakening of Nancy Kaye,
  The
Bill Pope: Portrait of a
  Native Son
Birthday Party at Repitition
  Cafe, The
Bitter Old Queens
Black People Get AIDS, Too
Blue
Both (De La Rosa, Vic)
Boy Who Fell In Love, The
Boys on the Side
Breast Exam

Bright Eyes
Broadcast Tapes of Dr. Peter, The
Buddies
Bumps
Cancer in Two Voices
Candlelight Vigil, A
Castro Cowboy
Chance of a Lifetime
Change
Chinaman's Peak: Walking the Mountain
Chuck Solomon: Coming of Age
Clinic, The
Closing Numbers
Clue
Cold Bath
Complaints of a Dutiful Daughter
Condomnation
Condoms Are a Girl's Best Friend
Cunt Dykula
Current Flow
Dadshuttle, The
Dancing Is Illegal
Deaf Heaven
Denajua: I Like My Name
DHPG Mon Amour
Diamanda Galas: Judgement Day
DiAna's Hair Ego: AIDS Info Up Front
Disappearing Act
Doctors, Liars and Women
Down on the River
Du Darst (Truth or Dare)
East River Park
Elegy in the Streets
Exits
Falling Through the Cracks
Family Values
Fast Trip, Long Drop
Fear of Disclosure
Fighting Chance
Fighting for Our Lives: Facing AIDS in San Francisco
Final Solutions
Finding Our Way Together
Flowing Hearts: Thailand Fights AIDS
Fly That Friendly Sky
Fresh Kill
From Dental Dams to Latex Gloves
Garden, The
Gay TV
Get It Girl: Lesbians Talk about Safe Sex
Girl's Best Friend, A
Girls Will Be Boys
Give AIDS the Freeze
Golden Gate Bridge Blockade, The
Grid-Lock: Women and the Politics of AIDS
Growing Up and I'm Fine
Hallowed
Hard Reign's Gonna Fall, A

Her Giveaway
Hero of My Own Life
Heroes
Homosexuality: What Science Understands
Housewife and the Plumber, The [Pout #3 excerpt]
I Will Not Think about Death Anymore
I'm Still Alive: A Person With AIDS Tells His Story
I'm You, You're Me
Ich Lebe Gern, Ich Sterbe Gern (Living And Dying)
(In)Visible Women
Jeffrey
Kore
Land Beyond Tomorrow
Last Supper, The
Latex—Step Out Smartly
Laura, Ingrid, and Rebecca
Living End, The
Living with AIDS
Living with AIDS: Women and AIDS
Longtime Companion
Memento Mori
Men In Love
My Brother's Keeper
N'oublie pas que tu vas mourir (Don't Forget You're Going To Die)
Night with Derek, A
No Fairy Tale
No Glove, No Love
No Regret (Non, Je ne Regrette Rien)
No Sad Songs
Nuit Sauvage, La (Savage Nights)
Ojos que No Ven (Eyes that Do Not See)
On the Safe Side
One Foot on a Banana Peel, the
Other Foot in the Grave
103 Degrees
Out On Four: Episodes 5 & 6
Out On Tuesday, Program 2
Over Our Dead Bodies
P.A.N.I.C. in Griffith Park
Package, The
Paradise Framed
Parting Glances
Philadelphia
Pink Pimpernel, The
Plague, A
Plague on You, A
Poison
Poisoned Blood
Political Funerals
Politics of Disco, The
Positive (Positiv)
Preservation of the Song
Rage & Desire
Ravissement, La
Ray Navarro Memorial Tape

Re Generation
Reframing AIDS
Relax
Right to Fight, The
Risk Group
Risk: Lesbians and AIDS
Room 303
Roy Cohn/Jack Smith
RSVP
Saddle Up
Safe Is Desire [excerpt]
Safe Sex is Fun
Safe Sex Is Hot Sex
Safe Sex: The Manual
Safe Soap
Safer Sister
Safety In Numbers
Saint Mulekicker
Schweigen=Tod (Silence=Death)
Sea of Time
Shot Through My Head
Silverlake Life: The View from Here
Snow Job: The Media Hysteria of AIDS
Song from an Angel
Sparky's Shoes
STD Cry CIA
Stephen
Stop the Church
Subject Is AIDS, The
Summer, 1993
Summer of Love— Art Against AIDS
Survivor, The
Tag Helms
Testing the Limits Guide to Safer Sex
This Is Not a Condom
This Is Not an AIDS Advertisement
Till Death Do Us Part
To Die For (Heaven's a Drag)
Together Alone
Tongues Untied
Too Little, Too Late
Two Men and a Baby
Under Heat
Untitled (Sanborn, John, and Mary Perillo)
Up In Arms Over Needle Exchange
Via Appia
Virus Kennt Keine Moral, Ein (Virus Has No Morals, A)
Viva Eu!
Voices from the Front
Voices of Life
Warrior Marks
We All Have Our Reasons
We're Talking Vulva
Welcome to the Dome
Well Sexy Women
World Is Sick (sic), The
Yearning For Sodom, A
You Little Devil, You
Zero Patience

Arts and Literature

Aesthetics and/or Transportation
Andy Makes a Movie
Andy Warhol
Angelic Conversation, The
Arlene Raven—April '79
Art of Mirrors, The
Assumption, The
Attendant, The
Ballad of Reading Gaol
Berenice Abbott: A View of
 the 20th Century
Bigger Splash, A
Boys in the Band, The
Carrington
Daddy and the Muscle Academy
David Hockney's Diaries
Day in the Life of Edmund
 White, A
Death of a Writer in Two Parts
 (A Comedy of Sorts)
Do You Think that a Candidate
 Should Live Like This?
Dream Machine, The
Eileen Myles: An American Poem
Erte
Fiction and Other Truths: A Film
 about Jane Rule
Flip Side, The
Forms and Motifs
Gertrude Stein and a Companion
Gertrude Stein: When This You
 See, Remember Me
Goblin Market
Good Dyke Gone Mad, A
Gracious Flab, Gracious Bone
Hotheads
I, The Worst of All
Is Mary Wings Coming?
Joe Joe
Last Paintings of Derek Jarman,
 The
Limités
Long Time Comin'
Looking for Langston
Louise Nevelson Takes a Bath
Mason's Life
Meteor and Shadow
 (Meteore et Ombre)
Mondays
My Courbet . . . Or, A
 Beaver's Tale
Narcissus
No More Nice Girls
Nobody's People
Nudes (A Sketchbook)
One Single Life
Our Trip
Paris Was a Woman
Pasolini, un delitto Italiano
 (Pasolini, an Italian Crime)
Portrait of a Marriage
Postcards from America
Proust's Favorite Fantasy
Querelle
Rage & Desire

Robert Mapplethorpe
Saint Genet
Salome
Sappho
Sphinxes Without Secrets
Standard of Living, The
Still Sane
Talk to Me Like the Rain
Tangled Garden, Act II,
 Scene II
Therese and Isabelle
To Tennessee with Love
Tom of Finland
Total Eclipse
Trojans
Uh-Oh!
Unzipped
Viva Eu!
Waiting
Waltz, The
What Can I Do with a Male
 Nude?
Whatever
Who Is Poetessa Fishhouse?
Wittgenstein
World of Light: A Portrait of
 May Sarton

Asian Images

After the Break
aletheia
Anguished Love
Anxiety of Inexpression and
 the Otherness Machine
Bare
Berlin Affair, The
Beyond/Body/Memory
Bi-Ways
Bottom
Chinaman's Peak: Walking
 the Mountain
Chinese Characters
Complete St. Veronica, The
Cut Sleeve
Destiny/Desire/Devotion
Displaced View, The
Dreamgirls
Eagle Shooting Hero
East Is Red, The
Eunuchs: India's Third Gender
Exposure
Farewell My Concubine
Ferdous (Paradise)
Fighting Chance
Flesh and Paper (see Out
 On Tuesday, Program 3)
Flowing Hearts: Thailand
 Fights AIDS
Fly That Friendly Sky
Foetal Gay's Nightmare, A
Fresh Kill
Funeral Parade of Roses
Give Me Body
Harold and Hiroshi
Hatachi No Binetsu
 (Slight Fever of a 20-Year-Old)

Her Sweetness Lingers
Hysterio Passio
I Am a Man
Iro Kaze (Colour Wind)
Irome (Colour Eyes)
Kazetachi No Gogo
 (Afternoon Breezes)
Khush
Kore
Koukei Dori
 (Landscape Catching)
Kuro Tokage (Black Lizard, The)
Ladyboys
Last Song, The
Legend of Fong Sai-Yuk, The
Lick
Loss of Heat
M. Butterfly
Macho Dancer
Malaysian Series, Part 1-6
Matsumae-Kun No Senritsu
 (Melody For Buddy Matsumae)
Maybe I Can Give You Sex ?
 Part One
Maybe I Can Give You Sex ?
 Part Two
Memory Pictures
Memsahib Rita
Midnight Dancers
Minoru and Me
More Love
Muscle
My Beautiful Laundrette
My Idol
My Sweet Peony
1999 - Nen No Natsu Yasumi
 (Summer Vacation: 1999)
Okoge
Orientations
Out On Tuesday, Program 2
Out On Tuesday, Program 3
Outsiders, The
Poisoned Blood
Rasen No Sobyo (Rough Sketch
 of a Spiral)
Revolutions Happen Like
 Refrains in a Song
Sari Red
Second Generation Once
 Removed
7 Steps to Sticky Heaven
Shisheng Huamei
 (Silent Thrush, The)
Skin Deep
Sleeping Subjects
Song of the Goddess
These Shoes Weren't Made
 For Walking
Thick Lips, Thin Lips
To Ride a Cow
Toc Storee
Tokyo Cowboy
Twin Bracelets, The
Twinkle
Two or Three Things I Know
 About Them

Vive L'Amour
Wedding Banquet, The
Wicked Radiance
Wild Woman of the Woods
You Thrive on Mistaken Identity

Biography

Absolutely Positive
Affengeil (Life Is Like a
    Cucumber)
Alleged, The
American Fabulous
An All-American Story
Andy Makes a Movie
Andy the Furniture Maker
Andy Warhol
Anxiety of Inexpression and the
    Otherness Machine
Aquavitae
Arlene Raven—April '79
Armistead Maupin Is a Man I
    Dreamt Up
Audience
Awakening of Nancy Kaye, The
Basic Necessities
Because This Is About Love
Bedtime Stories
Berenice Abbott: A View of the
    20th Century
Beyond Imagining: Margaret
    Anderson & the Little Review
Bigger Splash, A
Bill Pope: Portrait of a
    Native Son
Bitter Old Queens
Boy Next Door: A Profile of
    Boy George
Brincando El Charco: Portrait
    of a Puerto Rican
Broken Goddess
Bumps
Calamity Jane
Call Me Your Girlfriend
Can't Help Lovin Dat Man
Carrington
Castro Cowboy
Changing Our Minds: The Story
    Of Dr. Evelyn Hooker
Christopher Isherwood: Over
    There on a Visit
Chuck Solomon: Coming of Age
Coconut/Cane & Cutlass
Cold Bath
Communication from Weber
Complaints of a Dutiful Daughter
Confessions of a Pretty Lady
Daddy and the Muscle Academy
Darkness of My Language, The
David Hockney's Diaries
Day in the Life of Edmund
    White, A
Derek Jarman, Know What
    I Mean
DHPG Mon Amour
Do You Think that a Candidate
    Should Live Like This?

Doll House
Dorothy Arzner: A Profile
Dr. Paglia
Eileen Myles: An American Poem
Ein Mann Wie Eva
    (Man Like Eva, A)
Emergence
Erte
Execution: A Study of Mary
F2M (Female to Male)
Fast Trip, Long Drop
Fatboy Chronicles, The (Part
    One : Rene, Rene, Qu' est-ce-
    que c' est?)
Fearless: The Hunterwali Story
Fiction and Other Truths: A
    Film about Jane Rule
film, a
Flesh and Paper (see Out
    On Tuesday, Program 3)
Forward, Bound
Framing Lesbian Fashion
Frankie and Jocie
Friendly Witness
Gangtime
Ganze Leben, Das
    (The Whole of Life)
Geography of the Imagination
Gertrude Stein and a Companion
Gertrude Stein: When This You
    See, Remember Me
Glitterbug
Hail the New Puritan
Haircut
Hallowed
Henry and June
Hero of My Own Life
Home Movie
I Was I Am
Ich Bin Meine Eigene Frau
    (I Am My Own Woman)
Ich Lebe Gern, Ich Sterbe Gern
    (Living And Dying)
If Every Girl Had a Diary
International Sweethearts of
    Rhythm
It's the Look I'm After
Jean Genet
Joaquin
Jodie Promo
Joggernaught
John Lindquist: Photographer
    of the Dance
Juggling Gender
Last Paintings of Derek Jarman,
    The
Lesbians
Letter to My Grandma
Linda /Les and Annie
Living with AIDS
Looking for Langston
Lorenza
Louise Nevelson Takes a Bath
Ludwig
Ma Vie
Madame Simone

Madonna and Child
Maidens
Man of the Year
Massillon
Meet Johnny Eagle
Meteor and Shadow
    (Meteore et Ombre)
Millionaire
My Courbet . . . Or, A
    Beaver's Tale
New York Loft
Nico-Icon
Night with Derek, A
No Need to Repent
No Sad Songs
No Saintly Girl
Nobody's People
Not Like That: Diary of a
    Butch-A-Phobe
Off the Rails
One Foot on a Banana Peel, the
    Other Foot in the Grave
Ostia
Outlaw
P.A.R.A.N.O.R.M.A.L.
P(l)ain Truth
Pasolini, un delitto Italiano
    (Pasolini, an Italian Crime)
Paul Cadmus: Enfant Terrible
    at 80
Place Called Lovely, A
Place of Rage, A
Playing Poseidon
Please Decompose Slowly
Portrait of a Marriage
Portrait of Jason
Postcards from America
Prayer Before Birth, A
Prick Up Your Ears
Rainer Werner Fassbinder:
    The Last Works
Right to Fight, The
Robert Mapplethorpe
Rock Hudson's Home Movies
Roy Cohn/Jack Smith
Saint Genet
Saint Mulekicker
Sally Forth
Schweigen=Tod (Silence=Death)
Sergeant Matlovich Versus the
    U.S. Air Force
Sergei Eisenstein
Serving in Silence: The
    Margarethe Cammermeyer
    Story
Shirley Temple and Me
Shot Through My Head
Silverlake Life: The View
    from Here
Sink or Swim
Sis: The Perry Watkins Story
Sometimes
Spin Cycle
Stiller, Garbo & Jag (Stiller,
    Garbo & Me)
Storme: The Lady of the

Jewel Box
Strip Jack Naked
Suddenly Last Summer
Susana
Taxi Zum Klo
Tender Fictions
Terence Davies Trilogy, The
Terence Stark: Mythographer
These Shoes Weren't Made
   For Walking
Ties That Bind, The
Tim Miller: Loud and Queer
Times of Harvey Milk, The
Tiny & Ruby: Hell Divin' Women
To My Women Friends
Tom of Finland
Tongues Untied
Trojans
Turnabout
Untitled (Kossoff, Leslie)
Unzipped
Vanilla Sex
Verzaubert (Enchanted)
Video Album 5: The
   Thursday People
Waiting for the Moon
Whatever
Without You I'm Nothing
Wittgenstein
Woman's Heart, A
Woman's Place Is in the
   House, A
Women Like That
Women Like Us
Working Class Chronicle
World of Gilbert and George, The
World of Light: A Portrait of
   May Sarton
Yearning For Sodom, A
You Thrive on Mistaken Identity

Bisexual Images

Apartment Zero
Basic Instinct
Bisexual Kingdom, The
Blond Fury
Boy Next Door: A Profile of
   Boy George
Corps Perdu, A (Straight to
   the Heart)
Doom Generation, The
8mm Lesbian Love Film
History of Western Sexuality, The
In Plain View
Lesbians Who Date Men
Living with AIDS: Women
   and AIDS
Long Weekend (O'Despair), The
Minor Disturbances
My Dinner at Dan's
My Hustler
94 Arcana Drive
No Fairy Tale
No Ordinary Love
North of Vortex
Out On Tuesday, Program 1

Porcaria
Queers Among Queers:
   A Bay Area Perspective
Simple Facts
Sleeping Subjects
Something for Everyone
Sortie 234
Straight for the Money:
   Interviews with Queer Sex
   Workers
Strings
Stripped Bare: A Look at
   Erotic Dancers
Three Bewildered People in
   the Night
To Ride a Cow
Two Georges, The
   (Dos Jorges, Los)

Black Images

Ad, The
Affirmations
Among Good Christian Peoples
Anthem
Attendant, The
BD Women
Behind Every Good Man
Billy Turner's Secret
Bird In The Hand
Black and White in Color
Black Bag: Gender Bender
Black Body
Black People Get AIDS, Too
Bodily Functions
Borderline
Born In Flames
Boy! What A Girl!
Boys on the Side
Brown Sugar Licks Snow White
Central Park
Chasing the Moon
Cities of Lust
Coconut/Cane & Cutlass
Complicated Flesh
Cosmic Demonstration of
   Sexuality, A
Crying Game, The
Current Flow
Cutting the Edge of a Free Bird
Darker Side of Black, A
Darkness of My Language, The
DiAna's Hair Ego: AIDS Info
   Up Front
Disappearing Act
Drag in for Votes
Dreams of Passion
Edges
Emergence
Exposure
Fertile La Toyah Jackson
   Video Magazine
Flower Market, The
Frankie and Jocie
Gangtime
Ghost Body
Glad To Be Gay, Right?

Greta's Girls
Heaven, Earth and Hell
Here Be Dragons
I Am Your Sister
I Like Dreaming
I Never Danced the Way Girls
   Were Supposed To
I've Never
If She Grows Up Gay
Ifé
Incredibly True Adventures of
   Two Girls in Love, The
Infidel
International Sweethearts of
   Rhythm
Intro to Cultural Skit-Zo-Frenia
L-Shaped Room, The
Lady in Waiting, The
Lick Bush in '92
Long Time Comin'
Looking for Langston
Lord and Master
Male Gayze, The
Media Blackmale
Messiah at the City
Millionaire
Miss Ruby's House
Mother's Hands
My Sorrow Means Nothing to You
No Money, No Honey
No Regret
   (Non, Je ne regrette rien)
Nocturne
Norman, Is That You?
Odds and Ends (A New-Age
   Amazon Fable)
Our House: Lesbians and
   Gays in the Hood
Out in Africa (Symons, Johnny)
Out in South Africa
Out of the Shadows
Parallel Sons
Paris is Burning
Party
Passion of Remembrance, The
Peach
Place of Rage, A
Please Decompose Slowly
Portrait of Jason
Potluck and the Passion, The
Prayer Before Birth, A
Preservation of the Song
Rage & Desire
Shame
She Don't Fade
Sightings
Significant (Br)other
Silence . . . Broken
Sis: The Perry Watkins Story
Six Degrees of Separation
Sleeping Subjects
Spin Cycle
Splash
St. Louis Blues
Storme: The Lady of the
   Jewel Box

Story So Far: A Forgotten
Classic, The
Suburban Queen
Thick Lips, Thin Lips
This Is Not an AIDS
Advertisement
Three Faces of Women
Tiny & Ruby: Hell Divin' Women
Tongues Untied
24 Hours a Day
Two Men and a Baby
Untitled (Sanborn, John, and
Mary Perillo)
Vanilla Sex
Victor
Village Idiot, The
Vintage: Families of Value
Voguing: The Message
Warrior Marks
What Is a Line?
What's the Difference Between a
Yam and a Sweet Potato?
Whatever
Wild Thing: A Poem by Sapphire
Wolfgirl
Women In Love: Bonding
Strategies of Black Lesbians
Young Soul Rebels

Body Issues
Beyond/Body/Memory
Big Fat Slenderella
Breast Exam
Chubs & Bears [work in progress]
Divine Bodies
Fat Chance
Fatboy Chronicles, The (Part
One : Rene, Rene, Qu' est-ce-
que c' est?)
Give Me Body
Gracious Flab, Gracious Bone
Her Appetite
House of Pain
Life in the Kitchen
Limitless
On Becoming
Personal Best: Gay Body Culture
Pools
Sometimes
Tom's Flesh
Topsau, Die (The Top Pig)

Camp
Alfalfa
Algie the Miner
Always On Sunday
American Fabulous
Balcony, The
Beauties without a Cause
Because We Must
Big Time Wrestlers from
Hollywood
Bike Boy
Birthday Tribute to Dame Edna
Everage, A
Black Bag: Gender Bender

Brenda and Glenda Show, The
Bridgette
Bump and Grind It
Bust-Up
Caged
Calamity Jane
Can't Stop the Music
Carrie
Cat and the Canary, The
Cheap Skates: The Hardly-
Cardigan Affair
Chicken Elaine
Chickula: Teenage Vampire
Cliche in the Afternoon
Coal Miner's Granddaughter
Copenhagen: Gay Capitol of
Denmark
Daughters of Darkness
Desperate Remedies
Ding Dong
Dr. Jekyll and Sister Hyde
Drag on a Fag
Drag Queen Marathon, The
Dyketactics
East Is Red, The
Entre Tinieblas (Dark Habits)
ESP: Vision
Eurotrash
Even Cowgirls Get the Blues
Fabian's Freeak Show
Fairies, The
Female Impersonator, The
Fertile La Toyah Jackson
Video Magazine
Florida Enchantment, A
Frankenstein Created Woman
Frankfurter
Freebird
From Bejing to Brooklyn
Gay Deceivers, The
Gay San Francisco
Glen or Glenda?
(I Changed My Sex)
Grapefruit
Great Dykes of Holland, The
Halloweenie
Hi Mom!
"Home Movie"
Homicidal
Horror Vacui—Die Angst Vor Der
Leere (Horror Vacui—The Fear
of Emptiness)
Hustle with My Muscle
I Am a Man
I Want What I Want
In View of Her Fatal Inclination,
Lilo Wanders Gives Up
the Ghost
It's a Queer World
Jane Show, The
Joan Sees Stars
Joe Joe
John Sex: The True Story
Judy's Do
Kenneth Anger's Hollywood
Babylon

Laberinto de Pasiones
(Labyrinth of Passions)
Lavender Tortoise, The
Legend of Fong Sai-Yuk, The
Lost Lucy Episode, The
Madame Simone
Made for TV
Midwestern Skidmarks
Million Eyes of Su-Muru, The
Miss Otis
Mother Show, The
My Sister, My Love
Myra Breckenridge
976
Nude Inn
Ohrenwurm, Der
100 Seconds with Sasha
Out for Laughs
Pink Narcissus
Plastic Rap
Pout
Pouvoir Intime
Proust's Favorite Fantasy
Que He Hecho Yo Para Merecer
Esto? (What Have I Done to
Deserve This?)
Queen, The
Red Light, Green Light—
Meeting Strangers
Reflections in a Golden Eye
Remembrance
Right Stuff, The
Roman Springs on Mrs. Stone,
The
Salome
Sech Wie Pech & Schwefel
(Birds of a Feather)
Seven Women
She's a Talker
Singing Seas
Sisters of Darkness
Some of My Best Friends
Are . . .
Something for Everyone
Sparkle's Tavern
Stadt der Verlorenen Seelen
(City Of Lost Souls)
Sticky Moments
Strawberry Short Cut/Pickle
Surprise
Summer of Love—
Art Against AIDS
Swamp
"Sword Fight"
That Tender Touch
Their First Mistake
Theo und Thea
Touchables, The
Twin Cheeks: Who Killed the
Homecoming King?
Undercover Me!
. . . (Untitled) (Nicoletta,
Daniel)
Vicki Picks a Tie
Vivat Regina
What Really Happened to

Baby Jane?
Whatever Happened to
   Susan Jane?
Wigstock—The Movie
   (Rubnitz, Tom)
Wonderland
Yma Sumac: Hollywood's Inca
   Princess

Class

AIDS in the Barrio
Behind Glass
Born In Flames
Ernesto
Fried Green Tomatoes
Gerbroken Spiegels (Broken
   Mirrors)
Greetings from Out Here
I'm You, You're Me
If She Grows Up Gay
Jollies
Leather Boys, The
Macho Dancer
Maurice
More Than a Paycheck
Odd Girl Out
Out in Suburbia
Outlaw
Playing the Part
Prick Up Your Ears
Q.C. Girls, The
Reframing AIDS
Second Awakening of Christa
   Klages, The
Shasta Woman
Sister, My Sister
Six Degrees of Separation
Sum of Us, The
Taste of Honey, A
Working Class Dykes from Hell
You Can't Die from Not Sleeping

Coming Out

Afflicted
After the Game
After the Revolution
Avonden, De (Evenings, The)
Avskedet (Farewell, The)
Both of My Mom's Names Are
   Judy
Certain Grace, A
Claire of the Moon
Coming Out
Coming Out of the Iron Closet
Cumulus Nimbus
Cut Sleeve
Desert Hearts
Disco Years, The
Do You Know What I Mean
Does Your Mother Know?
Double Exposure
Double Trouble
Educate Your Attitude
   (Fresh Talk)
Family Affair, A
First Base

For a Lost Soldier
Fun Down There
Gangtime
Glad To Be Gay, Right?
Guess Who's Coming to Visit
Harlequin Exterminator
Homoteens
How He Goes
I Dream of Dorothy
I Was I Am
Kiev Blue
Kim
Kiss on the Cliff, The
L'Ingenue
Leather Boys, The
Lianna
Live to Tell: The First Gay
   Prom in America
Lost Heart, The
Lost Language of Cranes, The
Ma Vie
Maya
Me and Rubyfruit
Minoru and Me
Mondo Diviso, II (The
   Split World)
Monsters in the Closet
Montreal Main
Moscow Does Not Believe
   in Dreams
My First Suit
Odd Girl Out
Only the Brave
Oranges Are Not the Only Fruit
Orientations
Our Mom's a Dyke
Out in Suburbia
Personal Best
Playing the Part
Pride and Prejudice
Priest
Rosebud
Safe Place, A
Salmonberries
Sex and the Sandinistas
Shame
She Makes Love With Her
Sum of Us, The
Tell Me No Lies
Thin Ice
To My Women Friends
Tokyo Cowboy
Trevor
Truth About Alex, The
Truth Game, The
Twice a Woman
Vehlefanz
Veronica Four Rose
Vrouw Als Eva, Een
   (Woman Like Eve, A)
Waiting 'Round Wynyard
Want
War Widow, The
Wild Flowers
Wild Reeds
Word Is Out: Stories of Some
   of Our Lives

Differently Abled Images

Actions Speak Louder Than
   Words
aletheia
Awakening of Nancy Kaye, The
Cutting the Edge of a Free Bird
Double the Trouble, Twice the
   Fun
Lifetime Commitment:
   A Portrait of Karen Thompson
Lorenza
Loss of Heat
Margaret and Adele
Mermaids, Fish & Other
   Non-Bipeds
Minoru and Me
P.A.R.A.N.O.R.M.A.L.
Prayer Before Birth, A
Proof

Discrimination

Age of Dissent
Anders als die Anderen
   (Different from the Others)
Bachvirus, Het
   (Bach Virus, The)
Ballot Measure Nine
Before the Act
Black Body
Body of Dissent: Lesbian and
   Gay Mennonites and Brethren
Continue the Journey
Both of My Mom's Names
   Are Judy
Changing Our Minds: The Story
   Of Dr. Evelyn Hooker
Chicken Hawk
Choosing Children
Coming Out under Fire
Fantasy Island
Fighting in Southwest Louisiana
Fresa y Chocolate
   (Strawberry and Chocolate)
Good Dyke Gone Mad, A
Happy Gordons, The
Haven
History Will Accuse Me
Il Etait une Fois dans L'est
   (Once Upon a Time in the
   East)
In the Best Interest of the
   Children
Just Because of Who We Are
Kanada
Konsequenz, Die
   (Consequence, The)
Labor More Than Once
Last Island, The
Lifetime Commitment:
   A Portrait of Karen Thompson
Massillon
Maurice
No Porque Fidel Castro Lo Diga
   (Not Because Fidel Castro
   Says So)
Outcasts

P4W: Prison for Women
Pedagogue
Philadelphia
Raw Meet
Rights and Reactions
Sergeant Matlovich Versus the
   U.S. Air Force
Serving in Silence: The
   Margarethe Cammermeyer
   Story
Sis: The Perry Watkins Story
Verzaubert (Enchanted)
We Were Marked with a Big A
You Can Fight City Hall

Drag and
Transgender Images

Across the Rubicon
Adventures of Priscilla, Queen
   of the Desert, The
Afflicted
Algie the Miner
All Of Me
Alphabit Land: The Backyard
   Tour Featuring Wigstock '89
Always On Sunday
Angel
Aquavitae
Ballad of Little Jo, The
Basket Case
Bathroom Gender
Beauties without a Cause
Because We Must
Behind Every Good Man
Bette Walters Interviews Garbo
Betty Walters Show, The
Birthday Party
Birthday Tribute to Dame Edna
   Everage, A
Black Bag: Gender Bender
Boys from Brazil
Brenda and Glenda Show, The
Broken Goddess
Brown Sugar Licks Snow White
Butch Wax
Calamity Jane
Can You Say Androgynous?
Can't Help Lovin Dat Man
Changes
Cheap Skates: The Hardly-
   Cardigan Affair
Commercial for Murder
Conceicao
Crying Game, The
Cuz' It's Boy
Dandy Dust [trailer]
Danger Girl, The
Dare to Be Butch
DeAundra Peek's High Class Hall
   O'Fame Theater
Denajua: I Like My Name
Dialogo
Dinner with Malibu
Dorian Gray Im Spiegel Der
   Boulevardpresse (Dorian Gray
   in the Mirror of the Popular
Press)
Dr. Jekyll and Sister Hyde
Drag Attack
Drag in for Votes
Drag Queen Marathon, The
Drama in Blond
Dream Come True
Dreamgirls
Dual of the Senses
Eagle Shooting Hero
East Is Red, The
Ein Mann Wie Eva
   (Man Like Eva, A)
Elevator Girls in Bondage
Eunuchs: India's Third Gender
F2M (Female to Male)
Fairest of Them All
Farewell My Concubine
Female Impersonator, The
Female Misbehavior
Five Minutes, Ms. Lenska
Flaming Creatures
Florida Enchantment, A
Fontvella's Box
Forms and Motifs
Fortune and Men's Eyes
Frankenstein Created Woman
Fuji
Funeral Parade of Roses
Genderfuck
Girls Will Be Boys
Glen or Glenda?
   (I Changed My Sex)
Grapefruit
Guadalcanal Interlude
He-She Pee
Homicidal
I Changed My Sex [trailer]
I Don't Want to Be a Boy
I Want What I Want
Ich Bin Meine Eigene Frau
   (I Am My Own Woman)
Ich Mochte Kein Mann Sein!
   (I Don't Want To Be A Man!)
If They'd Asked for a Lion Tamer
Il Etait une Fois dans L'est
   (Once Upon a Time in the
   East)
In View of Her Fatal Inclination,
Lilo Wanders Gives Up the Ghost
It's a Queer World
Jane Show, The
Jewel's Darl
Joaquin
Judy's Do
Juggling Gender
Just Another Girl
Kiss of the Spider Woman
Kuro Tokage (Black Lizard, The)
Laberinto de Pasiones
   (Labyrinth of Passions)
Lady
Lady in Waiting, The
Ladyboys
Laundromat
Legend of Fong Sai-Yuk, The
Let Me Die, Again
Ley del Deseo, La
   (Law of Desire)
Lick Bush in '92
Like Mother, Like Son
Lillian's Dilemma
Linda /Les and Annie
Little Bit of Lippy, A
Love and Lashes
Lugar Sin Limites, El (A
Limitless Place/Hell Without
   Limits)
Luminous Procuress
M. Butterfly
Mad about the Boy
Madame Simone
Marta: Portrait of a Teen Activist
Men Like Me
Mi Pollo Loco
Midnight Dancers
Miracle on Sunset Boulevard
Mirror, Mirror
Miss Otis
Mister Sisters, The
Mothers
Muerte de Mikel, La
   (The Death of Mikel)
Myra Breckenridge
New Pupil, The
1999 - Nen No Natsu Yasumi
   (Summer Vacation: 1999)
94 Arcana Drive
No Money, No Honey
Not Like That: Diary of a
   Butch-A-Phobe
On Becoming
100 Seconds with Sasha
Orlando
Outlaw
P(I)ain Truth
Palace
Paris is Burning
Passing
Poodle-Poo-Poo Miracle Mask,
   The
Queen Christina
Queen, The
Queens of Columbus:
Performance Art & Art of Illusion
Revolutions Happen Like
Refrains in a Song
Right Stuff, The
Rites of Passage
Roman Springs on Mrs. Stone,
   The
Salt Mines, The
Sex Change—Shock! Horror!
   Probe!
Sex of the Stars
   (Le sexe des Etoiles)
She Even Chewed Tobacco!
Shit Fit
Silence of the Lambs, The
Sister Is (Not) A Mister, The
Skin Deep
Something Special

Sometimes
Song of the Goddess
Spy, The (Hester Reeve Does
  "The Doors")
Stafford's Story
Stonewall
Storme: The Lady of the Jewel
  Box
Strawberry Short Cut/Pickle
Surprise
Sylvia Scarlett
Three Faces of Women
To Die For (Heaven's a Drag)
To Wong Foo, Thanks for
  Everything, Julie Newmar
Tomboy!
Tomboychik
Tracce di Chlodo sul Muro
  (Tracks of Nail on the Wall)
Trans
Tricia's Wedding
21st Century Nuns
Two Spirits
Vera
Vestida de Azul
  (Dressed in Blue)
Viktor und Viktoria
  (Victor and Victoria)
Vivat Regina
Walk on the Wild Side
What Really Happened to
  Baby Jane?
Whatever Happened to Susan
Jane?
Wigstock—The Movie
  (Rubnitz, Tom)
Wigstock: The Movie
  (Shils, Barry)
Woman's Heart, A
Zoe la Boxeuse (Zoe the Boxer)

Erotica and Pornography
Airport
All You Can Eat
Analstahl (Anal Steel)
Baja Fantasy
Barely Human
Be Careful What Kind of Skin
  You Pull Back, You Never
  Know What Kind of Head Will
  Appear
Beefcake Cheesecake
Bi-Ways
Bike Boy
Bittersweet
Blicklust
Blow Job (Warhol, Andy)
Boys/Life
Cell Mates
Central Park
Chant d'amour, Un
Closet, The
Cunt Dykula
Current Flow
Dangerous Bliss
Dangerous When Wet

Djune/Idexa
Do You Mind?
Don't Touch (Hors Limite)
Down on the River
Dreams of Passion
Du Darst (Truth or Dare)
Dura Mater
Easy Garden, The
Ecce Homo
Erotic in Nature
Erotique
Evil Thoughts
Excerpts from the Far East
Fireworks
Five Naked Surfers
Flower Market, The
Foolish Things
From Dental Dams to
  Latex Gloves
Fruta, La
Fuck Film
Gay TV
Girls Will Be Boys
Golden Positions, The
Grey Hideaway
Hermes Bird
His Red Snow White Apple Lips
Holding
"Home Movie"
Housewife and the Plumber, The
  [Pout #3 excerpt]
I'm Gonna Eat Worms
Inevitable Love
Irome (Colour Eyes)
Jonathan and David
Kamikaze Hearts
Kathy
Keep Your Laws Off My Body
Latex—Step Out Smartly
Lick
Liebe, Eifersucht und Rache
  (Love, Jealousy and Revenge)
Limités
Loads
Lush Life
Maneaters
Men In Love
Mouse Klub Konfidential
Mulberry Bush, The
1970's Porn Trailers
No Fairy Tale
No Glove, No Love
No Help Needed
No Skin Off My Ass
Nobody's People
Now Playing
Nude Inn
Nudes (A Sketchbook)
Of Man; For Dad
Package, The
Peril or Pleasure? Feminist-
  Produced Pornography
Perilous Liaisons
Peter Fucking Wayne Fucking
Peter
Pink Narcissus

Pleasure Beach
Porn
Possession
Private Pleasures
Queer Love Poem, A
Querelle
Ravissement, La
Rove
Safe Is Desire
Safe Sex Is Hot Sex
Safer Sister
Sebastiane
See Saw
7 Steps to Sticky Heaven
Sex Bowl
Sex Fish
Sex Is . . .
Sex, Lies, Religion
Shadows
Solo
Solos Y Soledades
Stand By
Super 8 1/2
Sweet Dreams
Tex-Sex
Therese and Isabelle
Trojans
25 Year Old Man Loses His
  Virginity to a Woman, A
24 Hours a Day
Twin Cheeks: Who Killed the
  Homecoming King?
Verfuhrung: Die Grausame Frau
  (Seduction: The Cruel Woman)
Vice and the Badge, The
Well Sexy Women
Where There's Smoke
Why I Stopped Going to
  Foreign Films
You Little Devil, You
Young Physique, The :
  "Duals" & "A Day At
  Fire Island"

Family and Parenting
Adios, Roberto
Alicia Was Fainting
Alkali, Iowa
All Fall Down
Alleged, The
Alternative Conceptions
Amazing Grace
Amelia Rose Towers
Among Good Christian Peoples
Antonia's Line
Avskedet (Farewell, The)
Because This Is About Love
Birthday Party
Both of My Mom's Names
  Are Judy
Breaking the Silence
Bus Stops Here, The:
  Three Case Histories
Caesura
Cap Tourmente
Cat Nip

Change
Chicks in White Satin
Choosing Children
Closing Numbers
Coal Miner's Granddaughter
Conception, The
Cutting the Edge of a Free Bird
Dadshuttle, The
Dare to Be Butch
Destiny/Desire/Devotion
Dinner with Malibu
Domestic Bliss
Dona Herlinda Y Su Hijo
  (Dona Herlinda and Her Son)
Dottie Gets Spanked
Execution: A Study of Mary
Family Affair, A
Fanci's Persuasion
Flesh on Glass
Florence and Robin
Forms and Motifs
Frankie and Jocie
Fried Green Tomatoes
Gay Youth
Gazon Maudit (Bushwhacked)
Guess Who's Coming to Visit
If She Grows Up Gay
Immaculate Conception
In My Father's Bed
In the Best Interest of
  the Children
Incredibly True Adventures of
  Two Girls in Love, The
Inside Monkey Zetterland
Labor More Than Once
Letter to My Grandma
Lianna
Lifetime Commitment: A Portrait
  of Karen Thompson
Like Mother, Like Son
Love and Marriage
Love Makes a Family
Lune
Margaret and Adele
Maya
Memsahib Rita
Millionaire
More Love
Mother's Hands
Mothers
My Beautiful Laundrette
My Brother's Keeper
My Father is Coming
My Grandma's Lady Cabaret
My Mother's Secret
My Sister, My Love
Naomi's Legacy
Neapolitans, The
No Sad Songs
Nocturne
Norman, Is That You?
Nuclear Family
Of Man; For Dad
Only the Brave
Optic Nerve
Other Families (Chvatal, Dorothy)

Other Families (Jones, William)
Our Mom's a Dyke
Out: Stories of Lesbian and
  Gay Youth
Parents Come Out
Party Favor, The
Paso Doble
Passage a L'Acte
Pervola, Sporen in de Sneeuw
  (Pervola, Tracks in the Snow)
Playing the Part
Queer Son
Raising Nicholas
rising
Rites of Passage
Rocking the Cradle
Sandra's Garden
Sea of Time
Seams
Seth's Aunts
Sex of the Stars
  (Le sexe des Etoiles)
Shared Lives
Shell
Shot Through My Head
Sink or Swim
Sister Louise's Discovery
Six Degrees of Separation
Something for Everyone
Something Special
Stand By
Stephen
Straight from the Heart
Suburban Queen
Sum of Us, The
Terence Davies Trilogy, The
Terms of Conception
Terra Nullius
Thank You and Good Night
These Shoes Weren't Made
  For Walking
This Is Not a Very Blank
  Tape, Dear
Ties That Bind, The
Tom's Flesh
Too Little, Too Late
Tracce di Chlodo sul Muro
  (Tracks of Nail on the Wall)
Truth Game, The
Two Men and a Baby
Under Heat
Vintage: Families of Value
Waving Fork, The
We Are Family
Wedding Banquet, The
Withnail & I
World and Time Enough
You Just Love Your Children

History/Herstory

Achilles
After the War You Have to Tell
  Everyone about the Dutch
  Gay Resistance Fighters
AIDS Show, The
Algie the Miner

All the Time
Anatomy of Desire
Anders als die Anderen
  (Different from the Others)
Andy Warhol
Anita Bryant: Pie-in-the-Face
Antonia's Line
Army of Lovers: or Revolt of
  the Sex Perverts
Ballad of Little Jo, The
Ballad of Reading Gaol
Battle of Tuntenhaüs, The
BD Women
Bedtime Stories
Beefcake Cheesecake
Before Stonewall
Berenice Abbott: A View of
  the 20th Century
Berlin Affair, The
Big Time Wrestlers from
  Hollywood
Bit of Scarlett, A
Black and White in Color
Blue Boys
Bogjavlar (Damned Queers)
Boys in the Band, The
Can't Help Lovin Dat Man
Candlelight Vigil, A
Carrington
Cell Mates
Celluloid Closet, The
Changer, The: A Record of
  the Times
Changing Our Minds: The Story
  Of Dr. Evelyn Hooker
Chant d'amour, Un
Christopher Isherwood:
  Over There on a Visit
Clones In Love
Club des Femmes
  (Women's Club)
Coming Out under Fire
Communication from Weber
Comrades In Arms
Craig's Wife
Crimes Against Nature
Daddy and the Muscle Academy
Damned, The
Deaf Heaven
Desire
Desperate Remedies
Disco Years, The
Displaced View, The
Dorothy Arzner: A Profile
Dozens, The
Dream Come True
Dream Machine, The
Edward II
Elevator Girls in Bondage
Erte
Excess Is What I Came For
Execution: A Study of Mary
Fearless: The Hunterwali Story
Female Impersonator, The
Fireworks
Flaming Creatures

Florida Enchantment, A
For a Lost Soldier
Framing Lesbian Fashion
Funeral Parade of Roses
Gay Day, A
Gay Deceivers, The
Gay Freedom Day Parade 1976
Gay Olympics '82
Gay Rock 'N' Roll Years, The
Gay San Francisco
Gay USA
Gertrude Stein: When This
  You See, Remember Me
Glitterbug
Golden Gate Bridge Blockade,
  The
Greetings from Washington D.C.
Guadalcanal Interlude
Half a Million Strong
Harold and Hiroshi
Hazel's Photos
Henry and June
History of the World According
  to a Lesbian, The
Home Stories
Homicidal
Homosexual Desire in Minnesota
Hours And Times, The
I Changed My Sex [trailer]
I Want What I Want
Ich Mochte Kein Mann Sein!
  (I Don't Want To Be A Man!)
Interview With The Vampire
Invocation of My Demon Brother
Jean Genet
Jeanne & Hauviette
Joe Joe
John Lindquist: Photographer of
  the Dance
Journey to Avebury
Jungle Boy, The
Kenneth Anger's Hollywood
  Babylon
Killing of Sister George, The
Kustom Kar Kommandos
L Is for the Way You Look
Last Call at Maud's
Last of England, The
Lawless
Lot in Sodom
Ludwig
Luminous Procuress
Ma Vie
Mädchen In Uniform (1931)
Mädchen In Uniform (1957)
Making of "Monsters," The
Massillon
Meeting of Two Queens, The
Meteor and Shadow
  (Meteore et Ombre)
Mr. W's Little Game
Naomi's Legacy
Neighborhood Voices
New Pupil, The
Nico-Icon
1970's Porn Trailers

Nitrate Kisses
No Help Needed
No More Nice Girls
Nous Etions un Seul Homme
  (We Were One Man)
Novembermund (Novembermoon)
Nude Inn
Olivia (Pit of Loneliness)
Orlando
Out of Our Time
Out On Four: Episodes 3&4
Out On Four: Episodes 5&6
Outcasts
P4W: Prison for Women
Palace
Paris Was a Woman
Pasolini, un delitto Italiano
  (Pasolini, an Italian Crime)
Paul Cadmus: Enfant Terrible
  at 80
Pauline's Birthday, or The
  Beast of Notre Dame
Pink Narcissus
Pink Triangles
Politics of Disco, The
Poodle-Poo-Poo Miracle Mask,
  The
Portrait of a Marriage
Prick Up Your Ears
Proust's Favorite Fantasy
Psyclones on Heat
Puce Moment
Queen Christina
Queen, The
Queens of Columbus:
  Performance Art & Art of
  Illusion
Ray
Rhythm Divine: The Story
  of Disco, The
Robert Having His Nipple
  Pierced
Robert Mapplethorpe
Roman Springs on Mrs.
  Stone, The
Saint Genet
Salome
Sappho
Scorpio Rising
Sergei Eisenstein
She Even Chewed Tobacco!
Shirley Temple and Me
Shriek, The
Silent Pioneers
Sister, My Sister
Six Million and One
Some of My Best Friends
  Are . . .
Split Britches
Stonewall
Storm in a Teacup
Swoon
"Sword Fight"
Sylvia Scarlett
Taking Back The Dolls
That Tender Touch

Theatrical Collage
Their First Mistake
Times of Harvey Milk, The
Total Eclipse
Tras el Cristal (In a Glass Cage)
Triangle
Tricia's Wedding
Tricycle Race
Unity
Verzaubert (Enchanted)
Vice and the Badge, The
Victim
Viktor und Viktoria
  (Victor and Victoria)
Vingarne (Wings, The)
Voices from the Front
Waiting for the Moon
War Widow, The
We Were Marked with a Big A
Westler—East of the Wall
When Shirley Met Florence
Where the Cows Go
Where There Was Silence
White Justice (A case of
  diminished capacity)
Wild Reeds
Wittgenstein
Word Is Out: Stories of Some
  of Our Lives
Working Class Chronicle
Wrecked for Life: The Trip and
  Magic of the Trocadero Transfer
Yma Sumac: Hollywood's Inca
  Princess
Young Physique, The : "Duals"
  & "A Day At Fire Island"
Young Soul Rebels

Homophobia

American Shooting
  Numbers 1, 2 and 3
Anatomy of Desire
Anthem
Asa Branca (A Brazilian Dream)
Ballad of Reading Gaol
Bashing
Basic Instinct
Before Stonewall
Billy Turner's Secret
Blue Boys
Boot
Burden of Dykes
Can't Take That Way from Me
Celluloid Closet, The
Chaero
Coming Out under Fire
Crimes Against Nature
Darker Side of Black, A
Double the Trouble, Twice the
  Fun
Edward II
Fighting in Southwest Louisiana
Gay Lives and Culture Wars
Gay Youth
Green on Thursdays
Haven

History of Violence, A
Homophobia is Known to
  Cause Nightmares
Homosexuality: What Science
  Understands
Hotheads
Hunting Season, The
I'll Show You
Intro to Cultural Skit-Zo-Frenia
Jean Genet
Jungle Boy, The
Just Because of Who We Are
Just for Fun
Labor More Than Once
Making of "Monsters," The
Mauvaise Conduite
  (Improper Conduct)
Midnight Life and Death
One Nation Under God
Ostia
Our House: Lesbians and Gays
  in the Hood
Out for a Change: Addressing
  Homophobia in Women's Sports
Out On Tuesday, Program 1
Parents Come Out
Pedagogue
Pink Triangles
Pink Triangles
Placeros Ocultos, Los (Hidden
  Pleasures)
Pout
Pride and Prejudice
Q.C. Girls, The
Raid on a Peruvian Lesbian Bar
Resonance
Self Defense
Silence . . . Broken
Silence of the Lambs, The
Some of My Best Friends
  Are . . .
Staircase
Stick Figures
Straight from the Heart
Taxi to Cairo
Taxi Zum Klo
Thick Lips, Thin Lips
Time Off
Tough Love, Smart Weapons
Triangle
Urinal
Victim
Vivat Regina
Want
Wanted!
What's in a Name
When You Name Me
Where Are We?: Our Trip
  Through America
Where the Cows Go
Where There Was Silence
Why Not Love?/Get Used to It

Humor

Across the Rubicon
Ad, The

Adventures of Priscilla, Queen of
  the Desert, The
Affengeil
  (Life Is Like a Cucumber)
Agora
Airport
Alfalfa
All Out Comedy
All You Can Eat
Always On Sunday
American Fabulous
Anniversary, The
Assassination
Assassination of Anita Bryant,
  The
Assembly at Dyke High
Attention Cinemagoers
B.U.C.K.L.E.
Bar Girls
Bar Yoga
Basket Case
Bears in the Hall
Beauties without a Cause
Bete Noire
Betty Walters Show, The
Big Fat Slenderella
Bill and Ted's Homosexual
  Adventure
Billy Turner's Secret
Birthday Party
Birthday Tribute to Dame Edna
  Everage, A
Bisexual Kingdom, The
Bitter Old Queens
Blond Fury
Boy with Cat
Burden of Dykes
Butch Patrol!
Butch/Femme in Paradise
Camp Christmas
Can You Say Androgynous?
Can't You Take a Joke?
Carmelita Tropicana
Carrie
Cat and the Canary, The
Cat Nip
Catalina
Chance, The
Charming Mutt
Cheap Skates: The Hardly-
  Cardigan Affair
Cliche in the Afternoon
Comedy in Six Unnatural Acts, A
Commercial for Murder
Complaints
Connan the Waitress
Cunt Dykula
David Roche Talks to You
  about Love
Death of a Writer in Two Parts
  (A Comedy of Sorts)
DeAundra Peek's High Class
  Hall O'Fame Theater
Deflatable Man, The
Devotion
Dick Tricks

Dinner with Malibu
Don't Look Up My Skirt
  Unless You Mean It
Don't Make Me Up
Donna e Mobile, La
Drip: A Narcissistic Love Story
Dykes Rule
Dyketactics
Eggsplantsia
8mm Lesbian Love Film
Entre Tinieblas (Dark Habits)
Eurotrash
Fairest of Them All
Fanci's Persuasion
Fertile La Toyah Jackson
  Video Magazine
Fingered!
Five Minutes, Ms. Lenska
Five Ways to Kill Yourself
Fontvella's Box
Fun Down There
Fun with a Sausage
Gabriella on the Half Shell
Gay Day, A
Gazon Maudit (Bushwhacked)
Get Over It
Give AIDS the Freeze
Go Fish
Goat Named Tension, A
Good Dyke Gone Mad, A
He-She Pee
Hi Mom!
History of Western Sexuality, The
Home Movie
Housewife and the Plumber, The
  [Pout #3 excerpt]
How Many Lesbians Does It
  Take to Change a Lightbulb?
How to Seduce a Preppy
How to Turn Heads
Hysterio Passio
I Became a Lesbian and So
  Can You
I Need a Man Like You..
I Shot My W.O.D.
I Was I Am
I've Heard the Mermaids Singing
In the Cards
Innings
Inside Monkey Zetterland
Interior Decorator from Hell
Intrepidissima
Is Mary Wings Coming?
Is That All There Is to the
  Greenhouse Effect?
It's a Lezzie Life: A
  Dyke-U-Mentary
Jackie and the Beanstalk
Jeffrey
Joystick Blues
Ken Death Gets Out of Jail
Kipling Meets the Cowboy
L'Ingenue
Lady
Laundromat
Lavender Tortoise, The

Lawn Butch
Lesbian Bed Death: Myth or
   Epidemic. An investigative
   report.
Lesbian Impress Card, The
Lesbians Who Date Men
Liebe, Eifersucht und Rache
(Love, Jealousy and Revenge)
Life in the Kitchen
Like a Dog
Lillian's Dilemma
Little Bit of Lippy, A
London Story, The
Long Weekend (O'Despair), The
Lost Lucy Episode, The
Love and Lashes
Love Crisis
Love Machine, The
Loverville
Loverville 2: The Honeymoon
Mad about the Boy
Made for TV
Magic Cottage
Margaret Atwood and the
   Problem with Canada
Mark Called
Marta: Portrait of a Teen Activist
Men Behind Bars
Mi Pollo Loco
Midwestern Skidmarks
Miracle on Sunset Boulevard
Mirror, Mirror
Mister Reagan
Mister Sisters, The
Moscow Does Not Believe in
   Queers
Mothers
Mr. W's Little Game
Mr. Wonderful
Mulberry Bush, The
My Addiction
My First Suit
My Name Is Edwina Carerra
My New Friend
My Polish Waiter
My Sorrow Means Nothing to You
976
No Ordinary Love
No Skin Off My Ass
Norman, Is That You?
Order, The
Our Gay Brothers
Out for Laughs
Out in Comedy
"OUT" Takes
Party Favor, The
Performance Notes: A Bar is a
   Bar is a Bar
Pleasure Garden, The
PMS (Positioning My Sexuality)
Poodle-Poo-Poo Miracle Mask,
   The
Porcaria
Possession
Potluck and the Passion, The
Prague

Pubic Beard
Put Your Lips Around Yes
Queer Carpentry Seminar
Queer Christmas
Ray's Male Heterosexual
   Dance Hall
Revenge of the Wicked Witch
Safe Soap
San Fernando Valley
Searanch: The True Story
See Saw
Sex Bowl
Sexlock
Sexual I.D.
She Can Probably Fix It
Shit Fit
Snatch
Speaking in Riddles
Steal America
Steps, The
Sticky Moments
Surely to God
Taking Back The Dolls
Tales of an Exhausted Woman
Taxi to Cairo
Texas
That's Amore
Theo und Thea
Three Faces of Women
To Wong Foo, Thanks for
   Everything, Julie Newmar
Toe Heel Polka, The
Top Secret
True Blue
Twenty-Two
Two In Twenty
Two Quickies
Vacancy
Very Funny
Village Idiot, The
Wake Up, Jerk Off, Etc
Wanderer, The
Wavering Heterosexual Confronts
   the Pleasure Principle Head
   On and Is Forced to Decide, A
We're Talking Vulva
We've Only Just Begun
What Gets You Off
Who Is Poetessa Fishhouse?
Why I Masturbate
Wild Woman of the Woods
Withnail & I
Without You I'm Nothing
You Can Open Your Eyes Now
You Say Maria, I Say Mariah
You Taste American
Your Heart Is All Mine

Jewish Images

Anne Trister
Ash and Hatred
Babi-It (At Home)
Cancer in Two Voices
Chicks in White Satin
Complaints of a Dutiful Daughter
Costa Brava

Delius
Ernesto
Fast Trip, Long Drop
I Will Not Think about
   Death Anymore
It's a Mitzvah
Le Jupon Rouge
   (Manuela's Loves)
Margaret and Adele
Memento Mori
Nagua (Drifting)
Naomi's Legacy
Novembermund (Novembermoon)
Occupied Territories
Outcasts
Oy Gay
Party Favor, The
Searching for Contact
Separate Skin
Seth's Aunts
She Makes Love With Her
Six Million and One
Swoon
Time Off
Tomboychik
We Were Marked with a Big A
When Shirley Met Florence
Woman's Heart, A

Latino/a Images

Adios, Roberto
After the Break
AIDS in the Barrio
Al Margen del Margen
   (Beyond Outcasts)
Alicia Was Fainting
Aqueles Dois
Asa Branca (A Brazilian Dream)
Because Reality Isn't Black
   and White [work in progress]
Boys from Brazil
Brincando El Charco: Portrait
   of a Puerto Rican
Buscando un Espacio: Los
Homosexuales en Cuba
   (Looking for a Space)
Cana, Em
Carmelita Tropicana
Change the Frame
Cholo Joto
Cities of Lust
Clue
Conceicao
Cosas del Querer, Las
   (Affairs of Love, The)
Costa Brava
Cruel
Danny
Darkness of My Language, The
Date With Fate
Defect [unfinished]
Dialogo
Diputado, Il (Deputy, The)
Dona Herlinda Y Su Hijo
   (Dona Herlinda and Her Son)
East River Park

Esplada, A
Falling Through the Cracks
Frankie Goes Downtown
Fresa y Chocolate
  (Strawberry and Chocolate)
Fruta, La
Fuji
History of Violence, A
History Will Accuse Me
How to Kill Her
Hunting Season, The
I
I, The Worst of All
Illuminado las Aguas
In Plain View
(In)Visible Women
Intrepidissima
Kim
Kiss of the Spider Woman
Laberinto de Pasiones
  (Labyrinth of Passions)
Lily & Lulu Go to the March
Lorenza
Love Beneath a Neon Sky
Lugar Sin Limites, El
  (A Limitless Place/Hell
  Without Limits)
Mala Noche
Manuel Y Clemente
  (Manuel and Clemente)
Mauvaise Conduite
  (Improper Conduct)
Meridad Proscrita
Mi Pollo Loco
More Than a Paycheck
Mujeria: Olmeca Rap
No Porque Fidel Castro Lo Diga
  (Not Because Fidel Castro
  Says So)
Normal Life
Ojos que No Ven
  (Eyes that Do Not See)
Other Woman, The
  (Slane, Andrea)
P.A.R.A.N.O.R.M.A.L.
Paris is Burning
Placeros Ocultos, Los
  (Hidden Pleasures)
Porcaria
Primas
Primitive and Proud
Raid on a Peruvian Lesbian Bar
Ray Navarro Memorial Tape
Safer Sister
Salt Mines, The
Sano y Sanitario
Seams
Serial Clubber Killer
Sex and the Sandinistas
Silencis (Silent Moments)
Sisters of Darkness
Solos Y Soledades
Stonewall
Susana
To Be with You
Toys: Basic Technologies of

Devotion
Two Georges, The
  (Dos Jorges, Los)
Vera
Version de Marcial, La
  (Marcial's Version)
!Viva 16th!
Viva Eu!
Voguing: The Message
Wild Life

Media Studies

ADS Epidemic, The
All You Can Eat
Alleged, The
Angelic Conversation, The
Anita Bryant: Pie-in-the-Face
Art of Mirrors, The
At Home with the Stars
Attention Cinemagoers
Audience
Bette Walters Interviews Garbo
Bit of Scarlett, A
Black and White in Color
Blue
Bogjavlar (Damned Queers)
Both (Child, Abigail)
Bright Eyes
Camp Christmas
Celluloid Closet, The
Civil Enough
Coal Miner's Granddaughter
Commercial for Murder
Confessions of a Pretty Lady
Damned If You Don't
Dance Macabre
Dear Rock
Death of Dottie Love, The
Dedicated to Those Days
Derek Jarman, Know What I
  Mean
Dorian Gray Im Spiegel Der
  Boulevardpresse
  (Dorian Gray in the Mirror of
  the Popular Press)
Dorothy Arzner: A Profile
Dottie Gets Spanked
Dream Machine, The
Fabian's Freeak Show
Fearless: The Hunterwali Story
Food for Thought
Freebird
Friendly Witness
Gay Day, A
Gay San Francisco
Give AIDS the Freeze
Glen or Glenda?
  (I Changed My Sex)
Glitterbug
Guadalcanal Interlude
Hello-Goodbye
Hey Bud
Hollywood and Homophobia
Home Stories
Homophobia is Known to
  Cause Nightmares

Household
I Became a Lesbian and So
  Can You
I Changed My Sex [trailer]
I Didn't Know What Time It Was
I Object
Innings
It's a Queer World
Joan Sees Stars
Jodie Promo
Johnny
Journey to Avebury
Just Another Girl
Kamikaze Hearts
Kanada
Kipling Meets the Cowboy
L Is for the Way You Look
Lady
Last of England, The
Let's Play Prisoners
Liebe, Eifersucht und Rache
  (Love, Jealousy and Revenge)
London Story, The
Luscious Brite
Macumba
Madame X—Eine Absolute
  Herrscherin (Madame X—An
  Absolute Ruler)
Making of "Monsters," The
Making of "The Lost Language
  of Cranes," The
Man of the Year
Mark of Lilith, The
Media Blackmale
Meeting of Two Queens, The
Negative Man
Night with Derek, A
No No Nooky T.V.
Our Trip
Out On Four: Episodes 1 & 2
Out On Four: Episodes 3 & 4
Out On Four: Episodes 5 & 6
"OUT" Takes
Paris Was a Woman
Passage a L'Acte
Pink Pimpernel, The
Plague on You, A
Playing Poseidon
Poison
Projections
  (Pet Shop Boys compilation)
PSA
Put Your Lips Around Yes
Rainer Werner Fassbinder:
  The Last Works
Red Light, Green Light—
  Meeting Strangers
Remembrance
Remembrance of Things Fast
Rhythm Divine:
  The Story of Disco, The
Rock Hudson's Home Movies
San Fernando Valley
Secrets
Sergei Eisenstein
She Begins

She Must Be Seeing Things
Shirley Temple and Me
Snow Job: The Media Hysteria
of AIDS
Sparkle's Tavern
Sphinxes Without Secrets
Stand on Your Man
Steps, The
Sternenschauer
(Scattering Stars)
Stiller, Garbo & Jag (Stiller,
Garbo & Me)
Strange Love Affair, A
Suddenly Last Summer
Super 8 1/2
Sync Touch
T.V. Tart
Taking Back The Dolls
Tell Me Why: The Epistemology
of Disco
Tender Fictions
Thriller
Tortures That Laugh
Touch Me
Tourist
TV In Africa
Two Bad Daughters
Two Quickies
Undecided
Video Album 5: The Thursday
People
Voices of Life
Walk on the Wild Side
War on Lesbians
We've Been Framed
What Can I Do with a Male
Nude?
Where There Was Silence
Wrecked for Life: The Trip and
Magic of the Trocadero Transfer
Yearning For Sodom, A
Yma Sumac: Hollywood's Inca
Princess
You Taste American
Zero Patience

Music and Dance

ADS Epidemic, The
All Day Always
Ash and Hatred
Assembly at Dyke High
At Home with the Stars
Because We Must
Biennale Apollo
Bill and Ted's Homosexual
Adventure
Boy Next Door: A Profile of
Boy George
Breast Exam
Bridgette
Call Me Your Girlfriend
Can't Stop the Music
Casta Diva
Changer, The: A Record of
the Times
Complaint of the Empress, The

Complaints
Continuum 2
Count Me In
Cross Body Ride
Darker Side of Black, A
Defectors: My Vacation
Dreams of Passion
Drip: A Narcissistic Love Story
Dumbshit
8mm Lesbian Love Film
Excess Is What I Came For
Fabulous Dyketones Rock
Around the Clock, The
Fairy Who Didn't Want to Be a
Fairy Anymore, The
Free Love
Freebird
French Bitch
Frenzy
Friendly Witness
Gay Rock 'N' Roll Years, The
Hard Reign's Gonna Fall, A
Heaven, Earth and Hell
Hello-Goodbye
Her Sweetness Lingers
History of the World According to
a Lesbian, The
Holly Near
Hours And Times, The
I Didn't Know What Time It Was
Ich und Frau Berger
(Me & Mrs. Berger)
In Search of Margo-Go
John Lindquist: Photographer
of the Dance
Language of Boys, The
Last Supper, The
Let Me Die, Again
Long Time Comin'
Love Strikes Hard
Love Triangle
Lucifer Rising
Mad, Mad World Of Stella
Slick, The
Madonna In Me
Man I Love, The
Me and Mrs. Jones
Messiah at the City
Mujeria: Olmeca Rap
Nexus (Bond, Rose)
Nexus (Johns, Jennifer)
No Money, No Honey
Olivia Records: More
Than Music
One Fool
Our Trip
Out On Four: Episodes 3 & 4
Out on the Road with 2 Nice
Girls [trailer]
Patsy Cline: A Tribute
Pearl Harbor & the Explosions
Peter Fucking Wayne
Fucking Peter
Pleasure Garden, The
Projections
(Pet Shop Boys compilation)

Pull Your Finger Out:
Lesbians Rock
Queen is Dead, The
Rapture
Reservaat (Reservation)
Resonance
Rhythm Divine: The Story of
Disco, The
Rough Outrageous
She's Real: A Document of
Queer Rock
Shisheng Huamei
(Silent Thrush, The)
Show Me
Singing Seas
Snow White
Song from an Angel
Spy, The (Hester Reeve
Does "The Doors")
St. Louis Blues
Stadt der Verlorenen Seelen
(City Of Lost Souls)
Stand on Your Man
Tell Me Why: The Epistemology
of Disco
Tempted
Theatrical Collage
This Is Not an AIDS
Advertisement
Thriller
Times Square
Toe Heel Polka, The
Trevor
Turnabout
29 Effeminate Gestures
Undecided
Untitled (Sanborn, John, and
Mary Perillo)
Viktor und Viktoria
(Victor and Victoria)
Voguing: The Message
Walk on the Wild Side
Waltz, The
Wanderer, The
Wank Stallions
We've Only Just Begun
Why I Masturbate
Wigstock: The Movie
(Shils, Barry)
Wrecked for Life: The Trip and
Magic of the Trocadero
Transfer
Yma Sumac: Hollywood's
Inca Princess
You Can Open Your Eyes Now
Young Soul Rebels
Zanne: So Many Women
Zero Patience

Native American Images

Balancing Factor
Her Giveaway
Honored by the Moon
Land Beyond Tomorrow
Lawn Butch
Night Visions

Primitive and Proud
Shasta Woman
Two Spirit People
Two Spirits

Performing Arts
AIDS Show, The
All Of Me
All Out Comedy
Alphabit Land: The Backyard
  Tour Featuring Wigstock '89
Andy Makes a Movie
Annie
At Home with the Stars
Avskedet (Farewell, The)
Balcony, The

Politics
Across the Rubicon
ACT UP at the FDA
Acting Up for Prisoners
After the Revolution
After the War You Have to Tell
  Everyone about the Dutch Gay
  Resistance Fighters
Age of Dissent
AIDS: A Priest's Testament
AIDS/ARC Vigil
Al Margen del Margen
  (Beyond Outcasts)
All the Time
And the Band Played On
Anita Bryant: Pie-in-the-Face
Army of Lovers: or Revolt of the
  Sex Perverts
Assassination of Anita Bryant,
  The
Ballot Measure Nine
Bare
Be Careful What Kind of Skin
  You Pull Back, You Never
  Know What Kind of Head
  Will Appear
Before the Act
Bicentennial Movie, A
Breaking the Silence
Brincando El Charco: Portrait
  of a Puerto Rican
Broadcast Tapes of Dr. Peter,
  The
Buscando un Espacio: Los
  Homosexuales en Cuba
  (Looking for a Space)
Coming Out of the Iron Closet
Crying Game, The
Damned, The
Dancing in Dulais
Deadly Deception
Diputado, Il (Deputy, The)
Do You Think that a Candidate
  Should Live Like This?
Doll House
Egymasra Nezve (Another Way)
Empire State
Final Solutions
Fresa y Chocolate

(Strawberry and Chocolate)
Fresh Kill
Garden, The
Gay Freedom Day Parade 1976
Gay Lives and Culture Wars
Gloria's Point of View
Grid-Lock: Women and the
  Politics of AIDS
Happy Gordons, The
Haven
Homoteens
Imagining October
Kanada
Keep Your Laws Off My Body
Kiev Blue
Kiss of the Spider Woman
Last of England, The
Le Jupon Rouge
  (Manuela's Loves)
London Story, The
Love and Marriage
Mädchen In Uniform (1931)
Mädchen In Uniform (1957)
Margaret Atwood and the
  Problem with Canada
Mauvaise Conduite
  (Improper Conduct)
Mayhem
Mouse Klub Konfidential
Neighborhood Voices
Night Visions
No Porque Fidel Castro Lo Diga
  (Not Because Fidel Castro
  Says So)
Occupied Territories
Orlando
Paper Cranes
Peter Fucking Wayne
  Fucking Peter
Place of Rage, A
Political Funerals
Public
Ray
Risk: Lesbians and AIDS
Sacred Lies, Civil Truths
Sergeant Matlovich Versus the
  U.S. Air Force
Serving in Silence: The
  Margarethe Cammermeyer
  Story
Spikes and Heels
Straight Agenda, The
Tag Helms
Tourist
Wanted!
White Justice (A case of
  diminished capacity)
Wild Reeds
Woman's Place Is in the
  House, A
Working Class Dykes from Hell

Racism
Anthem
Bare
BD Women

Black Body
Cholo Joto
Cities of Lust
Complicated Flesh
Double the Trouble,
  Twice the Fun
Double Trouble
Fated to Be Queer
I've Never
Infidel
Maybe I Can Give You Sex ?
  Part One
Maybe I Can Give You Sex ?
  Part Two
Memsahib Rita
Moffie Called Simon, A
My Beautiful Laundrette
My Sweet Peony
Night Visions
Occupied Territories
Orientations
Our House: Lesbians and Gays
  in the Hood
Parallel Sons
Passion of Remembrance, The
Queers Are Not Enough
Reframing AIDS
Sari Red
Shasta Woman
Silence . . . Broken
Skin Complex
Splash
Toc Storee

Relationships
Affirmations
After the Game
Agora
Alternative Conceptions
Among Men
An Empty Bed
An Individual Desires Solution
Anastasia and the Queen of
  Hearts
Anders als die Anderen
  (Different from the Others)
Angel
Angel of Woolworths, The
Anne Trister
Anniversary, The
Aqueles Dois
Asa Branca (A Brazilian Dream)
Babi-It (At Home)
Ballad of Little Jo, The
Basic Necessities
Be My Valentine
Because The Dawn
Because This Is About Love
Behind Glass
Belle
Beloved Murderer
Berlin Affair, The
Bertrand Disparu
  (Bertrand Is Missing)
Bete Noire
Between Two Worlds

Beyond Gravity
Bird In The Hand
Black Widow
Borderline
Both (De La Rosa, Vic)
Boy Who Fell In Love, The
Breaking the Silence
Brinco, O (The Earring)
Buddies
Butterfly Kiss
Caged
Can't You Take a Joke?
Cancer in Two Voices
Cavale
Certain Grace, A
Change the Frame
Claire of the Moon
Clinic, The
Closing Numbers
Club des Femmes
   (Women's Club)
Common Flower, A
Complicated Flesh
Conception, The
Corps Perdu, A
   (Straight to the Heart)
Cosas del Querer, Las
   (Affairs of Love, The)
Costa Brava
Craig's Wife
Creation of Adam
Cross Your Heart
Cruel
Cupid's True Love
Dadshuttle, The
Dance, The
Danny
Death in Venice, CA
Death Watch
Desert of Love
Desperate Remedies
Destiny/Desire/Devotion
Devotion
Devotions
Domestic Bliss
Dona Herlinda Y Su Hijo
   (Dona Herlinda and Her Son)
Double Exposure
Double Strength
Dozens, The
Dream A40
Eclipse
Egymasra Nezve (Another Way)
Ein Mann Wie Eva (Man Like
   Eva, A)
Ernesto
Ernie and Rose
Fanci's Persuasion
Farewell My Concubine
Farewell to Charms
Fear of Disclosure
Fell
Film for Two
Fin Amour
Fingered!
First Comes Love

Flames of Passion
Flesh on Glass
Florence and Robin
Frankly, Shirley
Friend of Dorothy, A
Gazon Maudit (Bushwhacked)
Get Over It
Ghost Body
Glasses Break
Go Fish
Goat Named Tension, A
Greta's Girls
Grief
Growing Up and I'm Fine
Hallowed
Harlequin Exterminator
He Would Have Loved Me to
   Death
He's Like
Heatwave
Her Sweetness Lingers
Here Be Dragons
History of Western Sexuality, The
Home You Go
Hot and Cold
Hours And Times, The
How He Goes
How to Kill Her
I Didn't Know What Time It Was
I Like Girls for Friends
I Remember Running
I've Never
Ich und Frau Berger
   (Me & Mrs. Berger)
If Only
In Search of Margo-Go
Inside Monkey Zetterland
Is Mary Wings Coming?
It's a Mitzvah
It's That Age
Jackie and the Beanstalk
Jeanne & Hauviette
Jeffrey
Jellyfish Kiss [trailer]
Jewel's Darl
Joggernaught
Jonathan and David
Jumping the Gun
Just Friends
Kamikaze Hearts
Kathy
Kazetachi No Gogo
   (Afternoon Breezes)
Keeping the Faith
Killing of Sister George, The
Kiss on the Cliff, The
Kiss, The
Krokodillen in Amsterdam
   (Crocodiles in Amsterdam)
L'Usure (By Attrition)
La Couer Decouvert
   (Heart Exposed, The)
Last Supper, The
Le Poisson D' Amour
Letter of Introduction, The
Ley del Deseo, La

   (Law of Desire)
Lick
Lie Down with Dogs
Lieve Jongens (Dear Boys)
Life on Earth as I Know It
Lily & Lulu Go to the March
Lipotaktis (Deserter)
Liquor, Guns and Ammo
Longtime Companion
Loss of Heat
Lost Heart, The
Lost Love
Lost Sleep
Love and Human Remains
Love Like Any Other, A
Love Machine, The
Loverville
Loverville 2: The Honeymoon
Lune
Macumba
Madagascar Skin
Mala Noche
Man I Love, The
Manuel Y Clemente
   (Manuel and Clemente)
Mara
Mark of Lilith, The
Mason's Life
Matsumae-Kun No Senritsu
   (Melody For Buddy Matsumae)
Me and Mrs. Jones
Men In Love
Mermaids, Fish & Other
   Non-Bipeds
Midnight Life and Death
Minor Disturbances
Montreal Main
More Than a Paycheck
Muerte de Mikel, La
   (The Death of Mikel)
My Addiction
My Dinner at Dan's
My New Friend
My New Lover
My Own Private Idaho
My Polish Waiter
N'oublie pas que tu vas mourir
   (Don't Forget You're Going
   To Die)
Nagua (Drifting)
Naughty Boys
Neapolitans, The
Nightwork
Nineteen Nineteen
94 Arcana Drive
No Ordinary Love
Nocturne
North of Vortex
Nous Etions un Seul Homme
   (We Were One Man)
Now That It's Morning
Nuit Sauvage, La
   (Savage Nights)
Obelisk, The
Off the Rails
Okoge

Olivia (Pit of Loneliness)
On a Queer Day
One and the Other Time
One Sings
Other Half, The
Other Woman, The
Other Woman, The
  (Slane, Andrea)
Out of Our Time
Paper Cranes
Parallel Sons
Parting Glances
Paso Doble
Passion: A Letter in 16mm
Peach
Perils of Pedagogy, The
Personal Best
Personally Yours
Pervola, Sporen in de Sneeuw
(Pervola, Tracks in the Snow)
Place in the Sun, A
Politics of Disco, The
Pool Days
Potluck and the Passion, The
Prague
Prisonnieres
Proof
Que He Hecho Yo Para Merecer
Esto? (What Have I Done to
  Deserve This?)
Rainbow Serpent, The
Rasen No Sobyo
  (Rough Sketch of a Spiral)
Recent Sorrows
Reencounter
Reise, Eine (The Journey)
Remnants
RSVP
Rules of the Road
Sacred Lies, Civil Truths
Salmonberries
Salut Victor!
Scene from Frankie and
  Johnny, A
Scrubbers
Second Awakening of Christa
  Klages, The
Separate Skin
7 Steps to Sticky Heaven
Sex Wars
Shame
Shared Lives
She Can Probably Fix It
She Must Be Seeing Things
Shot Through My Head
Sightings
Simone
Simple Facts
Sisters of Darkness
Sleepin' Round
Smoke
Some of These Days
Somebody Else
Sortie 234
Souvenir
Sparky's Shoes

Sprinter, Der (Sprinter, The)
Staircase
Standard of Living, The
Strange Love Affair, A
Strings
Summer, 1993
Talk to Me Like the Rain
Tall Dark Stranger
Tempted
Ten Cents a Dance (Parallax)
Terms of Conception
That Tender Touch
That's Alright Mama
That's Amore
Thin Ice
Things We Said Today
Three Bewildered People in
  the Night
To Be with You
To Die For (Heaven's a Drag)
Toe Heel Polka, The
Together Alone
Token of Love
Total Eclipse
Transportations
Tras el Cristal (In a Glass Cage)
Tread Softly
Triche, La
Truth Game, The
Twice a Woman
Twin Bracelets, The
Twinkle
Two Georges, The
  (Dos Jorges, Los)
Two In Twenty
Two of Us
Vehlefanz
Vera
Version de Marcial, La
  (Marcial's Version)
Victor
Vive L'Amour
Vrouw Als Eva, Een
  (Woman Like Eve, A)
Waving Fork, The
Wedding Banquet, The
Wedding of the Year,
  Chuck & Vince
Weggehen um Anzukommen
  (Depart to Arrive)
Wendel
Westler—East of the Wall
What's the Difference Between a
  Yam and a Sweet Potato?
When Night is Falling
Where Are We?: Our Trip
  Through America
Withnail & I
Without Saying Goodbye
Wolfgirl
Women In Love: Bonding
  Strategies of Black Lesbians
World and Time Enough
You & I Will Play
Your Heart Is All Mine

Religion and Spirituality
AIDS: A Priest's Testament
Altered Habits
Among Good Christian Peoples
Balancing Factor
Body of Dissent: Lesbian and
  Gay Mennonites and Brethren
Continue the Journey
Change
Damned If You Don't
Exits
Extramuros
Ferdous (Paradise)
Flesh on Glass
Forsaken
Fuck the Pope
Garden, The
Holy Mary
I, The Worst of All
Images
Invocation of My Demon Brother
Jonathan and David
Journey to Avebury
Kain and Abel
Last Island, The
Les Amities Particulieres
  (This Special Friendship)
Lot in Sodom
Lucifer Rising
Madonna and Child
Manuel Y Clemente
  (Manuel and Clemente)
No Need to Repent
No Saintly Girl
Off the Rails
One Nation Under God
Oranges Are Not the Only Fruit
Our Lady of L.A.
Peccatum Mutum
  (The Silent Sin)
PSA
Public Opinion
Random Access
Religieuse, La (The Nun)
Rights and Reactions
Sea of Time
Search, The
Sebastiane
Sister Louise's Discovery
Smoke
Stop the Church
Terence Davies Trilogy, The
21st Century Nuns
Virgin, the Mother and the
  Crone, The
Way of the Wicked, The
Welcome to the Dome
Wicked Radiance
World and Time Enough

**S/M and Alternative
Sexuality**
Airport
Analstahl (Anal Steel)
Attendant, The
Bachvirus, Het

(Bach Virus, The)
Be Careful What Kind of Skin
 You Pull Back, You Never
 Know What Kind of Head
 Will Appear
Bears in the Hall
Bears Will Be Bears
Bitter Strength: Sadistic
 Response Version
Bittersweet
Blicklust
Blood Sisters: Leather, Dykes
 and Sadomasochism
Bondage
Chicken Hawk
Chubs & Bears [work in progress]
Cruising
Dance with a Body, A
Dandy Dust [trailer]
Dick Tricks
Djune/Idexa
Du Darst (Truth or Dare)
Elegant Spanking, The
Empire State
Erotique
Excerpts from the Far East
Fireworks Revisited
Frankfurter
Frisk
Fuck Film
House of Pain
In Loving Memory
Jungfrauenmaschine, Die
 (The Virgin Machine)
Kindling Point, The
Let Me Die, Again
Let's Play Prisoners
Lieve Jongens (Dear Boys)
Liquor, Guns and Ammo
Lord and Master
Lush Life
Malaysian Series, Part 1-6
Male Escorts of San Francisco:
 Raphael, the Call Bear
 [excerpt]
Mano Destra
Men Maniacs
Miguel
Muscle
No Skin Off My Ass
None of the Above
Other Woman, The
 (Slane, Andrea)
Pauline's Birthday, or The
 Beast of Notre Dame
Perilous Liaisons
Querelle
Rainbow Serpent, The
Rapture
Razor Head
Robert Having His
 Nipple Pierced
Rote Ohren Fetzen Durch Asche
 (Flaming Ears)
Saint Mulekicker
Scars

Scorpio Rising
Sewing on Breast
Sex, Lies, Religion
Shadows
Skin Deep
Snatch
Sonny
State of Mind
Stellium In Capricorn
Tom of Finland
Topsau, Die (The Top Pig)
Two Bad Daughters
Uh-Oh!
Verfuhrung: Die Grausame Frau
 (Seduction: The Cruel Woman)
Wicked Radiance

Sex Work

Alone Once Again
Andy the Furniture Maker
Angel
Annie
Being at Home with Claude
Bel Ragazzo
Boys from Brazil
Cold Bath
Diputado, Il (Deputy, The)
Easy Money
Empire State
Erotique
Everlasting Secret Family, The
Every Conceivable Position:
 Inside Gay Porn
From Bejing to Brooklyn
Gerbroken Spiegels
 (Broken Mirrors)
Hatachi No Binetsu
 (Slight Fever of a 20-Year-Old)
I Don't Want to Be e Boy
Jungfrauenmaschine, Die
 (The Virgin Machine)
Ladyboys
Macho Dancer
Magic Cottage
Male Escorts of San Francisco:
 Raphael, the Call Bear [excerpt]
Male Escorts of San Francisco,
 The
Maybe I Can Give You Sex ?
 Part One
Maybe I Can Give You Sex ?
 Part Two
Midnight Dancers
My Hustler
My Own Private Idaho
Not Angels but Angels
103 Degrees
Outlaw Poverty, Not Prostitutes
Poisoned Blood
Portrait of Jason
Prinz In Holleland
 (Prince In Hell)
Revolutions Happen Like
 Refrains in a Song
Salt Mines, The
Sex Is Sex

Sexual I.D.
Some of These Days
Straight for the Money:
 Interviews with Queer
 Sex Workers
Stripped Bare: A Look at
 Erotic Dancers
Trick or Treat
V Is for Violet
Vestida de Azul
 (Dressed in Blue)
Via Appia

Sexuality

A.I.D.S.C.R.E.A.M.
Abuse
Adrian's Montag
 (Adrian's Monday)
Adventures of Priscilla, Queen of
 the Desert, The
Affirmations
Age 12: Love With A Little L
Agora
Airport
aletheia
All Of Me
Alone Once Again
Analstahl (Anal Steel)
Annie
Attendant, The
Automonosexual
Awkward for Years
Bachvirus, Het
 (Bach Virus, The)
Basic Necessities
Be Careful What Kind of Skin
 You Pull Back, You Never
 Know What Kind of Head
 Will Appear
Be My Valentine
Bears in the Hall
Bears Will Be Bears
Beyond/Body/Memory
Bi-Ways
Bitter Strength: Sadistic
 Response Version
Bittersweet
Black Sheep Boy
Black Widow
Blicklust
Blood and Roses
Blood Sisters: Leather, Dykes
 and Sadomasochism
Bondage
Bottom
Boy with Cat
Butch Wax
Cap Tourmente
Caught Looking
Chance of a Lifetime
Chicken Hawk
Chinese Characters
Chubs & Bears [work in progress]
Clearing, The
Clips from Kelly's Porn Movie
Clones In Love

Coconut/Cane & Cutlass
Complaint of the Empress, The
Cost of Love, The
Covert Action
Cruising
Damned If You Don't
Dance with a Body, A
Dandy Dust [trailer]
Dangerous Bliss
David, Montgomery und Ich
Dead Dreams of Monochrome
    Men
Deflatable Man, The
Devotions
Dick Tricks
Djune/Idexa
Does Your Mother Know?
Doll Shop
Doom Generation, The
Double Entente
Du Darst (Truth or Dare)
Ecce Homo
Eclipse
Educate Your Attitude
    (Fresh Talk)
Elegant Spanking, The
Empire State
Erotic in Nature
Erotique
Even Cowgirls Get the Blues
Every Conceivable Position:
    Inside Gay Porn
Evolution Of a Sex Life
Excerpts from the Far East
Exposure
Fabian's Freeak Show
Faerie Tales
Fat Chance
Feed Them to the Cannibals
Female Misbehavior
Fireworks Revisited
Foetal Gay's Nightmare, A
Frankfurter
Frenzy [excerpt]
Frisk
Fuck Film
Gay Tape: Butch and Femme
Get It Girl: Lesbians Talk
    about Safe Sex
Girl Power (Part 1)
Go Fish
Goblin Market
Golden Positions, The
Grey Hideaway
Grief
Her Appetite
Hermes Bird
Horror Vacui—Die Angst Vor Der
    Leere (Horror Vacui—The Fear
    of Emptiness)
House of Pain
How to Seduce a Preppy
I Like Dreaming
I'm Gonna Eat Worms
Illegal Tender
In Loving Memory

In My Father's Bed
Inevitable Love
Interview With The Vampire
It Wasn't Love
Joggernaught
Jomasay
Jungfrauenmaschine, Die
    (The Virgin Machine)
Kachapati: Spray the Wall
Kindling Point, The
Konsequenz, Die
    (Consequence, The)
Kore
L'Amico Fried's Glamorous
    Friends
L'Hiver Approche
    (Winter Is Approaching)
L'Ingenue
Let Me Die, Again
Let's Play Prisoners
Lie Down with Dogs
Lieve Jongens (Dear Boys)
Limités
Liquor, Guns and Ammo
Living End, The
Loads
Look
Lord and Master
Love on the Line
Love/Sex
Lush Life
Madame X—Eine Absolute
    Herrscherin (Madame X—An
    Absolute Ruler)
Madonna In Me
Malaysian Series, Part 1-6
Male Escorts of San Francisco:
    Raphael, the Call Bear
    [excerpt]
Male Escorts of San Francisco
Maneaters
Mano Destra
    (Mas-ter-ba-shun)
Masturbation: 5 Women
Mayhem
Men Maniacs
Meridad Proscrita
Miguel
Mondo Diviso, Il
    (The Split World)
Monsters in the Closet
Muscle
My Addiction
My Father is Coming
Naughty Boys
Nice Girls Don't Do It
Nitrate Kisses
No Glove, No Love
No No Nooky T.V.
No Skin Off My Ass
None of the Above
Now Playing
Nudes (A Sketchbook)
Odd Girl Out
Off Our Chests
On the Safe Side

Other Woman, The
    (Slane, Andrea)
Our Gay Brothers
Outlaw Poverty, Not Prostitutes
Pauline's Birthday, or The
    Beast of Notre Dame
Pedagogue
Peril or Pleasure? Feminist-
    Produced Pornography
Perilous Liaisons
Playing Poseidon
Please Decompose Slowly
Pleasure Beach
Poison
Primas
Private Pleasures
Pubic Beard
Public
Public Opinion
Put Your Lips Around Yes
Queer Across Canada
Querelle
Rainbow Serpent, The
Rambles
Rapture
Razor Head
Reference
Reflections
Robert Having His Nipple
    Pierced
Rote Ohren Fetzen Durch Asche
    (Flaming Ears)
Safe Soap
Saint Mulekicker
Sandra's Garden
Sano y Sanitario
Scars
Scorpio Rising
Search, The
17 Rooms or, What Lesbians Do
    in Bed
Sewing on Breast
Sex Bowl
Sex Elvis Boy
Sex Is . . .
Sex, Lies, Religion
Shadows
Shaman Psalm
She Thrills Me
Show Me
Silencis (Silent Moments)
Skin Deep
Sluts and Goddesses Video
Workshop, The, or How To Be a
    Sex Goddess in 101
    Easy Ways
Snatch
Some of These Days
Son, Are You Down There?
Sonny
Stafford's Story
State of Mind
Stellium In Capricorn
Straight for the Money:
    Interviews with Queer Sex
    Workers

Super 8 1/2
Sweet Dreams
Sync Touch
Tangled Garden,
  Act II, Scene II
Taste of Kiwi, A
Taxi Zum Klo
Ten Cents a Dance (Parallax)
Texas
Tom of Finland
Topsau, Die (The Top Pig)
Totally F***ed Up
Touchables, The
Transeltown
25 Year Old Man Loses His
  Virginity to a Woman, A
Two Bad Daughters
Two Spirit People
Uh-Oh!
Venner for Altid (Friends Forever)
Verfuhrung: Die Grausame Frau
  (Seduction: The Cruel Woman)
Vive L'Amour
Walk the Dog
West Coast Crones: A Glimpse at
  the Lives Of Nine Old
  Lesbians
What Can I Do with a Male
  Nude?
What Gets You Off
What's the Difference Between a
  Yam and a Sweet Potato?
Where There's Smoke
Wicked Radiance

Sports and Leisure
After the Game
Bar Girls
Big Time Wrestlers from
  Hollywood
Divine Bodies
Feed Them to the Cannibals
Gay Olympics '82
Iowa City Women's Rugby
Last Call at Maud's
Limitless
Olympia
Out for a Change: Addressing
  Homophobia in Women's
  Sports
Personal Best: Gay Body Culture
Pools
Queers Are Not Enough
Running Gay
She Shoots, She Scores
Source, The
Spikes and Heels
Suddenly Last Summer
Thin Ice
Tricycle Race
Video Album: The Gaymes
Zoe la Boxeuse (Zoe the Boxer)

Violence
Abuse
All Fall Down

American Shooting
  Numbers 1, 2 and 3
Analstahl (Anal Steel)
Apartment Zero
Bashing
Basic Instinct
Being at Home with Claude
Bete Noire
Black Widow
Blond Fury
Built for Endurance
Butterfly Kiss
Can't Take That Way from Me
Cruising
Damned, The
Dandy Dust [trailer]
Descent
Dr. Jekyll and Sister Hyde
ESP: Vision
Fortune and Men's Eyes
Frisk
Green on Thursdays
Heavenly Creatures
Hey Bud
History of Violence, A
Hot and Cold
Hotheads
House of Pain
Hunting Season, The
I Remember Running
In My Father's Bed
In View of Her Fatal Inclination,
  Lilo Wanders Gives Up the
  Ghost
Just for Fun
Killer Babe
Last Island, The
Living End, The
Lost Heart, The
Magic Cottage
Million Eyes of Su-Muru, The
Mother's Hands
Muscle
New Year, A
One and the Other Time
Orgasm of Hot Blood
Place Called Lovely, A
Postcards from America
Prinz In Holleland
  (Prince In Hell)
Reflections
Reflections in a Golden Eye
Remnants
Resonance
Rote Ohren Fetzen Durch Asche
  (Flaming Ears)
S.S.
Sandra's Garden
Sari Red
Scrubbers
Self Defense
Sister, My Sister
Stick Figures
Still Sane
Terra Nullius
Tom's Flesh

Tough Love, Smart Weapons
Tras el Cristal (In a Glass Cage)
Triangle
Unity
Want
Warrior Marks [excerpt]
What's in a Name
When You Name Me
White Justice (A case of
  diminished capacity)
Why Not Love?/Get Used to It
Wild Thing: A Poem by Sapphire

Youth
Abuse
After the Break
Age 12: Love With A Little L
AIDS Movie, The
Alicia Was Fainting
Alkali, Iowa
Alone Once Again
Alone Together: Young Adults
  Living With HIV
Alpsee
Amblyopia (Points of View)
Amelia Rose Towers
Anxiety of Inexpression and the
  Otherness Machine
Awkward for Years
Bedtime Stories
Bertrand Disparu
  (Bertrand Is Missing)
Black Sheep Boy
Chaero
Chickula: Teenage Vampire
Crows
Dare to Be Butch
Death in Venice, CA
Delius
Does Your Mother Know?
Doom Generation, The
Dottie Gets Spanked
Educate Your Attitude
  (Fresh Talk)
Family Affair, A
Fatboy Chronicles, The
  (Part One : Rene, Rene, Qu'
  est-ce-que c' est?)
First Base
Forsaken
Framed Youth: The Revenge of
  the Teenage Perverts
Frisk
Fun Down There
Gay Lives and Culture Wars
Gay Youth
Girl Power (Part 1)
Growing Up and I'm Fine
Harold and Hiroshi
Hatachi No Binetsu (Slight
  Fever of a 20-Year-Old)
Heatwave
Heavenly Creatures
Homoteens
How He Goes
If Every Girl Had a Diary

If Only
Incredibly True Adventures of
   Two Girls in Love, The
Intrepidissima
Is-Slottet (Ice Palace, The)
It Wasn't Love
It's That Age
Jollies
Just for Fun
Kiss on the Cliff, The
Konsequenz, Die
   (Consequence, The)
Les Amities Particulieres
   (This Special Friendship)
Like Mother, Like Son
Live to Tell: The First Gay
   Prom in America
Lune
Mädchen In Uniform (1931)
Mädchen In Uniform (1957)
Mala Noche
Me and Rubyfruit
Mondo Diviso, II
   (The Split World)
Montreal Main
Moscow Does Not Believe in
   Queers
My First Suit
My Grandma's Lady Cabaret
My Mother's Secret
New Year, A
1999 - Nen No Natsu Yasumi
   (Summer Vacation: 1999)
No Saintly Girl
Not Angels but Angels
Olivia (Pit of Loneliness)
103 Degrees
Only the Brave
Out: Stories of Lesbian and
   Gay Youth
Perils of Pedagogy, The
Place Called Lovely, A
Placeros Ocultos, Los
   (Hidden Pleasures)
Primas
Prinz In Holleland
   (Prince In Hell)
Public
Queer Son
Re Generation
Red Light, Green Light—
   Meeting Strangers
Saddle Up
Safe Place, A
Sally Forth
Sex of the Stars
   (Le sexe des Etoiles)
Simone
Something Special
Straight from the Heart
Subject Is AIDS, The
Taste of Honey, A
Times Square
To Play or Die
To Ride a Cow
Tomboy!

Totally F***ed Up
Trevor
Truth About Alex, The
Two of Us
V Is for Violet
Venner for Altid (Friends Forever)
Veronica Four Rose
Village Idiot, The
Waiting
Weiner Brut
What's A Nice Kid Like
   You . . .
Wild Life
Wild Thing: A Poem by Sapphire
Wonderland

INDEX OF DIRECTORS

Adair, Peter
  Absolutely Positive
  Word Is Out
Akarasainee, Pisan
  Anguished Love
  Last Song, The
Alea, Tomas Gutierrez,
and Juan Carlos Tabio
  Fresa y Chocolate
  (Strawberry and Chocolate)
Almendros, Nestor,
and Orlando Jiminez Leal
  Mauvaise Conduite
  (Improper Conduct)
Almodovar, Pedro
  Entre Tinieblas (Dark Habits)
  Laberinto de Pasiones
  (Labyrinth of Passions)
  Ley del Deseo, La
  (Law of Desire)
  Que He Hecho Yo Para
  Merecer Esto?
  (What Have I Done to
  Deserve This?)
  Sisters of Darkness
Anger, Kenneth
  Fireworks
  Invocation of My Demon
  Brother
  Kustom Kar Kommandos
  Lucifer Rising
  Puce Moment
  Scorpio Rising
Araki, Gregg
  Doom Generation, The
  Living End, The
  Long Weekend (O'Despair),
  The
  Three Bewildered People
  in the Night
  Totally F***ed Up
Araki, Gregg, and Jaie Laplante
  Show Me
Arcand, Denys
  Love and Human Remains
Ardill, Susan
  Love and Marriage
  Stand on Your Man
  Talking Hairs
Armstrong, Gillian
  Satdee Night
Arzner, Dorothy
  Craig's Wife
Babenco, Hector
  Kiss of the Spider Woman
Balletbò-Coll, Marta
  Costa Brava
  Harlequin Exterminator
  Intrepidissima
Beatty, Maria
  Sphinxes Without Secrets
Beatty, Maria,
and Annie Sprinkle
  Sluts and Goddesses Video
  Workshop, The, or How To

Be a Sex Goddess in 101
  Easy Ways
Beatty, Maria
and Rosemary Delain
  Elegant Spanking, The
Beavan, Clare
  Dorothy Arzner: A Profile
  (BBC The Late Show)
  Every Conceivable Position:
  Inside Gay Porn
  Gay Rock 'n' Roll Years, The
  Hollywood and Homophobia
  Innings
  Suddenly Last Summer
Bemberg, Maria Luisa
  I, The Worst of All
Benning, Sadie
  Girl Power (Part 1)
  If Every Girl Had a Diary
  It Wasn't Love
  Jollies
  Me and Rubyfruit
  New Year, A
  Place Called Lovely, A
  Guess Who's Coming to Visit
Borden, Lizzie
  Born In Flames
Borden, Lizzie, Monika Treut,
and Clara Law
  Erotique
Bordowitz, Gregg
  Fast Trip, Long Drop
Boskovich, John
  Without You I'm Nothing
Boyle, Bernie
  Assassination of Anita
  Bryant, The
  Castro at 18th
  Etc.
  5
  How To Cook A Plantain,
  Properly
  Narcissus Lingerie—Screen
  Test of Lawanda Rose
  Untitled
Bressan, Arthur
  Abuse
  Gay USA
  Buddies
  Pleasure Beach
Brocka, Lino
  Macho Dancer
Broughton, James
  Devotions
  Golden Positions, The
  Hermes Bird
  Pleasure Garden, The
Broughton, James,
and Joel Singer
  Scattered Remains
  Shaman Psalm
Canalli, John
  Alphabit Land: The Backyard
  Tour Featuring Wigstock '89
  Heroes
  Human Still Life [Rough Cut]
  Me Show, The

One In Seven
One Sings
  Patsy Cline: A Tribute
  Right Stuff, The
Canalli, John, and Marty Monroe
  Nuclear Family
Carlomusto, Jean
  Current Flow
  L Is for the Way You Look
Carlomusto, Jean,
and Hilary Joy Kipnis
  Up In Arms Over Needle
  Exchange
Carlomusto, Jean,
and Maria Maggenti
  Doctors, Liars and Women
Castle, William
  Homicidal
Cavani, Lilliana
  Berlin Affair, The
Chasnoff, Debra
  Deadly Deception
Chasnoff, Debra
and Kim Klausner
  Choosing Children
Cheang, Shu Lea
  Fresh Kill
  Sex Bowl
  Sex Fish
Child, Abigail
  Both
  Covert Action
  Mayhem
  Swamp
Christopher, Mark
  Alkali, Iowa
  Dead Boys' Club, The
  Language of Boys, The
Clarke, Kris
  Armistead Maupin Is a Man
  I Dreamt Up
  Confessions of a Pretty Lady
  Sex Change—Shock! Horror!
  Probe! (BBC Arena)
Comstock, William
  Man I Love, The
  On the Sentimental Side
  Out in the Streets
  Pavane for a Dead Princess
  Voi Che Sapete
Cronenberg, David
  M. Butterfly
Cukor, George
  Sylvia Scarlett
Davies, Terence
  Madonna and Child
  Terence Davies Trilogy, The
De Kuyper, Eric
  Casta Diva
  Naughty Boys
  Pink Ulysses
De Kuyper, Eric,
and Paul Verstraaten
  Strange Love Affair, A
de la Iglesia, Eloy
  Diputado, Il (Deputy, The)

Placeros Ocultos, Los
  (Hidden Pleasures)
Deitch, Donna
  Desert Hearts
Demme, Jonathan
  Philadelphia
  Silence of the Lambs, The
Deocampo, Nick
  Revolutions Happen Like
    Refrains in a Song
Dong, Arthur
  Coming Out under Fire
  Public
Dougherty, Cecilia
  Coal Miner's Granddaughter
  Drama of the Gifted Child,
    The
  Gay Tape: Butch and Femme
  Grapefruit
  Kathy
  My Failure to Assimilate
  76 Trombones
Dougherty, Cecilia, and
Leslie Singer
  Joe Joe
Dunye, Cheryl
  Millionaire
  Potluck and the Passion, The
  She Don't Fade
  Vanilla Sex
  Wild Thing: A Poem by
    Sapphire
Dunye, Cheryl, and Kristina
Deutsch
  Complicated Flesh
Epstein, Robert
  Times of Harvey Milk, The
Epstein, Rob,
and Jeffrey Friedman
  Celluloid Closet, The
  Where Are We?: Our Trip
    Through America
Epstein, Robert and Peter Adair
  AIDS Show, The
Epstein, Robert, Frances Reid,
Greta Schiller, and Lucy Winer
  Greetings from Washington
    D.C.
Farthing, Cheryl
  Call Me Your Girlfriend
  It's a Queer World
  Rosebud
  We've Been Framed
Farthing, Cheryl,
and Penny Ashbrook
  Sex Wars
Fassbinder, Rainer Werner
  Querelle
Finch, Nigel
  Kenneth Anger's Hollywood
  Babylon (BBC Arena)
  Lost Language of Cranes, The
  Robert Mapplethorpe
    (BBC Arena)
  Saint Genet (BBC Arena)
  Stonewall

Fontaine, Richard
  Cell Mates
  Nude Inn
  Vice and the Badge, The
Frears, Stephen
  My Beautiful Laundrette
  Prick Up Your Ears
Friedkin, William
  Boys in the Band, The
  Cruising
Friedrich, Su
  Bedtime Stories
    [work in progress]
  But No One
  Cool Hands, Warm Heart
  Damned If You Don't
  First Comes Love
  Gently Down the Stream
  Rules of the Road
  Sink or Swim
  Ties That Bind, The
Fung, Richard
  Chinese Characters
  Fighting Chance
  Orientations
Gay Girls Riding Club
  Always On Sunday
  Roman Springs on
    Mrs. Stone, The
  What Really Happened
    to Baby Jane?
Genet, Jean
  Chant d'amour, Un
Giannaris, Constantine
  Caught Looking
  North of Vortex
  Place in the Sun, A
  Trojans
Godmilow, Jill
  Roy Cohn/Jack Smith
  Waiting for the Moon
Gorris, Marleen
  Antonia's Line
  Gerbroken Spiegels
    (Broken Mirrors)
  Last Island, The
Goss, John
  Flowing Hearts: Thailand
  Fights AIDS
  "OUT" Takes
  He's Like
  Virtual Cockpits of Tomorrow
  Wild Life
  Wrecked for Life: The Trip
    and Magic of the
  Trocadero Transfer
Greyson, John
  AIDS Epidemic, The
  Jungle Boy, The
  Kipling Meets the Cowboy
  Making of "Monsters," The
  Moffie Called Simon, A
  Moscow Does Not
    Believe in Queers
  Perils of Pedagogy, The
  Pink Pimpernel, The

Urinal
  World Is Sick (sic), The
  You Taste American
  Zero Patience
Grote, Alexandra Von
  Novembermund
    (Novembermoon)
  Weggehen um Anzukommen
    (Depart to Arrive)
Hammer, Barbara
  Audience
  Bedtime Stories
  Bent Time
  Doll House
  Double Strength
  Dyketactics
  Gay Day, A
  Haircut
  History of the World According
    to a Lesbian, The
  I Was I Am
  New York Loft
  Nitrate Kisses
  No No Nooky T.V.
  Optic Nerve
  Our Trip
  Out in South Africa
  Parisian Blinds Hammer,
    Barbara Pearl Diver
  Pictures for Barbara
  Psychosynthesis
  Sappho
  Shirley Temple and Me
  Snow Job: The Media
    Hysteria of AIDS
  Still Point
  Stone Circles
  Sync Touch
  T.V. Tart
  Tender Fictions
  Tourist
  Vital Signs
  Women I Love
Hammer, Barbara,
and Barbara Klutinis
  Pools
Hammer, Barbara,
and Paula Levine
  Two Bad Daughters]
Harris, Thomas Allen
  Black Body
  Heaven, Earth and Hell
  Splash
  Vintage: Families of Value
Haynes, Todd
  Dottie Gets Spanked
  Poison
Hermosillo, Jaime Humberto
  Dona Herlinda Y Su Hijo
    (Dona Herlinda and
    Her Son)
Hoffman, Deborah
  Complaints of a Dutiful
    Daughter
Hubbard, Jim
  Dance, The

Elegy in the Streets
Homosexual Desire in
  Minnesota [excerpt]
Memento Mori
Huestis, Marc
  Basket Case
  Bitter Old Queens
  [work in progress]
  Chuck Solomon:
    Coming of Age
  Cliche in the Afternoon
  Men In Love
  Miracle on Sunset Boulevard
  Poodle-Poo-Poo Miracle
    Mask, The
  Sex Is. . .
    [work in progress]
  Shriek, The
  Unity
  Whatever Happened
    to Susan Jane?
Ivory, James
  Maurice
Jarman, Derek
  Angelic Conversation, The
  Art of Mirrors, The
  Blue
  Edward II
  Garden, The
  Glitterbug
  Imagining October
  Journey to Avebury
  Last of England, The
  Projections
    (Pet Shop Boys compilation)
  Wittgenstein
Jarman, Derek,
and Paul Humfress
  Sebastiane
Jarman, Derek, Cerith Wyn
Evans, John Maybury,
and Michael Kostiff
  Dream Machine, The
Jarman, Derek, John Maybury,
and Richard Heslop
  Queen is Dead, The
Jones, William
  Massillon
  Other Families
Jordan, Neil
  Crying Game, The
  Interview with the Vampire
Julien, Isaac
  Attendant, The
  Black and White in Color
  Darker Side of Black, A
  Looking for Langston
  This Is Not an AIDS
    Advertisement
  Young Soul Rebels
Kaige, Chen
  Farewell My Concubine
Kalin, Tom
  Confirmed Bachelor
  Darling Child
  Finally Destroy Us

Nation
Nomads
Swoon
They Are Lost to
  Vision Altogether
Kalin, Tom,
and Stathis Lagoudakif
  News from Home
Kalmen, Michael
  Bar Time
Kidron, Beeban
  Oranges Are Not the
    Only Fruit
  To Wong Foo, Thanks for
    Everything, Julie Newmar
Kinney, Robert,
and Donald Kinney
  Agora
Stephen
  Talk to Me Like the Rain
Kuchar, George
  Video Album 5:
    The Thursday People
Kuchinskas, Susan
  Off Our Chests
Kwietniowski, Richard
  Actions Speak Louder
    Than Words
  Alfalfa
  Ballad of Reading Gaol
  Cost of Love, The
  Flames of Passion
  Guess Who's Coming
    to Dinner
  Night with Derek, A
  Personal Best:
    Gay Body Culture
Kwietniowski, Richard,
and Roger Clark
  Proust's Favorite Fantasy
LaBruce, Bruce
  No Skin Off My Ass
  Super 8 1/2
Lambert, Lothar
  Desert of Love
  Drama in Blond
  Paso Doble
Lee, Ang
  Wedding Banquet, The
Lee, Quentin
  Anxiety of Inexpression and
    the Otherness Machine
  Hysterio Passio
  Sleeping Subjects
Lee, Quentin, and Deeya Loran
  To Ride a Cow
Lindell, John
  Blue Hour, The
  Caress
  Put Your Lips Around Yes
  Sunray
  Watch Out for North Dakota
Livingston, Jennie
  Hotheads
  Paris is Burning
Lubitsch, Ernst

Ich Mochte Kein Mann Sein!
  (I Don't Want To Be
  A Man!)
Maggenti, Maria
  Donna e Mobile, La
  Incredibly True Adventures
    of Two Girls in Love, The
Marshall, Stuart
  Blue Boys
  Bright Eyes
  Comrades In Arms
  Desire
  Over Our Dead Bodies
  Pedagogue
Maybury, John
  Premonition of Absurd
    Perversion in Sexual
    Personae Part 1
  Remembrance of Things Fast
  Tortures That Laugh
McDowell, Curt
  Loads
  Nudes (A Sketchbook)
  Sparkle's Tavern
  Stand By
Metzger, Radley
  Cat and the Canary, The
  Therese and Isabelle
Mikesch, Elfi
  Blue Distance
  Execution: A Study of Mary
  Hyena's Breakfast, The
  Macumba
  Was Soll'n Wir Denn Machen
    Ohne Den Tod (What Shall
    We Do Without Death)
Mikesch, Elfi, and Monika Treut
  Verfuhrung: Die Grausame
    Frau (Seduction: The Cruel
    Woman)
Montgomery, Jennifer
  Age 12: Love With A Little L
  Do You Think that a Candidate
    Should Live Like This?
Mosbacher, Dee
  Out for a Change: Addressing
    Homophobia in Women's
    Sports
Mosbacher, Dee,
and Frances Reid
  Straight from the Heart
Mueller, Matthias
  Alpsee
  Home Stories
  Sleepy Haven
  Sternenschauer
    (Scattering Stars)
Newby, Chris
  Kiss
  Madagascar Skin
  Relax
Oki, Hiroyuki
  Iro Kaze (Colour Wind)
  Irome (Colour Eyes)
  Koukei Dori
    (Landscape Catching)

Matsumae-Kun No Senritsu
(Melody For Buddy
Matsumae)
Onodera, Midi
Displaced View, The
Skin Deep
Ten Cents a Dance (Parallax)
Oremland, Paul
Andy the Furniture Maker
If They'd Asked for a
Lion Tamer
Rhythm Divine:
The Story of Disco, The
Tall Dark Stranger
Ottinger, Ulrike
Dorian Gray Im Spiegel Der
Boulevardpresse (Dorian
Gray in the Mirror of the
Popular Press)
Johanna D'arc of Mongolia
Madame X—Eine Absolute
Herrscherin (Madame X—
An Absolute Ruler)
Oxenberg, Jan
Comedy in Six Unnatural
Acts, A
Home Movie
Thank You and Good Night
Paradis, Marc
Cage, La
Deliver Us from Evil
Voyage de l'Ogre, Le
Parkerson, Michelle
Odds and Ends
(A New-Age Amazon Fable)
Storme: The Lady of the
Jewel Box
Parmar, Pratibha
Double the Trouble,
Twice the Fun
Emergence
Flesh and Paper
(see Out On Tuesday,
Program 3)
Khush
Memory Pictures
Memsahib Rita
Place of Rage, A
Reframing AIDS
Sari Red
Warrior Marks [excerpt]
Peck, Ron
Empire State
Strip Jack Naked
What Can I Do with a
Male Nude?
Peck, Ron, and Paul Hallam
Nighthawks
Potter, Sally
London Story, The
Orlando
Thriller
Rajski,Peggy
Trevor
Reid, Frances and Dlugacz, Judy
Changer, The: A Record

of the Times
Reid, Frances,
and Elizabeth Stevens
We All Have Our Reasons
Richardson, Tony
Taste of Honey, A
Riggs, Marlon
Affirmations
Anthem
No Regret
(Non, Je ne regrette rien)
Tongues Untied
Ripploh, Frank
Taxi to Cairo
Taxi Zum Klo
Ripstein, Arturo
Lugar Sin Limites, El
(A Limitless Place/Hell
Without Limits)
Rivette, Jacques
Religieuse, La (The Nun)
Rozema, Paticia
Passion: A Letter in 16mm
I've Heard the
Mermaids Singing
When Night is Falling
Rubnitz, Tom
Bump and Grind It
Chicken Elaine
Drag Queen Marathon, The
Fairies, The
Hustle with My Muscle
John Sex: The True Story
Made for TV
Mother Show, The
Plastic Rap
Strawberry Short Cut/Pickle
Surprise
Summer of Love—
Art Against AIDS
Undercover Me!
Wigstock—The Movie
(Rubnitz, Tom)
Saalfield, Catherine
Among Good Christian
Peoples
Cuz' It's Boy
Infidel
Saalfield, Catherine,
and Cyrille Phipps
Sacred Lies, Civil Truths
Saalfield, Catherine,
and Debra Levine
I'm You, You're Me
Saalfield, Catherine,
and Gregg Bordowitz
Ray Navarro Memorial Tape
Saalfield, Catherine,
and Julie Tolentino
B.U.C.K.L.E.
Saalfield, Catherine,
and Zoe Leonard
Keep Your Laws Off My Body
Sankofa Black Film Workshop
Passion of Remembrance, The
Sayles, John

Lianna
Scheirl, A. Hans
Dandy Dust [trailer]
Scheirl, Angela Hans, Dietmar
Schipek, and Ursula Purrer
Rote Ohren Fetzen Durch
Asche (Flaming Ears)
Schiller, Greta
Greta's Girls
Paris Was a Woman
Tiny & Ruby: Hell Divin'
Women
Woman of the Wolf
Schiller, Greta,
and Robert Rosenberg
Before Stonewall
Schiller, Greta
and Andrea Weiss
International Sweethearts of
Rhythm
Schmiechen, Richard
Changing Our Minds: The
Story Of Dr. Evelyn Hooker
Sherwood, Bill
Parting Glances
Smith, Jack
Flaming Creatures
Snee, Patrick
Letter of Introduction, The
Love Machine, The
Prague
Village Idiot, The
Sonbert, Warren
Friendly Witness
Speck, Weiland
Westler—East of the Wall
Among Men
David, Montgomery und Ich
Gay TV
Room 303
Spiro, Ellen
ACT UP at the FDA
DiAna's Hair Ego:
AIDS Info Up Front
Greetings from Out Here
Video Album: The Gaymes
Spiro, Ellen, and Marina Alvarez
(In)Visible Women
Tartaglia, Jerry
A.I.D.S.C.R.E.A.M.
Ecce Homo
Final Solutions
Holy Mary
Lawless
Remembrance
Taylor, Jocelyn
Bodily Functions
[work in progress]
Frankie and Jocie
24 Hours a Day
Testing the Limits Collective
Testing the Limits Guide to
Safer Sex
Voices from the Front
Tiffenbach, Joe
Closet, The

Five Naked Surfers
  Solo
Treut, Monika
  Annie
  Bondage
  Dr. Paglia
  Female Misbehavior
  Jungfrauenmaschine, Die
    (The Virgin Machine)
  My Father is Coming
Treut, Monika and Elfi Mikesch
  Verfuhrung: Die Grausame
    Frau (Seduction: The Cruel
    Woman)
Troche, Rose
  Gabriella on the Half Shell
  Go Fish
Vadim, Roger
  Blood and Roses
Van Sant, Gus
  Even Cowgirls Get the Blues
  Five Ways to Kill Yourself
  Ken Death Gets Out of Jail
  Mala Noche
  My New Friend
  My Own Private Idaho
Verhoeven, Paul
  Basic Instinct
Verow, Todd
  Built for Endurance
  Death of Dottie Love, The
  Frisk
  V Is for Violet
Visconti, Luchino
  Damned, The
  Ludwig
von Praunheim, Rosa
  Affengeil (Life Is Like a
    Cucumber)
  Army of Lovers: or Revolt of
    the Sex Perverts
  Horror Vacui—Die Angst Vor
    Der Leere (Horror Vacui—
    The Fear of Emptiness)
  Ich Bin Meine Eigene Frau
    (I Am My Own Woman)
  Positive (Positiv)
  Schweigen=Tod
    (Silence=Death)
  Stadt der Verlorenen Seelen
    (City Of Lost Souls)
  Virus Kennt Keine Moral, Ein
    (Virus Has No Morals, A)
Von Trotta, Margarethe
  Second Awakening of Christa
    Klages, The
Walker, Nancy
  Can't Stop the Music
Wallin, Michael
  Black Sheep Boy
Walsh, Jack
  Dear Rock
  Working Class Chronicle
Walton, Pam
  Gay Youth
  Lesbians

Out in Suburbia
Warhol, Andy
  Bike Boy
  Blow Job (Warhol, Andy)
  My Hustler
Weiss, Andrea
  Bit of Scarlett, A
Weissman, Aerlyn,
and Lynne Fernie
  Forbidden Love
  Fiction and Other Truths:
    A Film about Jane Rule
Weissman, David
  Beauties without a Cause
  Complaints
  Mothers
  976
  Song from an Angel
  Steps, The
Wheelock , Martha
and Maria Simpson
  World of Light: A Portrait of
    May Sarton
Wheelock, Martha
and Kay Weaver
  Berenice Abbott: A View of
    the 20th Century
Whittaker, Stephen
  Closing Numbers
  Portrait of a Marriage
Wilhite, Ingrid
  Fun with a Sausage
  It's a Lezzie Life: A
    Dyke-U-Mentary Wilhite,
    Ingrid L'Ingenue
  Lesbian Impress Card, The
  Mister Sisters, The
Winer, Lucy
  Greetings from
    Washington D.C.
  Silent Pioneers
  Tales of an Exhausted Woman
Wood, Ed
  Glen or Glenda?
    (I Changed My Sex)
  I Changed My Sex [trailer]
Zando, Julie
  Hey Bud
  How Big Is Big?
  I Like Girls for Friends
  Let's Play Prisoners
  Uh-Oh!
Zando, Julie, and Jo Anstey
  Bus Stops Here, The: Three
    Case Histories

DISTRIBUTOR DIRECTORY

Do gay people move more than straight people? Who can say? Every effort has been made to obtain current addresses, phone and fax numbers (and some e-mail addresses) for all of the film and video makers and distributors whose works are described in this book. Please do send updates, corrections, and address changes to:

The Ultimate Guide,
c/o popcornQ
584 Castro St., #550 .
San Francisco, CA 94114
phone: (415) 252-6285
fax (415) 252-6287
email: popcornQ@aol.com

The following individual distributor listings include: name, address, phone, fax, and e-mail in that order (note that the phone number is listed first, followed by the fax number when available).

Because this volume is being published simultaneously in the U.S. and U.K. I have tried to list both distribution sources if there are separate distributors; if only a U.S. (or U.K.) source is listed, please contact that source to find out about distribution information for other territories. In some cases, the U.K. home video (sell-thru) source is listed when there is no U.K. nontheatrical distributor.

Consumers looking for titles available for individual purchase or rental should contact a home video company (see the appendixes of U.S. and U.K. lesbian and gay mail-order home video and sell-thru distributors) rather than contacting the distributors listed here which are primarily sources for nontheatrical exhibition (i.e. film festivals, colleges, community groups, museums).

While I was pleasantly surprised at the percentage of success I had in tracking down current distribution information, there were many titles where a disconnected phone number or "return to sender" label left no other tracking options and it was necessary to list the title as "n/a" (source "not available").

In the case of several feature films, I ran up against complicated questions around rights-holders, companies who have rights but no actual film prints, and companies that no longer exist. Sadly, some of the most interesting and historically significant films fall into these categories.

Programmers, please also see the Checklist for Programmers chapter for more information.

Acosta, Danny G.
1243 Armacost, #6
Los Angeles, CA 90025
USA
310 473-7171

ACPAV
1050 Blvd. Rene-Levesque est,
#200
Montreal, Quebec H2L 2L6
CANADA

Adair & Armstrong
900 23rd St.
San Francisco, CA 94107
USA
415 826-6500

Adams, Kevin
7510 Sunset Blvd., #203
Los Angeles, CA 90046
USA
213 850-5448

AIDS Community Television
12 Wooster St.
New York, NY 10013
USA
212 226-8147
212 966-5622

AIDS Films
50 W. 34th St., #6B6
New York, NY 10001
USA
212 629-6288
212 629-1069

Albany Video
The Albany, Douglas Way
London SE8 4AG
ENGLAND
44 171 498-6811
44 171 498-1494

Alfalfa Entertainments, Ltd.
21B Cliff Villas
London NW1 9AT
ENGLAND
44 171 284-3275
44 171 485-6843

Alive From Off Center
172 E. 4th St.
St. Paul, MN 55101
USA
612 229-1253

Allard, Martin
1300 Logan
Montreal, Quebec H2l 1X1
CANADA
514 524-8353

Alliance International
355 Place Royale

Montreal, Quebec H2Y 2V3
CANADA
514 878-2282
514 878-2419

Alliance Releasing
920 Yonge St., #400
Toronto, Ontario M4W 3C7
CANADA
416 967-1174
416 967-4358

Allyn, Jerri
573 9th Ave.
New York, NY 10036
USA

Altermedia
P. O. Box 010-084
St. George Station
Staten Island, NY 10301
USA
718 273-8829

American Federation of Arts
41 E. 65th St.
New York, NY 10021
USA

American Film Institute
PO Box 27999
2021 N. Western Ave.
Los Angeles, CA 90027
USA
213 856-7600
213 467-4578

American Red Cross
1900 25th Ave. S.
Seattle, WA 98144
USA

Anderlini, Ken
3-1785 Adanac St.
Vancouver, British Columbia V5L
2C8
CANADA
604 253-6605

Anderson, Kelly
200 Dean St.
Brooklyn, NY 11217
USA
718 243-0075
212 772-4088

Andree Duchaine Films
6 rue de Berne
Paris 75008 FRANCE
33 1 45 22 44 38
33 1 45 22 26 98

Andrews, Jan
PO Box 2813
Salt Lake City UT 84110
USA
801 355-3612

Anthex Film Co.
Ludwigkirchstrasse 6,
1000 Berlin 15
GERMANY
49 30 881 6554
49 30 883 2500

Appel, Lynn
3 E. 10th St., #4A
New York, NY 10003
USA
212 473-2863

Ariadne Film
Gustav Muller Strass 17,
1000 Berlin 62
GERMANY

Aries Releasing
322 W. 57th St., #35S
New York, NY 10019
USA
212 246-0528

Arnesen, Heidi
146 Downey St.
San Francisco, CA 94117
USA
415 665-7795

Arocha, Ivan and
Hernandez, David
21-66th St., #4 West
Newark, NJ 07093
USA
201 295-9483

Art Com Media Distribution
P.O. Box 193123
Rincon Center
San Francisco, CA 94119-3123
USA
415 431-7524
415 431-7841

Artisan Productions
1737 N. Gardner St.
Los Angeles, CA 90046
USA
213 954-9000
213 954-9009

Artistic License Films
444 Park Ave S., #303
New York, NY 10016 USA
212 779-0290
212 696-9546

Arts Council of Great Britain
14 Great Peter St.
London SW1 P3NQ
ENGLAND
44 171 333-0100
44 171 973-6590

Ashkenazi
4605 NW 3rd Ave.
Pompano Beach, FL 33064
USA
305 941-9652

Askinazi, Edward
128 Lincoln Place
Brooklyn, NY 11217
USA
718 783-4943

Atkins, Shawn
63 Avenue D, #4B
New York, NY 10009
USA
212 254-2631
212 302-0829

Atkol
912 South Ave.
Plainfield, NJ 07062
USA
908 756-2011
atkol@glitch.com

Aubert, Elisabeth
48 Rue Monsieur Le Prince
Paris 75006
FRANCE
33 1 435-4478
33 1 432-8950

Audubon Films
131 E. 74th St.
New York, NY 10012
USA
212 832-0427

Australian Film Commission
8 West St.
North Sydney, NSW 2060
AUSTRALIA
61 2 925 7333
61 2 954 4001

Australian Film, Television &
Radio School
PO Box 126
North Ryde, NSW 2113
AUSTRALIA
61 2 805 6455
61 2 887 1030

Aynes, Tony
91226 Campbell Pde
Bondi Beach, NSW 2026
AUSTRALIA
61 2 303716

B., Hima
P.O. Box 460697
San Francisco, CA 94146
USA
415 647-9680
415 647-9658

Back Porch Productions
113 E. Whiteman St.
Yellow Springs OH 45387
USA

Baker, Henry
127 Fourth Av., PH-A
New York, NY 10003
USA
212 777-0482

Baldwin, Craig
992 Valencia St.
San Francisco, CA 94110
USA
415 648-0654

Balletbò-Coll, Marta
Trebol 2, 2nd Floor
Barcelona 08032 SPAIN
34 3 456-1076
34 3 456-1076

Balzli, Res
Hauptstrasse 33
Nidau CH-2560
SWITZERLAND

BAMC
1501 Broadway, #1915
New York, NY 10036
USA

Bardsley, Gil
298 Collingwood St.
San Francisco, CA 94114
USA
415 863-9278

Barrish Films
869 Bryant St.
San Francisco, CA 94103
USA
415 863-5644

Bartoni, Doreen
2150 Lincoln Park W.
Chicago, IL 60614
USA
312 935-5258

Basilisk
31 Percy St.
London W1 9FG
ENGLAND
44 171 580-7222
44 171 631-0572

Baum, Jennifer
150 W. 96th St.
New York, NY 10025
USA

Baus, Janet
c/o Sang Froid,
588 Broadway, # 504

New York, NY 10012 USA
212 343-9337
212 343-9336

Bautista, Pablo
437 Urbano Dr.
San Francisco, CA 94127
USA
415 584-1992

BBC TV
80 Wood Lane
London W12 OTT
ENGLAND
44 181 743-8000
44 171 749-6075

Beatty, Maria
Chelsea Hotel
222 West 23rd St., #412
New York, NY 10011
USA
212 243-3700

Beck, Robert
717 E. 5th St.
New York, NY 10009
USA
212 995-1659

Behrens, Alec
707 Brouwersgracht
Amsterdam 1015 G7
NETHERLANDS
31 20 420-5414
31 20 420-6442

Belverio, Glenn
PO Box 20553
Tompkins Square Station
New York, NY 10009
USA

Bergen, Brian
3153 Broadway, #3A
New York, NY 10027
USA
212 316-1705

Bernard, Gene
14624 Hart St.
Van Nuys, CA 91405
USA
818 505-7786

Berrios, Javier Antonio
San Antonio de los Banos, Aptdo
40/41
Havana 73145
CUBA

Bessie, Dan
26873 Hester Creek Rd.
Los Gatos, CA 95030
USA
408 353-4253

Bettina Wilhelm Filmproduktion
Kottbusser Damm 2,
D-1000 Berlin 61
GERMANY

Beveridge, Scott
461A Sackville St.
Toronto, Ontario M4X 1T3
CANADA
416 944-0450

Bijou Video
1349 N. Wells St.
Chicago, IL 60610
800 932-7111

Binninger, John
65 Hartford St.
San Francisco, CA 94114
USA
415 626-1154

Biskup, Marianne
744 Oregon St.
Watsonville, CA 95076
USA
408 724-3326

Bistecis, Alexis
Avras 44 Kifissia
Athens 14562
GREECE
30 1 801 8872
30 1 801 8872

Black, Angie
44A Northchurch Rd., Islington
London N14 EJ
ENGLAND
44 171 254-1166

Black, Julie X.
73 Potomac End
San Francisco, CA
94117-3322
USA
415 552-1907

Black Planet Productions
PO Box 435
Cooper Station
New York, NY 10003-0435
USA
718 857-5685
212 420-8223

Blackwood Productions
251 W 57th St.
New York, NY 10019
USA
212 247-4710
212 247-4713

Blind Eye Films
3807 Loma Vista Ave.
Oakland, CA 94619

USA
510 482-3876
510 835-8393

Blumen, Rebecca
26 Olive St.
Northampton, MA 01060
USA
413 586-1989

Bo Productions
2912 24th St.
San Francisco, CA 94110
USA
415 826-8551

Bociurkiw, Marusia
4659A rue de Lanauderie
Montreal, Quebec H2J 3P6
CANADA
514 596-0354

Bohm, Daniel
Puerredon 2458, #11B
Buenos Aires
ARGENTINA
541 786-9065

Bond, Rose
925 NW 19th
Portland, OR 97209

Boudreau, Charlene
935 Marie Anne Est.
Montreal, Quebec H2J 2B2
CANADA
514 598-7653

Bournemouth Film School
Wallisdown Poole
Dorset BH12 5HH
ENGLAND
44 1202 537729

Bowen, Peter
PO Box 1655
Old Chelsea Station
New York, NY 10113
USA
212 995-8753
212 966-4701

Boyle, Brian
178 N. Main St.
Sharon MA 02067
USA
617 784-8575
617 339-0658

Brava! For Women in the Arts
P.O. Box 3122
San Francisco, CA 94103
USA
415 252-0187

Bremer Institut Film/Fernsehen
Dechanastrasse 13
2800 Bremer 1
GERMANY
49 421 327 931

Brenin, Richard
P.O. Box 1862
Evanston, IL 60204
USA

British Film Institute
21 Stephen St.
London W1P 1PL
ENGLAND
44 171 255-1444
44 171 580-5830

Brodsky & Treadway
P.O. Box 335
Rowley MA 01969
USA
508 948-7985

Broggi, Paolo
396 Connecticut St.
San Francisco, CA 94107
USA
415 550-6980
415 550-6980

Broussard, Rene
2010 Magazine St.
New Orleans, LA 70130
USA
504 288-1991
504 288-1991

Brownsey, Maureen
87 Ramona Ave
San Francisco, CA 94103
USA
415 864-6764

Bruno, Wendell
5370 Avenue du Parc, #15
Montreal, Quebec H2V 4G7
CANADA
514 276-5354

Brynntrup, Michael
Hermannstr. 64
Berlin 12049
GERMANY
49 30 621-7800
49 30 621-7800

Bull, Marilyn
3932 17th St.
San Francisco, CA 94114
USA
415 552-5117

Butler, Kenneth
20 Ongar Rd.
London SW6
ENGLAND

California Newsreel
149 9th St. #420
San Francisco, CA 94103
USA
415 621-6196
415 621-6522

Calliope Film Resources
35 Granite St.
Cambridge, MA 02139
USA

Cambridge Documentary Films
P. O. Box 385
Cambridge, MA 02139
USA
617 354-3677
617 492-7653

Canadian Broadcasting
Corporation (Montreal)
1400 Blvd. Rene-Levesque est
Montreal, Quebec H2L 2M2
CANADA
514 597-6000

Canadian Broadcasting
Corporation (Toronto)
P.O. Box 500, Station A
Toronto, Ontario M5W 1E6
CANADA
416 205-5633
416 205-8607

Canadian Film Centre
2489 Bayview Ave.
Toronto, Ontario M2L 1A8
CANADA
416 445-1446
416 445-9481

Canadian Filmmakers
Distribution Centre
67A Portland St.
Toronto, Ontario M5V 2M9
CANADA
416 593-1808
416 593-8661

Canalli, John
633 E. 11th St., #1
New York, NY 10009
USA

Canyon Cinema
2325 Third St., #338
San Francisco, CA 94107
USA
415 626-2255

Capella
9242 Beverly Blvd., #280
Beverly Hills, CA 90210
USA
310 247-4700
310 247-4701

Carlton, Wendy Jo
237 N. Sherman
Olympia WA 98502
USA
206 352-8538

Carr, Shan
P.O. Box 31860
San Francisco, CA 94131
USA
415 826-8339

Cartagena, Chiqui
15 E. 36th St., #3C
New York, NY 10016
USA
212 447-6242
212 447-6242

Caspersen, Randy
2523 E Webster, #15
Milwaukee, WI 53211
USA 414 962-9757

Castellaneta, P.J.
1326 N. Citrus Ave., #5
Los Angeles, CA 90028
USA
213 460-4339

Castle Hill Productions
1414 Avenue of the Americas,
15th Floor
New York, NY 10019
USA
212 888-0080

Castle, Jane and
Cheang, Shu Lea
594 Broadway, #908
New York, NY 10012
USA
212 431-5119
212 431-4608

Castro, Rick
1312 N. Stanley Ave.
Los Angeles, CA 90046
USA
213 830-0206
213 850-0206

Catamas, Scott
340 North Ferndale
Mill Valley, CA 94941
USA

Cecchi Gori Group
Via Valadier 42
Rome 00193
ITALY
39 6 3247-2251
39 6 3247-2300

Chamberlain, Anne
Dept. of Cinema & Photo,

Southern Illinois University
Carbondale, IL 62901
USA
618 453-2365

Channel 4 Television
60 Charlotte St.
London W1P 2AX
ENGLAND
44 171 631-4444
44 171 580-2617

Charman, Karen
4116 Argyle St., Fitzroy,
Melbourne, Victoria
AUSTRALIA
61 3 419 0585

Chicago Filmmakers
1229 W. Belmont Ave.
Chicago, IL 60657
USA
312 281-8788
312 281-0389

Child, Abigail
303 E. 8th St.
New York, NY 10009
USA

Chimpanzee Productions
Visual Arts #0327,
9500 Gilman Dr.
La Jolla, CA 92093
USA
619 534-1307
619 534-8651

Chiu, Terry
720A 14th St.
San Francisco, CA 94114
USA
415 558-9710

Chocolate Fish Productions
15 Newell St.
Pt Chevalier
NEW ZEALAND
64 9 846-7990
64 9 373-4830

Cholodenko, Lisa
434 W 120th St., #8L
New York, NY 10027
USA
212 932-9234

Chowdhry, Maya
18 Vickers Rd.
Sheffield 55 6UZ
ENGLAND
44 1742 443013
44 1742 795225

Christensen Productions
230 E. 44th St., #14D

New York, NY 10017
USA
212 983-1142
212 692-9116

Christmas Pictures Ltd.
34 Curzon St.
London W1Y 7AE
ENGLAND 4
4 171 493-4656
44 171 491-1687

Christopher, Mark
434 Lafayette, #C-2
New York, NY 10003
USA
212 677-4245
212 677-4245

Church, John
53 Landers St., #2
San Francisco, CA 94114
USA
415 552-6252

Cinecom
1290 Avenue of the Americas,
42nd floor
New York, NY 10104
USA
212 830-9700

Cinema Esperanca International
96 Spadina Ave., #301
Toronto, Ontario M5V 2J6
CANADA
416 865-1225
416 865-9223

Cinema Guild
1697 Broadway, #506
New York, NY 10019
USA
212 246-5522
212 246-5525

Cinema Libre
4067 Blvd. Saint-Laurent,
Bureau 403
Montreal, Quebec H2W 1Y7
CANADA
514 849-7888
514 849-1231

Cinemaginaire
5505 Blvd. St. Laurent, #3005
Montreal, Quebec H2T 1S6
CANADA
514 272-5505
514 272-9841

Cinematherapy, Inc.
839 14th St.
San Francisco, CA 94114
USA
415 863-3999

Cinemien
Entrepotdok 66
Amsterdam 1018 AD
NETHERLANDS
31 20 27 95 01

Cinenova
13 Roman Rd.
London E2 OHU
ENGLAND
44 181 981-6828
44 181 983-4441

Cinephile Productions
POB 20479
Tompkins Square Station
New York, NY 10009
USA
212 777-2497
212 353-0250

Cinepix Inc.
8275 Mayrand
Montreal, Quebec H4P 2C8
CANADA
514 342-2340
514 342-1922

Cinevista
1680 Michigan Ave.
Miami Beach, FL 33139
305 532-3400
305 532-0047

Cipelletti, Claudio
Via Abano 7
Milano 20131
ITALY
39 2 266-4621
39 2 839-4604

City Heights Closet Case Show
P.O. Box 790
New York, NY 10108
USA

Clark, Kathy
2119 NE 14th St., #14
Portland, OR 97212
USA

Clarke, Kris
12C Colvestone Crescent
London E8 2LH
ENGLAND
44 171 923-4105

Clash Pictures
2407 1/2 West Silverlake Dr.
Los Angeles, CA 90039
USA

Clinica Estetico
127 W 24th St., 7th floor
New York, NY 10011
USA

212 807-6800
212 807-6830

Cole, Jeff
1 Gorfton House, Aytoun Rd.
London SW9 OTX
ENGLAND
44 171 326-4859
44 171 793-0849

Cole, Julian
39 Navarino Rd.
London E8 1AD
ENGLAND
44 171 249-1945
44 171 249-1945

Collins, David
46 Sproatt Ave.
Toronto, Ontario M4M 1WY
CANADA
416 461-2451
416 638-7819

Collins, Lisa
504 W 111th St., #43
New York, NY 10025
USA
212 866-1952

Comstock, William
515 E. 12th St., #7B
New YorkNY 10009
USA
212 861-9797
212 628-0698

Conboy, Teresa
PO Box 27766
Los Angeles, CA 90027
USA
213 660-7748
213 660-2529

Concrete Foundation, A
73 5th Ave., 7th Floor
New York, NY 10003
USA

Connie Boy Productions
80 S. Sixth St.
San Jose, CA 95112
USA

Conroy, Dennis
3143 22nd St.
San Francisco, CA 94110
USA
415 648-8190
415 282-7280

Constantinou, Sophie
131 Albion St., #5
San Francisco, CA 94110
USA
415 431-7203

Converse Pictures
Bon Marche Building
444 Brixton Rd.
London SW9 8EJ
ENGLAND

Cooper, Aaron
490 Post St.
San Francisco, CA 94102
USA
415 587-5669

Copi, Susannah
220 Center, #3
Santa Cruz, CA 95060
USA
408 459-8309

Coray, Tony
158 Downey St.
San Francisco, CA 94117
USA
415 753-1822

Cory, Bill
601 Q St. NW
Washington DC 20001
USA
202 387-8096

Corzine, Georgina
22 Chenery St.
San Francisco, CA 94131
USA
415 550-6335

Cowan, Jeff
728 Great Highway, #2
San Francisco, CA 94121
USA
415 386-2002
415 752-0300

Cowell, Laura
37 Gorevale Ave.
Toronto, Ontario M6J 2R5
CANADA
416 861-8595

Craig, Scott
2434 Silver Lake Dr.
Los Angeles, CA 90039
USA
213 665-2069
213 665-2711

Crazy Heart Films
5261 Miles Ave.
Oakland, CA 94618
USA
510 655-4043

Crows/Big Girl
25 Ormy St.
Tel Aviv 69016
ISRAEL

Cutrone, Christopher
510 W. Fullerton, #301
Chicago, IL 60614
USA
312 472-7754

Cypriano, Tania
110 Bridge St.
Brooklyn, NY 11201
USA
718 643-1489

Czechoslovak Filmexport
Vaclavske nam. 28,
111 45 Prague
CZECH REPUBLIC
42 2 236-5385

D'Auria, Mark/Ancestor Films
21 W 46th St., 9th Floor
New York, NY 10036
USA
212 944-8539

Da Da Kamera
700 Shaw St.
Toronto, Ontario M6G 3L7
CANADA
416 535-4345
416 593-1616

Dabek, Nina
51 Fairfield St., #2
Cambridge, MA 02145
USA
617 491-8644

Dailey, Tom
1714 Bryant St.
San Francisco, CA 94110
USA

Dangerous to Know
66 Offley Road,
Kennington Oval
London SW9
ENGLAND
44 171 735-8330
44 171 793-8488

Danish Film Institute
Store Sonderwoldstroede 4
Copenhagen DK-1419
DENMARK
45 1 57 65 00
45 1 57 67 00

Dar, Zahid
Ground Floor Flat,
72 Southborough Rd.
London E9 7EE
ENGLAND
44 181 986-5436
44 1753 540542

Daschbach, John
301 E. 21st
New York, NY 10010
USA
212 475-2356

Day, Dennis
PO Box 737, Station C
Toronto, Ontario M6J 351
CANADA
416 504-0275
416 365-3332

de la Riva, T. Osa Hidalgo
2429 13th Ave., #4
Oakland, CA 94606
USA
510 533-6938

Deafvision Filmworks Inc.
PO Box 1858
New York, NY 10026
USA
212 932-0861

Dean, Margo
2510 San Mateo St.
Richmond, CA 94804
USA
510 525-9310

Decent, Dean R.
1510A Jackson St.
San Francisco, CA 94109
USA

DeepFocus Productions
4506 Palmero Dr.
Los Angeles, CA 90065
USA
213 254-7773
213 254-7974

DEFA
Milastrasse 2
Berlin 1058
GERMANY
49 30 440 08 01

del Valle, Desi/Chula Pictures
471 1/2 Sanchez St.
San Francisco, CA 94114
USA
415 703-0685
415 861-1404

Democracy Media
PO Box 82777
Portland, OR 97282
USA
503 452-6500

Derry, Charles
Wright State University,
Theater Department
Dayton, OH 45406

USA
Desperate Pictures
740 S. Detroit St., #1
Los Angeles, CA 90036
USA
213 845-9613

Develpment Education Centre
229 College St.
Toronto, Ontario M5T 1R4
CANADA

Deville, Noski
c/o Media and Communications
86 Ryyerdale Rd.
London N16 6PL
ENGLAND
44 181 806-6012
44 181 694-8911

Diaz, Ramona S.
704 Campus Dr., #270
Stanford, CA 94305
USA
415 497-3967

DiFeliciantonio, Tina/Naked Eye
Productions
211 E. 17th St., #1
New York, NY 10003
USA
212 254-8045
212 254-7468

Tom di Maria
830 Hayes St., #306
San Francisco, CA 94117
415 861-8085

Dimpfl, Susanne /DFFB
Pommernallee 1,
Theodor Heuss Pl.
Berlin 14052
GERMANY
49 30 303 7252
49 30 301 9875

Direct Cinema
Box 10003
Santa Monica, CA 90410
USA

Donahue, Elizabeth
66 Bridge St.
Northampton, MA 01060
USA
413 585-0837

Dougherty, Cecilia
520 E. 14th St., #32
New York, NY 10009
USA
212 533-7565

Dovi, Lori
2215R Market St., #804

San Francisco, CA 94114
USA
415 252-1312

Downs, Randa
3850 Pleasant Beach Dr.
Bainridge Island, WA 98110
USA
206 842-0635

Drift Distribution
150 W. 22nd St., Floor 10, #3
New York, NY 10011
USA
212 741-8681

Drift Releasing
611 Broadway, #742
New York, NY 10012
USA
212 254-4118
212 254-3154

Drinkrow, Lars and Uren, Jurgen
"Boys Entrance"
8/11 Teesdale Close
London E2 6PQ
ENGLAND
44 171 729-6302
44 171 873-0051

DuBowski, Sandi
33 Exeter St.
Brooklyn, NY 11235
USA
718 891-6045

Duesing, James
1908 Mills Ave.
Cincinnati, OH 45212
USA

Dumas, Chris
336 9th St., 3rd Floor
Brooklyn, NY 11215
USA
718 369-3307
212 854-2325

Durrin Films
1748 Kalorama Rd. NW
Washington, DC 20009
USA

Dutch Film and TV Academy
Ite Boeremastraat 1
Amsterdam 1054 PP
NETHERLANDS
31 20 683 0206
31 20 612 6266

Dvoracek, Ted
3501 W. School
Chicago, IL 60618
USA
312 463-5376

Ebersole, P. David
1048 Manzanita
Los Angeles, CA 90029
USA
213 666-4911
213 666-4911

Ebert, Matt
1001 SW Klickitat Way, #200C
Seattle, WA 98134
USA
206 292-9661
206 292-9326

EBS Productions
360 Ritch St.
San Francisco, CA 94107
USA
415 495-2327
415 495-2381

Edition Manfred Salzgeber
Schlosstr. 29
Berlin 12163
GERMANY
49 30 793 4181
49 30 793 3888

Ehorn, Scott
2 Cottage Row
San Francisco, CA 94115
USA
415 929-1506

Eichorn, Christoph
Adalbertsrasse 94
Berlin 36
GERMANY
49 30 614-3446
49 30 614-3446

Eidetix
379 Ridge Rd.
San Carlos, CA 94070
USA
415 369-8524

Elbert, Lawrence
921 Robinson St.
Los Angeles, CA 90026
USA
213 368-9606

Electronic Arts Intermix
536 Broadway, 9th floor
New York, NY 10012
USA
212 966-4605
212 941-6118

Ellsworth, Robert
1125 N. Gardner St.
Los Angeles, CA 90046
USA
213 876-0419

Em Gee Film Library
6924 Canby Ave., #103
Reseda, CA 91335
USA
818 881-8110

Embrafilme
rua Mayrink Veiga 28
Rio de Janeiro CEP 20.090
BRAZIL
55 21 223 2171

Engleman, Dorothy
3005 Man St, #407
Santa Monica, CA 90405
USA
310 399-5068

Esteves, Roberto
34 Caselli St.
San Francisco, CA 94114
USA
415 621-7541

Everly, Bart
823 Palms Blvd.
Venice, CA 90291
USA
310 823-3770

Exportfilm Bischoff &Co.
Isabellastr. 20,
D-8000 Munich 40
GERMANY
89 55 55 16-19

FACSEA
972 Fifth Ave.
New York, NY 10021
USA
212 439-1439
212 439-1449

Fanlight Productions
47 Halifax St.
Boston, MA 02130
USA
617 524-0980
617 524-8838

Fantom Film
Stumpergasse 7/14
Vienna A-1060
AUSTRIA

Farallon Films
548 Fifth St.
San Francisco, CA 94107
USA
415 495-3934

Fatale Video
1537 4th St., #193
San Rafael, CA 94901
415 454-3291

Fearless Productions Inc.
P.O. Box 8928
Atlanta, GA 30306 - 9998
USA
404 897-5218
404 897-5565

Ferrera-Balanquet, Raul/Latino
Midwest Video Collective
2616 N. Mozart St., #2
Chicago, IL
60647-1740
USA

Film Cinematografica
Rue Casa do Ator 390
Sao Paulo
BRAZIL

Film Four International
124 Horseferry Rd.
London SW1P 2TX
ENGLAND
44 171 396-4444
44 171 306-8363

Filmmaker's Cooperative
175 Lexington Ave
New York, NY 10016
USA
212 889-3820
212 477-2714

Filmmaker's Library
133 East 58th St.
New York, NY 10022
USA
212 808-4980
212 808-4983

Films Incorporated
5547 N. Ravenswood Ave.
Chicago, IL 60640
USA
800 323-4222
312 878-8648

Films Transit
402 est, rue Notre-Dame
Montreal, Quebec H2Y 1C8
CANADA
514 844-3358
514 844-7298

Filmschool Munich
Isartalstr. 44
Munich 80469
GERMANY
49 89 762 051
49 89 680 004

Fine Line Features
888 Seventh Ave.
New York, NY 10106
USA
212 649-4803
212 956-1942

Finnish Film Archive
Box 177
Helsinki SF-00151
FINLAND
358 171 417
358 171 544

Finnish Film Foundation
Kanavakatu 12
Helsinki SF-00160
FINLAND
358 0 17 77 27
358 0 17 71 13

Fireball Films
10144 Tabor Ave., #210
Los Angeles, CA 90034
USA

First Floor Features
Bolderweg 22, 1332 AV
Postbus 30086
Almere 1303 AB
HOLLAND
31 36 532 7003
31 36 532 7940

First Look Pictures
8800 Sunset Blvd., #302
Los Angeles, CA 90069
USA
310 855-1199
310 855-0719

First Run Features
153 Waverly Pl.
New York, NY 10014
USA
212 243-0600
212 989-7649

Fisher, Lisa
2535 2nd Ave. S., #2
Minneapolis, MN 55404
USA
612 874-3519

Foiles, Stacey
3706 22nd St.
San Francisco, CA 94114
USA
415 826-1889

Foley, Elizabeth
423 W. 120th St., #61
New York, NY 10027
USA
212 222-4472
212 865-0309

Fontaine, Richard
P.O. Box 1515
Hanford CA 93230-1515
USA
209 582-4448

Fontenot, Heyd
1403 E. 34th St.
Austin, TX 78722
USA
512 476-7709

Fort God Hell Cat Productions
228 Ronalds St.
Iowa City, IA 52245
USA

Fox/Lorber
482 Park Ave. S.
New York, NY 10016
USA

Frameline
346 Ninth St.
San Francisco, CA 94103
USA
415 703-8650
415 861-1404
Frameline@aol.com

Frameline Archive
346 Ninth St.
San Francisco, CA 94103
USA
415 703-8650
415 861-1404
Frameline@aol.com

Franchini, Frankie
818 Garfield St.
San Francisco, CA 94132
USA
415 739-6281

Franklin Media Distribution
211 W Broadway #5C
New York, NY 10013
USA
212 274-8480

Frauen Film Produktion
Gustav Muller -Str. 17
Berlin 1000
GERMANY
49 30 782 60 04

Freelance Video Star Route
Redway, CA 95560
USA

Freeman, Marilyn c/o Olympia
Pictures
PO Box 341
Olympia, WA 98507-0341
USA
206 438-9502
206 438-9502

Friedman, Peter Bat.
Les Collines A1,
Chateau-Sec
Marseille 13009
FRANCE

Friedrich, Su
222 E. 5th St. #6
New York, NY 10003
USA
212 475-7186
212 529-5078

Frilot, Shari
16 Ocean Park W., #C21
Brooklyn, NY 11218
USA
718 851-8395
212 431-1783

Fritsch, Luc
2 rue l'Esperance
Brunoy 91800
FRANCE

Frontroom
79 Wardour St.
London W1V 3TH
ENGLAND
44 181 653-9343
44 181 653-9343

Fry, Katherine
48 Fife St.
Westmore
Auckland
NEW ZEALAND
64 9 376 4481
64 9 373 2772

Fulcrum Productions
254 Goswell Rd.
London
EC1 VEB
ENGLAND
44 171 253-0353
44 171 490-0206

Fullman, Katrina
139-A Albion St.
San Francisco, CA 94110
USA
415 552-4543

Furious Films
73 5th Avenue, 7th floor
New York, NY 10003
USA
212 255-3326
212 255-3502

Gaffney, Cynthia
1022 Eighth Ave.
Helena, MT 59601
USA
406 449-3197
406 449-3197

Gaffney, Stuart
520 Shrader St., #3
San Francisco, CA 94117
USA

415 386-6710
415 399-3041

GANG c/o Mcalpin, Loring
39 Great Jones St., #7
New York, NY 10012
USA
212 598-4872
212 598-4872

Gant, Ella
3835 Griffin Rd.
Clinton, NY 13323
USA
315 853-6745

Garey, Melinda
26119 Bella Santa Dr.
Valencia, CA 91355
USA

Gaulke, Cheri
1336 N. Occidental Blvd.
Los Angeles, CA 90026
USA
213 662-3940

Gauthier, Paula
3653 Curlew St.
San Diego, CA 92103
USA
619 683-2754

Gay Men's Health Crisis
129 W 20th St.
New York, NY 10011 USA
212 807-7517
212 807-7036

Gee, Daven
4096 18th St., #35
San Francisco, CA 94114
USA
415 255-7844

Gelke, Hans
396 Connecticut St.
San Francisco, CA 94107
USA
415 550-6980
415 550-6980

George Eastman House
900 East Ave.
Rochester, NY 14607
USA
716 271-3361
716 271-3970

Giannaris, Constantine
29 Lorraine Rd.
London N7 6HB
ENGLAND

Gignac, Paula
305-54 Maitland St.

Toronto, Ontario N4Y 1C5
CANADA
416 928-2000
416 928-2000

Gilerman, Svetlana
24/112 Hall St.
Bondi, NSW 2026
AUSTRALIA
61 2 365-2315

Giorgio, Grace
307 Valencia St., #201
San Francisco, CA 94103
USA
415 255-7945

Girls In The Nose
P.O. Box 49828
Austin, TX 78765
USA
512 477-3134

GIV
3575 Blvd.. St-Laurent, Bureau
421
Montreal, Quebec H2X 2T7
CANADA
514 499-9840

GLAAD/SFBA
1360 Mission St., #200
San Francisco, CA 94103
USA
415 861-4588
415 861-4893

Glazier, Alison
4837 17th St.
San Francisco, CA 94117
USA
415 641-4848
415 641-5245

Gohman, Goo
1231 Navellier
El Cerrito, CA 94530
USA

Goldberg, Neil
95 E. 7th St., #19
New York, NY 10009
USA
212 982-6861

Golden, Anne
1965 Main St.
Vancouver, British Columbia V5T
3C1
CANADA
604 872-8449
604 876-1185

Gomez, Gabriel
512 W. Cornelia St., #101

Chicago, IL 60657
USA
312 404-7364

Gonzalez, Mari Keiko
122 Bond St.
Brooklyn, NY
USA
718 855-3461
212 251-8606

Goodman, Craig
3214-B Mission St.
San Francisco, CA 94110
USA
415 641-8278

Goodnight, Kate
441 Lincoln Way
San Francisco, CA 94122
USA

Goralsky, Michal
4674 A 18th St.
San Francisco, CA 94114
USA
415 621-4286

Gosney, Kristin
746 14th St., #1
San Francisco, CA 94114
USA
415 431-9787

Goss, John C.
1022 Keniston
Los Angeles, CA 90019
USA
213 938-9526

Governi, Valerio
Via Pontida 5
Milano 20121
ITALY
39 2 655 1318

Granada TV
Quam Street
Manchester M60 9EA
ENGLAND
44 161 832-7211

Grandell, Steve
212 N. 3rd Ave., #8
Minneapolis, MN 55401
USA
612 339-8342

Gray, Donna
135 Eastern Parkway, #15-I
Brooklyn, NY 11238
USA
718 622-9501

Great North Releasing
#012, 11523 - 100 Ave.

Edmonton, Alberta T5K OJ8
CANADA
403 482-2022
403 482-3036

Greek Film Centre
10 Panepistimiou Ave.
Athens, 106 71
GREECE
30 1 363 1733

Greenall, David
17 Haven St.,
Burnley, Lancashire BB10 4DQ
ENGLAND
44 181 282-3709

Grotell, David
315 E. 65th St.
New York, NY 10021
USA
212 249-8915

Group 1
9230 Robin Dr.
Los Angeles, CA 90069-1126
USA
310 550-7280
310 550-0830

Growing Up Productions
8721 Santa Monica Blvd., #208
West Hollywood, CA 90069
USA

Gundlach, Daniel
650A Guerrero St.
San Francisco, CA 94110 USA
415 431-7761
415 431-7761

Guy, Steve
312 Fillmore St., #1
San Francisco, CA 94117
USA
415 552-3896

Haeberli, Eric
1671 McAllister
San Francisco, CA 94115
USA
415 563-5036

Hammer, Barbara
55 Bethune St., #114G
New York, NY 10014
USA
212 645-9077
212 645-9077
BJHammer@aol.com

Handelman, Michelle
P.O. Box 170415
San Francisco, CA 94117
USA
510 245-1709
510 245-1709

Hands On Productions
633 Post Street, #500
San Francisco, CA 94109
USA

Hanlon, Terri
10 Beach St.
New York, NY 10013
USA

Hanno Baethe Video Production
Seelingstr. 14,
1000 Berlin 19
GERMANY

Harcourt Films
58 Camden Sq.
London NW1 9XE
ENGLAND

Harrison, James
492 Sunset Dr.
Asheville, NC 28804
USA
704 254-9938
704 253-3055

Harrison, Richard L.
725 Ste-Marguerite
Montreal, Quebec H4C 2X5
CANADA
514 932-4359

Hayes, Matt
Basement Flat,
65 Pemroke Rd.,
Ballsbridge, Dublin
IRELAND

Hayn, Stefan
Yorkstrasse 59
Berlin D-1000, 61
GERMANY
49 30 707 45 56
49 30 786 79 23

Hengst, Clifford
3264 17th St.
San Francisco, CA 94110
USA
415 552-1165

Hennessey, Halle and Willging,
Chris
2208 SE Ankeny
Portland, OR 97214
USA

Henszelman, Stefan
Mollegrade 38 3th
2200 Copenhagen
DENMARK
Herald Ace
5-11-1 Ginza, Chuo-ku
Tokyo 104
JAPAN

81 3 3248 1151
81 3 3248 1170

Herbert, Rachel
28A Cumberland St.
San Francisco, CA 94110
USA
415 824-6016

Hershey, Ann
4084 Lambert Rd.
El Sobrante, CA 94803
USA
510 222-6931
510 526-7234

Hetherman, Margaret
165 Garfield Place
Brooklyn, NY 11215
USA
718 369-3369
718 369-3369

HFF Munchen
Kesselbergstr. 14
Munich 81539
GERMANY
49 89 691-7737
49 89 680-0447

Hick, Jochen
332 Bleecker St., #P12
New York, NY 10014-2980
USA
212 228-7038
212 969-028

Hickson, Michelle
48B Montague Rd.
London E8 2HW
ENGLAND
44 171 275-7276
44 171 277-7303

Hildebran, Gretchen
1807 Market St.
San Francisco, CA 94103
USA
415 861-1293

Hill, Brent
P.O. Box 7926
Philadelphia, PA 19101
USA
215 472-7763
215 474-2931

Hill, Tom/Queer Action Figures
348 E. 9th St.
New York, NY 10003
USA
212 260-4622
Hindley, Emma
54A Glenarm Rd.
London E5 0LZ
ENGLAND

44 181 533-4350

Hirshorn, Harriet
20 Clinton St., #3E
New York, NY 10002
USA
212 343-9337
212 343-9336

Hoff, Robert
522 E. 5th St., #8
New York, NY 10009
USA
212 674-8381

Holdschmidt, Angela
Otto Karsh 15
Berlin 12105
GERMANY
49 30 751-9895
49 30 755-8210

Holland Film Promotion
Jan Luykenstraat 2
Amsterdam 1071 CM
NETHERLANDS
31 20 66 44 649
31 20 66 49 171

Hollibaugh, Amber
129 W. 20th St.
New York, NY 10011-0022
USA
212 337-3532

Hourglass Productions
6022 Wilshire Blvd., #201
Los Angeles, CA 90036
USA
213 656-3284
310 271-9632

House, Carrie H.
Box 945
St. Micheal, AZ 06511
USA

House O' Chicks
2215 R Market St., #813
San Francisco, CA 94114
USA
415 861-9849

House of Pain Production
130 W. Houston St., #2
New York, NY 10012
USA
212 982-3195
212 979-8786

Howe, Alyssa Cymene
66 Landers St.
San Francisco, CA 94114
USA
415 861-4168

Hoyt, Dale
650 Webster St.
San Francisco, CA 94117
USA
415 431-5329
415 864-2363

Hubbard, Jim
301 Cathedral Parkway #15A
New York, NY 10026
USA
212 865-1499

Humphrey, Daniel
3520 18th St., #2
San Francisco, CA 94110
USA
415 552-6019

Hungarofilm
Bathori utca 10
Budapest H-1054
HUNGARY
36 1 112-5425
36 1 153-1850

Hyanefilm
Geschw.-Scholl-Strasse 39,
Hamburg D-2000
GERMANY

Iberoamerica Films
RTVA-Peron,
40-D-Primero
Madrid 28020
SPAIN
34 1 581 7100
34 1 581 7125

ICA Projects
The Mall
London SW1Y 5AH
ENGLAND
44 171 930-0493
44 171 873-0051

Igelfilm GmbH
Filmhaus,
Friedensallee 7
Hamburg D 2000
GERMANY
49 40 390-2403

IKON Creative Pictures
3760 S. Robertson Blvd., #202
Culver City, CA 90232
USA
310 204-5711
310 204-4862

Image Forum, Tokyo
Fudosan,
Kaikan Bldg., 1,
6F 3-5, Yotsuya,
Shinjuku-ku Tokyo
JAPAN

81 3 3 3357 8023
81 3 3 3359 7532

Images en Stock
6331 St-Dominique
Montreal, Quebec H2S 3A6
CANADA
514 276-1803

Independent Television Service
190 E. 5th St., #200
St. Paul, MN 55101
USA
612 225-9035
612 225-9102

Instituto Mexicano de
Departamento de Eventos
Tepic No. 40
Col Roma Sur
D.F. C.P. 06760
MEXICO
52 584 72 83
52 564 41 87

Interama, Inc.
301 W. 53rd St., #19E
New York, NY 10019
USA
212 977-4830

Intercinema Agency
15 Druzhinnikivskaya St.
Moscow 123242
RUSSIA
7 095 255 9052
7 095 973 2029

International Film Circuit
P.O. Box 1151,
Old Chelsea Station
New York, NY 10011
USA
212 779-0660
212 779-9129

International Gay & Lesbian
Human Rights Commission
1360 Mission St., #200
San Francisco, CA 94103
USA
415 255-8680
415 255-8662
iglhrc@igc.apc.org

International Home Cinema
215 Broadway
Santa Monica, CA
USA
310 396-9898
310 396-9808

Interpictures
360 E. 65th St.
New York, NY 10021
USA

Intrepid Productions
8265 Sunset Blvd., #204
Los Angeles, CA 90046
USA
213 656-5472
213 654-0863

IRS Releasing
3520 Hayden Av
Los Angeles, CA 90232
USA
310 841-7402
310 838-7402

Ishtar Films
13564 Erwin St.
Van Nuys, CA 91401
USA
800 428-7136
818 781-1159

Jabaily, Barbara/KBDI-TV
1531 Stout St.
Denver CO 80202
USA

Jane Balfour Films
Burghley House,
35 Fortress Rd.
London NW5 1AD
ENGLAND
44 171 267-5392
44 171 267-4241

JBH Wadia/Wadia Movietone
First Floor,
Ballard House,
ADI Marazaban Path
Bombay 400038
INDIA
91 22 2619586
91 22 2626430

JEF/Film Classic Exchange
143 Hickory Hill Circle
Osterville, MA 02655
USA
508 428-7198

Jenkins, Henry/Massachusetts
Institute of Technology
617 253-3068
617 253-6105

Jezebel Productions
PO Box 1348
New York, NY 10011
USA
212 463-0578
212 535-5943

Johns, Jennifer
915 N. Westridge Dr., #1
Carbondale, IL 62901
USA
618 457-5803

Johnson, David E.
2211 Mission St., #C
San Francisco, CA 94110
USA
415 648-8190

Jones, Stephen
21 Smith St.
Fitzroy 3065
AUSTRALIA
61 2 419 8377
61 2 417 4472

Joritz, Cathy
Sternstr. 42
Dortmund D-4600
GERMANY

Jortner, Michael
391 San Jose Ave.
San Francisco, CA 94110
USA
415 647-5955

Jubela, Joan
P.O. Box 1966
New York, NY 10013
USA
212 219-1025

Jurgen Bruning Filmproduktion
Willmanndamm 12
Berlin 10827
GERMANY
49 30 782 8702
49 30 782 9760

Karpinski, Barbara
4/42 Cliffbrook Pde.
Clovelly, NSW 2031
AUSTRALIA
61 2 315 7587

Kates, Nancy
590 6th Ave.
Menlo Park, CA 94025
USA

Katsapetses, Nicholas
1714 Clay St., #6
San Francisco, CA 94109
USA
415 749-0966

Kaufman, Jennifer
125 S. Mansfield Ave.
Los Angeles, CA 90036
USA
213 939-5986

KD Productions
8 rue de la Chine
Paris 75020
FRANCE
33 1 42 71 69 45

Kehr, Walter
1800 Silverlake Blvd., #E
Los Angeles, CA 90026
USA
213 660-8025
213 271-7908

Keitel, John
8233 W First St., #2
Los Angeles, CA 90048
USA
213 653-0288

Keller, H. Len
P.O. Box 460295
San Francisco, CA 94146
USA
415 487-6290

Kelly, Alison
153 Norfolk St., #3E
New York, NY 10002
USA
212 228-3251

Kelly, Joe
58 E. 3rd St.
New York, NY 10003
USA
212 529-3821

Kendrick, Dean
534 E. North Ave.
Lake Bluff, IL 60044
USA
708 295-7837

Kidel, Mark
16 Sydenham Rd.,
Cotham
Bristol BS6 5SH
ENGLAND
44 1272 232026
44 1272 423256

Kijak, Stephen
1706 Fulton St.
San Francisco, CA 94117
USA
415 441-2484

Kim, Ingin
1932 Selby Ave., #402
Los Angeles, CA 90025
USA
310 474-8982

Kinesis Films
16 Colville Place
London W1
ENGLAND
Kino International
333 W. 39th St., #503
New York, NY 10018
USA
212 629-6880
212 714-0871

Kit Parker Films
1245 Tenth St.
Monterey, CA 93940
USA
408 393-0303
408 393-0304

Kitchen, The
512 W. 19th St.
New York, NY 10011
USA
212 255-5793
212 645-4258

Kllc, Aaron
215 Aldine St.
Rochester, NY 14619
USA
716 328-6531

Klymkiw, Greg
164 Bellwoods Av
Toronto, Ontario M6J 2P4
CANADA
416 603-9212
416 603-9444

Kot, Hagar
12 Arba-Artzot St.
Tel Aviv
ISRAEL

Kuchar, George
3434-A 19th St.
San Francisco, CA 94110
USA
415 431-8110

Kuchinskas, Susan
3016 Filbert #10
Oakland, CA 94608
USA

Kunja, Alexander
c/o Schuren,
Thierschstr. 40,
80538 Munchen
GERMANY
49 89 29 58 50

KVPI
625 Broadway, #7B
New York, NY 10012
USA
212 473-3950
212 473-6152

Kydd, Elspeth
3511 N. Reta
Chicago, IL 60657
USA
312 404-7364

L.C.P.D.T. Film and Video Dept.
10 Black Hill
London EC1R 5EN

ENGLAND
44 171 735-8484 ext. 172
44 171 833-8842

Laboratory for Icon and Idiom
135 Hudson St.
New York, NY 10013
USA
212 226-2462
212 226-2462

Lagestee Film BV
Haarlemmer Houttuinen 307
Amsterdam 1013 GM
NETHERLANDS
31 20 627 33 73
31 20 626 10 49

Lamble, David
2270 Market St.
San Franciso, CA 94114
USA
415 861-2996

Lance, Dean
1272 E. 56th St.
Brooklyn, NY 11234
USA
718 251-1240

Lang, Charley
848 Hilldale Ave.
Los Angeles, CA 90069
USA
310 657-0177

Lasbisch TV
c/o FAB
Nollendorfplatz 5,
1000 Berlin 30
GERMANY
49 30 216 77 07

Latino AIDS Project
2639 24th St.
San Francisco, CA 94110
USA
415 647-5450

Lawrence, Jacquie
Crack House,
1 Pink Lane
New Castle Upon Tyne NE1 5DW
ENGLAND
44 191 230-2585
44 191 230-4484

Lawson, Greg
Korte Leidsedwarsstraat 12
Amsterdam 1017 RC
NETHERLANDS
31 20 625 3197
31 20 620 6804

Leban, Lexi
120 Lundys Lane

San Francisco, CA 94110
USA
415 824-4330

Lebow, Alisa
320 1st Ave., #2E
New York, NY 10009
USA
212 673-6791

Leder, Evie
199 Riverside Drive
Northampton, MA 01060
USA
413 586-9012
413 582-5438

Lee, Karen
4738-1 Twining St.
Los Angeles, CA 90032
USA

Lee, Quentin
840 S. Serrano Ave. #608
Los Angeles, CA 90005
USA
213 654-0343

Leech, Marla
PO Box 460542
San Francisco, CA 94146
USA
415 281-0547

Lefkowitz, Karen
902 S. 48th St.
Philadelphia, PA 19143
USA
215 724-6548

Legler/Bashore Productions
Box 2285
Venice, CA 90294
USA
310 396-3600
310 396-5065

Leonor Films
8 rue Lincoln
Paris 75008
FRANCE
33 1 4225-8420
33 1 4225-6752

Les Films du Labyrinthe
15 rue Marcel Allegot
Meudon-Bellevue 92190
FRANCE

Lesbian and Gay Parents
Association
969 Hayes St., #4
San Francisco, CA 94117
USA

Library of Congress

Capitol Hill
Washington, DC 20540-1000
USA
202 707-5000

Light Box
2303 West 11th St.
Austin, TX 78703
USA
512 472-7465
512 472-7465

Light, Lauri
550 14th St., #203
San Francisco, CA 94103
USA
415 626-1746

Limelight
3 Bromley Place
London W1P 5HB
ENGLAND
44 171 255-3939
44 171 436-4334

Link, Matthew
1190 Adams St.,#C
Redwood City, CA 94061
USA
415 365-6245

Little Turk Films
P.O. Box 480475 Los Angeles,
CA 90048
USA
213 653-3187

Lofton, Charles
P.O. Box 2463
San Francisco, CA 94126
USA
415 995-4907

Logsdon, Dawn
430 Andover St.
San Francisco, CA 94110
USA
415 647-4754

London Film Makers Co-op
42 Gloucester Av.
London NW1
ENGLAND
44 171 586-4806
44 171 483-0068

London International Film
School
24 Shelton St.,
Covent Garden
London WC2H 9HP
ENGLAND
44 171 836-9642
44 171 497-3718

Lowy, Peter

P. O. Box 010-084,
St. George Station
Staten Island, NY 10301
USA
718 273-8829

Lunger, Jeff
259 W 15th St., #1D
New York, NY 10011
USA
212 243-3623

Lux, Billy
155 W. 15th St., #2A
New York, NY 10011
USA
212 989-5355

M & M Productions
POB 170415
San Franciso, CA 94117 USA
510 533-6474

Ma, Ming-Yuen S.
1530 N. Myra Ave.
Los Angeles, CA 90027
USA
213 666-5157
213 666-5157

MacDonald, Becky
899 Capp St., #3
San Francisco, CA 94110
USA
415 824-0119

MacLean, David
253 College St.,
Box 205
Toronto, Ontario M5T 1R5
CANADA

Maggenti, Maria/Smash Pictures
337 E. Tenth St., #3E
New York, NY 10009
USA
212 674-6520
212 995-4063

Mai Kiang/Artistic License Films
444 Park Av S, 3rd floor
New York, NY 10016
USA
212 779-0347
212 696-9546
artlic@aol.com

Mak, Anson
Flat A 13/F No 4,
Broadway Mei Foo Sun Chuen,
Kowloon, Hong Kong
TAIWAN
85 2 574 5660

Malkames, Marlise
2243 28th St., #D

Santa Monica, CA 90405
USA
301 396-7524

Mann, Shakila
2A Battishill St.
London N1 1TE
ENGLAND
44 171 359-1676

Manning, Caitlin
1243 Potrero Ave.
San Francisco, CA 94110
USA
415 641-5529
415 626-2685

Marcolina, Kirk
355 S. Cochran Ave., #201
Los Angeles, CA 90036
USA
213 934-5405
213 934-5405

Marnell, Lily
233 East 3rd St. #2C
New York, NY 10009
USA
212 475-4382

Marshall, Bertie
Fregeul,
44660 Rouge
Loire Atlantique
FRANCE

Martin, Carter
3169 Ripley Street
Lake Station, IN 46405
USA
312 784-1310

Marzi, Giampaolo
Via Cicco Simonetta 17
Milan 20123
ITALY
39 2 581-6204
39 2 551-6558

Mass Productions   #3
Hayes Court, Camberwell New
Road
London SE5 0TQ
ENGLAND
44 171 708-1716

Maxwell, Peter Edward
4 Bucareli Dr.
San Francisco, CA 94132
USA
415 333-7338
415 333-9610

Maya Vision
43 New Oxford St.
London WC1A 1BH

ENGLAND
44 171 836-1113
44 171 836-5169

McDowell, Peter
233 Hartford St.
San Francisco, CA 94114
USA
415 621-0634
415 978-9635

McMahon, Jeff
512 E. 11th St., #4B
New York, NY 10009
USA

McMurchy, Megan/Suitcase
Films
2 Buckland St., Top Floor
Chippendale NSW 2008
AUSTRALIA
61 2 211-2022
61 2 212-2350

Mead, Rebecca
Flat 7 - 112 Toorak Road West
South Yarra, Victoria 3141
AUSTRALIA
61 3 287-1200
61 3 344-1111

Mears, Ric
80 Ora Way, #303
San Francisco, CA 94131
USA
72772.1733@compuserve.com

Memory Lane
4004 N. Kenmore, #3S
Chicago, IL 60613
USA
312 404-6552

Mendías, Joel Román
400 N Genessee Ave.
Los Angeles, CA 90036
USA
213 652-1704
310 305-8576

Metcalf, Charlotte
34-38 Westbourne Rd. Grove
London W2 5SH
ENGLAND

Midbar Films
175 5th Ave., #2582
New York, NY 10010
USA
212 889-1704
Mikesch, Elfi
Gr. Bergstrasse 142,
2000 Hamburg 50
GERMANY
49 30 262-6492
49 39 215-2871

Miller, Tanya
31 Coso
San Francisco, CA 94110
USA
415 627-3127
415 627-3122

Miller-Monzon, John
200 E 15th St., #18H
New York, NY 10003
USA
718 599-9806
212 529-3330

Milstead, J.D. Salome
949 Fell St., #1
San Francisco, CA 94117
USA
415 255-4564

Minerba, Giovanni
Via T. Tasso 11
Torino 10122
ITALY
39 11 436-6855
39 11 521-3737

Minnesota AIDS Project
2025 Nicollet Ave. S.
Minneapolis, MN 55404
USA
612 341-2060

Miramax Films
375 Greenwich St.
New York, NY 10013
USA
212 941-3800
212 941-3949

MIX Brasil
av. Pedrosa de Morais, 89 cj. 5
Sao Paulo SP 05420-000
BRAZIL
55 11 211-4628

Mobley, Doug
326 Coleridge
San Francisco, CA 94110
USA
415 285-7129

Monozygote Productions
1050 University Ave., #103-310
San Diego, CA 92103
USA
619 337-0665

Montgomery, Jennifer
520 E. 14th St., #32
New York, NY 10009
USA
212 533-7565

Moore, David
26 St Mark's Pl., #5RE
New York, NY 10003
USA
212 254-4361

Moret, Alfonso
1321 San Bruno Ave.
San Francisco, CA 94110
USA
415 282-9028
415 648-4932

Morgan, Benjamin Jeremiah
3800 Cottonwood Dr.
Blackhawk, CA 94506
USA
510 736-1524

Morgan Creek Records
1875 Century Park East
Los Angeles, CA 90067
USA

Morgana, Aimee
132 Broadway
Brooklyn, NY 11211
USA
718 599-3860

Moriyasu, Ann Akiko
1833 Vancouver Place
Honolulu, HI 96822
USA
808 941-7801

Moser, Abby
138 Ludlow St., #25
New York, NY 10002
USA
212 677-5014

Mossanen, Moze
181 First Ave.
Toronto, Ontario M4M 1X3
CANADA
416 461-6717

Mosvold, Frank
8745 Delgany Ave., #104
Playa del Ray, CA 90293
USA
310 822-0130
310 822-0130

Motyl, H.D.
1633 W. Fargo
Chicago, IL 60626
USA
312 465-5305

Moving Images Distribution
402 W Pender St., #606
Vancouver, British Columbia V6B
1T6
CANADA
604 684-3014
604 684-7165

Muckerman, Ed
1704 20th St.
San Francisco, CA 94107
USA
415 641-1488

Mueller, Matthias
August-Bebel Strasse 104
Bielefeld D-4800
GERMANY
49 521 178363
49 521 178367

Multi Focus
1525 Franklin St.
San Francisco, CA 94109
USA
415 673-5100

Multicultural Prevention
Resource Center
1540 Market St., #320
San Francisco, CA 94102
USA

Multimedia Home Entertainment
Grosvenor House,
25 Boroughsfields,
Wooton Bassett
Swinton Mills SN4 7AX
ENGLAND
44 1793 854 949
44 1793 853 854

Murray, Alison/ARGUS
Boerenstraat 60
Brussels B-U040
BELGIUM
32 2 732 7687

Museo Contempo
419 S. Van Ness Av
San Francisco, CA 94103
USA
415 864-5453

Museum of Modern Art
11 W. 53rd St.
New York, NY 10019
USA
212 708-9530
212 708-9531

Myles, Eileen
86 E. 3rd St.
New York, NY 10009
USA
212 982-4703
Nadel, Arl Spencer
528 41st St.
Oakland, CA 94609
USA

Nagel, Marga
Stuhlmannstr. 5,
2000 Hamburg 50
GERMANY

Nakata, Toichi
9 Crossfield Rd.
London NW3 4NS
ENGLAND
44 171 483-1168

Naked Eye Cinema
POB 20260,
Tompkins Square Station
New York, NY 10009
USA
212 529-8815
212 353-0250

National Archives
8601 Adelphi Rd.
College Park, MD
USA
301 713-6800

National Film Board of Canada
1251 Avenue of the Americas
New York, NY 10020
USA
212 596-1770
212 596-1779

NBD Picture Ltd.
Remo House,
310-312 Regent Street
London W1R 5AJ
ENGLAND
44 171 499-9701
44 171 493-9587

Netherlands Information Service
NIS/RVD
Anna Paulownastraat 76
The Hague 2518 BJ
NETHERLANDS
31 70 356-4205
31 70 356-4681

Netherlands Ministry of Culture
P.O. Box 5406
Rijswijk 2280 HK
NETHERLANDS

New Line Cinema
575 8th Ave.
New York, NY 10018
USA

New Yorker Films
16 West 61st St.
New York, NY 10023
USA
212 247-6110

New Zealand Film Commission
1/2 Masons Ave.
Herne Bay, Auckland
NEW ZEALAND
64 9 360 2185
64 4 385 9754

Nguyen, Hoang Tan
1000 Physical Science Rd. B-6,
University of California
Irvine, CA 92717
USA
714 856-0541

Nicali Productions
3238 16th St., #C
San Francisco, CA 94103
USA
415 627-3127
415 627-3122

Nicoletta, Daniel
1493 20th Ave.
San Francisco, CA 94122
USA
415 665-5930

Nix, Laura
3570 18th St.
San Francisco, CA 94110
USA
415 552-5207

Nolan, Monica
3347 20th St.
San Francisco, CA 94110
USA
415 550-7412

Norsk Film A/S
PO Box 4
Jar N-1342
NORWAY
47 12 10 70
47 12 51 08

Northern Arts Entertainment
Northern Arts Studios
Williamsburg, MA 01096
USA
413 268-9301

Nurudin, Azian
PO Box 460376
San Francisco, CA 94146-0376
USA
415 586-9849
415 777-3088

O'Haver, Tommy
547 Venice Way
Venice, CA 90291
USA
310 301-4994

O'Shea, John
1839 Lucille Ave.
Los Angeles, CA 90026
USA
213 666-7857

Oberhausen Film Distribution
Christian Steger Strasse 10
Oberhausen 46042
GERMANY

49 208 807008
49 208 852691

October Films
65 Bleecker St.
New York, NY 10012
USA
800 628-6237
212 539-4099

ODN Productions
74 Varick St., #304
New York, NY 10013
USA

Off White Productions Inc.
212 969-8952

Olavarria, Juliette
121 E 12th St., #4H
New York, NY 10003
USA
212 982-2925

Olivé-Bellés, Núria
531 Main St., #1310
New York, NY 10044
USA
212 593-1054
212 727-3705

Oliver, Bill
265 Lafayette St., #A3
New York, NY 10012
USA
212 274-8939

Olivier, Felix
100 Hudson St., #2C
New York, NY 10013
USA
212 343-9763

Olson, Jenni
2978 Folsom St.
San Francisco, CA 94114
USA
415 285-2950
Jimbolnk@aol.com

Omni Productions
1117 Virginia St. E.
Charleston, WV 25301
USA

Once & Future Film Inc.
RR2 S-7, C-17
562 Cypress Place
Gibsons, British Columbia VON
1V0
CANADA
604 886-4209
604 886-4259

Oriental Films Ltd.
2025 W. Chestnut St.

Alhambra, CA 91803
USA

Orion Classics
711 Fifth Ave.
New York, NY 10022
USA
212 956-3800

Orr, Joe
12 Deloraine House,
Tanners Hill
London SE8 4PY
ENGLAND
44 181 694-1376

Osburg, Barbara
416 Sherwood Dr., #302
Sausalito, CA 94965
USA
415 331-4468

Oshiro, Resa
54 Rose #4
Venice, CA 90291
USA
310 396-7138
310 392-2021

Otterbach, Carolin
Nibelungenstrasse 24
Munich 80639
GERMANY
49 89 167 9964

Outsider Enterprises
2940 16th St., #200-1
San Francisco, CA 94103
USA
415 863-0611
415 863-0611

Paci, Myra
448 W. 37th Street #13B
New York, NY 10018
USA
212 629-5521

Pacific Film Archive
2625 Durant Av
Berkeley, CA 94720
USA
510 642-1412
510 642-4889

Paik, Esther Koohan
2348 Franklin
San Francisco, CA 94123
USA

Pandora Pictures Inc.
65 Northcote Ave.
Toronto, Ontario M6J 3K2
CANADA
416 534-3575
416 534-2309

Pansy Division
PO Box 460885
San Francisco, CA 94146-0885
USA
415 824-1615
415 206-0854

Parmar, Pratibha
78 Fonthill Rd.
London N4 3HT
ENGLAND
44 171 281-1310
44 171 281-3809

Patierno, Mary
20 Clinton St., #3E
New York, NY 10002
USA
212 343-9337
212 343-9336

Patten, Mary
1210 West Roscoe, #1E
Chicago, IL 60657
USA
312 871-6640

Pau, Ellen
22/F Flat E Block 1,
Chi Fu Fa Yuen, Pokfulam
HONG KONG
85 2 838 7527

Paull, Craig
66 Avenue A, #3I
New York, NY 10009
USA
212 473-4698
212 475-1148

Pearl Films
46 Ridgevale Dr.
Toronto, Ontario M6A 1L1
CANADA
416 784-0926

Pearl, Heather
546 Wisconsin St.
San Francisco, CA 94107
USA
415 206-9365
415 431-1456

Pearlstein, Feme
647 Montgomery School Lane
Wynwood, PA 19096
USA
215 664-9730

Peloso, Larry
1840 Bathurst St., #305
Toronto, Ontario M5P 3K7
CANADA
416 781-8870
416 785-0745

Persona Video
Box 14022
San Francisco, CA 94114-0022
USA
415 775-6143

Persuasion Productions
111A Cypress St.
San Francisco, CA 94110
USA
415 995-4667

Perzely, Mark
846 Commonwealth Ave.
Venice, CA 90291
USA
310 452-4272
310 452-4272

Petersen, Inka
Rosenhofstrasse 11,
2000 Hamburg 36
GERMANY
49 40 439 6802

PIA Corp.
5-19 Sanban-cho,
Chiyoda-ku
Tokyo 102
JAPAN
81 3 3265 1425
81 3 3265 5659

Picture Start
c/o Film Library
22-D Hollywood Ave.
Ho-Ho-Kus, NJ 07423
USA
800 343-5540
201 652-1973

Pig's Eye Productions
301 Cathedral Parkway #15A
New York, NY 10026
USA
212 865-1499
212 477-2714

Pike, Pamela
2491 Agricola St.
Halifax, Nova Scotia B3K 4C3
CANADA

Piranha Productions
United House, North Road
London N7 9DP
ENGLAND
44 171 607 3355
44 171 607 9980

Planet Eye Productions
2336 Market Street #28
San Francisco, CA 94114
USA
415 431-3691

Please Louise Productions
419 S. Van Ness Av
San Francisco, CA 94110
USA
415 864-5453

Plendl, Mat
6242 W. 6th St.
Los Angeles, CA 90048
USA
213 935-1923
213 874-3078

Poirier, Paris
32A Horizon Ave.
Venice, CA 90291
USA
310 392-1239

Polari Productions Ltd.
56-58 Clerkenwell Rd.
London EC1M 5PX
ENGLAND
44 171 250-1989
44 171 250-1985

PolygGram Film International
Oxford House, 76 Oxford St.
London W1N OHQ
ENGLAND
44 171 307-1300
44 171 307-1301

Porter, Andrew
118 Victoria St.,
Fitzroy
Melbourne,Victoria 3065
AUSTRALIA
61 3 419 8258

Press, Richard
50 Greenwich Ave.
New York City, NY 10011
USA
212 989-9297

Price, David A.
1224 N. Mansfield Ave., #5
Los Angeles, CA 90038
USA
213 962-2572

Pro Helvetia
Hirschengraben 22
Zurich CH-8024
SWITZERLAND
41 1 251 96 00
41 1 251 96 06

Production Pictures
337 W. 21st St. #5D
New York, NY 10011
USA
212 645-0658
212 645-0220

Project 1993 Productions
9175 Hammock Lake Dr.
Miami, FL 33156
USA
305 667-7346
305 667-7346

Prokopiuk, Cesary
22/52 Darling Point Rd.
Darling Point, NSW 2027
AUSTRALIA
61 2 327 8120
61 2 327 4361

Public Eye, Inc., The
P.O. Box 640402
San Francisco, CA 94164
USA

Pussy Tourette
584 Castro St. # 260
San Francisco, CA 94114
USA
415 648-8869

Pyewackett Productions
1312 N. Stanley Ave.
Los Angeles, CA 90046
USA
213 850-0206

Queer Shock Productions
1426 Waller St., #4
San Francisco, CA 94117
USA
415 578-3796

Rabarts, Marten
Retiefstraat 17 (11 Hoog)
Amsterdam 1092 W
NETHERLANDS
31 20 663-5626
31 20 612-4766

Rajski, Peggy
140 Riverside Dr., #5E
NewYork, NY 10024
USA
212 873-0279
212 721-3502

Rapid Film Group
P.O. Box 691725
West Hollywood, CA 90069
USA
213 930-2888
213 931-8836
adamfilm@aol.com

Rappaport, Mark
16 Crosby St.
New York, NY 10013
USA
212 966-7636
212 966-7636

Rauch, David
32 Domingo Ave., #5
Berkeley, CA 94705
USA
510 843-9930
drauch@adobe.com

Raymond, James
515 O'Farrell St., #82
San Francisco, CA 94102
USA
415 922-5079
415 922-5079

Reality Productions
P.O. Box 210256
San Francisco, CA 94121
USA
415 751-1659
415 751-1659
CarolLeigh@aol.com

Recorded Delivery Productions,
Ltd.
1 Elizabeth St.,
Whitewell Bottom,
Rossendale
Lancashire BB4 9LW
ENGLAND
44 171 621-6084
44 171 621-6084

Redding, Judith M.
311 W. Seymour St.
Philadelphia, PA 19144
USA
215 848-9341

Reeder, Andre
Toutenburgstraat 58
Amsterdam 1107 PW
NETHERLANDS
31 20 697 0074

Reeves, Jennifer Todd
121 MacDougal, #10
New York, NY 10012
USA
212 677-8692

Reid, David
P.O. Box 69991
W. Holywood, CA 90069
USA

Reinery Verlag Filmproduktion
Wassigertal 16
Remagen 5480
GERMANY

Reinke, Steve
5537 Gerrish St., #5
Halifax, Nova Scotia B3K 1G8
CANADA
902 425-6755

Reiter, Jill
P.O. Box 421912
San Francisco, CA 94142
USA
415 552-2763

Rey, Christina
P.O. Box 8928
Atlanta, GA 30306-9998
USA
404 897-5218
404 897-5565

Ribeiro, Flavio
Avenue Pasteur 403/502
Rio de Janeiro RJ 22290-240
BRAZIL
55 21 259 4829
55 21 259 0020

Rice, Teri/Egocentric Productions
738 E 6th St., #2B
New York, NY 10009
USA

Rich, B. Ruby
1736 Stockton St., #4
San Francisco, CA 94133
USA

Richards, Dick
1714 Adolphus St. NE
Atlanta, GA 30307
USA
404 377-2134

Richie, Donald
304 Shato Nezu Yanaka 1,
1-18, Taito-ku Tokyo
JAPAN

Richter, Suzy
94A Caroline Ave.
Toronto, Ontario M4M 2X7
CANADA
416 703-8650

Rim Film Distributors
9884 Santa Monica Blvd.
Beverly Hills, CA 90212
USA
310 203-8182
310 551-1530

Rinkenberger, Ginger
452- 15th St., #4L
Brooklyn, NY 11215
USA
718 768-0746
718 768-0746

Rita Moreira Producoes
Rua Rocha 119, apto 904,
Bela Vista
Sao Paulo Cep-10330
BRAZIL
55 11 284 9557

Ritschel-Cederbaum, Sherry
3302 S. Hudson, #108
Tulsa, OK 74135-5051
USA
918 622-5352

Rizzo, Teresa
8 John St.
Glebe, NSW 2037
AUSTRALIA
61 3 325-7466

RM Associates
46 Great Marlborough St.
London W1V 1DB
ENGLAND
44 171 439-2637

Robin, Jean
5631 Plantagenet
Montreal, Quebec H3T 1S3
CANADA
514 341-9802
514 985-2569

Robinson, Angela
108 Perry St., #4L
New York, NY 10014
USA
212 229-9288

Robinson, Jeff
33 Washington Square W
New York, NY 10011
USA
212 443-3794

Robles, Augie
920 Silverlake Blvd., #8
Los Angeles, CA 90026
USA
213 353-0645

Rod & Reel Films
812 N. Highland,
Los Angeles, CA 90038
USA

Rodriguez, Janelle
2441 Haste St., #19
Berkeley, CA
USA
510 204-9751

Rohauer Collection, The
209 S. High Street, Suite 310
Columbus, OH 43215
USA
614 469-0720
614 469-1607

Roques, Philippe
PO Box 411256
San Francisco, CA 94141
USA
415 861-7609

Rosenthal, Andrew/Sputnik
Productions
304 E 30th St., #2
New York, NY 10016
USA
212 213-6392
212 213-3539

Ross, Rock
30 Berry
San Francisco, CA 94107
USA
415 957-1153

Roth, Philip B.
130 W. Houston St.
New York, NY 10012-2512
USA
212 388-9223
212 982-2642

Rotman, Keith
135 Watts St.
New York, NY 10013
USA

Rowley, Patrick
#3, 93 Hornsey Rd.
London N7 6DJ
ENGLAND
44 171 700-7876

Roxie Releasing
3125 16th St.
San Francisco, CA 94103
USA
415 431-3611
415 431-2822

Rubicon Films
Sperlstrasse 42,
D-8000 Munich 71
GERMANY
49 89 755 1580

Rubio, R.X.
3143 22nd St.
San Francisco, CA 94110
USA
415 282-7280

Russell, Pamela August
75 Hartford St.
San Francisco, CA 94114
USA
415 255-0510

Russo, C.J.
206 Rutgers St., #3
Rochester, NY 14607
USA
716 244-5604

Rzeznik, Francine
1833 Edgecliffe Dr., #1
Los Angeles, CA 90026

USA
213 644-0577
213 644-0577

Saalfield, Catherine
136 Grand, #5EF
New York, NY 10013
USA
212 274-9782
212 274-0551

Sagalle, Jonathan
3 Eshkalot St.,
Mt. Carmel, Haifa 34 321
ISRAEL

Salandra, Eugene
145 4th Ave., #10-P
New York, NY 10003
USA
212 260-0738

Sales Company, The
62 Shaftesbury Ave.
London W1V 7AA
ENGLAND
44 171 434-9061
44 172 494-3293

Salzgeber & Co.
Schlossestrasse 29
Berlin 12163
GERMANY
49 30 793-4181
49 30 793-3888

Samuel Goldwyn Company
10203 Santa Monica Blvd.
Los Angeles, CA 90067
USA
310 284-9278
310 284-9124

San Francisco AIDS Foundation
Prevention Dept.
P.O. Box 426182
San Francisco, CA 94142
USA
415 487-3047
415 487-4019

Sandler, Arlene
218 E. 17th St., #4B
New York, NY 10003
USA
212 614-1424

Sandler, Carl
784 Dolores St.
San Francisco, CA 94110
USA
415 282-0338

Sankofa
Unit K,
32-34 Gordon House Rd.

London NW5 1LP
ENGLAND
44 171 485-0848
44 171 485-2869

Satori Films
330 W. 42nd St.
New York, NY 10036
USA

Scheirl, Angela Hans
c/o Escott,
1B East Lake Rd.,
Camberwell
London SE5
ENGLAND
44 171 737-4489

Scholastic Productions, Inc.
730 Broadway
New York, NY 10002
USA

Scovill, Ruth
8459 Bay Hill Blvd.
Orlando, FL 32819
USA
407 876-6998

Scratch & Sniff Videos
1044 Spaight St.
Madison, WI 53703 USA
608 251-8611
608 251-1715

Seaman, Gordon
44 Tennis Cres.
Toronto, Ontario M4K IJ3
CANADA
416 778-5574
416 778-0604

Sebastian
3108 Perlita Av
Los Angeles, CA 90039
USA
213 668-7777
213 660-1826

Seidler, Ellen
7746 Stockton Ave.
El Cerrito, CA 94530
USA
510 524-4098
510 524-4098

Seidler, Tamsin Orion
1272 Guerrero St.
San Francisco, CA 94110
USA
415 821-4357

Sensory Circus, Inc.
218 E. 17th St., #4B
New York, NY 10003
USA 212 714-7123

Seven Dimensions Pty. Ltd.
18 Armstrong St.
Middle Park, Victoria 3206
AUSTRALIA

Seventh Art Releasing
7551 Sunset Blvd., #104
Los Angeles, CA 90046
USA
213 845-1455
213 845-4717

Seyger, Israel
P. O. Box 3069,
7 Smadar St.
Savyon 56552
ISRAEL

Sheahan, Karen
3528 4th Ave. S
Minneapolis, MN 55408
USA
612 825-6600

Sheehan, Brian/Caspar Films
70b Ranelagh
Dublin 6
IRELAND
353 1 497-0981
353 1 497-0981

Sheffield Film Co-op
Brown St.
Sheffield S1 2BS
ENGLAND
44 1742 727170

Shmaeli, Nili
972 3 370 584

Shooting Star Film Company
Singel 395
1012 WN Amsterdam
NETHERLANDS
31 20 6247272
31 20 6268533

Shu Kei's Creative Workshop
Flat F, 18/F, Tonnochy Tower A,
272 Jaffe Rd.
Wanchai
HONG KONG
852 838-1129
852 519-9206

Sicular, Eve
520 E. 12th St.
New York, NY 10009
USA
212 475-4544

Sigal, David
30 Fifth Ave., #15H
New York, NY 10011
USA
212 475-6183

Simcom International
9570 Wilshire Blvd., PH
Los Angeles, CA 90067

Simmons, Aishah Shahidah
1618 Pine St., #3F
Philadelphia, PA 19103
USA
215 735-7372
215 241-7275

Simon, Karl
3235 NE 44th Av
Portland, OR 97213

Simpson, Steve
5311 Granada St.
Los Angeles, CA 90042
USA
213 258-2648

Singer, Leslie
520 E. 14th St., #32
New York, NY 10009
USA
212 533-7565

Sirus
P.O. Box 503
La Honda, CA 94020
USA

Sixpack Films
278 E 10th St., # 5B
New York, NY 10009
USA
212 353-8485

Slane, Andrea
750 Baldwin Av., #A6
Norfolk, VA 23517
USA
804 640-8658

Slater, John
496A Hudson St., #F25
New York, NY 10014
USA
212 505-9405

Sloan, Tamela
25 Dwight St.
Poughkeepsie, NY 12601
USA
914 471-7960

Smith, Jo
85 Coldharbour Lane,
Camberwell
London SE5 9NS
ENGLAND
44 171 274-5556

Snee, Patrick
151 7th Ave., #2
Brooklyn, NY 11215

USA
718 398-8609

Sobel, Lee Bennett /Garage Rock
Pictures
123 W. 93 St. #2C
New York, NY 10025
USA
212 865-8356

Soberon, Edgar
Escuela International de Cine y
TV,
Apartado Aereo 40 y 41
San Antonio de los banos
CUBA

Societe Temoins
12 Ave. Du Maine
Paris 75015
FRANCE

Soffa, Fred
395 Maple Ave.
Fond du Lac, WI 54935
USA
212 439-8753

Soldo, Mario
Wollzeile 17/5
Vienna 1010
AUSTRIA
431 512 7087
431 512 7086

Solinger, Michael
511 N. Puget St.
Olympia, WA 98506
USA

Sony Pictures Classics
550 Madison Ave
New York, NY 10022
USA
212 833-8833
212 833-8844
South Pacific Films
111 Pitt St.
Redfern, NSW 2016
AUSTRALIA

Spadola, Meema
211 Halsey St.
Newark, NJ 07102
USA
201 242-0831

Spanish Ministry of Culture
San Marcos 40
Madrid 28004
SPAIN
34 1 532-5089

Speck, Wieland
Grainauerstrasse 11,
1000 Berlin 30

GERMANY
49 30 2 548 9272

Spenger, Charles
840 S. Serrano Ave. #608
Los Angeles, CA 90005
USA
213 654-0343

Spero, Chuck
739 N Mariposa St.
Los Angeles, CA 90029-3485
USA
213 662-5221

Spiro, Ellen
P.O. Box 1970
New York, NY 10008
USA

Spitzer, John E.
1102 San Francisco NE
Olympia, WA 98506
USA
206 754-7930

Sprinkle, Annie
PO Box 435,
Prince Street Station
New York, NY 10012
USA
212 260-2431

Sputnik Productions
304 E 30th St., #2
New York, NY 10016
USA
212 213-6392
212 213-3539

St. Orr Healing Arts
427 E. 6th St., #2R
New York, NY 10009
USA
212 777-7199

Stagias, Nikolas/Sandler, Arlene
298 Collingwood
San Francisco, CA 94114
USA
415 863-9278

Stahlberg, Michael/Hocschule
Fur Fernsetter und Film
Franuenthalestr. 23
Munich 8000
GERMANY
49 89 680004 44
49 89 680004 36

Staley, Samantha
6608 N Newgrad, #2
Chicago, IL 60626
USA
312 338-8970
312 342-7532

Stambrini, Monica
Via Durini 20
Milan 20122
ITALY
39 2 760-02481
39 2 551-6558

Stanley, Anie
335 South St. #4
Brooklyn, NY 11211
USA
212 673-1467

Steger, Lawrence
1547 W. Chestnut
Chicago, IL 60622
USA
312 455-8675

Stephen Winter Filmworks
530 E. 13th St., #17
New York, NY 10009
USA
212 529-2894

Stephens, Elizabeth
111 First St.
Jersey City, NJ
07302
USA
201 420-8072

Stephens, Kathy
Flat 6, 594 Kingsland Road
London E8 4AH
ENGLAND
44 171 254-3896

Stevens, Ylonda
PO Box 6047
Olympia, WA 98502
USA
306 705-4219

Stevenson, Jack/Living Color
Productions
Blagardsgade 42TV
2 Copenhagen 2200 N
DENMARK
45 313 935 74
45 353 660 30

Stock, Michael
Adalbertstrasse 75
Berlin D-1000
GERMANY
49 30 614 -2379
49 30 615-2337

Storm, Harriet
422 Waller St.
San Francisco, CA 94117
USA
415 252-9030

Strand Releasing
8033 Sunset Blvd., # 4002
Los Angeles, CA 90046
USA
818 342-9006
818 342-9006

Stranger Than Fiction Films
155 W 70th St #12C
New York, NY 10023
USA
212 873-9013
212 873-9072

Stremmel, Michael
83 Horatio St.
New York, NY 10014
USA
212 229-2446
212 333-7552

Strongbow Marketing
15 Sir John Rogerson's Quay
Dublin 2
IRELAND

Struck, Andreas
1 Goldhawk Mews
London W12 8PA
ENGLAND
44 181 746-1566
44 181 746-1195

Suitcase Films
2 Buckland St., Top floor
Chippendale, NSW 2008
AUSTRALIA
61 2 211-2022
61 2 212-2350

Summit Films & Productions
112 Albion St
San Francisco, CA 94110
USA
415 252-0428

Surkis, Alisa
198 E. 7th St., #5
New York, NY 10009
USA
212 777-4406

Swank Motion Pictures
201 South Jefferson Ave.
St. Louis, MO 63103
USA
800 876-5577

Swedish Film Institute
Box 27-126
Stockholm S-102-52
SWEDEN
46 8 665 11 00
46 8 661 18 20

Sydney Filmmakers Cooperative
PO Box 217

Kings Cross, NSW 2011
AUSTRALIA
61 2 33-0721

Symons, Johnny
97 Coleridge St.
San Francisco, CA 94110
USA
415 642-1553
415 252-5352

Syrup Productions
Herrfruth strasse 4,
1000 Berlin 44
GERMANY

Take Off Productions
Reichenberger Str. 72a
Berlin 10999
GERMANY
49 30 612-7412

Tang, Sikay
5 Spring St., #13
New York, NY 10012
USA
212 219-9082
212 219-9082

Tapestry Productions
924 Broadway
New York, NY 10010
USA

Tara Releasing
124 Belevedere St., #5
San Rafael, CA 94901
USA
415 454-5838 415 454-5977

Tate, Jennifer
908 Amsterdam Ave., #5C
New York, NY 10025
USA
212 865-0123

Taylor, Amanda
1230 W Roselawn
St. Paul, MN 55113
USA
612 644-8632

Taylor, Christian
1206 North Clarke St.
West Hollywood, CA 90069
USA 310 657-5338

Taylor, Jennifer Maytorena
499 Alabama St., #116
San Francisco, CA 94110
USA
415 552-5856

Taylor, Jocelyn
272 Sackett St. #1-R
Brooklyn, NY 11231
USA

718 875-9010
212 941-1298

Taylor, Mark
8 W. 76th St., #4C
New York, NY 10023
USA
212 769-4975

Telefilm Canada
600 West de la Gauchetiere St.,
25th Floor
Montreal, Quebec H3B 4L2
CANADA
514 283-6363
514 283-8212

Terracino
512 E 12th St., Apt #A
New York, NY 10009
USA
212 473-0216

Testing the Limits
200 E. 10th St., #316
New York, NY 10003
USA
212 957-1909
212 957-1909
ttl@infohouse.com

Thai Motion Picture Producers
Association
514 Banmanangkasila Lanluang
Rd.
Bangkok 10300
THAILAND

Thane, Lucy
1106 Valencia St., #D
San Francisco, CA 94110
USA
415 206-1319

Third Ear, The
21 Sheinkin St.
Tel Aviv 65232
ISRAEL
972 3 526 3413

Third World Newsreel
335 W. 38th St.
New York, NY 10018
USA
212 947-9277
212 594-6417

This Side of Butch
4406 Harbor View Ave.
Oakland, CA 94619
USA
510 528-8397

Thomas, Brett
3 Ford St.

San Francisco, CA 94114
USA
415 431-7514
415 552-8704

Thorne, Kika
c/o LIFT
#505 - 345 Adelaide St. West
Toronto, Ontario M5V 1RS
CANADA
416 533-7398
416 596-8233

Three Fun Girls
307 Valencia St., #201
San Francisco, CA 94103
USA
415 255-7945
510 451-8796

Tiger Rose Distributing
P.O. Box 609
Cotati, CA 94928
USA

Tomboy, Texas
PO Box 14854
San Francisco, CA 94114
USA
415 553-3953

Topping, John
7985 Santa Monica Blvd.,
#109-348
Los Angeles, CA 90027
USA
213 669-8026

Torrice Productions
1455A Market St., #123
San Francisco, CA 94103
USA

Tremaglio Productions
7985 Santa Monica Blvd #109
West Hollywood, CA 90046
USA
213 659-4744

Troia, E.
1420 Polk St. #4
San Francisco, CA 94109
USA
415 673-2621

Tschetter, Sotera /Point of View
Films
1201 Currie Ave.
Minneapolis, MN 55403
USA
612 337-0000

Tuft, Sarah
47 W. 88th St., #35-A
New York, NY 10024
USA

Tupper, Krista
2-3290 Dumfries St.
Vancouver, British Columbia V5N
3S3
CANADA
604 879-7905
604 685-0252

Tuttle, Christien G.
615 Pheasant Dr.
Los Angeles, CA 90065-4005
USA
213 227-6062

Twinbrothers Filmproduktion
Fuhlsbuttler Str. 425
Hamburg 22309
GERMANY
49 40 6305260
49 40 394676

Two Faced Production
225 W. 13th St.
New York, NY 10011
USA
212 924-7665

Two In Twenty
P.O. Box 105
Somerville, MA 02114
USA

UCLA Film and Television
Archive
1015 N. Cahuenga
Los Angeles, CA 90038
USA
213 462-4921
213 461-6317

Umen, Alix
1143 Mariposa St.
San Francisco, CA 94107
USA
415 252-8044
Unifrance Film
114 Champs Elysees
Paris 75008
FRANCE

United States Holocaust
Memorial Museum
100 Raoul Wallenberg Place, SW
Washington, DC 20024-2150
USA
202 479-9726

Unity
P.O. Box 53617
Philadelphia, PA 19105
USA

University of Bristol
Cantocks Close, Woodland Rd.
Bristol BS8 1UP
ENGLAND

44 1272 303030
44 1272 288251

University of Southern
California—School of Cinema
University Park
Los Angeles, CA 90089
USA
213 740-2911

V-Tape
401 Richmond St. W., #452
Toronto, Ontario M5V 3A8
CANADA
416 351-1317
416 351-1509

Vallois, Philippe
3 rue Paul Lelong
Paris 75002
FRANCE

Vargas, Victor
956 North Wilcox, #11
Los Angeles, CA 90038
USA
213 465-9763

Vaughn, Alexis
185A Lexington St.
San Francisco, CA 94110
USA
415 552-3103

Veltri, Dan
38 Ord St.
San Francisco, CA 94114
USA
415 861-5810

Verow, Todd
1036 Natoma St.
San Francisco, CA 94103
USA
415 255-6761
Vestron Pictures
2029 Century Park East, #200
Los Angeles, CA 90067
USA

Video City Theatrical Distribution
4266 Broadway
Oakland, CA 94611
USA

Video Data Bank
37 S. Wabash Ave.
Chicago, IL 60603
USA
312 345-3550
312 541-8072

Video Free America
442 Shotwell
San Francisco, CA 94110
USA
415 648-3956

Video Out
1965 Main St.
Vancouver, British Columbia V5T
3C1
CANADA
604 872-8449
604 876-1185

Video Pool
300-100 Arthur St.
Winnipeg, Manitoba R3B 1H3
CANADA
204 949-9134
204 942-1555

Videographe, Inc.
4550 rue Garnier
Montreal, Quebec H2J 3S7
CANADA

Vidmark
2901 Ocean Park Blvd., #123
Santa Monica, CA 90405
USA

Vitale, Frank
45 Rosetown Rd.
Tomkins Cove, NY 10986
USA
914 786-3923

Vogelmann, Hilou
Arcisstrasse 57
Munich 80799
GERMANY
49 89 321 824 42

Voodoo Peep Productions
259 E. 35th St., #4D
New York, NY 10016
USA
212 685-0080

Wade Williams Distribution
13001 Wornall Rd.
Kansas City, MO 64145
USA
816 943-0855
816 941-7011

Wait, What? Productions
431 Van Ness
San Francisco, CA 94103
USA
415 626-4820

Wallin, Michael
22 Vicksburg
San Francisco, CA 94114
USA
415 826-1426

Walsh, Jack
654 Vermont St.
San Francisco, CA 94107
USA

415 826-5599
415 826-7023

Walters, Barry
273B Sanchez St.
San Francisco, CA 94114
USA
415 255-7239

Walters, Boyd
6 Kingston Road,
Riverside, Cardiff CF1 8HU
ENGLAND

Walton, Pam
P.O. Box 391025
Mountain View, CA 94039
USA
415 960-3414
415 962-8539

Waterer, Reid
115 S Detroit St.
Los Angeles, CA 90036
USA
213 936-1408
213 936-9109

Waugh, Thomas
4009, rue de Bullion
Montreal, Quebec H2W 2E3
CANADA
514 845-2512
514 848-8627

Wehling, Susan
47 Greenbrae Boardwalk
Greenbrae, CA 94904
USA
415 461-6490

Weissman, David
1659 Oak St.
San Francisco, CA 94117
USA
415 626-9349
415 626-7270

Wells, Peter
21 Curran St.
Auckland 2
NEW ZEALAND

West Glen Films
1430 Broadway
New York, NY 10018-3396
USA
212 921-2800
212 944-9055

Westmoreland, Joe
319 W. 14th St., #2
New York, NY 10014
USA
212 620-5958

Wet Spot Cinema
271 E 10th St.
New York, NY 10009
USA
212 714-7001
212 673-1467

Whitaker, Claire
1466 W. Pensacola
Chicago, IL 60613
USA
312 528-7412

Whiteley, Sara
P.O. Box 60934
Palo Alto, CA 94306
USA
415 637-1710

Wichterich, Beth
1902-B Robbins Place
Austin, TX 78705
USA
512 476-5400

Wild, Osker
2319 N. 45th St., #181
Seattle, WA 98103
USA
206 522-6064

Wilhite, Ingrid
608 Kernberry Dr.
San Rafael, CA 94903
USA
415 499-3412
415 252-7212

Wilson, Emjay
1426 Newcombe Ave.
San Francisco, CA 94124
USA
Winds of Change Productions
12 Grove Ave.
Toronto, Ontario M6J 3B6
CANADA

Wineland, Thom
326 Sanchez St.
San Francisco, CA 94117
USA
415 552-3457

Winkler, Robert
Am Kaiser Muhlendamm 103/36
Vienna 1223
AUSTRIA
43 222 239 575
43 222 4852 63515

WNYC-TV
One Centre St.
New York, NY 10007
USA

Wolfe Video

PO Box 64
New Almaden, CA 95042
USA
408 268-6782
408 268-0232

Wolfley, Brad
CPO 2502,
PO Box 700
New Brunswick, NJ 08903
USA
908 843-7727

Woman Vision Productions
3145 Geary Blvd., Box 421
San Francisco, CA 94118
USA
415 346-2336
415 346-1047

Women In Focus
#204-456 W. Broadway
Vancouver, British Columbia V5Y
1R3
CANADA

Women Make Movies
462 Broadway, 5th Floor
New York, NY 10013
USA
212 925-0606
212 925-2052

Wood, Brian
1 Eardesley Rd.
Liverpool L18 0HS
ENGLAND
44 151 737-1015

World Marketing Film
8 rue Lincoln
Paris 75008
FRANCE

Wright, Annie
Tuinstraat 203
Amsterdam 1015 PD
NETHERLANDS
31 20 6209032

Wright, Georgia B.
P.O. Box 29364
San Francisco, CA 94129
USA
415 978-0995

Wright, Patrick
2116 W. Potomac #2
Chicago, IL 60622
USA
312 235-5991

Wyman, Julie
31 Coso Ave.
San Francisco, CA 94110
USA
415 648-4140

Yahnke, John
1811 N. Whitely Ave., #503
Hollywood, CA 90028
USA
213 461-2141

Yankee-Oriole Company
28-02 36th Ave.
New York, NY 11106-3106
USA

Young, John G.
140 Fairmont Ave
Hastings-On-Hudson, NY 10706
USA
914 478-5903
914 747-0839

Youthwave
3315 Sacramento St., #351
San Francisco, CA 94118
USA
415 647-9283
415 647-0774

Yoyo Film Video & Theatre
Productions
108 Grove Park
London SE5
ENGLAND
44 171 735-3711
44 171 735-0795

Zachary, Bodhan
1376 Clayton St.
San Francisco, CA 94114
USA
415 621-6115
415 552-7723

Zando, Julie
PO Box 1612
Buffalo, NY 14205
USA

Zay, Julia
192 Spring St., #2
New York, NY 10012
USA
212 941-9357

Zeitgeist Films
200 Waverly Pl., #4
New York, NY 10014
USA
212 274-1989

Zepra International
6133 Pat Ave.
Woodland Hills, CA 91367
USA

Zoller, Claudia
Wissmanstr. 6
Berlin 12049
GERMANY

49 30 622-4231
49 30 694-7435

Zone Productions
Lighthouse Media Centre Art
Gallery,
Lichfield St.
Wolverhampton WV1 1DU
ENGLAND
44 1902 312033
Zwickler, Phil
330 3rd Ave., #16C
New York, NY 10010
USA

A CINEMA OF ONE'S OWN: A BRIEF HISTORY OF THE
SAN FRANCISCO INTERNATIONAL LESBIAN & GAY FILM FESTIVAL
by Susan Stryker

The San Francisco International Lesbian & Gay Film Festival turns 20 years old in 1996. For most of that time it has been the signature event of Frameline, a nonprofit, community-based media arts organization. As the festival grew from an impromptu screening of a dozen short films into an internationally significant cultural event, Frameline developed from a handful of activist artists into a complex operation with a professional staff. It oversees hundreds of volunteers each year, runs its own film/video distribution operation, and provides support to other festivals, all in addition to the year-round job of planning and presenting the oldest and largest lesbian and gay film festival in the world.

The Early Years
A sense of pride bolstered by hard-won gay political power and underpinned by the conviction that public art played an important role in the liberation movement helped launch the first festival in 1977. Filmmaker Marc Huestis remembered it as "a real Mickey and Judy affair. We got a space, rented a projector, threw up a sheet, and said 'Hey, kids! We're gonna put on a show!'" Huestis described himself and the other organizers as "a ragtag bunch of hippie fags," Haight-Ashbury denizens who lived on welfare and dabbled in a wide range of political and artistic activities. Cranking out no-budget Super-8s was for them just another cheap and easy means of self-expression. Taking the film to be developed at Harvey Milk's camera store on Castro Street, however, practically guaranteed the double exposure of art and gay liberation politics. Photographers Dan Nicoletta and David Waggoner, two other participants in the first Festival, worked in Milk's shop. Milk's long campaign to become the city's first openly gay elected official was well underway by the fall of 1976, when the idea for a festival gradually took shape among the young filmmakers who mingled with the political crowd that also frequented the camera store.

Huestis, Nicoletta, Waggoner, Greg Gonzales, postcard artist Berne Boyle (who had himself organized gay film screenings the year before), and a half-dozen other men took to the streets to publicize the Gay Film Festival of Super-8 Films on February 9 at the Gay Community Center at 32 Page Street. They plastered the city with handbills announcing a free screening of their work, and the event succeeded wildly. Two hundred people crowded into a room meant to accommodate a hundred twenty-five, and a hundred more were turned away at the door. A second expanded and equally well-attended show was scheduled for March 13 at the Pride Center at 330 Grove Street.

Viewers at these two virtually back-to-back, overflow-capacity "first" festivals witnessed an eclectic assortment of short films. Some dealt with such predictable fare as coming out or the pleasures of picking up a good trick. Others were vintage '70s period pieces. One offered a gay perspective on the recent national bicentennial celebrations, while another (with an obvious nod to underground icon John Waters) bore the title *Poodle Poo-Poo Miracle Mask*. Still other films seem curiously contemporary in retrospect: *Changes*, by a transsexual in transition from male to female, explored the intersection of feminism, personal identity, and state bureaucracy.

After two more screenings at 32 Page Street, the second annual festival (billed as The Super-8 Summer Festival) took place on June 22, 1978 at the Grove Street Center. It featured about a dozen short films, including a timely fantasy, *The Assassination of*

Anita Bryant. By then, a core group of the first festival's organizers led by Waggoner, Ric Mears, and Wayne Smolen had founded Persistence of Vision, a collective dedicated to building support for local gay artists interested in film. The short-lived group sponsored the second and third festivals, thus providing continuity between the first festival and all subsequent ones. It also moved the festival's date to the third week in June to make it part of San Francisco's yearly commemoration of the Stonewall uprising.

The Third Annual San Francisco Gay Film and Video Festival, with a volunteer staff of six drawn largely from veterans of the first two affairs, opened at the Roxie Cinema on June 19, 1979, with a repeat screening on June 22 at the Lumiere Theater. Public access television Channel 25 broadcast the program the next evening. Later that year Persistence of Vision changed its name to Frameline (a technical term that refers to the black bar separating each individual frame on a strip of film) and became a legally incorporated organization.

When a young film student at San Francisco State University named Michael Lumpkin responded to a call for volunteers and contacted Frameline in the fall of 1979, he had no idea he'd be running The Fourth Annual San Francisco Gay Film Festival the following summer, or that he had found his calling for many years to come. Burn-out was beginning to take its toll among the festival's founders, and Lumpkin's competence and enthusiasm gave the organization a much needed jolt of new energy. More than any other individual, he was responsible for the festival's remarkable transformation over the next decade. What had been primarily a forum for local film talent became, under his direction, a hip venue for film talent from around the world that drew an international audience, showcased the best work in queer film, and increasingly attracted the attention of the mainstream film industry.

At a time when Frameline could not hire paid staff, Lumpkin served as festival director as a labor of love. He began to increase the visibility and stature of the event by bringing out-of-town directors in to speak about their work, building personal contacts between the San Francisco festival and the newer gay film festival in New York, and securing funding from national grant-making organizations. Although Lumpkin would come under criticism for perpetuating the white gay male sensibility that some people felt dominated the festival for many years, he unquestionably reached out beyond the festival's overwhelmingly gay white roots to broaden the content of previous programming. The first festival he coordinated in 1980 was also the first one to feature work produced outside the United States, to substantially address interracial issues, and to include work by lesbians. Avant-garde lesbian filmmaker Barbara Hammer remembers arriving at her Oakland studio one morning to find Lumpkin waiting on her doorstep, eager to solicit one of her films. Hammer's work—along with that of Christine Wynne, Susana Blaustein, and Greta Schiller—appeared among the 11 titles featured in the 1980 Festival.

As a result of Lumpkin's efforts, The Fifth Annual San Francisco International Gay Film Festival in 1981 was a significantly bigger event than any of the previous ones. Making the Castro Theater the festival's main venue was the most obvious change. The Castro Theater first opened its doors in 1922, and had been one of America's grand movie palaces before World War II. By the mid-'70s it had fallen into disrepair and become a nondescript neighborhood movie house showing run-of-the-mill commercial features. Mel Novikoff, the art film exhibitor who had hooked San Franciscans on Bergman and Fellini at his historic Surf Theater in the early '60s, sensed a golden opportunity in restoring the

Castro to a semblance of its former glory. His timing was just right. The dramatic gay and lesbian migration to San Francisco that began around 1970 transformed the demographics of the formerly Irish working-class Castro neighborhood. Enough Judy Garland fans with disposable incomes settled there to insure the successful transformation of the old movie palace into the city's premier repertory film theater.

Given that the Castro Theater had become a fixture of local lesbian and gay culture by the late '70s, it made perfect sense to bring the festival there. Still, as long-time Castro film programmer (and liaison to Frameline) Bob Hawk explained, "Moving the festival required a leap of faith." The Castro's daunting 1500-seat capacity was four times the size of the Roxie Cinema, where the festival had played the year before, and could nearly swallow the audiences of all the previous festivals combined. Rising to the challenge, Lumpkin produced a festival designed to pack the house—not just for one night as in earlier years, but for a solid week. The festival opened with the world premiere of *Greetings From Washington, D.C.*, the ground-breaking documentary about the first March on Washington for Lesbian and Gay Rights in 1979. It continued with a revival screening of the classic 1931 lesbian film *Mädchen in Uniform*, a program of short documentaries about notable lesbian and gay artists, new dramatic works from Europe, and a weekend of experimental films at the Roxie. The indisputable highlight of the festival, however, was a sold-out lecture and clip show by film historian Vito Russo, whose book, *The Celluoid Closet* had just been published.

Frameline and the festival turned a corner in 1981. The addition of gala opening night festivities and champagne receptions where viewers could meet celebrities pointed towards the festival's future as a red-letter event on queer San Francisco's social calendar (it also fueled debates about the upwardly mobile assimilationist tendencies of lesbian and gay culture). While the festival continued to showcase experimental work by independent filmmakers and tried to cultivate an appreciation of aesthetically challenging visual arts among lesbians and gays, it increasingly responded to audience demands for more conventional and commercial films. It also became a vehicle for educating its audiences about the history and culture of marginalized sexualities and genders. One reason the festival grew so steadily throughout the '80s was Frameline's desire to be as many things to as many people as possible. Rather than narrow its focus, it expanded its scope in an effort to be inclusive of the wide range of queer communities.

Frameline Comes of Age

Frameline achieved another benchmark in 1986 with its 10th festival. Lumpkin credits his first visit to the massive, pace-setting Berlin Film Festival earlier that year with inspiring him to take Frameline and its San Francisco Festival to new levels of professionalism. Frameline hired Lumpkin as a full-time employee; other staff members were paid; and the Board of Directors began to serve more exclusively as a policy-making body. Audience awards had become a part of the festival two years before, and for the 10th anniversary, the Board inaugurated its annual Frameline Award for the year's outstanding contribution to queer filmmaking. Since then, recipients have included Vito Russo, filmmaker Marlon Riggs, actor Divine, director Pratibha Pramar, and producers Christine Vachon and Marcus Hu.

One other notable event in 1986 deeply affected Frameline and the festival—the so-called "lesbian riot" at the Roxie on June 25, when viewers offended by the depiction of gay male sex in one segment of a women's short film program stormed out in protest.

Discontent had simmered for years among some women viewers, many of whom felt that Frameline paid scant attention to lesbian concerns. The title of the festival had not included the word "lesbian" until 1982, and few feature-length films were by or about lesbians—though many fine short works by women artists played at the festival each year. This situation stemmed in part from the screening committee's reluctance to continue recommending the same handful of available high-quality lesbian features each year. The troubling shortage of lesbian features in turn reflected systemic gender-based economic inequalities in the film industry. Because more women worked in lower-budget media like video and in less commercial experimental forms, the best lesbian titles tended to show at the Roxie, the Festival's traditional venue for such works. Smaller and less prestigious than the Castro, the Roxie inadvertently functioned as a pink-collar ghetto and reinforced the impression that women's issues were of secondary importance.

Frameline responded by making meaningful institutional and philosophical changes in its organization. People in decision-making positions consciously chose to build structures capable of actively promoting diversity. Maria Kellet, who had served as Festival Assistant for several years, became a more visible spokesperson for the organization in the late '80s, as did some other women who had a long history of involvement behind the scenes at Frameline—most notably Phyllis Zusman and Susan Passino (both of whom served as Board President) Chris Olson, Sue Mitchell, Elizabeth Whipple, Karen Larsen, Kim Scala, Liz Rigali, and Mary Wings. Roberto Esteves, Shu Lee Ong, Hoa Tran and Lawrence Wong contributed to the ethnic diversity of the Board. To address the relative shortage of high-quality lesbian features, Frameline set up a completion fund designed to enable more women and people of color to realize their visions on the screen (Rose Troché and Guinevere Turner's break-through comedy *Go Fish* benefited from a completion fund grant in 1992).

By the late '80s Frameline had begun to hire guest curators who could lend their expertise to women's, minority, and issue-oriented programming. For example, at a time when a great deal of AIDS-related information was available only in the form of instructional videos, film scholar and Frameline video curator Daniel Mangin organized AIDS video symposia that ran concurrently with the festival. Annette Förster became Frameline's first guest curator for women's programming in 1991. Perhaps even more importantly, however, Frameline started hiring women for its highest permanent positions as staff needs continued to expand. Linda Farin became Frameline's first Executive Director in 1988, and since then Jill Jacobs and Tess Martin have also held that position.

Frameline Gets a Make-over

When Tom di Maria became Executive Director in 1990 he took seriously the Board of Directors's mandate to diversify the organization. The hiring of new personnel with a more multicultural view of queer media brought about a substantial change in Frameline's profile. Mark Finch of the British Film Institute had impressed di Maria while serving as Frameline's distribution manager in 1990, and he came on as the new Festival Director in 1992. Nancy Fishman became Distribution Manager in 1991, and Desi del Valle was hired as her assistant in 1992. Jenni Olson, women's guest curator in 1992, was hired as Festival Co-director in 1993, and directed Frameline's Archive and Resource Center in 1994.

A skillful fundraiser, Tom di Maria also pumped more cash into Frameline's completion fund. Women and people of color constituted majorities on the completion fund jury and festival screening committees, and after establishing a track record of multiculturally responsible programming at the festival, Frameline stepped-up its efforts to encourage a wide range of community-based organizations to co-sponsor programs of interest to those communities.

As president of the Board of Directors, Karl Knapper, a gregarious and articulate African-American, has become one of the most visible symbols of Frameline's image in the '90s. "I think lesbian and gay film festivals play a vital cultural role," Knapper says. "They create a place to be lesbian and gay. They provide validating representations. I wish I'd had a lesbian and gay film festival to go to when I was a kid in El Paso. I wish there was a lesbian and gay film festival in every hometown in America."

The San Francisco International Lesbian & Gay Film Festival has established itself as the place where programmers from most of the 80-plus other lesbian and gay festivals worldwide turn for ideas and information, making Frameline a strategically situated conduit between smaller local festivals and the international film community. Frameline's distribution service extends this function by making over 160 film and video titles available to festivals, community groups, schools, and universities. The myriad social events surrounding the annual festival have also become vital places for queer artists and film industry professionals from around the globe to congregate, talk shop, and build a sense of community. Gabriel Gonzales Vega, a regular festival guest and director of Costa Rica's state cinematheque, likened being in San Francisco for the festival to "being on another planet. At home my lover and I can scarcely go to public events together. I come here to be inspired about what is possible."

The undercurrent of excitement that charges the entire festival peaks when major new works hit the screen, and an enthusiastic response from audiences here can help catapult films into wider circulation. Over the years, festival-goers have advanced the fortunes of such films as Pedro Almodovar's *Law of Desire* and Gus Van Sant's *Mala Noche*, both of which had their U.S. festival premieres through Frameline. Festival screenings are often even more intoxicating for the filmmakers themselves than for their audiences. Recalling the west coast debut of *Paris is Burning* at the Castro in 1990, director Jennie Livingston says, "I can't imagine ever having that moment topped. I got a five minute standing ovation. Nothing more exciting than that has ever happened to me as a filmmaker."

By 1994, with nearly twenty years of experience behind it, Frameline had survived a bruising battle with the National Endowment for the Arts in 1992, when NEA grants awarded in previous years were suspended in the wake of the Robert Mapplethorpe controversy. Frameline seemed to emerge from this fray stronger than ever, looking somewhat heroic as it bashed back against federal homophobes. Although the NEA restored only part of the grants, Frameline's operating budget increased geometrically as money filtered in from the private sector. The budget practically doubled every year during the first half of the '90s, ballooning from just over $100,000 in 1991 to about $800,000 in 1994. The festival itself grew by similar proportions: under the direction of Mark Finch and Jenni Olson, attendance rose from 19,600 in 1991 to more than 55,000 in 1994. Over the same period the number of programs more than doubled, from 47 to 98.

Coping with Crisis

Late in 1994, Frameline seemed like a successful organization with a certain future, ideally positioned to amplify and benefit from the recent explosion of interest in the "new queer cinema." Mass media images play a powerful role in shaping identities, and Frameline was becoming an arbiter of queer sensibilities and self-conceptions around the world. At the request of Russian and Indian activists, Frameline worked with the San Francisco-based International Lesbian and Gay Human Rights Commission to present the first queer film festivals in those countries. These and other festivals from Australia to Zimbabwe received assistance from Frameline, raising complex questions about the cross-cultural and post-colonial politics of representation.

As a consequence of its prominent role in queer culture, Frameline struggled to meet conflicting demands. The organization's progamming consultant Bob Hawk, for example, felt that quality had sometimes taken a back seat to quantity during the dramatic expansion of festival programs in the early '90, and yet the number of films screened had swollen in response to audience demands for a wider range of representation. Similarly, the festival's historic commitment to provocative queer images hung in delicate balance with a tendency toward commercialization, a trend fostered by the Festival's increasing reliance on corporate sponsorship to replace dwindling government support for the arts.

A chronic but managable budget deficit had grown increasingly serious by April of 1994, and reached crisis proportions when the time came to pay the bills for the 18th festival, Frameline was flat broke with debts in the six-figure range. This situation reflected the paradoxes of explosive growth, but was also the result of serious structural problems and overhead costs that had sky-rocketed.

The crisis mentality that characterized Frameline at the end of 1994 deepened immeasurably on January 14, 1995, with the tragic suicide of Mark Finch. Finch had suffered his whole life with severe depression, and ended his life by jumping from the Golden Gate Bridge. A memorial service was held at the Castro Theater on February 26, 1995, and the 19th festival was dedicated to his memory. A special fund was also established in his name to help support the work of emerging queer filmmakers. Only 33 at the time of his death, Finch was regarded as an important cultural activist both in the United States and his native England, working tirelessly to secure venues for queer artists at a time when commerical movie houses and funders for the arts were leery of lesbian and gay images. He left a distinctive imprint on both Frameline and the San Francisco International Lesbian & Gay Film Festival.

In Finch's absence, Frameline and the film community rallied to ensure that the oldest and largest lesbian and gay film festival in the world would continue. Staff programmers Boone Nguyen and Jennifer Morris rose to the challenge of running the 1995 festival, and Frameline stalwarts Michael Lumpkin and Tom di Maria assisted Executive Director Tess Martin with festival administration and operations. Given the conditions under which the staff had to work, the 19th festival was a resounding success. Thirty-one of 84 programs were sold out during the 10-day run; attendance figures were only a few thousand tickets short of 1994's record of 55,000; and the level of financial sponsorship hit an all-time high. The festival had its artistic successes as well, opening with the crowd-pleasing *Incredibly True Story of Two Girls in Love*, and featuring dozens of fine short works.

Now in its 20th year, Frameline stands at a crossroads. The current level of visibility for queer issues in the United States and many other parts of the world was unthinkable when the decade began. The demand for queer interpretations of human experience is absolutely unprecedented. Frameline is still poised to fill a vital role in shaping global discourses on sexuality, gender, and artistic expression. And yet the events of the past two

.

years demonstrate the remarkable fragility of contemporary queer life. In spite of two rounds of lay-offs that decimated Frameline's paid staff, the organization maintains its committment to the importance of media arts in the lives of queer men and women the world over. It enjoys the support and patronage of tens of thousands of movie-goers. And year after year, the shows go on.

Thanks to the following people for their help with this brief history: Paul Bollwinkle, Desi Del Valle, Tom di Maria, Mark Finch, Nancy Fishman, Barbara Hammer, Bob Hawk, Marc Huestis, Karl Knapper, Jennie Livingston, Michael Lumpkin, Tess Martin, Jennifer Morris, Daniel Nicoletta, Boone Nguyen, Jenni Olson, Paul Thurston, Elizabeth Whipple, and Mary Wings.

CHECKLIST FOR PROGRAMMING

This chapter offers a task-oriented checklist on the how-to basics of film and video programming and publicity along with guidance and advice on program content and choosing films and videos to meet the needs of your audience; suggestions about such financial and practical considerations as venues, shipping, sponsorship, and negotiating rentals; and helpful hints and informational lists about organizations, books, and resources to further assist you in planning a successful film and video event.

For advice on how to plan, program, and promote film and video screenings in your community, this "Checklist for Programming" offers a few tips to help you plan your own gay and lesbian film and video program. When you read through this checklist you will want to think of each separate category in terms of:

1) Who is responsible for this? (organization)
2) When must it be done? (calendar)
3) How much will it cost? (budget)

Below, in the following order, you will find information on:
• Organizing and Producing Your Event
• Funding
• Staff and Volunteers
• Programming
• Scheduling
• Booking
• Shipping Films and Videos
• Theater/Space
• Promotional Materials
• Catalog/Program
• Mailing Lists and Mailings
• Advertising
• Sponsors
• Organizational Newsletters
• Press Releases and Public Service Announcements
• Specialized Letters to Community Groups
• Copresentations
• Follow up
• Press Screenings
• Distribution of Flyers and Posters
• Interviews
• Tickets
• Speakers
• Opening Night Reception
• After Your Event
• Programming and Publicity Resources
and more!

Organizing and Producing Your Event
Organization and production of a film and video festival or series should be by or in conjunction with a media group, movie theater, museum, exhibition space, or a gay and lesbian organization—or a group of such organizations working together. Local colleges or universities are a good possibility if they have film programs, theater space, and an active student

body. It helps if the organization has name recognition, experience in public programming, and something major to contribute to the program such as money, staff time, materials, or theater space. Cooperative organizing can lead to a multiplicity of program ideas, and it provides contacts and experience that can be mutually beneficial and lots more fun!

Funding

You must raise enough money to cover all your costs, or else sponsors must pick up the deficit; it's very important to draw up a detailed budget at the time you begin to organize your event. Projected expenses include, at a minimum: theater/space, film and video rentals, staff and overhead, shipping, and all promotional materials. Projected revenues may include box-office income (multiply ticket price times number of seats and number of programs for a high estimate, then divide by two for a more realistic estimate), grants, sponsorships, private donations, and income from an opening-night benefit you may have. Remember that box-office income rarely covers all of your expenses.

Staff and Volunteers

At least one or two people will need to work full time on the program in order to meet with sponsors, secure funding, book the theater/space as well as the films and videos, handle all press work and press screenings and the ad campaign, answer the phone, handle advance bookings and ticket sales, coordinate speakers and equipment, and be present at all screenings to manage unanticipated problems. Because of the large volume of work within a short period of time, the staff working on a festival or series will probably need several volunteers to assist with all of this. Good communication is essential between staff and volunteers; be clear about who is responsible for what and always remember to treat volunteers with gratitude and respect—the event would not be possible without them. Volunteers can be drawn from film studies departments at colleges, gay and lesbian organizations, and friends; they can do everything from typing lists, leafletting neighborhoods, coordinating special events, pursuing donations and moderating after-film discussions. To reward all of their hard work, you should have a guest list for volunteers, sponsors, and other people who helped with the program. A postfestival volunteer party is a good way to show appreciation and give people an opportunity to come together again a few weeks after the event.

Programming

Film and video showings can be exciting whether they are festivals that run over several consecutive days, series that run once a week over a one- to two-month period, or single-screenings such as gala premieres. Both variety and thematic continuity work when programming. For example, a festival could include dramas and documentaries, feature-length and short films, historical period pieces, and contemporary cinema. Series programs could focus on documentaries about HIV/AIDS, or new feature films focusing on gay and lesbian youth. Opening with an area premiere usually ensures a certain level of excitement. It's often difficult to balance imaginative and "risky" programming ideas with local audience expectations and community needs. Develop a clear program rationale. What are your goals and objectives, as an organization, in presenting this program? How, or to what degree, will this particular program accomplish these goals and objectives?

If you plan to show experimental or particularly challenging films and videos, encourage your audience to be open-minded. Audiences accustomed to Hollywood cinema generally expect films to be accessible; if you don't prepare them they may be impatient or irritated when confronted with nontraditional or difficult representations. If they are properly prepared they can enjoy the different sorts of viewing pleasures that experimental films and videos offer. Similarly, in the case of films and videos that are not overtly gay or lesbian or have minimal, subtextual, subtle, latent gay, or lesbian content, be sure to inform the audience in your publicity. Showing a film within the context of a gay or lesbian festival/series sets up certain expectations. If the film is about a strong nonlesbian female friendship, say so; an audience waiting for a kiss that never happens will be disappointed and unable to appreciate the film's other merits.

Presenting one or two older gay and lesbian-theme films can add depth to your program. These historical, and in the case of Hollywood, often "negative" portrayals are of interest inasmuch as they reflect the societal attitudes prevailing at the time of their production. With the passage of time, these cultural documents offer a valuable reminder of gay and lesbian history. Younger viewers are perhaps able to gain a sense of history from these films, and may also find them humorous in their dated homophobia, while older viewers may remember the reality around these representations quite clearly.

Short films and videos are an affordable way to expand the range of your programming and complement your feature programs. There are a number of independent distributors that handle a variety of contemporary comic, dramatic, and documentary shorts by gay and lesbian film and video makers.

Be sure to take into consideration the relative merits and drawbacks of film versus video programming. Depending on your theater/space you may be limited to one format or another, or you may be able to combine formats. Think through the issues of cost, availability, technical/setup, etc. When programming multiple formats in one program it's usually best to begin with the lower visual quality format and end with the higher quality format (i.e., video would precede 16mm film, which would precede 35mm film).

Lastly, a word of advice and encouragement: If there's a particular title you're having trouble finding a print of, be persistent in your search. When dealing with major Hollywood studio distributors you should continue to ask questions even if they say they can't help you. Ask them to explain the situation precisely or to refer you to someone who can. You want to know: Who originally owned the rights? Who owns them now? Is there someone else who owns the cable, home video, or other rights who might have a print? Is there a vault print in their archive? Is there a print at another archive, or possibly a foreign distributor? You can also try finding the director and asking whether they own a personal print of the film.

Scheduling
You can usually fit at least two evening shows in during the week. Try not to start too early or too late: 7:00, 7:15, or 7:30 may be good for your first show, and perhaps 9:15, 9:30, or 9:45 (psychologically better than 10:00 which sounds much later) for your second. Remember to leave enough time between shows to get the audience in and out (preferably at least half an hour). Depending on your venue expenses, you could also try a few weekend matinees or one late-night cult movie on a Friday or Saturday. Or if you're programming on campus, you might try some short lunchtime programs.

Booking
Note that film/video makers and distributors will have to be contacted at least four to six weeks prior to your playdate to ensure availability. Film and video rental fees will have to be negotiated individually on the basis of factors such as theater size, ticket price, and the nature of your presenting organization. Follow-up with distributors should be done again two weeks prior to your screening to ensure that the films have been sent to arrive on time.

Before calling distributors and film/videomakers, map out a provisional schedule with alternate dates (the film you want may not be available on the date you need it, so have an alternate date decided on when you call). Determine scheduling possibilities—prioritizing speakers or visiting directors (be sure of all other arrangements before you commit a speaker to a date).

You should also have a clear sense of what your film/video rental budget is in relation to the number of films and videos you want to present. You don't want to blow your whole budget by booking titles that you really can't afford early in the game. And don't forget to figure in your shipping and insurance costs (this is often an area where you'll find your budget slipping away from you).

You may want to try getting a number of titles from the same distributor and ask for a package deal with them. You might also offer to trade ads in your catalog in exchange for the rental, or to promote their home video line, etc. Be creative and don't forget to haggle—it never hurts to ask for a lower rental rate. In the case of feature film bookings, avoid percentage deals if you can, and try to get flat rate rentals. Also be prepared for the extra expense and hassles of overseas film bookings (the shipping is often as much or more as a domestic rental cost might be, and it can quite complicated to deal with pro forma invoices and getting things out of customs if you've never done it before).

Write everything down in one place (names, phone numbers, addresses, playdates, running times, rental and shipping costs, instructions and procedures, agreements and details to be taken care of). Be organized. Also be attentive to any special requirements around film projection formats (you will probably require special setups, often involving additional expense, to project: PAL or other foreign video formats, magnetic sound, wide-screen film formats, etc.). Be sure that your theater/space is capable of projecting what you're booking.

Shipping Films and Videos

When shipping films and videos within the U.S. be sure to allow enough transit time. Remember that films do sometimes get delayed or lost, so use a shipper that can track and trace shipments (don't send films by regular U.S. mail). To avoid nightmares, make follow-up calls to the film/video maker or distributor to confirm when the film was sent and when it is scheduled to arrive. Allow extra time—at least a few weeks—for shipping films in and out of the U.S. If you do get things from overseas, you may want to insist that they send it by door-to-door courier or you might end up having to go to the airport to clear it through customs. If it's not coming door-to-door, establish a connection early in your preparations with a customs broker at your nearest airport. The customs broker will help you clear films upon entry into the U.S. from abroad. Always insure your films to protect everyone from possible losses.

Theater/Space

Some of the considerations for selecting a space to present films include: capacity for 16mm, 35mm, and video projectors (many films and videos are only available in certain formats); price for rental; space for speaker forums; appropriate number of seats for projected audience size; location, public transportation, and access to theater; parking facilities; wheelchair accessibility; concessions; and quality of theater staff (projectionist, ushers, box-office staff, etc.). Be sure to meet or speak with the venue staff about all your anticipated program needs, be explicit about what you expect them to take care of and what you plan to be responsible for, don't assume anything.

Promotional Materials

Many weeks before your program begins you will be developing a set of materials that might include program notes, promotional flyers, posters, press packets, and advertising slicks, all with continuity of your festival/series title, style, and design. A simple and clean look works best because there is so much information to convey in print whether you're preparing for a single one-night screening, or a festival of thirty films and twenty programs over a ten-day period. It is essential that you prepare a calendar for the production of materials because deadlines become increasingly important as screening dates draw closer. If you're presenting a whole festival or series, you can produce and distribute individual flyers for upcoming screenings to your audience while they're waiting in line. If you receive a favorable review of an upcoming film, use it to create a flyer or blow it up and post it at your venue with an announcement that tickets are still available. Posters, lobby cards, photo stills, and previous reviews provided by distributors can also be used to create a display publicizing individual films at your venue.

Don't forget to request as many promotional materials from the distributor as you can get; you can also research film catalogs or books for graphics or photo images. For older titles, you can find original ad graphics and reviews from bound volumes of *New York Times Film Reviews* at your local library; or check bound volumes of *Variety* (also at your local library) for original reviews.

Catalog/Program
Depending on the size of your event you may want to produce a catalog or small program with descriptions, photos, dates, times, locations, ticket prices, and other information. Look at other film festival/series programs and publicity materials to get ideas. Design options include: a one-page insert in your local gay and lesbian newspaper (you can ask for an over-run so that you'll have extra copies for mailing and for giving to audiences at the venue); a small photocopied flyer or poster with your schedule on it; a fully designed and printed catalog. As always, think about your budget; and think about how you want your program to be distributed to reach your audience. Potential sponsors will want to know how widely distributed your program will be. Take some space in your program to thank all the people who helped with the event.

Mailing Lists and Mailings
Mailings can be an extremely effective means of promotion. They are more cost effective than ads, and more reliable than news stories (because you are in control of your message). The goals of a mailing four to six weeks in advance of a program are: 1) general promotion and 2) advance ticket sales. Determining target-audiences can be a highly creative task. Send about half of your flyers to specially targeted gay and lesbian groups. You might target such groups as: gay and lesbian studies programs, student organizations, or HIV/AIDS support organizations. Depending on your festival/series program, the second half of the mailing can go to media groups such as local film societies, film studies departments at colleges, and museums and galleries with an interest in identity-based art or media presentation. Your mailing may be done by mailing houses or by volunteers after you have compiled or obtained the list you will use. Ask your post office about procedures for bulk mail permits (and try to use a nonprofit bulk mail permit to decrease your costs!). If this is your first time, give yourself time to learn what is involved.

Advertising
The decision to take out paid display advertising will probably be based on your overall budget and should only be done to supplement your overall public relations campaign. You may first want to see if you can arrange an ad swap or a sponsorship arrangement to ensure maximum exposure. Quarter-page ads in the gay and lesbian press or alternative weeklies are good ideas; half-page ads in other local film festival catalogs are even better because you reach a more targeted movie-going audience. Specific ad placement on the upper-right-hand side of the page either in the entertainment section or toward the front of the paper is best. And don't forget about television and radio promotion (see below under Press Releases and Public Service Announcements (PSAs).

Sponsors

To ensure a solid financial base for your event you may want to pursue some business or corporate sponsorships. You might try for a "presenting sponsor" who would receive a very high profile in your materials in exchange for a cash or in-kind donation (this sponsor could be a newspaper that would print and distribute your festival catalogs, a liquor company that would offer a cash donation and provide free drinks for your opening party, or any company that wants to reach the gay and lesbian community). Other sponsor levels can be created in exchange for other donations: an individual "program sponsor" might sponsor a single screening for a smaller cash, food, or service donation; a number of "major sponsors" could be solicited underneath the "presenting sponsor." Be creative, and keep in mind what kind of image you want to convey about your festival—too much corporate sponsorship can have a negative impact on the feel of your program. Be appreciative of your sponsors and acknowledge them publicly in your prefilm introductions. If you're showing any foreign films and videos you can also try approaching cultural consulates for sponsorships or assistance with film shipping.

Organizational Newsletters

This form of free promotion can be extremely effective. To benefit you must provide your press release and other information to organizations in time for the deadlines of their monthly or quarterly mailings. Suggested targets for newsletter promotion include gay and lesbian, HIV/AIDS, women's, and arts organizations.

Press Releases and Public Service Announcements (PSAs)

Press releases and PSAs usually go out about three weeks prior to your opening to give you time for a follow-up call. Compile an accurate and up-to-date list of people working in the local media. Don't forget to include the alternative press and the major dailies, as well as your local public radio affiliate and public access cable channel. Press releases are preferred if they're typed on organizational letterhead with contact persons and phone numbers clearly visible at the top of the page. Brevity and clarity are essential. Develop contacts with specific arts writers at lesbian/gay and alternative newspapers. Be nice to them. Invite them to be on your festival guest list for screenings. Give them as much promotional material as possible (stills, press kits, posters).

Specialized Letters to Community Groups

Personalized letters to special interest organizations are another method of promotion and are often a good way to encourage advance group ticket sales to particular programs. The possibilities for community outreach parallel the issues raised in your individual films and videos: women's groups, senior centers, youth groups, HIV/AIDS service providers, lesbian and gay parenting groups, etc. With smaller groups, a phone call may be as effective as a letter.

Copresentations

Another way to ensure community involvement is to ask a specific group to "copresent" an individual film or video screening that is related to their constituency or area of interest. In exchange for lending their name to the program, the group will have an opportunity to distribute their literature at the screening and you may want to give them a few tickets for their staff or volunteers. You may also want to ask one of their staff to help introduce the program or participate in a postscreening discussion.

Followup

Media and Press: One week after you have sent out your press releases you will telephone to

a) find out if they have received the mailing; b) explain again briefly the what, where, and when of your event; c) invite them to a press screening or ask them to view a preview video-tape; d) ask if you can provide further materials such as press packets or photo stills; and e) ask for referrals to others who may be interested in covering the story. Community Groups: Likewise you will telephone to a) find out if they've received your letter; b) explain briefly the details of the event; c) ask if they're interested in advance-sale tickets at a discount for their group; and d) ask for referrals to others who may be interested. Theater/Space: In the week prior to your opening you will call to confirm all arrangements and verify the time and date of your screening, equipment needs, staffing, etc. Volunteers: Following up with volunteers is especially important. If a volunteer is supposed to be doing something at a certain time and place (taking tickets at the opening-night screening, helping cater the reception, flyer-ing at an event, picking up a filmmaker from the airport, etc.) call to remind them the night before.

Press Screenings

Determine from local theaters the usual hours and locations for press screenings in your community. Your screening, held sometime between two weeks and two days prior to your open-ing, is primarily for film critics and feature story writers, but it's common to also invite a few community leaders, possible speakers, and others who will generate "word of mouth" pro-motion through their networks. Try inviting the owner of your local gay bookstore, café or bar! Provide all critics and writers with a press packet that includes a summary, credit sheet, and past reviews of the specific film you are screening and of the other films in your series. It also helps to have photo stills available along with information about your organization. If the filmmaker is available for interviews (in person or by telephone) include this information in your press release and press packet, and also announce it when you introduce the press screening. Be sure to introduce yourself to all of the film critics and journalists who attend, impress upon them your appreciation of their coverage and your availability if they need any assistance or further information. Let them know any anecdotal information about the film or about the festival itself that might help add another angle to their coverage. Thank them for coming.

Distribution of Flyers and Posters

After the mailing goes out, your festival flyers and posters can be distributed and posted in visible places where your target audience regularly congregates such as: gay and lesbian and women's bookstores, gay and lesbian bars, cafés, restaurants, women's studies and gay and lesbian studies departments, etc.

Interviews

You may want to make one person responsible for liaison with the media and possible inter-views. It's critical that you know what you want to convey (and have practiced making it con-cise) before you sit down with your interviewer because more often than not the interviewer will not ask you the questions you're hoping for. Mention your concept, some individual films and videos by name and content, information about your organization, the date, time and place, and a telephone number where people can call to get more information. Handle the interview by expanding on the questions asked, or by asking and answering your own ques-tions! If possible, try to arrange for press interviews with individual film/videomakers in addi-tion to an interview with you about the program.

Tickets

Ticket prices should generally reflect the comparable rates in your community. Consider sell-ing a series pass at a discount and offering discounts for groups, seniors, and students. If you are selling advance tickets, mail-order forms should be available four weeks prior to your opening so that you have time to mail the tickets back to the buyer. For credit card orders that come in during the week prior to the opening tell the buyer the tickets will be held in their name at the box office. Phone reservations are NOT recommended as there is an unusually high percentage of no-shows for film screenings. Complimentary tickets are common for the press, speakers, and their guests, and a few others determined in advance at the sponsors' discretion.

Speakers

Speakers can add an illuminating and entertaining element to your presentation. If a dialogue with the audience takes place you will have an especially dynamic and exciting event. Draw on local film/video makers and film critics or professors, gay and lesbian community leaders, and activists, as well as experts or academics in fields of interest touched by the film or video. The degree of formality may vary—a single speaker with handheld microphone is quite different from a panel discussion with chairs and a table. The most stimulating and enlightening dialogues take place when "controversial" personalities are invited to participate in forums. Or you may want to have a "question and answer" session between the audience and the film/video maker after your screening. Don't forget to make sure that your microphones, chairs, and stage lights are all in good working condition prior to your opening.

Opening Night Reception

This is an optional event that can range from a small, quiet wine and cheese reception at a nearby home before the screening, to desserts and liqueurs at a neighborhood restaurant after the screening, to a light buffet in the theater lobby during intermission. Determine your budget, staff/volunteer support, and goals in order to shape the event. Do you want to create a small intimate setting to thank patrons, or a large bash in order to fund-raise and generate good public relations? Do you have the budget to design, print, and mail invitations, to order food and beverages, to pay for musicians? Do you have volunteers or friends who can solicit sponsor donations of wine and champagne, food and eating utensils, and flowers from local vendors? Who will prepare and clean up after the event? These are all things to consider before undertaking what can be an exciting way to open your event.

After Your Event

Evaluation of your program should incorporate audience feedback along with staff and volunteer analysis. You might want to have audience ballots available for people to offer their opinions on the films and videos and on the festival/series itself. Everyone who worked on the event should participate in a meeting to talk about any problems and issues that arose during the event. Putting on an event like this involves a lot of work; congratulate your staff and volunteers on their accomplishments, ask for their feedback, and incorporate it into your next event. What could be done differently next time? What went well this time? What improvements can be made in what areas? Cultivate your relationships with film/video makers and distributors by sending follow-up letters thanking them for their participation. Enclose a copy of your catalog or program as well as any reviews or mentions of their film or video.

FYI: While many of the films listed here are available on video from your local video store, these videos are licensed for home use only. You may not legally screen them in a public venue under any circumstances (except for classroom use, in some cases). Even if you actually own a tape, you do not own public performance rights. And even if you don't charge admission, you may not legally exhibit a tape without public performance rights.

Programming and Publicity Resources:

Film Resources at Your Local Library:
1) *Limbacher Guide to 16mm Films Available for Rental*—An alphabetical listing of 16mm films and their distributors.
2) *Index of Films Reviewed in Variety* (and bound volumes of *Variety* reviews)—An alphabetical reference lists the year and week of a review and where to find it.
3) *McGill's Cinema Annual*—An alphabetical catalog featuring descriptive reviews of American and foreign films.
4) Index and bound volumes of *New York Times Film Reviews.*
5) *Variety Year in Review Film Guide*—For country-by-country film listings and international distributor information.
6) The Dewey 900 section and the PN 1990 section is where you'll find other miscellaneous film books.

Information you should get for your files and for film ordering and publicity:
1) Title (year of release) country of origin, director; running time; format: (35mm, 16mm, 8mm, S8mm, 1/2" VHS, 3/4" U-matic, PAL 1/2" or 3/4"); (specify if b&w or silent); (if foreign language film specify in original language with English subtitles or dubbed); special print information: (specify if widescreen or magnetic sound print).
EXAMPLE: *Therese & Isabelle* (1968) Germany/USA
Dir. Radley Metzger 111 mins. 16mm b&w CinemaScope print
2) Distributor: name, address, phone/fax, contact person
3) Rental cost and shipping cost
4) Description: synopsis, stars/cast, awards, etc.

A Few Film Resource Organizations:

1) popcornQ
584 Castro St., #550
San Francisco, CA 94114
(415) 252-6285
fax (415) 252-6287
email: popcornQ@aol.com
This gay, lesbian, bis ual, and transgender film and video website offers a continually updated online database of titles, technical information, descriptions, and sources for thousands of films and videos. The website also includes a range of other resource information, including a networking area for film and videomakers, tips about film and video preservation, and a variety of film and video databases on everything from AIDS to queer youth.

2) Frameline
346 Ninth St.
San Francisco, CA 94103
(415) 703-8650
fax (415) 861-1404
Frameline provides information and distributes lesbian and gay film and video, produces the San Francisco International Lesbian & Gay Film Festival, offers Completion Grant funding for lesbian and gay film and video projects and is a focal point for international lesbian and gay film and video.

3) Acadamy of Motion Picture Arts & Sciences
Margaret Herrick Library
Center for Motion Picture Study

333 S. La Cienega Blvd.
Beverly Hills, CA 90211
(310) 247-3020—reference
(310) 247-3035—general
This reference library and film information service can help you find the distributor of a particular film, track down an actor or director you want to invite to your screening, or answer virtually any film-related question you can think of.

4) Association of Independent Video and Filmmakers
625 Broadway, 9th floor

New York, NY 10012
(212) 473-3400
Provides information, assistance, and services for independent makers. Publishes monthly magazine, *The Independent*, which has information about new and upcoming independent projects, including many gay and lesbian films.

5) National Gay & Lesbian Task Force
Campus Project
1517 U St. NW
Washington, DC 20009
(202) 332-6483.
Contact the Task Force for their *Guide to Using Gay & Lesbian Films on Campus*. This 28-page handbook offers useful and detailed information about exhibiting lesbian and gay films and videos, along with a substantial listing of films and videos and their distributors.

6) If there's a gay and lesbian film festival in your area, ask their advice or assistance (see the Directory of International Lesbian & Gay Film and Video Festivals at the end of this book).

7) Media Network
39 W. 14th St. #403
New York, NY 10011
(212) 929-2732
fax (212) 929-2732
National organization supporting alternative film and video producers. Programs and services include publications, information assistance, conferences, and fiscal sponsorships.

8) Lauri Rose Tanner
337 Nevada St.
San Francisco, CA 94110-6106
(415) 550-9445
fax: (415) 550-9445
Email: laurirose@aol.com
Lauri Rose Tanner is currently writing a nonprofit manual on *How to Start & Operate Film & Video Festivals* which will be published within the next 2 years by the American Council for the Arts. More than 400 hours of interviews with festival managers, directors, etc. around the country have already been processed, and Lauri is also available to consult with new or existing festivals.

This chapter was adapted from Deborah Kaufman's wonderfully concise "Check List for Programming" which first appeared in A Guide to Films Featured in the Jewish Film Festival.

INTERNATIONAL DIRECTORY OF LESBIAN & GAY FILM AND VIDEO FESTIVALS

Many festivals are annual events—the dates of their most recent, or upcoming, festival are listed here when available along with the festival name, address, phone, fax, e-mail, and contact person. Entry deadlines are usually one or two months prior to festival exhibition dates. Many festivals have entry fees or other requirements for submissions. Film/videomakers should inquire about submission guidelines before sending unsolicited work, and should be aware of international shipping requirements when sending films and videos overseas.

This directory is provided as an informal networking resource to facilitate contact between film/videomakers and festival programmers.

A listing of members of Projections: The International Alliance of Lesbian and Gay Film Festivals & Organizations is included here as well. Members and member organizations are indicated in the directory with an asterix. For further information about Projections please contact: Jim Hubbard at 341 Lafayette St., #169 New York, NY 10012 USA (212)539-1023/fax (212) 475-1399e-mail: jimhub@crl.com.

If you have updates or corrections, or want to receive a copy of this directory please contact popcornQ @Planet Out 584 Castro St., #550 San Francisco, CA 94114 USA. Telephone, (415) 252-6285; fax, (415) 252-6287; e-mail, popcornQ@aol.com; internet, http://www.popcornq.com/.

Atlanta Lesbian and Gay Film and Video Festival/Out on Film SAME Project 884 Monroe Drive, Atlanta, GA 30308, USA
(404) 733-6112
fax: (404) 897-1208/(404) 352-0173
Hubbell, Anne/Ranson, Rebecca
October 11-14, 1995

Austin Gay and Lesbian International Film Festival
P.O. Box K Austin, TX 78712, USA
(512) 472-3240
Dinger, Scott
September, 1995

Austrian Gay and Lesbian Film Festival
c/o Velvet Cinema Brunnlbadg.
7/11, A-1090 Vienna, AUSTRIA
43 1 402 6881
fax: 43 1 934683
April 15- May 8, 1994
*Schuttelkopf, Elke

Baltic International Sexual Equality Film and Video Festival
c/o The Baltic Observer Balasta dambis 3. Riga LV 1081, LATVIA
7 0132 462 9
fax: 7 0132 463 387
Juris, Laimons G.
January, 1995
Barcelona International

Exhibition of Gay and Lesbian Films
Carrer Ample 5 08002
Barcelona, SPAIN
34 3 412 72 72
fax: 34 3 412 74 76
Xavier, Daniel
October 23-29, 1995

Berlin, Lesbian Film Festival of Cinesisters c/o Lueschow,
Solmsstr. 24, 10961 Berlin
GERMANY
49 30 691 36 14
fax: 49 30 391 73 36
Michalski, Karin
October 3-8, 1995

Berlin Lesbian & Gay Film Festival c/o Lesbisches und schwules
Buro Film e.V. Kopenhagener Str. 14, 10437 Berlin, GERMANY
49 30 216 2134
fax: same
*Scheuch, Birgit/Wieler, Barbara/Hofner,
Michael/Bruning, Jurgen
July, 1995

Boston Lesbian and Gay Film Festival
Harvard Film Archive, 24 Quincy St., Cambridge, MA 02138, USA
(617) 496-6046
fax: (617) 495-8197

Mansour, George
January and June, 1995

Brussels International Lesbian and Gay Film Festival
v.z. w. AZIMUTH, Ijzerplein 8 b3, B-1210 Brussels, BELGIUM
32 2 201 53 45
Defurne, Bavo/Van Langenhof, Arthur
April, 1994 (every two years)

[Budapest] MELEG: Budapest Gay/Lesbian Film Festival BLUE Foundation,
c/o Ovegylet Foundation, Zichy Jenou. 29, H-1066 Budapest, HUNGARY
36 1 111-0651
fax: 36 1 112 58 44
Eisenstein, Adele
November 1995

[Budapest] POZITIV: World AIDS Day Film Programme BLUE Foundation,
c/o Ovegylet Foundation, Zichy Jenou. 29, H-1066 Budapest, HUNGARY
36 1 111 06 51
fax: 36 1 112 58 44
Eisenstein, Adele
December 1 - 2, 1995

Calgary Lesbian and Gay Film & Video Festival

P.O. Box 30089, Station B
Calgary, Alberta P2M 4N7
CANADA
(403) 277-1741
fax: (403) 277-8033
Chisholm, Barbara
June 21-24, 1995

[Cape Town] Out-In-Africa Film
Festival
P.O. Box 15707 Vlaeberg 8018,
Cape Town, SOUTH AFRICA
27 21 24 15 32
fax:same/e-mail:
nodi@icafe.co.za
Lewis, Jack/Murphy, Nodi
November 2-30, 1995

Chicago Lesbian and Gay
International Film Festival
1543 West Division Street,
Chicago IL 60622, USA
(312) 384-5533
fax (312) 384-5532 emailchi-
film@tezcat.com
Kybertas, Stashu
November 3-12, 1995

Connecticut Gay and Lesbian
Film and Video Festival
(Alternatives)
c/o Jason Plourde 123
Englewood Avenue, West
Hartford CT 06110, USA
(203) 523-1923/fax: same
Plourde, Jason
June, 1995

Copenhagen Gay and Lesbian
Film Festival
c/o Bulowsvej 50A, 1870
Frederiksberg C, DENMARK
45 3537 2507
fax: 45 3135 5758
Byrnit, Jill/Sunde, Lasse Soll
September 16 - 22, 1994

Dallas Lesbian and Gay Film
Festival
Dallas Gay & Lesbian Community
Center
2701 Reagan Dallas, TX 75205,
USA
(214) 528-4233
December 1995

Dayton Lesbian and Gay Film
Festival
c/o The New Neon Movies, 130
E 5th St., Dayton, OH 45402
USA
(513) 222-7469
fax: (513) 222-4119
Sebastian, Patrick
November 13-17, 1994

Dublin Lesbian and Gay Film
Festival c/o The Irish Film Center
6 Eustace St., Temple Bar,
Dublin 2 IRELAND
353 1 679 5744
fax: 353 1 677-8755/e-mail:
sexton@iol.ie
Sexyon, Kevin
August, 1996

[Finland] Turku Lesbian and Gay
Film Festival
c/o Turun Seudun SETA P.O. Box
288 20101 Turku FINLAND
358 21 2500 695
fax: 358 21 2512 905/e-mail:
festarit@smurf.seta.fi
Heiskanen, Outi
November 3-6, 1995

Florida Gay and Lesbian Film
Festival
1126 Kenwood Ave, Winter Park,
FL 32789, USA
(407) 236-9499
fax: (407) 644-4235
Arbogast, Brian
June, 1995

Frankfurt Gay and Lesbian
Festival Werkstattkino mal seh'n
Adlerflychtstr. 6H 6000
Frankfurt/MAIN GERMANY
49 69 5970 845
fax: 49 69 591533
*Gramann, Karola/Witte, Antje
April 13 - 17, 1994

Hamburg Lesbian and Gay Film
Festival METROPOLIS -
Kinemathek Hamburg e.V.
Dammtorstr. 30A D-20354
Hamburg GERMANY
49 40 34 23 53
fax: 49 40 35 40 90
*Wedding, Ludger
October 19-29, 1995

[Hannover] Schwule Filmtage
Kommunales Kino im
Kunstlerhaus, Sophienstr. 2,
30159 Hannover, GERMANY
49 511 1684731
fax: 49 511 306093
Hermes, Sigurd
October, 1995

[Holland] AIDS Film Festival
Hazenkampseweg 41 6531 NC
Nijmegen, NETHERLANDS
31 80 554 212
van den Broek, John
December, 1995 (every two
years)

Hong Kong Gay and Lesbian
Film Festival
Hong Kong Arts Center 2
Harbour Rd. Wanchai HONG
KONG
852 823 0200
fax: 852 865 0798
*Lam, Edward
January 1-24, 1994

[Honolulu] Adam Baran Gay and
Lesbian Film Festival
1877 Kalakaua Ave., Honolulu,
HI 96815, USA
(808) 941-0424
fax: (808) 943-1724
June 11-17, 1995

Icelandic Lesbian & Gay Film
Festival
Hinsegin Biodagar c.o. Samtokin
78 PO Box 1262 Reykjavik ICE-
LAND
354 1 552 8539
fax 354 1 552 7525
Olafsdottir, Margret Pala and
Sigurardottir, Lilja
March, 1996

Irish Lesbian and Gay Film
Festival
The Other Place, 8 South Main
Street, Cork, Ireland
353 21 278470 or 353 21
317660
fax: 353 21 965077
Twomey, Andrew/McAnallen,
Donna
October 5-8, 1995

Jerusalem Gay & Lesbian Film
Festival
Cinematheque, Wolfson Garden,
Hebron Road, Jerusalem,
ISRAEL
972 2 724 131
Shamir, Enulla
March 9-11, 1995

[London] Black Gay & Lesbian
Film/Video Exhibition
c/o PAF Company of Pride Trust,
28 Eurolink Centre 49 Effra
Rd, London SW2 1BZ ENGLAND
44 171 713 0386
fax: same
Ajalon, Jamika
June, 1996

London Lesbian and Gay Film
Festival
National Film Theatre,
Southbank, Waterloo, London
SE1 8XT ENGLAND
44 171 815 1323
fax: 44 171 633 0786

Smyth, Cherry/Baker, Robin
March 21-April 4, 1996

London Lesbian Film Festival -
Canada
956 Dundas St. E., PO Box
46014, London, Ontario N5W
3A1 CANADA
(519) 432-7348
Money, Janet
May 3-5, 1996

Long Beach International Gay
and Lesbian Film Festival
2017 E. 4th St., Long Beach,
CA 90814-1001, USA
(310) 434-9124
fax: (310) 433 6428
Cano, Robert
June 7 - 16, 1996

Los Angeles Gay & Lesbian Film
Festival, Outfest '96 c/o Out On
The Screen
8455 Beverly Blvd., #309, Los
Angeles, CA 90048, USA
(213) 951-1247
fax: (213) 951-0721
Cooper, John
July 11-21, 1996

Melbourne Queer Film and Video
Festival
1/35 Cato St., Prahran 3181
Victoria AUSTRALIA
61 39 510 5576
fax: 61 39 510 5699
Jungwith, Tamara
March 15-24, 1996

Michigan Gay and Lesbian Film
Festival
P.O. Box 1915, Royal Oak, M,
48068-1915, USA
(810) 825-6651
Lary, Michael
September 22-24, 1995

Milano Festival Internazionale di
Cinema Gaylesbico
Via Cicco, Simonetta 17, 20123
Milano, ITALY
39 2 58 10 6204
fax: 39 2 72 00 2942
Marzi, Giampaolo/Lo Manto,
Mariella/Schindler, James
June 20-26 1996 (Milano and
Bologna)

Milwaukee Lesbian and Gay Film
and Video Festival
Great Lakes Film & Video, P.O.
Box 413 Milwaukee, WI 53201,
USA
(414) 229-6971
Yelanjian, Mary
January, 1995

Minneapolis/St. Paul Lesbian,
Gay, Bi & Transgender Film
Festival
c/o U Film Society, 425 Ontario
St. S.E., Minneapolis, MN
55414, USA
(612) 627-4431
fax: (612) 627-4111
Strong, Bob/Olson, Jenni
March, 1995

Montreal Lesbian and Gay Film
Festival/Image & Nation
D.G.L.Q.,
C.P. 1595, succ. Place du Parc
Montreal, Quebec H2W 2R6,
CANADA
(514) 285-4467
fax: same
Golden, Anne/Boudreau, Charline
November 2-20, 1995

[Munich] Verzaubert Gay and
Lesbian Film Festival
Rosebud Entertainment,
Hans-Sachsstr. 22, D-80469
Munich, GERMANY
49 89 260 7354
fax: 49 89 260 7387
*Stefan, Rainer/Muller, Schorsch
November, 1994

New York Festival of Lesbian and
Gay Film/The New Festival
462 Broadway, 5th floor, New
York, N.Y. 10013, USA
(212) 343-2707
fax: (212) 343-0629
*Love, Wellington/Vachal, Robin
June 1-11, 1995

New York Lesbian & Gay
Experimental Film/Video Festival
- MIX
341 Lafayette St. #169, New
York, NY 10012, USA
(212) 539-1023
fax: (212) 475-1399/email:
mix@nyo.com
*Frilot, Shari/Hubbard, Jim
November 2-12, 1995

Northwest International Lesbian
and Gay Film Festival
The Evergreen State College,
Media Loan L2300 Olympia, WA
98505, USA
(206) 866-6000 ext. 6542
Frank, Marcus/Ford, Kathryn
April 29-May 1, 1994

[Nova Scotia] Peggy's Festival
c/o The Centre for Art Tapes
5663 Cornwallis St., Suite 104,
Halifax Nova Scotia, CANADA
B3K 1B6 (902) 429-7299

fax: same
Verrall, Anne
June, 1996

[Oregon] University of Oregon
Queer Film Festival
Student Activities Resource
Office,
U. of Oregon, Eugene, OR
97403, USA
(503) 345-4375
fax: (503) 346 4400
Martin, Debby
February 16 - 19 & 23-25,
1996

Oslo Gay and Lesbian Film
Festival/HomoFilmKlubben
Box 6838 St. Olavs Plass. 0130
Oslo NORWAY
47 22 20 19 60
fax: same
*Johnsen, Anne Mette
June 18-22, 1995

Paris International Gay and
Lesbian Film Festival
c/o American Center 51, Rue de
Bercy 75012, Paris FRANCE
33 1 44 73 7740
fax: 33 1 44 73 7755
Lebovici, Elisabeth/Laurent,
Bocahut/Brooks, Philip
December 12-17 1995

Paris Lesbian Film Festival
/Cineffable
37 Avenue Pasteur, 93100
Montreuil FRANCE
33 1 48 70 77 11
fax: same
Baruch, Dominique
October 26-30, 1995

Philadelphia International Gay &
Lesbian Film Festival
1520 Locust St., #200,
Philadelphia, PA 19102 USA
(215) 790-1510
fax: (215) 7901501
Murray, Ray
July 11-21, 1996

Pittsburgh International Lesbian
and Gay Film Festival
P.O. Box 9007, Pittsburgh PA
15224, USA
Cummings, Rich
October, 1995

Princeton Film and Video
Festival, Queer Articulations
1996
306 Aaron Burr Hall, Princeton,
NJ 08544, USA
(609) 258-4522

fax: (609) 258-3831
Handler, Jen/Jusick, Stephen Kent
February 22-24, 1996

Quee(r)n City Cinema
2236 Osler Street, Regina, SK
54P 1W8 CANADA
(306) 757-6637
Varro, Gary
February/March 1996

Rochester Lesbian & Gay Film & Video Festival,
c/o Gay Alliance of Genessee Valley,
179 Atlantic Ave., Rochester NY, 14607 USA
(716) 244-8640
Soleil, Susan/Emert, David T.
October 20-28, 1995

Sacramento Gay and Lesbian Film Festival
2214 Arden Way, #138, Sacramento, CA 95825, USA
(916) 484-5636
October 19-21, 1995

San Antonio's Annual Festival of Lesbian & Gay Films - Out at the Movies
P.O. Box 15705 San Antonio, TX 78212 USA
(210) 228-0201
fax: (210) 228-0000
Poplin, Dennis
September 25-28, 1996

San Francisco International Lesbian & Gay Film Festival
Frameline 346 Ninth St., San Francisco, CA 94103 USA
(415) 703-8650
fax: (415) 861-1404/email: frameline@aol.com
*Lumpkin, Michael/Morris, Jennifer
June, 1996

Santa Barbara Lesbian and Gay Film Festival
PO Box 21653, Santa Barbara, CA 93121 USA
(805) 963-3636
November, 1994

Santa Cruz Gay/Lesbian/Bi Film & Video Festival
c/o Kresge College, Programs Activities Office,
UCSC 1156 High St., Santa Cruz, CA 95064 USA
May, 1994

[Sao Paulo] MIX Brasil
av. Pedrosa de Morais, 89 cj. 5,
Sao Paulo, 05420-000, BRAZIL
55 11 851 0214
fax: 55 11 211-4628
Capo, Suzy
October 11 - 16, 1994

Seattle Lesbian & Gay Film Festival - Buzzsaw
1202 E. Pike Street, #1313. Seattle, WA 98122-3934, USA
(206) 728-6126
email: Buzzsaw96@aol.com
Jenkins, Crescentia/Fein, Robert Henry
October 25 - November 2, 1996

St. Louis International Lesbian and Gay Film Festival
P.O. Box 2929 St. Louis, MO 63130, USA
(314) 997 9897 Ext. 54
Serafini, Linda
September 8 - 14, 1995

St. Petersburg Lesbian and Gay Film Festival
Lilienthalstr. 16, 10965 Berlin, GERMANY
49 30 691 3384
*Mahidelein
May 16-25, 1994

[Stockholm] Gay and Lesbian Film Festival/Folkets Bio
Box 2068, S-10312 Stockholm, SWEDEN
46 8 6560601
fax: 46 8 402 08 27
*Ervasti, Marjut
December, 1996

Sydney Gay and Lesbian Film Festival/Queer Screen Ltd.
12A, 94 Oxford St. P.O. Box 1081. Darlinghurst NSW 2010 AUSTRALIA
61 2 332 4938
fax: 61 2 331 2988
Mitchell, Jeff
February, 1996

Sydney International Queer Film and Video Festival
P.O. Box 522, Paddington NSW 2021, AUSTRALIA
61 2 332 4150
fax: 61 2 332 2969
Robinson, Denise
September 24 - October 1, 1994

[Tampa] Pride Film Festival
1222 S. Dale Mabry Hwy, # 602, Tampa, FL 33629-5009,

USA
(813) 837-4485
fax: (813) 837-0810
Puig, Mark/Pettijohn, Patricia/Williams, Susan
October 4 - October 13, 1996

Tokyo International Lesbian and Gay Film and Video Festival
Toride Publ. 201 Hoyu Bldg. 2-11-9 YotsuyaShinjuku-ku Tokyo 160 JAPAN
81 3 3359 8779
fax: 81 3 3359 5856
Robertson, Dru
May 28, 1995

Toronto, Lesbian and Gay Film and Video Festival of c/o Inside Out Collective, P.O. Box 121 Station P Toronto, Ontario M5S 2S7, CANADA
(416) 977-6847
fax: (416) 977-8025
Cormack, Joanne
May 23-June 2, 1996

Turin International Gay and Lesbian Film Festival
Via T. TASSO 11 10122 Torino ITALY
39 11 534 888
fax: 39 11 521 37 37
or 39 11 535 796
*Minerba, Giovanni/Humouda, Elisabetta
April 15-21, 1996

Vancouver Lesbian and Gay Film Festival/Out on Screen
P.O. Box 521 1027 Davie Street Vancouver, BC V6E 4L2 CANADA
(604) 685-1159
fax: (604) 689-1459
Esguerra, Marilou/Amaranth, Kaz
July 19-24,1995

Vienna Gay Film Festival (HOSI Wien)
Novaragasse 40, A-1020 Vienna AUSTRIA
43 222 26 66 04
Krickler, Kurt
March, 1994

[Vienna] TRANS-X Film Festival
DV-8 Film c/o P.O. Box 208, A-1071, Vienna AUSTRIA
43 1 522 86 41
fax: 43 1 522 98 74
Reumuller, Barbara
September, 1996

Washington DC International Lesbian and Gay Film Festival
c/o One In Ten,

1555 Connecticut Avenue, NW,
Suite 200, Washington, DC
20036 USA
(202) 986-1119
fax: (202) 462-9043
Becker, Barry
October 2-12, 1995

Winnipeg Gay and Lesbian Film
Festival/Counterparts
P.O. Box 1661 Winnipeg,
Manitoba R3C 2Z6 CANADA
(204) 474-0212
April, 1994

Worcester Lesbian, Gay and
Bisexual Film Festival
c/o D. A. Watson, 46 Deerfield
St., #3, Worcester, MA 01602,
USA
Watson, D. A.
Fridays in April, 1994

U.S. HOME VIDEO DISTRIBUTORS

• To find lesbian and gay films available on home video, contact one of these lesbian/gay (or lesbian/gay friendly) mail-order video distributors. Or check your local lesbian/gay bookstore:

Gay & Lesbian
Lambda Rising Bookstore
1625 Connecticut Ave. NW
Washington DC 20009-1013
(202) 462-6969 or (800) 621-6969. Mail-order sales of gay/lesbian films on video. (No catalog)

TLA Video Management
332 South St.
Philadelphia, PA 19147
(215) 922-1014 or (800) 333-TLA1. Mail-order sales of gay/lesbian films on video. (72-page Gay & Lesbian Video Guide)

Wolfe Video
P.O. Box 64
New Almaden, CA 95042
(408) 268-6782. Mail-order sales of gay/lesbian independent shorts and features. (Catalog)

The MC Film Festival/54561
Corporation
P.O. Box 20071
Tampa, FL 33622-0071
(813) 972-7995 or (800) 445-7134. Mail-order sales of gay/lesbian films on video. (34-page catalog)

Facets Multimedia
1517 W Fullerton Ave.
Chicago, IL 60614
(800) 331-6197. Mail-order rental and sales of gay/lesbian films on video. (Catalog)

Gay
Cinevista
1680 Michigan Ave.
Miami Beach, FL 33139
305 532-3400. Mail-order sales of gay men's foreign and independent feature films on video. (Newsletter)

Lesbian
Charis Video
P.O. Box 797
Brooklyn, NY 11231 Mail-order rental and sales of lesbian, women's and some gay films on video. (Catalog)

Lesbian (Erotic/Porn)
Good Vibrations
1210 Valencia St.
San Francisco CA 94110
(415) 974-8980. Mail-order sales. (Small catalog of porn/erotic videos)

Gay (Erotic/Porn)
Bijou Video
1349 N Wells St.
Chicago, IL 60610
800 932-7111. Mail-order sales. (HUGE well-illustrated catalog of porn/erotic videos)

U.K. SELL-THRU DISTRIBUTORS

• To find lesbian and gay films available on sell-thru contact one of these lesbian/gay (or lesbian/gay friendly) video distributors. Or check your local lesbian/gay bookstore:

BFI/Connoisseur Video
Glenbuck House, Glenbuck Rd.
Surbiton, Surrey KT6 6BT
44 181 399-0022
(The Gay Connoisseur series releases gay and lesbian features and shorts.)

Dangerous To Know
20 Offley Rd.
Kennington Oval
London SW9 OLS
44 171 735-8330/fax 44 171 793-8488
(Releases lesbian and gay feature-length works and packages of shorts.)

Electric Pictures
22 Carol St.
London NW1 OHU
44 171 267-8418
(Gay and lesbian features.)

Metro Tartan
79 Wardour St.
London W1V 3TH
44 171 734-8508/fax 44 171 287-2112
(Gay and lesbian features.)

BIBLIOGRAPHY

This queer film and video bibliography includes books about gay, lesbian, bisexual or transgender moving images, as well as books by or about queer film and video makers. It is not comprehensive, but it offers a very thorough overview of material for further reading on the subject. A few of the most significant works available, which are highly recommended, are highlighted in the bibliography by an asterix. This bibliography was compiled by Tanta Miller.

*Bad Object-Choices, ed. *How Do I Look?: Queer Film and Video*. Seattle: Bay Press, 1991.

Bell-Metereau, Rebecca Louise. *Hollywood Androgyny*. New York: Columbia University Press, 1985, 1993.

Bernstorff, Madeleine, and Stefanie Hetze. *Frauen in Hosen: Hosenrollen im Film*. Munchen: Herausgegeben vom Munchner Filmzentrum e V., 1989.

Berry, Chris. *A Bit on the Side: East-West Topographies of Desire*. Sydney: Empress, 1994.

Bijou Video. *Bijou Video: The Complete Reference Guide to Gay Adult Films*. Chicago, IL: Images of the World, 1993.

Burston, Paul, and Colin Richardson. *A Queer Romance: Lesbians, Gay Men and Popular Culture*. London, New York: Routledge, 1995.

Burston, Paul. *What Are You Looking At?: Queer Sex, Style and Cinema*. London: Cassel, 1995.

Corber, Robert. *In The Name of National Security: Hitchcock, Homophobia, & the Political Construction of Gender in Post-War America*. Durham: Duke University Press, 1993.

Creekmur, Corey K., and Alexander Doty eds. *Out In Culture: Gay, Lesbian and Queer Essays in Popular Culture*. London: Cassel, 1995.

De Rome, Peter. *The Erotic World of Peter De Rome*. London: GMP, 1984.

*Dickens, Homer. *What a Drag: Men as Women and Women as Men in the Movies*. New York: Quill, 1984.

Drost, Elmar, and Rosa Linse. *Filme von Anderen Ufa(r): Schwulen-und Lesbenfilme aus BRD und DDR*. Munster: SatzBau, 1992.

Du Plessis, Michael. *Queer Pasts Now: Historical Fiction in Lesbian, Bisexual, and Gay Film*. University of Southern California: Dissertation, 1993.

Dubowski, Sandi. *(Ex)Posing the Frame: Displaying Gay Male Bodies in Hollywood & Gay Independent Film*. Harvard University: Dissertation, 1992.

*Dyer, Richard. *Gays & Film*. London: British Film Institute, 1977; New York: Zoetrope, 1984.

Dyer, Richard. *Heavenly Bodies: Film Stars and Society*. Houndmills, Basingstoke, Hampshire: Macmillan, 1987.

*Dyer, Richard. *Now You See It: Studies on Lesbian and Gay Film*. New York, London: Routledge, 1990.

Dyer, Richard. *The Matter of Images: Essays on Representations.* New York, London: Routledge, 1993.

Forster, Annette. *Macumba. Amsterdam: Feministisch Filmkollektief Cinemien,* 1982. [The films of Elfi Mikesch]

Garsi, Jean-Francois, ed. *Cinemas Homosexuals.* Paris: Papyrus, 1983.

Gatiss, Mark. *James Whale: A Biography.* London: Cassel, 1995.

*Gever, Martha, Pratibha Parmar, and John Greyson eds. *Queer Looks: Perspectives on Lesbian & Gay Film & Video.* New York: Routledge, 1993.

*Giles, Jane. *The Cinema of Jean Genet: Un Chant d'amour.* London: British Film Institute, 1991.

Hadleigh, Boze. *Conversations with My Elders.* New York: St. Martin's Press, 1986. [Interviews with Sal Mineo, Luchino Visconti, Cecil Beaton, George Cukor, Rainer Werner Fassbinder, and Rock Hudson]

Hadleigh, Boze. *Hollywood Lesbians: Conversations with Sandy Dennis, Barbara Stanwyck, Marjorie Main, Nancy Kulp, Patsy Kelly, Agnes Moorehead, Edith Head, Dorothy Arzner, Capucine, and Judith Anderson.* New York: Barricade Books, 1994.

*Boze Hadleigh. *The Lavender Screen: The Gay and Lesbian Films: Their Stars, Makers, Characters and Critics.* New York: Citadel Press, 1993.

Hetze, Stefanie. *Happy-ending fur Wen? Kino und Lesbische Frauen.* Frankfurt/Munich: Tende, 1986.

*Howes, Keith. *Broadcasting It: An Encyclopedia of Homosexual Film, Radio, and Television in the UK, 1923-1993.* London; New York: Cassell, 1994.

Huber, Hermann J. *Gewalt und Leidenschaft: Das Lexicon Homosexualitat in Film und Video.* Berlin: Bruno Gmunder, 1987.

Jackson, Earl. *Strategies of Deviance: Studies in Gay Male Representation.* Bloomington: Indiana University Press, 1995.

Jarman, Derek. *Blue.* Rotterdam: International Film Festival Rotterdam & Uitgeverij International Theatre & Film Books, 1993.

Jarman, Derek. *Dancing Ledge.* Woodstock, New York: Overlook Press, 1993.

Jarman, Derek. *Modern Nature: The Journals of Derek Jarman.* London: Century, 1991.

Jarman, Derek. *Queer Edward II.* London: British Film Institute, 1991.

*Mayne, Judith. *Directed By Dorothy Arzner.* Bloomington, Indianapolis: Indiana University Press, 1995.

McDonald, Boyd. *Cruising the Movies.* New York: Gay Presses of New York, 1985.

*Murray, Raymond. *Images in the Dark: An Encyclopedia of Gay and Lesbian Film and Video.* Philadelphia: TLA Publications, 1994.

Murray, Timothy. *Like a Film: Ideological Fantasy of Screen, Camera, and Canvas.* London, New York: Routledge, 1993.

O'Pray, Michael. *Andy Warhol: Film Factory*. London: British Film Institute, 1989.

*Parish, James Robert. *Gays and Lesbians in Mainstream Cinema: Plots, Critiques, Casts and Credits for 272 Theatrical and Made-for-Television Hollywood Releases*. Jefferson, North Carolina: McFarland & Co, 1993.

Patrick, John. *The Best of the Superstars (1991: The Year in Sex)*. Sarasota, Florida: STARbooks Press, 1991.

Philbert, Bertrand. *L'Homosexualite A L'Ecran*. Paris: H. Veyrier, 1984.

Price, Theodore. *Hitchcock and Homosexuality: His 50-Year Obsession with Jack the Ripper and the Superbitch Prostitute*. Metuchen, New Jersey: Scarecrow Press, 1992.

Roen, Paul. *High Camp: A Gay Guide To Camp & Cult Films*. San Francisco: Leyland Publications, 1994.

Rowberry, John. *Gay Video: A Guide to Erotica*. San Francisco: G.S. Press, 1986

*Russo, Vito. *The Celluloid Closet: Homosexuality in the Movies*. New York: Harper & Row, 1981, 1987.

Satkin, Jeff, ed. *Atkol Comprehensive Guide to Adult Male VIdeos*. Plainfield, New Jersey: Atkol, Inc., 1990.

Siebenand, Paul Alcuin. *The Beginnings of Gay Cinema in Los Angeles: The Industry and the Audience*. University of Southern California: Dissertation, 1975.

Smith, Paul Julian. *Laws of Desire: Questions of Homosexuality in Spanish Writing and Film, 1960-1990*. Oxford: Oxford University Press; New York: Clarendon Press, 1992.

Steven, Peter, ed. *Jump Cut: Hollywood, Politics, and Counter-Cinema*. Toronto: Between the Lines, 1985.

*Stewart, Stephen. *Gay Hollywood Film and Video Guide: Over 75 Years of Male Homosexuality in the Movies*. Laguna Hills: Companion Publications, 1993.

Tyler, Parker. *Screening the Sexes: Homosexuality in the Movies*. New York: Holt, Rinehart & Winston, 1972; New York: Da Capo Press, 1993.

Van Leer, David. *The Queening of America: Gay Culture in Straight Society*. New York: Routeldge, 1995.

Weiss, Andrea. *Before Stonewall: The Making of a Gay and Lesbian Community*. Tallahassee, FL: Naiad Press, 1988.

*Weiss, Andrea. Vampires and Violets. New York: Penguin Books, 1993.

Worth, Fabienne, ed. *Queer Theory: Desire, Authorship and Visibility*. Yverdon, Switzerland: Harwood, 1993.